Advanced DBA Certification Guide and Reference

for DB2® Universal Database™ v8
for Linux®, UNIX®, and Windows®

Advanced DBA Certification Guide and Reference

for DB2® Universal Database™ v8
for Linux®, UNIX®, and Windows®

DB2® **Information Management Software**

Dwaine R. Snow
Thomas X. Phan

PRENTICE HALL
Professional Technical Reference
Upper Saddle River, New Jersey 07458
www.phptr.com

Editorial/production supervision: *Jane Bonnell*
Cover design director: *Jerry Votta*
Cover design: *IBM Corporation*
Manufacturing manager: *Alexis Heydt-Long*
Publisher: *Jeffrey Pepper*
Editorial assistant: *Linda Ramagnano*
Marketing manager: *Debby vanDijk*
IBM Consulting Editor: *Susan Visser*

 Published by Pearson Education, Inc.
Publishing as Prentice Hall Professional Technical Reference
Upper Saddle River, NJ 07458

Prentice Hall PTR offers excellent discounts on this book when ordered in quantity for bulk purchases or special sales. For more information, please contact: U.S. Corporate and Government Sales, 1-800-382-3419, corpsales@pearsontechgroup.com. For sales outside of the U.S., please contact: International Sales, 1-317-581-3793, international@pearsontechgroup.com.

Printed in the United States of America

First Printing

ISBN   0-13-046388-4

Pearson Education LTD.
Pearson Education Australia PTY, Limited
Pearson Education Singapore, Pte. Ltd.
Pearson Education North Asia Ltd.
Pearson Education Canada, Ltd.
Pearson Educación de Mexico, S.A. de C.V.
Pearson Education — Japan
Pearson Education Malaysia, Pte. Ltd.

Contents _____

CHAPTER 2 **Data Manipulation**   77

CHAPTER 4   Database Security   297

Foreword

An ongoing challenge for today's computer professionals is reserving the time to develop new skills to keep up with changes in technology. Our value as technology professionals is increased as we learn and develop new skills with industry leading products. One of the most technologically advanced products in the industry is DB2 Universal Database, which is also the market leader on popular environments such as Linux.

More than 20 years ago, Relational database technology was invented in IBM Research delivering the first commercially available database in the early 1980s. This invention created the unique ability to represent data in a simple tabular form, access it through the powerful SQL query language, and make it readily available to the business community. Today, tens of thousands of businesses all over the world rely on DB2 databases to store key corporate data assets and run their business both traditionally and over the Web.

DB2 provides virtually unlimited scalability, industry leading performance, reliability, and availability. DB2 continues to lead the industry by focusing on autonomic computing that will make DBAs more productive and allow our customers without a DBA staff to manage their database environments effectively with a minimum of effort.

The demand for DB2 skills continues to grow. Certifications were awarded in over 60 countries around the world, more than 3000 institutions worldwide are teaching DB2-related courses, and over 100,000 download requests have been made from DBAs and Developers who have wanted to extend their skills from Microsoft, Sybase, and Oracle to DB2 UDB.

This Certification Guide is an excellent way to learn about DB2, to develop new skills, and to provide new opportunities for yourself in the computer industry. This book includes a trial copy of DB2 that will give you an opportunity to develop skills using hands-on experience, as well as a set of scripts to help you monitor and tune your databases. I hope you use this Certification Guide in advancing your skills and enjoy the benefits of being a certified DB2 professional.

Janet Perna
General Manager, IBM Information Management
IBM Software Group

Preface

This book is a complete guide to the advanced features of IBM DB2 Universal Database (UDB) Enterprise Server Edition (ESE) Version 8.1. DB2 UDB Version 8.1 is available on many operating systems, and the book has been written with this in mind. Any significant differences in the implementation of DB2 on the various operating systems are highlighted. Although this book was written as a study guide for the new Advanced DBA certification (DB2 Exam number 704), it can also be used as a reference by DBAs as they perform their day-to-day activities.

The Advanced DBA exam contains the following sections:

Advanced Administration	22%
Ability to design table spaces	1%
Ability to design buffer pools	5%
Ability to create buffer pools	4%
Ability to exploit inter-partition parallelism	12%
High Availability	**28%**
Ability to develop a logging strategy	5%
Ability to use advanced backup features	8%
Ability to use advanced recovery features	10%
Ability to implement a standby database	5%

Performance and Scalability	31%
Ability to identify and use DB2 registry variables that affect database system performance	1%
Ability to manage and tune memory and I/O	6%
Ability to analyze performance problems	1%
Ability to manage a large number of users and connections	3%
Ability to partition large amounts of data for performance	12%
Ability to manage the number of partitions in a database	8%
Networking and Security	**19%**
Ability to configure a partitioned database on multiple servers	8%
Ability to manage connections to host systems	3%
Ability to identify and resolve connection problems	5%
Knowledge of external authentication mechanisms	3%

DB2: ANY WORKLOAD, ANY DATA, ALL THE TIME

DB2 UDB ESE provides unparalleled performance and scalability to handle the most demanding workloads. Today, workloads are not strictly online transaction programming or data warehousing. More and more, customers are buying or building systems that combine both transaction processing and decision support workloads.

To satisfy the needs of your most complex databases and applications, IBM has extended the rich feature set of DB2 UDB to deliver unparalleled power and scalability to your entire enterprise. This has been accomplished through the features discussed below.

Intelligent Data Distribution

DB2 UDB supports parallel queries through intelligent database partitioning. When a DB2 UDB ESE database is partitioned, DB2 automatically distributes the data across the database partitions, or subsets of the database, which can reside on multiple servers or within a large SMP server. A unique partition map allows DB2 to manage the distribution and redistribution of the data as required.

DB2 UDB uses a shared-nothing architecture that has proven to provide superior scalability, maintenance, and optimization, compared with a shared-disk architecture. The shared-nothing architecture eliminates the overhead of distributed lock management and distributed views required by a shared-disk architecture.

Efficient Optimization

DB2's unrivaled cost-based SQL optimizer makes use of the database and system configuration information to evaluate the potential execution paths for an SQL query and choose the lowest-cost path for execution. DB2 UDB has an enhanced optimizer that supports SQL query rewrite, OLAP SQL extensions, Dynamic Bit Mapped Indexing, and star joins commonly used in data warehousing.

Parallel Everything

In DB2 UDB, access plans are automatically created for parallel execution with standard SQL, and no additional programming is needed. DB2's parallel execution applies to SELECT, INSERT, UPDATE, and DELETE functions. Data scans, joins, sorts, load balancing, table reorganization, data load, index creation, indexed access, backup, and restore can all be performed on all database partitions simultaneously.

Although DB2 can break a query into a number of pieces that can be executed in parallel, the scalability of DB2 with intra-partition parallelism only (i.e., using SMP-type parallelism with a single database image) can be limited or restricted by the underlying operating system or hardware.

Creating multiple database partitions within a larger SMP server (or across multiple servers) has proven to provide better scalability than intra-partition parallelism alone. As the number of CPUs grows, the scalability decreases when using intra-partition parallelism alone. By creating multiple database partitions within the SMP server, the scalability is able to remain almost linear.

Supreme Scalability

As you expand your data warehouse, accommodate more users, and move projects from pilot to production, you'll appreciate the predictably scalable performance of DB2 UDB. Its shared-nothing architecture allows parallel database queries with minimal data transfer between database partitions. Because the number of database partitions has little impact on inter-partition traffic, performance scales in a near-linear fashion when you add more servers to your cluster of servers or add SMP servers to an existing server cluster.

Multi-dimensional clustering (MDC) provides an elegant method of ensuring flexible, continuous, and automatic clustering of data based on multiple dimensions within a table. This can result in significant improvement in the performance of queries, as well as significant reduction—or even elimination—in the overhead of data maintenance operations such as table reorganization and index maintenance operations during INSERT, UPDATE, and DELETE operations.

In many of today's database servers, a process or thread is dedicated to each client that connects to a database. For a typical OLTP workload that handles large numbers of connected users who perform relatively short-lived transactions with some delay between subsequent transactions, this puts a heavy load on the database server because system resources are being tied up by client connections that are not performing any work. DB2 UDB Version 8.1 has implemented a connection multiplexing architecture called the *Connection Concentrator* that will allow users to move from a configuration where the number of connected users is constrained by the physical limitations of the underlying hardware to a scenario where the limiting factor will be based solely on the transaction load and the machine's ability to handle such a load.

Materialized query tables (previously ASTs) allow you to precompute some typical table joins, queries, aggregates, etc., that can be reused by other users. By reusing the result set and not having to rerun the statements each time, the response time is much faster and the resources required are drastically reduced.

Database Partitioning

The DB2 UDB Database Partitioning Feature (DPF) is required in order to partition your DB2 UDB ESE database, either within a single server or across multiple servers. The DPF is a license only and does not require any products additional to DB2 UDB ESE to be installed on your database server to support database partitioning.

In the past, database partitioning was provided by DB2 UDB Enterprise-Extended Edition (EEE), and to partition a database, this product needed to be installed. With DB2 UDB Version 8.1, if you already have DB2 UDB ESE installed and determine that it would be beneficial to partition the database, there is no need to remove or install any software. You need only purchase the DPF for the server(s) where you will create the database partitions.

CONVENTIONS USED THROUGHOUT THE BOOK

Many examples of SQL statements, DB2 commands, and operating system commands are included throughout the book. If SQL keywords are referred to in the text portion of the book, they will be written in CAPITALS. For example, the SELECT statement is used to retrieve data from a DB2 database.

DB2 commands will be shown using the same method as SQL keywords. For example, the CREATE DATABASE command allows you to define the initial location of database objects. DB2 UDB commands are issued from the Command Line Processor (CLP) utility. This utility will accept the commands in upper- and lowercase. The CLP program itself is an executable called db2.

In the UNIX operating systems, program names are case sensitive. Therefore, be careful to enter the program name using the proper case. On UNIX, *db2* must be entered in lowercase.

Displayed SQL statements and commands usually appear within a shaded box.

ACKNOWLEDGMENTS

Dwaine and Tom would like to thank Patti Cartwright and Bob Harbus for their dedication and going above and beyond our expectations. Their review of the book and suggestions were invaluable in ensuring that the material is useful, understandable, and meets the objectives of the test.

The following people also provided a great deal of assistance, either through contributions to the book, technical expertise, and/or comments:

John Hornibrook, *IBM Toronto Lab*
Ian Finlay, *IBM Toronto Lab*
Guy Lohman, *IBM Silicon Valley Lab*
Kelly Schlamb, *IBM Toronto Lab*
Dale McInnis, *IBM Toronto Lab*
Leslie Cranston, *IBM Toronto Lab*
Adriana Zubiri, *IBM Toronto Lab*
Calisto Zuzarte, *IBM Toronto Lab*
Steve Raspudic, *IBM Toronto Lab*
Peter Shum, *IBM Toronto Lab*
Larry Pay, *IBM Toronto Lab*
Jon Rubin, *IBM Silicon Valley Lab*

TRADEMARKS

Data Storage

In order for a database to perform well, it must be able to efficiently store and quickly retrieve, search, and manipulate large amounts of data. Within a DB2 database, data is stored on disk and must be read into memory in order to be searched and manipulated. On disk, the data is stored within table spaces, and when the data and/or indexes are needed to build the result set for a particular query, the required pages must be read from the table space(s) into the buffer pool before they can be manipulated or searched. When designing a database system, these two elements, I/O and memory, are two of the most important elements in ensuring the overall performance of the database system. This chapter will focus on the design and implementation of the physical storage model for the database. Chapter 2 will focus on the design of the database buffer pool(s) for optimal data access.

In order for DB2 to scan a table or an index, the pages of the table or index must be in the database's buffer pool(s). The buffer pool(s) are the work area for the database, and all searching for and manipulation of the data and indexes must take place within the buffer pool(s). In order for the data and index pages to be manipulated, they must be within the buffer pool. If the page is already in the buffer pool, then DB2 can start to work on the page immediately. If the page is not in the buffer pool, DB2 must read the page from disk and position it in the buffer pool(s). Therefore, the physical placement of the data (and indexes) will have a direct effect on the overall performance of the database system. To design and build a database that will meet performance expectations, the database administrator must understand the concepts of data placement and data manipulation in order to create an appropriate physical database design.

Within a DB2 database, the storage of the data and indexes is defined and controlled at four different levels. To accommodate partitioned databases, there is an abstract layer referred to as *partition groups,* as shown in Figure 1.1. A partition group is a grouping or collection of one or more data-

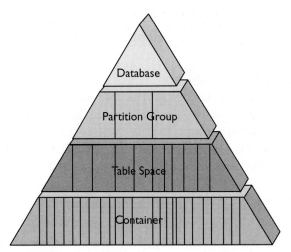

Figure 1.1
The DB2 storage triangle.

base partitions within a database. When a table space is created, it is assigned to a partition group and will be created only on the database partitions that are part of the partition group. Each table space must have one or more containers that define the physical storage for the table space. A container can be an operating system directory, a file with a predetermined size, or a raw device, such as an unformatted hard drive, a partition on the hard drive, or a logical volume.

> **N O T E**   LOB and Long Varchar columns are not manipulated in the database buffer pools. All access to LOB and Long Varchar data will occur directly to disk.

SOME TERMINOLOGY USED IN DB2

The terminology used to describe the database objects has changed again in DB2 for Linux, UNIX, and Windows Version 8, and this can lead to confusion for those experienced with previous versions of the product. This section will focus on the current terms but will point out where some of the old terminology may still be used.

A database can be described in the simplest terms as a collection of data. If you are familiar with DB2 or any other Relational Database Management Systems (RDBMSs), you'll know that data within a database is stored in tables. Tables are defined with a set of columns and the data is stored in rows within these tables. In DB2 Enterprise Server Edition (ESE), a database can be divided into several parts that are called *database partitions*. A database partition is a part of the database that has its own portion of the user data, indexes, configuration files, and transaction logs.

N O T E   To use more than one database partition, the Database
Partitioning Feature must be acquired from IBM.

In the past, the term *node* was used instead of *partition*; however, this was very confusing
because the term node was used to describe both the software and the hardware. A node in DB2
terminology is equivalent to a database partition, however, the computers involved in the database cluster were also referred to as *nodes*. This book will use the new terminology to avoid confusion, but a number of the DB2 commands and SQL statements also support the old
terminology to support scripts written for previous versions of DB2.

THE DEFAULT DATABASE

The CREATE DATABASE command allows a user to specify the drive or directory on which to
create the database, depending on the operating system. The Linux and UNIX operating systems
allow a user to specify the directory in which to create the database. On the Windows operating
system, a user can specify only the drive on which to create the database. If no drive or directory
is specified, the database will be created on the path specified by the DFTDBPATH instance
(database manager) configuration parameter.

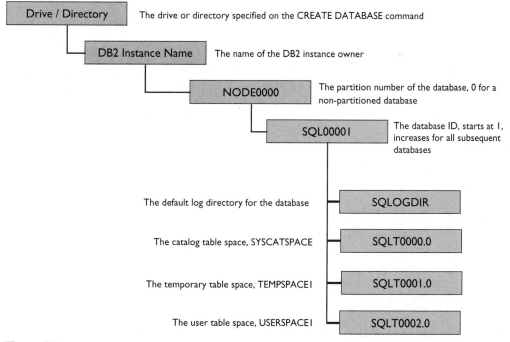

Figure 1.2
The default database structure.

On the drive or directory specified in the CREATE DATABASE command, DB2 will create a series of subdirectories, as shown in Figure 1.2. The first subdirectory is named after the instance owner for the instance in which the database was created. Under this subdirectory, DB2 will create a directory that indicates which database partition the database was created in. For a nonpartitioned database, the directory will be NODE0000. For a partitioned database, the directory will be named NODE*xxxx* where *xxxx* will be the database instance's four-digit partition number, as designated in the db2nodes.cfg file. For example, for partition number 43, this directory would be NODE0043.

> **N O T E**   In Windows, instances do not really have an instance owner, but the name of the instance, i.e., DB2, will be used in place of the instance owner's ID.

Because more than one database can be created on the same drive or directory, each database must have its own unique subdirectory. Under the NODE*xxxx* directory, there will be an SQL*xxxxx* directory for every database that was created on the drive/directory. For example, there are two databases, MYDB and SAMPLE, that were both created on the C: drive on Windows, so there will be two directories: SQL00001 and SQL00002.

To determine under which directory the database was created, enter the command LIST DATABASE DIRECTORY ON C:. This will produce output like the following:

```
Database 1 entry:

    Database alias                        = MYDB
    Database name                         = MYDB
    Database directory                    = SQL00002
    Database release level                = a.00
    Comment
    Directory entry type                  = Home
    Catalog database partition number     = 0
    Database partition number             = 0


Database 2 entry:

    Database alias                        = SAMPLE
    Database name                         = SAMPLE
    Database directory                    = SQL00001
    Database release level                = a.00
    Comment                               =
    Directory entry type                  = Home
    Catalog database partition number     = 0
    Database partition number             = 0
```

In the example above, the database SAMPLE would have been created in the SQL00001 directory, and the database MYDB would have been created in the SQL00002 directory under the NODE*xxxx* directory.

Under the database's SQL0000*x* directory, DB2 will create one directory for each of the three default table spaces, unless the table spaces were defined to use different containers in the CREATE DATABASE command.

By default, the system catalog table space will use the directory SQLT0000.0, the system temporary table space will use the directory SQLT0001.0, and the default user table space (USERSPACE1) will use the directory SQLT0002.0.

There is also a subdirectory named SQLOGDIR to hold the database log files. This location can be changed once the database has been created.

Given the following command, execute in the instance named *db2inst1*.

```
create database sample on /database
```

On the Linux or UNIX server where database partition 0 is defined, the following directory structures are created:

```
/database/db2inst1/NODE0000/sqldbdir
/database/db2inst1/NODE0000/SQL00001
```

On the server where database partition 1 is defined, the following directory structures are created:

```
/database/db2inst1/NODE0001/sqldbdir
/database/db2inst1/NODE0001/SQL00001
```

These directories would be created as illustrated in Figure 1.3.

If a second database is created in the same instance (i.e., db2inst1) on the same path using the command:

```
create database sample on /database
```

the directory structure would then look like Figure 1.4.

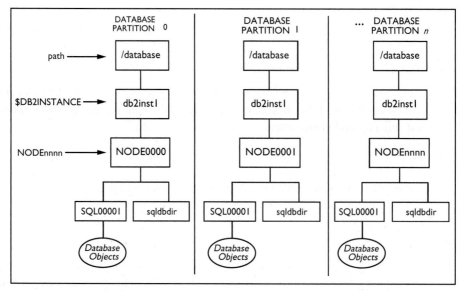

Figure 1.3
Directory structure for multi-partitioned database.

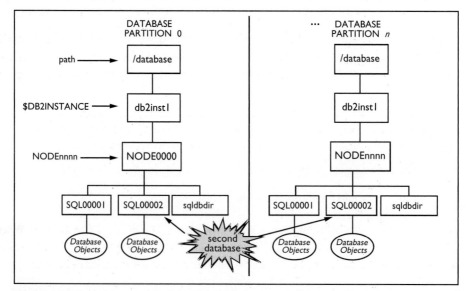

Figure 1.4
Directory structure for two databases in a multi-partitioned database.

> **N O T E**   The sqldbdir directory contains the database directory, i.e., a listing of all databases that are in the drive / path.

TABLE SPACES

A table space is a logical entity used to define where tables and indexes will be stored within a database. All DB2 tables and indexes reside in table spaces, allowing complete control over where the table and index data are physically stored.

A table space can be created using one or more underlying physical storage devices called *containers*. This provides the ability to create a physical database design that provides optimal performance in any physical environment.

Details about the table spaces in a database can be obtained using:

      1. GET SNAPSHOT FOR TABLESPACES ON <database name>
      2. LIST TABLESPACES

Containers

A table space is a logical database entity; table space containers are the physical storage associated with a table space. A container definition depends on the type of table space being created and can be defined as an operating system directory, a logical device/drive name, or a file.

When a table space is created, it must have at least one container associated with it. A single table space can contain multiple containers, but a container can belong to only one table space.

Details about a table space's containers can be obtained using the LIST TABLESPACE CONTAINERS FOR x command, where x is the table space's ID. A table space's ID can be found using the LIST TABLESPACES command and searching for the table space of interest.

> **N O T E** In general, containers must reside on local disks and cannot be created on LAN-redirected drives, NFS-mounted file systems, or GPFS file systems.

Extents

The basic unit of storage in a DB2 database is the page, and pages can be different sizes. When pages are written to disk, they are grouped into contiguous ranges called *extents*. The extent size for a table space is specified for the table space when it is created and cannot be changed.

The DFT_EXTENT_SZ database configuration parameter specifies the default extent size for all table spaces in the database. This value can be overridden when the table space is created, using the EXTENTSIZE parameter of the CREATE TABLESPACE statement.

When a table space is created with more than one container, DB2 will write the data to the containers in a round-robin fashion. DB2 will fill an extent in one container, then fill an extent in the next container, and so on, until it has written an extent in all of the containers in the table space. DB2 will then fill the second extent in the first container, and so on.

However, this may change if containers are added or removed using the ALTER TABLESPACE command.

In Figure 1.5, the first extent (Extent 0) is written to Container 0, Extent 1 is written to Container 1, Extent 2 is written to Container 2. At this point, there is one extent in each of the containers, so DB2 will go back to the first container and add the next extent. Therefore, Extent 3 is written to Container 0, Extent 4 is written to Container 1, and so on, as more data is added.

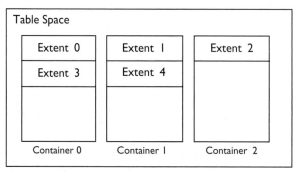

Figure 1.5
Extents written to containers.

> **N O T E** The first extent (extent 0) for each object can start in different containers. Not all objects start in container 0.

Creating Table Spaces

Creating a table space within a database assigns the specified containers to the table space and records the table space and container definitions and attributes in the database. When creating a table space, it is important to consider the following:

- What type of data the table space will hold
  - Regular data—Data or Index
  - Large/Long data
  - Temporary data

- What management type will be used
  - System Managed Space (SMS)
  - Database Managed Space (DMS)

- If using DMS, the type of container that will be used
  - File
  - Device

- What a good overhead and transfer rate would be, based on the underlying physical disks and/or disk subsystem being used for the container(s)
- The extent size and prefetch size that will best suit the workload and the underlying disks
- The page size that will be used for objects created within the table space
- The database partition group in which the table space will be placed
- The buffer pool(s) that will be used to manipulate data for the table space

The Table Space Types

There are three types of table spaces in DB2: regular, large, and temporary.

Regular Table Spaces

User-created tables are stored within regular table spaces. By default, every DB2 database has at least one regular table space called *USERSPACE1*. This table space is created when the CREATE DATABASE command is executed. In previous versions of DB2, indexes had to be stored in regular table spaces; however, in DB2 Version 8, indexes can be created in large table spaces, as well as in regular table spaces.

> **N O T E** In Version 7, large table spaces were known as *long table spaces* and could not hold indexes. Version 8 will recognize both the large and long keywords.

The system catalog tables are created and stored in a special regular table space called *SYSCATSPACE*. By default, the USERSPACE1 and SYSCATSPACE table spaces are created as SMS, but they can be created as DMS when the database is created.

The USERSPACE1 table space may be dropped once another user table space has been created; however, the SYSCATSPACE table space cannot be dropped because it holds the system catalog tables for the database.

The maximum size of a regular table space depends on the page size used for the table space. For a table space with 4-KB pages, the maximum size is 64 GB. For a table space with 32-KB pages, the maximum size is 512 GB.

The catalog table space   The DB2 system catalogs store all of the metadata about all of the DB2 objects in the database. The catalog table space is known as SYSCATSPACE and is created when the database is created. The system catalog table space is a regular table space, but it is used only to store the database catalog tables.

The system catalog table space contains many tables of varying sizes. When using a DMS table space, a minimum of two extents will be allocated for each table object. Depending on the table space's extent size, a significant amount of allocated and unused space may result. If using a

DMS table space for the system catalogs, use a small extent size (2–4 pages) to minimize the amount of wasted space.

The catalog tables contain large object data type columns. These columns must be read from disk each time they are needed and do not use the buffer pool. By using an SMS table space or a DMS table space with file containers, DB2 can take advantage of the file system cache to handle the read requests for this data more quickly.

> **N O T E**   In a partitioned database, there is only one set of system catalogs, and they will be located on the catalog partition for the database.

Large Table Spaces

If a table contains indexes, LongVarchar or Large Object (LOB) columns, the table may be split between table spaces. This must be done when the table is created and cannot be changed afterward. All columns not defined as LongVarchar or LOB must be stored in the regular table space; however, any indexes or LongVarchar or LOB columns can be stored in the regular table space or in a large table space, depending on how the table was created. To store indexes or LongVarchar and LOB objects in a separate table space from the other regular data columns, the LONG IN and/or INDEX IN options must be specified on the CREATE TABLE statement.

The maximum size of a large table space is 2 terabytes (TB).

> **N O T E**   In DB2 Version 7, large table spaces were called *long table spaces*.

Temporary Table Spaces

Temporary table spaces can be either system temporary table spaces or user temporary table spaces. System temporary table spaces are used by DB2 during SQL operations for holding transient data, such as intermediate tables, during sort operations, reorganizing tables, creating indexes, and joining tables. A database must have at least one system temporary table space. By default, an SMS table space called *TEMPSPACE1* is created when the database is created. It can be dropped after another temporary table space with the same page size has been created.

In the event that a temporary table is created, DB2 will create the temporary table in the system temporary table space with the largest buffer pool that has a page size large enough to hold the temporary table. The largest buffer pool is based on total size, not on the number of pages. For example: a 1,000-page, 4-KB buffer pool is smaller than a 1,000-page, 8-KB buffer pool. If there are multiple system temporary table spaces with the same page size and the same size buffer pool, DB2 will then choose the system temporary table space for the temporary table in a round-robin manner.

If applicatons or users will create declared global temporary tables while working with the database, a user temporary table space must exist in the database to hold the temporary table.

Temporary table spaces can be either SMS or DMS.

The maximum size of a temporary table space is 2 TB.

SMS Table Spaces

SMS table spaces use the file system manager provided by the operating system to allocate and manage the space where the tables are stored. Within an SMS table space, each container is an operating system directory, and the table objects are created as files within them. When creating an SMS table space, the user must specify the name of the directory for each of the containers. DB2 will create the tables within the directories used in the table space by using unique file names for each object.

If a table space is created with more than one container, DB2 will balance the amount of data written to the containers. Because containers cannot be dynamically added to an SMS table space once it has been created, it is important to know the size requirements of the table space and to create all required containers when the table space is created.

> **N O T E** Containers can be added to an SMS table space by first backing up the database, then performing a redirected restore. They cannot be added using the ALTER TABLESPACE statement.

An SMS table space can be created using the following command:

```
CREATE TABLESPACE <NAME>
MANAGED BY SYSTEM
USING ('<path1>', '<path2>', '<path3>')
```

When the path is specified for an SMS container, it can be either the absolute path or the relative path to the directory. If the directory does not exist, DB2 will create it. If the directory does exist, it cannot contain any files or subdirectories.

For example:

```
CREATE TABLESPACE ts1
MANAGED BY SYSTEM
USING ('D:\DIR1')
```

specifies the absolute path to the directory; therefore, DB2 would create the DIR1 directory on the D: drive on the database server if it does not already exist. The statement:

```
CREATE TABLESPACE ts2
MANAGED BY SYSTEM
USING ('DIR1')
```

specifies the relative path DIR1; therefore, DB2 would create the DIR1 directory under the database home directory. For this example, the table space will be created in the nonpartitioned database MYDB, which is the only database that was created in the default instance (DB2) on the D: drive on a Windows server. Therefore, the database will be created in the D:\DB2\NODE0000\SQL00001 directory. The three default table spaces will then use the following directories:

```
D:\DB2\NODE0000\SQL00001\SQLT0000.0        -        catalog table space
D:\DB2\NODE0000\SQL00001\SQLT0001.0        -        temp table space
D:\DB2\NODE0000\SQL00001\SQLT0002.0        -        userspace1
```

The table space TS2 would be created in the subdirectory DIR1 under the D:\DB2\NODE0000\SQL00001 directory, as shown below:

```
D:\DB2\NODE0000\SQL00001\DIR1
```

The following SQL statements create an SMS table space with three containers on three separate drives/file systems. Note that the table space name is the same in the examples, showing the differences between the UNIX/Linux and Windows table space definitions:

```
CREATE TABLESPACE smstbspc
MANAGED BY SYSTEM
USING ('d:\tbspc1', 'e:\tbspc2', 'f:\ tbspc3')


CREATE TABLESPACE smstbspc
MANAGED BY SYSTEM
USING ('/dbase/container1', '/dbase/container2', '/dbase/container3')
```

When an SMS table space is created, DB2 will create a tag file (SQLTAG.NAM) inside each container to uniquely identify the container. This file is called the *container tag*, and it contains information that identifies the container number, the table space the container belongs to, and the database to which the table space belongs. This is used to ensure that no other table space attempts to use the same container, even if it is in a different database.

For the table space TS1 created using:

```
CREATE TABLESPACE ts1
MANAGED BY SYSTEM
USING ('/mydir1', '/mydir2')
EXTENTSIZE 4
```

DB2 would create two directories, /mydir1 and /mydir2, and within each directory, DB2 will create the tag file SQLTAG.NAM.

With SMS containers, DB2 stores each database object in its own file.

- The file names are assigned by DB2, based on the table ID for the table that is assigned when it is created.
- The file name for the data part of the table will then be SQL<objectid>.DAT.
- The file name for the block map for any MDC table will be SQL<objectid>.BKM.
- The file name for the indexes for the table will be SQL<objectid>.INX.
- The file name for any LongVarchar columns in the table will be SQL<objectid>.LF.
- The file name for any LOB columns in the table will be SQL<objectid>.LB.
  - For each LOB object, there is also a LOB allocation object needed.
  - This will be stored in the file named SQL<objectid>.LBA.

For example, for a table with an object ID of 14, the following files may be created:

```
SQL00014.DAT    -    Normal data records
SQL00014.INX    -    Indexes
SQL00014.LF     -    Long varchar column data
SQL00014.LB     -    LOB column data
SQL00014.LBA    -    LOB allocation information
SQL00014.BKM    -    Block information for MDC tables
```

When the following SQL statements are run to create the tables T1 and T2, two additional files will be created, one for each table. The first table, T1, will be assigned object ID 2 and, therefore, will use the file SQL00002.DAT. The table T2 will be assigned object ID 3 and, therefore, will use the file SQL00003.DAT.

```
create table T1 (c1 int) in TS1
create table T2 (c1 float) in TS1
```

> **N O T E**   Object ID 1 is reserved and is not used for user-created tables.

As shown in Figure 1.6, the first extent of table TS1 is created in container 0 (mydir1), the second extent in container 1 (mydir2), the third extent will be back in container 0, and so on. The table T2 will have its first extent created in container 1, its second extent in container 0, and so on.

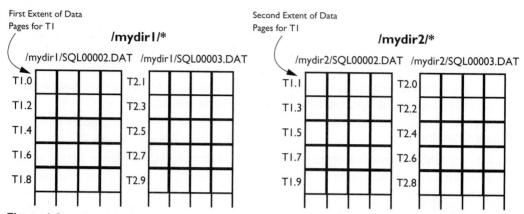

Figure 1.6
Tables in an SMS table space.

The initial empty file(s) will be created in one container only but will be written to subsequent containers as data is added to the table. The starting point for each table (i.e., the container where each table will have its first extent created) is determined using the following formula:

```
Start Container ID = Objectid % number of containers
```

> **N O T E**   % = modulus, which is the remainder after dividing the first number by the second number.

For the example above, table T1 has an objectid of 2; therefore, it will start in container:

```
Start Container ID = 2 % 2 = 0
```

Table T1 has an objectid of 3; therefore, it will start in container:

```
Start Container ID = 3 % 2 = 1
```

Enabling Multipage File Allocation

In an SMS table space, by default the object files are extended one page at a time as the object grows. Inserting a large number of rows into a table can result in a great deal of I/O that can have a negative impact on the database performance. The db2empfa tool enables DB2 to allocate or extend the object file by a full extent at a time. This tool is enabled at the database level, and when it is run, DB2 will allocate empty pages to fill up the last extent in all SMS table space containers within the specified database.

> **N O T E**   Once the db2empfa tool has been run, it cannot be undone.

DMS Table Spaces

When using DMS table spaces, the database manager controls the storage allocation within the table space. Within a DMS table space, a container can be either an operating system file or a raw logical volume or disk partition. With DMS table spaces, the space is preallocated when the table space is created. When creating a DMS table space, the user must specify the name of the file, logical volume or disk partition, as well as the size of the container(s).

Device Containers

In Linux and UNIX, a device container is mapped to an underlying logical volume. In Windows, a device container is mapped to an unformatted disk partition. The device that the container is created on cannot be used for any other purpose, i.e., it cannot contain any file systems and should not be formatted. When specifying the size of the container, make sure that all of the space on the device is used because no unused space will be available for any other use and will be unused. However, this space can be used at a later time if the table space containers are extended or resized. The size of the container can be specified in the number of pages, KB, MB, or GB.

For example:

```
create tablespace mytbspc managed by database using
   (device '/dev/rmydisk1' 20000)
create tablespace mytbspc managed by database using
   (device '\\.\G:' 20000)
create tablespace mytbspc managed by database using
   (device '/dev/rmydisk1' 200M)
create tablespace mytbspc managed by database using
   (device '\\.\G:' 200M)
```

File Containers

A file container is an operating system file of a given size and is created when the table space is created. The name used to define a file container can be the absolute path or the relative path to the file. If the file does not exist, DB2 will create the file and initialize it to the specific size. If the file does exist, DB2 will check the file to verify that it is not already used for some other purpose. If the file is not the size specified for the container, it will be either expanded or shrunk to match the specified container size. The size of the file can be specified in the number of pages, KB, MB, or GB.

For example:

```
create tablespace mytbspc managed by database using
   (file '/myfile1' 20000)
create tablespace mytbspc managed by database using
   (file 'G:\myfile1' 20000)
```

```
create tablespace mytbspc managed by database using
   (file '/myfile1' 200M)
create tablespace mytbspc managed by database using
   (file 'G:\myfile1' 200M)
```

Raw Logical Volumes vs. File Systems

Within the database community, there has been a long running debate surrounding the use of raw logical volumes (raw devices) versus file systems. Advocates of raw logical volumes stress the performance gains that can be realized through their use, whereas file system supporters emphasize the ease of use and manageability features of file systems. As with the other aspects of system design, a decision must be made as to which is more important: performance or manageability.

To understand the performance advantages associated with raw logical volumes better, it is helpful to have an understanding of the impact of the file system cache. Most UNIX file systems set aside an area of memory (the cache) to hold recently accessed files, which can subsequently allow physical I/O requests to be satisfied from memory instead of from disk. If DB2 requests data that is not already in the cache, the operating system will read the data from disk into the cache, then copy the data to the DB2 buffer pool so that it can be used. Therefore, each read request translates into a disk read, followed by a copy of the data from the cache to the database buffer pool.

When the data is read from the cache, I/O requests can be satisfied in nanoseconds instead of the milliseconds that would be required to retrieve the data from disk. In addition, most UNIX file systems employ the use of a sequential read-ahead mechanism to prefetch data into the cache when it detects that a file is being accessed sequentially.

In non-database environments, the UNIX file system cache can significantly reduce I/O wait time for heavily accessed files. However, the performance benefits of file system caching in database environments are not so clear. This is due to the fact that most RDBMS systems, including DB2, also allocate a region of memory for caching frequently accessed data (i.e., the database buffer pools). This results in double buffering of the data in the file system cache and the DB2 buffer pool.

In 64-bit systems, the memory used by the file system cache could be better utilized by the database buffer pools. In 32-bit systems, with their associated shared memory limits, the file system cache can provide benefit for some workloads.

The primary benefit of raw logical volumes is that they bypass the file system cache by directly accessing the underlying logical device. The extra memory saved by eliminating the file system cache can then be allocated to the database buffer pools. In addition, overall CPU utilization is decreased, due to the fact that the system no longer has to copy the data from the file system cache to the database buffer pools.

> **N O T E** Another benefit of raw logical volumes in AIX is that there is no inode management overhead, as opposed to file systems where the inode is locked when the file is accessed.

The Container Tag

When a DMS table space is created, the file or raw device containers will be preallocated by DB2. Within the first extent of each container, DB2 will create the container tag to identify the container.

In previous versions of DB2, the container tag for DMS containers was stored in a single page at the beginning of the container to minimize the space requirements. Large Storage Area Networks (SANs) and disk arrays using Redundant Array of Independent Disks (RAID) technology have become more popular, and many databases are being created on RAID protected disks. When using a one-page container tag, the beginning and end of an extent could not be made to line up with the beginning and end of a stripe on the underlying disks, and this could cause suboptimal I/O because each I/O would need to access more than one disk. If the extent size is set to be equal to or an integer multiple of the RAID strip size, by making the container tag a full extent in size, the I/Os would always line up with the underlying disk stripes. In DB2 Version 7, the container tag could be made a full extent using the DB2_STRIPED_CONTAINERS registry variable. Now, in DB2 Version 8, the container tag is created as a full extent in size by default for DMS table spaces.

To force DB2 to create the tag on a single page, the new registry variable, DB2_USE_PAGE_CONTAINER_TAG, should be set to ON.

> **N O T E** For databases migrated from Version 7 with page-sized container tags, the tag size will not change, regardless of the registry variable setting. DB2 will work fine in this case.

> **N O T E** A restore will respect the type of the containers and the size of the container tag in the backup image, whereas a redirected restore will respect the registry variable.

Overhead in DMS Table Spaces

There are some extents created within each DMS table space that are used by DB2 to control the allocation of the extents within the table space. The first extent in each container will be the container tag. There are three extents of overhead that will be used in addition to the container tag. In addition to these four extents required (the minimum if there is only one container), DB2 requires that there be a minimum of two additional extents so that at least one object can be created in the table space.

The overhead for a table space is summarized in Figure 1.7.

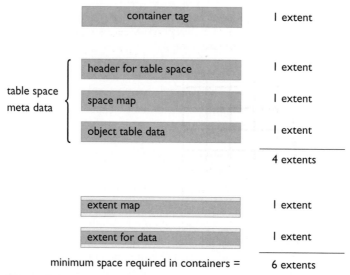

Figure 1.7
Overhead extents in a DMS table space.

For the table space TS1 created using:

```
create tablespace TS1
   managed by database using
   (file '/myfile' 10 M, device '/dev/rhd7' 20 M)
   extentsize 4
```

DB2 would create the file /myfile with a size of 10 MB and would also use 20 MB on the raw logical volume rhd7. The table space would logically look like Figure 1.8.

When the following SQL statements are run to create the tables T1 and T2, the first table, T1, will be assigned object ID 4, and the table T2 will be assigned object ID 5.

```
db2 create table T1 (c1 int ...) in TS1
db2 create table T2 (c1 float ...) in TS1
```

N O T E Object IDs start at 4 for DMS table spaces.

In a DMS table space, each object also needs an extent of overhead to be used to map the allocation of the object within the table space. Therefore, the logical view of the table space after the two tables have been created would look like Figure 1.9.

Table Space (Logical) Address Map

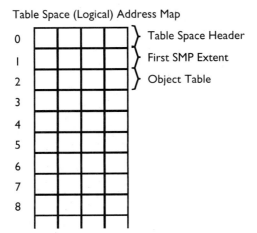

Figure 1.8
Logical view of the table space.

Table Space (Logical) Address Map

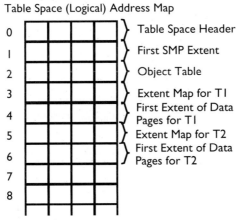

Figure 1.9
Logical view of the table space with tables T1 and T2.

Some important points to remember with regard to DMS table spaces are:

• An empty table space will always have at least four extents that cannot be used by data but are needed for the table space (because of the container tag, table space header, object table, and the SMP extent).

> **N O T E** The used pages shown in the table space snapshot do not count the pages used for the container tag.

- The minimum number of extents needed to hold a single table with no indexes or LOB/ Long Varchar columns is two (for the data object and the extent map for the data object).
- The smallest size allowed for a table space is six extents. Attempting to create a table space with a smaller number of extents available will result in a table space full error being returned.

Should the Temporary Table Space Be SMS or DMS?

Due to the extra overhead associated with creating an object in a DMS table space, the temporary table space should be SMS in most cases. This is especially true for Online Transaction Processing (OLTP) type workloads with very small, if any, sorts.

For a system that creates very large temporary tables that are flushed to disk and prefetched back into the buffer pool, a DMS temporary table space may provide better performance.

ADDITIONAL TABLE SPACE OPTIONS/PARAMETERS

When creating or altering a table space, there are a number of options or parameters that can be specified to control the placement and operation of the table space. The options that can be specified for a table space include:

- Page Size: Specifies the size of the pages that will be used in the table space. The page size can be 4 KB, 8 KB, 16 KB, or 32 KB. In order to create a table space with a page size other than 4 KB, there must already be a buffer pool with the same page size.
  - The default page size is 4096 bytes (4 KB).
  - By default, a buffer pool with a 4-KB page size is created when a database is created.

- Extent Size: Specifies the number of pages that will be written to a container before writing to the next container in the table space.
  - The default value is specified by the DFT_EXTENT_SZ database configuration parameter.
  - The default is good for most situations, but if using disk striping, try to match the extent size to the underlying disk or file system stripe size.

- Prefetch Size: Specifies the number of pages that will be read from the table space when data prefetching is being performed. Prefetching reads data for an SQL statement from disk into the buffer pool before it is used so that the statement need not wait for the I/O to be performed.
  - The default value is provided by the DFT_PREFETCH_SZ database configuration parameter.
  - As a general rule of thumb, use the following formula to determine the prefetch size for the table space:

```
Prefetch Size = min (512, number of containers * extent size)
```

- Buffer Pool: Specifies the name of the buffer pool used for manipulating data and index pages for tables in this table space. The buffer pool must exist, and the page size of the buffer pool must match the page size specified for the table space.
- Overhead: Specifies the I/O controller overhead and the disk seek and latency time, in milliseconds. This number should be an average for all containers that belong to the table space (if it is not the same for all of the containers). This value is used to determine the cost of I/O during query optimization.
- Transfer Rate: Specifies the time required to read one page into memory, in milliseconds. This number should be an average for all containers that belong to the table space (if it is not the same for all of the containers). This value is used to determine the I/O cost during query optimization.
- Dropped Table Recovery: Specifies whether tables in the table space that have been dropped can be recovered using the RECOVER TABLE ON option of the ROLLFORWARD command. This option can be specified only for a REGULAR table space.

> **N O T E**   Once a table space has been created, the page size and extent size cannot be changed.

Listing Table Spaces

Information about the table spaces within a database can be captured using the GET SNAPSHOT FOR TABLESPACES on <database name> command.

The basic information returned by the GET SNAPSHOT FOR TABLESPACES command includes the following:

- Table space ID, the internal ID that DB2 uses for the table space
- Table space storage type (DMS or SMS)
- Table space contents, which can be Regular (any data), Large, or Temporary
- Page size for the table space
- Extent size for the table space
- Prefetch size for the table space
- Current buffer pool used by the table space
- Buffer pool used at the next database startup
- State, a hexadecimal value indicating the current table space state, as well as a description of the state
- Size, in pages
- Number of useable pages
- Number of used pages
- Minimum point in time for roll forward recovery

- Number of table space quiescers
- Number of containers
- Container information, such as
  - Container name
  - Container ID
  - Container type
  - Total pages in the container
  - Number of useable pages in the container
  - Stripe set number
  - An indicator of whether the container is accessible
- The table space map for DMS table spaces

An example of the output of the GET SNAPSHOT FOR TABLESPACES command for an SMS table space is below.

```
Tablespace Snapshot

First database connect timestamp    = 01-07-2003 15:26:42.235201
Last reset timestamp                =
Snapshot timestamp                  = 01-07-2003 15:47:20.522435
Database name                       = W
Database path                       = C:\DB2\NODE0000\SQL00004\
Input database alias                = W
Number of accessed tablespaces      = 3

Tablespace name                     = SYSCATSPACE
   Tablespace ID                    = 0
   Tablespace Type                  = System managed space
   Tablespace Content Type          = Any data
   Tablespace Page size (bytes)     = 4096
   Tablespace Extent size (pages)   = 32
   Tablespace Prefetch size (pages) = 16
   Buffer pool ID currently in use  = 1
   Buffer pool ID next startup      = 1
   Tablespace State                 = 0x'00000000'
   Detailed explanation:
     Normal
   Total number of pages            = 0
   Number of usable pages           = 0
   Number of used pages             = 0
   Minimum Recovery Time            =
   Number of quiescers              = 0
   Number of containers             = 1
```

```
Container Name                      = C:\DB2\NODE0000\SQL00004\SQLT0000.0

Container ID                        = 0
Container Type                      = Path
Total Pages in Container            = 0
Usable Pages in Container           = 0
Stripe Set                          = 0
Container is accessible             = Yes
```

An example of the output of the GET SNAPSHOT FOR TABLESPACES command for a DMS table space is below.

```
Tablespace name                     = TS1
   Tablespace ID                    = 3
   Tablespace Type                  = Database managed space
   Tablespace Content Type          = Any data
   Tablespace Page size (bytes)     = 4096
   Tablespace Extent size (pages)   = 32
   Tablespace Prefetch size (pages) = 16
   Buffer pool ID currently in use  = 1
   Buffer pool ID next startup      = 1
   Tablespace State                 = 0x'00000000'
   Detailed explanation:
     Normal
   Total number of pages            = 5000
   Number of usable pages           = 4960
   Number of used pages             = 160
   Number of pending free pages     = 0
   Number of free pages             = 4800
   High water mark (pages)          = 160
   Rebalancer Mode                  = No Rebalancing
   Minimum Recovery Time            =
   Number of quiescers              = 0
   Number of containers             = 1
   Container Name                   = d:\ts1
      Container ID                  = 0
      Container Type                = File (extent sized tag)
      Total Pages in Container      = 5000
      Usable Pages in Container     = 4960
      Stripe Set                    = 0
      Container is accessible       = Yes

   Table space map:
   Range   Stripe Stripe  Max      Max   Start End    Adj.  Containers
   Number  Set    Offset  Extent   Page  Stripe Stripe
   [   0] [   0]     0     154      4959     0    154    0    1 (0)
```

The LIST TABLESPACES command can also be used to list the basic or detailed information about the table spaces within a database. The syntax for this command is:

```
LIST TABLESPACES [SHOW DETAIL]
```

The basic information returned by the LIST TABLESPACES command includes the following:

- Table space ID, the internal ID that DB2 uses for the table space
- Table space name
- Table space storage type (DMS or SMS)
- Table space contents, which can be Regular (any data), Large, or Temporary
- State, a hexadecimal value indicating the current table space state, as well as a description of the state

An example of the output of the LIST TABLESPACES command is below.

```
Tablespaces for Current Database

Tablespace ID                        = 0
Name                                 = SYSCATSPACE
Type                                 = System managed space
Contents                             = Any data
State                                = 0x0000
   Detailed explanation:
      Normal

Tablespace ID                        = 1
Name                                 = TEMPSPACE1
Type                                 = System managed space
Contents                             = System Temporary data
State                                = 0x0000
   Detailed explanation:
      Normal

Tablespace ID                        = 2
Name                                 = USERSPACE1
Type                                 = System managed space
Contents                             = Any data
State                                = 0x0000
   Detailed explanation:
      Normal
```

If the SHOW DETAIL option is specified, the following additional details will also be shown:

- Total number of pages
- Number of useable pages
- Number of used pages
- Number of free pages
- High water mark (in pages)
- Page size (in bytes)
- Extent size (in bytes)
- Prefetch size (in pages)
- Number of containers

An example of the output of the LIST TABLESPACES SHOW DETAIL command for the USERSPACE1 table space is shown below.

```
Tablespace ID                       = 2
Name                                = USERSPACE1
Type                                = Database managed space
Contents                            = Any data
State                               = 0x0000
   Detailed explanation:
      Normal
Total pages                         = 100000
Useable pages                       = 999968
Used pages                          = 5740
Free pages                          = Not applicable
High water mark (pages)             = Not applicable
Page size (bytes)                   = 4096
Extent size (pages)                 = 32
Prefetch size (pages)               = 16
Number of containers                = 1
```

This additional information is important in determining how full the table spaces are and whether any action is required, such as adding new containers, extending or resizing an existing container, sizing of database/table space backups, and so on.

> **N O T E**   For SMS table spaces, the information does not indicate how full the table space is.

SYSCAT.TABLESPACES View

This view contains a row for each table space defined in the database. It has the following columns:

    TBSPACE: The name of the table space
    DEFINER: The authorization ID of the user who created the table space
    CREATE_TIME: The timestamp when the table space was created
    TBSPACEID: The internal table space identifier
    TBSPACETYPE: The type of the table space:
        S = System managed space
        D = Database managed space
    DATATYPE: The type of data (contents) that can be stored in the table space:
        A = All types of permanent data
        L = Large data only
        T = Temporary tables only
        U = Declared global temporary tables
    EXTENTSIZE: The size of an extent, in pages
    PREFETCHSIZE: The number of pages to be read for each prefetch operation
    OVERHEAD: The disk controller overhead, seek time, and latency time, in milliseconds
    TRANSFERRATE: The time required to read one page into the buffer
    PAGESIZE: The size of the pages in the table space
    DBPGNAME: Name of the database partition group for the table space
    BUFFERPOOLID: ID of the buffer pool used by the table space
    DROP_RECOVERY: Specification of whether the tables in the table space are recoverable after a DROP TABLE statement:
        N = table is not recoverable
        Y = table is recoverable
    REMARKS: User-provided comments
    NGNAME: For compatibility with scripts and tools written for previous versions of DB2, specification of the database partition group for the table space

SYSCAT.TABLES View

The SYSCAT.TABLES catalog view also contains columns that indicate which table spaces are used to store the different table objects. The columns of interest are:

    TBSPACEID: The internal identifier of the table space where the table's data object is stored
    TBSPACE: The name of the table space where the table's data object is stored
    INDEX_TBSPACE: The name of the table space that holds all indexes for the table. If this is NULL, the indexes are stored in the TBSPACE table space.

LONG_TBSPACE: The name of the table space that holds all large/long data for the table. If this is NULL, the LOBs and Long Varchars are stored in the TBSPACE table space.

When Is a Table Space Full?

An SMS table space is considered full when any one of its containers becomes full.

To increase the amount of space allocated to an SMS table space:

- Add space to the underlying file systems or drives, using operating system commands or utilities.
- Perform a redirected restore, specifying more containers and/or larger file systems or drives.

A DMS table space is considered full when all of its containers are full and all of the extents within the containers have been used.

To increase the amount of space allocated to a DMS table space:

- Add new containers to the table space.
- Extend or resize the existing containers.
- Perform a redirected restore, specifying more and/or larger containers.

Table Space Maps and Table Space Extent Maps

When a DMS table space is created, an associated table space map and a table space extent map are also created. In the table space map, all of the initial containers are lined up so that they all start in stripe 0. This means that data will be striped evenly across all of the table space containers until the individual containers fill up.

The following example will illustrate this in more detail. A DMS table space is created with four containers, as follows:

```
CREATE TABLESPACE spc1
  MANAGED BY DATABASE
  USING (FILE 'c0' 15)
  USING (FILE 'c0' 11)
  USING (FILE 'c0' 15)
  USING (FILE 'c0' 17)
  EXTENTSIZE 2
```

In DB2 Version 8, the container tag will now use one full extent by default instead of the one page it used in DB2 Version 7. Therefore, the containers will contain the following number of useable extents:

```
container number 0 (cont0):        6 extents   [ (15 -2) / 2 ]
container number 1 (cont1):        4 extents   [ (11 -2) / 2 ]
container number 2 (cont2):        6 extents   [ (15 -2) / 2 ]
container number 3 (cont3):        7 extents   [ (17 -2) / 2 ]
```

> **N O T E**   The calculations above show the number of pages for the container, minus one extent for the container tag, divided by the extent size.

Before looking at the extent map for the table space, consider the following definitions:

Stripe: A contiguous number of extents spanning one or more containers without repeating

Range: A contiguous number of stripes sharing the same common set of containers

Stripe set: A contiguous number of ranges

Conceptually, the extent map would look like the following:

Containers

	0	1	2	3
0	0	1	2	3
1	4	5	6	7
2	8	9	10	11
3	12	13	14	15
4	16		17	18
5	19		20	21
6				22

(Stripes)

For example, Extent 0 can be found in Stripe 0 of Container 0, Extent 14 can be found in Stripe 3 of Container 2, and Extent 22 can be found in Stripe 6 of Container 3.

The table space map that would be created when the table space is created would look like:

Range Number	Stripe Set	Stripe Offset	Max Extent	Max Page	Start Stripe	End Stripe	Adj.	Containers
[0]	[0]	0	15	31	0	3	0	4(0, 1, 2, 3)
[1]	[0]	0	21	43	0	5	0	3(0, 2, 3)
[2]	[0]	0	22	45	0	6	0	1(3)

As shown, there are three ranges in this table space map. The first range maps from Extent 0 to Extent 15. The second range maps from Extent 16 to Extent 21. The third range maps only Extent 22.

The fields defined in the table space map are:

- **Range:** The range number. This always starts at zero (0).
- **Stripe Set:** The stripe set number. This always starts at zero (0).
- **Stripe Offset:** The extent number where the stripe set begins.
- **Max Extent:** The maximum extent number found in the range.
- **Max Page:** The maximum page number found in the range.
- **Start Stripe:** The number of the stripe where the range starts in the map.
- **End Stripe:** The number of the stripe where the range ends in the map.
- **Adj:** This is known as the adjustment, and it specifies how far a range is shifted during a rebalance.
- **Containers:** The array of containers that are part of the range.

For the table space created using:

```
CREATE TABLESPACE dmsfiletbspc
MANAGED BY DATABASE
USING
  (FILE '/tbspcs/cont1' 50, FILE '/tbspcs/cont2' 50, FILE '/tbspcs/cont3' 50)
EXTENTSIZE 10
PREFETCHSIZE 30
```

the extent map would look like the following:

Containers

	0	1	2
0	0	1	2
1	3	4	5
2	6	7	8
3	9	10	11

Stripes

The table space map would look like the following:

Range Number	Stripe Set	Stripe Offset	Max Extent	Max Page	Start Stripe	End Stripe	Adj.	Containers
[0]	[0]	0	11	119	0	3	0	3(0, 1, 2)

For the table space created using:

```
CREATE TABLESPACE dmsspc
MANAGED BY DATABASE
USING
  (FILE '/tbspcs/cont1' 50, FILE '/tbspcs/cont2' 30, FILE '/tbspcs/cont3' 40)
EXTENTSIZE 10
```

the extent map would look like the following:

Containers

The table space map would look like the following:

Range Number	Stripe Set	Stripe Offset	Max Extent	Max Page	Start Stripe	End Stripe	Adj.	Containers
[0]	[0]	0	5	59	0	1	0	3(0, 1, 2)
[1]	[0]	0	7	69	2	2	0	2(0, 2)
[2]	[0]	0	8	79	3	3	0	1(0)

Altering a Table Space

The ALTER TABLESPACE statement is used to modify the storage or I/O characteristics of an existing table space. Although the I/O characteristics can be modified for both SMS and DMS table spaces, the storage characteristics can generally be modified only for DMS table spaces.

The ALTER TABLESPACE statement can be used to add containers to existing DMS table spaces or to remove existing containers from a DMS table space. A container cannot be removed from an SMS table space and can be added to an SMS table space only on a partition where there are no existing containers for the table space using the *system container* clause.

With DMS table spaces, the containers can also be made larger or smaller using the ALTER TABLESPACE statement.

When a container is added to or removed from a table space, the existing data may need to be rebalanced among the new set of containers.

Alter Table Space Options

The following options can be used to alter a table space:

ADD: Used to add one or more containers to the specified table space. When adding a container to a table space, the container can be added to the last stripe set in the table space.

If the container is added to an existing stripe set, the stripe set can be explicitly specified using the ADD TO STRIPE SET option. Otherwise, it will be added to the existing table space, based on the size of the existing containers and the size of the new container. If the BEGIN NEW

STRIPE SET option is specified, the container will be added to the end of the table space in a new stripe set. This will avoid any potential data rebalance.

Consider a table space created with the following statement:

```
create tablespace ts1 managed by database using
   (file 'cont0' 60,
   file 'cont1' 60,
   file 'cont2' 40)
   extentsize 10
```

Because each container will have a tag consuming one extent, the containers will then be able to hold five extents, five extents, and three extents of data, respectively, for a total of 13 extents.

The extent map for the table space would look like the following:

Containers

	0	1	2	
0	0	1	2	
1	3	4	5	Range 1
2	6	7	8	
3	9	10		
4	11	12		Range 2

Stripes

The table space map would look like the following:

Range Number	Stripe Set	Stripe Offset	Max Extent	Max Page	Start Stripe	End Stripe	Adj.	Containers
[0]	[0]	0	8	89	0	2	0	3(0, 1, 2)
[1]	[0]	0	12	129	3	4	0	2(0, 1)

> **N O T E**   The following examples show containers of different sizes within a table space for the purposes of illustration. For performance reasons it is recommended that containers within a table space be the same size.

Using the table space created above, a container can be added in the following three ways.

Adding container with 3 extents

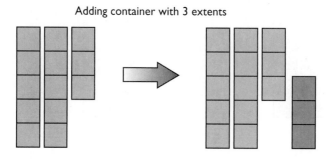

alter tablespace tsl add
(file 'cont3' 40)

Because the new container is not large enough to go from Stripe 0 to the end of the existing table space, it is added such that its last extent lines up with the highest stripe currently in the table space.

Adding container with 5 extents

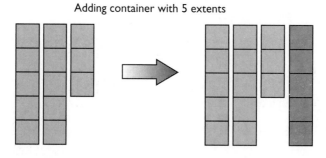

alter tablespace tsl add
(file 'cont3' 60)

In this case, the container is just large enough to go from Stripe 0 to the end of the existing table space, so it will be added and begin at Stripe 0.

Adding container with 6 extents

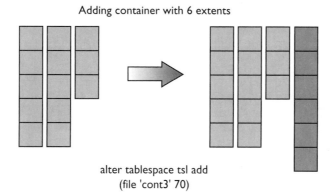

alter tablespace tsl add
(file 'cont3' 70)

In this case, the container is more than large enough to go from Stripe 0 to the end of the existing table space, so it will be added to begin at Stripe 0 and extend past the current last stripe for the table space.

When adding more than one container in the same ALTER TABLESPACE statement, the rules are applied to each new container individually. For example:

Adding 2 containers with 6 and 3 extents

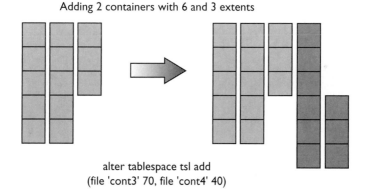

alter tablespace tsl add
(file 'cont3' 70, file 'cont4' 40)

In this case, the first new container is more than large enough to go from Stripe 0 to the end of the existing table space, so it will be added beginning at Stripe 0 and will extend past the current last stripe for the table space. The second new container is not large enough to go from Stripe 0 to the end of the existing table space, so it will be added such that its last extent lines up with the highest stripe in the table space, which would be the top of the first new container.

Adding 3 containers with 2, 3, and 4 extents

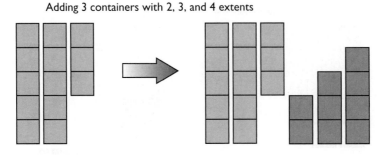

alter tablespace tsl add
(file 'cont3' 30, file 'cont4' 40, file 'cont5' 50)

In this case, none of the new extents are large enough to go from stripe zero to the end of the existing table space, so they will all be added such that their last extent lines up with the highest stripe currently in the table space.

Adding container with 3 extents

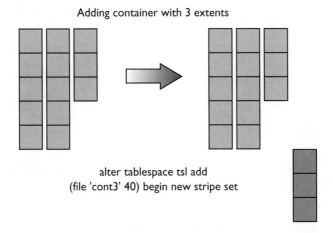

alter tablespace tsl add
(file 'cont3' 40) begin new stripe set

In the case where the BEGIN NEW STRIPE SET option is specified, the new container will be added to the table space, a new stripe will be created in the table space map, and the new container will start in this new stripe.

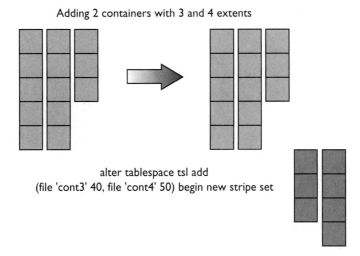

Adding 2 containers with 3 and 4 extents

alter tablespace tsl add
(file 'cont3' 40, file 'cont4' 50) begin new stripe set

When the BEGIN NEW STRIPE SET option is specified and there are multiple containers added in the same ALTER TABLESPACE statement, a new stripe set is created in the table space map, and the new containers are appended to the existing map. Each of the new containers will be positioned such that they start in the same stripe, regardless of their size.

DROP: Used to drop or remove one or more containers from the specified table space.

EXTEND: Used to increase the size of existing containers within a table space by a specified amount. This can be applied to a specific container or to all containers, using the ALL CONTAINERS clause.

REDUCE: Used to reduce the size of existing containers within a table space by a specified amount. This can be applied to a specific container or to all containers, using the ALL CONTAINERS clause.

RESIZE: Used to change the size of existing containers to the specified size. This can be applied to a specific container or to all containers, using the ALL CONTAINERS clause. When resizing more than one container, they must all be increased or decreased in size. It is not possible to increase the size of some containers while reducing the size of other containers.

When altering a table space, it is possible to perform multiple operations within the same command. However:

1. The BEGIN NEW STRIPE SET clause cannot be specified in the same ALTER TABLESPACE statement as ADD, DROP, EXTEND, REDUCE, and RESIZE (unless those options are being directed to different database partitions).
2. The stripe set value specified with the TO STRIPE SET clause must be within the valid range for the table space.

3. When adding or removing space from a table space, the following rules must be followed:

- ○ EXTEND and RESIZE can be used in the same statement, provided that the size of each specified container is increasing.
- ○ REDUCE and RESIZE can be used in the same statement, provided that the size of each specified container is decreasing.
- ○ EXTEND and REDUCE cannot be used in the same statement, unless they are being directed to different database partitions.
- ○ ADD cannot be used with REDUCE or DROP in the same statement, unless they are being directed to different database partitions.
- ○ DROP cannot be used with EXTEND or ADD in the same statement, unless they are being directed to different database partitions.

Adding Containers to a Table Space

When a container is added to a table space, the existing data typically will need to be rebalanced among the new set of containers unless the BEGIN NEW STRIPE SET option is specified. The process of rebalancing involves the moving of table space extents from one container to another in an attempt to keep the data striped evenly within the table space.

Adding containers to a table space and any potential rebalance operation is an online, asynchronous operation, but it will impact the overall performance of the server.

As a graphical example of this, consider a table space initially defined with two containers, as follows:

```
CREATE TABLESPACE ts1
MANAGED BY DATABASE
USING (FILE 'FILE1' 50)
USING (FILE 'FILE2' 50)
EXTENTSIZE 10
```

This table space would be graphically represented as follows:

File1	File2
tag	tag
Extent 0	Extent 1
Extent 2	Extent 3
Extent 4	Extent 5
Extent 6	Extent 7

Adding a third container of the same size to the table space using the following statement:

```
ALTER TABLESPACE ts1
ADD (FILE 'FILE3' 50)
```

may cause the table space to be rebalanced, depending on the amount of data in the table space. If no tables had yet been created in the table space, there would be no need to perform a rebalance; however, the table space map for the table space would still be changed and would then look like the following:

File1	File2	File3
tag	tag	tag
Extent 0	Extent 1	Extent 2
Extent 3	Extent 4	Extent 5
Extent 6	Extent 7	Extent 8
Extent 9	Extent 10	Extent 11

To show how DB2 would modify the internal table space extent maps and space maps, the following example will add a container with a length of 30 pages to the table space dmsspc, created previously with the following command:

```
ALTER TABLESPACE dmsspc
ADD (FILE '/tbspcs/cont4' 30)
```

This would add the container to the existing stripe set (because BEGIN NEW STRIPE SET was not specified) and would produce an extent map as shown below. If there were data in Extents 3 or higher before the container was added, the data would need to be rebalanced.

Containers

Stripes	0	1	2	3
0	0	1	2	3
1	4	5	6	7
2	8		9	
3	10			

The table space map would look like the following:

Range Number	Stripe Set	Stripe Offset	Max Extent	Max Page	Start Stripe	End Stripe	Adj.	Containers
[0]	[0]	0	7	79	0	1	0	4(0, 1, 2, 3)
[1]	[0]	2	9	99	2	2	0	2(0, 2)
[2]	[0]	3	10	109	3	3	0	1(0)

```
ALTER TABLESPACE dmsspc
   ADD (FILE '/tbspcs/cont4' 30)
   BEGIN NEW STRIPE SET
```

Adding a 30-page container to the table space dmsfiletbspc, created previously, with the BEGIN NEW STRIPE SET option specified, as above, would produce the extent map below.

Containers

Stripes	0	1	2	3
0	0	1	2	
1	3	4	5	
2	6	7	8	
3	9	10	11	
4				12
5				13

The table space map would look like the following:

```
Range   Stripe Stripe Max    Max   Start  End    Adj.  Containers
Number  Set    Offset Extent Page  Stripe Stripe
[0]     [0]    0      11     119   0      3      0     3 (0, 1, 2)
[1]     [1]    0      13     139   4      5      0     1 (3)
```

Dropping Containers from a Table Space

In DB2 Version 8, containers can be removed, or dropped, from an existing DMS table space. This can allow unused space to be freed back to the system for other file systems, or can also allow the reuse of the space for containers in another table space.

A container cannot be dropped from a table space if there will not be enough space in the table space to hold the existing data. Therefore, before dropping a container from a table space, it is a good idea to examine the table space high water mark and also to determine how much space is used and how much space is available to ensure that there is enough free space on the remainder of the containers to hold the data.

For the table space created using:

```
CREATE TABLESPACE tblspc
MANAGED BY DATABASE
USING (FILE '/tblspcs/cont1' 50,
       FILE '/tblspcs/cont2' 40,
       FILE '/tblspcs/cont3' 40)
EXTENTSIZE 10
```

The extent map would look like the following:

Containers

	0	1	2
0	0	1	2
1	3	4	5
2	6	7	8
3	9		

(Stripes)

The table space map would look like the following:

Range Number	Stripe Set	Stripe Offset	Max Extent	Max Page	Start Stripe	End Stripe	Adj.	Containers
[0]	[0]	0	8	89	0	2	0	3 (0, 1, 2)
[1]	[0]	0	9	99	3	3	0	1 (0)

To free up disk space back to the file system, the third container in the table space could be dropped with the following command:

```
ALTER TABLESPACE tblspc
   DROP (FILE '/tblspcs/cont3')
```

This would remove the container from the existing stripe set and would produce an extent map as shown below.

Containers

	0	1
0	0	1
1	2	3
2	4	5
3	6	

(Stripes)

If there were data in any of the extents in the container, the data would need to be rebalanced before the container can be physically removed from the table space. Once the rebalance has completed, the table space map would look like the following:

Range Number	Stripe Set	Stripe Offset	Max Extent	Max Page	Start Stripe	End Stripe	Adj.	Containers
[0]	[0]	0	5	59	0	2	0	2 (0, 1)
[1]	[0]	0	6	69	3	3	0	1 (0)

For a table space with five containers created using the following command:

```
CREATE TABLESPACE 5contspc
MANAGED BY DATABASE
USING (FILE 'd:\cont0' 5000,
       FILE 'e:\cont1' 5000,
       FILE 'f:\cont2' 5000,
       FILE 'g:\cont3' 5000,
       FILE 'h:\cont4' 5000)
```

removing Containers 2 and 4 from the table space could be done in two ways. The ALTER TABLESPACE statement could be called twice, once for each container, as follows:

```
ALTER TABLESPACE 5contspc
DROP (FILE 'f:\cont2')

ALTER TABLESPACE 5contspc
DROP (FILE 'f:\cont2')
```

Or the ALTER TABLESPACE statement could be called once, specifying both containers in the same statement, as follows:

```
ALTER TABLESPACE 5contspc
DROP (FILE 'f:\cont2', FILE 'f:\cont4')
```

In the second case, calling the ALTER TABLESPACE statement once and specifying both containers to be dropped would be the best option because DB2 would need to do two complete rebalances if the containers were dropped one at a time. By dropping both containers in the same statement, DB2 builds a new extent map for the table space and has to do only one rebalance.

The table space high water mark   The table space high water mark is very important when dropping containers from a table space or shrinking the containers within a table space. The high water mark is relevant only for DMS table spaces, and it represents the first page after the highest page number that has been allocated within the table space. The high water mark is not necessarily the same as the number of used pages because some objects may have been deleted from within the table space, and these unused pages do not have an effect on the high water mark. To illustrate this concept further, consider the following example.

- A table space has 100 useable pages, and its extent size is 10 (i.e., there are 10 extents available in the table space, not including the container tag).
- By default, extents 0, 1, and 2 will be used for the table space overhead.
- Create table T1.
  - Extent 3 will be allocated for the object map.
  - Extent 4 will be allocated for the table object.
- Create table T2.
  - Extent 5 will be allocated for the object map.
  - Extent 6 will be allocated for the table object.

- Drop table T1.
- Extents 3 and 4 will be freed up for reuse.
- There will be four extents in use, which means that the total number of pages used by the tables would be 40.
- The highest allocated page number in this table space is 69, which means that the high water mark is 70 (69 + 1).

Figure 1.10 illustrates the example above and shows the high water mark for the table space. As shown, Extents 3 and 4 are empty because the table (T1) was dropped and its extents freed up to be reused within the table space. However, the extents for table T2 still occupy Extents 5 and 6, so the high water mark is page 70.

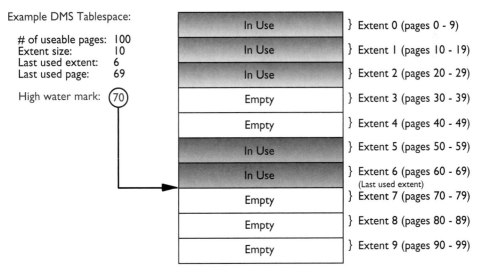

Figure 1.10
The table space high water mark.

Lowering the table space high water mark   If there are no unused extents below the current high water mark for a table space, the high water mark cannot be lowered without dropping one or more objects stored in the table space.

In the example in Figure 1.10, the high water mark is at page 70; however, there are 20 pages (two extents) of empty space below the high water mark. The table space high water mark could be lowered by reorganizing an existing table or by exporting an existing table, dropping it, recreating the table, then importing or loading the data into the new table. However, in both of these cases, it is important to know which object is holding the high water mark so that it can be reorganized or unloaded/dropped/loaded. This information can be found using DB2DART with the /DHWM option. This option will provide the following information:

- A map of the extents in the table space, showing the objects owning the extents
- The object ID and object type of the object holding the high water mark extent
- Information about the high water mark extent
- The number of free and used extents below the high water mark

The /LHWM option of DB2DART helps in lowering the high water mark for the table space. When this option is specified, the table space ID and a desired high water mark for the table space must also be specified. Although there is no guarantee that the current high water mark will be able to be lowered to the desired value, using a value of zero tells DB2 to determine the lowest possible value. The output of the DB2DART tool will then be a list of the required actions that must be executed (i.e., reorg, export, load). For each step in the above list, there will be an estimate of the number of used and free extents below the high water mark so that a DBA can determine the benefit of each step in the process and determine whether to perform all of the steps. The DB2DART tool makes some assumptions about the affects of the suggested operations, so the resulting high water mark may be higher or lower than the specified value.

> **N O T E**   For a partitioned database, DB2DART knows about the table space information and high water mark on only the partition where it is being run.

The /RHWM option of DB2DART can be used to remove space map extents within a table space that are no longer required. Within a DMS table space, DB2 places a space map extent at regular intervals in the table space to record the extent usage for a set of extents within the table space. If a table space has had a lot of data deleted from it, there may be space map pages that no longer point to used pages in the table space; however, they are not removed when the data is deleted. The /RHWM option of DB2DART will look for any unneeded space map pages and remove them from the table space to potentially reduce the high water mark.

Figure 1.11 shows a graphical example where there are two table space map extents that have been allocated but are no longer being used because the pages above the table space map extent are not in use. The /RHWM option of DB2DART would remove the last two table space map extents and, therefore, move the high water mark up to the end of the used space.

The dropping of existing table space containers is only allowed if the number of extents in the container(s) being dropped is less than or equal to the number of free extents above the high water mark in the table space. The number of free extents above the high water mark in the table space is important because all extents up to and including the high water mark must be able to fit in the same logical position within the table space. The altered table space must have enough space to hold all of the data.

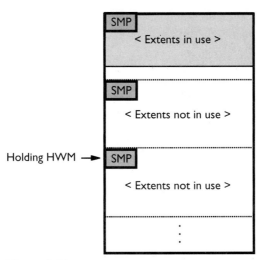

Figure 1.11
Space map extent holding high water mark.

Extending/Enlarging Containers in a Table Space

Although an existing table space can be made larger by adding one or more containers, this may require a rebalance of the existing data. Another way to make the table space larger without adding containers is to make the existing containers larger. This can be done using the EXTEND or RESIZE options on the ALTER TABLESPACE statement.

Extending a table space container increases the size of the container by the specified amount. Resizing a table space container changes the size of the container to the specified size.

The EXTEND or RESIZE options on the ALTER TABLESPACE statement will not require a table space rebalance under the following conditions:

1. The existing containers are all the same size.
2. The existing containers are not the same size, but none of the existing containers have filled so that there is data in one or more containers above the highest stripe in any other container in the table space.

For the table space created using:

```
CREATE TABLESPACE tblspc
MANAGED BY DATABASE
USING (FILE '/tblspcs/cont1' 50,
       FILE '/tblspcs/cont2' 40,
       FILE '/tblspcs/cont3' 40)
EXTENTSIZE 10
```

The extent map would look like the following:

Containers

	0	1	2
0	0	1	2
1	3	4	5
2	6	7	8
3	9		

(Stripes)

The table space map would look like the following:

Range Number	Stripe Set	Stripe Offset	Max Extent	Max Page	Start Stripe	End Stripe	Adj.	Containers
[0]	[0]	0	8	89	0	2	0	3 (0, 1, 2)
[1]	[0]	0	9	99	3	3	0	1 (0)

To add more space to the table space, containers cont2 and cont3 can be increased in size by one extent. This adds space above the existing high water mark, coincidentally ensuring that no rebalance takes place. This could be done using either of the following statements:

```
ALTER TABLESPACE tblspc
EXTEND (FILE '/tblspcs/cont2' 10,
        FILE '/tblspcs/cont3' 10)


ALTER TABLESPACE tblspc
RESIZE  (FILE '/tblspcs/cont2' 50,
         FILE '/tblspcs/cont3' 50)
```

This would cause DB2 to build a new table space extent map, as shown below.

Containers

	0	1	2
0	0	1	2
1	3	4	5
2	6	7	8
3	9	10	11

(Stripes)

The new table space map would look like the following:

Range Number	Stripe Set	Stripe Offset	Max Extent	Max Page	Start Stripe	End Stripe	Adj.	Containers
[0]	[0]	0	11	119	0	4	0	3 (0, 1, 2)

The following examples use the table space created by the statement:

```
CREATE TABLESPACE TS1
MANAGED BY DATABASE
     USING (FILE 'cont0' 1000,
     DEVICE '/dev/rcont1' 2000)
```

There are two ways in which to change the size of the file container (cont0) from 1,000 pages to 2,500 pages.

```
ALTER TABLESPACE TS1 EXTEND (FILE 'cont0' 1500)    [2500-1000=1500]


ALTER TABLESPACE TS1 RESIZE (FILE 'cont0' 2500)
```

To change the size of the device container from 2,000 pages to 3,000 pages, either of the following statements could be used:

```
ALTER TABLESPACE TS1 EXTEND (DEVICE '/dev/rcont1' 1000)[3000-2000=1000]


ALTER TABLESPACE TS1 RESIZE (DEVICE '/dev/rcont1' 3000)
```

To increase the sizes of both containers in the table space by 1,000 pages, any of the following statements can be used:

```
ALTER TABLESPACE TS1 EXTEND
     (FILE 'cont0' 1000,
     DEVICE '/dev/rcont1' 1000)
ALTER TABLESPACE TS1 EXTEND (ALL 1000)
ALTER TABLESPACE TS1 EXTEND (ALL CONTAINERS 1000)
ALTER TABLESPACE TS1 RESIZE
     (FILE 'cont0' 2000,                             [1000+1000=2000]
     DEVICE '/dev/rcont1' 3000)                      [2000+1000=3000]
```

To extend all of the containers in the table space by 100 MB, the following statement could be used:

```
ALTER TABLESPACE TS1 EXTEND (ALL CONTAINERS 100 M)
```

To change the size of both containers in the table space to 4,000 pages, any of the following statements can be used:

```
ALTER TABLESPACE TS1 RESIZE
     (FILE '/dir/c0' 4000,
     DEVICE '/dev/rdev1' 4000)
ALTER TABLESPACE TS1 RESIZE (ALL 4000)
ALTER TABLESPACE TS1 RESIZE (ALL CONTAINERS 4000)
ALTER TABLESPACE TS1 EXTEND
     (FILE 'cont0' 3000,                             [4000-1000=3000]
     DEVICE '/dev/rcont1' 2000)                      [4000-2000=2000]
```

To change the size for all of the containers in the table space to 100 MB, the following statement could be used:

```
ALTER TABLESPACE TS1 RESIZE (ALL CONTAINERS 100 M)
```

Reducing/Shrinking Containers in a Table Space

An existing table space may be made smaller by dropping one or more containers from the table space. However, for performance reasons, this may not be the best option. Normally, the containers in a table space are placed on separate physical disks to take advantage of the maximum amount of I/O parallelism. By removing a container, the underlying disk is no longer used by the table space, and the I/O is then spread over a smaller number of disks. This can adversely affect the performance of the database.

To overcome this, DB2 Version 8 allows containers within a table space to be shrunk. This can be done using either the RESIZE or REDUCE options on the ALTER TABLESPACE statement.

Reducing a table space container decreases the size of the container by the specified amount. Resizing a table space container changes the size of the container to the specified size, which can be larger or smaller than the original size.

For the table space created using:

```
CREATE TABLESPACE tblspc
MANAGED BY DATABASE
USING (FILE '/tblspcs/cont1' 50,
       FILE '/tblspcs/cont2' 40,
       FILE '/tblspcs/cont3' 40)
EXTENTSIZE 10
```

The extent map would look like the following:

Containers

	0	1	2
0	0	1	2
1	3	4	5
2	6	7	8
3	9		

(rows labeled on left: Stripes 0, 1, 2, 3)

The table space map would look like the following:

Range Number	Stripe Set	Stripe Offset	Max Extent	Max Page	Start Stripe	End Stripe	Adj.	Containers
[0]	[0]	0	8	89	0	2	0	3 (0, 1, 2)
[1]	[0]	0	9	99	3	3	0	1 (0)

To reduce the size of the table space, containers cont2 and cont3 can be reduced in size by one extent. This could be done using either of the following statements:

```
ALTER TABLESPACE tblspc
REDUCE (FILE '/tblspcs/cont2' 10,
        FILE '/tblspcs/cont3' 10)


ALTER TABLESPACE tblspc
RESIZE  (FILE '/tblspcs/cont2' 30,
         FILE '/tblspcs/cont3' 30)
```

This would cause DB2 to build a new table space extent map, as shown below.

Containers

	0	1	2
0	0	1	2
1	3	4	5
2	6		
3	7		

Stripes

The new table space map would look like the following:

Range Number	Stripe Set	Stripe Offset	Max Extent	Max Page	Start Stripe	End Stripe	Adj.	Containers
[0]	[0]	0	5	59	0	1	0	3 (0, 1, 2)
[1]	[0]	2	7	79	0	3	0	1 (0)

The following examples use the table space created by:

```
CREATE TABLESPACE TS1
MANAGED BY DATABASE
    USING (FILE 'cont0' 100 M,
    DEVICE '/dev/rcont1' 200 M)
```

There are two ways in which to change the size of the file container (cont0) from 100 MB pages to 50 MB.

```
ALTER TABLESPACE TS1 REDUCE (FILE 'cont0' 50 M)
ALTER TABLESPACE TS1 RESIZE (FILE 'cont0' 50 M)
```

To change the size of the device container from 200 MB to 100 MB, either of the following statements could be used:

```
ALTER TABLESPACE TS1 REDUCE (DEVICE '/dev/rcont1' 100 M)

ALTER TABLESPACE TS1 RESIZE (DEVICE '/dev/rcont1' 100 M)
```

To decrease the sizes of both containers in the table space by 25 MB, any of the following statements can be used:

```
ALTER TABLESPACE TS1 RESIZE
    (FILE 'cont0' 75 M,
    DEVICE '/dev/rcont1' 175 M )
ALTER TABLESPACE TS1 REDUCE
    (FILE 'cont0' 25 M,
    DEVICE '/dev/rcont1' 25 M
ALTER TABLESPACE TS1 REDUCE (ALL 25 M)
ALTER TABLESPACE TS1 REDUCE (ALL CONTAINERS 25 M)
```

To reduce the size for all of the containers in the table space to 40 MB, the following statement could be used:

```
ALTER TABLESPACE TS1 RESIZE (ALL CONTAINERS 40 M)
```

The reduction in size of existing containers is allowed only if the number of extents that the containers are being reduced by is less than or equal to the number of free extents above the high water mark in the table space.

Table Space Rebalance

Access to a table space is not restricted during rebalancing; tables and indexes can be dropped and created, and the data can be inserted, updated, deleted, and queried as usual. Based on the amount of data that must be moved during the rebalace, the rebalancing operation may have an impact on performance.

> **N O T E**   If there is a need to add or remove more than one container to a table space, it is best practice to add or remove them at the same time within a single ALTER TABLESPACE statement to prevent the database manager from having to rebalance the data more than once.

As discussed previously, the table space high water mark plays a key part in the rebalancing process. The high water mark is the page number of the highest page number allocated in the table space.

When space is added to a table space and a rebalance is necessary, a forward rebalance will take place. When space is removed from a table space and a rebalance is necessary, a reverse rebalance will take place.

Before the rebalance process starts, DB2 must first build a new table space map to reflect the changes made to the table space. (This will be referred to in the follwing sections as the new table space map.) The current table space map is the original table space map as it existed prior to making the container changes with the ALTER TABLESPACE statement. The rebalancer will move extents from their location in the current table space map to the location in the new table space map.

For a forward rebalance, the rebalancer will start at the first extent for the table space (Extent 0) and will move the data one extent at a time until the extent holding the high water mark for the table space has been moved. As each extent is moved, the current table space map is altered to represent the new location of the extent. After all of the extents have been moved, the current table space extent map will be the same as the new table space map, up to the stripe where the high water mark is located. The remainder of the current table space map is then changed to look like the new table space map, and the rebalancing process is complete.

For a reverse rebalance, the rebalancer will start at the extent holding the high water mark for the table space and will move the data one extent at a time until Extent 0 is moved. As each extent is moved, the current table space map is altered to represent the new location of the extent. After all extents have been moved, the current table space extent map will be the same as the new table space map.

For performance reasons, when the location of an extent in the current table space map is the same as its location in the new table space map, the extent is not moved, and no I/O takes place.

> **N O T E**   The following examples show containers of different sizes within a table space for the purposes of illustration. For performance reasons, it is recommended that containers within a table space be the same size.

Monitoring a Table Space Rebalance

The table space snapshot has been enhanced with DB2 Version 8 to include information about any table space rebalancing that may be occurring. This information includes:

- The method of rebalance
  - forward or reverse
- The time the rebalance started
  - and was restarted, if the database was brought down during the rebalance process
- How many extents have been processed and how many extents still need to be processed
- The table space map for the table space

```
Number of usable pages            = 6000
Number of used pages              = 3000
Number of pending free pages      = 0
Number of free pages              = 0
High water mark (pages)           = 3000
```

```
Rebalancer Mode                          = Forward
  Start Time                             = 03-06-2002 11:55:39.000000
  Restart Time                           = 03-06-2002 12:16:14.000000
  Number of extents processed            = 137
  Number of extents remaining            = 163
  Last extent moved                      = 137


Table space map:
```

Range Number	Stripe Set	Stripe Offset	Max Extent	Max Page	Start Stripe	End Stripe	Adj.	Containers
[0]	[0]	0	136	1369	0	22	0	6(0,1,2,3,4,5)
[1]	[0]	0	137	1379	45	45	0	1 (2)
[2]	[0]	0	299	2999	46	99	0	3 (0,1,2)

In addition, when the diagnostic level for the DB2 instance is set to level 4, DB2 will periodically write status messages about the rebalance progress to the db2diag.log and the administration notification log files.

The /DTSF option for DB2DART will also dump the table space extent map for the specified table space. The extent that is currently being relocated will have a range that is only one extent long. By running the DB2DART tool at set intervals and examining the currently moving extents, it is possible to estimate the rate at which the rebalance is progressing and to estimate how much time is left. For example, in the following table space extent map, Extent 70 is currently being rebalanced.

Range	MaxPage	MaxExtent	StartStripe	EndStripe	Adj	Containers
[0]	2239	69	0	17	0	4 (0,1,2,3)
[1]	2271	70	17	17	0	1 (2)
[2]	5599	174	23	58	2	3 (0,1,2)
[3]	5887	183	59	61	3	4 (0,1,2,3)

Rebalance Example 1

A table space has three containers of size 70, 50, and 90 pages, and an extent size of 10. Removing one extent from each of the containers for the container tag makes the space available for data in each container 6, 4, and 8 extents in size. The current table space extent map for this table space would then be:

Containers

Stripes	0	1	2
0	0	1	2
1	3	4	5
2	6	7	8
3	9	10	11
4	12		13
5	14		15
6			16
7			17

The corresponding table space map, as shown in a table space snapshot, looks like this:

Range Number	Stripe Set	Stripe Offset	Max Extent	Max Page	Start Stripe	End Stripe	Adj.	Containers
[0]	[0]	0	11	119	0	3	0	3 (0, 1, 2)
[1]	[0]	0	15	159	4	5	0	2 (0, 2)
[2]	[0]	0	17	179	6	7	0	1 (2)

A container with a size of 90 pages is added to the table space. The new table space extent map would look like the following:

Containers

Stripes	0	1	2	3
0	0	1	2	3
1	4	5	6	7
2	8	9	10	11
3	12	13	14	15
4	16		17	18
5	19		20	21
6			22	23
7			24	25

The corresponding table space map, as shown in a table space snapshot, will look like:

Range Number	Stripe Set	Stripe Offset	Max Extent	Max Page	Start Stripe	End Stripe	Adj.	Containers
[0]	[0]	0	15	159	0	3	0	4 (0, 1, 2, 3)
[1]	[0]	0	21	219	4	5	0	3 (0, 2, 3)
[2]	[0]	0	25	259	6	7	0	2 (2, 3)

If the current high water mark is located in Extent 12, the rebalancer will start working with Extent zero and will move every extent up to and including Extent 12. The location of Extent 0 is the same in both of the table space extent maps; therefore, this extent does not need to be moved. In this case, Extents 1 and 2 will also remain in the same place, so they will not need to be moved. In this example, Extent 3 will need to move, so the extent will be read from its old location (the second extent within Container 0) and written to its new location (the first extent within Container 3). Every extent from Extent 3, up to and including Extent 12, will also be moved. Once Extent 12 has been moved, there will be no more extents that need to be moved, the remainder of the current table space map will be made to look like the new table space map, and the rebalancer will terminate.

If the table space is altered such that the space is added to the new table space extent map above the high water mark, for example, using the BEGIN NEW STRIPE SET option, a rebalance will not be necessary, and all of the newly added extents in the table space will be available for use. If the table space is altered such that the space is added to the table space extent map with some of the data being below the high water mark, a rebalance will be necessary. During a rebalance, any extent above the high water mark will be available for use. The extents up to and including the high water mark will not be available until the rebalance is complete.

The function of the rebalancer is the same if a container is extended, resized, or reduced. If a container is extended such that it extends beyond the last stripe in its stripe set, the stripe set will expand to fit this, and the following stripe sets will be shifted out accordingly. The result is that the container will not extend into any stripe sets following it.

Rebalance Example 2

Using the original table space from Rebalance Example 1 above, if Container 1 is resized from 50 to 90 pages, the new table space extent map will look like the following:

Containers

Stripes	0	1	2
0	0	1	2
1	3	4	5
2	6	7	8
3	9	10	11
4	12	13	14
5	15	16	17
6		18	19
7		20	21

The corresponding table space map, as shown in a table space snapshot, will look like this:

Range Number	Stripe Set	Stripe Offset	Max Extent	Max Page	Start Stripe	End Stripe	Adj.	Containers
[0]	[0]	0	15	179	0	5	0	3 (0, 1, 2)
[1]	[0]	0	21	219	6	7	0	2 (1, 2)

When adding a container to a table space that has more than one stripe set, the container can be added to any of the existing stripe sets, using the ADD TO STRIPE SET option on the ALTER TABLE SPACE statement. If a stripe set is not specified, the container will be added to the most recently created stripe set in the table space. Any changes to an existing stripe set in a table space may require a rebalance. In this case, only the changed stripe set and any stripe sets following it in the table space map would need to be rebalanced.

The BEGIN NEW STRIPE SET option on the ALTER TABLE SPACE statement allows a container to be added to a table space without requiring a rebalance. This eliminates the work and overhead involved in performing the rebalance; it also makes the extents in the new container available for immediate use.

When extending or resizing containers in a table space, the rebalance can be avoided by adding space to containers that are above the high water mark. If the containers in the table space are the same size and they are all extended at the same time, the relative positions of the extents within the table space will not change, and a rebalance will not be needed.

The Table Space's Partition Group

The CREATE TABLESPACE statement creates a new table space within a specified partition group in the database, creates and assigns the defined containers to the table space, and records the table space definition and attributes in the database system catalog tables.

When a table space is created, the partition group in which the table space will be created can be specified. The table space will then be created on all of the database partitions that are defined in the partition group. If a partition group is not specified, the table space will be created in the default partition group (IBMDEFAULTGROUP).

> **N O T E**   The partition group must exist for the table space to be created.

A table space can belong to only one partition group, but a partition group can contain more than one table space. Figure 1.12 shows the one-to-many relationship between partition groups and table spaces.

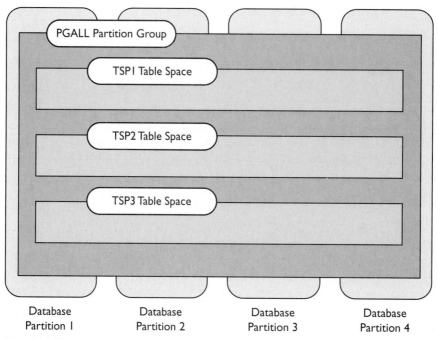

Figure 1.12
Table spaces and partition groups.

Database Partition Groups

A database instance is a logical database manager environment, and a database is created within a database instance. With DB2, the database may either be partitioned or nonpartitioned. There are no partition group design considerations if you are using a nonpartitioned database.

If the database is partitioned, the function and data can then be distributed among all of the database partitions in the DB2 instance.

A *partition group* is a set of one or more database partitions that have been defined within a database, as shown in Figure 1.12. Each database partition that is part of the database system configuration must already be defined in the partition configuration file called *db2nodes.cfg*.

The db2nodes.cfg file will be explained in more detail later in this chapter in the section Database Node Configuration File (db2nodes.cfg).

Partition Group Classes

There are two classes of partition groups: one is based on the number of database partitions in the partition group and another based on how the partition group is created.

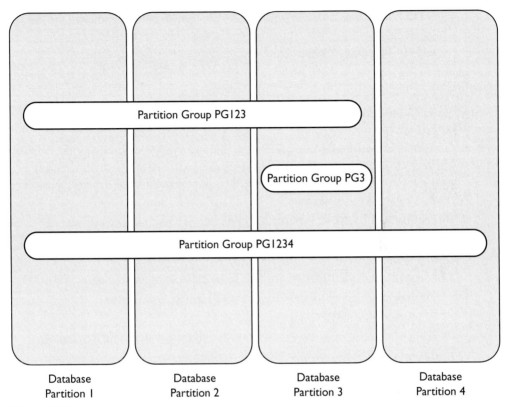

Figure 1.13
Single- and multi-partition groups.

Single- and Multi-Partition Partition Groups

There are two types of partition groups, depending on the number of database partitions that the partition group contains.

1. **Single-partition partition groups:** Partition groups that contain only one database partition

2. **Multi-partition partition groups:** Partition groups that contain more than one database partition.

Figure 1.13 illustrates a database with three partition groups, pg123, pg3, and pg1234. Partition group pg3 is a single-partition partition group, because only database partition 3 is contained in it. Partition groups pg123 and pg1234 are multi-partition partition groups. In this example, pg123 spans partitions 1, 2, and 3; pg1234 spans all four database partitions.

> **N O T E**   Database partitions can be in more than one partition
> group. For example, database partition 3 is found in all three partition
> groups, pg123, pg3, and pg1234.

User-Defined and System-Defined Partition Groups

Partition groups are also be classified by the way they were created:

1. **User-defined partition groups:** These partition groups are created after the database has been created using the CREATE DATABASE PARTITION GROUP statement. The user must have either SYSADM or SYSCTRL authority within the database instance to create a database partition group.

2. **System-defined partition groups:** These partition groups are created when the database is created. There are three system-defined partition groups in every database:

- IBMDEFAULTGROUP
  - By default, spans all database partitions listed in the db2nodes.cfg file
  - Default partition group for the CREATE TABLESPACE statement
  - Can be altered to add or remove database partitions
  - Cannot be dropped using the DROP DATABASE PARTITION GROUP statement
- IBMTEMPGROUP
  - Spans all database partitions listed in the db2nodes.cfg file
  - Holds temporary tables created during database processing on each database partition
  - Cannot be dropped using the DROP DATABASE PARTITION GROUP statement
- IBMCATGROUP
  - Restricted to the catalog partition. The catalog partition is the partition where the CREATE DATABASE command was executed
  - Contains all of the system catalog tables
  - Cannot be altered to span more partitions
  - Cannot be dropped using the DROP DATABASE PARTITION GROUP statement

> **N O T E**   To remain compatible with scripts and programs written
> for previous versions of DB2, NODEGROUP can be used in place of
> DATABASE PARTITION GROUP.

> **N O T E**   If a user temporary table space is created, it must be
> created in the IBMDEFAULTGROUP or another user-created
> partition group. It cannot be created in the IBMTEMPGROUP.

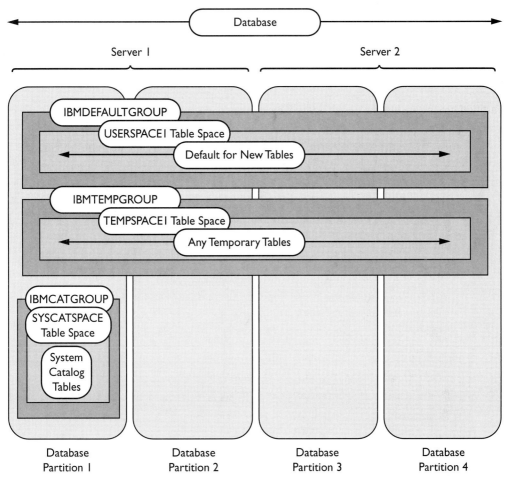

Figure 1.14
The default partition groups and table spaces.

In Figure 1.14, the database is distributed among four database partitions. The partition groups IBMDEFAULTGROUP and IBMTEMPGROUP are defined on all database partitions. IBMCATGROUP is defined on only the first database partition because the CREATE DATABASE command was executed from the first database partition.

Database Node Configuration File (db2nodes.cfg)

The db2nodes.cfg file is a configuration file used by DB2 that defines the partitions that are part of the database instance. The db2nodes.cfg file can contain up to four columns on UNIX and Linux, and five columns on Windows. The first column identifies the partition number used to identify the partition within DB2. The second column is the TCP/IP hostname of the server where the instance is created. The third column is optional but must be used if there are multiple partitions on the same server. This column specifies the logical port for the partitions within the server. The fourth column is also optional and is used to identify the network interface to use for interpartition communication.

Table 1.1 is an example db2nodes.cfg file for a database with four database partitions on different servers, as shown in Figure 1.15. Database partition 0 is located on Server1; partition 1 is located on Server2, and so on. Because there is only one partition per server, all partitions will use logical port zero (0) on their server.

Table 1.1   A db2nodes.cfg File for Four Partitions on Different Servers

0	Server1	0
1	Server2	0
2	Server3	0
3	Server4	0

N O T E   Because there is only one partition on each server in the above example, the logical port is optional in the db2nodes.cfg file. It is required only when there are multiple partitions on the same server.

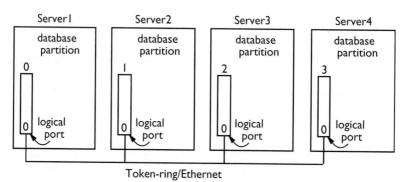

Token-ring/Ethernet

Figure 1.15
A partitioned database configuration.

With the various hardware vendors producing larger and larger symmetric multiprocessor (SMP) machines, the creation of multiple database partitions within a server is becoming more prevalent. DB2 works equally well within a single SMP server as it does across multiple servers.

To have multiple partitions on the same server, the database partitions must have unique logical ports assigned within the server. Table 1.2 is an example db2nodes.cfg file for a database with eight database partitions on the same server.

Table 1.2 db2nodes.cfg File for Eight Partitions on the Same Server

0	Server1	0
1	Server1	1
2	Server1	2
3	Server1	3
4	Server1	4
5	Server1	5
6	Server1	6
7	Server1	7

On UNIX and Linux, the db2nodes.cfg file can be edited directly with any ASCII editor, or entries can be added to or removed from the file using DB2 commands.

On Windows, the DB2NCRT and DB2NDROP commands should be used to create and drop database partitions; the db2nodes.cfg file should not be edited directly.

The DB2START command includes options for both adding and removing a database partition from the db2nodes.cfg file.

- DB2START ADD DBPARTITIONNUM will add a partition to the database and insert an entry in the db2nodes.cfg file.
- DB2START DROP DBPARTITIONNUM will remove a partition from the database and delete its entry from the db2nodes.cfg file.

In addition, the ADD DBPARTITIONNUM command will add a partition to the database if its entry already exists in the db2nodes.cfg file. The DROP DBPARTITIONNUM command will remove a partition from the database but will not remove its entry from the db2nodes.cfg file.

Creating a Database Partition Group

The CREATE DATABASE PARTITION GROUP statement will create a new database partition group within the database, assign the defined database partitions to the partition group, then record the partition group's definition in the database system catalog tables.

Table 1.3   Sample Eight-Partition db2nodes.cfg File

0	Server1	0
1	Server1	1
2	Server2	0
3	Server2	1
4	Server3	0
5	Server3	1
6	Server4	0
7	Server4	1

Given the db2nodes.cfg file as shown in Table 1.3, to create a partition group named pgrp1 that spans partitions 2–5, the CREATE DATABASE PARTITION GROUP statements would be:

```
create database partition group pgrp1 on dbpartitionnums (2,3,4,5)
```

To create a partition group named pgrpall that spans all partitions, the CREATE DATABASE PARTITION GROUP statement could be either of the following:

```
create database partition group pgrpall on all dbpartitionnums

create database partition group pgrpall on dbpartitionnums
(0,1,2,3,4,5,6,7)
```

Modifying a Database Partition Group

The ALTER DATABASE PARTITION GROUP statement can be used to add or remove database partitions from an existing partition group. When adding new partitions, the database partitions must be defined in the db2nodes.cfg file before modifying the partition group.

To add partition 6 to pgrp as created above, the ALTER DATABASE PARTITION GROUP statement would be:

```
alter database partition group pgrp add dbpartitionnum (6)
```

To remove partition 6 from pgrp, the ALTER DATABASE PARTITION GROUP statement would be:

```
alter database partition group pgrp drop dbpartitionnum (6)
```

To remove partitions 4–6 from pgrp, the ALTER DATABASE PARTITION GROUP statement could be either of the following:

```
alter database partition group pgrp drop dbpartitionnums (4 to 6)

alter database partition group pgrp drop dbpartitionnums (4,5,6)
```

To remove partitions 4 and 6 from pgrp, the ALTER DATABASE PARTITION GROUP statement would be:

```
alter database partition group pgrp drop dbpartitionnums (4,6)
```

> **N O T E**   To maintain compatibility with earlier versions of DB2, the following terms are interchangeable:
>
> NODE and DBPARTITIONNUM
> NODES and DBPARTITIONNUMS
> NODEGROUP and DATABASE PARTITION GROUP

Considerations When Creating Table Spaces on Multiple Database Partitions

When creating table spaces in a partitioned database, the partition group in which the table space is created determines on which partition the table space will be physically created. Due to the increased popularity of disk subsystems and SANs, as well as the trend to create multiple database partitions within large SMP servers, it is important to identify the database partition that the table space containers belong to. To do this, DB2 allows the use of a database partition expression in the container name when creating either SMS or DMS containers. This helps to ensure that container names are unique across the database partitions.

A database partition expression can be used anywhere in a container name. In addition, multiple database partition expressions can be specified within a container name. To use a partition expression, there must be a space after the container name, followed by the expression. The result of the expression following the space will then be appended to the container name. If there is no space character in the container name after the database partition expression, it is assumed that the rest of the string is part of the expression. The argument can be used in only one of the following forms:

```
[blank]$N
[blank]$N+[number]
[blank]$N%[number]
[blank]$N+[number]% [number]
[blank]$N%[number]+ [number]
```

For example, for partition 4, the expressions above would be as shown in Table 1.4.

Table 1.4   Expressions for Partition 4

Syntax	Example	Value
[blank]$N	" $N"	4
[blank]$N+[number]	" $N +6"	10
[blank]$N%[number]	" $N%11"	4
[blank]$N+[number]% [number]	" $N+6%11"	10
[blank]$N%[number]+ [number]	" $N%11+6"	10

For example:

```
CREATE TABLESPACE dmsfiletbspc
MANAGED BY DATABASE
USING (FILE '/tbspcs/cont1P $N' 25000)
```

If run on a database with five partitions, numbered 0–4, the containers would be:

```
/tbspcs/cont1P0              –         For Database Partition 0
/tbspcs/cont1P1              –         For Database Partition 1
/tbspcs/cont1P2              –         For Database Partition 2
/tbspcs/cont1P3              –         For Database Partition 3
/tbspcs/cont1P4              –         For Database Partition 4
```

The statement:

```
CREATE TABLESPACE ts1
MANAGED BY DATABASE
USING
  (device '/dev/rcont1p  $N+100' 50000, device '/dev/rcont2p  $N+100' 50000)
```

would create the following containers if it is run on a database with three partitions, numbered 0–2.

```
/dev/rcont1p100             –         For Database Partition 0
/dev/rcont2p100             –         For Database Partition 0
/dev/rcont1p101             –         For Database Partition 1
/dev/rcont2p101             –         For Database Partition 1
/dev/rcont1p102             –         For Database Partition 2
/dev/rcont2p102             –         For Database Partition 2
```

The statement:

```
CREATE TABLESPACE ts2
MANAGED BY DATABASE
USING (FILE '/tbspcs/p $N cont1' 25000)
```

would create the following container if it is run on a database with six partitions, numbered 0–5.

```
/tbspcs/p0cont1              -              For Database Partition 0
/tbspcs/p1cont1              -              For Database Partition 1
/tbspcs/p2cont1              -              For Database Partition 2
/tbspcs/p3cont1              -              For Database Partition 3
/tbspcs/p4cont1              -              For Database Partition 4
/tbspcs/p5cont1              -              For Database Partition 5
```

In addition, DB2 allows an administrator individually to control the creation and placement of containers within the database partitions, using the ON DBPARTITIONNUM parameter. For example:

```
CREATE TABLESPACE dmsfiletbspc
MANAGED BY DATABASE
USING (FILE '/tbspcs/cont1' 25000) on dbpartitonnum(0)
USING (FILE '/tbspcs/cont1' 25000) on dbpartitonnum(1)
USING (FILE '/tbspcs/cont1' 25000) on dbpartitonnum(2)
USING (FILE '/tbspcs/cont1' 25000) on dbpartitonnum(3)
```

Listing Existing Database Partition Groups

To get a list of the partition groups in a database, use the LIST DATABASE PARTITION GROUPS command. The output of this command lists all partition groups that are defined in the database, regardless of the partition on which the command is run. The output of the LIST DATABASE PARTITION GROUPS command for a database with the partition groups defined above would be:

```
DATABASE PARTITION GROUP
------------------------
IBMCATGROUP
IBMDEFAULTGROUP
IBMTEMPGROUP
PGRP
PGRPALL
```

The LIST DATABASE PARTITION GROUPS SHOW DETAIL command provides additional information about the existing partition groups in the database. This information includes:

- PMAP_ID: The partitioning map associated with the partition group
- NODE_NUMBER: The database partition number, as defined in the db2nodes.cfg file
- IN_USE: The status of the database partition

The output that follows shows that there is one row for each database partition to which the partition group belongs. Also notice that IBMTEMPGROUP is not displayed in the output when using the SHOW DETAIL parameter.

DATABASE PARTITION GROUP	PMAP_ID	DATABASE PARTITION NUMBER	IN_USE
IBMCATGROUP	0	0	Y
IBMDEFAULTGROUP	1	0	Y
IBMDEFAULTGROUP	1	1	Y
IBMDEFAULTGROUP	1	2	Y
IBMDEFAULTGROUP	1	3	Y
IBMDEFAULTGROUP	1	4	Y
IBMDEFAULTGROUP	1	5	Y
IBMDEFAULTGROUP	1	6	Y
IBMDEFAULTGROUP	1	7	Y
PGRP	2	2	Y
PGRP	2	3	Y
PGRP	2	4	Y
PGRP	2	5	Y
PGRPALL	3	0	Y
PGRPALL	3	1	Y
PGRPALL	3	2	Y
PGRPALL	3	3	Y
PGRPALL	3	4	Y
PGRPALL	3	5	Y
PGRPALL	3	6	Y
PGRPALL	3	7	Y

N O T E   This information is also available in the system catalog tables.

System Catalog Views Relating to Database Partition Groups

There are three system catalog views that can be used to retrieve information about partition groups and partitioning maps:

- SYSCAT.DBPARTITIONGROUPDEF
- SYSCAT. DBPARTITIONGROUPS
- SYSCAT.PARTITIONMAPS

SYSCAT.DBPARTITIONGROUPDEF view   This view contains a row for each database partition that belongs to the partition group. It has the following columns:

- DBPGNAME: The name of the database partition group. This name is defined when the partition group is created using the CREATE DATABASE PARTITION GROUP statement.

- DBPARTITIONNUM: The partition numbers of the database partitions that belong to the partition group. Each database partition has a unique database partition number, as defined in the db2nodes.cfg file.
- IN_USE: The status of the database partition. The status can be one of the following values:
  - A: Indicates that the database partition has been created but is not in the partitioning map. The containers for the table spaces in the partition group have been created. The database partition will be added to the partitioning map when a REDISTRIBUTE DATABASE PARTITION GROUP operation is successfully completed
  - D: Indicates that the database partition will be dropped when a REDISTRIBUTE DATABASE PARTITION GROUP operation is completed
  - T: Indicates that the database partition has been created using the WITHOUT TABLESPACES clause. Containers must be specifically added to the table spaces for the partition group using the ALTER TABLESPACE statement.
  - Y: The database partition is in the partition map

Below is an example of the contents of the SYSCAT.DBPARTITIONGROUPDEF view:

```
select * from SYSCAT.DBPARTITIONGROUPDEF

DBPGNAME                          DBPARTITIONNUM           IN_USE
------------------------------    ------------------       ------------------
IBMCATGROUP                              1                    Y
IBMDEFAULTGROUP                          1                    Y
IBMDEFAULTGROUP                          2                    Y
IBMDEFAULTGROUP                          3                    Y
IBMDEFAULTGROUP                          4                    Y

5 record(s) selected.
```

The output above shows that the IBMCATGROUP is defined in database partition 1 and is in use. IBMDEFAULTGROUP is defined in database partitions 1, 2, 3, and 4 and is also in use.

SYSCAT.DBPARTITIONGROUPS view   This view contains a row for each partition group defined in the database. It has the following columns:

- DBPGNAME: The name of the partition group. This name is defined when the partition group is created with the CREATE DATABASE PARTITION GROUP statement
- DEFINER: The Authorization ID of the creator of the partition group
- PMAP_ID: The identifier of the partitioning map
- REDISTRIBUTE_PMAP_ID: The identifier of the partitioning map created during redistribution
- CREATE_TIME: The date and time that the partition group was created
- REMARKS: Comments specified for the partition group

The following is an example of the contents of the first four columns of this table:

```
select NGNAME, DEFINER, PMAP_ID, REDISTRIBUTE_PMAP_ID from
SYSCAT.DBPARTITIONGROUPS


DBPGNAME                DEFINER             PMAP_ID    REDISTRIBUTE_PMAP_ID
---------------------------------------------------------------------------
IBMCATGROUP             SYSIBM                 0                         -1
IBMDEFAULTGROUP         SYSIBM                 1                         -1
IBMTEMPGROUP            SYSIBM                 2                         -1

3 record(s) selected.
```

SYSCAT.PARTITIONMAPS view   This view contains a row for each partitioning map created in a database. It has the following columns:

- PMAP_ID: This is the identifier of the partitioning map.
- PARTITIONMAP: The actual partitioning map is stored as a binary large object (BLOB). This is an array with 4096 entries for a multi-partition partition group. For a single-partition partition group, each element of the array will have the same value that specifies the database partition number.

Database Partition Groups Summary

Below are some of the main characteristics of partition groups.

- A partition group is a subset of the database partitions in a database.
- A partition group cannot span databases.
- A database may contain both single-partition and multi-partition partition groups.
- A database partition can be a member of more than one partition group.
- Three system-defined partition groups are created by default:
  ○ IBMCATGROUP
  ○ IBMDEFAULTGROUP
  ○ IBMTEMPGROUP
- SYSADM or SYSCTRL authority is required to create a partition group.
- There is only one partitioning map for each partition group (except during redistribution).
- A database can have a maximum of 32,768 partition groups.

Disk Layout

The design and physical layout of the table spaces within a database will have a very big impact on the overall performance of the database and its applications. The type, design, and physical location of the table spaces will ultimately determine the efficiency of the I/O performed against that table space.

Data Placement Considerations

It is important to understand the following before beginning the physical design of a database.

Workload considerations   The type of workload that will be executed against the database must be taken into account when designing the physical layout of the database and its table spaces. To understand the performance issues associated with a database, it is helpful to have an understanding of the different database profiles and their unique workload characteristics.

- Online Transaction Processing (OLTP)
- Reporting/Decision Support Systems (DSSs)

OLTP databases are among the most mission-critical and widely deployed of any of the database types. Literally, millions of transactions encompassing billions of dollars are processed on OLTP systems around the world on a daily basis. The primary defining characteristic of OLTP systems is that the transactions are processed in real time, or online, and often require immediate response back to the user.

From a workload perspective, OLTP databases typically:

- Process a large number of concurrent user sessions
- Process a large number of transactions using simple SQL statements
- Process a single database row at a time
- Are expected to complete transactions in seconds, not minutes or hours

Reporting/DSS systems differ from the typical transaction-oriented systems in that they most often consist of data extracted from multiple-source systems for the purpose of supporting the end user:

- Data analysis applications using predefined queries
- Application-generated queries
- Ad-hoc user queries
- Reporting requirements

DSS systems typically deal with substantially larger volumes of data than do OLTP systems, due to their role in supplying users with large amounts of historical data. Whereas a database of a couple hundred GB would be considered large for an OLTP system, a large DSS system is normally many TB. The increased storage requirements of DSS systems can also be attributed to the fact that they often contain multiple, aggregated views of the same data.

Whereas OLTP queries tend to be centered around one specific business function, DSS queries are often substantially more complex. The need to process large amounts data results in many

CPU-intensive database sort and join operations. The complexity and variability of these types of queries must be given special consideration when designing a DSS system for performance.

Available disk space   As a rule of thumb, the following formula can be used to determine the minimum amount of disk space required to support a database:

```
Disk Space Required = Expected Size of Raw Data * 4
```

The space is required for the following:

- Data and indexes
- Database logs
- Backup images
- System paging space
- Data export and staging space
- Fudge factor

Although it is important to ensure that there is enough disk space to hold the database, the amount of disk space available does not have a significant impact on the performance of the database.

Number of physical disks available for the database   As a rule of thumb, there should be a minimum of six to ten disks per CPU for the database. This does not include the disks required for paging space, backup images, etc.

An OLTP database will typically scan an index, then retrieve a small number of rows from a table. Because a typical OLTP database will have a number of applications connected, in order to make the index scans as efficient as possible and to attempt to avoid any contention when reading the indexes and data, it is important to have the database spread across enough physical disks.

A reporting/DSS system will typically scan large amounts of data and retrieve a number of rows from one or more tables. Although there are normally few users accessing the system, the number of tables that are normally scanned within a single SQL statement will normally result in a heavy I/O load on the system.

The best way to ensure that the database is able to retrieve the data as quickly as possible is to spread the database across a large number of physical disks to take advantage of the I/O parallelism.

> **N O T E**   There are also practical limits to the number of disks that a disk adapter can effectively handle. Use multiple disk adapters when using a large number of disks.

Rate of growth   For tables that will become very large, it is important to consider the maximum sizes of table spaces within DB2. The maximum size of a table space is determined by the page size used for the table space. The maximum table space sizes are shown in Table 1.5.

Table 1.5   Maximum Table Space Sizes

Page Size	Table Space Size
4 KB	64 GB
8 KB	128 GB
16 KB	256 GB
32 KB	512 GB

However, each page in DB2 can hold only 255 rows of data, regardless of the page size. There-fore, tables with short row lengths should be placed in a table space with 4-KB or 8-KB pages to avoid having pages with a lot of empty space.

Log placement   The factors that affect logging performance, such as log file size, the number of logs, and the type of underlying disks used for logs, will be discussed in a later chapter; however, before any log files ever exist, the database administrator must decide on the following factors:

On which disks are the logs to be placed?   In a highly active database, the log files will have a great deal of I/O. It is recommended that the log files reside on their own physical disk(s), sep-arate from the rest of the database. These disks should be dedicated to DB2 logging to avoid the possibility of any other processes accessing or writing to these disks and causing contention.

Availability   Whether the database is configured to use circular or archive logging, the logs must be available and accessible at all times. In previous versions of DB2, this typically required operating system or disk mirroring or striping. However, in DB2 Version 7.2, the concept of dual logging (also known as *mirrored logging*) was built into DB2.

In DB2 Version 7.2, the registry variable DB2_NEWLOGPATH2 had to be set to Y to enable dual logging. In DB2 Version 8, there is a new database configuration parameter, mirror log path (MIRRORLOGPATH), which is used to specify the path for the mirrored logs.

Table-to-table space assignments   When deciding which table space that a table should be created in, consider the following:

- Place tables that have referential constraints within the same table space.
- Place tables that are related through the use of triggers in the same table space.
- Place tables that share structured data types in the same table space.
- Place tables that are used by the same applications in the same table space.
- Place tables in the same table space for backup and recovery reasons.
- Tables do NOT need to be put into different table spaces.

With DB2 Version 8, there is no need to place tables into separate table spaces simply to use the LOAD utility. The LOAD utility will now work online and no longer locks the entire table space.

Because an OLTP-type system normally scans an index, then retrieves individual rows, there is little chance of I/O contention. In a DSS system, DB2 will typically scan the indexes and build a RID list that is then used to retrieve the data. Because these are separate operations, there is little chance of I/O contention. Therefore, there is no need to separate a table's data and indexes into different table spaces, unless they will be assigned to use different buffer pools. However, in order to place the data and indexes on different physical disks, they must be placed in separate table spaces.

Data Placement Summary

Designing the physical layout of the database on disk is one of the most important decisions a database administrator will make, and it will have a big impact on the throughput of the database system.

There is a common misconception that, in order to get the best performance from a database, its indexes and data need to be put into different table spaces, and the table spaces need to be created on separate disks. Although separating data and indexes into separate table spaces does allow the table and index to be assigned to different buffer pools, there is no need to separate them onto different physical disks, especially if the server does not have a lot of physical disks. In fact, separating the data and indexes onto different disks can limit performance if the server does not have enough physical disks to parallelize the I/O adequately.

There are three general guidelines to consider when determining how to place the table spaces on the available physical disks:

- Spread the table spaces across as many separate physical disks as possible
- If there are only a small number of disks available (i.e., less than 6–10 disks per CPU), it is better to spread *all* of the table spaces across *all* of the available physical disks, rather than to attempt to carve up the disks for different table spaces.
- If there are enough physical disks (i.e., at least 6–10 disks per CPU), place heavily accessed tables on different physical disks.

Configuration Considerations for DB2 with IBM ESS (Shark)

The following general guidelines will ensure the optimal use of IBM ESS (Shark) disk systems with DB2.

- Know where the data resides. Understand how DB2 containers map to ESS logical disks and how those logical disks map to RAID arrays.
- Spread DB2 data across as many RAID arrays as possible.
- Balance the workload across ESS resources. Establish a storage allocation policy that allows for a balanced workload activity across RAID arrays. Take advantage of the inherent balanced activity and parallelism within DB2, spreading the work for database partitions and containers across those arrays.

- Use the inherent striping of DB2, placing containers for a table space on separate ESS logical disks that reside on separate ESS RAID arrays. This will usually eliminate the need for using underlying operating system or logical volume manager striping.
- Select an ESS logical disk size that allows for granularity and growth without proliferating the number of logical disks. Approximately eight logical disks per ESS RAID array works well for most environments.
- Use ESS multi-pathing, along with DB2 striping, to ensure balanced use of fibre channel or SCSI paths.
- Consider isolating log files on separate arrays for high-volume, write-intensive OLTP environments but only if there are plenty of other RAID arrays allocated for data files. For example, if there are seven RAID arrays allocated for data files, isolating one for logging makes sense. However, if there are only two RAID arrays for the entire database application, do not isolate the log files. Data warehousing environments normally have high read content and do not stress the log files, so it is normally better to mix the logs and data on the same RAID arrays.

Know where the data resides   To get optimal performance from an ESS subsystem, it cannot be treated as a "black box." Establish a storage allocation policy that uses as many RAID arrays as possible. Understand how DB2 tables map to underlying logical disks and how the logical disks map to RAID arrays. One way to simplify this process is to maintain a modest number of ESS logical disks and maintain a simple mapping of logical volumes (such as one logical volume for every ESS logical disk).

Balance workload across ESS resources   Use the inherent parallelism and balanced approach of DB2 to help balance I/O workload across the ESS resources. When the I/O is balanced across enough ESS resources, many of the other decisions become secondary.

- DB2 uses query and I/O parallelism to help balance the workload within the server.
- DB2 query parallelism allows workload to be balanced across both CPUs and database partitions.
- I/O parallelism within DB2 allows workload to be balanced across containers.

These features allow for the workload to be balanced across the ESS resources by applying the following methodologies:

- Intermix data, indexes, and temporary table spaces on the RAID arrays.
- Do not attempt to isolate these components on separate arrays, because this will only skew activity to some of the arrays and lead to unbalance.

Establish a policy that allows partitions and containers within partitions to be spread evenly across ESS resources. This can be done using either a horizontal mapping, in which every database partition has containers on every available ESS array, or a vertical mapping, in which database partitions are isolated to specific arrays, with containers spread evenly across those arrays. Performance tests have proven that both approaches work well and achieve comparable performance.

Selection of a horizontal or vertical mapping approach will be influenced by:

- The number of database partitions
- The number of arrays
- How future growth will influence these factors

The vertical mapping approach works well, as long as the number of ESS RAID arrays is an even multiple of the number of database partitions. The horizontal approach should be used if these conditions are not met.

The following rules should be used when defining table space containers on ESS:

1. Span ESS cabinets first.
2. Span clusters within a cabinet next.
3. Span disk adapters next.
4. Engage as many arrays as possible.

Use DB2 to stripe across containers   Figure 1.16 shows how containers should be striped across arrays, across disk adapters, across clusters, and across ESS cabinets. This is done using the striping capabilities of DB2.

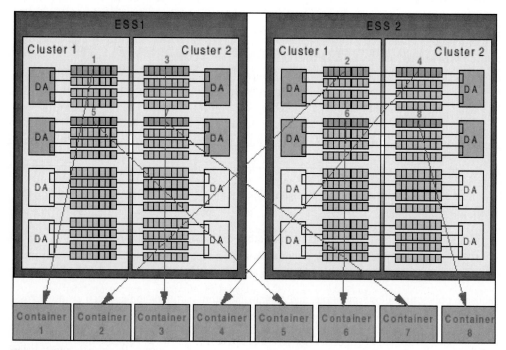

Figure 1.16
Container placement on IBM ESS.

Extent size for ESS   To stripe across multiple arrays in the ESS, assign a logical disk from each array to be used as a DB2 container. During writes, DB2 will write one extent to the first container, the next extent to the second container, and so on, until all eight containers have been addressed before cycling back to the first container.

DB2 stripes across containers at the extent level, and the stripe size is specified as the extent size of the table space.

Because the underlying ESS stripe size is 32 KB, using an extent size that is an integer multiple of 32 KB allows multiple ESS disks to be used within an array when a DB2 prefetch occurs. However, tests have shown that I/O performance is fairly insensitive to the selection of extent sizes, mostly due to the fact that ESS employs internal sequential detection and prefetch.

Prefetch size for ESS   The table space prefetch size determines the degree to which separate containers can operate in parallel to handle I/O requests. Although larger prefetch sizes can enhance throughput of individual queries, mixed applications generally work best with moderately sized prefetch and extent sizes.

To obtain maximum throughput, it is important to engage as many arrays as possible in the prefetch.

What about logs on ESS?   Some database specialists and consultants recommend not using RAID-5 to store database log files. Although this may be true with some RAID-5 implementations, it is not the same with IBM ESS. Some other RAID-5 implementations have not been able to handle database logging efficiently, due to a lack of one or more of the following:

- **Lack of a nonvolatile write cache**. A write cache is essential in eliminating the service time penalty associated with writes and allowing optimization of sequential write handling between the cache and the physical disks.
- **Software RAID.** Software RAID implementations usually lack the benefits of write cache, as well as other hardware optimizations, such as XOR (exclusive OR) engines for handling the parity manipulation. This can cause excessive processor overhead.
- **Striping granularity.** Some RAID-5 implementations use a very coarse striping technique that prevents implementation of full stripe writes. The ESS design includes hardware RAID, striping, and non-volatile cache that make its implementation of RAID-5 a very good logging architecture.

Database logging normally consists of sequences of synchronous sequential writes to disk. These patterns may not be purely sequential, meaning that they may periodically rewrite certain physical records, but they do have a generally sequential trend. The physical record sizes are normally small and typically range between 4 and 64 KB, depending on the frequency of commit points and other factors. Log archiving functions, where an entire log file is copied to an archived space, also tend to consist of simple sequential read and write operations.

When DB2 writes a log record, the ESS stores two copies of the log record in its cache (one in the cluster cache and the other in nonvolatile storage). The ESS will immediately indicate that the write is complete, once both copies have been stored safely. At this point, the log record is doubly protected. After a number of log records have been written, ESS will determine that this is a sequential write pattern.

When data is moved asynchronously to disk, the cache manager sends one or more full stripes of data to the SSA disk adapter. The ESS cache manager and disk adapter write data to each of the disks in parallel, while at the same time internally calculating the parity and sending it to disk. This technique eliminates the traditional RAID-5 write penalty.

Criteria for selecting ESS logical disk sizes   IBM ESS can support a high degree of parallelism and concurrency within a single logical disk. Performance tests have indicated that a single logical disk consuming an entire array achieves the same performance as many smaller logical disks on the same array. However, logical disk size also affects systems management.

Smaller logical disks allow for more granularity when managing storage, although they increase the number of logical disks seen by the operating system. Select an ESS logical disk size that allows for granularity and growth without proliferating the number of logical disks.

> **T I P**   Make the DB2 table space prefetch size a multiple of the extent size multiplied by the number of containers in the table space, but do not make it more than 512 pages.

```
Prefetch Size = min (512, Extent Size * Number of Containers)
```

> **T I P**   Allocate the table space containers on separate RAID arrays to ensure that multiple arrays can be used in parallel.

> **T I P**   Try to strike a reasonable balance between flexibility and manageability. A general recommendation is that there should be no fewer than two logical disks in an array, and a minimum logical disk size should be around 16 GB. Use a single logical disk size throughout the ESS. Eight logical disks per RAID array can be a reasonable balance.

Smaller logical disks have the following attributes:

Advantages:

• They allow an administrator to assign storage to different applications and hosts.

- They allow greater flexibility in performance reporting. For example, ESS Expert reports statistics for logical disks.
- They allow greater flexibility in use of Copy Services.

Disadvantages:

- Small logical disk sizes can contribute to many logical disks, particularly in SAN environments and large configurations.

Larger logical disks have the following attributes:

Advantages:

- They simplify the understanding of how data maps to arrays.
- They reduce the number of disks that appear to the operating system and storage administrators.

Disadvantages:

- Less granular storage administration

Use ESS multi-pathing   Multi-pathing is the use of hardware and supporting software to provide multiple access paths to the underlying disks from the host computer. When using ESS, this means that there needs to be at least two fibre or SCSI connections to each host computer from any component being multi-pathed. It also involves internal configuration of the ESS host adapters and volumes.

Multi-pathing also requires installation of the IBM subsystem device driver (SDD) software on the host computer. Without this software, a single logical disk on multiple paths will appear as multiple different disks to the operating system.

There are several benefits from using multi-pathing, including high availability, high bandwidth, and ease of performance management. A high-availability implementation is one in which an application can still access storage through an alternate path if a component on one path should fail. Multi-pathing for bandwidth means that there are enough access paths to the data so that the total bandwidth is not bound by the data throughput that other components of the system (i.e., CPUs) can sustain. Multi-pathing for ease of performance management means allowing multi-pathing software to balance the I/O workload across multiple available access paths automatically.

SUMMARY

DB2 Version 8 relies on the ability to store and retrieve data quickly and efficiently in order to respond as efficiently as possible to application requests. The main component of the storage and retrieval of the data is the manner in which the database is physically created on disk. Building a database to allow for maximum I/O parallelism by creating table spaces and containers on enough physical disks will help to ensure the performance of the system.

It is important to spend the time and attempt to build a database correctly the first time. However, if there are problems with performance or I/O at a later time, it is often worth the effort to rebuild the database, either by using a redirected restore or by exporting the data and reloading it into a database with a new table space definition.

## CHAPTER 2

Data Manipulation

All regular table data and indexes for a database are manipulated within the database's buffer pool area. A database must have at least one buffer pool associated with it but can use multiple buffer pools. The buffer pools are the work area for the database, and all searching for and manipulation of the data and indexes must take place within the buffer pools. In order for DB2 to scan a table or an index, the pages of the table or index must be in the database's buffer pool (or buffer pools). If the required page is already in the buffer pool, DB2 can start to work on the page immediately. If the page is not in the buffer pool, DB2 must read the page from disk and position it in the buffer pool(s) before it can be manipulated. Because most data manipulation takes place in the database buffer pools, configuring the buffer pools is the single most important tuning area for DB2 Universal Database (UDB) databases.

The database buffer pools have a profound effect on the overall performance of the database and, as such, there have been a number of enhancements to the manner in which buffer pools can be created and managed in DB2 UDB Version 8. This chapter will focus on the creation, management, and monitoring of buffer pools in DB2 UDB Version 8 to provide optimal performance for the database.

THE BUFFER POOLS

The database buffer pool area is a piece of memory used to cache a table's index and data pages as they are being read from disk to be scanned or modified. The buffer pool area helps to improve database system performance by allowing data to be accessed from memory instead of from disk. Because memory access is much faster than disk access, the less often that DB2 needs to read from or write to a disk, the better the system will perform.

When a database is created, there will be one default buffer pool created for the database. This buffer pool is named IBMDEFAULTBP; it has a page size of 4 KB; and it will be sized depending on the operating system. For Windows, the default buffer pool will be 250 pages or 1 MB, whereas for UNIX, the default buffer pool will be 1,000 pages or 4 MB. The default buffer pool cannot be dropped; however, the size of the default buffer pool can be changed, using the ALTER BUFFERPOOL statement.

A database's buffer pool(s) are allocated in memory when the database is activated or when the first application connects to the database. When all applications disconnect from the database and it is deactivated, the buffer pool memory is deallocated and freed back to the operating system. With DB2 UDB Version 8, buffer pools can now be created, dropped, and resized while the database is active.

Buffer Pool Usage

When a DB2 agent acting on behalf of an application retrieves a row in a table for the first time, DB2 UDB must first read the page containing that row from disk and place it in the buffer pool. The next time any application requests data, DB2 UDB will look for it in the buffer pool. If the requested data is in the buffer pool, it can be retrieved without disk access, resulting in faster performance.

Once a page is read into the buffer pool, it will remain in the buffer pool until the database is stopped or until the space used by the page in the buffer pool is needed to read another page into the buffer pool. When reading a page into the buffer pool, it will be placed into an empty buffer pool page if one exists. If the buffer pool is full (i.e., there are no empty pages available), DB2 will choose a victim page, based on the following:

- How recently the page was last accessed
- The probability that the page will be read again by the last agent that accessed it
- The type of data on the page (i.e., index or data)
- Whether the page was changed in the buffer pool but has not yet been written to disk

To guarantee the integrity of the data and transactions, changed pages must first be written to disk before they can be replaced in the buffer pool. Because the transaction must wait for the page to be written to disk, this can slow down the performance of the system. To overcome this condition and improve performance, DB2 UDB uses buffer pool cleaners periodically to scan the buffer pool for dirty pages (i.e., pages that have changed since being read into the buffer pool) and asynchronously write them to disk. To optimize the access to the data on these pages, they will not be removed from the buffer pool after they have been written to disk; however, they will no longer be dirty, so they can be replaced in the buffer pool without the need to write them to disk.

Reading pages from disk is an expensive, time-consuming operation. Reading several consecutive pages into the buffer pool using a single I/O operation can greatly reduce this overhead and allow applications to process their work faster. In addition, multiple parallel I/O operations to read several ranges of pages into the buffer pool can help reduce I/O wait time. In DB2 UDB this is accomplished using I/O prefetchers to read pages from disk into the buffer pool in the expectation that they will be required by an application. Prefetching of index and data pages into the buffer pool can help improve performance by reducing the I/O wait time and further taking advantage of parallel I/O operations.

> **N O T E** Prefetching and buffer pool cleaning will be discussed in more detail later in this chapter.

Creating Buffer Pools

The CREATE BUFFERPOOL statement will create a buffer pool for the database that the user is connected to. In previous versions of DB2 UDB, the buffer pool would not be allocated until the database was stopped and restarted (i.e., all current applications were disconnected from the database and another connection was established). With DB2 UDB Version 8, the buffer pool can be allocated immediately, if there is enough memory available to handle the request.

The CREATE BUFFERPOOL statement has options to specify the following:

- **bufferpool-name:** Specifies the name of the buffer pool. The name cannot be used for any other buffer pools and cannot begin with the characters SYS or IBM.
- **IMMEDIATE:** Specifies that the buffer pool will be created immediately if there is enough memory available on the system. If there is not enough reserved space in the database shared memory to allocate the new buffer pool, a warning is returned, and buffer pool creation will be DEFERRED, as described below.
  - ○ This is the default.
- **DEFERRED:** Specifies that the buffer pool will be created the next time the database is stopped and restarted.
- **ALL DBPARTITIONNUMS:** Specifies that the buffer pool will be created on all partitions in the database. This is the default if no database partition group is specified.
- **DATABASE PARTITION GROUP:** Specifies the database partition group(s) on which the buffer pool will be created. The buffer pool will be created on all database partitions that are part of the specified database partition groups.
- **SIZE:** Specifies the size of the buffer pool and is defined in number of pages. In a partitioned database, this will be the default size for all database partitions where the buffer pool exists.
  - ○ The EXCEPT ON DBPARTITIONNUMS clause described below allows the buffer pool to have different sizes on the different database partitions.
- **EXCEPT ON DBPARTITIONNUMS:** Specifies the database partition or partitions where the buffer pool will be sized differently than specified by the SIZES clause. This can be specified as a single partition, a list of partitions, or a range of partitions. To specify a list of partitions, separate the database partitions in the list by commas. To

specify a range of partitions, use the TO clause between the partition numbers. When specifying a range of partitions, the second database partition number must be higher than the first database partition number, and the buffer pool must exist on all of the database partitions. After the partitions or partitions have been specified, their *size* must also be specified.

- **NUMBLOCKPAGES:** Specifies the number of pages to be created in the block-based area of the buffer pool. The actual value of NUMBLOCKPAGES may differ from what was specified because the size must be a multiple of the BLOCKSIZE. The block-based area of the buffer pool cannot be more than 98% of the total buffer pool size. Specifying a value of 0 will disable block I/O for the buffer pool.
- **BLOCKSIZE:** Specifies the number of pages within a given block in the block-based area of the buffer pool. The block size must be between two and 256 pages, and the default value is 32 pages.
- **PAGESIZE:** Specifies the page size used for the buffer pool. The default page size is 4 KB, or 4096 bytes. The page size can be specified in both bytes and KB.
- **EXTENDED STORAGE/NOT EXTENDED STORAGE:** Specifies whether buffer pool victim pages will be copied to a secondary cache called *extended storage.* Extended storage is more efficient than retrieving data from disk but less efficient than retrieving data from the buffer pool, so it is not applicable to 64-bit environments.

> **N O T E**   Once defined for a buffer pool, the page size and buffer pool name cannot be altered.

Enabling block-based I/O by setting NUMBLOCKPAGES to a value greater than 0 can help performance for applications that do sequential prefetching. If the applications do not perform sequential prefetching of pages into the buffer pool, this area of the buffer pool will be wasted.

> **N O T E**   NUMBLOCKPAGES does not need to be set to allow prefetching to occur.

Block-based buffer pools have the following limitations:

- A buffer pool cannot be made block-based and also use extended storage.
- A buffer pool cannot be made block-based and also support Address Windowing Extensions (AWE) on Windows.
- If a buffer pool is enabled for AWE support and block-based I/O is enabled, the block-based I/O support will be disabled.

The following statement:

```
CREATE BUFFERPOOL BP1
SIZE 25000
```

will create a buffer pool named BP1 with a size of 100 MB (25,000 4-KB pages = 100 MB). Because the page size is not specified, the buffer pool will use the default page size of 4 KB. Because the IMMEDIATE option is the default, the buffer pool will be allocated immediately and available for use, as long as there is enough memory available to fulfill the request.

The following statement:

```
CREATE BUFFERPOOL BP2
SIZE 25000
PAGESIZE 8 K
```

will create a buffer pool named BP2 with a size of 200 MB (25,000 8-KB pages = 200 MB). The buffer pool will use an 8-KB page size. Because the IMMEDIATE option is the default, the buffer pool will be allocated immediately and available for use, as long as there is enough memory available to fulfill the request.

The following statement:

```
CREATE BUFFERPOOL BP3
DEFERRED
SIZE 1000000
```

will create a buffer pool named BP3 with a size of 4 GB (1,000,000 4-KB pages = 4 GB). Because the page size is not specified, the buffer pool will use the default page size of 4 KB. Because the DEFERRED option is specified, the buffer pool will not be allocated until the database is stopped and restarted.

The following statement:

```
CREATE BUFFERPOOL BP4
IMMEDIATE
SIZE 100000
NUMBLOCKPAGES 32000
BLOCKSIZE 256
```

will create a buffer pool named BP4 with a size of 400 MB (100,000 4-KB pages = 400 MB). Because the page size is not specified, the buffer pool will use the default page size of 4 KB. The buffer pool will have 128 MB set aside for block-based I/O to help optimize sequential prefetch activity. Because the IMMEDIATE option is specified, the buffer pool will be allocated immediately and available for use, as long as there is enough memory available to fulfill the request. Because the block size is set to 256 pages, it is recommended that the extent size for the table spaces assigned to this buffer pool also be set to 256 pages.

> **N O T E**   This may not always be possible, because several table spaces with different extent sizes may be bound to the same block-based buffer pool.

The proportions of the page area and block area are not maintained. The block-based area of the buffer pool will be altered only if:

- NUMBLOCKPAGES is specified in the ALTER BUFFERPOOL statement
- The buffer pool SIZE is altered to something that would cause NUMBLOCKPAGES to be greater than 98% of SIZE.

> **N O T E**   Altering the buffer pool size to a value less than the NUMBLOCKPAGES is not allowed, unless the BUFFPAGE parameter is used.

For example. Consider the buffer pool BP1, defined as:

```
create bufferpool BP1 size 9600 numblockpages 4800 blocksize 32
```

This gives a page-based area of 4,800 pages and a block-based area of 4,800 pages.

The statement:

```
alter bufferpool BP1 size 6400
```

would change the buffer pool to have a page-based area of 1,600 pages and a block-based area of 4,800 pages.

In the following statement, the specified SIZE is less than the current NUMBLOCKPAGES value of 4,800:

```
alter bufferpool BP1 size 3200
```

This would cause the following error to be returned.

```
DB21034E  The command was processed as an SQL statement because it was
not a valid Command Line Processor command.  During SQL processing it
returned: SQL20150N  The number of block pages for a buffer pool is
too large for the size of the buffer pool.  SQLSTATE=54052
```

In the following statement, the specified SIZE is less than the current NUMBLOCKPAGES value of 4,800. However, because the BUFFPAGE parameter is used, the buffer pool will be reduced in size, but the block-based area will have to be reduced accordingly. This is done to allow for a certain number of pages to exist in the page-based area for workloads that do not consist of sequential prefetching. Use this statement:

```
update db cfg for TEST using BUFFPAGE 3200
alter bufferpool BP1 size -1
```

for a partitioned database with 12 partitions and partition group DPG1 defined to include database partitions 0, 1, 2, 3, 4, 5, 6, and 7. To create a buffer pool named BP5 with a size of 25,000 pages and a page size of 32 KB that will be allocated only on the partitions where DPG1 is defined, use the following statement:

```
CREATE BUFFERPOOL BP5
DATABASEPARTITIONGROUP DPG1
SIZE 25000
PAGESIZE 32K
```

For the same database and partition groups as described above, to create a buffer pool named BP6 with a page size of 32 KB and a size of 25,000 pages on partitions 0, 1, 2, 3, 4, and 5 and a size of 35,000 pages on partitions 6 and 7, use either of the following statements:

```
CREATE BUFFERPOOL BP6
DATABASEPARTITIONGROUP DPG1
SIZE 25000
PAGESIZE 32K
EXCEPT ON DBPARTITIONNUMS 6 TO 7 SIZE 35000

CREATE BUFFERPOOL BP6
DATABASEPARTITIONGROUP DPG1
SIZE 25000
PAGESIZE 32K
EXCEPT ON DBPARTITIONNUM 6 SIZE 35000
EXCEPT ON DBPARTITIONNUM 7 SIZE 35000
```

How Many Buffer Pools Should a Database Have?

There are two main schools of thought regarding the number of buffer pools that should be configured for a database:

- Use one big buffer pool and let DB2's aging algorithm take care of which pages are in the buffer pool.
- Use multiple buffer pools and assign them to specific table spaces to ensure that highly active pages are kept in the buffer pool.

If DB2 is installed in 32-bit mode, there are limitations on the maximum amount of shared memory that can be addressed by a process. Because the buffer pool is allocated in shared memory, there are limits on the maximum size of the buffer pool(s) that can be created for a database, regardless of the amount of physical memory on the system. If DB2 is installed in 64-bit mode, the shared memory limit is much higher, and most systems will run out of real memory before hitting the operating system limit.

If they are properly sized and assigned to the right table spaces, multiple buffer pools will out-perform a single buffer pool. However, multiple buffer pools will require constant monitoring and tuning in order to keep them performing optimally.

Other than its size, a single buffer pool needs no tuning. DB2 has a highly optimized algorithm for aging pages in the buffer pool that uses several techniques designed to optimize the buffer pool hit ratio by:

- Favoring important pages, such as index pages
- Placing pages that are unlikely to be accessed again on "Hate stacks," which are used to identify victim pages quickly

When to Consider Multiple Buffer Pools

Multiple buffer pools should be considered under the following conditions:

- There are multiple applications accessing the database, and the user wants to favor a particular application.
- Certain tables do not need large buffer pools, for example:
  - Tables that are always appended to, such as journal or history tables.
  - Huge tables (i.e., bigger than the buffer pool) that are only ever fully scanned.
    - These tables will likely always require disk I/O, regardless of buffer pool size.
    - Assign these tables to a dedicated buffer pool; otherwise, when they are scanned, they will likely cause other important pages to be flushed from the buffer pool.
    - Be careful to make these tables' dedicated buffer pool large enough for effective prefetching.
- If tables are usually scanned concurrently, separate them into their own dedicated buffer pools.
  - UDB will try to keep these pages in memory; but in aggregate, this could swamp the buffer pool and interfere with the access to other objects.
- To isolate high-priority or high-usage tables or indexes from other database activity.
- If people occasionally run large reports on OLTP systems and the reports do large joins, sorts, etc. that cause large temporary tables to be created.
  - These temporary tables can sometimes overwhelm the buffer pool, so it can be beneficial to create a buffer pool for the temporary table space.
  - Size this buffer pool according to the typical overflow sorts, if there are any, under normal operations.
  - This buffer pool typically does not need to be large because it is normally accessed sequentially.

o This way, the reports have less impact on the overall performance of the online system.

Buffer Pool Overhead

For every page of buffer pool space and/or extended storage, DB2 creates a 100-byte descriptor in the database heap to store a descriptor of the page. Before creating large buffer pools, it may be necessary to increase the size of the database heap (dbheap) configuration parameter to hold the descriptors for the buffer pool pages.

For a 1-GB buffer pool with a page size of 4 KB, there must be 262,144 pointers allocated in the database heap. This will use up approximately 25 MB of database heap.

For a 32-GB buffer pool with a page size of 4 KB, there must be 8,388,608 pointers allocated in the database heap. This will use up approximately 800 MB of database heap.

32- and 64-bit Considerations

DB2 UDB Version 8 can be installed as a 32-bit or a 64-bit application. When DB2 is installed on the 64-bit version of UNIX, setting the DATABASE_MEMORY configuration parameter to AUTOMATIC allows DB2 to grow its memory usage as needed, when the buffer pools grow, or when additional memory is needed for database control blocks.

When DB2 is installed in 32-bit mode, the amount of shared memory available and the memory management options are more limited than in 64-bit mode. To guarantee that memory is available to create a new buffer pool or enlarge an existing buffer pool with the IMMEDIATE option, memory must be reserved when the database is started. If the database configuration parameter DATABASE_MEMORY is set to a numeric value, when the database is activated, DB2 will allocate the minimum of the following:

- The total shared memory used by the buffer pools, lock list, database heap, shared sort heap threshold, package cache, and utility heap.
- The amount of memory specified by DATABASE_MEMORY.

> **N O T E**   The db2level command now displays whether DB2 is installed in 32- or 64-bit mode, in addition to the version and fixpack level.

Shared Memory/Buffer Pool Limits

When DB2 is installed in 32-bit mode, there are operating system limitations to the maximum size of a shared memory that a process can allocate. Because each database will have all of its shared memory allocated in the same segment, there is a maximum amount of shared memory that can be allocated per database.

It is important to note that the limitation is on the total amount of shared memory that can be allocated/addressed, and the buffer pool is just one of the items that gets allocated in the database's shared memory. The following items are allocated in shared memory:

- Buffer pools (buffpage or BP size)
- Lock list (locklist)
- Package cache (pckcachesz)
- Shared sorts
  - If intra-partition parallelism is enabled, reserve the shared sort heap threshold (SHEAPTHRES_SHR).
- Database heap (dbheap)
  - Log buffer (logbufsz)
  - Catalog cache (catalogcache_sz)
- Utility heap (util_heap_sz)

In 32-bit AIX, there are a maximum of 16, 256 MB memory segments addressable by a process. Of these, only seven can be used by DB2 for shared memory. Of these seven segments (or 1.75 GB), one is used for memory mapped I/O, and one may be used by the fast communications manager (FCM) for inter- or intra-partition communication (if there are multiple database partitions or intra-partition parallelism is enabled). To maximize the amount of shared memory that can be used for the buffer pool, memory-mapped I/O can be disabled, and the FCM can be forced to use the network instead of shared memory.

To disable memory mapped I/O, set the following DB2 registry variables to no.

- DB2_MMAP_READ
- DB2_MMAP_WRITE

Using memory-mapped I/O is most beneficial for systems that contain table spaces with few file containers, i.e., SMS or DMS files. Memory-mapped I/O helps to avoid i-node latching by spreading the I/Os across more files (and more underlying i-nodes). If memory-mapped I/O is turned off, make sure that any SMS table space (or DMS table space using file containers) has enough containers (i.e., 3+ per file system) to avoid i-node contention. Otherwise, any performance gain from the extra memory will be lost due to contention on disk.

To force the FCM to use the network instead of shared memory, set the following DB2 registry variable to no.

- DB2_FORCE_FCM_BP

The maximum addressable amount of shared memory for the 32-bit version of DB2 varies, depending on the operating system. Table 2.1 shows shared memory limits.

Table 2.1   Operating System Shared Memory Limits

Operating System	Shared Memory Limit
AIX	1.75 GB
Solaris	3.35 GB
Windows NT/2000/XP	2 GB
	3 GB if using Advanced Server and /3GB set in boot.ini
	64 GB with AWE support; requires that DB2_AWE registry variable be set
Linux	Kernel 2.3 or earlier:
	768 KB if less than 2 GB of real memory
	1.1GB if 2 GB or more of real memory
	Kernel 2.4 or higher
	1.75 GB
HP/UX	800 KB

Maximizing Buffer Pool Size on Windows

When working with Windows 2000, the total addressable memory can be up to 64 GB; therefore, the maximum buffer pool sizes that can be created on Windows equals 64 GB minus the memory used by the operating system and other DB2 memory allocations, assuming that the server is dedicated to DB2. The support for large memory addressing on Windows is provided by the Microsoft Address Windowing Extensions (AWE). Through AWE, Windows 2000 Advanced Server provides support for up to 8 GB of memory addressing, whereas Windows 2000 Data Center Server provides support for up to 64 GB of memory.

To take advantage of memory addresses above 2 GB, both DB2 and Windows 2000 must be configured correctly to support AWE. To be able to address up to 3 GB of memory, the /3GB Windows 2000 boot option must be set. To enable access to more than 4 GB of memory via the AWE memory interface, the /PAE Windows 2000 boot option must be set. To verify that you have the correct boot option selected, under Control Panel, select System, then select "Startup and Recovery." From the drop-down list, you can see the available boot options. If the boot option (/3GB or /PAE) you want is selected, you are ready to proceed to the next task in setting up AWE support. If the option you want is not available for selection, you must add the option to the boot.ini file on the system drive. The boot.ini file contains a list of actions to be done when the operating system is started. Add /3GB or /PAE, or both (separated by blanks), at the end of the list of existing parameters. Once you have saved this changed file, you can verify and select the correct boot option, as mentioned above.

Windows 2000 also has to be modified to associate the right to "lock pages in memory" with the userid that was used to install DB2. To set the "lock pages in memory" correctly, once you have logged on to Windows 2000 as the user who installed DB2, under the Start menu on Windows 2000, select the "Administrative Tools" folder, then the "Local Security Policy" program. Under the local policies, you can select the user rights assignment for "lock pages in memory."

DB2 also requires the setting of the DB2_AWE registry variable to be able to take advantage of the larger memory addressing. This registry variable must be set to the buffer pool ID of the buffer pool that will be larger than 3 GB and have a need for AWE support, as well as the number of physical pages and the address window pages to be allocated for the buffer pool.

The buffer pool ID is found in the BUFFERPOOLID column in the catalog view SYSCAT.BUFFERPOOLS. The number of physical pages to allocate should be less than the total number of available pages of memory, and the actual number chosen will depend on the working environment. For example, in an environment where only DB2 UDB and database applications are used on the server, normally select a value between one-half of the available memory up to 1 GB less than the available memory. In an environment where other nondatabase applications are also running on the server, these values will need to be reduced to leave memory available for the other applications. The number used in the DB2_AWE registry variable is the number of physical pages to be used in support of AWE and for use by DB2. The upper limit on the address window pages is 1.5 GB, or 2.5 GB when the /3GB Windows 2000 boot option is in effect.

Hidden Buffer Pools

When a database is activated or started (i.e., during the first connection to the database), DB2 automatically creates four hidden buffer pools for the database, in addition to the IBMDEFAULTBP and any user created buffer pools. These buffer pools are hidden and do not have entries in the system catalog tables. In addition, these buffer pools cannot be used directly by assigning table spaces to them and cannot be altered.

There will be one hidden buffer pool per page size (i.e., 4 KB, 8 KB, 16 KB, and 32 KB) to ensure that there is a buffer pool available under all circumstances. DB2 UDB will use these buffer pools under the following conditions:

- When the CREATE BUFFERPOOL statement is executed and the IMMEDIATE option is specified, but there is not enough memory available to allocate the buffer pool.
  - If this occurs, a message is written to the administration notification log.
  - Any table spaces that are using the buffer pool will be remapped to the hidden buffer pool with the same page size.
- When the IBMDEFAULTBP and/or any of the user-created buffer pools cannot be allocated when the database is activated or started.
  - If this occurs, a message is written to the administration notification log.

- ○ Any table space that is using a buffer pool that was not allocated will be remapped to the hidden buffer pool with the same page size.
  - ○ DB2 will be fully functional because of the hidden buffer pools, but performance will be drastically reduced.
- When a table space is created and its page size does not correspond to the page size of any of the user created buffer pools.
- During a roll forward operation if a buffer pool is created and the DEFERRED option is specified.
  - ○ Any user-created table spaces that are assigned to this buffer pool will be remapped to the hidden buffer pool with the same page size for the duration of the roll forward operation.

By default, the hidden buffer pools will be created with a size of 16 pages. This can be changed, using the DB2_OVERRIDE_BPF registry variable. To change the size of the hidden buffer pools to use 64 pages each, set the registry variable as follows:

```
DB2SET DB2_OVERRIDE_BPF=64
```

Altering Buffer Pools

The ALTER BUFFERPOOL statement will change the defined attributes for the specified buffer pool in the database that the user is connected to. In previous versions of DB2 UDB, the buffer pool size could not be changed until the database was stopped and restarted (i.e., all current applications were disconnected from the database and another connection was established).

With DB2 UDB Version 8, the buffer pool size can be changed immediately, provided that there is enough memory available to handle the request. However, changes to any other buffer pool configuration parameters will be deferred until the database is stopped and restarted.

The ALTER BUFFERPOOL statement has options to specify the following:

- **bufferpool-name:** Specifies the name of the buffer pool. The name cannot be used for any other buffer pools and cannot begin with the characters SYS or IBM.
- **IMMEDIATE:** Specifies that the buffer pool will be created immediately if there is enough memory available on the system. If there is not enough reserved space in the database shared memory to allocate the new buffer pool, a warning is returned, and buffer pool creation will be DEFERRED. This is the default.
- **DEFERRED:** Specifies that the buffer pool will be created the next time that the database is stopped and restarted
- **DBPARTITIONNUM:** Specifies the database partition group on which the ALTER BUFFERPOOL statement will take effect.
- **SIZE:** Specifies the size of the buffer pool and is defined in number of pages. In a partitioned database, this will be the default size for all database partitions where the

buffer pool exists. The EXCEPT ON DBPARTITIONNUMS clause allows the buffer pool to have different sizes on the different database partitions.

- **EXTENDED STORAGE/NOT EXTENDED STORAGE:** Specifies whether buffer pool victim pages will be copied to a secondary cache called *extended storage*. Extended storage is more efficient than retrieving data from disk but less efficient than retrieving data from the buffer pool so is not applicable to 64-bit environments.
- **ADD DATABASE PARTITION GROUP:** Specifies the database partition group(s) to which the buffer pool will be added. The buffer pool will be created on all database partitions that are part of the specified database partition group(s).
- **NUMBLOCKPAGES:** Specifies the number of pages to be created in the block-based portion of the buffer pool. The actual value of NUMBLOCKPAGES may differ from what was specified because the size must be a multiple of the BLOCKSIZE. The block-based portion of the buffer pool cannot be more than 98% of the total buffer pool size. Specifying a value of 0 will disable block I/O for the table space.
- **BLOCKSIZE:** Specifies the number of pages used for the block-based I/O. The block size must be between 2 and 256 pages, and the default value is 32 pages.

A buffer pool cannot be altered to use both block-based I/O and extended storage at the same time.

> **N O T E**   Before altering the number of pages in a buffer pool, it is important to understand and assess the impact on applications accessing the database. A change in buffer pool size may result in a different access plan.

For the buffer pool created with the following statement:

```
CREATE BUFFERPOOL BP1
SIZE 25000
```

In order to change the size of the buffer pool to 200 MB use the following statement:

```
ALTER BUFFERPOOL BP1
SIZE 50000
```

For the buffer pool created with the following statement:

```
CREATE BUFFERPOOL BP2
IMMEDIATE
SIZE 100000
NUMBLOCKPAGES 32000
BLOCKSIZE 256
```

In order to change the size of the block-based area of the buffer pool to 200 MB use the following statement:

```
ALTER BUFFERPOOL BP2
NUMBLOCKPAGES 50000
```

> **N O T E**   Changes to the size of the block-based area of the buffer pool will not take effect immediately. They will take effect when the database is stopped and restarted.

For the buffer pool created with the following statement:

```
CREATE BUFFERPOOL BP3
DATABASEPARTITIONGROUP DPG1
SIZE 25000
PAGESIZE 32K
```

In order to allocate this buffer pool on the database partitions in the partition group DPG2, use the following statement:

```
ALTER BUFFERPOOL BP3
ADD DATABASEPARTITIONGROUP DPG2
```

For the buffer pool created with the following statement:

```
CREATE BUFFERPOOL BP4
IMMEDIATE
SIZE 100000
NUMBLOCKPAGES 32000
BLOCKSIZE 256
```

the following statement:

```
ALTER BUFFERPOOL BP4
EXTENDED STORAGE
```

would produce an error because block-based I/O and extended storage cannot both be enabled at the same time.

Block-Based Buffer Pools Can Improve Sequential Prefetching

The DB2 UDB buffer pools are page-based; therefore, when contiguous pages on disk are prefetched into the buffer pool, they likely will be placed into noncontiguous pages within the buffer pool. Sequential prefetching can be enhanced if contiguous pages can be read from disk into contiguous pages within the buffer pool.

This can be accomplished by enabling block-based I/O for the buffer pool, using the NUMBLOCKPAGES and BLOCKSIZE parameters for the buffer pool. A block-based buffer pool will contain a page-based area, as well as a block-based area, with sizes based on the NUMBLOCKPAGES parameter. The page-based area will be used for any I/O operation that is not performed using sequential prefetching. The block-based area of the buffer pool will be made up of a number of "blocks," where each block will contain a set number of contiguous pages, defined by the BLOCKSIZE.

To make the block-based I/O as efficient as possible, it is important to try to match the extent size for the table spaces, using the buffer pool with the block size for the buffer pool. Because the prefetch operation will attempt to read an extent from the table space into a block in the buffer pool, having these use the same size allows for the most optimal use of the memory. DB2 will still use the block-based area of the buffer pool for prefetching if the extent size is larger than the block size of the buffer pool. If the extent size is smaller than the block size, DB2 may still use the block-based area for prefetching, but if there is too much difference between the extent and block sizes, DB2 may chose to use the page-based area of the buffer pool, depending on the size difference.

If some of the pages that have been requested in the prefetch request have already been read into the page-based area of the buffer pool, using page-based I/O, the prefetcher may or may not read the data into the block-based area, depending on how much of the block would be wasted. The I/O server allows some wasted pages in each buffer pool block, but if too much of a block would be wasted, the I/O server will prefetch the data into the page-based area of the buffer pool. Space is considered as wasted under the following conditions:

- The page would be empty because the extent size is smaller than the block size
- The page already exists in the page-based area of the buffer pool

System Catalog Views Relating to Buffer Pools

There are two system catalog views that can be used to retrieve information about the buffer pools defined within a database:

- SYSCAT.BUFFERPOOLS
- SYSCAT. BUFFERPOOLDBPARTITIONS

SYSCAT.BUFFERPOOLS View

This view contains a row for each buffer pool defined in each database partition group in the database. It contains the following columns:

- BPNAME: Name of the buffer pool. The name is defined when you create the buffer pool with the CREATE BUFFERPOOL statement.
- BUFFERPOOLID: The unique identifier assigned to the buffer pool when it is created

- DBPGNAME: The name of the database partition group where the buffer pool is defined. Will be blank if the buffer pool is on all partitions.
- NPAGES: The size of the buffer pool, in number of pages.
- PAGESIZE: The page size for the buffer pool.
- ESTORE: Indicates whether the buffer pool is using extended storage as a secondary cache.
  - Y = Yes
  - N = No
- NUMBLOCKPAGES: The number of pages in the buffer pool set aside for block-based I/O, in number of pages.
  - Zero if block-based I/O is not enabled
- BLOCKSIZE: The block size of a given block in the block-based area of the buffer pool.
  - Zero if block-based I/O is not enabled

The following is an example of the contents of this view:

```
select * from SYSCAT.BUFFERPOOLS

BPNAME          BUFFERPOOLID  DBPGNAME  NPAGES  PAGESIZE  ESTORE  NUMBLOCKAPGES  BLOCKSIZE
--------------  ------------  --------  ------  --------  ------  -------------  ---------
IBMDEFAULTBP         1            -       250     4096       N          0             0
BP3                 2           PG2     25000    32768       N          0             0
BP4                 3            -      10000     4096       N         3200           256

3 record(s) selected.
```

To calculate the sizes of the buffer pools in MB, use the following statement:

```
select BPNAME, NPAGES*PAGESIZE/1024/1024 AS SIZE_in_MB from
SYSCAT.BUFFERPOOLS
```

The following is an example of the output of this statement:

```
BPNAME                                       SIZE_in_MB
-------------------------------------------  ----------
IBMDEFAULTBP                                     9
BP3                                             781
BP4                                             39

3 record(s) selected.
```

SYSCAT.BUFFERPOOLDBPARTITIONS View

This view contains a row for each database partition in the database partition group, where the size of the buffer pool is different from the default size specified in the column NPAGES in the SYSCAT.BUFFERPOOLS view. It contains the following columns:

- **BUFFERPOOLID:** The unique identifier assigned to the buffer pool when it is created
- **DBPARTITIONNUM:** The database partition number where the buffer pool has a different size.
- **NPAGES:** The size of the buffer pool, in number of pages on the specified database partition.

The following is an example of the contents of this view:

```
select * from SYSCAT.BUFFERPOOLDBPARTITIONS


BUFFERPOOLID                DBPARTITIONNUM              NPAGES
------------------------------------------------------------
2                           3                           30000


1 record(s) selected.
```

What Is Prefetching?

When an agent acting on behalf of an application needs to access table or index pages, it will first look for the pages in the database buffer pool area. If the page cannot be found in the buffer pool area, it will be read from disk into the buffer pool. I/O is very expensive, and in this case, the agent cannot do anything but wait for the read request to finish before it can access the page. These page reads are typically done one page at a time, and if the application also needs to access subsequent pages within the table or index, this is not an efficient method for reading the pages into the buffer pool.

In many situations, DB2 UDB can anticipate the pages that will be requested by an application and read them into the buffer pool before the agent actually attempts to access them. This is referred to as *prefetching*. Prefetching can improve the database performance because the pages will be found in the buffer pool when the agent accesses them, reducing or eliminating the time the application must wait for the page to be read from disk into the buffer pool. This is more relevant to DSS-type workloads that scan large indexes and tables than for OLTP-type workloads that involve less scanning and more random insert/update/delete activity.

Prefetching can be enabled by the DB2 optimizer when it is building the access plan for a statement and determines that it will be scanning a large portion of a table or index. It can also be enabled or triggered when DB2 is executing an access plan and detects that it has read a number of pages in sequence and will likely continue to do so. This is known as *sequential detection* and can be enabled or disabled, using the database configuration parameter SEQDETECT.

Restart recovery will automatically use the prefetchers to improve restart time; however, prefetching can be disabled during restart recovery by setting the DB2 registry variable DB2_AVOID_PREFETCH to ON.

How Does Prefetching Work?

Prefetching will be requested by a DB2 agent if the access plan has specified that prefetching should be done or if sequential detection is enabled and a number of pages are read in sequence. The DB2 agent will make prefetch requests that will be examined by the prefetch manager and assigned to the DB2 I/O servers (also known as *prefetchers*).

The prefetch requests are sent to a queue where they are examined by the prefetch manager. The prefetch manager examines the requests to determine whether any of the prefetch requests from different applications can be combined and handled more efficiently in one prefetch operation. If no prefetch requests can be combined, the queue acts in a first in-first out (FIFO) manner.

To ensure that the prefetchers do not work too aggressively, reading data into the buffer pool and overwriting pages before they can be accessed, the amount of prefetching is controlled by the size of the buffer pool, as well as the prefetch size and the access plan generated by the optimizer. For smaller buffer pools, prefetching may be scaled back to ensure that prefetched pages do not flood the buffer pool and kick out pages that are currently being used or have been prefetched into the buffer pool and have not been accessed.

Within DB2 UDB, there are two main types of data and index prefetch requests handled by the prefetchers: range and list prefetching.

Range prefetching is used to prefetch a sequential range of pages from a database object and is used during table scans and when triggered by sequential detection. If a block-based area is set aside in the buffer pool, DB2 will perform a "big block" read to read a contiguous series of pages into a single private memory buffer, then will copy the block of pages to the block-based area of the buffer pool with one memory copy operation.

Internally, the mechanism used is big block read or "vectored" read (on platforms that support an efficient vectored read API). A big block read involves reading a contiguous block of pages into a single, private memory buffer. Each individual page is then copied into its own buffer pool slot (and all of these slots are likely to be scattered throughout the buffer pool). A vectored read API will read a contiguous block of pages from disk into different memory buffers (a different memory buffer for each page of the block). In this case, those memory buffers can actually be the individual buffer pool slots, and the overhead of the copy from one memory buffer to another is avoided (hence, an efficient vectored read API is preferred over big block read). The block-based area of the buffer pool overcomes this by setting aside contiguous blocks of the buffer pool equal in size to the extent size to make prefetching more efficient, especially on operating systems that do not support vectored reads.

List prefetching is used to prefetch a list of pages into the buffer pool area when an index scan produces a list of record IDs (RIDs) that must be prefetched into the buffer pool. List prefetching is normally decided on and specified in the access plan when the SQL statement is optimized. A list prefetch request may get converted to a range prefetch request if the pages are found to be sequential.

There is one *prefetch queue* that is monitored by the prefetch manager and shared between all of the configured prefetchers. The prefetch queue can handle up to 100 prefetch requests.

When a prefetch request is made, the request will be broken up into a number of smaller I/O requests. By default, the number of I/O requests will be determined by the number of containers that are in the table space. However, if the DB2_PARALLEL_IO registry variable is set, DB2 will start up a number of prefetchers equal to the prefetch size divided by the extent size. This allows multiple prefetchers to be working on the requests in parallel.

Choosing the optimal prefetch size   The prefetch size for a table space can be changed using the ALTER TABLESPACE statement so it can be adjusted if the prefetchers are either over-prefetching or under-prefetching. Over-prefetching results in wasted space in the buffer pool and/or overwriting pages in the buffer pool that are likely to be reused by other applications. Under-prefetching results in high prefetch wait times and usually causes the DB2 agents to perform the I/O themselves.

As a general rule of thumb, set the prefetch size as follows:

For a table space with multiple containers:

```
prefetch size = extent size * number of containers
```

For a table space with a single container on a Redundant Array of Independent Disks (RAID) or striped disk with the DB2_PARALLEL_IO variable set:

```
prefetch size = extent size * number of disks in the stripe set
```

If the containers are on separate physical disks, this will allow parallel I/O that will enable the prefetchers to read all extents simultaneously. The prefetching can be made more aggressive by increasing the prefetch size to be an integer multiple of the above formula. However, for this to be effective, there must be sufficient disk bandwidth to support it. In addition, the number of prefetchers may need to be increased (but only if the registry variable DB2_PARALLEL_IO is enabled, because the number of requests will be (prefetch size/extent size). With the registry variable DB2_PARALLEL_IO disabled (which is the default), the number of requests will be based on the number of containers in the table space, so increasing the prefetch size will not result in more prefetch requests and will increase the amount of I/O requested in each request.

Consider the following example:

A table space has two containers with a prefetch size set to twice the extent size. With the registry variable DB2_PARALLEL_IO disabled, there will be two prefetch requests since there are two containers in the table space, and each prefetch request will be for one extent. With the registry variable DB2_PARALLEL_IO enabled, there will be two prefetch requests because the prefetch size divided by the extent size equals 2, and each prefetch request will be for one extent.

If the prefetch size is increased to be four times the extent size, with the registry variable DB2_PARALLEL_IO disabled, there will still only be two prefetch requests because there are two containers in the table space. However, each prefetch request will now be for two extents. With the registry variable DB2_PARALLEL_IO enabled, there will be four prefetch requests because the prefetch size divided by the extent size equals 4, and each prefetch request will still be for one extent.

Increasing the prefetch size when the registry variable DB2_PARALLEL_IO is disabled will normally result in the same number of prefetch requests but with more I/O assigned to each request.

Choosing the number of prefetchers   If prefetch size is set as suggested above (i.e., prefetch size = extent size × number of containers) for all of the table spaces in the database, and all of the table spaces are being scanned at the same time, then the number of prefetchers should be equal to the number of disks belonging to the database. However, if one or more of the table spaces has been set up using more aggressive prefetching (i.e., the prefetch size is a multiple of this value) and/or some of the table spaces are not being scanned at the same time as the others, then the calculation becomes more complicated. To determine the number of prefetchers required in this case:

- Determine the number of table spaces that will potentially be scanned at the same time.
- For each of these table spaces, determine the number of prefetchers required to service a scan of it (based on the formulas above).
- Sum these values to determine the total number of prefetchers required.

Prefetching example   When the optimizer determines that a table scan can benefit from prefetching, DB2 will not prefetch the entire table in at once because this could potentially flood the buffer pool and result in important pages being removed; it does the prefetching in stages.

In the example shown in Figure 2.1, the prefetch size is equal to four times the extent size. Each block represents an extent.

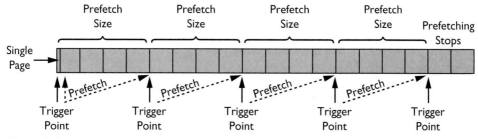

Figure 2.1
DB2 prefetching.

New prefetch requests are made each time a trigger-point page is read by the agent. Trigger-point pages are located at every multiple of the prefetch size within the table.

When the table scan starts, the first trigger point will be hit when the first page in the table is read. The first trigger point will request that DB2 prefetch the first two prefetch-sized blocks in the table. The first block will actually be one page less than the regular prefetch size and will start on the second page in the table to avoid prefetcher/agent contention on that first page. All subsequent trigger points will make a prefetch request to bring in the next prefetch-sized block of pages. If the system is configured and tuned properly, the agent should never have to wait on I/O because the prefetcher will have already read the page into the buffer pool.

If there is more than one container in the table space and/or DB2_PARALLEL_IO is enabled, it will be much more efficient to have multiple prefetchers performing the I/O, rather than one prefetcher. In this case, the prefetch request is broken up into smaller requests, and each of the requests is placed onto the prefetch queue. The prefetchers can then service the requests in parallel, potentially performing much faster than a single prefetcher doing all of the work.

In the example above, if DB2_PARALLEL_IO is enabled, the larger request would be broken into four (prefetch size / extent size = 4) smaller prefetch requests. If DB2_PARALLEL_IO is disabled (which is the default), the number of prefetch requests would be based on the number of containers in the table space.

In the example, the last trigger point will not result in prefetching because there are not enough pages remaining to fill an entire prefetch request.

Other roles of the prefetchers   In addition to the true prefetching work, prefetchers have some other key functions. These functions include:

1. **DROPPING TEMPORARY OBJECTS:** During query processing, one or more system temporary tables may be created to hold intermediate or final result sets. When a system temporary table is no longer required, it is dropped. This involves purging (removing) its pages from the buffer pool, and this can take a relatively long time. So, rather than having the agent drop the table and wait for it to complete, it instead makes a prefetcher request that will handle the drop table work. This reduces the agent's response time because it does not have to do the work itself.

2. **ADDING DMS CONTAINERS:** When more than one container is added to a DMS table space in a single ALTER TABLESPACE statement, the prefetchers assist the agent in allocating the disk space for those containers. The agent handles the allocation for one container, and for each of the remaining containers it creates a prefetch request to add the container. This allows the container allocation to be done in parallel, speeding up the process.

3. **RESIZING DMS CONTAINERS:** This request type is similar to adding DMS containers, but it handles allocation of new space when the RESIZE or EXTEND options of the ALTER TABLESPACE statement are used.

4. **TRAVERSING INDEX LEAF PAGES:** This request type is mainly used by the REORG utility when scanning an index object. Given the root page of an index, the leaf level is traversed using the prefetchers.

What Is Page Cleaning?

When an agent acting on behalf of an application needs to access table or index pages, it will first look for the pages in the database buffer pool area. If the page cannot be found in the buffer pool area, it will be read from disk into the buffer pool. If the buffer pool is full, DB2 must select a "victim" page to be overwritten in the buffer pool. If the victim page is dirty (i.e., it was changed since it was read into the buffer pool and has not been written to disk), it must first be written to disk before it can be overwritten. During the write operation, the application must wait. To reduce the likelihood that the victim page will be dirty, DB2 uses page cleaners to write dirty pages asynchronously to disk before they are chosen as victims.

An additional benefit of the page cleaners writing the dirty pages to disk is the reduction in the amount of work required in the event that there is a problem with DB2 and a database restart or recovery is required.

Each buffer pool has what is called a "dirty list" that contains a list of all dirty pages contained in the buffer pool. When the page cleaners are triggered, they will read the dirty lists for all table spaces in the database and will asynchronously write the dirty pages to disk.

How Are the Page Cleaners Triggered?

The page cleaners can be triggered in three different manners.

Dirty Page Threshold

When a page in the buffer pool is changed, it is added to the buffer pool's dirty list. At this time, DB2 checks to see whether this addition to the dirty list exceeds the changed page threshold (aka dirty page threshold) for the buffer pool. If the changed page threshold is exceeded, the page cleaners will be triggered.

The changed page threshold database configuration parameter (CHNGPGS_THRESH) represents the percentage of the buffer pool that can be dirty before the page cleaners are triggered.

LSN Gap

When transactions are occurring against the database, they will be logged. To reduce the amount of work required in the event of a problem, DB2 will trigger the page cleaners as it writes to the log file(s).

The percentage of the log file reclaimed before soft checkpoint database configuration parameter (SOFTMAX) represents the percentage of a log file that is written before the page cleaners are triggered.

Dirty Page Steals

When an agent requests a page that must be read from disk and DB2 chooses the victim page, if the page is dirty, the page must first be written to disk before it can be used to read the new page that the agent has requested. After a number of dirty victim pages have been selected, DB2 will automatically trigger the page cleaners to write the dirty pages to disk.

How the Page Cleaners Work

When the page cleaners are triggered, all of the page cleaners are triggered at the same time. They will each gather up to 400 pages from the dirty lists for the database buffer pools. The pages from the dirty list will then be written to disk one page at a time until the page cleaner has processed its assigned dirty pages. Once it has written all of the pages, it will check to see whether there are more pages to be written or whether there have been any new triggers. If so, it will gather a new list of pages to process; if not, it will wait for the next page cleaner to trigger.

Choosing the Number of Page Cleaners

Because all page cleaners are started whenever a page cleaner trigger is hit, having too many page cleaners can overwhelm the run queue on the server and cause a significant performance impact on the system. Therefore, as a rule of thumb, set the number of page cleaners equal to the number of CPUs in the database server.

Changed Page Threshold Tuning

The default value for the changed page threshold is 60%. For systems with large buffer pools, this can cause a noticeable slowdown of the system when the page cleaners are triggered. For example, with a 2-GB buffer pool, the changed page threshold will trigger the page cleaners when there is 1.2 GB of dirty pages in the buffer pool. Starting up a number of page cleaners to write out 1.2 GB of data to disk can cause a very noticeable slowdown. Setting the changed page threshold to a smaller value (i.e., 20–30%) will trigger the page cleaners more frequently, but they will have a smaller amount of data to write to disk and will have a much smaller impact on the performance of the system.

Monitoring Buffer Pool Activity

The database monitor can be used to monitor the various buffer pool and prefetching activities. The following entries in the buffer pool snapshot and/or the table space snapshot provide information about the page reads and writes occurring in the database:

- **Buffer Pool Data Physical Reads:** The number of data pages that were physically read from disk into the buffer pool. This includes synchronous reads done by the agents, as well as asynchronous reads that are done by the prefetchers.
- **Buffer Pool Data Logical Reads:** The number of data pages that were read from the buffer pool and from disk. To determine the number of read requests that were satisfied by the buffer pool, subtract the buffer pool data physical reads from the buffer pool data logical reads.
- **Buffer Pool Asynchronous Data Reads:** The number of data pages that were read into the buffer pool asynchronously by the prefetchers.
- **Buffer Pool Index Physical Reads:** The number of index pages that were physically read from disk into the buffer pool. This includes synchronous reads done by the agents, as well as asynchronous reads that are done by the prefetchers.
- **Buffer Pool Index Logical Reads:** The number of index pages that were read from the buffer pool and from disk. To determine the number of read requests that were satisfied by the buffer pool, subtract the buffer pool index physical reads from the buffer pool index logical reads.
- **Buffer Pool Asynchronous Index Reads:** The number of index pages that were read into the buffer pool asynchronously by the prefetchers.
- **Buffer Pool Data Writes:** The number of data pages that were written out from the buffer pool to disk. This includes synchronous writes done by the agents, as well as asynchronous writes done by the page cleaners and agents as a result of victim selection.
- **Buffer Pool Asynchronous Data Writes:** The number of data pages that were written out from the buffer pool to disk asynchronously by the page cleaners as a result of victim selection.
- **Buffer Pool Index Writes:** The number of index pages that were written out from the buffer pool to disk. This includes synchronous writes done by the agents, as well as asynchronous writes done by the page cleaners as a result of victim selection.
- **Buffer Pool Asynchronous Index Writes:** The number of index pages that were written out from the buffer pool to disk asynchronously by the page cleaners as a result of victim selection.
- **Total Buffer Pool Physical Read Time:** The total elapsed time spent processing read requests that caused data or index pages to be physically read from disk into the buffer pool. This includes synchronous reads done by the agents, as well as asynchronous reads done by the prefetchers.
- **Buffer Pool Asynchronous Read Time:** The total elapsed time spent by the prefetchers processing read requests that caused data or index pages to be physically read from disk into the buffer pool.
- **Total Buffer Pool Physical Write Time:** The total elapsed time spent processing write requests that caused data or index pages to be written out from the buffer pool to disk.

This includes synchronous writes done by the agents, as well as asynchronous writes done by the page cleaners as a result of victim selection.

- **Buffer Pool Asynchronous Write Time:** The total elapsed time spent writing data or index pages from the buffer pool to disk by page cleaners as a result of victim selection.
- **Buffer Pool Asynchronous Read Requests:** The total number of asynchronous read requests handled by the prefetchers.
- **Time Waited for Prefetch:** The total elapsed time that an agent spent waiting for a prefetcher to finish reading pages into the buffer pool.

In DB2 Version 8, the snapshot information can also be captured using SQL table functions. For each of the database snapshot monitors, there is an equivalent snapshot table function that can be used to obtain the same information. The SQL table functions normally require two input parameters, the database name and the database partition number. However, the database manager snapshot SQL table functions require only the partition number.

If no value is specified for the database name, the information will be captured for the database to which the application is currently connected. If a value of negative one (−1) is specified for the database partition number, the information will be captured for the database partition to which the application is currently connected. If a value of negative two (−2) is specified for the database partition number, the information will be captured for all of the database partitions in the database.

For example:

```
select BP_NAME,
(((1 - ((FLOAT(pool_Index_P_Reads + pool_data_P_Reads)) /
(FLOAT(Pool_Index_L_Reads + Pool_data_L_Reads)))) * 100)) AS
BPool_Hit_Ratio FROM TABLE(SNAPSHOT_BP('SAMPLE',-1 ))
as SNAPSHOT_BP;
```

will capture the snapshot information for the database partition the application is connected to, and

```
select BP_NAME,
(((1 - ((FLOAT(pool_Index_P_Reads + pool_data_P_Reads)) /
(FLOAT(Pool_Index_L_Reads + Pool_data_L_Reads)))) * 100)) AS
BPool_Hit_Ratio FROM TABLE(SNAPSHOT_BP('SAMPLE',-2 ))
as SNAPSHOT_BP;
```

will capture the snapshot information for all database partitions in the database.

Buffer Pool Tuning

After obtaining a buffer pool and/or table space snapshot for the database, the entries described above need to be analyzed to determine whether the database is operating efficiently. The information can also be examined using SQL table functions.

The buffer pool hit ratios are measures of the effectiveness of the buffer pool. The hits ratios reflect the number of times that a page request was able to be handled by the buffer pool directly without the need to read the page from disk. The more often that the request for a page can be satisfied from the buffer pool, the better that the overall performance of the system will be.

The following is a sample of the output of the buffer pool snapshot:

```
                    Database Snapshot
Database name                        = SAMPLE
Database path                        = /v1/db2/NODE0000/SQL00001/
Input database alias                 = SAMPLE
Database status                      = Active
Catalog database partition number    = 0
Catalog network node name            =
Operating system running at database = NT
   server
Location of the database             = Local
First database connect timestamp     = 09-04-2002 13:21:52.797473
Last reset timestamp                 =
Last backup timestamp                =
Snapshot timestamp                   = 09-04-2002 13:22:16.333042


                   Bufferpool Snapshot

Bufferpool name                      = IBMDEFAULTBP
Database name                        = SAMPLE
Database path                        = /v1/db2/NODE0000/SQL00001/
Input database alias                 = SAMPLE
Buffer pool data logical reads       = 523956
Buffer pool data physical reads      = 33542
Buffer pool data writes              = 288
Buffer pool index logical reads      = 257949
Buffer pool index physical reads     = 11323
Total buffer pool read time (ms      = 12012
Total buffer pool write time (ms)    = 720
Asynchronous pool data page reads    = 5227
Asynchronous pool data page writes   = 276
Buffer pool index writes             = 255
Asynchronous pool index page reads   = 451
Asynchronous pool index page writes  = 239
Total elapsed asynchronous read time = 819
Total elapsed asynchronous write time = 663
Asynchronous read requests           = 3553
Direct reads                         = 69664
```

```
Direct writes                          = 16902
Direct read requests                   = 2780
Direct write requests                  = 411
Direct reads elapsed time (ms)         = 4830
Direct write elapsed time (ms)         = 979
Database files closed                  = 17
Data pages copied to extended storage  = 0
Index pages copied to extended storage = 0
Data pages copied from extended storage = 0
Index pages copied from extended       = 0
   storage
Unread prefetch pages                  = 0
Vectored IOs                           = 0
Pages from vectored IOs                = 0
Block IOs                              = 0
Pages from block IOs                   = 0
Physical page maps                     = 0
```

Buffer Pool Hit Ratio

If DB2 needs to read an index or data page and the page is already in the buffer pool, the ability to access the page will be much faster than if the page has to be read from disk. The buffer pool hit ratio describes how frequently a request for an index or data page is handled directly from the buffer pool. The buffer pool hit ratio is calculated using the following formula:

```
BPHR = (1 - ((Data Physical Reads + Index Physical Reads) /
((Data Logical Reads + Index Logical Reads))) * 100%
```

Based on the above buffer pool snapshot, the buffer pool hit ratio would be:

```
BPHR = (1 - ((33542 + 11323) / (523956 + 257949))) * 100%
BPHR = 94.26%
```

In this case, 94.26% of the data and index page requests were able to be handled by the buffer pool, without the need for a physical I/O request.

The buffer pool hit ratio can also be calculated using the SQL table function as follows:

```
select BP_NAME,
(((1 - ((FLOAT(pool_Index_P_Reads + pool_data_P_Reads)) /
(FLOAT(Pool_Index_L_Reads + Pool_data_L_Reads)))) * 100)) AS
BPool_Hit_Ratio FROM TABLE(SNAPSHOT_BP('SAMPLE',-1 ))
as SNAPSHOT_BP;
```

The output of this statement would be the following:

```
BP_NAME                              BPOOL_HIT_RATIO
-------------------------------      --------------------
IBMDEFAULTBP                         +9.42652009389671E+001

1 record(s) selected.
```

To make the output more readable, the buffer pool hit ratio can be cast as an integer. This will round the value to the integer portion of its value but is close enough for most purposes. In this case, the SQL statement to calculate the buffer pool hit ratio can be changed to:

```
select BP_NAME,
(INT((1 - ((FLOAT(pool_Index_P_Reads + pool_data_P_Reads)) /
(FLOAT(Pool_Index_L_Reads + Pool_data_L_Reads)))) * 100)) AS
BPool_Hit_Ratio
FROM TABLE(SNAPSHOT_BP('SAMPLE',-1 ))
as SNAPSHOT_BP;
```

The output of this statement would be the following:

```
BP_NAME                              BPOOL_HIT_RATIO
-------------------------------      ----------------
IBMDEFAULTBP                         94

1 record(s) selected.
```

Index Hit Ratio

It is also important to examine the individual hit ratios, such as the data and index hit ratios. The index hit ratio is calculated using the following formula:

```
IHR = (1 - (Index Physical Reads / Index Logical Reads)) * 100%
```

The index hit ratio can also be calculated using the SQL table function as follows:

```
select BP_NAME,
(INT((1 - ((FLOAT(Pool_Index_P_Reads)) /
(FLOAT(Pool_Index_L_Reads)))) * 100))
AS Index_Hit_Ratio
FROM TABLE(SNAPSHOT_BP('SAMPLE',-1 ))
as SNAPSHOT_BP;
```

Data Hit Ratio

The data hit ratio is calculated using the following formula:

```
DHR = (1 - (Data Physical Reads / Data Logical Reads)) * 100%
```

The data hit ratio can also be calculated using the SQL table function as follows:

```
select BP_NAME,
(INT((1 - ((FLOAT(pool_Data_P_Reads)) /
(FLOAT(Pool_Data_L_Reads)))) * 100))
AS Data_Hit_Ratio
FROM TABLE(SNAPSHOT_BP('SAMPLE',-1 ))
as SNAPSHOT_BP;
```

Based on the above buffer pool snapshot, the index and data hit ratios would be:

```
IHR = (1 - (11323) / 257949)) * 100%
IHR = 95.61%


DHR = (1 - (33542) / 523956)) * 100%
DHR = 93.60%
```

In general, a buffer pool hit ratio above 80% is considered good. However, for an OLTP system, it is important to have the buffer pool hit ratio as high as possible (especially the index hit ratio) to be able to respond to requests efficiently and quickly. For large DSS systems, it is very unlikely that the buffer pool hit ratio will be high, due to the vast amounts of data that are normally read. Therefore, it is important to understand the workload on the system when analyzing the buffer pool hit ratios, so that they can be examined in the right context.

Asynchronous Read Ratio

Another important aspect of the buffer pool performance that can be analyzed using the snapshot information is the amount of synchronous versus asynchronous I/O. The percentage of asynchronous read requests (or Asynchronous Read Ratio) is calculated using the following formula:

```
ARR = ((Asynch Data Reads + Asynch Index Reads) /
((Data Logical Reads + Index Logical Reads)) * 100%
```

The asynchronous read ratio can also be calculated using the SQL table function as follows:

```
select BP_NAME,
(INT(((FLOAT(pool_Async_data_Reads + pool_async_index_Reads)) /
(FLOAT(Pool_Index_L_Reads + Pool_data_L_Reads))) * 100))
AS Asynch_Read_Ratio
FROM TABLE(SNAPSHOT_BP('SAMPLE',-1 ))
as SNAPSHOT_BP;
```

Based on the above buffer pool snapshot, the asynchronous read ratio would be:

```
ARR = ((5227 + 451) / (523956 + 257949)) * 100%
ARR = 0.73%
```

This is a very small value and would indicate that there is very little prefetch activity occurring for this database. This could be due to a number of reasons, such as:

1. The workload is reading and writing single rows, so it cannot take advantage of prefetching.
2. There are too few prefetchers configured for the database.
3. The table spaces in the database are set up with only one container each so that prefetching cannot normally take place.

> **N O T E** When DB2_PARALLEL_IO is set to YES, prefetching can occur within a single container table space if the prefetch size is a multiple of the extent size.

For a system with multiple buffer pools, it is normally a good idea to separate tables with a high percentage of asynchronous reads from those with a low percentage of asynchronous reads. The asynchronous read ratio can also be examined for each table space to help separate the table spaces with high and low asynchronous read ratios. For the following table space snapshot information, we see that there are four table spaces with different access patterns:

```
Tablespace name                             = TSPC1
   Buffer pool data logical reads           = 1200
   Asynchronous pool data page reads        = 32
   Buffer pool index logical reads          = 3400
   Asynchronous pool index page reads       = 128

Tablespace name                             = TSPC2
   Buffer pool data logical reads           = 15000
   Asynchronous pool data page reads        = 14000
   Buffer pool index logical reads          = 90000
   Asynchronous pool index page reads       = 86000

Tablespace name                             = TSPC3
   Buffer pool data logical reads           = 9000
   Asynchronous pool data page reads        = 8600
   Buffer pool index logical reads          = 6250
   Asynchronous pool index page reads       = 5975

Tablespace name                             = TSPC4
   Buffer pool data logical reads           = 7200
   Asynchronous pool data page reads        = 1400
   Buffer pool index logical reads          = 800
   Asynchronous pool index page reads       = 770
```

In this case, the asynchronous read ratios would be:

```
TBSPC1        3.5%
TBSPC2        95.2%
TBSCP3        95.6%
TBSPC4        27.1%
```

Because the table spaces TBSPC1 and TBSPC4 both have low asynchronous read ratios, they should not be placed in the same buffer pool as table space TBSPC2 or TBSPC3. Because the table spaces TBSPC2 and TBSPC3 both have a high asynchronous read ratio, they could be placed in the same buffer pool; however, because DB2 places an internal limit on the number of pages that can be prefetched into a buffer pool before they are accessed by a DB2 agent, having two table spaces with a high asynchronous read ratio in the same buffer pool may have an adverse effect. It may be more optimal to place the table spaces TBSPC2 and TBSPC3 in their own buffer pools.

Physical Read Rate

Also important is the rate at which DB2 is reading pages from disk. This should be calculated for all table spaces and, when compared, will show whether the I/O is spread evenly across all table spaces or whether the workload on certain table spaces is causing more I/O than in other table spaces.

The rate at which pages are read from disk (or Page Read Rate) is calculated using the following formula:

```
PRR = (Data Physical Reads + Index Physical Reads) /
(Time since monitor switches reset or activated)
```

Based on the above buffer pool snapshot, the page read rate would be:

```
PRR = (33542 + 11323) / (23.53 seconds)
PRR = 1906.7 reads per second
```

Examining the table space snapshot for the table spaces using the identified buffer pool may provide additional information to help determine which table space(s) is being read most often. Any table space(s) with a significantly higher I/O rate than other table spaces can be examined to determine whether the performance could be improved by assigning the table space to its own buffer pool or by adding containers to the table space to improve the I/O bandwidth.

Read Time

For every millisecond that a DB2 agent spends waiting for a page to be read into the buffer pool, the application is also waiting. The database snapshots do not provide information on the amount of time taken by each read request; however, they do provide enough information to calculate the average time taken per read request. The average read time is calculated using the following formula:

```
ART = (Total Buffer Pool Read Time) /
(Data Physical Reads + Index Physical Reads)
```

The average read time can also be calculated using the SQL table function as follows:

```
select BP_NAME,
(INT(((FLOAT(pool_read_time)) / (FLOAT(Pool_Index_p_Reads +
Pool_data_p_Reads))) * 100))
AS Avg_Read_Time_in_ms
FROM TABLE(SNAPSHOT_BP('SAMPLE',-1 ))
as SNAPSHOT_BP;
```

The SQL table function can also be used to calculate the buffer pool, data and index hit ratios, as well as the asynchronous read ratio and average read time in one SQL statement. This can be done using the following statement:

```
select BP_NAME,
(INT((1 - ((FLOAT(pool_Index_P_Reads + pool_data_P_Reads)) /
(FLOAT(Pool_Index_L_Reads + Pool_data_L_Reads)))) * 100))
AS BPool_Hit_Ratio,
(INT((1 - ((FLOAT(pool_Data_P_Reads)) /
(FLOAT(Pool_Data_L_Reads)))) * 100))
AS Data_Hit_Ratio,
(INT((1 - ((FLOAT(pool_Index_P_Reads)) / (FLOAT(Pool_Index_L_Reads))))
* 100))
AS Index_Hit_Ratio,
(INT(((FLOAT(pool_Async_data_Reads + pool_async_index_Reads)) /
(FLOAT(Pool_Index_L_Reads + Pool_data_L_Reads))) * 100))
AS Asynch_Read_Ratio,
(INT(((FLOAT(pool_read_time)) / (FLOAT(Pool_Index_p_Reads +
Pool_data_p_Reads))) * 100))
AS Avg_Read_Time_in_ms
FROM TABLE(SNAPSHOT_BP('SAMPLE',-1 ))
as SNAPSHOT_BP;
```

The output of this statement looks like the following:

```
BP_NAME        BPOOL_HIT_RATIO DATA_HIT_RATIO  INDEX_HIT_RATIO ASYNCH_READ_RATIO  AVG_READ_TIME_IN_MS
-------------  --------------- --------------  --------------- -----------------  -------------------
IBMDEFAULTBP                69             78               63                 0                  362

1 record(s) selected.
```

Page Cleaner Triggers

It is also important to understand which of the three triggers is causing the page cleaners to be activated and write the dirty pages from the buffer pools to disk. This information is available in the database snapshot information or through an SQL table function. The entries that describe the page cleaner triggers in the database snapshot are:

```
LSN Gap cleaner triggers              = 142
Dirty page steal cleaner triggers     = 2
Dirty page threshold cleaner triggers = 396
```

The SQL table function that will return the page cleaner triggers would look like the following:

```
SELECT DB_NAME,
POOL_LSN_GAP_CLNS,
POOL_DRTY_PG_STEAL_CLNS,
POOL_DRTY_PG_THRSH_CLNS
FROM TABLE(SNAPSHOT_DATABASE('SAMPLE',-1 ))
as SNAPSHOT_DATABASE
```

The output of the SQL function would look like the following:

DB_NAME	POOL_LSN_GAP_CLNS	POOL_DRTY_PG_STEAL_CLNS	POOL_DRTY_PG_THRSH_CLNS
SAMPLE	142	2	396

```
1 record(s) selected.
```

In this case, the page cleaners have been triggered by the "good" triggers, i.e., changed page threshold or LSN gap (softmax) well over 99% of the time. As was explained earlier, a dirty page steal trigger is done only after a number of pages have been synchronously written to disk and their associated clients forced to wait. If the number of "bad" page cleaner triggers (i.e., dirty page steal triggers) is more than a small percentage of the total number of triggers, the values set for changed page threshold and softmax, as well as the number of page cleaners, should be examined.

The percentage of bad page cleaner triggers is calculated as follows:

```
PBPCT = ((Dirty page steal cleaner triggers) /
(Dirty page steal cleaner triggers + Dirty page threshold cleaner
triggers + LSN Gap Cleaner Triggers)) * 100%
```

Based on the snapshot information above, the percentage of bad page cleaner triggers equals:

```
PBPCT = ((2) / (142 + 396 + 2)) * 100%
PBPCT = 0.37%
```

This ratio is very good and indicates that the system is primarily writing dirty pages to disk, using the asynchronous page cleaners.

However, based on the following snapshot information for the page cleaner triggers, the percentage of bad page cleaner triggers is much higher.

```
DB_NAME                    POOL_LSN_GAP_CLNS     POOL_DRTY_PG_STEAL_CLNS   POOL_DRTY_PG_THRSH_CLNS

-----------------------    -----------------     ----------------------    ----------------------

SAMPLE                                    17                       2034                      1192

1 record(s) selected.
```

The percentage of bad page cleaner triggers equals:

```
PBPCT = ((2034) / (17 + 1192 + 2034)) * 100%
PBPCT = 62.7%
```

In this case, the page cleaners are rarely being triggered by the pool LSN gap trigger, which indicates that the database configuration parameter softmax may be set too high. To determine the value of the softmax configuration variable, use the command:

```
get db cfg for sample | grep -i softmax
```

This returns the following:

```
Percent log file reclaimed before soft chckpt (SOFTMAX) = 100
```

In this case, the page cleaners are being triggered each time a log file is filled. Because this value is not abnormally high, next examine the log file size, using the command:

```
get db cfg for sample | grep -i logfilsiz
```

This returns the following:

```
Log file size (4KB)                    (LOGFILSIZ) = 250000
```

The log file size for this database is 250,000 4-KB pages, or 1 GB. Therefore, the page cleaners are being triggered only after 1 GB of log information has been written. If the log file size cannot be reduced, the softmax configuration parameter can be reduced to cause the page cleaners to be triggered more frequently. To update the softmax configuration parameter to cause the page cleaners to trigger after 10% of a log has been written, use the following command:

```
update db cfg for sample using softmax 10
```

If the log files do not need to be this large and can be reduced, the log file size can be changed to 250 4-KB pages, or 1 MB, using the following command:

```
update db cfg for sample using logfilsiz 250
```

Asynchronous Pages per Write

When the page cleaners are triggered, it is important that they be writing to disk as efficiently as possible. Having the page cleaners triggered too infrequently and writing a large number of pages to disk will cause the system to slow down. Likewise, having the page cleaners triggered frequently but writing a small number of pages to disk is also inefficient.

The number of pages written per page cleaner trigger is not captured in any of the DB2 snapshots; however, the average number of pages written per asynchronous write request can be calculated using the database base and buffer pool snapshot information. The average pages per asynchronous write can be calculated using the formula:

```
APPAW = ((Asynchronous pool data page writes + Asynchronous pool index
page writes) / (Dirty page steal cleaner triggers + Dirty page
threshold cleaner triggers + LSN Gap Cleaner Triggers))
```

Based on the following information from the database and buffer pool snapshots:

```
LSN Gap cleaner triggers                    = 142
Dirty page steal cleaner triggers           = 2
Dirty page threshold cleaner triggers       = 396
Asynchronous pool data page writes          = 167660
Asynchronous pool index page writes         = 178944
```

the average pages per asynchronous write would be:

```
APPAW = (167660 + 178944) / (142 + 2 + 396)
APPAW = 641.9
```

In this case, the page cleaners wrote an average of 641.9 pages, or 2.5 MB, each time they were triggered. This value needs to be examined in the context of the size of the buffer pool that is being examined. For a 1-GB buffer pool, this is a small value, and perhaps the page cleaners are being triggered too aggressively. For a 100-MB buffer pool, this value is much more reasonable.

PARALLELISM

The exploitation of parallelism within a database and within an application accessing a database can also have a significant benefit for overall database performance, as well as the normal administrative tasks. There are two types of query parallelism that are available with DB2 UDB: *inter-query* parallelism and *intra-query* parallelism.

Inter-query parallelism refers to the ability of multiple applications to query a database at the same time. Each query will execute independently of the others, but DB2 UDB will execute them at the same time.

Intra-query parallelism refers to the ability to break a single query into a number of pieces and replicate them at the same time using either *intra-partition* parallelism or *inter-partition* parallelism, or both.

Intra-Partition Parallelism

Intra-partition parallelism refers to the ability to break up a query into multiple parts within a single database partition and execute these parts at the same time. This type of parallelism subdivides what is usually considered a single database operation, such as index creation, database load, or SQL queries into multiple parts, many or all of which can be executed in parallel within a single database partition. Intra-partition parallelism can be used to take advantage of multiple processors of a symmetric multiprocessor (SMP) server.

Intra-partition parallelism can take advantage of either data parallelism or pipeline parallelism. Data parallelism is normally used when scanning large indexes or tables. When data parallelism is used as part of the access plan for an SQL statement, the index or data will be dynamically partitioned, and each of the executing parts of the query (known as *package parts*) is assigned a range of data to act on. For an index scan, the data will be partitioned based on the key values, whereas for a table scan, the data will be partitioned based on the actual data pages.

Pipeline parallelism is normally used when distinct operations on the data can be executed in parallel. For example, a table is being scanned and the scan is immediately feeding into a sort operation that is executing in parallel to sort the data as it is being scanned.

Figure 2.2 shows a query that is broken into four pieces that can be executed in parallel, each working with a subset of the data. When this happens, the results can be returned more quickly than if the query was run serially. To utilize intra-partition parallelism, the database must be configured appropriately.

Intra-partition parallelism must be enabled for the DB2 instance before the queries can be executed in parallel. Once intra-partition parallelism is enabled, the degree of parallelism, or number of pieces of the query that can execute in parallel, can be controlled using database configuration parameters.

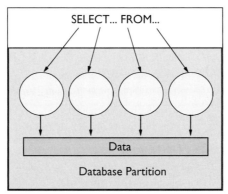

Figure 2.2
Intra-partition parallelism.

Configuring Intra-Partition Parallelism

Intra-partition parallelism in DB2 UDB is enabled or disabled using the database manager configuration parameter INTRA_PARALLEL. To enable intra-partition parallelism in DB2 UDB, the INTRA_PARALLEL configuration must be set to YES. This can be done using the following command:

```
UPDATE DBM CFG USING INTRA_PARALLEL YES
```

The degree of parallelism can then be controlled at the instance level, the database level, the application, or the statement level. The degree of parallelism can be set to a specific value or to ANY. If the degree of parallelism is set to ANY, the optimizer will determine the degree of parallelism for each individual SQL query that is submitted, based on the query itself and the number of CPUs available to the database or database partition.

Table 2.2 gives an overview of the parameters and options that are related to intra-partition parallelism in DB2 UDB.

Table 2.2   Controlling Intra-Partition Parallelism in DB2 UDB

Parameter	Value
INTRA_PARALLEL	YES/NO
	Defaults to NO on uni-processor machine
	Defaults to YES on SMP machine
	If changed, packages already bound will automatically be rebound at next execution.
MAX_QUERYDEGREE	1–32767, ANY
	Defaults to ANY; allows optimizer to choose degree of parallelism based on cost.
	No SQL executed on a database in this instance can use a degree of parallelism higher than this value.
DFT_DEGREE	1–32767, ANY
	Defaults to 1 (no parallelism)
	Provides the default value for:
	CURRENT DEGREE special register
	DEGREE bind option
	Maximum for any SQL in this database
CURRENT DEGREE	1–32767, ANY
	Sets degree of parallelism for dynamic SQL
	Defaults to DFT_DEGREE

Table 2.2   Controlling Intra-Partition Parallelism in DB2 UDB (Continued)

Parameter	Value
DEGREE	1–32767, ANY
	Sets degree of parallelism for static SQL
	Defaults to DFT_DEGREE
	To change: *PREP STATIC.SQL DEGREE n*
RUNTIME DEGREE	1–32767, ANY
(SET RUNTIME DEGREE	Sets degree of parallelism for running applications
command)	To change:
	SET RUNTIME DEGREE FOR (appid) to n
	Affects only queries issued after SET RUNTIME is executed
DB2DEGREE	1–32767, ANY
(CLI configuration file)	Default is 1
	Sets degree of parallelism for CLI applications
	CLI application issues a SET CURRENT DEGREE statement after database connection

The maximum degree of parallelism for an active application can be specified using the SET RUNTIME DEGREE command. The application can set its own run time degree of parallelism by using the SET CURRENT DEGREE statement. The actual run time degree used is the lower of:

- MAX_QUERYDEGREE instance configuration parameter
- Application run time degree
- SQL statement compilation degree

More information on parallelism support in DB2 Universal Database can be found in the *DB2 UDB Administration Guide: Performance.*

For a multi-partitioned database on a large SMP server, the maximum degree of parallelism for each partition should be limited so that each partition does not attempt to use all of the CPUs on the server. This can be done using the MAX_QUERYDEGREE instance configuration parameter. For a 32-way SMP server with eight database partitions, the maximum degree of parallelism for each partition could be limited to four, as follows:

```
UPDATE DBM CFG USING MAX_QUERYDEGREE 4
```

For an SMP server with 16 CPUs, running two separate DB2 instances, the maximum degree of parallelism for each partition could be limited to eight, as follows:

```
UPDATE DBM CFG USING MAX_QUERYDEGREE 8
```

for a DB2 instance with two databases that has intra-partition parallelism enabled. The benefit of intra-partition parallelism is very different if one database is a data mart or data warehouse and has large, complex queries scanning a large amount of data and the other database is used as a journal and is accessed using only INSERT statements. In this case, the default degree of parallelism can be set to different values for each database. If the databases are named DMDB and JRNLDB, this can be done as follows:

```
UPDATE DB CFG for DMDB USING DFT_DEGREE 8
UPDATE DB CFG for JRNLDB USING DFT_DEGREE 1
```

For CLI, ODBC, and JDBC applications, the degree of parallelism is controlled using the db2cli.ini file. The following is an example db2cli.ini file where any application that connects to the SAMPLE database will use a degree of parallelism of four.

```
[common]
TRACE=1                              Turn the trace on
TRACECOMM=1                          Trace communications costs as well
TRACEFLUSH=1                         Flush the trace as it happens
TRACEPATHNAME=d:\trace               Directory for the trace.


; Comment lines start with a
semi-colon.


[sample]
DBALIAS=MYSAMP
DB2DEGREE=4
autocommit=0
```

To change the degree of parallelism for a currently executing SQL statement, the SYSADM can change the run time degree for an application. For an application with an application ID of 130, to change the degree of parallelism to 2, the following command can be used:

```
SET RUNTIME DEGREE FOR (130) to 2
```

> **N O T E**   This change cannot affect the currently executing SQL statement but will be effective for all subsequent SQL statements.

Applications and Intra-Partition Parallelism

When an application connects to a nonpartitioned database, the connection is assigned to a coordinating agent, and all subsequent SQL statements and DB2 commands are executed by the coordinating agent on behalf of the application. If intra-partition parallelism is enabled, when an SQL statement is executed, the coordinating agent will determine the degree of parallelism to be used to execute the statement based on the access plan and the database and instance configura-

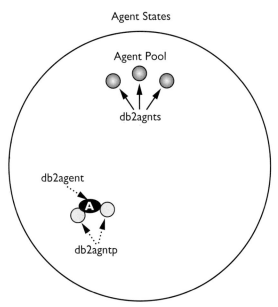

Figure 2.3
Agent states with intra-parallel enabled.

tion parameters. The coordinating agent will then make *n* copies of the access plan, where *n* is the degree of parallelism and will execute each copy of the plan on its own subagent. Therefore, for an access plan with a degree of parallelism of eight, there will be eight subagents and one coordinating agent used to execute the plan and return the data.

On a UNIX system, the coordinating agent and subagent processes will have different names. The coordinating agent process will be named *db2agent*, and the subagent process will be named either *db2agntp* or *db2agnts*, depending on whether the process is currently idle or working. An idle subagent will be named *db2agnts*, and a working subagent will be named *db2agntp*. In Figure 2.3, coordinating agent A has two subagents associated to it; therefore, the statement that it is currently executing has a degree of parallelism of 2. If coordinating agent A next runs an SQL statement with a degree of parallelism of 3, it must acquire another subagent in order to execute the access plan, as depicted in Figure 2.4.

If another application connects to the database and executes an SQL statement that has a degree of parallelism of 1, the agent pool would look like Figure 2.5. In this case, there will be three subagent processes associated with coordinating agent A and one subagent process associated with coordinating agent B.

The subagents are called *associated* because they have an affiliation with the coordinating agent and have control blocks and shared inter process communication (IPC) blocks set up to communicate between the coordinating agent and its associated subagents.

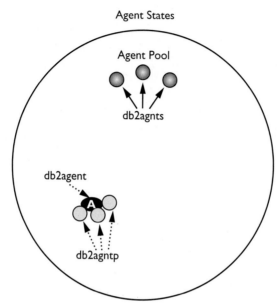

Figure 2.4
Degree of parallelism of 3.

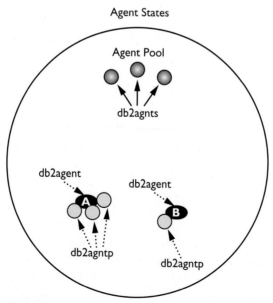

Figure 2.5
Two applications executing with varying degrees of parallelism.

If the application that is connected to coordinating agent B finishes its current SQL statement, its associated subagent will become idle but will remain associated with its coordinating agent. It remains associated because there is a chance that it may be needed in the future for a subsequent statement, and it is inefficient to break its association to release it back to the idle agent pool if it may be needed again.

If the application connected to coordinating agent A completes the current statement and runs a subsequent statement with a degree of parallelism of 2, one of its subagents will become idle but will remain associated with coordinating agent A. The agent pool would then look like that in Figure 2.6.

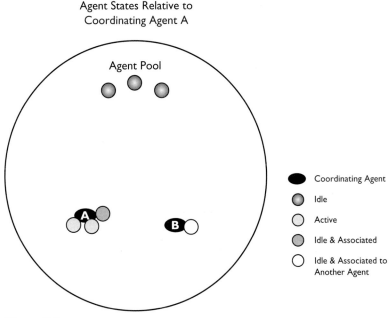

Figure 2.6
Summary of agent states.

Figure 2.6 shows all of the states that agents and subagents can be in within the agent pool. Within the pool, there are three idle agents waiting to be called on by either of the existing coordinating agents or by a subsequent application connecting to the database. Coordinating agent B is idle, but its application has not yet disconnected from the database, so the agent and its associated subagents will remain to service any subsequent SQL statements or until the application disconnects. If the application disconnects, the coordinating agent and its subagents will be returned to the agent pool as idle agents.

Coordinating agent A is currently executing an SQL statement with a degree of parallelism of 2; therefore, the coordinating agent and two of its associated subagents are busy. The third subagent is idle but remains associated to coordinating agent A.

If the current statement executing in coordinating agent A completes and the next SQL statement has a degree of parallelism of 8, the coordinating agent must make active and/or acquire a number of additional subagents. The activation and acquiring of these subagents will be done in an order that helps ensure the optimal usage of the agents and available resources. The agents will be acquired in the following order:

1. Convert any idle subagents currently associated to the coordinating agent to active.
2. Convert any idle subagents not currently associated to another coordinating agent to active (i.e., in the idle agent pool).
3. Convert any idle subagents currently associated to another coordinating agent to active.
4. Create a new agent process.

For this example, the idle subagent currently associated with coordinating agent A would be converted to active. The three idle agents in the pool would be associated with coordinating agent A and made active. The idle subagent currently associated with coordinating agent B would be unassociated from coordinating agent B, associated with coordinating agent A, and made active. One additional agent process would need to be created, associated with coordinating agent A and made active; then the SQL statement could be processed.

For a large, complex query, intra-partition parallelism is good, and the result set can normally be returned much quicker this way. However, an insert of a single does not require nine (eight subagents plus the coordinating agent) agents. In a typical OLTP environment, there are normally hundreds (if not more) of applications running in parallel. If each of them were assigned nine agent processes to handle their simple tasks, there would be far too many agent processes running on the system, causing a great deal more system overhead than is required.

In addition, when intra-partition parallelism is enabled, an instance level control block is set up by DB2, and each statement that is performed on any database in the DB2 instance will require a check of this control block during the statement's optimization and execution. Even if intra-partition parallelism is disabled for a database by setting the maximum degree of parallelism or default degree of parallelism to 1, this control block will still be checked during the optimization and execution of each statement. Therefore, it is best to disable intra-partition parallelism, using the database manager configuration parameter INTRA_PARALLEL.

Inter-Partition Parallelism

Inter-partition parallelism refers to the ability to break up a query into multiple parts across multiple partitions of a partitioned database on a single server or between multiple servers. The query will be executed in parallel on all of the database partitions. Inter-partition parallelism can

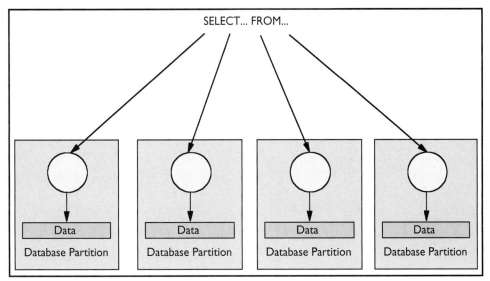

Figure 2.7
Inter-partition parallelism.

be used to take advantage of multiple processors of an SMP server or multiple processors spread across a number of servers.

Figure 2.7 shows a query that is broken into four pieces that can be executed in parallel, with the results returned more quickly than if the query was run in a serial fashion in a single partition. In this case, the degree of parallelism for the query is limited by the number of database partitions.

Combined Intra-Partition Parallelism and Inter-Partition Parallelism

In a partitioned database, intra-partition parallelism and inter-partition parallelism can be combined and used at the same time (Figure 2.8). This combination provides, in effect, two dimensions of parallelism. This results in an even more dramatic increase in the speed at which queries are processed. Combined intra-partition and inter-partition parallelism can be used to take advantage of multiple processors of a single or multiple SMP servers.

Why Partition a Database on a Large SMP Server?

Although DB2 can break a query into a number of pieces that can be executed in parallel, the scalability of DB2 with intra-partition parallelism can be limited or restricted only by the operating system and hardware on which DB2 is installed.

Creating multiple database partitions within a larger SMP server has proven to provide better scalability than intra-partition parallelism alone. As the number of CPUs grows, the scalability

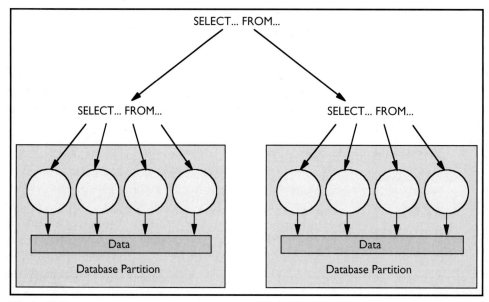

Figure 2.8
Combined intra-partition and inter-partition parallelism.

decreases when using intra-partition parallelism alone. By creating multiple database partitions within the SMP server, the scalability will remain almost linear. In a recent test of DB2 with multiple database partitions on a single SMP server growing from 6 to 24 CPUs (Figure 2.9), DB2 was able to deliver a speedup of 23.9 times on query response time.

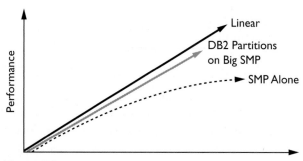

Figure 2.9
Comparing query scaling on large SMP servers.

Considerations with Multiple Database Partitions

In a partitioned database, the partition or partitions that will accept connection requests from clients are known as *coordinator partitions*. Because DB2 will automatically route all requests to the underlying database partitions, not all partitions need to be configured as coordinator partitions. In fact, when DB2 is configured with multiple database partitions within a single server, only one database partition per server can be a coordinator. The first database partition on the server listed in the db2nodes.cfg file is the only database partition that can be a coordinator partition.

Because the database partitions share a common install path and home directory, the listener port for the partitions, as defined in the database manager configuration, is the same for all database partitions on the same server. Because the database partitions cannot use the same listener process, only one partition per server can be a coordinator.

This should be taken into consideration when choosing where to create database partition groups within the database. Database partition groups that will be created on a single partition may benefit from being placed on database partitions that can be coordinators. Accessing tables in a single partitioned database partition group that is not a coordinator requires the coordinator to receive the SQL statement, then to pass it to the database partition where the SQL statement will be executed. The extra overhead of the coordinator partition "handling" the request and sending it to the affected database partition is not significant if the operation is complex and accesses a large amount of data. A transactional environment, where only a single row may be updated, can result in increased response time. However, DB2 provides a method to achieve maximum scalability and throughput, even for single-row selects or updates, known as *local bypass*.

Local Bypass

There is an API that can be called within the application to determine on which database partition the particular row is stored so that the application can then call another API to connect directly to the identified partition and read/update/delete the row.

These APIs are:

- **sqlugtpi** – Get partition information for the table being worked on
- **sqlugrpn** – Determine the partition to connect to

There are some important considerations when using these APIs that need to be noted:

1. As noted previously, only one database partition per server can be a coordinator; therefore, even if the application is directed to another partition on the server, it will be handled by the first database partition on the server. The communication between partitions within the same server uses shared memory to reduce the overhead associated with TPC/IP.

2. These APIs can be invoked from only one of the servers identified in the db2nodes.cfg file.
   a. They cannot be called in an application running on Windows if the database is on a UNIX server.
   b. The application must be running on the same server as one of the database partitions.

Some pseudo-code to show the use of the above APIs:

```
//create an array of connections as the connection pool to use.
SQLHDBC hDbc[NumOfNodes];    // will have one connection for each
logical node
SQLAllocEnv(&hEnv);

for (NodeNum=0; NodeNum < NumOfNodes; NodeNum++)
{
SQLAllocHandle(SQL_HANDLE_DBC, henv, hdbc);    // used to be
SQLAllocConnect
SQLSetConnectAttr(hDbc[NodeNum], SQL_ATTR_CONNECT_NODE, NodeNum);
SQLConnect(hDbc[NodeNum], "Your_DB_NAME");
} // Now you have one connection for each logical node ready.


//  Need to get the partition information for the table you are
working on
//  See last sample for more information about this part
strcpy(table_name, dbname);
strcat(table_name, "table_name");

sqlugtpi( table_name, &part_info, &sqlca_inst );
if(check_error("sqlugtpi failed", &sqlca_inst)!=0){
exit(-1);
}
// Say you got your primary key value and want to see which node you
want to connect and do your SQL
// See last sample for more information about this part

key_value[0] = malloc(10);
sprintf(key_value[0],"%d", YouKeyValue);
key_len[0] = strlen(key_value[0]);

sqlugrpn( part_info.sqld, key_value, key_len, ctrycode, codepage,
&part_info,
&part_number, &node_number, chklvl, &sqlca_inst,
SQL_CHARSTRING_FORMAT,
(void*)0, (void *)0 );
if(check_error("sqlugrpn failed", &sqlca_inst)!=0){
exit(-1);
}
```

```
// node_number is the node you need to connect
// Then you just need to use the connection handle hDbc[node_number]
// here is more CLI stuff for running your sql, consulting the CLI
documentation

SQLAllocStmt(hDbc[node_number], & hStmt);
SQLPrepare(hStmt, "Your SQL Statement String like select * from
....");
<< ... more statement specific calls to bind the columns and
parameters, etc. >>
SQLExect(hStmt);
SQLFetch(.....)
SQLFreeStmt(....)
```

Multiple Database Partitions within a Single Server

When configuring multiple database partitions on the same server, it is important that each database partition have sufficient resources in order to perform optimally. Each database partition contains a number of processes (or threads on Windows), and it is important to ensure that there are enough CPU cycles available to execute these processes. To ensure that there are sufficient CPU resources available, it is recommended that the ratio of database partitions to CPUs not exceed 1:1, i.e., do not create more database partitions on a server than there are CPUs in the server.

Depending on the speed and relative processing power of the CPUs on the server, a ratio of CPUs to database partitions of 1:1 or 2:1 will normally give the best performance. For most servers, a ratio of CPUs to database partitions of 2:1 will provide the best performance; however, with faster processors, such as the IBM pSeries P690 (Regatta), it is possible to reduce this ratio to 1:1 if needed.

For a database with multiple database partitions on the same server, DB2 UDB can use shared memory to communicate between the database partitions instead of using the network interconnect. The use of shared memory improves the performance of inter-partition communication but must be enabled using the DB2 registry variable DB2_FORCE_FCM_BP. Any inter-partition communication between database partitions on different servers will still use the dedicated interconnect; however, all inter-partition communication between database partitions on the same server will use shared memory, as shown in Figure 2.10.

One of the features available with the IBM pSeries P690 server is the ability to create logical servers within a large SMP server, using logical partitions (LPARs). This is a good way to separate different DB2 UDB instances within a single server and ensure that each partition gets dedicated resources. However, it may not be an optimal way of separating database partitions for the

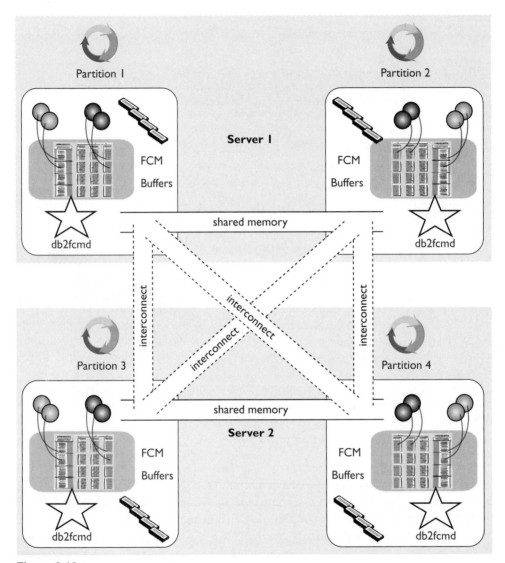

Figure 2.10
Inter-partition communication within and between servers.

same database within a server. Currently, the only way to communicate between LPARs on the same server is using a network interconnect because the LPARs cannot currently communicate using any optimized methods, such as shared memory. Therefore, when creating multiple database partitions on the same IBM pSeries P690 server, it is normally best not to use LPARs so that the inter-partition communication can benefit from the use of shared memory.

An additional benefit of this approach is that when some database partitions are not as busy as others, they can take advantage of all of the resources available on the server and not be constrained to the resources assigned to the LPAR.

> **N O T E**   This is also true with the Sun E10000 and E15000 servers that support a concept similar to LPARs, called *domains*.

TYPES OF DATABASE OBJECTS

A DB2 database is composed of data, indexes, and LOB and Long Varchar objects. When a table is created, the data object for the table is automatically created by DB2. If there are any indexes, primary keys, or unique constraints defined on the table, an index object will also be created. If the table contains one or more LOB columns, a LOB object will be created, and if the table contains one or more Long Varchar columns, a Long Varchar object will be created.

Tables

A table consists of data logically arranged in columns and rows. Users access the data by referring to its content instead of its location or organization in storage.

As we discussed early in this chapter, database partition groups are created within a database. Table spaces are created within database partition groups, and when tables are created, the name of the table space where the table objects will be created can be specified. If the database is partitioned, the rows of the table are distributed across the database partitions, based on the partition group's partitioning map, via a hashing algorithm.

Partition Maps

As shown in Figure 2.11, DB2 uses a hashing algorithm to assign a given row of a table to a corresponding database partition. When a table is created, a partitioning key is defined for that table. This partitioning key consists of one or many columns. (See "Partitioning Keys," later in this chapter for more details.) DB2 uses the value of the partitioning key for a given row as the input for the hashing function, and the output of the hashing function is a displacement into the partitioning map. The partitioning map is an array of 4,096 entries, each entry containing a database partition ID. The value at the specified position (displacement) in the partition map is the database partition ID where the row will be stored. Figure 2.11 shows an example of this process.

Based on the example above, a row is inserted into the table with a partitioning key value of 10004. This value is then used as input for the hashing algorithm. When the value of 10004 is hashed, the output of the algorithm is 514. DB2 then selects the value at offset 514 in the partitioning map as the database partition where the row will be stored. In this case, the row will be stored in database partition number 3.

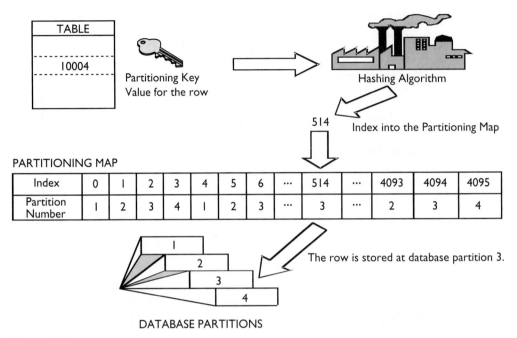

Figure 2.11
Hashing data rows using a partitioning map.

A partitioning map is an array (or vector) of 4,096 database partition numbers. Each partitioning map corresponds to only one database partition group and is created when the database partition group is created (or when data is redistributed).

> **N O T E**   All tables in a database partition group will use the same partitioning map.

Figure 2.12 shows three additional examples of partitioning maps. A partitioning map normally consists of an array of 4,096 elements (starting at element number 0) and is formed of two rows: The first row represents the element of the array—which ranges from 0 to 4,095—and the second row is the value at that element in the array, which is a database partition number.

In the first example, partition group PG123 is created on database partitions 1, 2, and 3. Therefore, the default partitioning map is created containing only these database partitions.

In the second example, a single-partition partition group is created. The partition map, therefore, has only one entry because all of the data rows will be stored in the same database partition. In this example, this is database partition 3.

1. create database partition group PG123 on dbpartitionnums (1,2,3)

Index	0	1	2	3	4	5	6	7	...	...	...	4093	4094	4095
Partition Number	1	2	3	1	2	3	1	2	...	...	...	3	1	2

2. create database partition group PG3 on dbpartitionnum (3)

Index	0
Partition Number	3

3. create database partition group PG1234 on all dbpartitionnums

Index	0	1	2	3	4	5	6	7	...	...	...	4093	4094	4095
Partition Number	1	2	3	4	1	2	3	4	...	...	...	2	3	4

Figure 2.12
Database partition map examples.

In the third example, a partition group is created, spanning all partitions in the database (i.e., database partitions 1, 2, 3, and 4). The partitioning map associated with this partition group will then contain all of these database partition numbers.

The partitioning map is created when a partition group is created, and it is stored in the SYSCAT.PARTITIONMAPS catalog view.

The default partitioning map contains the database partition numbers of the partition group assigned in a round-robin fashion, as shown in Figure 2.12. It is also possible to create and use partitioning maps that do not use this round-robin system. These maps are known as *customized partitioning maps* and may be required to achieve an even distribution of the table's data across the database partitions used by the table.

The utility db2gmap can be used to extract and display the partitioning map of a partition group from the SYSCAT.PARTITIONMAPS catalog view. To extract the partitioning map for the partition group PG123 depicted in Figure 2.12 and write it to the file PG123map.txt, use the following command:

```
db2gpmap -d <database_name> -g PG123 -m PG123map.txt
```

The first eight lines of the output file (PG123map.txt) generated by the db2gpmap utility would look like the following:

```
1 2 3 1 2 3 1 2 3 1 2 3 1 2 3 1 2 3 1 2 3 1 2 3 1 2 3 1 2 3
1 2 3 1 2 3 1 2 3 1 2 3 1 2 3 1 2 3 1 2 3 1 2 3 1 2 3 1 2 3
1 2 3 1 2 3 1 2 3 1 2 3 1 2 3 1 2 3 1 2 3 1 2 3 1 2 3 1 2 3
1 2 3 1 2 3 1 2 3 1 2 3 1 2 3 1 2 3 1 2 3 1 2 3 1 2 3 1 2 3
1 2 3 1 2 3 1 2 3 1 2 3 1 2 3 1 2 3 1 2 3 1 2 3 1 2 3 1 2 3
1 2 3 1 2 3 1 2 3 1 2 3 1 2 3 1 2 3 1 2 3 1 2 3 1 2 3 1 2 3
1 2 3 1 2 3 1 2 3 1 2 3 1 2 3 1 2 3 1 2 3 1 2 3 1 2 3 1 2 3
1 2 3 1 2 3 1 2 3 1 2 3 1 2 3 1 2 3 1 2 3 1 2 3 1 2 3 1 2 3
```

The upper left corner corresponds to the partition ID at element 0 of the partitioning map. The map is read by moving to the right and down, line by line.

The Relationship Between Partition Groups, Table Spaces, and Tables

In a partition database, a table will span all of the database partitions in its partition group. A table cannot span more than one partition group, but multiple tables can exist in the same partition group. Figure 2.13 shows the relationship between partition groups, table spaces, and tables.

The figure shows that the tables T2 and T3 are in the table space TS2, and the table space TS2 is in the partition group PG1234. The table spaces TS1 and TS2 both span all four database partitions, because the partition group PG1234 is created on all four database partitions.

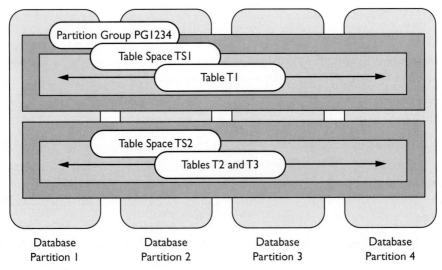

Figure 2.13
Tables, table spaces, and partition groups.

Partitioning Keys

The element that determines how the rows in a table are allocated among the database partitions is the table's partitioning key. The partitioning key for a table is a subset of the columns of the table and is defined when a table is created within a partitioned database.

For tables created in database partition groups containing more than one database partition, the partition key cannot be changed. If no partitioning key is explicitly specified, the first column that is not a Long Varchar or LOB will be used as the partitioning key.

> **N O T E**   Tables containing only LOB and/or Long Varchar columns cannot have partitioning keys and can be placed into only single-partition partition groups.

Choosing a Partitioning Key

The following considerations should be taken into account when choosing a partitioning key for a table:

- Include frequently used join columns.
- Use the smallest number of columns possible.
- The column(s) should have a high proportion of different values.
- Integer columns are more efficient than character columns, which are more efficient than decimal columns.
- Long Varchar and LOB columns fields cannot be part of the partitioning key.
- The primary key or any unique index must include the partitioning key.

Specifying the Partitioning Key

If the partitioning key is not explicitly specified in the create table statement and the table is being created in a multiple-partition database partition group, the partitioning key will be defined as follows:

- If a primary key is specified, the first column of the primary key is the partitioning key.
- If the table is a typed table, the object identifier column will be the primary key.
- Otherwise, the first column whose data type is not a LOB, LONG VARCHAR, LONG VARGRAPHIC, DATALINK column, distinct type based on one of these types, or structured type column is the partitioning key.

If none of the columns satisfy the requirements described above, the table will be created without a partitioning key, and it can be created only in a table space defined on single-partition database partition groups.

For tables in table spaces defined on single-partition database partition groups, any collection of non-long (i.e., not Long Varchar, not LOB) columns can be used to define the partitioning key. If the partitioning key is not explicitly specified, no partitioning key will be created.

Partitioning Key Examples

To determine the partitioning key used for an existing table, use the following statement:

```
select colname, partkeyseq
from syscat.columns
where tabname='<table_name>'
order by partkeyseq
```

The following examples will show how the partitioning key for a table can be specified, and if not specified, how DB2 will choose the partitioning key. The examples will show the create table statement, followed by the partitioning key.

```
create table <table_name>
(c1 varchar(30), c2 int, c3 char(10), c4 int) partitioning key (c2)
```

partitioning key c2

```
create table <table_name>
(name char(30), ID int, email varchar(50)) partitioning key (ID)
```

partitioning key ID

```
create table <table_name> (name char(30), ID int, email varchar(50))
```

partitioning key name

```
create table <table_name>
(description longvarchar(3000), ID int, email varchar(50))
```

partitioning key ID

```
create table <table_name>
(name char(30) not null, ID int not null, email varchar(50),
primary key (ID))
```

partitioning key ID

```
create table <table_name>
(name char(30) not null, ID int not null, email varchar(50),
primary key (ID, name))
```

partitioning key ID

For tables T1 and T2 with the following columns:

```
T1                              T2
-----------                     -----------
C1 int                          C1 char(10)
C2 char(10)                     C2 int
C3 real                         C3 real
```

To support the following SQL statement without needing to send data between partitions:

```
select t1.c, t1.c3 from t1, t2
where t1.c2=t2.c1
```

The partitioning key for table T1 should be c2, and the partitioning key for table T2 should be c1. To create the tables with these partitioning keys, the following statements can be used:

```
create table T1  (c1 int, c2 char(10), c3 real) partitioning key (c2)
create table T2  ( c1 char(10), c2 int, c3 real) partitioning key (c1)
```

Because the column c1 would be the default partitioning key for table T2, the partitioning key does not need to be explicitly specified. However, it is always good practice to explicitly specify the partitioning key when a table is created.

Changing the Partitioning Key

Once a partitioning key has been specified for a partitioned table, it cannot be changed. To change it, the table's data would need to be exported, the table dropped and recreated, and the data reloaded. For a table in a single-partition database partition group, the partitioning key can be changed by dropping the existing partitioning key and creating a new partitioning key, as follows:

```
alter table <table_name> drop partitioning key
alter table <table_name> add partitioning key(<column,column,...>)
```

For example, for the following table in a nonpartitioned database partition group:

```
create table T2  ( c1 char(10), c2 int, c3 real) partitioning key (c1)
```

To change the partitioning key to be column c2, use the following statements:

```
alter table T2 drop partitioning key
alter table T2 add partitioning key(c2)
```

If an attempt is made to drop the partitioning key of a table created in a multi-partition database partition group, the following error will be returned:

```
SQL0264N Partitioning key cannot be added or dropped because
    table resides in a table space defined on the
    multi-node nodegroup "<name>".
```

Indexes and Partitioning Keys

The indexes defined on a table are partitioned based on the partitioning key of the underlying table. When an index is created, it will be created in all of the database partitions where the table was created. In each database partition, the entries in the index will have entries only for the rows of the table that are located in the same database partition.

Non-unique indexes can be created on any columns of a table, regardless of whether it is partitioned. However, any unique index or primary key created on a partitioned table must include the columns in the partitioning key.

Collocated Tables

Often in a database, there will be tables that are frequently joined by applications. If the database is partitioned, it is good practice to try to avoid sending data between the partitions to satisfy these joins. This can be achieved in DB2 by exploiting table collocation. Collocation between two joined tables occurs when the matching rows of the two tables are stored in the same database partitions, so that no data needs to be sent between partitions. Figure 2.14 shows an example where tables T1 and T2 are collocated. A join made between these two tables is satisfied without the need for rows to be sent from one database partition to another.

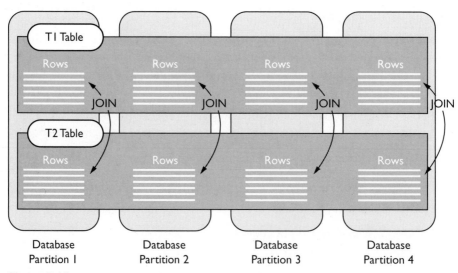

Figure 2.14
Collocated tables.

Two tables are collocated when they satisfy all of the following conditions:

- The partition groups of both tables must have the same partitioning map.
- The partitioning key from both tables must have the same number of columns.

- Corresponding partitioning key columns must be partition-compatible (the same or similar base data type).
- For tables in multi-partition partition groups:
  - The two tables must be in the same partition group.
- For tables in single-partition partition groups:
  - The tables can be in different partition groups, but these partition groups must include the same (single) database partition.

A collocated join will occur if two collocated tables are joined using all of the columns in the partitioning key.

If two tables can be joined using a collocated join, the query can be performed much more efficiently, compared with a join that sends data between database partitions.

SUMMARY

DB2 UDB Version 8 must read and update data rows in the database buffer pools. To be able to do this as efficiently and effectively as possible, it is important that the buffer pools be sized correctly and assigned to the correct table spaces. DB2 UDB V8 can manipulate the data in parallel, using intra-partition parallelism, inter-partition parallelism, or a combination of both.

It is important to remember that parallelism will not help all database workloads and that it should be enabled only where appropriate.

Database Availability

his chapter discusses the following concepts related to database availability with DB2:

1. Ability to manage logs
2. Ability to use advanced backup and recovery features
3. Ability to back up and recover in a partition environment
4. Ability to implement a standby database using: log shipping, replication, automated high availability cluster, etc.
5. Ability to use db2dart

ABILITY TO MANAGE LOGS

All databases have logs associated with them. These logs keep records of database changes. If a database needs to be restored and the transactions recovered to a point beyond the time of the last full, offline backup, the logs are required to roll the data forward to that point in time. There are two types of DB2 logging, and each provides a different level of recovery capability: circular logging and archive logging.

Circular logging is the default method when a new database is created.

- In the database configuration, the LOGRETAIN and USEREXIT parameters are set to NO. It is set to OFF by default.
- When circular logging is used, only full, offline backups of the database are allowed.
- The database must be offline (no connections to the database) when a full backup is taken.

- This logging method does not allow the database to roll forward through transactions performed after the last full backup operation.
- All changes occurring since the last backup operation are lost if the database is restored.
- It is also known as version recovery, i.e., you can recover the database as it existed when the backup was taken.

```
db2 get db cfg for sample | grep -i "log retain"

Log retain for recovery status                              = NO
Log retain for recovery enabled              (LOGRETAIN)    = OFF

db2 get db cfg for sample | grep -i "user exit"

User exit for logging status                               = NO
User exit for logging enabled                (USEREXIT)     = OFF

You can combine the above commands if egrep is compatible on Windows:
db2 get db cfg for sample | egrep -i "log retain|user exit"
```

Archive logging is used to enable rollforward recovery of a database to ensure that transactions performed after the backup images were taken are not lost in the event that the database needs to be restored.

- Enabling either LOGRETAIN or USEREXIT in the database configuration parameter will result in archive logging method.
- Online backups of the database are allowed.
- Table space backups are allowed.
- Rollforward recovery can use both archived logs and active logs to rebuild a database, either to the end of the logs or to a specific point in time.
- To archive logs, you can choose to have DB2 leave the log files in the active log path, then manually archive them (LOGRETAIN=ON), or you can edit and build one of the sample user exit programs to automate the archiving (USEREXIT=ON).
- Archived logs are logs that were active but are no longer required for crash recovery.
- The archived log files can be used to recover changes made after the backup was taken.

```
db2 update db cfg for sample using logretain ON userexit ON

db2 get db cfg for sample | egrep -i "log retain|user exit"

Log retain for recovery status                             = NO
Log retain for recovery enabled              (LOGRETAIN)    = RECOVERY

User exit for logging status                               = NO
User exit for logging enabled                (USEREXIT)     = ON
```

> **N O T E** You must take a full database backup right after enabling LOGRETAIN and USEREXIT to avoid the following error message on the subsequent connection to the database.

```
SQL1116N  A connection to or activation of database "SAMPLE" cannot be
made because of BACKUP PENDING.  SQLSTATE=57019
```

After the database has been successfully backed up, the "Log retain for recovery status" will change from NO to RECOVERY.

```
db2 get db cfg for sample | egrep -i "log retain|user exit"

Log retain for recovery status                              = RECOVERY
Log retain for recovery enabled            (LOGRETAIN)      = RECOVERY


User exit for logging status                                = YES
User exit for logging enabled              (USEREXIT)       = ON
```

Without infinite active log files enabled, active logs are:

- Used during crash recovery to prevent a system failure (such as a system power or application error) from leaving a database in an inconsistent state.
- Located in the database log path directory.

> **N O T E** We will discuss infinite active logs later.

The RESTART DATABASE command uses the active logs to apply or undo the necessary transactions to change the database to a consistent and usable state. During crash recovery, all uncommitted changes recorded in the logs are rolled back, and changes that were committed but not yet written from the buffer pool to table space containers are redone. These actions ensure the integrity of the database and guarantee that no transactions will be lost.

Online archival log files contain information related to completed transactions no longer required for crash recovery. They reside in the same subdirectory path as the active log files.

Offline archival log files have been moved from the active log file directory. The method of moving these files could be either manual or a process that is invoked through a user exit program or a shell script. Archived log files can be placed offline simply by moving them to another directory, storing them on tape or elsewhere.

Taking online backups is supported only if the database is configured for archive logging. During an online backup operation, all activities against the database are logged. When an online backup image is restored, the logs must be rolled forward at least to the point in time at which the backup operation completed to guarantee the integrity of the data. For this to happen, the logs must be available when the database is restored. After an online backup is complete, DB2 forces the currently active log to be closed, and as a result, it will be archived (if USEREXIT is set to YES or ON). This ensures that your online backup has a complete set of archived logs available for recovery.

```
db2 backup database sample online to c:\dbbackup

Backup successful. The timestamp for this backup image is : 20020714115137
```

The USEREXIT database configuration parameter allows you to change where archived logs are stored. Changing the NEWLOGPATH parameter affects only where active logs are stored. To determine which log files in the database log path directory are archived logs, check the value of the "First active log file" in the database configuration. This field indicates the lowest numbered log file that is active. Those logs with sequence numbers less than the value displayed in the "First active log file" are archived logs and can be moved. You can check the value of this parameter by using the Control Center or by using the following command:

```
db2 get db cfg for sample | grep -i "first active log"

First active log file                                        = S0000000.LOG
Percent of max active log space by transaction    (MAX_LOG)       = 0
Num. of active log files for 1 active UOW         (NUM_LOG_SPAN)  = 0
```

Primary Logs (LOGPRIMARY)

This parameter specifies the number of primary logs of size LOGFILSIZ that will be created. As you select the number of logs to configure, you must consider the size you make each log and whether your application can handle a log-full condition.

- A primary log requires the same amount of disk space, whether it is full or empty.
- You can waste disk space if you configure more logs than you need.
- You can encounter a log-full condition if you configure too few logs.
- The total log file size default limit on active log space is 256 GB (it is UNLIMITED if the LOGSECOND is set to −1).

```
db2 get db cfg for sample | grep -i logprimary

Number of primary log files                        (LOGPRIMARY) = 3
```

Secondary Logs (LOGSECOND)

This parameter specifies the maximum number of secondary log files that can be created and used for recovery, if needed.

- If the primary log files become full, secondary log files are allocated, one at a time as needed, up to the maximum number specified by this parameter.
- Once allocated, they are not deleted until the database is deactivated.
- If this parameter is set to −1, the database is configured with infinite active log space.
- There is no limit on the size or number of in-flight transactions running on the database when infinite active logs is set.

```
db2 get db cfg for sample | grep -i logsecond

Number of secondary log files               (LOGSECOND)   = 2
```

> **NOTE**
>
> 1. The USEREXIT database configuration parameter must be set to YES or ON in order to set LOGSECOND parameter to −1.
> 2. If this parameter is set to −1, crash recovery time may be increased because DB2 may need to retrieve archived log files.

Log File Size (LOGFILSIZ)

This parameter specifies the size of each configured log, in number of 4-KB pages. The maximum log file size is 262,144 pages.

```
db2 get db cfg for sample | grep -i logfilsiz

Log file size (4KB)                          (LOGFILSIZ)   = 250
```

> **NOTE** Prior to Version 7, there was a 4-GB logical limit on the total active log space that you can configure. In Version 7, the upper limit for the active log space is 32 GB. In Version 8, there is no limit on the active log space.

The size of the log file has an impact on performance because there is a cost for switching from one log to another. So, from a pure performance perspective, the larger the log file size, the better. This parameter also indicates the log file size for archiving. In this case, a larger log file size is not necessarily better, because a larger log file size may increase the chance of failure or cause a delay in log shipping scenarios. When considering the active log space, it may be better to have a larger number of smaller log files. For example, if there are two very large log files and a transaction starts close to the end of one log file, only half of the log space remains available.

Assuming that you have an application that keeps the database open or that the DBA has activated the database, to minimize processing time when opening the database, the log file size should be determined by the amount of time it takes to make offline archived log copies. When LOGRETAIN is set to YES or ON, minimizing log file loss is also an important consideration when setting the log size.

Log archiving will copy an entire log file. If you use a single large log file, you increase the time between archiving, and if the disk(s) containing the log fails, some transaction information will probably be lost. Decreasing the log file size increases the frequency of archiving but can reduce the amount of information loss in case of a media failure because the logs will be archived more frequently and will contain less work.

Log Buffer Size (LOGBUFSZ)

This parameter allows you to specify the amount of memory to use as a buffer for log records before writing these records to disk. The log buffer is written to disk when the first of the following events occurs:

- A transaction commits.
- The log buffer becomes full.
- Every one second interval.

```
db2 get db cfg for sample | grep -i logbufsz

Log buffer size (4KB)                          (LOGBUFSZ)   = 8
```

Increasing the log buffer size results in more efficient I/O activity associated with logging, because the log records are written to disk less frequently, and more records are written each time.

Number of Commits to Group (MINCOMMIT)

This parameter allows you to delay the writing of the log buffer log records to disk until a minimum number of commits have been performed, when the buffer is filled, or at one second intervals. This can

- Reduce the database manager overhead associated with writing log records.
- Improve performance when you have multiple applications running against a database and many commits are requested by the applications within a very short period of time.

> **N O T E**   This can slow down very short transactions, because each one will likely take up to 1 second to return.

The grouping of commits occurs only if the value of this parameter is greater than 1 and if the number of applications connected to the database is greater than the value of this parameter.

When commit grouping is in effect, application commit requests are held until either one second has elapsed or the number of commit requests equals the value of this parameter.

```
db2 get db cfg for sample | grep -i mincommit

Group commit count                        (MINCOMMIT) = 1
```

New Log Path (NEWLOGPATH)

The database logs are initially created in SQLOGDIR, which is a subdirectory under the database directory.

- You can change the location in which active logs and future online archive logs are placed/stored by changing the value of this configuration parameter to point to a different directory or to a device.
- Active logs that are stored in the database log path directory are not moved to the new location if the database is configured for rollforward recovery. It will be moved only once the database is stopped and reactivated.

```
db2 get db cfg for sample | grep -i path

Changed path to log files     (NEWLOGPATH) =
Path to log files                 = C:\DB2\NODE0000\SQL00002\SQLOGDIR\
Overflow log path            (OVERFLOWLOGPATH)                =
Mirror log path             (MIRRORLOGPATH)                  =

db2 update db cfg for sample using newlogpath c:\dblog\SAMPLE

db2 get db cfg for sample | grep -i path

Changed path to log files     (NEWLOGPATH) = c:\dblog\SAMPLE\NODE0000\
Path to log files                 = C:\DB2\NODE0000\SQL00002\SQLOGDIR\
Overflow log path            (OVERFLOWLOGPATH)                =
Mirror log path             (MIRRORLOGPATH)                  =
```

Because you can change the log path location, the logs needed for rollforward recovery may exist in different directories or on different devices. The OVERFLOWLOGPATH can be used to specify the location of the logs during a rollforward operation to allow you to access logs in multiple locations.

Overflow Log Path (OVERFLOWLOGPATH)

This parameter can be used for several functions, depending on your logging requirements. You can specify a location for DB2 to find log files that are needed for a rollforward operation. It is similar to the OVERFLOWLOGPATH option of the ROLLFORWARD command.

```
db2 update db cfg for sample using overflowlogpath e:\dblogo\SAMPLE

db2 get db cfg for sample | grep -i path

Changed path to log files     (NEWLOGPATH) = c:\dblog\SAMPLE\NODE0000\
Path to log files                     = C:\DB2\NODE0000\SQL00002\SQLOGDIR\
Overflow log path            (OVERFLOWLOGPATH) = e:\dblogo\SAMPLE\NODE0000\
Mirror log path              (MIRRORLOGPATH) = d:\dblogm\SAMPLE\NODE0000\
```

However, instead of specifying the OVERFLOWLOGPATH option for every ROLLFORWARD command issued, you can set this configuration parameter once. If both are used, the OVERFLOWLOGPATH option on the rollforward command will overwrite the OVERFLOWLOGPATH configuration parameter for that rollforward operation.

If LOGSECOND is set to −1, you can specify a directory for DB2 to store active log files retrieved from the archive. Active log files must be retrieved for rollback operations if they are no longer in the active log path.

If OVERFLOWLOGPATH is not specified, DB2 will retrieve the log files into the active log path. By specifying this parameter, you can provide additional resource for DB2 to store the retrieved log files. The benefit includes spreading the I/O cost to different disks and allowing more log files to be stored in the active log path.

If you have configured a raw device for the active log path, OVERFLOWLOGPATH must be configured if you want to enable infinite active log space.

> **N O T E**   In a partitioned database environment, the database partition number is automatically appended to the path. This is done to maintain the uniqueness of the path in a multi-partitioned database configuration.

Log Mirroring

At the database level, mirroring log files helps protect a database from:

- Accidental deletion of an active log
- File corruption caused by hardware failure

Since the logs for a database can be a single point of failure, you should consider using the DB2 database configuration parameter, MIRRORLOGPATH, to specify a secondary path for the database to manage copies of the active log file; or you can use the operating system or hardware to mirror the volumes on which the logs are stored.

The MIRRORLOGPATH configuration parameter allows the database to write an identical second copy of log files to a different path. It is recommended that you place the secondary log path on a physically separate disk (preferably one that is also on a different disk controller). That way, the disk controller cannot be a single point of failure.

When MIRRORLOGPATH is first enabled, it will not actually be used until the database is stopped and reactivated. This is similar to the NEWLOGPATH configuration parameter. If there is an error writing to either the active log path or the mirror log path, the database will mark the failing path as *bad*, write a message to the administration notification log, and write subsequent log records only to the remaining *good* log path.

DB2 will not attempt to use the *bad* path again until the current log file is completed. When DB2 needs to open the next log file, it will again try writing to both locations, and if there are no errors, it will continue to use both log paths. If not, DB2 will not attempt to use the path again until the next log file is accessed for the first time. There is no attempt to synchronize the log paths, but DB2 keeps information about access errors that occur, so that the correct paths are used when log files are archived. If a failure occurs while writing to the remaining *good* path, the database will be shut down.

- Active logs that are currently stored in the mirrored log path directory are not moved to the new location if the database is configured for rollforward recovery.
- Since you can change the log path location, the logs needed for rollforward recovery may exist in different directories. You can change the value of this configuration parameter during a rollforward operation to allow you to access logs in multiple locations.
- You must keep track of the location of the logs. Changes are not applied until the database is in a consistent state. The configuration parameter "Database is consistent" displays the status of the database.
- To turn this configuration parameter off, set its value to DEFAULT.

```
db2 update db cfg for sample using mirrorlogpath d:\dblogm\SAMPLE

db2 get db cfg for sample | grep -i path

Changed path to log files    (NEWLOGPATH) = c:\dblog\SAMPLE\NODE0000\
Path to log files                        = C:\DB2\NODE0000\SQL00002\SQLOGDIR\
Overflow log path            (OVERFLOWLOGPATH)                        =
Mirror log path              (MIRRORLOGPATH) = d:\dblogm\SAMPLE\NODE0000\
```

NOTE

1. This configuration parameter is not supported if the primary log path is a raw device.

2. The value specified for this parameter cannot be a raw device.

Reducing Logging with the NOT LOGGED INITIALLY Parameter Option

If your application creates and populates work tables from master tables and you are not concerned about the recoverability of these work tables because they can be easily recreated from the master tables, you may want to create the work tables specifying the NOT LOGGED INITIALLY parameter on the CREATE TABLE statement. You can achieve the same result for existing tables by using the ALTER TABLE statement with the NOT LOGGED INITIALLY parameter (if and only if they were created with the NOT LOGGED INITIALLY option).

Advantages of using the NOT LOGGED INITIALLY:

- Any changes made on the table (including insert, delete, update, or create index operations) in the same unit of work that creates the table will not be logged or in the UOW after the table is altered with the NOT LOGGED option.
- Increases the performance of your application.

```
db2 connect to sample

db2 "create table tab_1 (col1 int, col2 char(20) not logged initially"
db2 "alter table tab_1 activate not logged initially"

db2 "insert into tab_1 values (1,'MICHAEL')"
db2 "insert into tab_1 values (2,'TIFFANY')"
db2 "insert into tab_1 values (3,'JONATHAN')"
db2 "insert into tab_1 values (4,'JENNIFER')"
db2 "insert into tab_1 values (5,'DWAINE')"
db2 "insert into tab_1 values (6,'TOM')"
db2 COMMIT
db2 "delete from tab_1 where col1=6"
db2 ROLLBACK
```

NOTE

1. You can create more than one table with the NOT LOGGED INITIALLY parameter in the same unit of work.

2. Changes to the catalog tables and other user tables are still logged.

Because changes to the table are not logged, you should consider the following when deciding whether to use the NOT LOGGED INITIALLY table attribute:

- All changes to the table will be flushed to disk at commit time. This means that the commit may take longer.
- If the NOT LOGGED INITIALLY attribute is activated and an activity occurs that is not logged, the entire unit of work will be rolled back if a statement fails or a ROLLBACK TO SAVEPOINT is executed.
- You cannot recover these tables when rolling forward. If the rollforward operation encounters a table that was created or altered with the NOT LOGGED INITIALLY option, the table is marked as unavailable. After the database is recovered, any attempt to access the table returns SQL1477N.
- When a table is created, row locks are held on the catalog tables until a COMMIT is done. To take advantage of the no logging behavior, you must populate the table in the same unit of work in which it is created (or altered). This has implications for concurrency.

Reducing Logging with
Declared Global Temporary Tables (DGTTs)

DGTTs can now be logged. It is the default. If you plan to use DGTTs as work tables, note the following:

- The create DGTT statement defines a temporary table for the current session.
- The DGTT description does not appear in the system catalog.
- The DGTT is not persistent and cannot be shared with other sessions.
- Each session that defines a DGTT of the same name has its own unique description of the temporary table.
- When the session terminates, the rows of the table are deleted, and the description of the temporary table is dropped.
- Errors in operation during a unit of work using a DGTT do not cause the unit of work to be completely rolled back. However, an error in operation in a statement changing the contents of a DGTT will delete all the rows in that table.
- A rollback of the unit of work (or a savepoint) will delete all rows in declared temporary tables that were modified in that unit of work (or savepoint).
- Changes to the DGTT are not logged if you created the DGTT with the NOT LOGGED option.

```
db2 connect to sample

db2 "create user temporary tablespace global_temp_ts managed by system
    using ('c:\data\global_temp_ts') extentsize 16 prefetchsize 64"

Application …

declared global temporary table gtab_1 (col1 int, col2 char(20))
    with replace in global_temp_ts NOT LOGGED;

insert into gtab_1 values (1,'SAN FRANCISCO');
update gtab_1 set col2='TIBURON' where col1=1;

… Application.
```

Managing Log Files

Consider the following when managing database logs:

- The numbering scheme for archived logs starts with S0000000.LOG, and continues through S9999999.LOG.
- DB2 may reuse log names after restoring a database (with or without rollforward recovery).
    - There is an exception if you roll forward to end of logs.
- The database manager ensures that an incorrect log is not applied during rollforward recovery, but it cannot detect the location of the required log if it has been archived.
- You must ensure that the correct logs are available for rollforward recovery. When a rollforward operation completes successfully, the last log that was used is truncated, and logging begins with the next sequential log file.
- Any log in the log path directory with a sequence number greater than the last log used for rollforward recovery is reused.
- Any entries in the truncated log following the truncation point are lost.
- If a database has not been activated, DB2 truncates the current log file when all applications have disconnected from the database. The next time an application connects to the database, DB2 starts logging to a new log file. If many small log files (i.e., smaller than the configured LOGFILSIZ) are being produced on your system, you may want to consider using the ACTIVATE DATABASE command. This not only saves the overhead of having to initialize the database when applications connect, but it also saves the overhead of having to allocate a large log file, truncate it, then allocate a new log file.

Archiving Log Files with a User Exit Program

The USEREXIT database parameter causes the database manager to call a user exit program to archive and retrieve log files. The log files are archived in a location that is different from the active log path. If USEREXIT is set to ON, rollforward recovery is automatically enabled.

```
db2 get db cfg for sample | grep -i "user exit"

User exit for logging status                              = YES
User exit for logging enabled              (USEREXIT)     = ON
```

Consider the following when deciding whether to enable user exits:

- The data transfer speed of the device you use to store offline archived logs and the software used to make the copies should, at a minimum, match the average rate at which the database manager fills log files. If the transfer speed cannot keep up with new log files being generated, you may run out of disk space if logging activity continues for a sufficient period of time. The amount of time it takes to run out of disk space is determined by the amount of free disk space. If this happens, DB2 database processing stops.
  - Unless the BLK_LOG_DSK_FUL variable is set.
- The data transfer speed is most significant when using tape or an optical medium. Some tape devices require the same amount of time to copy a file, regardless of its size. You must determine the capabilities of your archiving device. Tape devices have other considerations. The frequency of the archiving request is important. For example, if the time taken to complete any copy operation is 5 minutes, the log should be large enough to hold 5 minutes of log data during your peak workload.
- The tape device may have design limits that restrict the number of operations per day. This is very important when you determine the log file size.

The following considerations apply to calling a user exit program for archiving and retrieving log files:

- The database configuration file parameter USEREXIT specifies whether the database manager invokes a user exit program to archive log files automatically or to retrieve log files during rollforward recovery of databases. A request to the user exit program to retrieve a log file is also made when the rollforward command needs a log file that is not found in the active log path.
- When archiving, a log file name is passed to the user exit program when it is full, even if the log file is still active and is needed for normal processing. This allows copies of the log file to be moved away from volatile media as quickly as possible. The log file that was passed to the user exit program is retained in the log path directory until it is no longer needed for normal processing. At this point, the disk space is reused.
- DB2 opens a log file in read mode when it starts a user exit program to archive the log file. A user exit program should never delete a log file after it is archived, because the

file could still be active and needed for crash recovery. DB2 manages disk space reuse when log files are archived.

- When a log file has been archived and is inactive, DB2 does not delete the file but renames it as the next log file in sequence when such a file is needed. This results in a performance gain, because creating a new log file (instead of renaming the file) causes all pages to be written out to guarantee the disk space. It is more efficient to reuse than to free up and then reacquire the necessary pages on disk.

- DB2 will not invoke the user exit program to retrieve the log file during crash recovery or rollback unless the logsecond database configuration parameter is set to −1 (i.e., infinite active log space is enabled).

- A user exit program does not guarantee rollforward recovery to the point of failure but attempts only to make the failure window smaller. As log files fill, they are queued for the user exit program. Should the disk containing the log fail before a log file is filled, the data in that log file is lost (unless it is mirrored). Also, because the files are queued for archiving, the disk can fail before all the files are copied, causing any log files in the queue to be lost.

- The configured size of each individual log file has a direct bearing on the user exit program. If each log file is very large, a large amount of data can be lost if a disk fails. A database configured with small log files causes the data to be passed to the user exit program more often.

An archive request to the user exit program occurs each time an active log file is filled, only if USEREXIT is set to YES or ON. It is possible that an active log file is not full when the last disconnection from the database occurs and the user exit program is also called for the last truncated log file.

- A copy of the log should be made to another physical device so that the offline log file can be used by rollforward recovery if the device containing the log file experiences a media failure. This should not be the same device containing database data files.

- If you have enabled user exit programs and are using a tape drive as a storage device for logs and backup images, you need to ensure that the destination for the backup images and the archived logs is not the same tape drive. Because some log archiving may take place while a backup operation is in progress, an error may occur when the two processes are trying to write to the same tape drive at the same time.

- In some cases, if a database is closed before a positive response has been received from a user exit program for an archive request, the database manager will send another request when the database is opened. Thus, a log file may be archived more than once.

> **NOTE**   To free unused log space, the log file is truncated before it is archived.

- If a user exit program receives a request to archive a file that does not exist (because there were multiple requests to archive and the file was deleted after the first successful archiving operation) or to retrieve a file that does not exist (because it is located in another directory or the end of the logs has been reached), it should ignore this request and pass a successful return code.
- The user exit program should allow for the existence of different log files with the same name after a point in time recovery; it should be written to preserve both log files and to associate those log files with the correct recovery path.
- When a user exit program is enabled for two or more databases that are using the same tape device to archive log files and a rollforward operation is taking place on one of the databases, if the other database(s) is active, it can impact the performance of the rollforward. If another database tries to archive a log file while the rollforward operation is in progress, the logs required for the rollforward operation may not be found or the new log file archived to the tape device might overwrite the log files previously stored on that tape device.

To prevent either situation from occurring, you can ensure that no other databases on the server that calls the user exit program are open during the rollforward operation or write a user exit program to handle this situation.

When a database is restarted, the minimum number of logs in the database log directory will equal the number of primary logs that can be configured using the LOGPRIMARY database configuration parameter. More logs than the number of primary logs might be found in the log directory if, at the time of shutdown, the number of empty logs in the log directory is greater than the primary log configuration parameter at the time of database restart. This will happen if, between shutdown and restart, the primary log configuration parameter was changed or if secondary logs were allocated and never used.

Each time that a database is restarted, DB2 examines the database log directory. If fewer logs than the number of primary logs are found, the difference will be allocated. If more empty logs than primary logs are available in the database directory, DB2 will allow the database to be restarted with as many available empty logs as are found in the database directory.

As well, after database shutdown, secondary log files that have been created will remain in the active log path at restart time.

How Truncated Logs Are Handled

If a log file is truncated as a result of an online backup or force archive command (ARCHIVE LOG), DB2 does not rename the log file. Instead, a truncated log file is deleted when it becomes inactive. A new log file will be created when the application needs one. As a result, it may appear as though there are fewer log files in the log directory than LOGPRIMARY. You can avoid generating truncated logs altogether by setting the DB2 registry variable

DB2_DISABLE_FLUSH_LOG registry variable to ON. However, this may cause online backups to be unusable if the log is not flushed after the backup completes.

DB2 checks whenever the first active log changes. As a result, information is recorded to disk earlier and more often. The benefit of this change is that if the system crashes, the information stored on disk (related to which log files are successfully archived) is more accurate, and DB2 does not have to reissue the archive request for log files that are already archived.

There is no change to what DB2 does after detecting the successful archive of a particular log file. DB2 now detects the completion of log archives earlier and will rename them earlier. Inactive truncated log files are deleted. As a result, the number of log files remaining in the active log path can be fewer than the LOGPRIMARY database configuration value. In this case, DB2 will create new log files when needed.

Before this change, restarting the database reduced the number of logs to equal the value of LOGPRIMARY. Now, when you restart a database, DB2 first examines the database log directory. If the number of empty logs is fewer than the number of primary logs, DB2 will allocate new logs to make up the difference. If more empty logs are available than there are primary logs in the database directory, DB2 will allow the database to be restarted with all the available empty logs in the database directory.

After database shutdown, any secondary log files in existence will remain in the active log path at restart time. To clear out the active log path, the ARCHIVE LOG command may be used.

Log File Allocation and Removal

If the LOGRETAIN is set to YES or ON, archived logs are kept in the database log path directory, and the database is considered to be recoverable, meaning that rollforward recovery is enabled.

- Log files in the database log directory are never removed if they may be required for crash recovery.
- When the USEREXIT database configuration parameter is enabled, a full log file becomes a candidate for removal only after it has been archived and is no longer required for crash recovery.
- A log file that is required for crash recovery is called an *active log*.
- A log file that is not required for crash recovery is called an *archived log*.

```
db2 get db cfg for sample | grep -i "log retain"


Log retain for recovery status                              = RECOVERY
Log retain for recovery enabled           (LOGRETAIN)       = RECOVERY
```

The process of allocating new log files and removing old log files is dependent on the settings of the USEREXIT and LOGRETAIN database configuration parameters.

When both LOGRETAIN and USEREXIT are set to OFF:

- Circular logging will be used.
- Rollforward recovery is not supported with circular logging.
- Crash recovery is always supported.
- During circular logging, new log files other than secondary logs are not generated, and old log files are not deleted.
- Log files are handled in a circular fashion. That is, when the last log file is full, DB2 begins writing to the first log file.
- A log full situation can occur if all of the log files are active and the circular logging process cannot wrap to the first log file.
- Secondary log files are created when all the primary log files are active and full. Once a secondary log is created, it is not deleted until the database is restarted.

When LOGRETAIN is set to ON and USEREXIT is set to OFF:

- Both rollforward recovery and crash recovery are enabled.
- The database is known to be recoverable.
- When USEREXIT is set to OFF, DB2 does not move log files from the active log directory.
- Each time a log file becomes full, DB2 begins writing records to another log file and creates a new log file.

When USEREXIT is set to ON:

- This also turns LOGRETAIN ON.
- When both LOGRETAIN and USEREXIT are set to ON, both rollforward recovery and crash recovery are enabled.
- When a log file becomes full, it is automatically archived, using the user-supplied user exit program.
- Log files are usually not deleted. Instead, when a new log file is required and one is not available, an archived log file is renamed and used again.
- An archived log file is not deleted or renamed once it has been closed and copied to the log archive directory.
- DB2 waits until a new log file is needed, then renames the oldest archived log.
- A log file that has been moved to the database directory during recovery is removed during the recovery process when it is no longer needed. Until DB2 runs out of log space, you will see old log files in the database directory.

If an error is encountered while archiving a log file, archiving of log files will be suspended for 5 minutes before being attempted again. DB2 will then continue archiving log files as they become full. Log files that became full during the 5-minute waiting period will not be archived immediately after the delay; DB2 will spread the archive of these files over time.

Blocking Transactions When the Log Directory File Is Full

This configuration parameter can be set to prevent disk full errors from causing DB2 to stop processing when it cannot create a new log file in the active log path.

- If BLK_LOG_DSK_FUL is set to NO, a transaction that receives a log disk full error will fail and be rolled back. In addition, DB2 will stop processing.
- Setting BLK_LOG_DSK_FUL to YES causes applications to wait when DB2 encounters a log disk full error. You are then able to resolve the error, and the transaction can continue.
- A disk full situation can be resolved by moving old log files to another file system or by increasing the size of the file system so that hanging applications can complete.
- DB2 will attempt to create a log file every 5 minutes until it succeeds and will write a message to the administration notification log.
- Frequently monitor the administration notification log to confirm that your application is hanging because of a log disk full condition.
- Until the log file is successfully created, no user application that attempts to update table data will be able to commit transactions.
- Read-only queries may not be directly affected; however, if a query needs to access data that is locked by an update request or a data page that is fixed in the buffer pool by the updating application, read-only queries will also appear to hang.

```
db2 get db cfg for sample | grep -i "block log"

Block log on disk full              (BLK_LOG_DSK_FUL) = NO

db2 update db cfg for sample using blk_log_dsk_ful on
db2 get db cfg for sample | grep -i "block log"

Block log on disk full              (BLK_LOG_DSK_FUL) = ON
```

On Demand Log Archive

DB2 now supports closing the active log for a recoverable database at any time. This allows you to collect a complete set of log files up to a known point, then to use these log files to update a standby database. You can initiate on demand log archiving by invoking the ARCHIVE LOG command.

```
db2 archive log for database sample
```

> **N O T E**
> • The issuer of this command cannot have a connection to the specified database, although other users may be connected.
> • Performance may be impacted during execution of the command, due to the activities writing from the log buffer to disk.
>   ○ If USEREXIT is set to ON, an archive request is issued after the logs are closed and truncated. The completion of the archive command does not guarantee that the logs have been moved to the archive directory.

Using Raw Logs

There are some advantages and disadvantages when a raw device is used for the database logs.

Advantages:

- You can attach more than 26 physical drives to a system.
- The file I/O path length is shorter. This may improve performance on your system. You should conduct benchmarks to evaluate whether there are measurable benefits for your workload.

Disadvantages:

- The device cannot be shared by other applications; i.e., the entire device must be assigned to DB2.
- The device cannot be operated on by any operating system utility or third-party tool that would backup or copy from the device.

You can easily wipe out the file system on an existing drive if you specify the wrong physical drive number.

You can configure a raw log with the NEWLOGPATH database configuration parameter. Before doing so, however, consider the advantages and disadvantages listed above and the additional considerations listed below:

- Only one PATH device is allowed. You can define the PATH device over multiple disks at the operating system level. DB2 will make an operating system call to determine the size of the device in 4-KB pages.
- If you use multiple disks, this will provide a larger device, and the striping that results can improve performance and increase I/O throughput speed.

In this situation, DB2 will attempt to use all pages, up to the supported limit. Information about the size of the device is used to indicate the size of the device (in 4-KB pages) available to DB2 under the support of the operating system. The amount of disk space that DB2 can write to is referred to as the *device size available*. The first 4-KB page of the device is not used by DB2 (it is generally used by the operating system). This means that the total space available to DB2 is *device size = device size available* − 1.

When using raw devices for the logs, secondary logs are not used. The size of active log space is the number of 4-KB pages that result from (LOGPRIMARY × LOGFILSIZ).

Log records are still grouped into log extents, each with a log file size of 4-KB pages. Log extents are placed in the raw device, one after another. Each extent also consists of an extra two pages for the extent header. This means that the number of available log extents on the device is device-size / (LOGFILSIZ + 2).

The device must be large enough to support the active log space. That is, the number of available log extents must be greater than (or equal to) the value specified for the LOGPRIMARY database configuration parameter. If the USEREXIT database configuration parameter is set to ON, ensure that the raw device can contain more logs than the value specified for the LOGPRIMARY database configuration parameter. This will compensate for the delay incurred when the user exit program is archiving a log file.

If you are using circular logging, the LOGPRIMARY database configuration parameter will determine the number of log extents that are written to the device. This may result in unused space on the device.

If you are using LOGRETAIN without a user exit program, after the number of available log extents are all used up, all operations that result in an update will receive a log full error. At this time, you must shut down the database and take an offline backup of it to ensure recoverability. After the database backup operation, the log records written to the device are lost. This means that you cannot use an earlier database backup image to restore the database, then roll it forward. If you take a database backup before the number of available log extents are all used up, you can restore and roll the database forward.

If you are using LOGRETAIN with a user exit program, the user exit program is called for each log extent as it is filled with log records. The user exit program must be able to read the device and to store the archived log as a file. DB2 will not call a user exit program to retrieve log files to a raw device. Instead, during rollforward recovery, DB2 will read the extent headers to determine when the raw device contains the required log file. If the required log file is not found in the raw device, DB2 will search the overflow log path. If the log file is still not found, DB2 will call the user exit program to retrieve the log file into the overflow log path. If you do not specify an overflow log path for the rollforward operation, DB2 will not call the user exit program to retrieve the log file.

If you have configured a raw device for logging and are using DataPropagator or another application that calls the **db2ReadLog API**, the OVERFLOWLOGPATH database configuration parameter must be configured. DB2 may call a user exit program to retrieve the log file and return the log data requested by the **db2ReadLog API**. The retrieved log file will be placed in the path specified by the OVERFLOWLOGPATH database configuration parameter.

How to Prevent Losing Log Files

When a database is restored and rolled forward to a point in time prior to the end of logs, a new set of logs is generated. Therefore, the currently archived logs will no longer be useable for this new database.

Consider the following scenarios:

Scenario #1: Drop a Database

If you plan to drop a database prior to a restore operation, you need to save the log files in the active log path before issuing the DROP DATABASE command. After the database has been restored, these log files may be required for rollforward recovery because some of them may not have been archived before the database was dropped. Normally, you are not required to drop a database prior to issuing the RESTORE command.

Scenario #2: Rollforward a Database

If you are rolling a database forward to a specific point in time, log data after the timestamp you specify will be overwritten. If, after you have completed the point-in-time rollforward operation and reconnected to the database, you determine that you actually needed to roll the database forward to a later point in time, you will not be able to because the logs may already have been overwritten, if they were not saved to a different path or using a utility such as TSM.

It is possible that the original set of log files may have been archived; however, DB2 may be calling a user exit program to automatically archive the newly generated log files automatically. Depending on how the user exit program is written, this could cause the original set of log files in the archive log directory to be overwritten. Even if both the original and new set of log files exist in the archive log directory, you may have to determine which set of logs should be used for future recovery operations.

Review Session

Let's manage log files for the database SAMPLE.

First, you must create SAMPLE database using the db2sampl program. After this database has been successfully created, the default primary log files (3) with the size of 250 4-KB pages will be created in the directory:

```
Path to log files           = C:\DB2\NODE0000\SQL00002\SQLOGDIR\
```

By default, all databases use circular logging. We need to enable archive logging by updating the LOGRETAIN and/or USEREXIT database configuration parameters. Then we will need to modify the DB2 user exit program to archive and retrieve logs. The log files are archived in a location that is different from the active log path.

How to Enable Archive Log for the Database

Step 1.   Create sample database and get the database configuration

```
db2sampl
db2 connect to sample
db2 get db cfg for sample | grep -i log

Log retain for recovery status = NO
User exit for logging status =
Catalog cache size (4KB)      (CATALOGCACHE_SZ) = (MAXAPPLS*4)
Log buffer size (4KB)         (LOGBUFSZ) = 8
Log file size (4KB)           (LOGFILSIZ) = 250
Number of primary log files   (LOGPRIMARY) = 3
Number of secondary log files (LOGSECOND) = 2
Changed path to log files     (NEWLOGPATH) =
Path to log files             = C:\DB2\NODE0000\SQL00002\SQLOGDIR\
Overflow log path             (OVERFLOWLOGPATH) =
Mirror log path               (MIRRORLOGPATH) =
First active log file         =
Block log on disk full        (BLK_LOG_DSK_FUL) = NO
Percent of max active log space by transaction (MAX_LOG) = 0
Num. of active log files for 1 active UOW (NUM_LOG_SPAN) = 0
Percent log file reclaimed before soft chckpt (SOFTMAX) = 100
Log retain for recovery enabled (LOGRETAIN) = OFF
User exit for logging enabled (USEREXIT) = OFF
```

For this example, we will change the log file size to a smaller size in order to make the log fill up quickly. By doing that, we will need to reduce the logfilsiz to 16 4-KB pages.

For recovery reasons, we will need to change the active log directory to c:\dblog\SAMPLE. This directory structure must match with the definition defined in the db2uext2.c program.

Step 2.   Reduce log file size

```
db2 update db cfg for sample using logfilsiz 16 logprimary 2 logsecond 10
db2 get db cfg for sample | grep -i log

Log retain for recovery status        = NO
User exit for logging status          =
Catalog cache size (4KB)              (CATALOGCACHE_SZ) = (MAXAPPLS*4)
Log buffer size (4KB)                 (LOGBUFSZ) = 8
Log file size (4KB)                   (LOGFILSIZ) = 16
Number of primary log files           (LOGPRIMARY) = 2
Number of secondary log files         (LOGSECOND) = 10
Changed path to log files             (NEWLOGPATH) =
Path to log files                     = C:\DB2\NODE0000\SQL00002\SQLOGDIR\
Overflow log path                     (OVERFLOWLOGPATH) =
Mirror log path                       (MIRRORLOGPATH) =
First active log file                 =
Block log on disk full                (BLK_LOG_DSK_FUL) = NO
Percent of max active log space by transaction (MAX_LOG) = 0
Num. of active log files for 1 active UOW (NUM_LOG_SPAN) = 0
Percent log file reclaimed before soft chckpt (SOFTMAX) = 100
Log retain for recovery enabled       (LOGRETAIN) = OFF
User exit for logging enabled         (USEREXIT) = OFF
```

By default, the first database is SQL00001, and the active log files reside under C:\DB2\NODE0000\SQL00002\SQLOGDIR\. After the database was updated with the NEWLOGPATH parameter, the active log files will be allocated under the new log path directory when last users disconnect from the database and the first user connects to the database.

```
ls -altr c:\DB2\NODE0000\SQL00002\SQLOGDIR\
total 6048
drwxrwxrwx   1 Administrators   None      0 Jul 14 22:12 ..
drwxrwxrwx   1 Administrators   None      0 Jul 14 22:12 .
-rwxrwxrwa   1 Administrators   None 1032192 Jul 14 22:15 S0000002.LOG
-rwxrwxrwa   1 Administrators   None 1032192 Jul 14 22:15 S0000001.LOG
-rwxrwxrwa   1 Administrators   None 1032192 Jul 14 22:16 S0000000.LOG
```

```
db2 update db cfg for sample using newlogpath c:\dblog\SAMPLE
db2 connect to sample
db2 get db cfg for sample | grep -i log

Log retain for recovery status          = NO
User exit for logging status            =
Catalog cache size (4KB)                (CATALOGCACHE_SZ) = (MAXAPPLS*4)
Log buffer size (4KB)                   (LOGBUFSZ) = 8
Log file size (4KB)                     (LOGFILSIZ) = 16
Number of primary log files             (LOGPRIMARY) = 2
Number of secondary log files           (LOGSECOND) = 10
Changed path to log files               (NEWLOGPATH) =
Path to log files                       = c:\dblog\SAMPLE\NODE0000\
Overflow log path                       (OVERFLOWLOGPATH) =
Mirror log path                         (MIRRORLOGPATH) =
First active log file                   =
Block log on disk full                  (BLK_LOG_DSK_FUL) = NO
Percent of max active log space by      (MAX_LOG) = 0
   transaction
Num. of active log files for 1          (NUM_LOG_SPAN) = 0
   active UOW
Percent log file reclaimed before       (SOFTMAX) = 100
   soft chckpt
Log retain for recovery enabled         (LOGRETAIN) = OFF
User exit for logging enabled           (USEREXIT) = OFF
```

```
ls -altr c:\DB2\NODE0000\SQL00002\SQLOGDIR\
total 0
drwxrwxrwx   1 Administrators   None   0 Jul 14 22:28 ..
drwxrwxrwx   1 Administrators   None   0 Jul 14 22:28 .

ls -altr c:\dblog\sample\NODE0000\
total 289
-rwxrwxrwa   1 Administrators   None     512 Jul 14 22:28 SQLLPATH.TAG
-rwxrwxrwa   1 Administrators   None   73728 Jul 14 22:28 S0000001.LOG
-rwxrwxrwa   1 Administrators   None   73728 Jul 14 22:28 S0000000.LOG
drwxrwxrwx   1 Administrators   None       0 Jul 14 22:28 ..
drwxrwxrwx   1 Administrators   None       0 Jul 14 22:28 .
```

Now, we need to enable archive logging by updating the LOGRETAIN and USEREXIT database configuration parameters.

Step 3.   Enable archive logging

Right after the database changed from circular log to archive log, we must take a full database backup to reset backup pending state.

```
db2 update db cfg for sample using logretain on userexit on
db2 connect to sample

SQL1116N  A connection to or activation of database "SAMPLE" cannot be
made because of BACKUP PENDING.  SQLSTATE=57019
```

> **N O T E**   We need to modify the user exit program, db2uext2.cdisk, to archive inactive log files from the active log directory. See the next section on how to set up user exits.

Step 4.   Take a full database backup

```
db2 backup database sample to c:\dbbackup

Backup successful. The timestamp for this backup image is:
    20020714224710

db2 connect to sample

  Database Connection Information

Database server            = DB2/NT 8.1.0
SQL authorization ID       = TPHAN
Local database alias       = SAMPLE

db2 get db cfg for sample | grep -i log

Log retain for recovery status    = RECOVERY
User exit for logging status      =
Catalog cache size (4KB)          (CATALOGCACHE_SZ) = (MAXAPPLS*4)
Log buffer size (4KB)             (LOGBUFSZ) = 8
Log file size (4KB)               (LOGFILSIZ) = 16
Number of primary log files       (LOGPRIMARY) = 2
Number of secondary log files     (LOGSECOND) = 10
Changed path to log files         (NEWLOGPATH) =
Path to log files                 = c:\dblog\SAMPLE\NODE0000\
Overflow log path                 (OVERFLOWLOGPATH) =
Mirror log path                   (MIRRORLOGPATH) =
First active log file             = S0000000.LOG
```

```
Block log on disk full              (BLK_LOG_DSK_FUL) = NO
Percent of max active log space by transaction (MAX_LOG) = 0
Num. of active log files for 1 active UOW (NUM_LOG_SPAN) = 0
Percent log file reclaimed before soft chckpt (SOFTMAX) = 100
Log retain for recovery enabled     (LOGRETAIN) = RECOVERY
User exit for logging enabled       (USEREXIT) = ON
```

Step 5.   Create a test table

```
db2 connect to sample

   Database Connection Information

Database server                   = DB2/NT 8.1.0
SQL authorization ID              = TPHAN
Local database alias              = SAMPLE

db2 "create table tab_1 (c1 int, c2 int)"

DB20000I  The SQL command completed successfully.

db2 terminate

DB20000I  The SQL command completed successfully.
```

Step 6.   Populate test data

From the command line, we will write a short interactive command to insert 5,000 rows into tab_1 table. Or we can write a short script to generate 5,000 rows into a data_file and invoke db2 –tvf data_file to insert them.

We will need to open four sessions (or command prompts): The first session (or command prompt) will list all files in the active log directory; the second session will list all files in the archive log directory; the third session will tell which is the first active log; and the fourth session will insert data into the tab_1 table.

N O T E   The DB2 user exit program must be enabled.

Session #1: List all active log files   The following command will list all active log files in the current directory indefinitely, then will go to sleep for 10 seconds. When the test is complete, press Ctrl+C to terminate.

```
cd c:\dblog\SAMPLE\NODE0000\

while true
do
    ls -altr *LOG
    sleep 10
    echo
done

Output from the above command:

-rwxrwxrwa   1 Administrators   None    73728 Jul 14 22:46 S0000001.LOG
-rwxrwxrwa   1 Administrators   None    73728 Jul 14 22:47 S0000002.LOG
```

Session #2: List all archived log files   The following command will list all archived log files in the current directory indefinitely, then will go to sleep for 10 seconds. When the test is complete, press Ctrl+C to terminate.

```
cd c:\dbarch\SAMPLE\NODE0000\

while true
do
    ls -altr *LOG
    sleep 10
    echo
done

Output from the above command:

-rwxrwxrwa   1 Administrators   None    88 Jul 14 22:49 S0000000.LOG
```

Session #3: Display first active log file   On UNIX or Linux, the following command will display the first active log file. When the test is complete, press Ctrl+C to terminate.

```
while true
do
    db2 get db cfg for sample | grep -i "first active log"
    sleep 10
    echo
done

Output from the above command:

First active log file                  = S0000001.LOG
```

Session #4: Insert test data   The following command will insert 5,000 rows into table tab_1. When the test is complete, press Ctrl+C to terminate.

```
db2 connect to sample

i=0
while [ $i -lt 5000 ]
do
     print "db2 insert into tab_1 values ($i, $RANDOM)"
     db2 "insert into tab_1 values ($i, $RANDOM)"
     let i=i+1
done

Output from the above command:

insert into tab_1 values(0, 18362);
DB20000I  The SQL command completed successfully.
insert into tab_1 values(1, 18171);
DB20000I  The SQL command completed successfully.
insert into tab_1 values(2, 32302);
...
insert into tab_1 values(4998, 5103);
DB20000I  The SQL command completed successfully.
insert into tab_1 values(4999, 32514);
DB20000I  The SQL command completed successfully.

db2 terminate

DB20000I  The SQL command completed successfully.
```

You can generate the data into a file and invoke db2 –tvf data_file to insert data into tab_1 table:

```
db2 connect to sample

i=0
while [ $i - lt 5000 ]
do
     print "db2 insert into tab_1 values ($i, $RANDOM)" >> tab_1.dat
     let i=i+1
done

db2 -tvf tab_1.dat -z tab_1.out

db2 terminate
```

Observation

It will take approximately six log files to insert 5,000 rows into tab_1 table. During insert rows into table tab_1, the files are archived to the dbarch directory as follows:

num_rec	first_active_log	active_log_dir	archive_log_dir
0000 - 2000	S0000001.LOG	S0000001.LOG	S0000000.LOG
		S0000002.LOG	
		S0000003.LOG	
2000 - 2800	S0000002.LOG	S0000002.LOG	S0000000.LOG
		S0000003.LOG	S0000001.LOG
		S0000004.LOG	
2800 - 3600	S0000003.LOG	S0000003.LOG	S0000000.LOG
		S0000004.LOG	S0000001.LOG
		S0000005.LOG	S0000002.LOG
3600 - 4500	S0000004.LOG	S0000004.LOG	S0000000.LOG
		S0000005.LOG	S0000001.LOG
		S0000006.LOG	S0000002.LOG
			S0000003.LOG
4500 - 5000	S0000005.LOG	S0000005.LOG	S0000000.LOG
		S0000006.LOG	S0000001.LOG
		S0000007.LOG	S0000002.LOG
			S0000003.LOG
			S0000004.LOG

How to Set Up DB2 User Exits

Step 1. Copy sample user exit program

```
cd c:\work
cp c:\sqllib\sample\c\db2uext2.cdisk    db2uext2.c
chmod 755 db2uext2.c
```

Step 2. Edit db2uext2.c

```
cd c:\work
vi db2uext2.c

#define ARCHIVE_PATH            "c:\\dbarch\\"
#define RETRIEVE_PATH           "c:\\dblog\\"
#define AUDIT_ERROR_PATH        "c:\\dblog\\"
```

Step 3.   Create subdirectories

```
cd c:\dbarch
mkdir -p SAMPLE\NODE0000
cd c:\dblog
mkdir SAMPLE
```

Step 4.   Compile db2uext2.c program

```
cd c:\work
cp c:\work\db2uext2.c   c:\sqllib\bin
cd c:\sqllib\bin
cl -o db2uext2.exe db2uext2.c

Microsoft (R) 32-bit C/C++ Optimizing Compiler Version 12.00.8168 for
80x86
Copyright (C) Microsoft Corp 1984-1998. All rights reserved.

db2uext2.c
Microsoft (R) Incremental Linker Version 6.00.8168
Copyright (C) Microsoft Corp 1992-1998. All rights reserved.

/out:db2uext2.exe
/out:db2uext2.exe
db2uext2.obj

For UNIX or Linux:
cc -o db2uext2 db2uext2.c
chmod +s db2uext2
```

Debug: If, for some reason, the db2uext2 user exit program did not work properly, we would need to examine the c:\dblog\ARCHIVE.LOG or USEREXIT.ERR. Here is the content of the ARCHIVE.LOG file:

```
************************************************************************
Time Started:       Sun Jul 14 22:49:19 2002
Parameter Count:    8
Parameters
  Passed:
Database name:      SAMPLE
Logfile name:       S0000000.LOG
Logfile path:       c:\dblog\SAMPLE\NODE0000\
Node number:        NODE0000
Operating           NT
  system:
Release:            SQL08010
Request:            ARCHIVE
System Action:      ARCHIVE c:\dblog\SAMPLE\NODE0000\S0000000.LOG to
                    c:\dbarch\SAMPLE
Media Type:         disk
User Exit RC:       0
Time Completed:     Sun Jul 14 22:49:19 2002


************************************************************************
Time Started:       Sun Jul 14 23:14:42 2002
Parameter Count:    8
Parameters
  Passed:
Database name:      SAMPLE
Logfile name:       S0000001.LOG
Logfile path:       c:\dblog\SAMPLE\NODE0000\
Node number:        NODE0000
Operating           NT
  system:
Release:            SQL08010
Request:            ARCHIVE
System Action:      ARCHIVE c:\dblog\SAMPLE\NODE0000\S0000001.LOG to
                    c:\dbarch\SAMPLE
Media Type:         disk
User Exit RC:       0
Time Completed:     Sun Jul 14 23:14:42 2002
```

```
*******************************************************************
Time Started:      Sun Jul 14 23:16:37 2002
Parameter Count:   8
Parameters
  Passed:
Database name:     SAMPLE
Logfile name:      S0000002.LOG
Logfile path:      c:\dblog\SAMPLE\NODE0000\
Node number:       NODE0000
Operating          NT
  system:
Release:           SQL08010
Request:           ARCHIVE
System Action:     ARCHIVE c:\dblog\SAMPLE\NODE0000\S0000002.LOG to
                   c:\dbarch\SAMPLE
Media Type:        disk
User Exit RC:      0
Time Completed:    Sun Jul 14 23:16:37 2002


*******************************************************************
Time Started:      Sun Jul 14 23:18:32 2002
Parameter Count:   8
Parameters
  Passed:
Database name:     SAMPLE
Logfile name:      S0000003.LOG
Logfile path:      c:\dblog\SAMPLE\NODE0000\
Node number:       NODE0000
Operating          NT
  system:
Release:           SQL08010
Request:           ARCHIVE
System Action:     ARCHIVE c:\dblog\SAMPLE\NODE0000\S0000003.LOG to
                   c:\dbarch\SAMPLE
Media Type:        disk
User Exit RC:      0
Time Completed:    Sun Jul 14 23:18:32 2002


*******************************************************************
Time Started:      Sun Jul 14 23:20:34 2002
Parameter Count:   8
Parameters
  Passed:
Database name:     SAMPLE
Logfile name:      S0000004.LOG
```

```
Logfile path:        c:\dblog\SAMPLE\NODE0000\
Node number:         NODE0000
Operating            NT
   system:
Release:             SQL08010
Request:             ARCHIVE
System Action:       ARCHIVE c:\dblog\SAMPLE\NODE0000\S0000004.LOG to
                     c:\dbarch\SAMPLE
Media Type:          disk
User Exit RC:        0
Time Completed:      Sun Jul 14 23:20:34 2002
                     ARCHIVE c:\dblog\SAMPLE\NODE0000\S0000004.LOG to
                     c:\dbarch\SAMPLE
**********************************************************************
Time Started:        Sun Jul 14 23:22:17 2002
Parameter Count:     8
Parameters
   Passed:
Database name:       SAMPLE
Logfile name:        S0000005.LOG
Logfile path:        c:\dblog\SAMPLE\NODE0000\
Node number:         NODE0000
Operating            NT
   system:
Release:             SQL08010
Request:             ARCHIVE
System Action:       ARCHIVE c:\dblog\SAMPLE\NODE0000\S0000005.LOG to
                     c:\dbarch\SAMPLE
Media Type:          disk
User Exit RC:        0
Time Completed:      Sun Jul 14 23:22:17 2002
```

Check list:

- Restart DB2 (db2stop and db2start)
- Verify file permission on the executable file db2uext2
- Check directory permission for c:\dblog and c:\dbarch
- For additional information, view c:\dblog\ARCHIVE.LOG or
  c:\dblog\USEREXIT.ERR

DEVELOPING A BACKUP AND RECOVERY STRATEGY

A database can become unusable because of hardware or software failure, or both. You may, at one time or another, encounter storage problems, power interruptions, application failures, and different failure scenarios that require different recovery actions. It is important to protect your data against the possibility of loss by having a well-rehearsed recovery strategy in place. Some of the questions that you should answer when developing your recovery strategy are:

- Will the database be recoverable?
- Is version recovery sufficient, or must the database allow rollforward recovery?
- How much time can be spent recovering the database?
- How much time will pass between backup operations?
- How much storage space can be allocated for backup copies and archived logs?
- Will table space level backups be sufficient, or will full database backups be necessary?

Now the question is, Why back up? What are you trying to protect? What failures do you expect?

You should:

- Always have a recovery plan in place (make sure the plan is well documented and practiced).
- Identify failures that can occur and how to prevent/react to the failures.
    ○ Disk failure: Use disk mirroring or Redundant Array of Independent Disks (RAID)
    ○ CPU failure: Use a standby machine or failover machine
    ○ Application failure: Use a backup image
- Use DB2's backup and recovery utilities.

A database recovery strategy should ensure that all information is available when it is required for database recovery. It should include a regular schedule for taking backups and, in the case of partitioned database systems, should include backups when the system is scaled (when database partitions are added or dropped).

The overall strategy should also include procedures for recovering command scripts, applications, user-defined functions (UDFs), as well as stored procedure code in the operating system libraries, and load copies.

Different recovery methods are discussed in the sections that follow, and you will discover which recovery method is best suited to your business environment.

The concept of a database backup is the same as any other data backup: taking a copy of the data, then storing it on a different medium in case of failure or damage to the original. The simplest case of a backup involves shutting down the database to ensure that no further transactions occur, then simply backing it up. You can then rebuild the database if it becomes damaged or corrupted in some way.

The rebuilding of the database is called *recovery*.

- Crash recovery is the automatic recovery of the database if a failure occurs before all of the changes that are part of one or more units of work are completed and committed or rolled back. This is done by rolling back incomplete transactions and ensuring completion of committed transactions that were still in memory when the crash occurred.

- Version recovery is the restoration of a previous version of the database, using an image that was created during a backup operation.
- Disaster recovery is the restoration of the entire database on another machine, using the full database backup and all of the archived logs for the database.
- Rollforward recovery is the reapplication of transactions recorded in the database log files after a database or a table space backup image has been restored.

Each database includes logs, which are used to recover from application or system errors. In combination with the database backups, they are used to recover the consistency of the database right up to the point in time when the error occurred.

Data that is easily recreated can be stored in a non-recoverable database. This includes data from an outside source that is used for read-only applications and tables that are not often updated, for which the small amount of logging does not justify the added complexity of managing log files and rolling forward after a restore operation. Non-recoverable databases have both the LOGRETAIN and the USEREXIT database configuration parameters turned off. This means that the only logs that are kept are those required for crash recovery.

These logs are known as *active logs*, and they contain current transaction data. Version recovery using offline backups is the primary means of recovery for a non-recoverable database. An offline backup means that no other application can use the database when the backup operation is in progress. Such a database can be restored only offline. It is restored to the state it was in when the backup image was taken, and rollforward recovery is not supported.

Data that cannot be easily recreated should be stored in a recoverable database. This includes data whose source is destroyed after the data is loaded, data that is manually entered into tables, and data that is modified by application programs or users after it is loaded into the database. Recoverable databases have either the LOGRETAIN database configuration parameter set to RECOVERY, the USEREXIT database configuration parameter set to YES, or both.

Active logs are still available for crash recovery, but when the database is configured as a recoverable database, you also have the archived logs, which contain committed transaction data. Such a database can be restored only offline. It is restored to the state it was in when the backup image was taken. However, with rollforward recovery, you can roll the database forward (that is, past the time when the backup image was taken) by using the active and archived logs either to a specific point in time or to the end of the active logs.

Recoverable database backup operations can be performed either offline or online. An online backup means that other applications can connect to the database when the backup operation is in progress. Database restore and rollforward operations must always be performed offline. During an online backup operation, rollforward recovery ensures that all changes are captured and reapplied if that backup is restored.

If you have a recoverable database, you can back up, restore, and roll individual table spaces forward, rather than the entire database. When you back up a table space online, it is still available for use, and simultaneous updates are recorded in the logs. When you perform an online restore or rollforward operation on a table space, the table space itself is not available for use until the operation completes, but users can be allowed to access tables in other table spaces.

The Recovery History File

The recovery history file contains certain historical information about major actions that have been performed against a database. The information recorded in the recovery history file is used to assist with the recovery of the database in the event of a failure. The following is a list of the actions that will generate an entry in the history file:

- Backing up the database or a table space
- Restoring the database or a table space from a backup image
- Performing a rollforward recovery operation on the database or a table space
- Loading a table
- Altering a table space's definition
- Quiescing a table space
- Reorganizing a table (REORG)
- Updating statistics for a table (RUNSTATS)
- Dropping a table

A recovery history file is also created automatically when a database is created. This file is located in the database directory. You cannot directly modify a recovery history file; however, you can delete entries from the recovery history file using the PRUNE HISTORY command. You can also use the REC_HIS_RETENTN database configuration parameter to specify the number of days that the recovery history file will be retained.

Recovery history file related to backup information for the database SAMPLE:

```
db2 list history backup all for sample


                      List History File for sample
Number of matching file entries = 1
Op   Obj  Timestamp+Sequence  Type  Dev  Earliest Log  Current Log  Backup ID
---  ---  ----------------    ----  ---  ------------  -----------  ---------
B    D    20020829090733001   F     D    S0000000.LOG  S0000000.LOG
----------------------------------------------------------------------------
Contains 2 tablespace(s):
00001 SYSCATSPACE
00002 USERSPACE1
----------------------------------------------------------------------------
```

```
       Comment: DB2 BACKUP SAMPLE OFFLINE
   Start Time: 20020829090733
     End Time: 20020829090756
   ----------------------------------------------------------------------
   00001 Location: /data/dbbackup
```

Deciding How Often to Back Up

Your recovery plan should allow for regularly scheduled backup operations, because backing up a database requires time and system resources. Your plan may include a combination of full database backups, table space backups, and incremental backup operations.

You should take full database backups regularly, even if you archive the logs (which allows for rollforward recovery). It is more time consuming to rebuild a database from a collection of table space backup images than it is to recover the database from a full database backup image. Table space backup images are useful for recovering from an isolated disk failure or an application error.

You should also consider not overwriting backup images and logs, saving at least two full database backup images and their associated logs as an extra precaution.

If the amount of time needed to apply archived logs when recovering and rolling a very active database forward is a major concern, consider the cost of backing up the database more frequently. This reduces the number of archived logs you need to apply when rolling forward. You can initiate a backup operation while the database is either online or offline. If it is online, other applications or processes can connect to the database, as well as read and modify data while the backup operation is running. If the backup operation is running offline, other applications cannot connect to the database.

To reduce the amount of time that the database is not available, consider using online backup operations. Online backup operations are supported only if rollforward recovery is enabled. If rollforward recovery is enabled and you have a complete set of recovery logs, you can rebuild the database, should the need arise. You can use an online backup image for recovery only if you have the logs that span the time during which the backup operation was running.

Offline backup operations can be faster than online backup operations, because there is no contention for the data files.

The backup utility lets you back up selected table spaces. If you use DMS table spaces, you can store different types of data in their own table spaces to reduce the time required for backup operations. You can keep table data in one table space, long field and large object (LOB) data in another table space, and indexes in yet another table space. If you do this and a disk failure occurs, it is likely to affect only one of the table spaces. Restoring or rolling forward one of these table spaces will take less time than it would have taken to restore a single table space containing all of the data.

> **NOTE**   If a table is split among table spaces, you must restore all
> of the table spaces for the table to roll forward to a point in time
> prior to the end of the logs.

You can also save time by taking backups of different table spaces at different times, as long as the frequency of changes to them are not the same. If long field or LOB data is not changed as frequently as the other data, you can back up these table spaces less frequently. If long field and LOB data are not required for recovery, you can also consider not backing up the table space that contains that data. If the LOB data can be reproduced from a separate source, choose the NOT LOGGED column option when creating or altering a table to include LOB columns.

When formulating a recovery plan, you should take these recovery costs and their impact on your business operations into account. Testing your overall recovery plan will assist you in determining whether the time required to recover the database is reasonable, given your business requirements. Following each test, you should determine whether the recovery time required is acceptable; if it is too long, you may want to increase the frequency with which you take a backup. If rollforward recovery is part of your strategy, this will reduce the number of logs that are archived between backups and, as a result, reduce the time required to roll the database forward after a restore operation.

Storage Considerations

When deciding which recovery method to use, consider the storage space required.

The version recovery method requires space to hold the backup copy of the database and the restored database. The rollforward recovery method requires space to hold the backup copy of the database or table spaces, the restored database, and the archived database logs.

If a table contains long field or LOB columns, you should consider placing this data into a separate table space. This will affect your storage space considerations, as well as your plan for recovery, as mentioned above. With a separate table space for long field and LOB data, and knowing the time required to back up long field and LOB data, you may decide to use a recovery plan that only occasionally saves a backup of this table space. You may also choose, when creating or altering a table, to include LOB columns, not to log changes to those columns. This will reduce the size of the required log space and the corresponding log archive space.

To prevent media failure from destroying a database and your ability to rebuild it, keep the database backup, the database logs, and the database itself on different devices. For this reason, it is highly recommended that you use the NEWLOGPATH configuration parameter to put database logs on a separate device, once the database is created.

The database logs can use up a large amount of storage. If you plan to use the rollforward recovery method, you must decide how to manage the archived logs. Your choices are the following:

- Use a user exit program to copy these logs to another storage device in your environment.
- Manually copy the logs to a storage device or directory other than the database log path directory after they are no longer in the active set of logs.

Keeping Related Data Together

As part of your database design, you will know the relationships that exist between tables. These relationships can be expressed at the application level, when transactions update more than one table; at the database level, where referential integrity exists between tables; or where triggers on one table affect another table. You should consider these relationships when developing a recovery plan. You will want to back up related sets of data together. Such sets can be established at either the table space or the database level. By keeping related sets of data together, you can recover to a point where all of the data is consistent. This is especially important if you want to be able to perform point-in-time rollforward recovery on table spaces.

Using Different Operating Systems

When working in an environment that has more than one operating system, you must consider that you cannot back up a database on one operating system, then restore that database on another operating system (such as UNIX to/from Linux or Windows).

In such cases, you should keep the recovery plans for each operating system separate and independent. There is, however, support for cross-platform backup and restore operations between operating systems with similar architectures, such as AIX, HP/UX, and Sun Solaris, and between 32-bit and 64-bit operating systems.

When you transfer the backup image between systems, you must transfer it in binary mode. The target system must have the same (or later) version of DB2 as the source system. Restore operations to a down-level system are not supported.

If you must move tables from one operating system to another and cross-platform backup and restore support is not available in your environment, you can use the *db2move* command, or the *export* utility followed by the *import* or the *load* utility.

Crash Recovery

Transactions or units of work against a database can be interrupted unexpectedly. If a failure occurs before all of the changes that are part of the unit of work are completed and committed, the database is left in an inconsistent and unusable state. Crash recovery is the process by which the database is moved back to a consistent and usable state. This is done by rolling back incomplete transactions and completing committed transactions that were still in memory when the crash occurred. When a database is in a consistent and usable state, it has attained what is known as a *point of consistency*.

If you want the rollback of incomplete units of work to be done automatically by the database manager, enable the automatic restart (AUTORESTART) database configuration parameter by setting it to ON; this is the default value. If you do not want automatic restart behavior, set the AUTORESTART database configuration parameter to OFF. As a result, you will need to issue the RESTART DATABASE command when a database failure occurs. If the database I/O was suspended before the crash occurred, you must specify the WRITE RESUME option of the RESTART DATABASE command in order for the crash recovery to continue. The administration notification log records when the database restart operation begins.

If crash recovery is applied to a database that is enabled for forward recovery (that is, the LOGRETAIN configuration parameter is set to RECOVERY, or the USEREXIT configuration parameter is set to ON) and an error occurs during crash recovery that is attributable to an individual table space, that table space will be taken offline and cannot be accessed until it is repaired. Crash recovery continues. At the completion of crash recovery, the other table spaces in the database will be accessible, and connections to the database can be established. However, if the table space that is taken offline is the table space that contains the system catalogs, it must be repaired before any connections will be permitted.

Recovering Damaged Table Spaces

A damaged table space has one or more containers that cannot be accessed. This is often caused by media problems that are either permanent (a bad disk) or temporary (an offline disk or an unmounted file system).

If the damaged table space is the system catalog table space, the database cannot be restarted. If the container problems cannot be fixed, leaving the original data intact, the only available options are:

- To restore the database.
- To restore the catalog table space. Table space restore is valid only for recoverable databases, because the database must be rolled forward.

If the damaged table space is not the system catalog table space, DB2 attempts to make as much of the database available as possible.

If the damaged table space is the only temporary table space, you should create a new temporary table space as soon as a connection to the database can be made. Once created, the new temporary table space can be used, and normal database operations requiring a temporary table space can resume.

You can, if you wish, drop the offline temporary table space. There are special considerations for table reorganization using a system temporary table space:

- If the database or the database manager configuration parameter INDEXREC is set to RESTART, all invalid indexes must be rebuilt during database activation; this includes indexes from a reorganization that crashed during the build phase.

- If there are incomplete reorganization requests in a damaged temporary table space, you may have to set the INDEXREC configuration parameter to ACCESS to avoid restart failures.

Recovering Table Spaces in Recoverable Databases

When crash recovery is necessary, a damaged table space will be taken offline and will not be accessible. It will be placed in rollforward pending state. A restart operation will succeed if there are no additional problems, and the damaged table space can be used again once you:

- Fix the damaged containers without losing the original data (i.e., mount the file systems), then perform a table space rollforward operation to the end of the logs. The rollforward operation will first attempt to bring it from offline to normal state.
- Perform a table space restore operation after fixing the damaged containers (with or without losing the original data), then a rollforward operation to the end of the logs or to a point in time.

Reducing the Impact of Media Failure

To reduce the probability of media failure causing a database problem and to simplify recovery from this type of failure if it does occur:

- Mirror or duplicate the disks that hold the data and logs for important databases.
- Use a RAID configuration, such as RAID level 5.
- In a partitioned database environment, set up a procedure for handling the data and the logs on the catalog partition. Because this catalog partition is critical for maintaining the database:
  - Ensure that it resides on redundant disks, i.e., mirrored or RAID-protected.
  - Mirror or duplicate the disk as needed.
  - Make frequent backups.
  - Consider not placing user data on the catalog partition.

Protecting Against Disk Failure

If you are concerned about the possibility of damaged data or logs due to a disk crash, consider the use of some form of disk fault tolerance. Generally, this is accomplished through the use of a disk array or disk/file system mirroring.

A disk array is sometimes referred to simply as a RAID. Disk arrays can also be provided through hardware or software at the operating system or application level. The point of distinction between hardware and software disk arrays is how processing of I/O requests is handled.

For hardware disk arrays, I/O activity is managed by the disk controllers; for software disk arrays, this is done by the operating system/file system.

Hardware Disk Arrays

In a hardware disk array, multiple disks are used and managed by a disk controller (or controllers), complete with its own memory/storage. All of the logic required to manage the disks forming the array is contained on the disk controller; therefore, this implementation is independent of the operating system.

There are several types of RAID architecture, differing in function and performance, but RAID levels 1 and 5 are the most commonly used today.

RAID level 1 is also known as *disk mirroring* or *duplexing*.

- Disk mirroring copies data from one disk to a second disk, using a single disk controller.
- Disk duplexing is similar to disk mirroring, except that disks are attached to a second disk controller (such as two adapters).
- With either of these technologies, data protection is very good: Either disk can fail, and data is still accessible from the other disk. With disk duplexing, a disk controller can also fail without compromising data protection.
- Performance is also good, but this implementation requires twice the usual number of disks.

RAID level 5 involves data and parity striping by sectors, across a set of disks. Parity is interleaved with the data, rather than being stored on a dedicated drive. With this technology, data protection is also good: If any disk fails, the data can still be accessed by using the parity information from the other disks. Read performance is good, but write performance can be adversely affected. A RAID level 5 configuration requires a minimum of three identical disks. The amount of disk space required for overhead varies with the number of disks in the array. In the case of a RAID level 5 configuration with 5 disks, the space overhead is 20% (i.e., five disks plus a parity disk).

When using a RAID (but not a RAID level 0) disk array, a disk failure will not prevent you from accessing data on the array. When hot-pluggable or hot-swappable disks are used in the array, a replacement disk can be swapped with the failed disk while the array is in use. With RAID level 5, if two disks fail at the same time, all data is lost (but the probability of simultaneous disk failures is very small).

You might consider using a RAID level 1 hardware disk array or a software disk array for your logs, because this provides recoverability to the point of failure and offers good write performance, which is important for logs. In cases where reliability is critical (because time cannot be lost recovering data following a disk failure) and write performance is not so critical, consider using a RAID level 5 hardware disk array. Alternatively, if write performance is critical and the cost of additional disk space is not significant, consider a RAID level 1 hardware disk array for your data, as well as for your logs.

> **NOTE** You should consider using MIRRORLOGPATH to specify a secondary log path for the database to manage copies of the active log. It is recommended that you place the secondary log path on a separate physical disk (preferably one that is also on a different disk controller). That way, the disk controller cannot be a single point of failure.

Stripe Set

A software disk array accomplishes much the same as does a hardware disk array, but disk traffic is managed either by the operating system or by an application program running on the server. Like other programs, the software array must compete for CPU and system resources. This is not a good option for a CPU-constrained system, and it should be remembered that overall disk array performance is dependent on the server's CPU load and capacity.

A typical software disk array provides disk mirroring. Although redundant disks are required, a software disk array is comparatively inexpensive to implement, because costly disk controllers are not required.

> **CAUTION** Having the operating system boot drive in the disk array prevents your system from starting if that drive fails. If the drive fails before the disk array is running, the disk array cannot allow access to the drive. A boot drive should be separate from the disk array.

Reducing the Potential of Transaction Failure

To reduce the potential of a transaction failure, try to ensure:

- Adequate disk space for the database logs.
- Reliable communication links among the database partitions in a partitioned database environment.
- Synchronization of the system clocks in a partitioned database environment.

Recovering from Transaction Failures in a Partitioned Database Environment

If a transaction failure occurs in a partitioned database environment, database recovery is usually necessary on both the failed database partition and any other database partitions that were participating in the transaction:

- Crash recovery occurs on the failed database partition after the failure condition is corrected.
- Database partition failure recovery on the other (still active) database partitions occurs immediately after the failure has been detected.

In a partitioned database environment, the database partition on which an application is submitted is the coordinator partition, and the first agent that works for the application is the coordinator agent. The coordinator agent is responsible for distributing work to other database partitions, and it keeps track of which ones are involved in the transaction. When the application issues a COMMIT statement for a transaction, the coordinator agent commits the transaction by using a two-phase commit protocol.

During the first phase, the coordinator partition distributes a PREPARE request to all the other database partitions that are participating in the transaction. These database partitions then respond with one of the following:

- **READ-ONLY** indicates that no data change occurred at this database partition.
- **YES** indicates that data change occurred at this database partition.
- **NO** indicates that there is an error and the database partition is not prepared to commit.

If one of the database partitions responds with a NO, the transaction is rolled back. Otherwise, the coordinator partition begins the second phase.

During the second phase, the coordinator partition writes a COMMIT log record, then distributes a COMMIT request to all the database partitions that responded with a YES. After all the other database partitions have committed, they send an acknowledgement of the COMMIT to the coordinator partition. The transaction is complete when the coordinator agent has received all COMMIT acknowledgements from all the participating partitions. At this point, the coordinator agent writes a FORGET log record.

Transaction Failure Recovery on an Active Database Partition

If any database partition detects that another database partition is down, all work that is associated with the failed database partition is stopped:

- If the still active database partition is the coordinator partition for an application and the application was running on the failed database partition (and not ready to COMMIT), the coordinator agent is interrupted to do failure recovery. If the coordinator agent is in the second phase of COMMIT processing, SQL0279N is returned to the application, which in turn loses its database connection. Otherwise, the coordinator agent distributes a ROLLBACK request to all other partitions participating in the transaction, and SQL1229N is returned to the application.
- If the failed database partition was the coordinator partition for the application, agents that are still working for the application on the active partitions are interrupted to do failure recovery. The current transaction is rolled back locally on each database partition, unless it has been prepared and is waiting for the transaction outcome. In this situation, the transaction is left in doubt on the active database partitions, and the coordinator partition is not aware of this (because it is not available).

- If the application was connected to the failed database partition (before it failed) but neither the local database partition nor the failed database partition is the coordinator partition, agents working for this application are interrupted. The coordinator partition will send either a ROLLBACK or a disconnect message to the other database partitions.

The transaction will be indoubt only on database partitions that are still active if the coordinator partition returns an SQL0279N.

Any process (such as an agent or deadlock detector) that attempts to send a request to the failed partition is informed that it cannot send the request.

Transaction Failure Recovery on the Failed Database Partition

If the transaction failure causes the database manager to end abnormally, you can issue the *db2start* command with the RESTART option to restart the database manager, once the database partition has been restarted. If you cannot restart the database partition, you can issue *db2start* to restart the database manager on a different partition.

If the database manager ends abnormally, database partitions may be left in an inconsistent state. To make them usable, crash recovery can be triggered on a database partition:

- Explicitly, through the RESTART DATABASE command
- Implicitly, through a CONNECT request when the AUTORESTART database configuration parameter has been set to ON

Crash recovery reapplies the log records in the active log files to ensure that the effects of all complete transactions are in the database. After the changes have been reapplied, all uncommitted transactions are rolled back locally, except for indoubt transactions. There are two types of indoubt transaction in a partitioned database environment:

- On a database partition that is not the coordinator partition, a transaction is indoubt if it is prepared but not yet committed.
- On the coordinator partition, a transaction is indoubt if it is committed but not yet logged as complete (that is, the FORGET record is not yet written). This situation occurs when the coordinator agent has not received all the COMMIT acknowledgements from all the database partitions that worked for the application.

Crash recovery attempts to resolve all the indoubt transactions by doing one of the following. The action that is taken depends on whether the database partition was the coordinator partition for an application:

- If the database partition that restarted is not the coordinator partition for the application, it sends a query message to the coordinator agent to discover the outcome of the transaction.

- If the database partition that restarted is the coordinator partition for the application, it sends a message to all the other agents (subordinate agents) that the coordinator agent is still waiting for COMMIT acknowledgements.

It is possible that crash recovery may not be able to resolve all the indoubt transactions (for example, some of the database partitions may not be available). In this situation, the SQL warning message SQL1061W is returned. Because indoubt transactions hold resources, such as locks and active log space, it is possible to get to a point where no changes can be made to the database because the active log space is being held up by indoubt transactions. For this reason, you should determine whether indoubt transactions remain after crash recovery and recover all database partitions that are required to resolve the indoubt transactions as quickly as possible.

If one or more partitions that are required to resolve an indoubt transaction cannot be recovered in time, and access is required to database partitions, you can manually resolve the indoubt transaction by making a heuristic decision. You can use the LIST INDOUBT TRANSACTIONS command to query, commit, and roll back the indoubt transaction on the database partition.

Identifying the Failed Database Partition

When a database partition fails, the application will typically receive one of the following SQLCODEs. The method for detecting which database manager failed depends on the SQLCODE received:

- **SQL0279N**—This SQLCODE is received when a database partition involved in a transaction is terminated during COMMIT processing.
- **SQL1224N**—This SQLCODE is received when the database partition that failed is the coordinator partition for the transaction.
- **SQL1229N**—This SQLCODE is received when the database partition that failed is not the coordinator partition for the transaction.

Determining which database partition failed is a two-step process. The SQLCA associated with SQLCODE SQL1229N contains the database partition number of the server that detected the error in the sixth array position of the sqlerrd field.

> **NOTE** If multiple logical database partitions are being used on a single server, the failure of one logical database partition may cause other logical database partitions on the same single server to fail.

Recovering from the Failure of a Database Partition

To recover from the failure of a database partition:

- Correct the problem that caused the failure.

- Restart the database manager by issuing the *db2start* command from any database partition.
- Restart the database by issuing the RESTART DATABASE command on the failed database partition.

Disaster Recovery

The term *disaster recovery* is used to describe the activities that need to be done to restore the database (in a remote location) in the event of a fire, earthquake, vandalism, or other catastrophic events. A plan for disaster recovery can include one or more of the following:

- A remote site to be used in the event of an emergency
- A different server on which to recover the database
- Off-site storage of database backups and archived logs

If your plan for disaster recovery is to recover the entire database on another machine, you require at least one full database backup and all the archived logs for the database. You may choose to keep a standby database up to date by applying the logs to it as they are archived. Or you may choose to keep the database backup and log archives in the standby site and to perform the restore and rollforward operations only after a disaster has occurred. With a disaster, however, it is generally not possible to recover all of the transactions up to the time of the disaster, i.e., some of the active log files may be lost.

The usefulness of a table space backup for disaster recovery depends on the scope of the failure. Typically, disaster recovery requires that you restore the entire database; therefore, a full database backup should be kept at a standby site. Even if you have a separate backup image of every table space, you cannot use them to recover the database.

Both table space backups and full database backups can have a role to play in any disaster recovery plan. The DB2 facilities available for backing up, restoring, and rolling data forward provide a foundation for a disaster recovery plan. You should ensure that you have tested recovery procedures in place to protect your business.

Version Recovery

Version recovery is the restoration of a previous version of the database, using an image that was created during an offline database backup operation. You use this recovery method with non-recoverable databases (that is, databases for which you do not have archived logs). You can also use this method with recoverable databases by using the WITHOUT ROLLING FORWARD option on the RESTORE DATABASE command.

A database restore operation will rebuild the entire database, using a backup image created earlier. A database backup allows you to restore a database to a state identical to the state at the time that the backup was made. However, every unit of work from the time of the backup to the time of the failure is lost.

Using the version recovery method, you must schedule and perform full offline backups of the database on a regular basis.

In a partitioned database environment, the database is located across many database partitions. You must restore all partitions, and the backup images that you use for the restore database operation must all have been taken at the same time. Each database partition is backed up and restored separately. A backup of each database partition taken at the same time is known as a *version backup.*

> **N O T E**   You need to restore the catalog partition first, then the remaining database partitions.

Rollforward Recovery

To use the rollforward recovery method, you must have taken a backup of the database and archived the logs (by setting to YES either the LOGRETAIN or the USEREXIT database configuration parameters, or both). Restoring the database and specifying the WITHOUT ROLLING FORWARD option is equivalent to using the version recovery method. The database is restored to a state identical to the one at the time that the offline backup image was made. If you restore the database and do not specify the WITHOUT ROLLING FORWARD option for the restore database operation, the database will be in rollforward pending state at the end of the restore operation. This allows rollforward recovery to take place.

> **N O T E**   The WITHOUT ROLLING FORWARD option cannot be used if the database backup was taken online.

The two types of rollforward recovery to consider are:

1. Database rollforward recovery. In this type of rollforward recovery, transactions recorded in database logs are applied following the database restore operation. The database logs record all changes made to the database. This method completes the recovery of the database to its state at a particular point in time or to its state immediately before the failure (i.e., to the end of the active logs).
   In a partitioned database environment, the database is located across many database partitions. If you are performing point-in-time rollforward recovery, all database partitions must be rolled forward to ensure that all partitions are at the same level. If you need to restore a single database partition, you can perform rollforward recovery to the end of the logs to bring it up to the same level as the other partitions in the database.

Only recovery to the end of the logs can be used if one database partition is being rolled forward. Point-in-time recovery applies to all database partitions.

2. Table space rollforward recovery. If the database is enabled for forward recovery, it is also possible to back up, restore, and roll table spaces forward. To perform a table space restore and rollforward operation, you need a backup image of either the entire database (i.e., all of the table spaces) or one or more individual table spaces. You also need the log records that affect the table spaces that are to be recovered.

You can roll forward through the logs to one of two points:

- The end of the logs
- A particular point in time (called *point-in-time recovery*)

Table space rollforward recovery can be used in the following two situations:

- After a table space restore operation, the table space is always in rollforward pending state, and it must be rolled forward. Invoke the ROLLFORWARD DATABASE command to apply the logs against the table spaces either to a point in time or to the end of the logs.

- If one or more table spaces are in rollforward pending state after crash recovery, first correct the table space problem. In some cases, correcting the table space problem does not involve a restore database operation. For example, a power loss could leave the table space in rollforward pending state. A restore database operation is not required in this case. Once the problem with the table space is corrected, you can use the ROLLFORWARD DATABASE command to apply the logs against the table spaces to the end of the logs. If the problem is corrected before crash recovery, crash recovery may be sufficient to take the database to a consistent, usable state.

> **N O T E**   If the table space in error contains the system catalog tables, you will not be able to start the database. You must restore the SYSCATSPACE table space, then perform rollforward recovery to the end of the logs.

In a partitioned database environment:

- If you are rolling a table space forward to a point in time, you do not have to supply the list of database partitions on which the table space resides. DB2 submits the rollforward request to all partitions. This means the table space must be restored on all database partitions on which the table space resides.

- If you are rolling a table space forward to the end of the logs, you must supply the list of database partitions if you do not want to roll the table space forward on all partitions. If you want to roll all table spaces (on all partitions) that are in rollforward pending state forward to the end of the logs, you do not have to supply the list of database partitions. By default, the database rollforward request is sent to all partitions.

• You must restore catalog partition first.

Incremental Backup and Recovery

As the size of databases, and particularly data warehouses, continues to expand into the tens and hundreds of terabytes time and hardware resources required to back up and recover these databases are also growing substantially.

Full database and table space backups are not always the best approach when dealing with large databases, because the storage requirements for multiple copies of such databases are enormous. When only a small percentage of the data in a warehouse changes, it should not be necessary to back up the entire database or table space.

An incremental backup is a backup image that contains only pages that have been updated since the previous backup was taken. In addition to updated data and index pages, each incremental backup image also contains all of the initial database metadata (such as database configuration, table space definitions, database history, and so on) that is normally stored in full backup images.

Two types of incremental backup are supported:

• **Incremental**—An incremental backup image is a copy of all database data that has changed since the most recent, successful, full backup operation. This is also known as a *cumulative backup image*, because a series of incremental backups taken over time will each have the contents of the previous incremental backup image. The predecessor of an incremental backup image is always the most recent successful full backup of the same object.

• **Delta**—A delta, or incremental delta, backup image is a copy of all database data that has changed since the last successful backup (full, incremental, or delta) of the database or table space in question.

The key difference between incremental and delta backup images is their behavior when successive backups are taken of an object that is continually changing over time. Each successive incremental image contains the entire contents of the previous incremental image, plus any data that has changed or is new since the previous full backup was produced. Delta backup images contain only the pages that have changed since the previous image of any type was produced.

Combinations of database and table space incremental backups are permitted in both online and offline modes of operation. Be careful when planning your backup strategy, because combining database and table space incremental backups implies that the predecessor of a database backup (or a table space backup of multiple table spaces) is not necessarily a single image but could be a unique set of previous database and table space backups taken at different times.

To rebuild the database or the table space to a consistent state, the recovery process must begin with a consistent image of the entire object (database or table space) to be restored and must then apply each of the appropriate incremental backup images in the order described below.

To enable the tracking of database updates, DB2 supports a database configuration parameter, TRACKMOD, which can have one of two accepted values:

- Set TRACKMOD to NO—incremental backup is not permitted with this configuration. Database page updates are not tracked or recorded in any way. This is the default value.
- Set TRACKMOD to YES—incremental backup is permitted with this configuration. When update tracking is enabled, the change becomes effective at the first successful connection to the database. Before an incremental backup can be taken on a particular table space, a full backup of that table space is necessary.

> **N O T E**   The tracking of updates to the database can have an impact on the runtime performance of transactions that update or insert data.

For SMS and DMS table spaces, the granularity of this tracking is at the table space level. In table space level tracking, a flag for each table space indicates whether there are pages in that table space that need to be backed up.

If no pages in a table space need to be backed up, the backup operation can skip that table space altogether.

Restoring from Incremental Backup Images

A restore operation from incremental backup images always consists of the following steps:

1. Identifying the incremental target image or the last image to be restored and request an incremental restore operation from the DB2 restore utility. The incremental target image is specified using the TAKEN AT parameter in the RESTORE DATABASE command.
2. Restoring the most recent full database or table space image to establish a baseline against which each of the subsequent incremental backup images can be applied.
3. Restoring each of the required full or table space incremental backup images, in the order in which they were produced, on top of the baseline image restored in Step 2.
4. Repeating Step 3 until the target image from Step 1 is read a second time. The target image is accessed twice during a complete incremental restore operation to ensure that the database is initially configured with the correct history, database configuration, and table space definitions for the database that will be created during the restore operation.

There are two ways to restore incremental backup images.

1. For a manual incremental restore, the RESTORE command must be issued once for each backup image that needs to be restored (as outlined in the steps above).
2. For an automatic incremental restore, the RESTORE command is issued only once, specifying the target image to be used. DB2 then uses the database history to determine the remaining required backup images and restores them.

Manual Incremental Restore Example

To restore a set of incremental backup images, using manual incremental restore, specify the target image using the TAKEN AT timestamp option of the RESTORE DATABASE command and follow the steps outlined above.

For example:

```
db2 restore db sample incremental taken at 20020829102021
```

1. db2 restore database sample incremental taken at <timestamp_1>
   where <timestamp_1> points to the last incremental backup image (the target image) to be restored
2. db2 restore database sample incremental taken at <timestamp_2>
   where <timestamp_2> points to the initial full database (or table space) image
3. db2 restore database sample incremental taken at <timestamp_X>
   where <timestamp_X> points to each incremental backup image in creation sequence
4. Repeat Step 3, restoring each incremental backup image up to and including image <timestamp_1>

If you are using manual incremental restore for a database restore operation, and table space backup images have been produced, the table space images must be restored in the chronological order of their backup timestamps.

If you want to use manual incremental restore, the *db2ckrst* utility can be used to query the database history and generate a list of backup image timestamps needed for an incremental restore. A simplified restore syntax for a manual incremental restore is also generated. It is recommended that you keep a complete record of backups and use this utility only as a guide.

Automatic Incremental Restore Example

To restore a set of incremental backup images using automatic incremental restore, specify the TAKEN AT timestamp option on the RESTORE DATABASE command. Use the timestamp for the last image that you want to restore.

For example:

```
db2 restore db sample incremental automatic taken at 20020829102037
```

1. This will result in the restore utility performing each of the steps described at the beginning of this section, automatically and in sequence. During the initial phase of processing, the backup image with timestamp 20020829102037 is read, and the restore utility verifies that the database, its history, and the table space definitions exist and are valid.

2. During the second phase of processing, the database history is queried to build a chain of backup images required to perform the requested restore operation. If, for some reason, this is not possible, and DB2 is unable to build a complete chain of required images, the restore operation terminates, and an error message is returned. In this case, an automatic incremental restore will not be possible, and you will have to issue the RESTORE DATABASE command with the INCREMENTAL ABORT option. This will clean up any remaining resources so that you can proceed with a manual incremental restore.

3. During the third phase of processing, DB2 will restore each of the remaining backup images in the generated chain. If an error occurs during this phase, you will have to issue the RESTORE DATABASE command with the INCREMENTAL ABORT option to clean up any remaining resources. You will then have to determine whether the error can be resolved before you reissue the RESTORE command or attempt the manual incremental restore again.

> **NOTE** It is highly recommended that you not use the FORCE option of the PRUNE HISTORY command. The default operation of the PRUNE HISTORY command prevents you from deleting history entries that may be required for recovery from the most recent, full database backup image; but with the FORCE option, it is possible to delete entries that are required for an automatic restore operation.

Limitations to Automatic Incremental Restore

Scenario #1: Automatic incremental restore is unable to proceed   When a table space name has been changed since the backup operation you want to restore from the backup images, and you use the new name when you issue a table space level restore operation, the required chain of backup images from the database history will not be generated correctly with automatic incremental restore, and an error will occur (SQL2571N).

Example restore procedure:

- Step #1: db2 backup db sample
- Step #2: db2 backup db sample incremental
- Step #3: db2 rename tablespace userspace1 to ts1
- Step #4: db2 restore db sample tablespace (ts1) incremental automatic taken at <step #2 timestamp>

Limitation:

- SQL2571N Automatic incremental restore is unable to proceed. Reason code: "3".

Solution:

- Check restore order sequence.
- Use manual incremental restore.

The following is sample output from automatic incremental restore:

```
db2 update db cfg for sample using trackmod

DB20000I  The UPDATE DATABASE CONFIGURATION command completed successfully.

db2 backup db sample to /data/dbbackup

Backup successful. The timestamp for this backup image is : 20020829090733
➔ This is the first timestamp

db2 list history backup all for sample

                          List History File for sample
Number of matching file entries = 1
Op       Obj    Timestamp+Sequence  Type      Dev   Earliest Log Current Log Backup ID
---      ---    ---------------     ----      ---   --------- --------- ---------
                ---
B        D      20020829090733001   F         D     S0000000.LOG S0000000.LOG
--------------------------------------------------------------------------
Contains 2 tablespace(s):
00001 SYSCATSPACE
00002 USERSPACE1
--------------------------------------------------------------------------
   Comment: DB2 BACKUP SAMPLE OFFLINE
Start Time: 20020829090733
  End Time: 20020829090756
--------------------------------------------------------------------------
 00001 Location: /data/dbbackup

db2 connect to sample

  Database Connection Information
Database server          = DB2/6000 8.1.0
SQL authorization ID     = V8INST
Local database alias     = SAMPLE

db2 "create table t1 (c1 int)"

DB20000I  The SQL command completed successfully.

db2 backup db sample incremental to /data/dbbackup

Backup successful. The timestamp for this backup image is : 20020829091526
➔ This is the second timestamp
```

```
db2 list history backup all for sample

                      List History File for sample
Number of matching file entries = 2
Op        Obj     Timestamp+Sequence  Type      Dev   Earliest Log  Current Log  Backup ID
---       ---     ------------------  ----      ---   ------------  -----------  ----------
B         D       20020829090733001   F         D     S0000000.LOG  S0000000.LOG
 ------------------------------------------------------------------------
Contains 2 tablespace(s):
00001 SYSCATSPACE
00002 USERSPACE1
 ------------------------------------------------------------------------
   Comment: DB2 BACKUP SAMPLE OFFLINE
Start Time: 20020829090733
  End Time: 20020829090756
 ------------------------------------------------------------------------
00001 Location: /data/dbbackup

Op        Obj     Timestamp+Sequence  Type      Dev   Earliest Log  Current Log  Backup ID
---       ---     ------------------  ----      ---   ------------  -----------  ----------
B         D       20020829091526001   I         D     S0000000.LOG  S0000000.LOG
 ------------------------------------------------------------------------
Contains 2 tablespace(s):
00001 SYSCATSPACE
00002 USERSPACE1
 ------------------------------------------------------------------------
   Comment: DB2 BACKUP SAMPLE OFFLINE
Start Time: 20020829091526
  End Time: 20020829091548
 ------------------------------------------------------------------------
00002 Location: /data/dbbackup

db2 connect to sample

  Database Connection Information
Database server             = DB2/6000 8.1.0
SQL authorization ID        = V8INST
Local database alias        = SAMPLE

db2 rename tablespace userspace1 to ts1
DB20000I  The SQL command completed successfully.
```

```
db2 list tablespaces

                    Tablespaces for Current Database

Tablespace ID                       = 0
Name                                = SYSCATSPACE
Type                                = System managed space
Contents                            = Any data
State                               = 0x0000
   Detailed explanation:
     Normal


Tablespace ID                       = 1
Name                                = TEMPSPACE1
Type                                = System managed space
Contents                            = System Temporary data
State                               = 0x0000
   Detailed explanation:
     Normal


Tablespace ID                       = 2
Name                                = TS1
Type                                = System managed space
Contents                            = Any data
State                               = 0x0000
   Detailed explanation:
     Normal


DB21011I  In a partitioned database server environment, only the table
spaces on the current node are listed.


ls

SAMPLE.0.v8inst.NODE0000.CATN0000.20020829090733.001
SAMPLE.0.v8inst.NODE0000.CATN0000.20020829091526.001


db2ckrst -d sample -t 20020829090733 -r database

Suggested restore order of images using timestamp 20020829090733 for
database sample.
===========================================================================
 restore db sample incremental taken at 20020829090733
 restore db sample incremental taken at 20020829090733
===========================================================================
```

```
db2ckrst -d sample -t 20020829091526 -r database

Suggested restore order of images using timestamp 20020829091526 for
database sample.
=======================================================================
restore db sample incremental taken at 20020829091526
restore db sample incremental taken at 20020829090733
restore db sample incremental taken at 20020829091526
=======================================================================

db2 "restore db sample tablespace (ts1) incremental automatic taken at
20020829091526"
SQL1260N  Database "SAMPLE" is not configured for roll-forward recovery on
node(s) "0".

db2 update db cfg for sample using logretain on
DB20000I  The UPDATE DATABASE CONFIGURATION command completed successfully.

db2 backup db sample to /data/dbbackup
Backup successful. The timestamp for this backup image is : 20020829093112

db2 "restore db sample tablespace (ts1) incremental automatic taken at
20020829091526"
SQL2571N  Automatic incremental restore is unable to proceed.  Reason code:
"3".

To resolve this limitation using manual incremental restore:
db2 "restore db sample tablespace (ts1) incremental taken at 20020829090733"
DB20000I  The RESTORE DATABASE command completed successfully.

db2 connect to sample

   Database Connection Information
Database server         = DB2/6000 8.1.0
SQL authorization ID    = V8INST
Local database alias    = SAMPLE

db2 list tables
Table/View      Schema       Type          Creation time
-----------     -----------  ------------  ------------------------------
CL_SCHED        V8INST       T             2002-08-29-09.06.14.645927
DEPARTMENT      V8INST       T             2002-08-29-09.05.57.363049
EMP_ACT         V8INST       T             2002-08-29-09.06.00.583974
EMP_PHOTO       V8INST       T             2002-08-29-09.06.06.356846
EMP_RESUME      V8INST       T             2002-08-29-09.06.10.105601
EMPLOYEE        V8INST       T             2002-08-29-09.05.58.127094
```

```
IN_TRAY        V8INST          T            2002-08-29-09.06.14.892679
ORG            V8INST          T            2002-08-29-09.05.52.642463
PROJECT        V8INST          T            2002-08-29-09.06.04.996372
SALES          V8INST          T            2002-08-29-09.06.12.433438
STAFF          V8INST          T            2002-08-29-09.05.55.331102
T1             V8INST          T            2002-08-29-09.15.14.026532

 12 record(s) selected.
```

Scenario #2: Automatic incremental restore is out of sequence   When you drop a database, the database history will be deleted. If you restore the dropped database, the database history will be restored to its state at the time of the restored backup, and all history entries after that time will be lost. If you then attempt to perform an automatic incremental restore that would need to use any of these lost history entries, the RESTORE utility will attempt to restore an incorrect chain of backups and will return an "out of sequence" error (SQL2572N).

Example Restore Procedure:

  • Step #1: db2 backup db sample
  • Step #2: db2 backup db sample incremental
  • Step #3: db2 backup db sample incremental delta
  • Step #4: db2 backup db sample incremental delta
  • Step #5: db2 drop db sample
  • Step #6: db2 restore db sample incremental automatic taken at <step #2 timestamp>
  • Step #7: db2 restore db sample incremental automatic taken at <step #4 timestamp>

Limitation:

  • SQL2572N—Attempted an incremental restore of an out-of-order image.

Solution:

  • Restore backup history file.
  • Check restore order sequence.
  • Use manual incremental restore.

The following is sample output from automatic incremental restore:

```
db2 update db cfg for sample using on trackmod on

DB20000I  The UPDATE DATABASE CONFIGURATION command completed successfully.

db2 backup db sample to /data/dbbackup

Backup successful. The timestamp for this backup image is : 20020829101746

db2 list history backup all for sample
```

```
                         List History File for sample
Number of matching file entries = 1
Op   Obj   Timestamp+Sequence    Type   Dev    Earliest Log    Current Log    Backup ID
---  ---   ------------------    ----   ---    ------------    -----------    ---------
B    D     20020829101746001     F      D      S0000000.LOG    S0000000.LOG
--------------------------------------------------------------------------------
Contains 2 tablespace(s):
00001 SYSCATSPACE
00002 USERSPACE1
--------------------------------------------------------------------------------
    Comment: DB2 BACKUP SAMPLE OFFLINE
Start Time: 20020829101746
  End Time: 20020829101808
--------------------------------------------------------------------------------
00001 Location: /data/dbbackup


db2 connect to sample

                      Database Connection Information
Database server          = DB2/6000 8.1.0
SQL authorization ID     = V8INST
Local database alias     = SAMPL


db2 "create table t1 (c1 int)"
DB20000I  The SQL command completed successfully.

db2 backup db sample incremental to /data/dbbackup

Backup successful. The timestamp for this backup image is : 20020829102037

db2 list history backup all for sample

                         List History File for sample
Number of matching file entries = 2
...
Op   Obj   Timestamp+Sequence    Type   Dev    Earliest Log    Current Log    Backup ID
---  ---   ------------------    ----   ----   ------------    -----------    -------
B    D     20020829102037001     I      D      S0000000.LOG    S0000000.LOG
--------------------------------------------------------------------------------
Contains 2 tablespace(s):
00001 SYSCATSPACE
00002 USERSPACE1
--------------------------------------------------------------------------------
    Comment: DB2 BACKUP SAMPLE OFFLINE
Start Time: 20020829102037
  End Time: 20020829102050
--------------------------------------------------------------------------------
```

```
00002 Location: /data/dbbackup

db2 connect to sample

                    Database Connection Information
Database server          = DB2/6000 8.1.0
SQL authorization ID     = V8INST
Local database alias     = SAMPLE


db2 "create table t2 (c1 int)"

DB20000I  The SQL command completed successfully.

db2 backup db sample incremental delta to /data/dbbackup

Backup successful. The timestamp for this backup image is : 20020829102219

db2 list history backup all for sample

                    List History File for sample
Number of matching file entries = 3
...
Op    Obj   Timestamp+Sequence   Type  Dev    Earliest Log   Current Log   Backup ID
---   ---   ------------------   ----  ----   ------------   -----------   ---------
 B    D     20020829102219001    D     D      S0000000.LOG   S0000000.LOG
----------------------------------------------------------------------------
Contains 2 tablespace(s):
00001 SYSCATSPACE
00002 USERSPACE1
----------------------------------------------------------------------------
Comment: DB2 BACKUP SAMPLE OFFLINE
Start Time: 20020829102219
End Time: 20020829102232
----------------------------------------------------------------------------
00003 Location: /data/dbbackup

db2 connect to sample

Database Connection Information
Database server          = DB2/6000 8.1.0
SQL authorization ID     = V8INST
Local database alias     = SAMPLE


db2 "create table t3 (c1 int)"

DB20000I  The SQL command completed successfully.

db2 backup db sample incremental delta to /data/dbbackup

Backup successful. The timestamp for this backup image is : 20020829094439
```

```
db2 list history backup all for sample

                          List History File for sample
Number of matching file entries = 4
...

 Op   Obj   Timestamp+Sequence     Type   Dev    Earliest Log   Current Log    Backup ID
 ---   ---   ------------------     ----   ----   ------------   -----------    ---------
  B    D     20020829094439001       D      D     S0000002.LOG   S0000002.LOG
-------------------------------------------------------------------------------------
Contains 2 tablespace(s):
00001 SYSCATSPACE
00002 USERSPACE1
-------------------------------------------------------------------------------------
    Comment: DB2 BACKUP SAMPLE OFFLINE
Start Time: 20020829094439
  End Time: 20020829094451
-------------------------------------------------------------------------------------
00003 Location: /data/dbbackup

db2 connect to sample

                     Database Connection Information
Database server          = DB2/6000 8.1.0
SQL authorization ID     = V8INST
Local database alias     = SAMPLE

db2 "create table t4 (c1 int)"
DB20000I  The SQL command completed successfully.

db2 backup db sample incremental delta to /data/dbbackup
Backup successful. The timestamp for this backup image is : 20020829094737

db2 drop db sample
DB20000I  The DROP DATABASE command completed successfully.

db2 list history backup all for sample
SQL1013N  The database alias name or database name "sample" could not be
found.  SQLSTATE=42705

db2 restore db sample history file taken at 20020829094737
DB20000I  The RESTORE DATABASE command completed successfully.

db2 list history backup all for sample

                          List History File for sample
Number of matching file entries = 4
 Op   Obj   Timestamp+Sequence     Type   Dev    Earliest Log   Current Log    Backup ID
 ---   ---   ------------------     ----   ----   ------------   -----------    ---------
  B    D     20020829094045001       F      D     S0000000.LOG   S0000000.LOG
-------------------------------------------------------------------------------------
```

```
Contains 2 tablespace(s):
00001 SYSCATSPACE
00002 USERSPACE1
-------------------------------------------------------------------------
   Comment: DB2 BACKUP SAMPLE OFFLINE
Start Time: 20020829094045
  End Time: 20020829094057
-------------------------------------------------------------------------
00001 Location: /data/dbbackup

Op   Obj   Timestamp+Sequence      Type   Dev   Earliest Log   Current Log   Backup ID
---  ---   ------------------      ----   ----  ------------   -----------   ---------
 B    D    20020829094208001        I      D    S0000001.LOG   S0000001.LOG
-------------------------------------------------------------------------
Contains 2 tablespace(s):
00001 SYSCATSPACE
00002 USERSPACE1
-------------------------------------------------------------------------
   Comment: DB2 BACKUP SAMPLE OFFLINE
Start Time: 20020829094208
  End Time: 20020829094220
-------------------------------------------------------------------------
00002 Location: /data/dbbackup

Op   Obj   Timestamp+Sequence      Type   Dev   Earliest Log   Current Log   Backup ID
---  ---   ------------------      ----   ----  ------------   -----------   ---------
 B    D    20020829094439001        D      D    S0000002.LOG   S0000002.LOG
-------------------------------------------------------------------------
Contains 2 tablespace(s):
00001 SYSCATSPACE
00002 USERSPACE1
-------------------------------------------------------------------------
Comment: DB2 BACKUP SAMPLE OFFLINE
Start Time: 20020829094439
End Time: 20020829094451
-------------------------------------------------------------------------
00003 Location: /data/dbbackup

Op   Obj   Timestamp+Sequence      Type   Dev   Earliest Log   Current Log   Backup ID
---  ---   ------------------      ----   ----  ------------   -----------   ---------
 B    D    20020829094737001               D         D
-------------------------------------------------------------------------
Contains 2 tablespace(s):
00001 SYSCATSPACE
00002 USERSPACE1
-------------------------------------------------------------------------
```

```
    Comment: DB2 BACKUP SAMPLE OFFLINE
Start Time: 20020829094737
  End Time:
--------------------------------------------------------------------
00004 Location: /data/dbbackup

db2 connect to sample

Database Connection Information
 Database server        = DB2/6000 8.1.0
 SQL authorization ID    = V8INST
 Local database alias    = SAMPLE

db2 "create table t4 (c1 int)"

DB20000I  The SQL command completed successfully.

db2 backup db sample incremental delta to /data/dbbackup
Backup successful. The timestamp for this backup image is : 20020829102509

db2 list history backup all for sample

                    List History File for sample

...
 Op  Obj  Timestamp+Sequence   Type  Dev   Earliest Log   Current Log   Backup ID
--- ---  ------------------   ----  ---   ------------   -----------   ---------
  B  D    20020829102509001    D     D     S0000000.LOG   S0000000.LOG
--------------------------------------------------------------------
Contains 2 tablespace(s):
00001 SYSCATSPACE
00002 USERSPACE1
--------------------------------------------------------------------
    Comment: DB2 BACKUP SAMPLE OFFLINE
Start Time: 20020829102509
  End Time: 20020829102522
--------------------------------------------------------------------
00004 Location: /data/dbbackup

db2 drop db sample
DB20000I  The DROP DATABASE command completed successfully.

db2 "restore db sample incremental automatic taken at 20020829102037"
DB20000I  The RESTORE DATABASE command completed successfully.

db2 "restore db sample incremental automatic taken at 20020829102509"
SQL2539W  Warning!  Restoring to an existing database that is the same as
the backup image database.  The database files will be deleted.

Do you want to continue ? (y/n) y

SQL2572N  Attempted an incremental restore of an out of order image.  The
restore of tablespace "USERSPACE" encountered an error because the backup
image with timestamp "20020829102219" must be restored before the image
that was just attempted.
```

```
To resolve this limitation:

db2 restore db sample history file taken at 20020829102509
DB20000I  The RESTORE DATABASE command completed successfully.

db2ckrst -d sample -t 20020829102509 -r database

Suggested restore order of images using timestamp 20020829102509 for
database sample.
======================================================================
restore db sample incremental taken at 20020829102509
restore db sample incremental taken at 20020829101746
restore db sample incremental taken at 20020829102037
restore db sample incremental taken at 20020829102219
restore db sample incremental taken at 20020829102509
======================================================================

db2 "restore db sample incremental taken at 20020829102509"
SQL2523W  Warning!  Restoring to an existing database that is different
from the database on the backup image, but have matching names. The target
database will be overwritten by the backup version.  The Roll-forward
recovery logs associated with the target database will be deleted.

Do you want to continue ? (y/n) y

DB20000I  The RESTORE DATABASE command completed successfully.

db2 "restore db sample incremental taken at  20020829101746"
DB20000I  The RESTORE DATABASE command completed successfully.

db2 "restore db sample incremental taken at  20020829102037"
DB20000I  The RESTORE DATABASE command completed successfully.

db2 "restore db sample incremental taken at  20020829102219"
DB20000I  The RESTORE DATABASE command completed successfully.

db2 "restore db sample incremental taken at  20020829102509"
DB20000I  The RESTORE DATABASE command completed successfully.

db2 connect to sample

                    Database Connection Information
Database server          = DB2/6000 8.1.0
SQL authorization ID     = V8INST
Local database alias     = SAMPLE
```

Scenario #3: Automatic incremental restore is different from the backup image database
When you restore a backup image from one database into another database, then do an incremental (delta) backup, you can no longer use automatic incremental restore to restore this backup image, and an error will occur (SQL2542N).

Example Restore Procedure:

- Step #1: db2 create db test1
- Step #2: db2 create db test2
- Step #3: db2 backup db test1
- Step #4: db2 restore db test1 taken at <step #3 timestamp> into test2
- Step #5: db2 update db cfg for test2 using trackmod on
- Step #6: db2 backup db test2
- Step #7: db2 backup db test2 incremental
- Step #8: db2 restore db test2 incremental automatic taken at <step #7 timestamp>

Limitation:

- SQL2572N—No match for test1 database image file was found based on the source database alias "TEST2" and timestamp <step #7 timestamp> provided.

Solution:

- Check restore order sequence.
- Use manual incremental restore:
  - db2 restore db test2 incremental taken at <step #7 timestamp)
  - db2 restore db test1 incremental taken at <step #3 timestamp) into test2
  - db2 restore db test2 incremental taken at <step #7 timestamp)
- Perform a full database backup to start a new incremental chain
  - db2 backup db test2

BACKUP OVERVIEW

The simplest form of the BACKUP DATABASE command requires only that you specify the alias or name of the database that you want to back up.

For example:

```
db2 backup db sample
```

If the command completes successfully, you will have acquired a new backup image that is located in the path or the directory from which the command was issued. It is located in this directory because the command in this example does not explicitly specify a target location for the backup image.

On the Windows operating systems, for example, this command (when issued from the root directory of the D: drive) creates an image that appears in a directory listing as follows:

```
Windows:

Directory of D:\SAMPLE.0\DB2\NODE0000\CATN0000\20020829
08/29/2002 15:26p <DIR> .
08/29/2002 15:26p <DIR> ..
08/29/2002 15:26p 12,615,680 122644.001
```

On UNIX, the backup image name will be of the form below:

```
UNIX:

SAMPLE.0.v8inst.NODE0000.CATN0000.20020829152626.001
```

> **N O T E** If the DB2 client and server are not located on the same system, the default target directory for the backup image is the current working directory on the client system where the command was issued, unless a path for the backup image is specified. This target directory or device must exist on the server system.

You have the option to specify the backup target location when you invoke the backup utility. This backup target location can be:

- A directory (for backups to disk or diskette)
- A device (for backups to tape)
- A Tivoli Storage Manager (TSM) server
- Another vendor's server, such as VERITAS, etc....

The recovery history file is updated automatically with summary information whenever you invoke a database backup operation. This file is created in the same directory as the database configuration file.

On UNIX-based systems, file names for backup images created on disk consist of a concatenation of several elements, separated by periods:

```
DB_alias.Type.Inst_name.NODEnnnn.CATNnnnn.timestamp.Seq_num
```

On Windows operating systems, a five-level subdirectory tree is used:

```
DB_alias.Type\Inst_name\NODEnnnn\CATNnnnn\yyyymmdd\hhmmss.Seq_num

For example:

D:\SAMPLE.0\DB2\NODE0000\CATN0000\20020829\122644.001
```

DB_alias: A 1- to 8-character database alias name that was specified when the backup utility was invoked.

Type: Type of backup operation, where:
- 0 represents a full database-level backup
- 3 represents a table space level backup
- 4 represents a backup image generated by the LOAD...COPY TO command.

Inst_ name: A 1- to 8-character name of the current instance that is taken from the **DB2INSTANCE** environment variable.

NODE*nnnn***:** The database partition number. In non-partitioned database systems, this is always NODE0000. In partitioned database systems, it is NODE*xxxx*, where *xxxx* is the number assigned to the database partition in the db2nodes.cfg file.

CATN*nnnn***:** The database partition number of the catalog partition for the database. In non-partitioned database systems, this is always CATN0000. In partitioned database systems, it is CATN*nnnn*, where *nnnn* is the number assigned to the database partition in the db2nodes.cfg file.

Date: An 8-character representation of the date at which the backup operation was performed. The date is in the form *yyyymmdd*, where:
- *yyyy* represents the year (1995 to 9999)
- *mm* represents the month (01 to 12)
- *dd* represents the day of the month (01 to 31)

Time: A 6-character representation of the time at which the backup operation was performed. The time is in the form *hhmmss*, where:
- *hh* represents the hour (00 to 23)
- *mm* represents the minutes (00 to 59)
- *ss* represents the seconds (00 to 59)

Seq_num: is a 3-digit number used as a file extension.

When a backup image is written to tape:

- File names are not created, but the information described above is stored in the backup header for verification purposes.
- A tape device must be available through the standard operating system interface. On a large partitioned database system, however, it may not be practical to have a tape device dedicated to each database partition. You can connect the tape devices to one or more TSM servers, so that access to these tape devices is provided to each database partition.
- On a partitioned database system, you can also use products that provide virtual tape device functions, such as CLIO/S. You can use these products to access the tape device connected to other database partitions through a pseudo tape device. Access to the remote tape device is provided transparently, and the pseudo tape device can be accessed through the standard operating system interface.

You cannot back up a database that is in an inconsistent state. If any table space is in an abnormal state, you cannot back up the database or that table space, unless it is in backup pending state.

If a database or a table space is in a partially restored state because a system crash occurred during the restore operation, you must complete the restore of the database or the table space before you can back it up.

A table space level backup operation will fail if a list of the table spaces to be backed up contains the name of a temporary table space.

If you are using the backup utility for concurrent backup operations to tape, ensure that the processes do not target the same tape.

Displaying Backup Information

You can use *db2ckbkp* to display information about existing backup images.

This utility allows you to:

- Test the integrity of a backup image and determine whether it can be restored.
- Display information that is stored in the backup header.
- Display information about the objects and the log file header in the backup image.

Authorities Required to Use Backup

Privileges enable users to create or access database resources. Authority levels provide a method of grouping privileges and higher level database manager maintenance and utility operations. Together, these act to control access to the database manager and its database objects. Users can access only those objects for which they have the appropriate authorization, i.e., the required privilege or authority. You must have SYSADM, SYSCTRL, or SYSMAINT authority to use the backup utility.

Using Backup

You should not be connected to the database that is to be backed up. The backup utility automatically establishes a connection to the specified database, and this connection is terminated at the completion of the backup operation. Offline backup gets an exclusive connection to the database.

The database can be local or remote. The backup image remains on the database server, unless you are using a storage management product, such as TSM.

On a partitioned database system, database partitions are backed up individually. The operation is local to the database partition on which you invoke the utility. You can, however, issue *db2_all* from one of the database partitions in the instance to invoke the backup utility on a list of servers (or all servers), which you identify by database partition number. (Use the LIST DBPARTITIONNUMS command to identify the database partitions that have user tables on them.) If you do this, you must back up the catalog partition first, then back up the other database partitions.

> **N O T E**   You should also keep a copy of the db2nodes.cfg file with any backup copies you take as protection against possible damage to this file.

On a distributed request system, backup operations apply to the distributed request database and the metadata stored in the database catalog (wrappers, servers, nicknames, and so on). Data source objects (tables and views) are not backed up, unless they are stored in the distributed request database.

If a database was created with a previous release of the database manager, and the database has not been migrated, you must migrate the database before you can back it up.

The following restrictions apply to the backup utility:

- A table space backup operation and a table space restore operation cannot be run at the same time, even if different table spaces are involved.
- If you want to be able to do rollforward recovery in a partitioned database environment, you must regularly back up the database on the list of database partitions, and you must have at least one backup image of the rest of the database partitions in the system (even those that do not contain user data for that database).

Two situations require the backed-up image of a database partition at a database partition that does not contain user data for the database:

1. You added a database partition to the database system after taking the last backup, and you need to do forward recovery on this database partition.
2. Point-in-time recovery is used, which requires that all database partitions in the system are in rollforward pending state.

The backup utility can be invoked through the command line processor (CLP), the database Backup Wizard in the Control Center, or the *db2Backup* API.

Following is an example of the BACKUP DATABASE command issued through the CLP:

```
db2 backup database sample to c:\DB2Backups
```

To open the database Backup Wizard:

1. From the Control Center, expand the object tree until you find the Databases folder.
2. Click on the Databases folder. Any existing databases are displayed in the pane on the right side of the window.
3. Click the right mouse button on the database you want in the contents pane, and select Backup Wizard from the pop-up menu. The database Backup Wizard opens.

> **N O T E**   Detailed information is provided through the online help facility within the Control Center.

Backing Up to Tape

When you back up your database or table space to tape, you must correctly set your block size and your buffer size. This is particularly true if you are using a variable block size (on AIX, for example, if the block size has been set to zero).

There is a restriction on the number of fixed block sizes that can be used when backing up. This restriction exists because DB2 writes out the backup image header as a 4-KB block. The only fixed block sizes DB2 supports are 512, 1024, 2048, and 4096 bytes. If you are using a fixed block size, you can specify any backup buffer size. However, you may find that your backup operation will not complete successfully if the fixed block size is not one of the sizes that DB2 supports.

An example of backing up and restoring the database to and from an attached tape drive:

```
db2 backup database sample to /dev/rmt0 with 2 buffers buffer 512
db2 restore database sample from /dev/rmt0 taken at <timestamp>
    with 2 buffers buffer 512
```

Backing Up to Named Pipes

DB2 supports database backup to (and database restore from) local named pipes on UNIX-based systems. Both the writer and the reader of the named pipe must be on the same machine. The pipe must exist and be located on a local file system. Because the named pipe is treated as a local device, there is no need to specify that the target is a named pipe.

Following is an example:

1. Create a named pipe:

```
cd /data/dbbackup/
mkfifo mypipe
ls -altr mypipe

prw-r--r--   1 v8inst    sys          0 Aug 29 01:09 mypipe
```

2. If this backup image is going to be used by the restore utility, the restore operation must be invoked before the backup operation, so that it will not miss any data:

```
db2 restore database sample from /data/dbbackup/mypipe into newdb &
```

3. Use this pipe as the target for a database backup operation:

```
db2 backup db sample to /data/dbbackup/mypipe
```

Backup Database: Examples

In the following example, the database SAMPLE is defined on all four partitions, numbered 0 through 3. The path /data/dbbackup is accessible from all partitions. Partition 0 is the catalog partition and needs to be backed up separately because this is an offline backup. To perform an offline backup of all the SAMPLE database partitions to /data/dbbackup, issue the following commands from one of the database partitions:

```
db2_all '<<+0< db2 backup db sample to /data/dbbackup'
Backup successful. The timestamp for this backup image is : 20020829012853
phantom: db2 backup database ... completed ok

db2_all '<<-0< db2 backup db sample to /data/dbbackup'
rah: omitting logical node 0
Backup successful. The timestamp for this backup image is : 20020829012956
phantom: db2 backup database ... completed ok

Backup successful. The timestamp for this backup image is : 20020829013012
phantom: db2 backup database ... completed ok

Backup successful. The timestamp for this backup image is : 20020829013028
phantom: db2 backup database ... completed ok

ls /data/dbbackup/

SAMPLE.0.v8inst.NODE0000.CATN0000.20020829012853.001
SAMPLE.0.v8inst.NODE0001.CATN0000.20020829012956.001
SAMPLE.0.v8inst.NODE0002.CATN0000.20020829013012.001
SAMPLE.0.v8inst.NODE0003.CATN0000.20020829013028.001
```

In the second command, the db2_all utility will issue the same backup command to each database partition in turn (except partition 0). All four database partition backup images will be stored in the /data/dbbackup directory.

In the following example, database SAMPLE is backed up to a TSM server using two concurrent TSM client sessions. The backup utility will use four buffers, which are of the default buffer size (1024 × 4-KB pages).

```
db2 backup database sample use tsm open 2 sessions with 4 buffers

or

db2 backup database sample use tsm open 2 sessions with 4 buffers
     buffer 1024
```

If the util_heap_sz < ((number of buffers × buffer size) × number of data partitions), then an error (SQL2009C) will occur. The SQL2009C error indicates that there is not enough memory available to run the utility. You must increase the utility heap size (util_heap_sz).

```
db2 backup database sample with 4 buffers buffer 4096
SQL2009C  There is not enough memory available to run the utility.
```

Following is a sample weekly incremental backup strategy for a recoverable database. It includes a weekly full database backup operation, a daily non-cumulative (delta) backup operation, and a mid-week cumulative (incremental) backup operation:

```
Day of week        Backup Operation
Sunday             Full
Monday             Online incremental delta
Tuesday            Online incremental delta
Wednesday          Online incremental
Thursday           Online incremental delta
Friday             Online incremental delta
Saturday           Online incremental

db2 backup db sample use tsm
db2 backup db sample online incremental delta use tsm
db2 backup db sample online incremental delta use tsm
db2 backup db sample online incremental use tsm
db2 backup db sample online incremental delta use tsm
db2 backup db sample online incremental delta use tsm
db2 backup db sample online incremental use tsm
```

The following command failed because an online backup allows other transactions to be changing the database simultaneously. Therefore, only a database configured for rollforward recovery can support an online backup.

```
User A connects to the database and selects a table
db2 connect to sample
db2 "select count(*) from employee"
```

```
This database is configured as circular logging, and you want to take
an online backup

db2_all "db2 backup db sample online to /data/backup"

→ the utility did not complete
```

Now, you want to take an offline backup, and the utility still failed because an offline backup requires exclusive use of the database. User A is already connected to the database earlier. To resolve this problem and perform the backup again, you must do the following.

```
Now you want to perform an offline backup
db2_all "db2 backup db sample to /data/backup"

→ the utility did not complete

To resolve, you must do
db2 terminate
db2 force application all
db2_all "db2 backup db sample to /data/backup"

→ the utility complete successfully
```

Optimizing Backup Performance

To reduce the amount of time required to complete a backup operation:

- Specify table space backup. You can back up (and subsequently recover) part of a database by using the TABLESPACE option on the BACKUP DATABASE command. This facilitates the management of table data, indexes, and long field or LOB data in separate table spaces.
- Increase the value of the PARALLELISM parameter on the BACKUP DATABASE command so that it reflects the number of table spaces being backed up. The PARALLELISM parameter defines the number of processes or threads that are started when reading data from the database. Each process or thread is assigned to a specific table space. When it finishes backing up this table space, it requests another. Note, however, that each process or thread requires both memory and CPU overhead: On a heavily loaded system, keep the PARALLELISM parameter at its default value of 1.
- Increase the backup buffer size. The ideal backup buffer size is a multiple of the table space extent size. If you have multiple table spaces with different extent sizes, specify a value that is a multiple of the largest extent size.
- Increase the number of buffers. If you use multiple buffers and I/O channels, you should use at least twice as many buffers as channels to ensure that the channels do not have to wait for data.
- Use multiple target devices, and the backup images must be directed to local devices.

Offline versus Online Backup

Database backup can be performed either offline or online:

Offline Backup

- If the backup is performed offline, then only the backup task can be connected to the database partition.
- An offline backup is the only backup supported when circular logging is used.
- No connection is allowed when the backup task is running.
- Concurrent offline backup of both catalog partition and non-catalog partitions is not possible.

Online Backup

- If the backup is performed online, other applications or processes can continue to connect to the database while the backup task is running.
- An online backup is supported when archive logging is enabled.
- While the online backup operation is running, changes can be performed on the tables.
- At the end of an online backup, the current archive log is truncated and made available for offline archival.

Backup Considerations

There are a number of points to consider when planning the use of BACKUP command:

- For disaster recovery support, it is necessary to perform a full database backup as the starting point for recovery.
- It is best to take table space level backups of the DB2 catalog table space (SYSCATSPACE). This will allow the restore of a damaged DB2 catalog to be as quick as possible.
- Online backup, either table space level or full database, requires the retention of the archive DB2 logs at the time of the backup, for use in the restore and rollforward process. If the logs are not available, the database or table space cannot be recovered using that backup.
- Selected table space backup that includes all of the table spaces related to a single application could be useful to perform point-in-time recovery of an application to a point prior to the execution of an erroneous application process.
- Using the DB2 incremental backup options can reduce the size and duration of periodic DB2 backups by including only the changed portion of the database or table space.

RESTORE OVERVIEW

The simplest form of the RESTORE DATABASE command requires only that you specify the alias name of the database that you want to restore.

For example:

```
db2 restore db sample
```

> **NOTE** This will restore the image from the path the restore command is run from.

In this example, because the SAMPLE database exists, the following message is returned:

```
SQL2539W Warning! Restoring to an existing database that is the same
as the backup image database. The database files will be deleted.

Do you want to continue ? (y/n)
```

If you enter Y, and a backup image for the SAMPLE database exists in the directory, the restore operation will be performed.

A database restore operation requires an exclusive connection: That is, no applications can be running against the database when the operation starts, and the restore utility prevents other applications from accessing the database until the restore operation completes successfully. A table space restore operation, however, can be done online.

A table space is not usable until the restore operation (followed by rollforward recovery) completes successfully.

If you have tables that span more than one table space, you should back up and restore the set of table spaces together.

When doing a partial or subset restore operation, you can use either a table space level backup image or a full database-level backup image and choose one or more table spaces from that image. All the log files associated with these table spaces from the time that the backup image was created must exist and will be rolled forward.

Authorities Required to Use Restore

Privileges enable users to create or access database resources. Authority levels provide a method of grouping privileges and higher level database manager maintenance and utility operations. Together, these act to control access to the database manager and its database objects. Users can access only those objects for which they have the appropriate authorization; that is, the required privilege or authority.

You must have SYSADM, SYSCTRL, or SYSMAINT authority to restore to an existing database from a full database backup. To restore to a new database, you must have SYSADM or SYSCTRL authority.

Using Restore

When restoring to an existing database, you should not be connected to the database that is to be restored: The restore utility automatically establishes a connection to the specified database, and this connection is terminated at the completion of the restore operation. When restoring to a new database, an instance attachment is required to create the database. When restoring to a new remote database, you must first attach to the instance where the new database will reside. If the target database does not exist, it will be created using the INTO target-database-alias clause.

The following restrictions apply to the restore utility:

- You can use the restore utility only if the database has been previously backed up using the DB2 backup utility.
- A database restore operation cannot be started while the rollforward process is running.
- You can restore a table space only if the table space currently exists, and if it is the same table space. For example, the table space was not dropped and then recreated between the backup and the restore operation.
- You cannot restore a table space level backup to a new database.
- You cannot perform an online table space level restore operation involving the system catalog tables.

The restore utility can be invoked through the CLP, the database Restore Wizard in the Control Center, or the *db2Restore* API.

Following is an example of the RESTORE DATABASE command issued through the CLP:

```
db2 restore db sample from D:\DB2Backups taken at 20020829152626
```

To open the database Restore Wizard:

1. From the Control Center, expand the object tree until you find the Databases folder.
2. Click on the Databases folder. Any existing databases are displayed in the pane on the right side of the window.
3. Click the right mouse button on the database you want in the contents pane, and select Restore Wizard from the pop-up menu. The database Restore Wizard opens.

Using Incremental Restore in a Test and Production Environment

Once a production database is enabled for incremental backup and recovery, you can use an incremental or delta backup image to create or refresh a test database. You can do this by using either manual or automatic incremental restore. To restore the backup image from the production

database to the test database, use the INTO target-database-alias option on the RESTORE
DATABASE command.

For example, in a production database with the following backup images:

```
db2 backup db proddb
Backup successful. The timestamp for this backup image is : 20020829021740

The backup will fail if the TRACKMOD is not set:

db2 backup db proddb incremental
SQL2426N  The database has not been configured to allow the incremental
backup operation. Reason code = "1".

Now, the TRACKMOD is set to ON, the database backup complete successfully

db2 update db cfg for proddb using trackmod on
DB20000I  The UPDATE DATABASE CONFIGURATION command completed successfully.

db2 backup db proddb
Backup successful. The timestamp for this backup image is : 20020829021853

db2 backup db proddb incremental
Backup successful. The timestamp for this backup image is : 20020829022152

db2ckrst -d proddb -t 20020829022152 -r database

Suggested restore order of images using timestamp 20020829022152 for
database proddb
=========================================================================
 restore db proddb incremental taken at 20020829022152
 restore db proddb incremental taken at 20020829021853
 restore db proddb incremental taken at 20020829022152
=========================================================================
```

An example of a manual incremental restore would be:

```
restore db proddb incremental taken at 20020829022152 into testdb without
     prompting
DB20000I The RESTORE DATABASE command completed successfully.

restore db proddb incremental taken at 20020829021853 into testdb without
     prompting
DB20000I The RESTORE DATABASE command completed successfully.

restore db proddb incremental taken at 20020829022152 into testdb without
     prompting
DB20000I  The RESTORE DATABASE command completed successfully.
```

If the database TESTDB already exists, the restore operation will overwrite any data that is already there. If the database TESTDB does not exist, the restore utility will create it, then will populate it with the data from the backup images.

Because automatic incremental restore operations are dependent on the database history, the restore steps change slightly, based on whether the test database exists. To perform an automatic incremental restore to the database TESTDB, its history must contain the backup image history for database PRODDB.

The database history for the backup image will replace any database history that already exists for database TESTDB if:

- the database TESTDB does not exist when the RESTORE DATABASE command is issued

or

- the database TESTDB exists when the RESTORE DATABASE command is issued, and the database TESTDB history contains no records.

The following example shows an automatic incremental restore to database TESTDB which does not exist:

```
restore db proddb incremental automatic taken at 20020829021853
    into testdb without prompting
DB20000I The RESTORE DATABASE command completed successfully.
```

The restore utility will create the TESTDB database and populate it.

If the database TESTDB does exist and the database history is not empty, you must drop the database before the automatic incremental restore operation as follows:

```
drop db testdb
DB20000I The DROP DATABASE command completed successfully.

restore db proddb incremental automatic taken at 20020829021853
    into testdb without prompting
DB20000I The RESTORE DATABASE command completed successfully.
```

If you do not want to drop the database, you can issue the PRUNE HISTORY command using a timestamp far into the future and the WITH FORCE OPTION parameter before issuing the RESTORE DATABASE command:

```
connect to testdb

Database Connection Information
Database server = DB2/6000 8.1.0
SQL authorization ID = V8INST
Local database alias = TESTDB
```

```
prune history 9999 with force option
DB20000I The PRUNE command completed successfully.

connect reset
DB20000I The SQL command completed successfully.

restore db proddb incremental automatic taken at 20020829022152
    into testdb without prompting
SQL2540W Restore is successful, however a warning "2528" was
    encountered during Database Restore while processing in No
    Interrupt mode.
```

In this case, the RESTORE DATABASE command will act in the same manner as when the database TESTDB did not exist.

You can continue taking incremental or delta backups of the test database without first taking a full database backup. However, if you ever need to restore one of the incremental or delta images, you will have to perform a manual incremental restore. This is because automatic incremental restore operations require that each of the backup images restored during an automatic incremental restore be created from the same database alias.

If you make a full database backup of the test database after you complete the restore operation using the production backup image, you can take incremental or delta backups and can restore them using either manual or automatic mode.

Redefining Table Space Containers
During a Restore Operation (Redirected Restore)

During a database backup operation, a record is kept of all the table space containers associated with the table spaces that are being backed up. During a restore operation, all containers listed in the backup image are checked to determine if they exist and whether they are accessible. If one or more of these containers is inaccessible because of media failure (or for any other reason), the restore operation will fail. A successful restore operation in this case requires redirection to different containers. DB2 supports adding, changing, or removing table space containers.

You can redefine table space containers by invoking the RESTORE DATABASE command and specifying the REDIRECT parameter or by using the Containers page of the database Restore Wizard in the Control Center.

The following example using the redirected restore from the table space ID 3 containers /db00/ts1/c0 and /db00/ts1/c1 to /db01/ts1/con00 and /db01/ts1/con01 of 2,000 4-KB pages per container. The database SAMPLE is defined on all two partitions, numbered 0 through 1. A table space TS1 is created on two containers /db00/ts1/c0 and /db00/ts1/c1 of 1,000 4-KB pages per container:

```
1. Connect to the database

db2 connect to sample

Database Connection Information
Database server                  = DB2/6000 8.1.0
SQL authorization ID             = V8INST
Local database alias             = SAMPLE

2. Create tablespace ts1 with two containers, 1,000 4-KB pages each
   container

db2 "create tablespace ts1 managed by database using
     (file '/db00/ts1/c $N' 1000)"
DB20000I  The SQL command completed successfully.

db2 terminate
DB20000I  The TERMINATE command completed successfully.

3. Backup sample database (catalog partition first, then the remaining
   database partition)

db2_all '<<+0< db2 backup db sample to /data/dbbackup'
Backup successful. The timestamp for this backup image is:
    20030108231322
phantom: db2 backup database ... completed ok

db2_all '<<-0< db2 backup db sample to /data/dbbackup'
rah: omitting logical node 0
Backup successful. The timestamp for this backup image is:
    20030108231410
phantom: db2 backup database ... completed ok

4. Show the database backup images

ls /data/dbbackup/
SAMPLE.0.v8inst.NODE0000.CATN0000.20030108231322.001
SAMPLE.0.v8inst.NODE0001.CATN0000.20030108231410.001

5. Show the containers for tablespace ID 3

db2_all "db2 connect to sample; db2 list tablespace containers for 3
    show detail"| egrep -i "name|total"

Name              = /db00/ts1/c0
Total pages       = 1000
Name              = /db00/ts1/c1
Total pages       = 1000
```

6. Restore from the last database backup images using redirected
   restore. Replace existing containers for tablespace ts1 to new
   containers /db01/ts1/con00 and /db01/ts1/con01 with 2,000 4-KB
   pages per container.

At the catalog partition:

```
export DB2NODE=0
db2 terminate
DB20000I  The TERMINATE command completed successfully.

db2 restore db sample taken at 20030108231322 replace existing
    redirect
SQL2539W  Warning! Restoring to an existing database that is the same
    as the backup image database. The database files will be deleted.
SQL1277N  Restore has detected that one or more table space containers
    are inaccessible, or has set their state to 'storage must be
    defined'.
DB20000I  The RESTORE DATABASE command completed successfully.

db2 "set tablespace containers for 3
    using (file '/db01/ts/con00' 2000)"
DB20000I  The SET TABLESPACE CONTAINERS command completed
    successfully.
```

At the non-catalog partition (database partition number 1)

```
export DB2NODE=1
db2 terminate
DB20000I  The TERMINATE command completed successfully.

db2 restore db sample taken at 20030108231410 replace existing
    redirect
SQL2539W  Warning! Restoring to an existing database that is the same
    as the backup image database. The database files will be deleted.
SQL1277N  Restore has detected that one or more table space containers
    are inaccessible, or has set their state to 'storage must be
    defined'.
DB20000I  The RESTORE DATABASE command completed successfully.

db2 "set tablespace containers for 3 using (file '/db01/ts/con01'
    2000)"
DB20000I  The SET TABLESPACE CONTAINERS command completed
    successfully.
```

```
7. Continue restore

At the catalog partition:

db2 restore db testdb continue
DB20000I  The RESTORE DATABASE command completed successfully.

At the non-catalog partition (database partition number 1):

db2 restore db testdb continue
DB20000I  The RESTORE DATABASE command completed successfully.

8. Verify the tablespace ts1

db2_all "db2 connect to sample; db2 list tablespace containers for 3
    show detail" | egrep -i "name|total"

Name                    = /db01/ts1/con00
Total pages             = 2000
Name                    = /db01/ts1/con01
Total pages             = 2000
```

The process for invoking a redirected restore of an incremental backup image is similar to the process for a non-incremental backup image: Call the RESTORE DATABASE command with the REDIRECT parameter and specify the backup image from which the database should be incrementally restored. During a redirected restore operation, directory and file containers are automatically created if they do not already exist. The database manager does not automatically create device containers.

Container redirection provides considerable flexibility for managing table space containers. For example, even though adding containers to SMS table spaces is not supported, you could accomplish this by specifying additional containers when invoking a redirected restore operation.

Restoring to an Existing Database

You can restore a full database backup image to an existing database. The backup image may differ from the existing database in its alias name, its database name, or its database seed.

A database seed is a unique identifier for a database that does not change during the life of the database. The seed is assigned by the database manager when the database is created. DB2 always uses the seed from the backup image.

When restoring to an existing database, the restore utility:

- Deletes table, index, and long field data from the existing database and replaces it with data from the backup image.
- Replaces table entries for each table space being restored.
- Retains the current recovery history file, unless it is damaged or has no entries. If the recovery history file is damaged, the database manager copies the file from the backup image.

- Retains the authentication type for the existing database.
- Retains the database directories for the existing database. The directories define where the database resides and how it is cataloged.
- Compares the database seeds. If the seeds are different:
    - Deletes the logs associated with the existing database.
    - Copies the database configuration file from the backup image.
    - Specifies the NEWLOGPATH if the log path in the backup image is not suitable to be used after the restore (i.e., the path is no longer valid or is currently used by a different database).
- If the database seeds are the same:
    - Deletes the logs if the image is for a non-recoverable database.
    - Retains the current database configuration file, unless the file has been corrupted, in which case, the file is copied from the backup image.
    - Specifies the NEWLOGPATH if the log path in the backup image is not suitable to be used after the restore (i.e., the path is no longer valid or is currently used by a different database).

Restoring to a New Database

You can create a new database, then restore a full database backup image to it. If you do not create a new database, the restore utility will create one.

When restoring to a new database, the restore utility:

- Creates a new database, using the database alias name that was specified through the target database alias parameter. If a target database alias was not specified, the restore utility creates the database with an alias that is the same as that specified through the source database alias parameter.
- Restores the database configuration file from the backup image.
- Specifies the NEWLOGPATH if the log path in the backup image is not suitable to be used after the restore (i.e., the path is no longer valid or is currently used by different a database).
- Restores the authentication type from the backup image.
- Restores the comments from the database directories in the backup image.
- Restores the recovery history file for the database.

Restore Database: Examples

The RESTORE DATABASE utility rebuilds a damaged or corrupted database that has been backed up using the DB2 backup utility. The restored database is in the same state it was in when the backup copy was made. This utility can also restore to a database with a name different from the database name in the backup image (in addition to being able to restore to a new database).

This utility can also be used to restore offline backup images, which were produced by the previous two versions of DB2. If a migration is required, it will be invoked automatically at the end of the restore operation. If, at the time of the backup operation, the database was enabled for rollforward recovery, the database can be brought to the state it was in prior to the occurrence of the damage or corruption by invoking the rollforward utility after successful completion of a restore operation.

This utility can also restore from a table space level backup.

When working in an environment that has more than one operating system, you must consider that you cannot back up a database on one operation system, then restore that database on another operating system (such as UNIX to/from Linux). In this case, you can use the db2move utility. There is more cross-operating system backup/restore allowed—any UNIX to any UNIX, Linux to Linux, and Windows to Windows.

In the following example, the database SAMPLE is defined on all four database partitions, numbered 0 through 3 (catalog partition is 0). The path /data/dbbackup is accessible from all database partitions. The following offline backup images are available from /data/dbbackup:

```
cd /data/dbbackup
ls

SAMPLE.0.v8inst.NODE0000.CATN0000.20020829013314.001
SAMPLE.0.v8inst.NODE0001.CATN0000.20020829013401.001
SAMPLE.0.v8inst.NODE0002.CATN0000.20020829013012.001
SAMPLE.0.v8inst.NODE0003.CATN0000.20020829013028.001
```

To restore the catalog partition first, then all other database partitions of the NEWDB database from the /data/dbbackup directory (one at a time), issue the following commands from one of the database partitions:

```
db2_all '<<+0< db2 restore db sample from /data/dbbackup taken at
    20020829013314 into newdb replace existing'
db2_all '<<+1< db2 restore db sample from /data/dbbackup taken at
    20020829013401 into newdb replace existing'
db2_all '<<+2< db2 restore db sample from /data/dbbackup taken at
    20020829013012 into newdb replace existing'
db2_all '<<+3< db2 restore db sample from /data/dbbackup taken at
    20020829013028 into newdb replace existing'
```

NOTE   The db2_all utility issues the restore command to each specified database partition.

The following example using redirected restore from the tablespace id 3 container ts1.dat to newts:

```
db2 connect to testdb

Database Connection Information
Database server        = DB2/6000 8.1.0
SQL authorization ID   = V8INST
Local database alias   = TESTDB

db2 "create tablespace ts1 managed by database
    using (file '/data/ts/ts1.dat' 1024)"
DB20000I  The SQL command completed successfully.

db2 list tablespace containers for 3 show detail | grep ts1

Name                   = /data/ts/ts1.dat

db2 backup database testdb
Backup successful. The timestamp for this backup image is :
    20020829125126

db2 restore db testdb taken at 20020829125126 into newdb replace
    existing redirect
SQL1277N  Restore has detected that one or more table space containers
    are inaccessible, or has set their state to 'storage must be
    defined'.
DB20000I  The RESTORE DATABASE command completed successfully.

db2 "set tablespace containers for 3
    using (file '/data/ts/newts' 1024)"
DB20000I  The SET TABLESPACE CONTAINERS command completed
    successfully.

db2 restore db testdb continue
DB20000I  The RESTORE DATABASE command completed successfully.

db2 connect to newdb

Database Connection Information
Database server        = DB2/6000 8.1.0
SQL authorization ID   = V8INST
Local database alias   = NEWDB

db2 list tablespace containers for 3 show detail | grep newts

Name                   = /data/ts/newts
```

Following is a sample weekly incremental backup strategy for a recoverable database. It includes a weekly full database backup operation, a daily non-cumulative (delta) backup operation, and a mid-week cumulative (incremental) backup operation:

```
Day of week      Backup Operation
Sunday           Full
Monday           Online incremental delta
Tuesday          Online incremental delta
Wednesday        Online incremental
Thursday         Online incremental delta
Friday           Online incremental delta
Saturday         Online incremental


For an automatic database restore of the images created on Friday
    morning, issue:


restore db mydb incremental automatic taken at <Friday timestamp>


For a manual database restore of the images created on Friday morning,
    issue:


restore db mydb incremental taken at <Friday timestamp>
restore db mydb incremental taken at <Sunday timestamp>
restore db mydb incremental taken at <Wednesday timestamp>
restore db mydb incremental taken at <Thursday timestamp>
restore db mydb incremental taken at <Friday timestamp>
```

Optimizing Restore Performance

To reduce the amount of time required to complete a restore operation:

- Increase the restore buffer size. The restore buffer size must be a positive integer multiple of the backup buffer size specified during the backup operation. If an incorrect buffer size is specified, the buffers allocated will be the smallest acceptable size.
- Increase the number of buffers. The value you specify must be a multiple of the number of pages that you specified for the backup buffer. The minimum number of pages is 16.
- Increase the value of the PARALLELISM option. This will increase the number of buffer manipulators (BM) that will be used to write to the database during the restore operation. The default value is 1.

Restore Considerations

There are a number of points to consider when planning the use of RESTORE command:

- A full database backup image can be used to create a new DB2 database that can be used for disaster recovery at a remote location or as a source for running read-only queries.
- The restore command must read the entire backup image to complete the processing.
- If the archive logging is enabled, selected table space can be restored from either a full database backup or a table space backup that contains the select subset of table space.
- The DB2 catalog table space must be restored in offline mode; then it must be rolled forward to the end of logs to maintain a consistent database (restoring the catalog partition first, then all other partitions in parallel).
- A dropped table space cannot be recovered from a previous backup image with a RESTORE command in table space mode, even if the table space was recreated with a new CREATE TABLESPACE command.
- Use the REDIRECT restore option to allocate additional space or to bypass disk media failures.

Restore to a Damaged Partition

If the database is damaged at a partition level, normally you can use RESTORE and ROLLFORWARD utilities to recover the database partition. If for some reasons you cannot connect to this database partition, the restore will fail. First you must drop the database at the database partition number, create a database at the database partition number, then restore the database from the last backup.

- Determine which database partition is damaged.
- Capture the database configuration.
- Drop the database at the database partition number.
- Create a database at the database partition number.
- Update the database configuration.
- The database partition is placed in restore pending condition.
- Run DB2 restore to recreate the database partition.

ROLLFORWARD OVERVIEW

This utility recovers a database by applying transactions recorded in the database log files. It is invoked after a database or table space backup has been restored. The database must be recoverable before the database can be recovered with rollforward recovery.

In a multi-partitioned database environment, the rollforward database command can be issued only from the catalog partition.

```
db2 rollforward db sample to end of logs


                                            Rollforward Status
Input database alias                      = sample
Number of nodes have returned status      = 1
Node number                               = 0
Rollforward status                        = not pending
Next log file to be read                  =
Log files processed                       = S0000000.LOG - S0000001.LOG
Last committed transaction                = 2002-08-29-17.31.53.000000


DB20000I  The ROLLFORWARD command completed successfully.
```

The general approach to rollforward recovery involves:

1. Invoking the rollforward utility without the STOP option.

2. Invoking the rollforward utility with the QUERY STATUS option.

- If you specify recovery to the end of the logs, the QUERY STATUS option can indicate that one or more log files is missing, if the returned point in time is earlier than you expect.

- If you specify point-in-time recovery, the QUERY STATUS option will help you to ensure that the rollforward operation has completed at the correct point.

3. Invoking the rollforward utility with the STOP option. After the operation stops, it is not possible to roll additional changes forward.

When the rollforward utility is invoked:

- If the database is in rollforward pending state, the database is rolled forward. If table spaces are also in rollforward pending state, you must invoke the rollforward utility again after the database rollforward operation completes to roll the table spaces forward.

- If the database is *not* in rollforward pending state but table spaces in the database *are* in rollforward pending state:
  - If you specify a list of table spaces, only those table spaces are rolled forward.
  - If you do not specify a list of table spaces, all table spaces that are in rollforward pending state are rolled forward.

A database rollforward operation runs offline. The database is not available for use until the rollforward operation completes successfully, and the operation cannot complete unless the STOP option was specified when the utility was invoked.

A table space rollforward operation can run offline. The database is not available for use until the rollforward operation completes successfully. This occurs if the end of the logs is reached or if the STOP option was specified when the utility was invoked.

You can perform an online rollforward operation on table spaces, as long as SYSCATSPACE is not included. When you perform an online rollforward operation on a table space, the table space is not available for use, but the other table spaces in the database are available.

When you first create a database, it is enabled for circular logging only. This means that logs are reused, rather than being saved or archived. With circular logging, rollforward recovery is not possible: Only crash recovery or version recovery can be done. Archived logs document changes to a database that occur after a backup was taken. You enable log archiving (and rollforward recovery) by setting the logretain database configuration parameter to RECOVERY or setting the userexit database configuration parameter to YES, or both. The default value for both of these parameters is NO, because initially, there is no backup image that you can use to recover the database. When you change the value of one or both of these parameters, the database is put into backup pending state, and you must take an offline backup of the database before it can be used again.

Authorities Required to Use Rollforward

Privileges enable users to create or access database resources. Authority levels provide a method of grouping privileges and higher level database manager maintenance and utility operations. Together, these act to control access to the database manager and its database objects. Users can access only those objects for which they have the appropriate authorization, i.e., the required privilege or authority.

You must have SYSADM, SYSCTRL, or SYSMAINT authority to use the rollforward utility.

Using Rollforward

You should not be connected to the database that is to be rollforward recovered: The rollforward utility automatically establishes a connection to the specified database, and this connection is terminated at the completion of the rollforward operation.

Do not restore table spaces without canceling a rollforward operation that is in progress; otherwise, you may have a table space set in which some table spaces are in rollforward in-progress state and some table spaces are in rollforward pending state. A rollforward operation that is in progress will operate only on the table spaces that are in rollforward in-progress state.

The following restrictions apply to the rollforward utility:

- You can invoke only one rollforward operation at a time. If there are many table spaces to recover, you can specify all of them in the same operation.

- If you have renamed a table space following the most recent backup operation, ensure that you use the new name when rolling the table space forward. The previous table space name will not be recognized.
- You cannot cancel a rollforward operation that is running. You can cancel only a rollforward operation that has completed but for which the STOP option has not been specified or a rollforward operation that has failed before completing.
- You cannot continue a table space rollforward operation to a point in time, specifying a time stamp that is less than the previous one. If a point in time is not specified, the previous one is used. You can initiate a rollforward operation to a point in time by just specifying STOP, but this is allowed only if the table spaces involved were all restored from the same offline backup image. In this case, no log processing is required. If you start another rollforward operation with a different table space list before the in-progress rollforward operation is either completed or cancelled, an error message (SQL4908) is returned. Invoke the LIST TABLESPACES SHOW DETAIL or get snapshot for TABLESPACES command on all database partitions to determine which table spaces are currently being rolled forward (rollforward in-progress state) and which table spaces are ready to be rolled forward (rollforward pending state). You have three options:
  - ◦ Finish the in-progress rollforward operation on all table spaces.
  - ◦ Finish the in-progress rollforward operation on a subset of table spaces. This may not be possible if the rollforward operation is to continue to a specific point in time, which requires the participation of all database partitions.
  - ◦ Cancel the in-progress rollforward operation.
- In a partitioned database environment, the rollforward utility must be invoked from the catalog partition of the database.

The rollforward utility can be invoked through the command line processor (CLP), the database Rollforward Wizard in the Control Center, or the db2Rollforward API.

Rollforward Database: Examples

The ROLLFORWARD DATABASE command permits specification of multiple operations at once, each being separated with the key word AND.

For example, to roll forward to the end of logs and complete, use the separate commands:

```
db2 rollforward db sample to end of logs
db2 rollforward db sample complete
```

The above commands can be combined as follows:

```
db2 rollforward db sample to end of logs and complete
```

Although the two are equivalent, it is recommended that such operations be done in two steps. It is important to verify that the rollforward operation has progressed as expected before stopping it and possibly missing logs. This is especially important if a bad log is found during rollforward recovery, and the bad log is interpreted to mean the "end of logs." In such cases, an undamaged backup copy of that log could be used to continue the rollforward operation through more logs.

After restoring the database, roll forward to a point in time, using OVERFLOW LOG PATH to specify the directory where the user exit saves archived logs:

```
db2 "rollforward db sample to end of logs and stop overflow log path
(/data/archlog)"


                                       Rollforward Status
Input database alias                 = sample
Number of nodes have returned status = 1
Node number                          = 0
Rollforward status                   = not pending
Next log file to be read             =
Log files processed                  = S0000000.LOG - S0000000.LOG
Last committed transaction           = 2002-08-29-17.31.53.000000

DB20000I  The ROLLFORWARD command completed successfully.
```

An example of rolling forward a table space (tscustomer) that resides on a single-partition database partition group (on database partition number 2):

```
db2 rollforward db dwtest to end of logs on dbpartitionnum (2)
tablespace(tscustomer)
```

HIGH AVAILABILITY CLUSTERING

High availability (HA) is the term that is used to describe systems that run and are available to customers more or less all the time.

Failover protection can be achieved by keeping a copy of your database on another machine that is perpetually rolling the log files forward. Log shipping is the process of copying whole log files to a standby machine, either from an archive device or through a user exit program running against the primary database. With this approach, the primary database is restored to the standby machine, using either the DB2 restore utility or the split mirror function. You can use the new suspended I/O support to initialize the new database quickly. The secondary database on the standby machine continuously rolls the log files forward.

If the primary database fails, any remaining log files are copied over to the standby machine. After a rollforward to the end of the logs and stop operation, all clients are reconnected to the secondary database on the standby machine.

Failover strategies are usually based on clusters of systems. A cluster is a group of connected systems that work together as a single system. Clustering allows servers to back each other up when failures occur by picking up the workload of the failed server.

IP address takeover (or IP takeover) is the ability to transfer a server IP address from one machine to another when a server goes down; to a client application, the two machines appear at different times to be the same server.

Failover software may use heartbeat monitoring or keepalive packets between systems to confirm availability. Heartbeat monitoring involves system services that maintain constant communication between all the servers in a cluster. If a heartbeat is not detected, failover to a backup system starts. End users are usually not aware that a system has failed.

> **N O T E**   For clarification and consistency with the naming convention throughout the book, a database node is now called a *database partition*, and when referencing a node name in the cluster, we refer to it as a *server*.

The two most common failover strategies on the market are known as idle standby and mutual takeover, although the configurations associated with these terms may also be associated with different terms that depend on the vendor.

Idle Standby

In this configuration, one system is used to run a DB2 instance, and the second system is *idle*, or in standby mode, ready to take over the instance if there is an operating system or hardware failure involving the first system. Overall system performance is not impacted, because the standby system is idle until needed.

Mutual Takeover

In this configuration, each system is the designated backup for another system. Overall system performance may be impacted, because the backup system must do extra work following a failover: It must do its own work plus the work that was being done by the failed system.

Failover strategies can be used to failover an instance, a partition, or multiple database partitions.

When designing and testing a cluster:

1. Ensure that the administrator of the cluster is familiar with the system and what should happen when a failover occurs.

2. Ensure that each part of the cluster is truly redundant and can be replaced quickly if it fails.

3. Force a test system to fail in a controlled environment, and make sure that it fails over correctly each time.

4. Keep track of the reasons for each failover. Although this should not happen often, it is important to address any issues that make the cluster unstable. For example, if one piece of the cluster caused a failover five times in one month, find out why and fix it.

5. Ensure that the support staff for the cluster is notified when a failover occurs.

6. Do not overload the cluster. Ensure that the remaining systems can still handle the workload at an acceptable level after a failover.

7. Check failure-prone components (such as disks) often, so that they can be replaced before problems occur.

In order to implement a split mirror scenario with DB2 Universal Database (UDB) Enterprise Server Edition, it is very important to understand the following three concepts.

Split Mirror

Split mirror is an identical and independent copy of disk volumes that can be attached to a different system and can be used in various ways, e.g., to populate a test system, as a warm standby copy of the database, and to offload backups from the primary machine.

A split mirror of a database includes the entire contents of the database directory, all the table space containers, the local database directory, and the active log directory, if it does not reside on the database directory. The active log directory needs to be split *only* for creating a clone database using the "snapshot" option of the "db2inidb" tool.

Suspend I/O Feature

When splitting the mirror, it is important to ensure that there is no page write occurring on the source database. One way to ensure this is to bring the database offline. But, due to the required downtime, this method is not a feasible solution in a true 24x7 production environment.

In an effort to provide continuous system availability during the split mirror process, DB2 UDB Enterprise Server Edition (ESE) provides a feature known as suspend I/O, which allows online split mirroring without shutting down the database. The suspend I/O feature ensures the prevention of any partial page write by suspending all write operations on the source database. While the database is in write suspend mode, all of the table space states change to a new state SUSPEND_WRITE, and all operations function normally.

However, some transactions may wait if they require disk I/O, such as flushing dirty pages from the buffer pool or flushing logs from the log buffer. These transactions will proceed normally, once the write operations on the database are resumed. The following command is used to suspend or resume write operations on the source database:

```
db2 set write <suspend | resume> for database
```

The db2inidb Tool

The split mirror created using the suspend I/O feature continues to stay in a write-suspend mode until it is initialized to a useable state. To initialize the split mirror, you can invoke the db2inidb tool.

This tool can either perform a crash recovery on a split mirror image or can put it in a rollforward pending state, depending on the options provided in the db2inidb command, the syntax of which is as follows:

```
db2inidb <database_alias> as < snapshot | standby |mirror >[ relocate
    using <config_file> ]
```

The *snapshot* option clones the primary database to offload work from the source database, such as running reports, analysis, or populating a target system.

The *standby* option continues rolling forward through the log, and even new logs that are created by the source database are constantly fetched from the source system.

The *mirror* uses the mirrored system as a backup image to restore over the source system.

The *relocate* option allows the split mirror to be relocated in terms of the database name, database directory path, container path, log path, and the instance name associated with the database.

Common Usage of Suspend I/O and db2inidb

The combination of the suspend I/O feature and the db2inidb tool is necessary to bring the split mirror database into a functional state. With the functionalities of the three options (snapshot, standby, mirror) provided in the db2inidb tool, in conjunction with the suspend I/O feature, it is possible to create a fast snapshot of a database, which can be used to:

- Populate a test system by making a copy of the current data.
- Create a standby database that can be used as a warm standby (DB2 backup can be taken if the database contains DMS only table spaces).
- Provide a quick file system level recovery option.
- Take database backups that can be restored on the database server.

The suspend I/O feature is necessary to ensure that all DB2 data gets written out to the disk consistently (no partial page write) before splitting the mirror. This assures a well-defined state where the database can be recovered to later, using the db2inidb tool.

The db2inidb tool can either force the database to perform a crash recovery (when the snapshot option is specified) or put the database into a rollforward pending state (when the standby or mirror option is specified) to allow processing of additional log files.

High Availability through Log Shipping

Log shipping is the process of copying whole log files to a standby machine, either from an archive device or through a user exit program running against the primary database. The standby database is continuously rolling forward through the log files produced by the production machine. When the production machine fails, a switch over occurs, and the following takes place:

- The remaining logs are transferred over to the standby machine, if possible.
- The standby database rolls forward to the end of the logs and stops.
- The clients reconnect to the standby database and resume operations.

The standby machine has its own resources (i.e., disks) but must have the same physical and logical definitions as the production database. When using this approach, the primary database is restored to the standby machine by using the restore utility or the split mirror function.

To ensure that you are able to recover your database in a disaster recovery situation, consider the following:

- The archive location should be geographically separate from the primary site.
- Remotely mirror the log at the standby database site.
- Use a synchronous mirror for no loss support. You can do this through:
  - DB2 log mirroring or modern disk subsystems, such as ESS and EMC.
  - NVRAM cache (both local and remote) is also recommended to minimize the performance impact of a disaster recovery situation.

> **NOTE**
>
> 1. When the standby database processes a log record indicating that an index rebuild took place on the primary database, the indexes on the standby server are not automatically rebuilt. The index will be rebuilt on the standby server, either at the first connection to the database or at the first attempt to access the index after the standby server is taken out of rollforward pending state. It is recommended that the standby server be resynchronized with the primary server if any indexes on the primary server are rebuilt.
>
> 2. If the load utility is run on the primary database with the COPY YES option specified, the standby database must have access to the copy image.
>
> 3. If the load utility is run on the primary database with the COPY NO option specified, the standby database should be resynchronized; otherwise the table space will be placed in restore pending state.

4. There are two ways to initialize a standby machine:
   a. Restoring it from a backup image
   b. Creating a split mirror of the production system and issuing the db2inidb command with the STANDBY option (only after the standby machine has been initialized and you issue the ROLLFORWARD command on the standby system)

5. Operations that are not logged (i.e., activities performed on a table created with NOT LOGGED INITIALLY) will not be replayed on the standby database. As a result, it is recommended that you resync the standby database after such operations. You can do this through online split mirror and suspended I/O support.

High Availability through Online Split Mirror and Suspended I/O Support

Suspended I/O supports continuous system availability by providing a full implementation for online split mirror handling; that is, splitting a mirror without shutting down the database. A split mirror is an "instantaneous" copy of the database that can be made by mirroring the disks containing the data and splitting the mirror when a copy is required. Disk mirroring is the process of writing all of your data to two separate hard disks; one is the mirror of the other. Splitting a mirror is the process of separating the primary and secondary copies of the database.

If you would rather not back up a large database using the DB2 backup utility, you can make copies from a mirrored image by using suspended I/O and the split mirror function. This approach also:

- Eliminates backup operation overhead from the production machine.
- Represents a fast way to clone systems.
- Represents a fast implementation of idle standby failover. There is no initial restore operation, and if a rollforward operation proves to be too slow or encounters errors, reinitialization is very quick.

The *db2inidb* command initializes the split mirror so that it can be used:

- As a clone database
- As a standby database
- As a backup image

In a partitioned database environment, you do not have to suspend I/O writes on all partitions simultaneously. You can suspend a subset of one or more partitions to create split mirrors for performing offline backups. If the catalog partition is included in the subset, it must be the last partition to be suspended.

In a partitioned database environment, the *db2inidb* command must be run on every partition before the split image from any of the partitions can be used. The tool can be run on all partitions simultaneously, using the *db2_all* command.

> **N O T E** Ensure that the split mirror contains all containers and directories that comprise the database, including the volume directory (each autonumbered directory within a volume).

Split Mirror to Clone a Database

Clone the primary database to offload work from source database, such as running reports, analysis, or populating a target system.

The following scenario shows how to create a clone database on the target system, using the suspend I/O feature. In this scenario, the split mirror database goes through a crash recovery initiated by the *db2inidb* tool with the *snapshot* parameter. A clone database generated in this manner can be used to populate a test database or to generate reports. Due to crash recovery, the clone database will start a new log chain; therefore, it will not be able to replay any future log files from the source database. A database backup taken from this clone database can be restored to the source database. However, it will not be able to roll forward through any log records generated after the database was split. Thus, it will be a version-level copy only.

1. Suspend I/O on the source system.

The following commands will suspend I/O (all write activities from DB2 clients) on the source database so that the mirrors of the database containers can be split without the possibility of a partial page write occurring. Please note that suspending I/O on a database will not disconnect the existing connections to the database, and all operations would function normally. However, some transactions may wait if they require disk I/O. But as soon as the I/O has been resumed on the database, the transactions will proceed normally.

```
db2 connect to <source-database>
db2 set write suspend for database
```

2. Use appropriate operating system-level commands to split the mirror or mirrors from the source database.

The process to split a mirror differs from vendor to vendor. Please consult the storage vendor documentation applicable to your device on how to create a split mirror. Regardless of the variations on the split mirror process, the entire contents of the database directory, all the table space containers, the local database directory, and the active log directory (if it does not reside on the database directory) must be split at the same time.

3. Resume I/O on the source system.

The following command will resume I/O (all write activities from DB2 clients) on the source database, and the currently running transactions will proceed as normal. It is essential that the same database connection that was used to issue the db2 set write suspend command be used to issue the write resume command.

```
db2 set write resume for database
```

4. Attach to the mirrored database from the target machine.

After the split of the mirror, the administrator for the target machine must use the facilities of the storage vendor to provide access to the split mirror copy, to be referred to as *mount*. For initial setup, the following steps need to be taken on the target system:

- Create the same database instance as it is on the source machine.
- Catalog the database (system database directory).
- Mount the database directory into the same directory as it is on the source machine.
- Mount all of the containers to the same paths as they are on the source machine. If the containers are located in several directories, all container directories must be mounted.
- If the log files are located in a directory other than the database directory, the log directory should also be mounted into the same directory as it is on the source machine.

5. Start the database instance on the target system.

Start the database manager on the target machine, assuming that the DB2 registry variable DB2INSTANCE is set to the instance name the same as the source machine.

```
db2start
```

6. Bring the clone database into a consistent state.

The following command will initiate a crash recovery and will roll back all uncommitted transactions, making the database consistent. It is essential to have all the log files that were active at the time of the split. The active log directory should not contain any log file that is not a part of the split mirror. After the crash recovery a new log chain will be started; therefore, the database will not be able to roll forward through any of the logs from the source database. The database will now be available for any operation.

```
db2inidb <dbname> as snapshot
```

> **N O T E** This command will roll back transactions that were in flight when the split occured and start a new log chain sequence so that any logs from the primary database cannot be replayed on the cloned database.

Split Mirror as a Standby Database

Continue to roll forward through the logs and even new logs that are created by the source database are constantly fetched from the source system.

The following scenario shows how to create a standby database on the target system, using the suspend I/O feature. In a warm standby database scenario, the log files of the source database will be applied on the target (standby) database. The standby database will be kept in a rollforward pending state until the rollforward has been stopped. A DB2 backup image taken on the clone database (DMS only) can be used for restoring on the source database for the purpose of performing a rollforward recovery by using the log files produced on the source database after the mirror was split. Please see the following steps:

1. Suspend I/O on the source system.

The following commands will suspend the I/O (all write activities from DB2 clients) on the database so that the mirrors of the database containers can be split without the possibility of a partial page write occurring. Please note that suspending I/O on a database will not disconnect the existing connections to the database, and all operations would function normally. However, some transactions may wait if they require disk I/O. But as soon as the I/O has been resumed on the database, the transactions will proceed normally.

```
db2 connect to <source-database>
db2 set write suspend for database
```

2. Use appropriate operating system-level commands to split the mirror or mirrors from the source database.

The process to split a mirror differs from vendor to vendor. Please consult the storage vendor documentation applicable to your device on how to create a split mirror. Regardless of the variations on the split mirroring process, the entire contents of the database directory, all the table space containers, and the local database directory must be split at the same time. It is NOT necessary to split the active log directory in this case.

3. Resume I/O on the source system.

The following command will resume I/O (all write activities from DB2 clients) on the source database, and the currently running transactions will proceed as normal. It is essential that the same database connection that was used to issue the db2 set write suspend command be used to issue the write resume command.

```
db2 set write resume for database
```

4. Attach to the mirrored database from the target machine.

After the split of the mirror, the administrator for the target machine must use the facilities of the storage vendor to provide access to the split mirror copy, to be referred to as *mount*. For initial setup, the following steps need to be taken on the target system:

- Create the same database instance as it is on the source machine.
- Catalog the database (system database directory).
- Mount the database directory into the same directory as it is on the source machine.
- Mount all of the containers to the same paths as they are on the source machine. If the containers are located in several directories, all container directories must be mounted.
- If the log files are located in a directory other than the database directory, the log directory should also be mounted into the same directory as it is on the source machine.

5. Start the database instance on the target system.

Start the database manager on the target machine, assuming that the DB2 registry variable DB2INSTANCE is set to the instance name the same as the source machine.

```
db2start
```

6. Put the mirrored database in rollforward mode.

This places the split mirror database into a rollforward pending state. Crash recovery is not performed, and the database remains inconsistent.

```
db2inidb <dbname> as standby
```

7. Continually copy over the log files and roll forward.

Once the database is placed into a rollforward pending state, the log files from the source database can be used to roll forward the target database. A user exit program can be used in this case to automate the continuous archival of the inactive log files. If user exit is used, both source and target databases must be configured with the same user exit program.

```
db2 rollforward db <dbname> to end of logs
```

8. Activate the standby database.

If the source database crashes, the standby database on the target machine can be activated for user access. The user applications will have to make new connections to this standby database. In order to activate, the standby database needs to be taken out of the rollforward pending state. The users should issue the rollforward command with the "stop" or "complete" option to bring the database into a consistent state. Once the database is in consistent state, the users can switch over to the standby database to continue their work. The log files generated on the standby database cannot be applied on the source database.

While the target database is in rollforward pending state, it is possible to perform an offline backup if the database has DMS only table spaces.

```
db2 rollforward db <dbname> stop
```

> **N O T E** If you have only DMS table spaces, you can take a full database backup to offload the overhead of taking a backup on the production database.

Split Mirror as a Backup Image

Use the mirrored system as a backup image to restore over the source system.

The following scenario shows how to create a mirror database on the target system, using the suspend I/O feature. The purpose of this option is to provide the possibility of using a split mirror database for restoring on top of the source database, then to roll forward the log files of the source database. It is important to note that the split mirror must remain in the SUSPEND_WRITE state until it has been copied over on top of the source database.

Split Mirror

1. Suspend I/O on the source database.

The following commands will suspend I/O (all write activities from DB2 clients) on the database so that the mirrors of the database containers can be split without the possibility of a partial page write occurring. Please note that suspending I/O on a database will not disconnect the existing connections to the database, and all operations would function normally. However, some transactions may wait if they require disk I/O. But as soon as the I/O has been resumed on the database, the transactions will proceed normally.

```
db2 connect to <source-database>
db2 set write suspend for database
```

2. Split the mirror.

The process to split the mirror differs from vendor to vendor. Please consult the storage vendor documentation applicable to your device on how to create a split mirror. Regardless of the variations on the split mirroring process, the entire contents of the database directory, all the table space containers, and the local database directory must be split at the same time. It is not necessary to split the active log directory in this case.

3. Resume I/O on the source database.

The following command will resume I/O (all write activities from DB2 clients) on the source database, and the currently running transactions will proceed as normal. It is essential that the same database connection that was used to issue the db2 set write suspend command be used to issue the write resume command.

```
db2 set write resume for database
```

Restore the Split Mirror Image

There is no "target" database in this scenario. The intent of this scenario is to use the mirror copy to restore on top of the "source" database to recover from a disk failure. The split mirror cannot be backed up using the DB2 backup utility, but it can be backed up using operating system tools. If the source database happens to crash, it can be restored with the split mirror image by copying it on top of the source database. Please see the following steps:

1. Stop the source database instance.

The database instance needs to be shut down using the following DB2 command before restoring the split mirror image into it.

```
db2stop
```

2. Restore the split mirror image.

Using the storage vendor utilities, copy the data files of the split mirror database over the original database. Please *do not* use the operating system utilities in this case because the operating system does not have any knowledge of this split image.

3. Start the source database instance after restoring the split mirror image.

```
db2start
```

4. Initialize the mirror copy on the source database.

This step will replace the source database with the mirror copy of the database and will place it into a rollforward pending state. No crash recovery is initiated, and the database will remain inconsistent until it has been rolled forward to the end of logs.

```
db2inidb <database> as mirror
```

5. Rollforward to end of logs.

The log files from the source database must be used to roll forward the database.

```
db2 rollforward database <database> to end of logs and complete
```

In a multi-partitioned database environment, every database partition is treated as a separate database. Therefore, the I/O on each partition needs to be suspended during the split mirror process and should be resumed afterward. The same applies to the *db2inidb* tool and needs to be run on each mirrored partition before using the database.

Following are some examples of how to issue the commands simultaneously on all partitions.

```
db2_all "db2 connect to <source-database>; db2 set write resume for
    database"
db2_all "db2inidb <target-database> as <options>"
```

High Availability on AIX

Enhanced scalability (ES) is a feature of High Availability Cluster Multi-Processing (HACMP) for AIX. This feature provides the same failover recovery and has the same event structure as HACMP. Enhanced scalability also has other provisions:

- Larger clusters.
- Additional error coverage through user-defined events.
- Monitored areas can trigger user-defined events, which can be as diverse as the death of a process or the fact that paging space is nearing capacity. Such events include pre- and post-events that can be added to the failover recovery process, if needed. Extra functions that are specific to the different implementations can be placed within the HACMP pre-event and post-event streams.
- A rules file (/usr/sbin/cluster/events/rules.hacmprd) contains the HACMP events. User-defined events are added to this file. The script files that are to be run when events occur are part of this definition.
- HACMP client utilities for monitoring and detecting status changes (in one or more clusters) from AIX physical server outside of the HACMP cluster.

The servers in HACMP ES clusters exchange messages called *heartbeats* or *keepalive packets*, by which each server informs the other server about its availability. A server that has stopped responding causes the remaining servers in the cluster to invoke recovery. The recovery process is called a *server-down-event* and may also be referred to as *failover*. The completion of the recovery process is followed by the reintegration of the server into the cluster. This is called a *server-up-event*.

There are two types of events: standard events that are anticipated within the operations of HACMP ES and user-defined events that are associated with the monitoring of parameters in hardware and software components. One of the standard events is the *server-down-event*. When planning what should be done as part of the recovery process, HACMP allows two failover options: hot (or idle) standby and mutual takeover.

> **N O T E**   When using HACMP, ensure that DB2 instances are not started at boot time by using the *db2iauto* utility, as follows:
>
> ```
> db2iauto -off InstName
> ```
> where InstName is the login name of the instance.

Cluster Configuration

In a hot-standby configuration, the AIX server that is the takeover server is not running any other workload. In a mutual takeover configuration, the AIX server that is the takeover server is running other workloads.

Generally, in a partitioned database environment, DB2 UDB runs in mutual takeover mode with multiple database partitions on each server. One exception is a scenario in which the catalog partition is part of a hot-standby configuration.

When planning a large DB2 installation on an RS/6000 SP using HACMP ES, you need to consider how to divide the servers of the cluster within or between the RS/6000 SP frames. Having a server and its backup in different SP frames allows takeover in the event that one frame goes down (that is, the frame power/switch board fails). However, such failures are expected to be exceedingly rare because there are N+1 power supplies in each SP frame, and each SP switch has redundant paths, along with N+1 fans and power. In the case of a frame failure, manual intervention may be required to recover the remaining frames. This recovery procedure is documented in the SP Administration Guide. HACMP ES provides for recovery of SP server failures; recovery of frame failures is dependent on the proper layout of clusters within one or more SP frames.

Another planning consideration is how to manage big clusters. It is easier to manage a small cluster than a big one; however, it is also easier to manage one big cluster than many smaller ones. When planning, consider how your applications will be used in your cluster environment.

If there is a single, large, homogeneous application running, for example, on 16 servers, it is probably easier to manage the configuration as a single cluster, rather than as eight two-server clusters. If the same 16 servers contain many different applications with different networks, disks, and server relationships, it is probably better to group the servers into smaller clusters. Keep in mind that servers integrate into an HACMP cluster one at a time; it will be faster to start a configuration of multiple clusters, rather than one large cluster. HACMP ES supports both single and multiple clusters, as long as a server and its backup are in the same cluster.

HACMP ES failover recovery allows predefined (also known as *cascading*) assignment of a resource group to a physical server. The failover recovery procedure also allows floating (or rotating) assignment of a resource group to a physical server. IP addresses and external disk volume groups, file systems, or NFS file systems, as well as application servers within each resource group specify either an application or an application component, which can be manipulated by HACMP ES between physical servers by failover and reintegration. Failover and reintegration behavior is specified by the type of resource group created and by the number of servers placed in the resource group.

For example, consider a partitioned database environment, if its log and table space containers were placed on external disks and other servers were linked to those disks, it would be possible for those other servers to access these disks and to restart the database partition (on a takeover server). It is this type of operation that is automated by HACMP. HACMP ES can also be used to recover NFS file systems used by DB2 instance main user directories.

Read the HACMP ES documentation thoroughly as part of your planning for recovery with DB2 UDB in a partitioned database environment. You should read the Concepts, Planning, Installation, and Administration guides, then build the recovery architecture for your environment. For each subsystem that you have identified for recovery, based on known points of failure, identify the HACMP clusters that you need, as well as the recovery servers (either hot standby or mutual takeover).

It is strongly recommended that both disks and adapters be mirrored in your external disk configuration. For DB2 servers that are configured for HACMP, care is required to ensure that servers on the volume group can vary from the shared external disks. In a mutual takeover configuration, this arrangement requires some additional planning, so that the paired servers can access each other's volume groups without conflicts. In a partitioned database environment, this means that all container names must be unique across all databases.

One way to achieve uniqueness is to include the partition number as part of the name. You can specify a database partition expression for container string syntax when creating either SMS or DMS containers. When you specify the expression, the database partition number can be part of the container name or, if you specify additional arguments, the results of those arguments can be part of the container name. Use the argument $N ([blank]$N) to indicate the database partition expression. The argument must occur at the end of the container string.

Following are some examples of how to create containers using this special argument:

- Creating containers for use on a two-database partition system

The following containers would be used:

```
CREATE TABLESPACE TS1 MANAGED BY DATABASE USING (device '/dev/rcont
    $N' 20000)
/dev/rcont0—on DATABASE PARTITION 0
/dev/rcont1—on DATABASE PARTITION 1
```

- Creating containers for use on a four-database partition system

The following containers would be used:

```
CREATE TABLESPACE TS2 MANAGED BY DATABASE USING (file '/DB2/
    containers/TS2/container $N+100' 10000)
/DB2/containers/TS2/container100—on DATABASE PARTITION 0
/DB2/containers/TS2/container101—on DATABASE PARTITION 1
/DB2/containers/TS2/container102—on DATABASE PARTITION 2
/DB2/containers/TS2/container103—on DATABASE PARTITION 3
```

- Creating containers for use on a two-database partition system

The following containers would be used:

```
CREATE TABLESPACE TS3 MANAGED BY SYSTEM USING ('/TS3/cont  $N%2, '/
    TS3/cont  $N%2+2')
/TS3/cont0—on DATABASE PARTITION 0
/TS3/cont2—on DATABASE PARTITION 0
/TS3/cont1—on DATABASE PARTITION 1
/TS3/cont3—on DATABASE PARTITION 1
```

A script file, rc.db2pe, is packaged with DB2 UDB Enterprise Server Edition (and installed on each server in /usr/bin) to assist in configuring for HACMP ES failover or recovery in either hot standby or mutual takeover servers. In addition, DB2 buffer pool sizes can be customized during failover in mutual takeover configurations from within rc.db2pe. Buffer pool sizes can be configured to ensure proper resource allocation when two database partitions run on one physical server.

HACMP ES Event Monitoring and User-Defined Events

Initiating a failover operation if a process dies on a given server is an example of a user-defined event. Examples that illustrate user-defined events, such as shutting down a database partition and forcing a transaction abort to free paging space, can be found in the sqllib/samples/hacmp/es subdirectory.

A rules file, /usr/sbin/cluster/events/rules.hacmprd, contains HACMP events. Each event description in this file has the following nine components:

- Event name, which must be unique.
- State, or qualifier for the event. The event name and state are the rule triggers. HACMP ES Cluster Manager initiates recovery only if it finds a rule with a trigger corresponding to the event name and state.
- Resource program path, a full path specification of the xxx.rp file containing the recovery program.
- Recovery type. This is reserved for future use.
- Recovery level. This is reserved for future use.
- Resource variable name, which is used for Event Manager events.
- Instance vector, which is used for Event Manager events. This is a set of elements of the form *name=value*. The values uniquely identify the copy of the resource in the system and, by extension, the copy of the resource variable.
- Predicate, which is used for Event Manager events. This is a relational expression between a resource variable and other elements. When this expression is true, the Event Management subsystem generates an event to notify the Cluster Manager and the appropriate application.
- Rearm predicate, which is used for Event Manager events. This is a predicate used to generate an event that alters the status of the primary predicate. This predicate is typically the inverse of the primary predicate. It can also be used with the event predicate to establish an upper and a lower boundary for a condition of interest.

Each object requires one line in the event definition, even if the line is not used. If these lines are removed, HACMP ES Cluster Manager cannot parse the event definition properly, and this may cause the system to hang. Any line beginning with "#" is treated as a comment line.

> **N O T E** The rules file requires exactly nine lines for each event definition, not counting any comment lines. When adding a user-defined event at the bottom of the rules file, it is important to remove the unnecessary empty line at the end of the file, or the server will hang.

HACMP ES uses PSSP event detection to treat user-defined events. The PSSP Event Management subsystem provides comprehensive event detection by monitoring various hardware and software resources.

The process can be summarized as follows:

1. Either Group Services/ES (for predefined events) or Event Management (for user-defined events) notifies HACMP ES Cluster Manager of the event.

2. Cluster Manager reads the rules.hacmprd file and determines the recovery program that is mapped to the event.

3. Cluster Manager runs the recovery program, which consists of a sequence of recovery commands.

4. The recovery program executes the recovery commands, which may be shell scripts or binary commands. (In HACMP for AIX, the recovery commands are the same as the HACMP event scripts.)

5. Cluster Manager receives the return status from the recovery commands. An unexpected status "hangs" the cluster until manual intervention (using smit cm_rec_aids or the /usr/sbin/cluster/utilities/clruncmd command) is carried out.

In Figure 3.1, both servers have access to the installation directory, the instance directory, and the database directory. The database instance db2inst is being actively executed on server 1. Server 2 is not active and is being used as a hot standby. A failure occurs on server 1, and the instance is taken over by server 2. Once the failover is complete, both remote and local applications can access the database within instance db2inst. The database will have to be manually

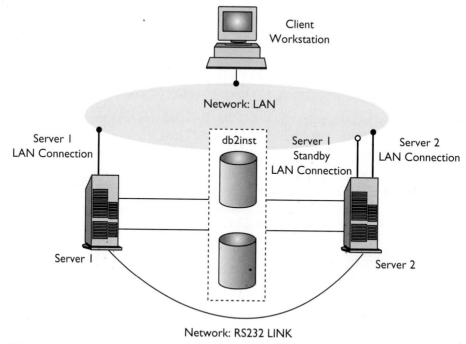

Figure 3.1
Failover on a two-server HACMP cluster.

restarted or, if AUTORESTART is on, the first connection to the database will initiate a restart operation. In the sample script provided, it is assumed that AUTORESTART is off and that the failover script performs the restart for the database.

Partition Failover (Hot Standby)

In the following hot-standby failover scenario, we are using an instance partition instead of the entire instance. The scenario includes a two-server HACMP cluster as in the previous example, but the machine represents one of the partitions of a partitioned database server. Server 1 is running a single partition of the overall configuration, and server 2 is being used as the failover server. When server 1 fails, the partition is restarted on the second server. The failover updates the db2nodes.cfg file, pointing to server 2's host name and net name, then restarts the partition on the new server.

Following is a portion of the *db2nodes.cfg* file, both before and after the failover. In this example, database partition number 2 is running on server 1 of the HACMP machine, which has both a host name and a net name of *srvr201*. The server 2 *srvr202* is running as a hot standby, ready to take over the execution of the partition if there is a failure on *srvr201*. After the failover, database partition number 2 is running on server 2 of the HACMP machine, which has both a host name and a net name of *srvr202*.

```
Before:
    1 srvr101 0 srvr101
    2 srvr201 0 srvr201 <= HACMP running on primary server

db2start dbpartitionnum 2 restart hostname srvr202 port 0 netname
    srvr202

After:
    1 srvr101 0 srvr101
    2 srvr202 0 srvr202 <= HACMP running on standby server
```

Multiple Logical Partition Database Failover

A more complex variation on the previous example involves the failover of multiple logical partition databases from one server to another. Again, we are using the same two server HACMP cluster configuration as above. However, in this scenario, server 1, *srvr201*, is actively running three logical database partitions while server 2, *srvr202,* is running as a hot standby, ready to take over the execution of the partition if there is a failure on *srvr201*. The setup is the same as that for the simple database partition failover scenario but in this case, when server 1 fails, each of the logical database partitions must be started on server 2. It is critical that each logical database partition must be started in the order that is defined in the db2nodes.cfg file: The logical database partition with port number 0 must always be started first.

Following is a portion of the *db2nodes.cfg* file, both before and after the failover. In this example, there are three logical database partitions defined on server 1 of a two-server HACMP cluster. After the failover, database partitions 2, 3, and 4 are running on server 2 of the HACMP machine, which has both a host name and a net name of *srvr202*.

```
Before:
    1 srvr101 0 srvr101
    2 srvr201 0 srvr201 <= HACMP running on the primary server
    3 srvr201 1 srvr201 <= HACMP
    4 srvr201 2 srvr201 <= HACMP

db2start dbpartitionnum 2 restart hostname srvr202 port 0 netname
    srvr202
db2start dbpartitionnum 3 restart hostname srvr202 port 1 netname
    srvr202
db2start dbpartitionnum 4 restart hostname srvr202 port 2 netname
    srvr202

After:
    1 srvr101 0 srvr101
    2 srvr202 0 srvr202 <= HACMP running on the standby server
    3 srvr202 1 srvr202 <= HACMP
    4 srvr202 2 srvr202 <= HACMP
```

Partition Failover (Mutual Takeover)

In this example, we are running two of the partitions of a multi-partitioned database system on the two separate servers of an HACMP configuration. The database partition for each server is created on the path /db2, which is not shared with other partitions. The following is the contents of the *db2nodes.cfg* file associated with the overall multi-partition instance before and after the failover. The *srvr201* crashes and fails over to *srvr202*. After the failover, the database partition that was executing on *srvr201*, which is defined as database partition number 2, starts up on *srvr202*. Because *srvr202* is already running a database partition number 3 for this database, therefore, database partition number 2 will be started as a logical database partition number on *srvr202* with the logical port 1.

```
Before:
    1 srvr101 0 srvr101
    2 srvr201 0 srvr201 <= HACMP failover server
    3 srvr202 0 srvr202 <= HACMP

db2start dbpartitionnum 2 restart hostname srvr202 port 1 netname
    srvr202

After:
    1 srvr101 0 srvr101
    2 srvr202 1 srvr202 <= srvr201 failover to srvr202
    3 srvr202 0 srvr202 <= HACMP
```

Scenario #1: Hot Standby with a Cascading Resource Group

In this HACMP configuration (hot standby with a cascading resource group), we use HACMP/ES 4.3 and DB2 UDB Enterprise Server Edition running on AIX 4.3.3. The cluster being defined is called *dbcluster*. This cluster has two servers (*dbserv1* and *dbserv2*), one resource group (*db2grp*), and one application server (*db2as*). Because we want the resource group and the application server to be active on the *dbserv1* server when there are no failovers, we will define the *dbserv1* server in the resource group first. Each of these servers will have two network adapters and one serial port. The servers will have a shared external disk, with only one server accessing the disk at a time. Both servers will have access to a volume group (*havg*), three file systems (/home/db2inst1, /db1, and /home/db2fenc1), and a logical volume (/dev/udbdata).

If the *dbserv1* server has a hardware or software failure, the *dbserv2* server will acquire the resources that are defined in the resource group. The application server is then started on the *dbserv2* server. In our case, the application server that is started is DB2 UDB ESE for the instance *db2inst1*. There are failures that would not cause the application to move to the *dbserv2* server; these include a disk failure or a network adapter failure.

Here is one example of a failover: DB2 UDB ESE is running on a server called *dbserv1*; it has a home directory of /home/db2inst1, a database located on the /db1 file system, and a /dev/udbdata logical volume. These two file systems and logical volume are in a volume group called *havg*. The *dbserv2* server is currently not running any application except HACMP, but it is ready to take over from the *dbserv1* server, if necessary. Suppose someone unplugs the *dbserv1* server. The *dbserv2* server detects this event and begins taking over resources from the *dbserv1* server. These resources include the havg volume group, the three file systems, the logical volume, and the hostname dbs1.

Once the resources are available on the *dbserv2* server, the application server start script runs. The instance ID can log on to the *dbserv2* server (now called *dbs1*) and connect to the database. Remote clients can also connect to the database, because the hostname *dbs1* is now located on the *db2serv2* server.

Follow these steps to set up shared disk drives and the logical volume manager:

1. Set up the disk drives.
2. Create the volume group (VG). The VG must have a unique name and a major number for all servers in the cluster.
3. Create a JFSLog.
4. Create the LVs and the JFSs.
5. Unmount all of the file systems and deactivate the VG. The volume is varied off on the dbserv1 server before it is activated on the dbserver server.
6. Import the VG on the dbserv2.
7. Move the active VG to the dbserv1 server.

User Setup and DB2 Installation

Now that the components of the LVM are set up, DB2 can be installed. The *db2setup* utility can be used to install and configure DB2. To understand the configuration better, we will define some of the components manually and use the *db2setup* utility to install only the DB2 product and license.

All commands described in this chapter must be invoked by the root user. Although the steps used to install DB2 are outlined below, for complete details, please refer to the DB2 for UNIX Quick Beginnings guide and the DB2 Client Installation Guide.

> **N O T E**   Before any groups or IDs are created, ensure that the volume group is activated and that the file systems /home/db2inst1 and /home/db2fenc1 are mounted.

To install and configure DB2 on the dbserv1 server:

1. Create the group for the DB2 instance.
2. Create the user ID for the DB2 instance.
3. Create the group and user ID for the DB2 fenced ID.
4. Mount the CD-ROM.
5. Install DB2 and set up the license key.
6. Create the DB2 instance.
7. Install the DB2 HACMP scripts.
   To copy the HACMP scripts to /usr/bin from /usr/opt/db2_08_01/samples/hacmp/es, use the db2_inst_ha.local command. The db2_inst_ha.local script also copies over the HACMP/ES event stanzas. These events are defined in the db2_event_stanzas file.
8. Failover $HOME to the dbserv2 server. Repeat steps 1 to 7 on the dbserv2 server.

> **N O T E**   Once DB2 HACMP is configured and set up, any changes made (for example, to the IDs, groups, AIX system parameters, or the level of DB2 code) must be done on both servers.

Following are some examples:

- The HACMP cluster is active on the *dbserv1* server, and the password is changed on that server. When failover happens to the *dbserv2* server and the user tries to log on, the new password will not work. Therefore, the administrator must ensure that passwords are kept synchronized.
- If the *ulimit* parameter on the *dbserv1* server is changed, it must also be changed on the *dbserv2* server. For example, suppose the file size is set to unlimited on the *dbserv1*

server. When a failover happens to the *dbserv2* server and the user tries to access a file that is greater than the default size of 1 GB, an error is returned.

- If the AIX parameter *maxuproc* is changed on the *dbserv1* server, it also must be changed on the *dbserv2* server. When a failover occurs, and DB2 is now running on the *dbserv2* server, it may hit the *maxuproc* value and return errors.
- If non-DB2 software is installed or a DB2 upgrade is installed on the *dbserv1* server but not on the *dbserv2* server, the new software will not be available when a failover takes place.
- Suppose that the database manager configuration parameter *svcename* is used and that /etc/services is updated on the *dbserv1* server. If the *dbserv2* server does not receive the same update, DB2 clients will report errors after a failover.

The testing procedure itself is simple. First, connect to the cluster from a client machine; next, cause one of the points of failure to fail; then watch to ensure that the failover takes place properly to make sure that the application is available and properly configured after failover. If the cluster is built using a cascading cluster configuration, check again after service has been restored to the original server. If the cluster is built using a rotating cluster configuration, bring up the original server again, then cause the second server to fail, which should restore the system to its original server.

When testing the availability of the application, be sure that accounts and passwords work as expected, that hostnames and IP addresses work as expected, that the data is complete and up to date, and that the hangover is essentially transparent to the user.

Configure a remote machine to be able to connect to the highly available DB2 UDB database. A script can be easily written that will connect to our database, select some data from a table, record the results, and disconnect from the database. If these steps are set inside a loop that will run until interrupted by the operator, the procedure can be used to monitor the state of the cluster.

Keep in mind that the script should continue even if the database cannot be contacted. This way, when the database restarts, it will provide a benchmark for the length of time failover is expected to take. Here is a brief sample script that may be useful for testing an HACMP cluster:

```
while true
   do
   db2 connect to database
   db2 "select count(*) from syscat.tables"
   db2 terminate
   sleep 60

   done
```

Scenario #2: Mutual Takeover with a Cascading Resource Group

This configuration involves a six-database partitions and two clusters, each with mutual takeover and cascading resource groups. It uses HACMP/ES 4.3 and DB2 UDB ESE running on AIX 4.3.3.

The clusters being defined are named *cl1314* and *cl1516*, with cluster IDs of 1314 and 1516, respectively. We arbitrarily selected these numbers because we are using SP servers 13,14,15, and 16.

- The *cl1314* cluster has two servers (*bf01n013* and *bf01n014*), two cluster server names (*clsrv13* and *clsrv14*), two resource groups (*rg1314* and *rg1413*), and two application servers (*as1314* and *as1413*).
- The *cl1516* cluster has two servers (*bf01n015* and *bf01n016*), two cluster server names (*clsrv15* and *clsrv16*), two resource groups (*rg1516* and *rg1615*), and two application servers (*as1516* and *as1615*).
- Each of these servers will have one SP switch and one Ethernet adapter.

The servers within a cluster will have a shared external disk (Table 3.1).

- The *cl1314* cluster will have access to two volume groups, *havg1314* and *havg1413*.
- The *cl1516* cluster will have access to two volume groups, *havg1516* and *havg1615*.

Table 3.1   Scenario #2 Configuration

Cluster	Cluster Server	Ethernet	Switch	Resource Group	Volume Group	File System
cl1314	clsrv13	bf01n13	b_sw_013	rg1314	havg1314	/homehalocal
						/db1ha/svtha1/SRV130
						/db1ha/svtha1/SRV131
	clsrv14	bf01n14	b_sw_014	rg1413	havg1413	/db1ha/svtha1/SRV140
cl1516	clsrv15	bf01n15	b_sw_015	rg1516	havg1516	/db1ha/svtha1/SRV150
	clsrv16	bf01n16	b_sw_016	rg1615	havg1615	/db1ha/svtha1/SRV160
						/db1ha/svtha1/SRV161

In the initial target configuration, the db2nodes.cfg will have the following entries:

```
130 b_sw_013 0 b_sw_013
131 b_sw_013 1 b_sw_013
140 b_sw_014 0 b_sw_014
150 b_sw_015 0 b_sw_015
160 b_sw_016 0 b_sw_016
161 b_sw_016 1 b_sw_016
```

If one of the two servers within the cluster (for example, *cl1314*) has a failure, the other server in the cluster will acquire the resources that are defined in the resource group. The application server is then started on the server that has taken over the resource group. In our case, the application server that is started is DB2 UDB ESE for the instance *svtha1*.

In our example of a failover, DB2 UDB ESE is running on a server *clsrv13*; it has an NFS mounted home directory and a database located on the /db1ha/svtha1/SRV130 and /db1ha/svtha1/SRV131 file systems. This file system is in a volume group called *havg1314*. The *clsrv14* server is currently running DB2 for partition 140 and is ready to take over from the *clsrv13* server, if necessary. Suppose someone unplugs the *clsrv13* server.

The *clsrv14* server detects this event and begins taking over resources from the *clsrv13* server. These resources include the *havg1314* volume group, the file system, and the hostname *swserv13*. Once the resources are available on the *clsrv14* server, the application server start script runs. The instance ID can log on to the *clsrv14* server (now with an additional hostname *swserv13*) and can connect to the database. Remote clients can also connect to the database, because the hostname *swserv13* is now located on the *clsrv14* server.

User Setup and DB2 Installation

Now that the components of the LVM are set up, DB2 can be installed. The *db2setup* utility can be used to install and configure DB2. To illustrate the configuration better, we will define some of the components manually and will use the db2setup utility to install only the DB2 product and license.

All commands described in this chapter must be invoked by the root user. Although the steps used to install DB2 are outlined below, for complete details, refer to the DB2 UDB ESE for UNIX Quick Beginnings guide and to the DB2 UDB ESE Installation and Configuration Supplement guide.

Before running *db2icrt*, make sure that the $HOME directory for the instance is available and the *svtha1* id can write to the directory. Also make sure that a .profile file exists, because *db2icrt* will append to the file but will not create a new one.

For this example, we are using the *svtha1* id that already exists on the SP complex.

1. Mount the CD-ROM.

```
# crfs -v cdrfs -p ro -d'cd0' -m'/cdrom'
```

2. Install DB2 and set up the license key.

```
# cd /cdrom
# ./db2setup
Note: Select DB2 UDB Enterprise Server Edition and install.
```

3. Create the DB2 instance.

```
# cd /usr/opt/db2_08_01/instance
# ./db2icrt -u svtha1 svtha1
```

4. Test db2start and file system setup.

Because *db2icrt* adds only one line to the $HOME/sqllib/db2nodes.cfg file, we are required to update the file and add the other servers, such that the db2nodes.cfg file would look like the following:

```
130 b_sw_013 0 b_sw_013
131 b_sw_013 1 b_sw_013
140 b_sw_014 0 b_sw_014
150 b_sw_015 0 b_sw_015
160 b_sw_016 0 b_sw_016
161 b_sw_016 1 b_sw_016
```

We must also create the $HOME/.rhosts file because *db2start* and other DB2 programs require it to run remote shells from one server to another. The .rhosts file would look like the following in our example:

```
swserv13 svtha1
swserv14 svtha1
swserv15 svtha1
swserv16 svtha1
b_sw_013 svtha1
b_sw_014 svtha1
b_sw_015 svtha1
b_sw_016 svtha1
bf01n013 svtha1
bf01n014 svtha1
bf01n015 svtha1
bf01n016 svtha1
```

N O T E   Ensure the permissions on the $HOME/.rhosts files are correct (i.e., run chmod 600 .rhosts).

This is a good place to see whether *db2start* will work. Log on as the *svtha1* instance and run the *db2start* command. To test the file system setup on each server, try creating a database. Be sure to create it on /db1ha and not in $HOME, which is the default. Use the following command to create the database:

```
$ db2 create database testdb on /db1ha
```

Ensure that all errors are corrected before proceeding to the next step; also be sure to stop DB2 using the *db2stop* command before proceeding to the next step.

5. Install the DB2 HACMP scripts.

DB2 UDB EEE supplies sample scripts for failover and user-defined events. These files are located in the /usr/opt/db2_08_01/samples/hacmp/es directory.

In our example, we copied this directory to a special directory on the control workstation of the SP complex. Our example used /spdata/sys1/hacmp on the control workstation.

The *db2_inst_ha.local* script is the tool used for installing scripts and events on multiple database partitions in an HACMP ESE environment. It was used in the following manner for our examples:

```
# cd /spdata/sys1/hacmp
# db2_inst_ha.local svtha1 . 15-16 TESTDB
```

This will install the scripts in the directory /usr/bin to all the servers listed (i.e., servers 15 and 16) and prepare them to work with the database TESTDB. Note that the database name needs to be in uppercase. The server selection can also be written in the form "15,16" if you want to copy the files to specific servers.

When the application server is set up and the start and stop scripts are defined, they will call /usr/bin/rc.db2pe with a number of parameters.

> **N O T E** The start and stop scripts that are called from the application server must exist on both servers and have the same name. They do not need to have the same content if, for example, some customizing is needed.

The *db2_inst_ha.local* script also copies over the HACMP/ES event stanzas. These events are defined in the db2_event_stanzas file. One example is the DB2_PROC_DOWN event, which will restart DB2 if it terminates for some reason.

> **N O T E** DB2 will also restart if terminated by the *db2stop* or *db2stop force* commands. To stop DB2 without triggering a failure event, use the *ha_db2stop* command.

6. Test a failover of the resources on *bf01n015* to *bf01n016*.

On the *bf01n015* server:

```
# unmount /db1ha/svtha1/SRV150
# varyoffvg havg1516
```

On the *bf01n016* server:

```
# varyonvg havg1516
# mount /db1ha/svtha1/SRV150
```

> **N O T E** These are the actual steps that the HACMP software takes during failover of the necessary file systems.

Once DB2 HACMP is configured and set up, any changes made (for example, to the ID, groups, AIX system parameters, or the level of DB2 code) must be done on all servers. Following are some examples:

- The HACMP cluster is active on the *bf01n015* server, and the password is changed on that server. When failover happens to the *bf01n016* server and the user tries to log on, the new password will not work. Therefore, the administrator must ensure that passwords are kept synchronized.
- If the ulimit parameter on the *bf01n015* server is changed, it must also be changed on the *bf01n016* server. For example, suppose the file size is set to unlimited on the *bf01n015* server. When a failover happens to the *bf01n016* server and the user tries to access a file that is greater than the default size of 1 GB, an error is returned.
- If the AIX parameter *maxuproc* is changed on the *bf01n015* server, it also must be changed on the *bf01n016* server. When a failover occurs and DB2 begins running on the *bf01n016* server, it may reach the *maxuproc* value and return errors.
- If non-DB2 software is installed on the *bf01n015* server but not on the *bf01n016* server, the software will not be available when a failover takes place.
- Suppose that the database manager configuration parameter *svcename* is used, and that /etc/services is updated on the *bf01n015* server. If the *bf01n016* server does not receive the same update and a failover occurs, the DB2 server will report warnings during *db2start*, and will not start up the TCP/IP communications listeners, and DB2 clients will report errors.

High Availability on the Windows Operating System

Microsoft Cluster Service (MSCS) is a feature of Windows NT Server, Windows 2000 Server, and Windows .NET Server operating systems. It is the software that supports the connection of two servers (up to four servers in DataCenter Server) into a cluster for high availability and easier management of data and applications.

MSCS can also automatically detect and recover from server or application failures. It can be used to move server workloads to balance machine utilization and to provide for planned maintenance without downtime.

DB2 MSCS Components

A cluster is a configuration of two or more servers, each of which is an independent computer system. The cluster appears to network clients as a single server.

The servers in an MSCS cluster are connected using one or more shared storage buses and one or more physically independent networks. A network that connects only the servers but does not connect the clients to the cluster is referred to as a *private network*. The network that supports client connections is referred to as the public network. There are one or more local disks on each server. Each shared storage bus attaches to one or more disks. Each disk on the shared bus is owned by only one server of the cluster at a time. The DB2 software resides on the local disk. DB2 database files (tables, indexes, log files, etc.) reside on the shared disks. Because MSCS does not support the use of raw partitions in a cluster, it is not possible to configure DB2 to use raw devices in an MSCS environment.

The DB2 Resource

In an MSCS environment, a resource is an entity that is managed by the clustering software. For example, a disk, an IP address, or a generic service can be managed as a resource. DB2 integrates with MSCS by creating its own resource type called *DB2*. Each DB2 resource manages a DB2 instance and when running in a partitioned database environment, each DB2 resource manages a database partition. The name of the DB2 resource is the instance name, although in the case of a partitioned database environment, the name of the DB2 resource consists of both the instance name and the partition number.

Pre-Online and Post-Online Scripts

You can run scripts both before and after a DB2 resource is brought online. These scripts are referred to as *pre-online* and *post-online scripts*. Pre-online and post-online scripts are .BAT files that can run DB2 and system commands.

In a situation when multiple instances of DB2 may be running on the same machine, you can use the pre-online and post-online scripts to adjust the configuration so that both instances can be started successfully. In the event of a failover, you can use the post-online script to perform manual database recovery. Post-online scripts can also be used to start any applications or services that depend on DB2.

The DB2 Group

Related or dependent resources are organized into resource groups. All resources in a group move between cluster servers as a unit. For example, in a typical DB2 single-partition cluster environment, there will be a DB2 group that contains the following resources:

1. DB2 resource. The DB2 resource manages the DB2 instance.
2. IP Address resource. The IP Address resource allows client applications to connect to the DB2 server.
3. Network Name resource. The Network Name resource allows client applications to connect to the DB2 server by using a name, rather than an IP address. The Network Name resource has a dependency on the IP Address resource. The Network Name

resource is optional. (Configuring a Network Name resource may affect the failover performance.)

4. One or more Physical Disk resources. Each Physical Disk resource manages a shared disk in the cluster.

> **N O T E**   The DB2 resource is configured to depend on all other resources in the same group, so the DB2 server can be started only after all other resources are online.

Two types of configuration are available:

- Hot standby
- Mutual takeover

In a partitioned database environment, the clusters do not all have to have the same type of configuration. You can have some clusters that are set up to use hot standby and others that are set up for mutual takeover. For example, if your DB2 instance consists of five workstations, you can have two machines set up to use a mutual takeover configuration, two to use a hot-standby configuration, and one machine not configured for failover support.

Hot standby configuration   In a hot standby configuration, one machine in the MSCS cluster provides dedicated failover support, and the other machine participates in the database system. If the machine participating in the database system fails, the database server on it will be started on the failover machine. If, in a partitioned database system, you are running multiple logical database partitions on a machine and it fails, the logical database partitions will be started on the failover machine.

Mutual takeover configuration   In a mutual takeover configuration, both workstations participate in the database system (i.e., each machine has at least one database server running on it). If one of the workstations in the MSCS cluster fails, the database server on the failing machine will be started to run on the other machine. In a mutual takeover configuration, a database server on one machine can fail independently of the database server on another machine.

Clustered Servers for High Availability

In this example, we define a dbclust cluster. The members of the cluster are serv1 and serv2. Clients communicate over the public network to the cluster through the IP address assigned to the cluster's host name. The cluster's host name can be assigned to only one member of the cluster at any given time but can move to any member of the cluster. The shared storage is accessible to all members in the cluster but can be assigned to only one member server at any given time. The member servers use a private network to check on the vitality of other members in the cluster (it is called the server's *heartbeat*).

The basic components consist of two servers that establish a cluster when MSCS software is installed and configured on both servers. Prior to installing the MSCS software, these two servers must be able to communicate with each other over a network.

Highly recommended is a dedicated private network between the two servers that can be used to communicate their heartbeats without interference from traffic on the public network. Both servers must also have access to shared storage.

The MSCS software configuration process will create several default cluster resource types. These include a network name, an IP address, and at least one physical disk that is referred to as the *quorum drive* and usually assigned the Q: drive letter. The network name represents the cluster's host name that is registered in DNS and assigned the IP address. The primary purpose of the cluster's network name is to manage the cluster by a DNS name.

Before Installing Microsoft Cluster Service

Prior to installing and configuring the MSCS software, there are a number of pre-installation tasks that need to be addressed.

- Verify the hardware compatibility list prior to performing the install.
- Verify that your system or components are on the Hardware Compatibility List (HCL) as part of your planning effort. (Microsoft maintains a HCL specifically for cluster implementations. The HCL includes both complete systems and system components that are certified for MSCS.)
- Verify that each server can access the storage once shared storage is physically connected to all servers in the cluster.
- Verify that all of the shared disks that will be used in the cluster are defined as type basic, have a drive letter assigned, are formatted, and contain no mounted volumes because MSCS does not support dynamic disk volumes, physical disk names, mounted volumes, or raw devices.
- Verify that you are not using Network Adapter Fault Tolerance or Load Balancing for the Private Network adapters because MSCS does not support this type of configuration for private heartbeat communications and provides for fault tolerance by using one or more public networks as a backup to the private heartbeat network.
- Verify the order in which your network connections are accessed by DNS and network services. Select Start, Setting, Control Panel, Network and Dial-up Connections, Advanced, Advanced Settings. Verify that the public network connections are listed first.
- Verify that no other client, service, or protocol network components are used by the private network connection except Internet Protocol (TCP/IP). Select Start, Setting, Control Panel, Network and Dial-up Connections, Private LAN, Properties and scroll the list found on the properties dialog.

- Verify that your private network connection has a static TCP/IP address. Select Start, Setting, Control Panel, Network and Dial-up Connections, Private LAN, Properties, Internet Protocol (TCP/IP), Properties.
- Verify that NetBIOS over TCP/IP is disabled. Select Start, Setting, Control Panel, Network and Dial-up Connections, Private LAN, Properties, Internet Protocol (TCP/IP), Properties, Advanced, WINS.
- Verify that the Link Speed & Duplex on the private network adapter is set to 10Mbps/Half Duplex. Select Start, Setting, Control Panel, Network and Dial-up Connections, Private LAN, Properties, Configure, Advanced, Link Speed & Duplex.

Installing Microsoft Cluster Service

If the MSCS was installed as part of the initial operating system load, you can start the Cluster Service Configuration Wizard by selecting the Control Panel, Add/Remove Programs, Add/Remove Windows Components, Configure.

If the MSCS was not installed as part of the initial operating system load, you can install it by selecting Control Panel, Add/Remove Programs, Add/Remove Windows Components, Components, and the Cluster Service Configuration Wizard will start as part of this installation process.

Tasks to be performed during the installation and configuration using the Cluster Service Configuration Wizard:

- Create a new cluster or join an existing cluster. Because this is the first node in the cluster, we will create a new cluster.
- Define the cluster name, in this case, dbclust. This will be the name we use to manage the cluster, either locally or remotely, with the MSCS Cluster Administrator.
- Create a domain user account that will be used to run the Cluster Service and add this account to the local Administrators Group. If possible, set the account password to never expire. Otherwise, be aware that you will need to change the password within the Services Microsoft Management Console (MMC) when the account password expires.
- The Cluster Service Configuration Wizard presents a list of all disks on the shared storage that are supported by the Clustering Service. If your storage does not appear as expected, go back to the preinstall tasks and verify that the storage is configured correctly.
- Select the disk partition that will be used for the quorum drive.
- Select the network connection that will be used for the private heartbeat communications.
- Select All communications (mixed network). This will enable the public network connection to work as a backup to the private heartbeat network.
- Verify that the private network connection has the priority for internal cluster communication.

- Assign a TCP/IP address to the cluster. This address will be used to manage the cluster over the public network. As the cluster moves from one server to another, this address, along with the cluster name, moves as well.
- If the Cluster Service Configuration Wizard is successful, you will see this final confirmation that the cluster service has successfully started. At this point, the shared storage is managed by the Cluster Service, and the other servers can be booted.
- Once the cluster has been created, you can open the Cluster Administrator MMC and see the default Cluster Group containing the Cluster Name, Cluster IP Address, and Disk Q: quorum drive.
- Start the Cluster Service Configuration Wizard on the next server that will be added to the cluster.
- Joining an existing cluster requires that we enter the cluster name.
- Enter the password for the domain user account that was created to run the MSCS service and added to the local Administrators group.

As each individual node is added to the cluster, it will appear within the MSCS Cluster Administrator. We can see that both serv1 and serv2 are now members of the cluster dbclust from the left panel.

After Installing Microsoft Cluster Service

Once the MSCS software has been installed on all servers within the cluster, we need to perform post-install tasks to verify that everything is in working order. To prepare for these tasks, we will consolidate all of the resources into one group and rename the clusters quorum drive from Disk Q: to a more meaningful name.

- Consolidating the Physical Disks resources
- Renaming the quorum drive resource
- Moving the Cluster Group
- Initiating failure on the Cluster Group resources
- Testing the Cluster Group

The following is a list of tests that can be performed to verify that the Cluster Service is working properly.

Test 1   Logon to the first server in the cluster, verify that the Cluster Group is currently online at this server, and open a Windows command prompt. Verify that you can ping the Cluster Group by IP address and name. Verify that you can access the quorum drive (Disk Q:). Move the Cluster Group to another member in the cluster and repeat.

- Ping 192.168.1.51
- Ping DBCLUST
- DIR Q:

Test 2   Logon to a server that is not a member of the cluster, verify that the Cluster Group is currently online at the primary server, and open a Windows command prompt. Verify that you can ping the Cluster Group by IP address and name. Verify that you can access the quorum drive. Do this while moving the Cluster Group from one member of the cluster to another.

- Ping 192.168.1.51 –t
- Ping DBCLUST –t
- NET USE Q: \\dbclust\q$

Test 3   Logon to a client that will use the resources of this cluster, verify that the Cluster Group is currently online at the primary server, and open a Windows command prompt. Verify that you can ping the Cluster Group by IP Address and Cluster Name. Verify that you can access the quorum drive.

- Ping 192.168.1.51 –t
- Ping DBCLUST –t
- NET USE Q: \\dbclust\q$

Before Enabling DB2 MSCS Support

There are tasks that should be performed prior to enabling DB2 UDB HA support with MSCS.

- Install DB2 on a local (non-clustered) drive on all servers that will participate in the cluster.
- Create DB2 instance on the shared storage.
- Configure the DB2 instance that will be clustered to start manually in the Windows Services dialog.
- Enable DB2 to fall back to the primary server as soon as the primary server is available. You may also want DB2 to move back and forth between servers for testing purposes only. To accomplish this, you must set the DB2 registry variable DB2_FALLBACK to YES.

```
db2set DB2_FALLBACK=YES
```

- Create database on the shared storage.

Enabling DB2 MSCS Support

Enabling DB2 MSCS support includes the following:

- Enable a DB2 instance
- Modify the DB2 MSCS configuration file
- Modify DB2 dependencies
- Modify DAS restart option
- Implement pre-online and post-online scripts

High Availability on Sun Solaris

Although there are a number of methods to increase availability for a data service, the most common is an HA cluster. A cluster, when used for HA, consists of two or more machines, a set of private network interfaces, one or more public network interfaces, and some shared disks. This special configuration allows a data service to be moved from one machine to another. By moving the data service to another machine in the cluster, it should be able to continue providing access to its data. Moving a data service from one machine to another is called a *failover*.

The private network interfaces are used to send heartbeat messages, as well as control messages, among the machines in the cluster. The public network interfaces are used to communicate directly with clients of the HA cluster. The disks in an HA cluster are connected to two or more machines in the cluster, so that if one machine fails, another machine has access to them.

A data service running on an HA cluster has one or more logical public network interfaces and a set of disks associated with it. The clients of an HA data service connect via TCP/IP to the logical network interfaces of the data service only. If a failover occurs, the data service, along with its logical network interfaces and set of disks, are moved to another machine.

One of the benefits of an HA cluster is that a data service can recover without the aid of support staff, and it can do so at any time. Another benefit is redundancy. All of the parts in the cluster should be redundant, including the machines themselves. The cluster should be able to survive any single point of failure.

Even though HA data services can be very different in nature, they have some common requirements. Clients of an HA data service expect the network address and host name of the data service to remain the same and expect to be able to make requests in the same way, regardless of which machine the data service is on.

Consider a Web browser that is accessing an HA Web server. The request is issued with a URL (Uniform Resource Locator), which contains both a host name and the path to a file on the Web server. The browser expects both the host name and the path to remain the same after a failover of the Web server. If the browser is downloading a file from the Web server and the server is failed over, the browser will need to reissue the request.

Availability of a data service is measured by the amount of time the data service is available to its users. The most common unit of measurement for availability is the percentage of "up time"; this is often referred to as the *number of nines*:

> 99.99% => service is down for (at most) 52.6 minutes/year
> 99.999% => service is down for (at most) 5.26 minutes/year
> 99.9999% => service is down for (at most) 31.5 seconds/year

Hot Standby

Hot standby is the simplest HA cluster topology. In this scenario, the primary machine is hosting the production database instance and associated resources. A second idle machine is available to host the production database instance and associated resources, should a failure occur on the primary machine. The second machine can also be running a workload (perhaps another DB2 instance) in order to maximize resource use.

Mutual Takeover

In the mutual takeover case, you envision a cluster of N servers as $N/2$ pairs of servers. Server number N is responsible for failover support of server number $N+1$; server number $N+2$ is responsible for failover support of server number $N+3$; and so on until you reach the Nth server.

Note that this scenario requires that N be an even number.

The advantage of this configuration is that in the normal (non-failure) case, all machines are hosting database resources and are performing productive work. The primary disadvantage is that, during the failure period (the period after one of the hardware resources has failed and before its repair), there is one server that is required to support, on average, twice the workload of any other physical server.

Mutual takeover $(N + 1)$ *Single defined server serves as standby.* This case relies on an N server cluster, with one defined server as the standby for all N servers. The advantage of this scenario is that there is no performance degradation during the failure (the period after one of the hardware resources has failed and before its repair). The primary disadvantage is that approximately $1 / (N + 1)$ of the aggregate physical computing resource goes unused during the normal operation.

Pair + M $(N + M)$ *M defined servers serve as the hot standby for each N server.* This case relies on an N server cluster, with M defined servers as the hot standby for each of the N servers. Essentially, this is the default cluster topology configured by the regdb2udb, where N is equal to the number of physical servers in the cluster and M is equal to $N - 1$. The prime advantage of this configuration is that the environment is fully redundant; up to $N - 1$ server failures can be tolerated while still maintaining full database access (subject, of course, to increased query response times due to capacity constraints when there are fewer than N servers in the cluster). In this way, DB2 UDB ESE, used in conjunction with Sun Cluster 3.0, ensures full database software redundancy and is most appropriate for environments requiring the highest degree of availability.

Fault Tolerance

Another way to increase the availability of a data service is fault tolerance. A fault tolerant machine has all of its redundancy built in and should be able to withstand a single failure of any part, including CPU and memory. Fault-tolerant machines are most often used in niche markets and are usually expensive to implement. An HA cluster with machines in different geographical locations has the added advantage of being able to recover from a disaster affecting only a subset of those locations.

An HA cluster is the most common solution to increase availability because it is scalable, easy to use, and relatively inexpensive to implement.

Failover

Sun Cluster 3.0 provides HA by enabling application failover. Each server is periodically monitored, and the cluster software automatically relocates a cluster-aware application from a failed primary server to a designated secondary server. When a failover occurs, clients may experience a brief interruption in service and may have to reconnect to the server.

However, they will not be aware of the physical server from which they are accessing the application and the data. By allowing other servers in a cluster automatically to host workloads when the primary server fails, Sun Cluster 3.0 can significantly reduce downtime and increase productivity.

Multihost Disks

Sun Cluster 3.0 requires multihost disk storage. This means that disks can be connected to more than one server at a time. In the Sun Cluster 3.0 environment, multihost storage allows disk devices to become highly available. Disk devices that reside on multihost storage can tolerate single-server failures because there is still a physical path to the data through the alternate server. Multihost disks can be accessed globally through a primary server. If client requests are accessing the data through one server and that server fails, the requests are switched over to another server that has a direct connection to the same disks. A volume manager provides for mirrored or RAID 5 configurations for data redundancy of the multihost disks.

Currently, Sun Cluster 3.0 supports Solstice DiskSuite and VERITAS Volume Manager as volume managers. Combining multihost disks with disk mirroring and striping protects against both server failure and individual disk failure.

Global Devices

Global devices are used to provide cluster-wide HA access to any device in a cluster, from any server, regardless of the physical device location. All disks are included in the global namespace with an assigned device ID (DID) and are configured as global devices. Therefore, the disks themselves are visible from all cluster servers.

File Systems/Global File Systems

A cluster or global file system is a proxy between the kernel (on one server) and the underlying file system volume manager (on a server that has a physical connection to one or more disks). Cluster file systems are dependent on global devices with physical connections to one or more servers. They are independent of the underlying file system and volume manager. Currently, cluster file systems can be built on UFS, using either Solstice DiskSuite or VERITAS Volume Manager. The data becomes available to all servers only if the file systems on the disks are mounted globally as a cluster file system.

Device Group

All multihost disks must be controlled by the Sun Cluster framework. Disk groups, managed by either Solstice DiskSuite or VERITAS Volume Manager, are first created on the multihost disk. Then they are registered as Sun Cluster disk device groups. A disk device group is a type of global device.

Multihost device groups are HA. Disks are accessible through an alternate path if the server currently mastering the device group fails. The failure of the server mastering the device group does not affect access to the device group, except for the time required to perform the recovery and consistency checks. During this time, all requests are blocked (transparently to the application) until the system makes the device group available.

Resource Group Manager

The Resource Group Manager (RGM) provides the mechanism for HA and runs as a daemon on each cluster server. It automatically starts and stops resources on selected servers according to preconfigured policies. The RGM allows a resource to be highly available in the event of a server failure or to reboot by stopping the resource on the affected server and starting it on another. The RGM also automatically starts and stops resource-specific monitors that can detect resource failures and relocate failing resources onto another server.

Data Services

The term *data service* is used to describe a third-party application that has been configured to run on a cluster, rather than on a single server. A data service includes the application software and Sun Cluster 3.0 software that starts, stops, and monitors the application. Sun Cluster 3.0 supplies data service methods that are used to control and monitor the application within the cluster. These methods run under the control of the RGM, which uses them to start, stop, and monitor the application on the cluster servers. These methods, along with the cluster framework software and multihost disks, enable applications to become HA data services. As HA data services, they can prevent significant application interruptions after any single failure within the cluster, regardless of whether the failure is on a server, on an interface component, or in the application itself. The RGM also manages resources in the cluster, including network resources (logical host names and shared addresses) and application instances.

Resource Type, Resource, and Resource Group

A resource type is made up of the following:

1. A software application to be run on the cluster.
2. Control programs used as callback methods by the RGM to manage the application as a cluster resource.
3. A set of properties that form part of the static configuration of a cluster.

The RGM uses resource type properties to manage resources of a particular type.

A resource inherits the properties and values of its resource type. It is an instance of the underlying application running on the cluster. Each instance requires a unique name within the cluster. Each resource must be configured in a resource group. The RGM brings all resources in a group, online and offline, together on the same server. When the RGM brings a resource group online or offline, it invokes callback methods on the individual resources in the group.

The servers on which a resource group is currently online are called its *primary servers*, or its *primaries*. A resource group is mastered by each of its primaries. Each resource group has an associated server list property, set by the cluster administrator, to identify all potential primaries or masters of the resource group.

High Availability with VERITAS Cluster Server

VERITAS Cluster Server (VCS) can be used to eliminate both planned and unplanned downtime. It can facilitate server consolidation and effectively manage a wide range of applications in heterogeneous environments.

VCS supports up to 32 server clusters in both Storage Area Network (SAN) and traditional client/server environments. VCS can protect everything from a single critical database instance, to very large multi-application clusters in networked storage environments. This section provides a brief summary of the features of VCS.

Failover

VCS is an availability clustering solution that manages the availability of application services, such as DB2 UDB, by enabling application failover. The states of each individual cluster server and its associated software services are regularly monitored. When a failure occurs that disrupts the application service (in this case, the DB2 UDB service), VCS and/or the VCS HA-DB2 Agent detect the failure and automatically take steps to restore the service. This can include restarting DB2 UDB on the same server or moving DB2 UDB to another server in the cluster and restarting it on that server. If an application needs to be migrated to a new server, VCS moves everything associated with the application (i.e., network IP addresses, ownership of underlying storage) to the new server so that users will not be aware that the service is actually running on another server. They will still access the service using the same IP addresses, but those addresses will now point to a different cluster server.

When a failover occurs with VCS, users may or may not see a disruption in service. This will be based on the type of connection (stateful or stateless) that the client has with the application service. In application environments with stateful connections (such as DB2 UDB), users may see a brief interruption in service and may need to reconnect after the failover has completed. In application environments with stateless connections (such as NFS), users may see a brief delay in service but generally will not see a disruption and will not need to log back on.

By supporting an application as a service that can be automatically migrated between cluster servers, VCS can not only reduce unplanned downtime, but can also shorten the duration of outages associated with planned downtime (i.e., for maintenance and upgrades). Failovers can also be initiated manually. If a hardware or operating system upgrade must be performed on a particular server, DB2 UDB can be migrated to another server in the cluster, the upgrade can be performed, and DB2 UDB can then be migrated back to the original server.

Applications recommended for use in these types of clustering environments should be crash tolerant. A crash tolerant application can recover from an unexpected crash while still maintaining the integrity of committed data.

Crash tolerant applications are sometimes referred to as *cluster friendly applications*. DB2 UDB is a crash tolerant application.

Shared Storage

When used with the VCS HA-DB2 Agent, VCS requires shared storage. Shared storage is storage that has a physical connection to multiple servers in the cluster. Disk devices resident on shared storage can tolerate server failures because a physical path to the disk devices still exists through one or more alternate cluster servers.

Through the control of VCS, cluster servers can access shared storage through a logical construct called *disk groups*. Disk groups represent a collection of logically defined storage devices whose ownership can be atomically migrated between servers in a cluster. A disk group can be imported to only a single server at any given time. For example, if Disk Group A is imported to Server1 and Server1 fails, Disk Group A can be exported from the failed server and imported to a new server in the cluster. VCS can simultaneously control multiple disk groups within a single cluster.

In addition to allowing disk group definition, a volume manager can provide for redundant data configurations, using mirroring or RAID 5, on shared storage. VCS supports VERITAS Volume Manager and Solstice DiskSuite as logical volume managers. Combining shared storage with disk mirroring and striping can protect against both server failure and individual disk or controller failure.

VERITAS Cluster Server Global Atomic Broadcast and Low Latency Transport

An interserver communication mechanism is required in cluster configurations so that servers can exchange information concerning hardware and software status, keep track of cluster membership, and keep this information synchronized across all cluster servers. The Global Atomic Broadcast (GAB) facility, running across a low-latency transport (LLT), provides the high-speed, low-latency mechanism used by VCS to do this. GAB is loaded as a kernel module on each cluster server and provides an atomic broadcast mechanism that ensures that all servers get status update information at the same time.

By leveraging kernel-to-kernel communication capabilities, LLT provides high-speed LLT for all information that needs to be exchanged and synchronized between cluster servers. GAB runs on top of LLT. VCS does not use IP as a heartbeat mechanism but offers two other, more reliable options. GAB with LLT can be configured to act as a heartbeat mechanism, or a GABdisk can be configured as a disk-based heartbeat. The heartbeat must run over redundant connections. These connections can either be two private Ethernet connections between cluster servers or one private Ethernet connection and one GABdisk connection. The use of two GABdisks is not a supported configuration because the exchange of cluster status between servers requires a private Ethernet connection.

For more information about GAB or LLT, or how to configure them in VCS configurations, please consult the VERITAS Cluster Server User's Guide for Solaris.

Bundled and Enterprise Agents

An agent is a program that is designed to manage the availability of a particular resource or application. When an agent is started, it obtains the necessary configuration information from VCS, then periodically monitors the resource or application and updates VCS with the status. In general, agents are used to bring resources online, take resources offline, or monitor resources and provide four types of services: start, stop, monitor, and clean.

Start and stop are used to bring resources online or offline, monitor is used to test a particular resource or application for its status, and clean is used in the recovery process.

A variety of bundled agents are included as part of VCS and are installed when VCS is installed. The bundled agents are VCS processes that manage predefined resource types commonly found in cluster configurations (i.e., IP, mount, process, and share), and they help to simplify cluster installation and configuration considerably. There are over 20 bundled agents with VCS.

Enterprise agents tend to focus on specific applications, such as DB2 UDB. The VCS HA-DB2 Agent can be considered an Enterprise Agent, and it interfaces with VCS through the VCS Agent framework.

VCS Resources, Resource Types, and Resource Groups

A resource type is an object definition used to define resources within a VCS cluster that will be monitored. A resource type includes the resource type name and a set of properties associated with the resource that are salient from an HA point of view. A resource inherits the properties and values of its resource type, and resource names must be unique on a cluster-wide basis.

There are two types of resources: persistent and standard (non-persistent). Persistent resources are resources such as network interface controllers (NICs) that are monitored but are not brought online or taken offline by VCS. Standard resources are those whose online and offline status is controlled by VCS.

The lowest level object that is monitored is a resource, and there are various resource types (e.g., share, mount). Each resource must be configured into a resource group, and VCS will bring all resources in a particular resource group online and offline together. To bring a resource group online or offline, VCS will invoke the start or stop methods for each of the resources in the group. There are two types of resource groups: failover and parallel. An HA DB2 UDB configuration, regardless of whether it is partitioned or not, will use failover resource groups.

A "primary" or "master" server is a server that can potentially host a resource. A resource group attribute called *systemlist* is used to specify which servers within a cluster can be primaries for a particular resource group. In a two-server cluster, usually both servers are included in the systemlist, but in larger, multiserver clusters that may be hosting several HA applications, there may be a requirement to ensure that certain application services (defined by their resources at the lowest level) can never fail over to certain servers.

Dependencies can be defined between resource groups, and VCS depends on this resource group dependence hierarchy in assessing the impact of various resource failures and in managing recovery. For example, if the resource group ClientApp1 cannot be brought online unless the resource group DB2 has already been successfully started, resource group ClientApp1 is considered dependent on resource group DB2.

Logical Hostname/IP Failover

A logical hostname, together with the IP address to which it maps, must be associated with a particular DB2 UDB ESE instance. Client programs will access the DB2 database instance using this logical hostname instead of the physical hostname of a server in the cluster. This logical hostname is the entry point to the cluster, and it shields the client program from addressing the physical servers directly. That is, this logical hostname/IP address is cataloged from the DB2 TCP/IP clients (via the catalog TCP/IP node DB2 command).

This logical hostname is configured as a logical hostname resource and must be added to the same resource group as the instance resource. In the case of a failure, the entire resource group, including the instance and the logical host name, will be failed over to the backup server. This floating IP setup provides HA DB2 service to client programs.

Ensure that this hostname maps to an IP address and that this name-to-IP address mapping is configured on all servers in the cluster, preferably in /etc/inet/hosts on each server. More information on configuration for public IP addresses can be found in the Sun Cluster 3.0 Installation Guide.

Considerations for High Availability with DB2 ESE

- The logical hostname/IP must be collocated with the instance to ensure that it will always be local to the DB2 instance.
- Ensure that the instance is not autostarted; the instance start and stop should be under the control of the Sun Cluster infrastructure.
- The DB2 registry setting DB2SYSTEM should refer to the logical hostname, rather than the physical hostname.
- Configure the $INSTHOME/sqllib/db2nodes.cfg file and the /etc/services file in order to allow for communications between databases partition.
- Ensure that the port range in the /etc/services file is sufficiently large to support all failover scenarios envisioned.
- File containers of DMS table spaces and containers of SMS table spaces need to reside on mounted file systems.
- The disks for the file system must be in a disk group of the logical host responsible for the database partitions that need them.

One Logical Hostname

The DB2-HA package will create one logical hostname resource for a particular DB2 UDB ESE instance, and this logical hostname resource is added to the same resource group as the first partition in the instance (as defined by the first entry in the $INSTHOME/sqllib/db2nodes.cfg). In this case, client programs will use the logical hostname to access this DB2 UDB ESE instance. Therefore, this partition will be the coordinator partition (regardless of where that particular DB2 partition is physically hosted). This is the default install behavior of the DB2-HA package and is the most common configuration scenario.

DB2 UDB ESE is designed with symmetrical data access across partitions in the sense that client programs may access any database partition as an entry point to the DB2 UDB ESE instance and receive the same result sets from their queries, regardless of the coordinator partition used to process the query. Thus, a DB2 UDB ESE installation provides access redundancy (when the DB2 UDB ESE instance exists initially on more than one physical server). Here, the client program can access the DB2 UDB ESE instance through a round-robin selection of all available physical server names for the instance (or for a subset, provided that the subset contains at least two distinct physical servers). In the case of a failover, the DB2 UDB ESE instance can be accessed through any of the remaining healthy host names/IP addresses.

N Logical Hostnames

If the demands of the application require access to a particular DB2 UDB ESE partition, a logical hostname can be associated with each partition. Using Sun Cluster 3.0 administrative commands, each logical hostname resource can be added and grouped with its corresponding DB2 partition resource.

Consequently, the logical hostname/IP address will failover, together with its associated DB2 UDB ESE partition resource. Thus, connections to a logical hostname/IP address will always be associated with a connection to a particular DB2 UDB ESE coordinator partition.

Sun Cluster 3.0 DB2-HA Agent—Packages

There are four methods that are used to control the way DB2 UDB is registered, removed, brought online, or taken offline in a Sun Cluster 3.0 environment. Note that, although there exist a number of other components in the package, only these four can be called directly.

`regdb2udb`

This method will register appropriate resources and resource groups for a specified instance. Note that it will not attempt to bring online any resources. This will usually be the first script called, because it will perform all necessary steps to prepare DB2 UDB for Sun Cluster 3.0 control.

`unregdb2udb`

This method will execute required Sun Cluster 3.0 commands in order to remove DB2-HA (including resources and groups registered for this instance) from the cluster. Essentially, this method is the inverse of *regdb2udb* and will be generally called if the instance is no longer required to be HA.

`onlinedb2udb`

This method will execute required Sun Cluster 3.0 commands in order to bring a DB2-HA instance online. It will not create any resources or resource groups.

`offlinedb2udb`

This method will execute required Sun Cluster 3.0 commands in order to bring a DB2-HA instance offline. It will not remove any resources or groups from the Sun Cluster 3.0 infrastructure.

Note the naming convention of the resources and resource groups and their structure. The instance we have made HA is clearly a two-database partition DB2 UDB instance. The partition numbers (also referred to as *DB2 logical database partition numbers*) are 0 and 1, and the instance name is db2inst1. For each partition, we can see that exactly one resource group is created, and within that resource group, there is exactly one resource (the HA hostname/IP address has been discussed earlier). This allows for fine-grained control of the movement of the DB2 UDB across the physical servers of the complex.

The naming system is rather mechanical and is chosen to ensure name uniqueness, regardless of the number of instances or partitions that are to be made HA.

The naming convention is as follows:

- The string "db2_"
- Followed by the name of the instance (in this case "db2inst1")
- Followed by the string "_"
- Followed by the partition number of the instance (note that, for a single-database partitioned instance, the partition number will be represented as the number 0)
- Followed by the string "_"
- Followed by the string "rs" to represent a resource, or the string "rg" to represent a resource group.

Note the one-to-one mapping of DB2 resources to DB2 resource groups (and of a particular DB2 instance's logical partition resources and the Sun Cluster 3.0 resources).

In addition, there is one HA hostname/IP address. This is the address that, for example, will be used by clients to catalog the databases in this instance. This hostname/IP address (if present) is always associated with the first DB2 resources group for the instance (first when reading the db2nodes.cfg file top to bottom). For the single-database partitioned, the address is associated with the only DB2 resource group defined for that instance.

Sample Configuration Sun Cluster 3.x and DB2 UDB

We will create a simple DB2 UDB environment on a Sun Cluster platform. The DB2 UDB instance name is *db2inst1*, and the HA hostname is *sc30*.

Assumptions

It is presumed that:

- The reader is familiar with the motivation for the implementation of an HA solution.
- The reader is familiar with the basic terminology in this field.
- The reader has some experience with DB2 UDB and with Sun Cluster.

> **N O T E**   When using Sun Cluster 3.0 or VCS, ensure that DB2 instances are not started at boot time by using the db2iauto utility, as follows:
>
> ```
> db2iauto -off InstName
> ```
>
> where InstName is the login name of the instance.

Installation of DB2 binary   The DB2 Universal Database setup utility will install the executable file on the path /opt/IBM/db2.

Prior to performing the install, you must ensure that this mount point is on a global device. This can be accomplished by mounting this path directly or by providing a symbolic link from this path to a global mount point.

For example, on one cluster server, run:

```
mkdir /global/scdg2/scdg2/opt/IBM/db2
```

On remaining cluster servers, run:

```
ln -s /global/scdg2/scdg2/opt/IBM/db2 /opt/IBM/db2
```

Besides /opt/IBM/db2, /var/db2 can also be placed on a global file system. Some profile registry values and environment variables are stored in the files in /var/db2. Use the db2setup tool to create the instance. Ensure that the instance is not autostarted; the instance start and stop should be under the control of the Sun Cluster infrastructure. Additionally, the DB2 registry setting DB2SYSTEM should refer to the logical hostname, rather than the physical hostname.

The DB2 binary should be installed on a global shared file system. You must also take steps to ensure that the license key is available in the case of failover. You can achieve this in one of two ways:

1. Install the license key of each machine in the cluster using the db2licm tool.
2. Mount the license key location as a global mount point (this location, at the time of writing, is /var/lum) and, afterward, install the license key on exactly one server in the cluster.

The /etc/services file reserves a range of ports required for DB2 UDB communications. Ensure that the port range is sufficiently large to support all failover scenarios envisioned. For simplicity, we recommend that you configure the port range to be as large as the number of database partitions in the instance. You must configure the same port range for all cluster servers in the cluster.

The entries that compose the db2node.cfg determine the logical-to-physical mapping of the DB2 logical database partition to the appropriate physical host.

For each database partition that is expected to be subjected to significant disk activity, it is strongly recommended that each partition exist on a physical server with at least one local cluster file system mount point (i.e., for which that physical server is the primary of the cluster file system mount point). The cluster must be configured to give the user remote shell access from every server in the cluster to every server in the cluster (this step is required for multiple database partitions only). Generally, this is accomplished through the creation of a .rhosts file in the instance home directory. When this is completed, remote shell commands should proceed unprompted, and the db2_all command should execute without error.

As instance owner, issue the following command:

```
db2_all date
```

This should return the correct date and time from each server. If not, you'll have to troubleshoot and solve this problem before proceeding.

For the instance in question, issue the following command (again, as the instance owner):

```
db2start
```

This should complete successfully. If it does not complete successfully at all servers, that likely means a configuration error. You must review the DB2 UDB ESE Quick Beginnings guide and resolve the problem before proceeding.

Next, attempt to stop the instance with the following command (again, as the instance owner):

```
db2stop
```

This should also complete successfully. Again, if for DB2 UDB ESE it does not complete successfully at all servers, that likely means a configuration error. You must review the DB2 UDB Quick Beginnings guide and resolve the problem before proceeding.

Once you've verified that the instance can be started and stopped, attempt to create the sample database (or an empty test database, if you prefer). Create the database on the path of the global device you plan to use for storage of the actual production database. When you're certain the create database command has completed successfully, remove the test or sample database, using the drop database command.

The instance is now ready to be made HA. Steps to configure:

Step #1   First, use the regdb2udb utility to register the instance with the Sun Cluster 3.0 infrastructure. Use the scstat commands to investigate the status of the cluster. We should see the necessary resources and resource groups registered.

```
sun-ha1 # /opt/IBM/db2/V8.1/ha/sc30/util/regdb2udb -a db2inst1 -h sc30
sun-ha1 # scstat -p
```

> **N O T E**   The result of the regdb2udb processing is that the appropriate DB2 resources and resource groups are created and registered with Sun Cluster 3.0.

Step #2 Next, use the onlinedb2udb utility to bring these registered resources online. Use the scstat commands to investigate the status of the cluster. We should see the necessary resources and resource groups registered.

```
sun-ha1 # /opt/IBM/db2/V8.1/ha/sc30/util/onlinedb2udb -a db2inst1 -h sc30
sun-ha1 # scstat -p
```

> **NOTE** The result of the online processing is that the db2inst1 instance (and its associated HA IP address) is online and under the control of Sun Cluster 3.0.

As a result of this, you should see the resources brought online at the appropriate server (for example, on the physical hostname sun-ha1, you should see that it hosts the HA IP address for sc30, as well as the processes for the instance db2inst1, database partition 0).

There are two more supplied scripts that we will now discuss: offlinedb2udb and unregdb2udb.

Typically, you may wish to take a DB2 instance offline in order to remove the DB2 resources from Sun Cluster 3.0 control. For example, you may wish to bring the database engine down for an extended period of time. Directly issuing the appropriate DB2 commands (for example, db2start, db2stop) will be ineffective, because Sun Cluster 3.0 will interpret the absence of resources caused by the successful completion of the db2stop command as a failure and attempt to restart the appropriate database instance resources.

Instead, you must bring the resources offline as follows:

```
sun-ha1 # offlinedb2udb -a db2inst1 -h sc30
sun-ha1 # scstat -p
```

As you can see from the scstat output, all resources are now offline. No resources associated with the instance db2inst1 should be present on either server, nor will Sun Cluster 3.0 take any action to protect this instance, should it be brought online manually (i.e., via db2start) and a failure occur.

Let's assume that you've decided to remove this instance permanently from Sun Cluster 3.0 monitoring and control. For this task, you may use the unregdb2udb method. Note that this method merely interfaces with Sun Cluster 3.0 in order to perform these tasks; the instance itself is neither dropped nor removed.

```
sun-ha1 # unregdb2udb -a db2inst1 -h sc30
sun-ha1 # scstat -p
```

Configuration of Multiple DB2 Instances

For each additional instance, including the DAS that you wish to make HA, you are required to execute the regdb2udb command to register the instance with Sun Cluster 3.0. If it is desired to enable multiple HA DB2 instances, each HA DB2 instance will require a distinct HA hostname/IP address. This HA hostname/IP address is identified uniquely with exactly one instance.

For the DAS instance, the DAS instance name is used as the instance name argument when running the regdb2udb command. For example:

```
sun-ha1 # /opt/IBM/db2/V8.1/ha/sc30/util/regdb2udb -a db2as -h
daslogicalhostname
```

Cluster Verification Testing

Testing is an important aspect of an HA cluster. The purpose of testing is to gain some confidence that the HA cluster will function as envisioned for various failure scenarios. What follows is a set of minimum recommended scenarios for cluster testing and verification. These tests should be run regularly to ensure that the cluster continues to function as expected. Timing will vary, depending on production schedules, the degree to which the cluster state evolves over time, and management diligence.

Test 1   In this test, we're performing Sun Cluster 3.0 management commands to ensure that the db2inst1 instance can be controlled correctly.

First, verify that the instance is accessible from the clients (or locally) and that various database commands complete successfully (for example, create database).

Take the db2_db2inst1_0-rs and sc30 resources offline, using the following:

```
scswitch -n -j db2_db2inst1_0-rs
scswitch -n -j sc30
```

Observe that the DB2 instance resources no longer exist on any server in the cluster, and the HA hostname sc30 is likewise inaccessible.

From the perspective of a client of this instance, the existing DB2 connections are closed, and new ones start up, pending the process to bring online the appropriate DB2 and IP resources.

Test 2   To return the resources to their previous states, bring them online with the following SC30 commands:

```
scswitch -e -j sc30
scswitch -e -j db2_db2inst1_0-rs
```

DB2 clients waiting in the previous test mode will be able to connect and resubmit transactions to pick up from the last failure. The client program must send retries to accomplish this.

Test 3   Test the failover of the DB2 instance and associated resources from sun-ha1 onto sun-ha2. At this point, the cluster is again at its initial state.

Bring the resources contained within the resource group db2_db2inst1_0-rg offline, using the commands described in Test 1.

Then move the containing resource group to the secondary server, using the following Sun Cluster 3.0 command:

```
scswitch -z -g db2_db2inst1_0-rg -h sun-ha2
```

Now attempt to enable the relevant resources, using the same commands described in Test 2.

You should see the DB2 resource for db2inst1 and the associated hostname/IP address now hosted by the secondary machine, sun-ha2. Verify by executing the scstat -p command.

Test 4   Here, test the failover capabilities of the Sun Cluster 3.0 software itself. Bring the resources back into their initial state (i.e., have the db2_db2inst1_0-rg hosted on sun-ha1).

Once the instance and its associated resources are hosted on the sun-ha1 machine, perform a power-off operation on that physical server. This will cause the internal heartbeat mechanism to detect a physical server failure, and the DB2 resources will be restarted on the surviving server.

Verify that the results are identical to those seen in Test 3 (i.e., the DB2 resources should be hosted on sun-ha2, and the clients should behave similarly in both cases).

Test 5   Bring the cluster back to its initial state. In this test, verify that the software monitoring is working as expected. To perform this test, you may issue commands as follows:

```
ps -ef | grep db2sysc
kill -9 <pid>
or
ps -ef | grep db2tcpcm
kill -9 <pid>
```

The Sun Cluster 3.0 monitor should detect that a required process is not running and attempt to restart the instance on the same server. Verify that this, in fact, does occur. The client connections should experience a brief delay in service while the restart process continues.

Note that there is a high number of distinct testing scenarios that can be executed, limited only by your resources and imagination. Those discussed here are the minimum you should run to test the correct functioning of the cluster.

High Availability on HP/UX

HP MC/ServiceGuard monitors the health of each server and quickly responds to failures in a way that minimizes or eliminates application downtime. MC/ServiceGuard is able to detect and respond automatically to failures in the following components:

- System processors
- System memory
- LAN media and adapters
- System processes
- Application processes

Application Packages

With HP MC/ServiceGuard, application services and all the resources needed to support the application are bundled into special entities called *application packages*. These application packages are the basic units that are managed and moved within an enterprise cluster. Packages simplify the creation and management of HA services and provide outstanding levels of flexibility for workload balancing.

Fast Detection of Failure, Fast Restoration of Applications

Within an enterprise cluster, HP MC/ServiceGuard monitors hardware and software components, detects failures, and responds by promptly allocating new resources to support mission-critical applications. The process of detecting the failure and restoring the application service is completely automated—no operator intervention is needed.

Recovery times for failures requiring the switch of an application to an alternate server will vary, depending on the software services being used by the application. For example, a database application that is using a logging facility would need to perform transaction rollbacks as part of the recovery process. The time needed to perform this transaction rollback would be part of the total time to recover the application. MC/ServiceGuard will detect the server failure, reconfigure the cluster, and begin executing the startup script for the application package on an alternate server in a short period of time.

Installation Outline for DB2 and MC/ServiceGuard

The following steps outline the installation process and configuration changes required for DB2 in an HA environment and summarize the full installation as documented.

- Create a volume group to put the shared logical volumes on /dev/db2.
- Create a logical volume on the new volume group, with a mountpoint, mounted under the shared logical volume /db2.
- Mount the shared logical volume.
- Install DB2 on the shared disk mounted as detailed in the DB2 UDB ESE Installation guide.
- Unmount the shared directories.
- Issue a "vgchange –a n /dev/db2"
- Issue a "vgchange –c y /dev/db2"
- Issue a "vgexport –m db2.map –s –p –v /dev/db2"

- Issue a "vgexport –m db2.map –s –p –v /dev/db2"
- FTP the db2.map file to the adoptive server.
- Telnet into the adoptive server.
- Create the /dev/db2 directory and group file with the name major and minor numbers.
- Issue a "vgimport –m db2.map –s –v /dev/db2"
- Mount /db2 to confirm the import was successful.
- Install DB2 UDB ESE.
- Once the shared file system can be mounted on both systems, set up and configure the MC/ServiceGuard scripts for DB2.

Configuring the Cluster

All of the MC/ServiceGuard scripts developed during the certification process have been provided in this document. The following section describes the creation and use of these scripts.

Create the ASCII cluster template file:

```
cmquerycl -v -C /etc/cmcluster/cluster.ascii -n ptac171 -n ptac178
```

Modify the template (cluster.ascii) to reflect the environment and to verify the cluster configuration:

```
cmcheckconf -v -C /etc/cmcluster/cluster.ascii
```

Create the cluster by applying the configuration file. This will create the binary file cmclconfig and automatically distribute it among the servers defined in the cluster:

```
cmapplyconf -v -C /etc/cmcluster/cluster.ascii
```

Start the cluster and check the cluster status. Test the cluster halt also:

```
cmruncl -v -n ptac171 -n ptac178
cmviewcl -v
cmhaltcl -f -v
cmruncl -n ptac171 -n ptac178
```

Configuring a ServiceGuard Package (on a Single Server)

Create the db2inst1 package configuration file and tailor to the test environment. Do not include the second server at this stage.

```
cd /etc/cmcluster
mkdir db2inst1
cmmakepkg -p db2inst1.conf          # Edit db2inst1.conf
```

Create the db2inst1 package control script and tailor to the test environment. Do not include application startup/shutdown, service monitoring, or relocatable IP address at this stage.

```
cd db2inst1
cmmakepkg -s db2inst1.cntl
```

Shut down cluster; verify and distribute the binary configuration files

```
cmhaltcl -f -v
cmapplyconf -v -C /etc/cmcluster/cluster.ascii -P \
/etc/cmcluster/db2inst1/db2inst1.conf
```

Test cluster and package startup. Shut down DB2 if running, unmount all logical volumes on /dev/db2, and deactivate the volume group first. Copy the db2inst1.cntl and db2inst1.ascii scripts into the /etc/cmcluster/db2inst1 directory.

```
cmruncl                     # Start cluster and package
cmviewcl -v                 # Check that package has started
```

Edit db2inst1.cntl and assign the dynamic IP address of the db2inst1 package.

```
cmhaltpkg db2inst1
vi db2inst1.cntl            # Edit to add package IP
cmrunpkg -v db2inst1        # Start DB2 Package
cmviewcl -v                 # Check package has started and clients
```

Enable switching to a local standby LAN card.

```
vi db2inst1.conf                    # Net switching enabled = YES
cmapplyconf -v -C /etc/cmcluster/cluster.ascii -P db2inst1.ascii
cmhaltcl -f -v
cmruncl -v
```

Configuring a ServiceGuard Package (Adding a Second Server)

Enable db2inst1 to switch to a second server by editing the package control file:

```
vi db2inst1.conf                    # add SERVER_NAME ptac178
cmapplyconf -v -C /etc/cmcluster/cluster.ascii -P db2inst1/
db2inst1.conf
cmhaltcl -f -v
cmruncl -v
```

Test package switch to ptac178 and back to ptac171

```
cmhaltpkg db2inst1
cmrunpkg -n ptac178 db2inst1        # Run package on Ptac178 and
cmmodpkg -e db2inst1                # run DB2 and check application
```

```
cmhaltpkg db2inst1                  # Enable package switching
cmrunpkg -n ptac171 db2inst1        # Run package on ptac171 and test
cmmodpkg -e db2inst1                # DB2 runs here
```

Configuring DB2 in the MC/ServiceGuard Environment

Once DB2 is installed and configured in the MC/ServiceGuard cluster, the DB2 package scripts can be configured.

In testing the MC/ServiceGuard integration with IBM engineers, the db2inst1.cntl file was configured such that the db2inst1 service has 0 restarts and will failover to the adoptive server in the case of a software or hardware failure. This number can be changed to suit the needs of each install. It is recommended that the restart value be left at 0. DB2 is a robust product, and if there is a failure, the probability of a successful restart is low. To ensure a stable DB2 operating environment, it is suggested that MC/ServiceGuard be allowed to move the db2inst1 package to an adoptive server in the case of any failure.

The DB2 daemons that are monitored are db2sysc, db2tcpcm, db2srvlst, db2resyn, db2gds, and db2ipccm. Testing was performed where the list of processes above was monitored, and just db2sysc was monitored. The testing results were the same. If any of the other DB2 processes failed, db2sysc failed, as well. Because the MC/ServiceGuard monitor script for db2inst1 was monitoring the db2sysc process, the db2inst1 package was moved to the adoptive server in the case of any DB2 process failing.

AVAILABILITY ENHANCEMENTS

In this section we will discuss the online utilities like table load, index rebuild, index create and the incremental maintenance of materialized query table during load append.

Online Table Load

When loading data into a table in Version 8, the table space in which the table resides will no longer be locked. Users have full read and write access to all the tables in the table space, except for the table being loaded. For the table being loaded, the existing data in the table will be available for read access if the load is appending data to the table.

These new load features significantly improve the availability of the data and help customers deal with the maintenance of large data volumes and shrinking maintenance windows.

ALLOW READ ACCESS

Load will lock the target table in a share mode. The table state will be set to both LOAD IN PROGRESS and READ ACCESS. Readers may access the non-delta portion of the data while the table is being loaded.

In other words, data that existed before the start of the load will be accessible by readers to the table; data that is being loaded is not available until the load is complete. LOAD TERMINATE or LOAD RESTART of an ALLOW READ ACCESS load may use this option; LOAD TERMINATE or LOAD RESTART of an ALLOW NO ACCESS load may not use this option. Furthermore, this option is not valid if the indexes on the target table are marked as requiring a rebuild.

When there are constraints on the table, the table state will be set to CHECK PENDING, as well as LOAD IN PROGRESS and READ ACCESS. At the end of the load, the table state LOAD IN PROGRESS will be removed but the table states CHECK PENDING and READ ACCESS will remain. The SET INTEGRITY command must be used to take the table out of CHECK PENDING. While the table is in CHECK PENDING and READ ACCESS, the non-delta portion of the data is still accessible to readers; the new (delta) portion of the data will remain inaccessible until the SET INTEGRITY command has completed. A user may perform multiple loads on the same table without issuing a SET INTEGRITY command. Only the original (checked) data will remain visible, however, until the SET INTEGRITY command is issued.

ALLOW READ ACCESS also supports modifiers. The load utility provides two options that control the amount of access that other applications have to a table being loaded.

1. The ALLOW NO ACCESS option locks the table exclusively and allows no access to the table data while the table is being loaded. This is the default.
2. The ALLOW READ ACCESS option prevents all write access to the table by other applications but allows read access to preloaded data. This section deals with the ALLOW READ ACCESS option.

> **N O T E**   Table data and index data that exist prior to the start of a load operation are visible to queries while the load operation is in progress.

The ALLOW READ ACCESS option is very useful when loading large amounts of data because it gives users access to table data at all times, even when the load operation is in progress. The behavior of a load operation in ALLOW READ ACCESS mode is independent of the isolation level of the application. That is, readers with any isolation level can always read the pre-existing data while the load operation is in progress. They will not be able to read the newly loaded data until the load operation has finished.

Read access is provided throughout the load operation, except at the very end.

Before data is committed, the load utility acquires an exclusive lock on the table. The load utility will wait until all applications that have locks on the table release them. This may cause a delay before the data can be committed. The LOCK WITH FORCE option may be used to force off conflicting applications and allow the load operation to proceed without having to wait.

Usually, a load operation in ALLOW READ ACCESS mode acquires an exclusive lock for a short amount of time; however, if the USE <tablespaceName> option is specified, the exclusive lock will last for the entire period of the index copy phase.

> **NOTE**
>
> 1. If a load operation is aborted, it remains at the same access level that was specified when the load operation was issued. So if a load operation in ALLOW NO ACCESS mode aborts, the table data is inaccessible until a load terminate or a load restart is issued. If a load operation in ALLOW READ ACCESS mode aborts, the pre-loaded table data is still accessible for read access.
> 2. If the ALLOW READ ACCESS option was specified for a load operation, it can also be specified for a load restart or load terminate operation. However, if the original load operation specified the ALLOW READ ACCESS option, the ALLOW NO ACCESS option cannot be specified for a load restart or load terminate operation.

The ALLOW READ ACCESS option is not supported if:

- The REPLACE option is specified. Because a load replace operation truncates the existing table data before loading the new data, there is no preexisting data to query until after the load operation is complete.
- The indexes have been marked invalid and are waiting to be rebuilt. Indexes can be marked invalid in a rollforward scenario or through the use of the db2dart command.
- The INDEXING MODE DEFERRED option is specified. This mode marks the indexes as requiring a rebuild.
- An ALLOW NO ACCESS load operation is being restarted or terminated. Until it is brought fully online, a load operation in ALLOW READ ACCESS mode cannot take place on the table.
- A load operation is taking place to a table that is in check-pending state and is not in read access state. This is also the case for multiple load operations on tables with constraints. A table is not brought online until the SET INTEGRITY statement is issued.

Generally, if table data is taken offline, read access is not available during a load operation until the table data is back online.

Building Indexes

Indexes are built during the build phase of a load operation. There are four indexing modes that can be specified in the LOAD command:

1. REBUILD. All indexes will be rebuilt.
2. INCREMENTAL. Indexes will be extended with new data.
3. AUTOSELECT. The load utility will automatically decide between REBUILD or INCREMENTAL mode. This is the default.
4. DEFERRED. The load utility will not attempt index creation if this mode is specified. Indexes will be marked as needing a refresh. The first access to such indexes that is unrelated to a load operation may force a rebuild. This option is not compatible with the ALLOW READ ACCESS option because it does not maintain the indexes, and index scanners require a valid index.

> **N O T E** You may decide to choose an indexing mode explicitly because the behavior of the REBUILD and INCREMENTAL modes are quite different.

Load operations that specify the ALLOW READ ACCESS option require special considerations in terms of space usage and logging, depending on the type of indexing mode chosen. The load utility keeps indexes available for queries, even while building new indexes.

When a load operation in ALLOW READ ACCESS mode specifies the INDEXING MODE INCREMENTAL option, the load utility will write some log records that protect the integrity of the index tree. The number of log records written is a fraction of the number of inserted keys and is a number considerably less than would be needed by a similar SQL insert operation. A load operation in ALLOW NO ACCESS mode with the INDEXING MODE INCREMENTAL option specified writes only a small log record beyond the normal space allocation logs.

When a load operation in ALLOW READ ACCESS mode specifies the INDEXING MODE REBUILD option, new indexes are built as a shadow, either in the same table space as the original index or in a system temporary table space. The original indexes remain intact and are available during the load operation, and they are replaced by the new indexes only at the end of the load operation, while the table is exclusively locked.

Incremental Maintenance of Materialized Query Tables During Load Append

A materialized query table is a dependent of an underlying table. Before Version 8, if data was appended to the underlying table during a load operation, the materialized query table was unavailable until the load completed and the materialized query table was maintained. Furthermore, the materialized query table was completely rebuilt, which was often a lengthy operation.

With Version 8, the materialized query table can remain available during the load append operation on the underlying table. When the load of the appended rows in the underlying table is complete, the materialized query table may be refreshed incrementally, using only the appended data, which significantly reduces the time to update it.

For example, if the materialized query table is an aggregate (automatic summary table), for rows appended to the underlying table that correspond to new groups in the aggregate, new summary rows will be inserted.

For appended rows that correspond to existing groups in the aggregate, existing rows will be updated. Although the aggregate table remains unavailable during this maintenance phase, when a small number of rows are appended to the underlying table (when compared with the size of the table), the time the aggregate is unavailable is reduced.

The ability to incrementally maintain a materialized query table is not restricted to aggregates. Many materialized query tables can be incrementally maintained.

These changes significantly improve the availability of materialized query tables to your users.

If the underlying table of an immediate refresh materialized query table is loaded using the INSERT option, executing the SET INTEGRITY statement on the dependent materialized query tables defined with REFRESH IMMEDIATE will result in an incremental refresh of the materialized query table. During an incremental refresh, the rows corresponding to the appended rows in the underlying tables are updated and inserted into the materialized query tables.

Incremental refresh is faster in the case of large underlying tables with small amounts of appended data. There are cases in which incremental refresh is not allowed, and full refresh (that is, recomputation of the materialized query table definition query) will be used.

When the INCREMENTAL option is specified but incremental processing of the materialized query table is not possible, an error is returned if:

- A load replace operation has taken place into an underlying table of the materialized query table or the NOT LOGGED INITIALLY WITH EMPTY TABLE option has been activated since the last integrity check on the underlying table. The materialized query table has been loaded (in either REPLACE or INSERT mode).
- An underlying table has been taken out of check-pending state before the materialized query table is refreshed by using the FULL ACCESS option during integrity checking.
- An underlying table of the materialized query table has been checked for integrity non-incrementally.
- The materialized query table was in check-pending state before migration.

- The table space containing the materialized query table or its underlying table has been rolled forward to a point in time, and the materialized query table and its underlying table reside in different table spaces.

If the materialized query table has one or more W values in the CONST_CHECKED column of the SYSCAT.TABLES catalog, and if the NOT INCREMENTAL option is not specified in the SET INTEGRITY statement, the table will be incrementally refreshed and the CONST_CHECKED column of SYSCAT.TABLES will be marked U to indicate that not all data has been verified by the system.

Online Table Reorganization

DB2 now provides two methods of reorganizing tables: online and offline.

- The online table reorganization allows applications to access the table during the reorganization. In addition, online table reorganization can be paused and resumed later by anyone with the appropriate authority by using the schema and table name.

  Online table reorganization is allowed only on tables with type-2 indexes and without extended indexes.
- The offline method provides faster table reorganization, especially if you do not need to reorganize LOB or LONG data. LOBS and LONG data are no longer reorganized unless specifically requested. In addition, indexes are rebuilt in order after the table is reorganized.

  Read-only applications can access the original copy of the table, except during the last phases of the reorganization, when the "shadow copy" replaces the original copy and the indexes are rebuilt.

Both online and offline reorganizations have been enhanced to improve support for multi-partition databases. You can reorganize a single partition, a set of partitions, or all partitions.

Online Index Reorganization

New for DB2 Version 8 is the ability to read and update a table and its existing indexes during an index reorganization, using the new REORG INDEXES command.

During online index reorganization, the entire index object (that is, all indexes on the table) is rebuilt. A "shadow copy" of the index object is made, leaving the original indexes and the table available for read and write access. Any concurrent transactions that update the table are logged. Once the logged table changes have been forward-fitted and the new index (the shadow copy) is ready, the new index is made available. While the new index is being made available, all access to the table is prohibited.

The default behavior of the REORG INDEXES command is ALLOW NO ACCESS, which places an exclusive lock on the table during the reorganization process, but you can also specify

ALLOW READ ACCESS or ALLOW WRITE ACCESS to permit other transactions to read from or update the table.

Indexes can now be created in large table spaces (formerly long table spaces). In situations where the existing indexes consume more than 32 GB, this will allow you to allocate sufficient space to accommodate the two sets of indexes that will exist during the online index reorganization process.

INDEXES ALL FOR TABLE table-name

This option specifies the table whose indexes are to be reorganized. The table can be in a local or a remote database.

ALLOW NO ACCESS

This option specifies that no other users can access the table while the indexes are being reorganized. This is the default.

ALLOW READ ACCESS

This option specifies that other users can have read-only access to the table while the indexes are being reorganized.

ALLOW WRITE ACCESS

This option specifies that other users can read from and write to the table while the indexes are being reorganized.

CLEANUP ONLY

When CLEANUP ONLY is requested, a cleanup rather than a full reorganization will be done. The indexes will not be rebuilt, and any pages freed up will be available for reuse by indexes defined on this table only.

The CLEANUP ONLY PAGES option will search for and free committed pseudo empty pages. A committed pseudo empty page is one where all the keys on the page are marked as deleted, and all these deletions are known to be committed.

The number of pseudo empty pages in an index can be determined by running runstats and looking at the NUM EMPTY LEAFS column in SYSCAT.INDEXES. The PAGES option will clean the NUM EMPTY LEAFS if they are determined to be committed.

The CLEANUP ONLY ALL option will free committed pseudo empty pages, as well as remove committed pseudo deleted keys from pages that are not pseudo empty. This option will also try to merge adjacent leaf pages if doing so will result in a merged leaf page that has at least PCTFREE free space on the merged leaf page, where PCTFREE is the percentage of free space defined for the index at index creation time. The default PCTFREE is 10%. If two pages can be merged, one of the pages will be freed. The number of pseudo deleted keys in an index, excluding those on pseudo empty pages, can be determined by running runstats, then selecting the NUMRIDS DELETED from SYSCAT.INDEXES. The ALL option will clean the NUM-RIDS DELETED and the NUM EMPTY LEAFS if they are determined to be committed.

Use the ALLOW READ ACCESS or ALLOW WRITE ACCESS option to allow other transactions either read-only or read-write access to the table while the indexes are being reorganized. Note that, while ALLOW READ ACCESS and ALLOW WRITE ACCESS allow access to the table, during the period in which the reorganized copies of the indexes are made available, no access to the table is allowed.

TABLE table-name

This option specifies the table to reorganize. The table can be in a local or a remote database. The name or alias in the form: schema.table-name may be used. The schema is the user name under which the table was created. If you omit the schema name, the default schema is assumed.

> **N O T E**   For typed tables, the specified table name must be the name of the hierarchy's root table.

You cannot specify an index for the reorganization of a multidimensional clustering (MDC) table. Also note that in-place reorganization of tables cannot be used for MDC tables.

INDEX index-name

This option specifies the index to use when reorganizing the table. If you do not specify the fully qualified name in the form schema.index-name, the default schema is assumed. The schema is the user name under which the index was created. The database manager uses the index to physically reorder the records in the table it is reorganizing.

For an inplace table reorg, if a clustering index is defined on the table and an index is specified, it must be a clustering index.

If the inplace option is not specified, any index specified will be used. If you do not specify the name of an index, the records are reorganized without regard to order. If the table has a clustering index defined, however, and no index is specified, the clustering index is used to cluster the table.

You cannot specify an index if you are reorganizing an MDC table.

INPLACE

Reorganize the table while permitting user access. Inplace table reorganization is allowed only on tables with type-2 indexes and without extended indexes.

ALLOW READ ACCESS

Allow only read access to the table during reorganization.

ALLOW WRITE ACCESS

Allow write access to the table during reorganization. This is the default behavior.

NOTRUNCATE TABLE

Do not truncate the table after inplace reorganization. During truncation, the table is S-locked.

START

Start the inplace REORG processing. Because this is the default, this keyword is optional.

STOP

Stop the inplace REORG processing at its current point.

PAUSE

Suspend or pause inplace REORG for the time being.

RESUME

Continue or resume a previously paused inplace table reorganization.

To clean up the pseudo empty pages in all the indexes on the EMPLOYEE table while allowing other transactions to read and update the table, enter:

```
db2 reorg indexes all for table homer.employee allow write access
    cleanup only pages
```

ABILITY TO USE db2dart

The db2dart is used to verify that the architectural integrity of a database is correct.

For example, this tool confirms that:

- The control information is correct.
- There are no discrepancies in the format of the data.
- The data pages are the correct size and contain the correct column types.
- Indexes are valid.

> **NOTE** If db2dart reports a problem with an index, use the tool's /MI option to mark the index as invalid. The index is rebuilt based on the value of the indexrec database and database manager configuration parameters.

You must run this tool on the DB2 server where the database resides. You must also ensure that there are no active connections to the database. (Use the LIST APPLICATIONS FOR DATABASE database-alias command and disconnect any applications that are listed.)

In a DB2 UDB Enterprise Server Edition (ESE) with multiple database partitions, db2dart must be run on each database partition. For information on db2dart options, type db2dart without any options.

```
db2dart
```

Help screen from db2dart:

```
                      DB2 V810    DB2DART HELP
Syntax:

                DB2DART <DB Alias> <option>  ...


Help:
/H                 Help. This help text.


Inspect Action:
/DB                (default) Inspects entire database.
/T                 Inspects a single table.  (See notes 1, 3)
/TSF               Inspects only the tablespace files and containers.
/TSC               Inspects a tablespace's constructs (but not its tables).
/TS                Inspects a single tablespace and its tables.
                   (/TSC and /TS require a tablespace id.  See notes 1, 2)
/ATSC              Inspect constructs of all tablespaces (but not their
                   tables).


Data Format Action:
/DD                Dumps formatted table data.  (See notes 1, 4)
/DM                Dumps formatted block map data (See notes 1, 4)
/DI                Dumps formatted index data.  (See notes 1, 4)
/DP                Dumps pages in hex format.   (See notes 1, 7)
/DTSF              Dumps formatted tablespace file information.
/DEMP              Dumps formatted EMP information for a DMS table.
                   (See notes 1, 3)
/DDEL              Dumps formatted table data in delimited ASCII format.
/DHWM              Dumps highwater mark information.  (See notes 1, 2)
/LHWM              Suggests ways of lowering highwater mark.
                   (See notes 1, 8)


(press <enter> for more text)
```

```
Repair Action: (MAKE SURE DATABASE IS OFFLINE)
/MI                 Mark index as invalid (make sure db is offline)
                    (See notes 1, 5)
/MT                 Mark table with drop-pending (unavailable) state.
                    (See notes 1, 6, 9.  Make sure db is offline.)
/IP                 Initialize data page of a table as empty.
                    (See note 9.  Make sure db is offline.)
/UBPF               Updates the bufferpool file with a new specification.


Change State Action: (MAKE SURE DATABASE IS OFFLINE)
/CHST               Change a state of the database.


(press <enter> for more text)


Input values options:
/OI object-id       Object ID
/TN table-name      Table name
/TSI tablespace-id  Tablespace ID
/ROW sum            (2) Check LF/LOB descriptors
                    (1) Check control info of varying types in rows
                    (see note 10)
/PS number          Page number to start with
                    (suffix page number with 'p' for pool relative)
/NP number          Number of pages
/V Y/N              Y or N for verbose option
/PW password        Contact DB2 service for valid password
/RPT path           Optional path to place report output file
/RPTN file-name     Optional name for report file
/CONN Y/N           Specify whether DB2DART processing includes operations
                    that connect to database (Y) or not (N).  Default (Y)
/SCR Y/M/N          (Y) normal output produced to screen
                    (M) minimize output to screen
                    (N) no output to screen
/RPTF Y/E/N         (Y) normal output produced to report file
                    (E) only error information to report file
                    (N) no report file output
/ERR Y/N/E          (Y) normal error log DART.ERR file
                    (N) minimize output to error log DART.ERR file
                    (E) minimize DART.ERR file output, minimize screen
                    output, only error information to report file
                    Default (Y)
/WHAT DBBP OFF/ON   Database backup pending state
                    (OFF) off state
                    (ON) on state
```

```
(press <enter> for more text)

Notes:
1. For actions that require additional input values for identifying the data
   to act on, the input values can be specified as arguments along with the
   action, or if not specified then you will be prompted for input values.
   This does not apply for actions /DDEL and /IP, the input values required
   will be prompted for.
2. Actions /TSC, /TS, /ETS, and /DHWM require 1 input value—the tablespace ID.
3. Actions /T and /DEMP require two input values consisting of tablespace ID,
   and either of table object ID or table name.
4. Actions /DD and /DI require five input values consisting of either table
   object ID or table name, tablespace ID, page number to start with, number
   of pages, and verbose choice.
5. Action /MI requires two input values consisting of tablespace ID and index
   object ID.
6. Action /MT requires three input values consisting of either table object
   ID or table name, tablespace ID, and password.
7. Action /DP requires three input values consisting of tablespace ID (DMS
   tablespace only), page number to start with, and number of pages.
8. Action /LHWM requires a tablespace ID and the number of pages for the
   desired highwater mark after lowering it.
9. For password required by some actions, please contact DB2 service.
10.For value options where unique values identify different choices for the
   option, sum up the values to get the combination of choices.
11.Default location for report output file is the current directory in a non-
   MPP environment, and in the db2dump directory in a MPP environment.
12.The scope of db2dart is single node.
13.In a MPP environment, you can use dart_all to invoke db2dart at all DB2
   logical nodes in a single invocation. As well, db2_all can be used.
_____
        D A R T   P R O C E S S I N G   C O M P L E T E   _____
```

You can use the db2dart tool to obtain information about a database's tables and table space. While many of the dump or inspection options can be run while a connection to the database exists, it is good practice to ensure that you have terminated all connections to the database prior to running db2dart.

The syntax of the db2dart command is:

```
db2dart database dart_command [command parameters] [global options ]
```

If you select a command that requires one or more parameters but do not specify them on the command line, db2dart will prompt you for the appropriate values.

Some of the more common command actions you will want to run:

`/DEMP`

This command dumps all the EMP pages for all data types (DAT, INX, LF, LOB, LOBA) for a given table. This command requires that you specify the table space ID (parameter /TSI) and either the table name (parameter /TN) or the table object ID (parameter /OI). Note that, if a table spans multiple table spaces (for example, longs or indices are in a different table space), you have to specify the "main" table space, not the "secondary" ones.

`/DTSF`

This command dumps formatted information on all the table spaces in the database. It doesn't require any options.

`/DP`

This command dumps a range of pages from a table space. It requires three parameters:

- the table space ID
- the starting page to dump
- the number of pages to dump

These are the command parameters that you would be likely to use:

`/OI <object ID>`

Object ID of the table.

`/TN <table name>`

Name of the table. This should match what's listed in SYSTABLES.

`/TSI <tablespace ID>`

The tablespace ID.

`/PS <page number>`

The page number at which to start dumping. For DMS table spaces, you can add the suffix p to signify a pool-relative page number.

`/NP <number of pages>`

The number of pages to dump.

By default, db2dart outputs to a file called *X.RPT* in the current directory:

```
On Windows NT/2000:
driver:\..\SQLLIB\<instance_name>\DARTnnnn\
On UNIX:
$DB2INSTANCE_HOME/sqllib/db2dump/DARTnnnn/
```

```
where
nnnn is the partition number, such as 0000, 0001, etc.
X is the name of the database being inspected.
```

You can change the name of this file by using the /RPTN option and adding /RPTN <filename> to the command line.

For example, to dump the information for the table TEST_1 in table space 9 in the TESTDB database and save the result in a file called MYDB.RPT:

```
db2dart TESTDB /DEMP /TN TEST_1 /TSI 9 /RPTN MYDB.RPT
```

Assuming that the table TEST_1 has an object ID of 6, the following command does the same thing:

```
db2dart TESTDB /DEMP /OI 6 /TSI 9 /RPTN MYDB.RPT
```

To dump 100 pages from table space ID 2 in the database TESTDB, starting from pool-relative page number 1000, with output going to MYDB.RPT:

```
db2dart TESTDB /DP /TSI 2 /PS 1000p /NP 100 /RPTN MYDB.RPT
```

To verify that a container was created as a striped container, you can use the /DTSF option of DB2DART to dump table space and container information, then look at the type field for the container in question.

If the container type is file, the DMS table space was created without striping or DB2_STRIPED_CONTAINERS is not set. If the container type is striped file, the DMS table space was created with striping or the DB2_STRIPED_CONTAINERS is already set to ON.

Container Type	DB2_STRIPED_CONTAINERS	DMS Table Space
file	Registry is not set	Without striping
striped file	Registry is set to ON	Striping

As an example, a table space ts1 is created without striping:

```
db2 connect to sample
db2 "create tablespace ts1 managed by database
    using (file '/data/v8inst/dms/ts1.dat' 1000)"
db2 terminate

db2dart sample /DTSF
pg SAMPLE.RPT
...
```

```
Container list:
#            Total         Useable       Container     Container
             Pages         Pages         Type          Name
=======================================================================
0            1000          992           file          /data/v8inst/dsm/ts1.dat
Container checksum for disk space: 641033847
```

Now, table space ts2 is created with striping:

```
  db2set DB2_STRIPED_CONTAINERS=ON
  db2stop
  db2start
  db2 connect to sample
  db2 "create tablespace ts2 managed by database
      using (file '/data/v8inst/dms/ts2.dat' 1000)"
  db2 terminate

  db2dart sample /DTSF
  pg SAMPLE.RPT
  ...
Container list:
#            Total         Useable       Container     Container
             Pages         Pages         Type          Name
=======================================================================
0            1000          960           striped file  /data/v8inst/dsm/ts2.dat
Container checksum for disk space: 641168976
```

Let's take a look at a potential problem with corrupt indexes in DB2. In order to avoid this problem, you should go through the following steps:

Scenario #1: With rebuild all indexes Option

If you have run the db2uiddl optional migration step to rebuild all indexes immediately after migration, you should run:

```
db2dart <dbname> /ts /tsi 0
```

In the <DBNAME>.RPT file, there will be errors reported if there are any indexes that need to be rebuilt. There will also be the commands reported to the <DBNAME>.RPT file to mark the indexes as bad:

```
db2dart <dbname> /MI .....
```

The exact steps to follow are:

1. db2stop
2. db2dart <dbname> /ts /tsi 0

3. Check the <DBNAME>.RPT file for any errors and the commands to mark indexes as bad.

4. Run the db2dart <dbname> /mi ... commands as printed in the <DBNAME>.RPT file.

5. db2start

6. db2 restart database <dbname>

Scenario #2: Without rebuild all indexes Option

If you have not run db2uiddl immediately after migration:

```
db2dart <dbname> /db
```

Any indexes that db2dart identifies errors in should be marked as bad and rebuilt.

As above, there will be errors reported to the <DBNAME>.RPT file, as well as the commands to rebuild the offending indexes.

The exact steps to follow are:

1. db2stop

2. db2dart <dbname> /db

3. Check the <DBNAME>.RPT file for any errors and the commands to mark indexes as bad.

4. Run the db2dart <dbname> /mi ... commands as printed in the <DBNAME>.RPT file.

5. db2start

6. db2 restart database <dbname>

SUMMARY

With many features as discussed in this chapter, DB2's built-in planned and unplanned availability capabilities ensure that your business applications are available whenever you need them. Whether switching to a standby database server if an unexpected database failure occurs or carrying out online maintenance, DB2 makes sure all of your business applications remain available.

When defining a backup strategy, do not neglect planning for and testing your recovery from a backup image. It is a good practice to develop a recovery plan as part of the database development rather than after the first failure has occurred.

Database Security

This chapter discusses the following:

    1. Knowledge of external authentication mechanisms (LDAP, active server, etc.)
    2. Ability to implement data encryption

One of the most important responsibilities of the database administrator and the system administrator is database security. Securing your database involves the following activities:

- Preventing accidental loss of data or data integrity through equipment or system malfunction.
- Preventing unauthorized access to valuable data.
- Preventing unauthorized persons from committing mischief through malicious deletion or tampering with data.
- Monitoring data access by users.

You should start planning for security by:

- Defining your objectives for a database access control plan.
- Specifying who shall have access to what and under what circumstances.

SELECTING USER NAMES AND GROUP NAMES FOR DB2 INSTALLATION

Security issues are important to the DB2 Administrator from the moment the product is installed. During the installation process, DB2 requires a user name, a group name, and a password.

Recommendations

To control the proliferation of user names and group names that are able to modify the instance environment, you should change the default privileges granted to users after the installation because during the installation process, System Administration (SYSADM) privileges are granted by default to the users on the specific operating system.

- You should create new groups and passwords before creating the instances where the databases will reside.
- You should add only the required user(s) to the SYSADM group.
- To control the scope and authority of the actions that can be performed by user-defined functions (UDFs) and stored procedures, you should create a new user name in which fenced UDFs will execute differently than those of the DB2 instance or other database users.
- Because SYSADM privileges are the most powerful set of privileges available within DB2, you must check the following guidelines before creating any groups or user IDs:
  ○ Create a separate instance owner group per instance.
  ○ Create an instance owner user ID and define this user ID as a member of the instance owner group. For UNIX, you specify the instance owner when you create the instance.
  ○ Do not add new users to the instance owner group. (It is sometimes a good idea to have two or three, but not more than that.)
  ○ The user ID should always be associated with a password to enforce user authentication.
  ○ Do not use the instance owner user ID as the fenced ID.

> **N O T E**   On UNIX, user names must be in lower case.

For example, suppose you already created a user ID *dsnow* under a group called *dntsadm* (this is the DB2 instance owner ID and instance owner group), then later you decided to grant SYSADM authority to *tphan*. First, you must add the user tphan to the group *dntsadm*, then update the dbm cfg SYSADM_GROUP to *dntsadm* as needed (on UNIX, the database manager configuration for SYSADM_GROUP is automatically set to the instance owner group at instance creation time):

```
cat /etc/group | grep dntsadm

dntsadm:!:5000:dsnow

Now the system administrator just added tphan to the group dntsadm

cat /etc/group | grep dntsadm

dntsadm:!:5000:dsnow,tphan
```

```
db2 get dbm cfg | grep SYS

SYSADM group name               (SYSADM_GROUP)    =
SYSCTRL group name              (SYSCTRL_GROUP)   =
SYSMAINT group name             (SYSMAINT_GROUP)  =
Priority of agents              (AGENTPRI)        = SYSTEM

db2 update dbm cfg using SYSADM_GROUP dntsadm
db2 get dbm cfg | grep SYS

SYSADM group name               (SYSADM_GROUP)    = DNTSADM
SYSCTRL group name              (SYSCTRL_GROUP)   =
SYSMAINT group name             (SYSMAINT_GROUP)  =
Priority of agents              (AGENTPRI)        = SYSTEM
```

Table 4.1 shows a list of group names.

Table 4.1   Group Names Defined

Group Name	GID	Description
dntsadm	5000	DB2 Instance Owner Group
dntsas	5100	DB2 Administration Server Group
dntfadm	5200	DB2 Fence Administration Group
dntsdba	5300	DB2 DBA Group
dntabc	5400	DB2 User Group for Application abc
dntxyz	5500	DB2 User Group for Application xyz

Table 4.2 shows a list of user names.

Table 4.2   User Names Defined

User Name	UID	Default Shell	Home Directory	Group Primary	Group Secondary
dsnow	8000	/usr/bin/ksh	/dbhome/dsnow	dntsadm	dntsas, dntfadm
tphan	8001	/usr/bin/ksh	/dbhome/tphan	dntsadm	
dntas	8100	/usr/bin/ksh	/dbhome/dntas	dntsas	
dntudf	8200	/usr/bin/ksh	/dbhome/dntudf	dntfadm	

Table 4.2   User Names Defined (Continued)

User Name	UID	Default Shell	Home Directory	Group Primary	Group Secondary
dntdba	8300	/usr/bin/ksh	/dbhome/dntdba	dntsdba	
abcuser1	8400	/usr/bin/ksh	/apphome/abcuser1	dntabc	
xyzuser1	8500	/usr/bin/ksh	/apphome/xyzuser1	dntxyz	

User and Group Naming Rules

- Group names can contain up to 8 bytes.
- User IDs on UNIX-based systems can contain up to 8 characters.
- User names on Windows can contain up to 30 characters.
- When not using Client authentication, non-Windows 32-bit clients connecting to Windows NT, Windows 2000, Windows XP, and Windows .NET with user names longer than 8 characters are supported when the user name and password are specified explicitly.
- User IDs cannot:
  - Be USERS, ADMINS, GUESTS, PUBLIC, LOCAL, or any SQL reserved word.
  - Begin with IBM, SQL, or SYS.
  - Include accented characters.

> **N O T E**   Windows .NET Server is also known as Windows 2003 Server.

AUTHENTICATION METHODS

Access to an instance or a database first requires that the user be authenticated. The authentication type for each instance:

- Is set when the instance is created.
- Determines how and where a user will be authenticated.
- Is stored in the database manager configuration file at the server.
- Is set as one authentication type per instance, which covers access to all the databases under its control.

> **N O T E**   If you intend to access data sources from a federated database, you must consider data source authentication processing and definitions for federated authentication types.

The following authentication types are provided.

SERVER

- This is the default security mechanism.
- Authentication occurs on the server using local operating system security.
- If a user ID and password are specified during the connection or attachment attempt, they are compared with the valid user ID and password combinations at the server to determine whether the user is permitted to access the instance.
- If a user ID and password are not specified and the client OS is a trusted OS, then the user ID and password that you used to log on to the client is sent to the server for authentication.

SERVER_ENCRYPT

- Specifies that the server accepts encrypted SERVER authentication schemes.
- If the client authentication is SERVER_ENCRYPT, the client is authenticated by passing an unencrypted user ID and an encrypted password to the server.
- If the client authentication is SERVER, the client is authenticated by passing an unencrypted user ID and an unencrypted password to the server.

CLIENT

- Specifies that authentication occurs on the server/client where the application is invoked using operating system security.
- The user ID and password specified during a connection or attachment attempt are compared with the valid user ID and password combinations on the client node to determine whether the user ID is permitted access to the instance. No further authentication will take place on the database server.
- If the user performs a local or client login, the user is known only to that local client workstation.
- If the remote instance has CLIENT authentication, two other parameters determine the final authentication type: TRUST_ALLCLNTS and TRUST_CLNTAUTH.

TRUST_ALLCLNTS

- Trusted clients are clients that have a reliable, local security system. Specifically, all clients are trusted clients except for the Windows 95, 98, and ME operating systems.
- To protect against unsecured clients accessing the databases, you can select Trusted Client Authentication by setting the TRUST_ALLCLNTS parameter to NO. This implies that only trusted platforms can authenticate the user on behalf of the server. The default for this parameter is YES.
- In this case, the untrusted clients are authenticated on the server and must provide a valid user ID and password.

- It is possible to trust all clients (TRUST_ALLCLNTS is YES) yet have some of those clients as those who do not have a native safe security system for authentication.
- To protect against all clients except DRDA clients from DB2 for OS/390 and z/OS, DB2 for VM and VSE, and DB2 for iSeries, set the TRUST_ALLCLNTS parameter to DRDAONLY. Only these clients can be trusted to perform client-side authentication. All other clients must provide a user ID and password to be authenticated by the server.

TRUST_CLNTAUTH

- The TRUST_CLNTAUTH parameter is used to determine where the above clients are authenticated:
  - If TRUST_CLNTAUTH is *client*, authentication takes place at the client.
  - If TRUST_CLNTAUTH is *server*, authentication takes place at the client when no password is provided and at the server when a password is provided.

Let's look at Table 4.3: If you set TRUST_ALLCLNTS=YES and TRUST_CLNTAUTH=SERVER, then authentication for Trusted non-DRDA Client Authentication with password is at SERVER and Trusted non-DRDA Client Authentication no password is at CLIENT.

Table 4.3   Authentication Types

Parameter	Authentication Type					
TRUST_ALLCLNTS	YES	YES	NO	NO	DRDAONLY	DRDAONLY
TRUST_CLNTAUTH	CLIENT	SERVER	CLIENT	SERVER	CLIENT	SERVER
Untrusted non-DRDA Client Authentication no password	CLIENT	CLIENT	SERVER	SERVER	SERVER	SERVER
Untrusted non-DRDA Client Authentication with password	CLIENT	SERVER	SERVER	SERVER	SERVER	SERVER
Trusted non-DRDA Client Authentication no password	CLIENT	CLIENT	CLIENT	CLIENT	SERVER	SERVER
Trusted non-DRDA Client Authentication with password	CLIENT	SERVER	CLIENT	SERVER	SERVER	SERVER
DRDA Client Authentication no password	CLIENT	CLIENT	CLIENT	CLIENT	CLIENT	CLIENT
DRDA Client Authentication with password	CLIENT	SERVER	CLIENT	SERVER	CLIENT	SERVER

KERBEROS Authentication

When dealing with authentication and Kerberos, three entities are involved:

1. the *client*, who is requesting service from
2. a *server*, the second entity, and
3. the Key Distribution Center (KDC) or Kerberos server, which is a machine that manages the database where all the authentication data is kept and maintained

- Kerberos is used when both the DB2 client and server are on operating systems that support the Kerberos security protocol. Kerberos security protocol enables the use of a single sign-on to a remote DB2 server.
- Kerberos is a third-party authentication service that uses conventional cryptography to create a shared secret key. It is a 56-bit encrypted key using the Data Encryption Standard (DES) algorithm. This key becomes a user's credential and is used to verify the identity of users during all occasions when local or network services and DB2 services are requested. The key eliminates the need to pass the user name and password across the network as clear text. This key is stored in the Kerberos server database.
- When a client needs the services of a server, the client must prove its identity to the server so that the server knows to whom it is talking.
- Tickets are the means the Kerberos server gives to clients to authenticate themselves to the service providers and to get work done on their behalf on the service's servers. Tickets have a finite life, known as the *ticket life span*.

The Kerberos authentication types are supported only on clients and servers running Windows 2000, Windows XP, and Windows .NET operating systems. In addition, both the client and server machines must either belong to the same Windows domain or belong to trusted domains.

In Kerberos terms, making a Kerberos authenticated service provider work on the behalf of a client is a three-step process:

1. Get a *ticket-granting ticket* (TGT).
2. Get a *service ticket* (ST).
3. Get the work done on the service provider.

The main role of the *ticket-granting* ticket service is to avoid unnecessary password traffic over the network, so the user should issue his or her password only once per session. What this *ticket-granting* ticket service does is to give the client systems a ticket that has a certain time span, whose purpose is to allow the clients to get *service tickets* (STs) to be used with other servers without the need to give them the password every time they request services.

Every service that uses Kerberos is registered with the Kerberos service. To use a kerberized service, you must request a ticket for that service from Kerberos. To request tickets, you must have a special ticket called a *ticket-granting ticket* (TGT). You get a Kerberos TGT by running the *kinit* program. Once you have a TGT, you don't have to enter your password anymore when you want to get other Kerberos tickets.

Once a user has a TGT, if the user requests a kerberized service, he or she has to get an ST for it. To get one, the kerberized command sends an encrypted message containing the requested service name, the machine's name, and a timestamp to the Kerberos server. The Kerberos server decrypts the message, checks whether everything is in order, and if so, sends back an ST encrypted with the service's private key, so that only the requested service can decrypt it. The client sends a request, along with the just-received ticket, to the service provider, who in turn decrypts and checks authorization, and, if it is in order, provides the requested service to the client.

An example of how Kerberos authentication works in a Windows environment:

1. A user logging on to the client machine using a domain account authenticates to the Kerberos KDC at the Windows domain controller. The KDC issues a TGT to the client.
2. During the first phase of the connection, the server sends the target principal name, which is the service account name for the DB2 server service, to the client. Using the server's target principal name and the TGT, the client requests an ST from the *ticket-granting* service that also resides at the domain controller. If both the client's TGT and the server's target principal name are valid, the ticket-granting service issues a ST to the client.
3. The client sends this ST to the server via the communication channel.
4. The server validates the client's ST. If the client's ST is valid, the authentication is completed.

> **N O T E** It is possible to catalog the databases on the client machine and explicitly specify the Kerberos authentication type with the server's target principal name. In this way, the first phase of the connection can be bypassed. If a user ID and a password are specified, the client will request the TGT for that user account and use it for authentication.

KRB_SERVER_ENCRYPT

One of the values of KERBEROS authentication is that the userid and password verification can be performed at a Kerberos server using the Kerberos security protocol for authentication. With an authentication type of KRB_SERVER_ENCRYPT at the server and clients that support the Kerberos security system, the effective system authentication type is KERBEROS. If the clients do not support the Kerberos security system, the effective system authentication type is equivalent to SERVER_ENCRYPT.

NOTE

1. The type of authentication you choose is most important when you have remote database clients accessing the database or when you are using federated database functionality. Most users accessing the database through local clients (i.e., running on the same server as the DB2 instance) are always authenticated on the same machine as the database.

2. Do not inadvertently lock yourself out of your instance when you are changing the authentication information, because access to the configuration file itself is protected by information in the configuration file. The following database manager configuration parameters control access to the instance:

   - SYSADM_GROUP
   - SYSCTRL_GROUP
   - SYSMAINT_GROUP
   - AUTHENTICATION
   - TRUST_ALLCLNTS
   - TRUST_CLNTAUTH

Authentication Considerations for Remote Clients

When cataloging a database for remote access, the authentication type may be specified in the database directory entry.

- SERVER authentication is assumed if a value is not specified for database accessed using DB2 Connect.
- The authentication type is not required. If it is not specified, the client will default to SERVER_ENCRYPT. If the server does not support SERVER_ENCRYPT, the client attempts to retry using a value supported by the server. If the server supports multiple authentication types, the client will not choose among them but will instead return an error. This is done to ensure that the correct authentication type is used. In this case, the client must catalog the database using a supported authentication type.
- If an authentication type is specified, authentication can begin immediately, provided that the value specified matches that at the server. If a mismatch is detected, DB2 attempts to recover. Recovery may result in more flows to reconcile the difference or in an error if DB2 cannot recover. In the case of a mismatch, the value at the server is assumed to be correct.

Partitioned Database Authentication Considerations

In a partitioned database, each partition of the database must have the same set of users and groups defined. If the definitions are not the same, the user may be authorized to do different things on different partitions. Consistency across all partitions is highly recommended.

PRIVILEGES, AUTHORITIES, AND AUTHORIZATIONS

Privileges enable users to create, delete, or access database resources. Authority levels provide a method of grouping privileges and higher-level database manager maintenance and utility operations. Together, these act to control access to the database manager and its database objects. Users can access only those objects for which they have the appropriate authorization, i.e., the required privilege or authority.

A user or group can have one or more of the following levels of authorization and privileges:

- Administrative authority (SYSADM or DBADM) gives full privileges for a set of objects.
- System authority (SYSCTRL or SYSMAINT) gives full privileges for managing the system but does not allow access to the data.
- LOAD authority (LOAD) gives LOAD utility privileges to load data into tables.
- Ownership privilege (also called *CONTROL privilege* in some cases) gives full privileges for a specific object.
- Individual privileges may be granted to allow a user to carry out specific functions on specific objects.
- Implicit privileges may be granted to a user who has the privilege to execute a package. Although users can run the application, they do not necessarily require explicit privileges on the data objects used within the package.

Users with administrative authority (SYSADM or DBADM) or ownership privileges (CONTROL) can grant and revoke privileges to and from others, using the GRANT and REVOKE statements. It is also possible to grant a table, view, or schema privilege to another user if that privilege is held with the WITH GRANT OPTION. However, the WITH GRANT OPTION does not allow the person granting the privilege to revoke the privilege, once granted. You must have SYSADM authority, DBADM authority, or CONTROL privilege to revoke the privilege.

A user or group can be authorized for any combination of individual privileges or authorities. When a privilege is associated with a resource, that resource must already exist. For example, a user cannot be given the SELECT privilege on a table unless that table has previously been created.

> **NOTE**   Care must be taken when an authorization name is given authorities and privileges and no user exists with that authorization name. At some later time, a user can be created with that authorization name and automatically receive all of the authorities and privileges associated with that authorization name.

Tasks and Required Authorizations

Not all organizations divide job responsibilities in the same manner. Table 4.4 lists some other common job responsibilities by titles, the tasks that usually accompany them, and the authorities or privileges that are needed to carry out those tasks.

Table 4.4   Common Job Responsibilities

Job Title	Tasks	Required Authorization
Department Administrator	Oversees the departmental system; creates databases	SYSCTRL authority. SYSADM authority if the department has its own instance
Security Administrator	Authorizes other users for some or all authorizations and privileges	SYSADM or DBADM authority
Database Administrator	Designs, develops, operates, safeguards, and maintains one or more databases	DBADM and SYSMAINT authority over one or more databases; SYSCTRL authority in some cases
System Operator	Monitors the database and carries out backup functions	SYSMAINT authority
Application Programmer	Develops and tests the database manager application programs; may also create tables of test data	BINDADD, BIND on an existing package; CONNECT and CREATETAB on one or more databases; some specific schema privileges; and a list of privileges on some tables
User Analyst	Defines the data requirements for an application program by examining the system catalog views	SELECT on the catalog views; CONNECT on one or more databases
Program End User	Executes an application program	EXECUTE on the package; CONNECT on one or more databases (See the note following this table.)
Information Center Consultant	Defines the data requirements for a query user; provides the data by creating tables and views and by granting access to database objects	DBADM authority over one or more databases
Query User	Issues SQL statements to retrieve, add, delete, or change data; may save results as tables	CONNECT on one or more databases; CREATEIN on the schema of the tables and views being created; and SELECT, INSERT, UPDATE, DELETE on some tables and views

> **N O T E**   If an application program contains dynamic SQL statements, the program end user may need additional privileges to EXECUTE and CONNECT (such as SELECT, INSERT, DELETE, and UPDATE).

Using the System Catalog for Security Issues

Information about each database is automatically maintained in a set of views called the *system catalog*, which is created when the database is generated. This system catalog describes tables, columns, indexes, programs, privileges, and other objects. The system catalog views list the privileges held by users and the identity of the user granting each privilege, as described in Table 4.5.

Table 4.5   System Catalog Views

System Catalog	Description
SYSCAT.DBAUTH	Lists the database privileges
SYSCAT.TABAUTH	Lists the table and view privileges
SYSCAT.COLAUTH	Lists the column privileges
SYSCAT.PACKAGEAUTH	Lists the package privileges
SYSCAT.INDEXAUTH	Lists the index privileges
SYSCAT.SCHEMAAUTH	Lists the schema privileges
SYSCAT.PASSTHRUAUTH	Lists the server privileges
SYSCAT.ROUTINEAUTH	Lists the routine (functions, methods, and stored procedures) privileges

Considerations:

* SYSADM, SYSMAINT, and SYSCTRL are not listed in the system catalog.
* The CREATE and GRANT statements place privileges in the system catalog.
* Privileges granted to users by the system will have SYSIBM as the grantor.
* Users with SYSADM and DBADM authorities can grant and revoke SELECT privilege on the system catalog views.

The following statement retrieves all authorization names with privileges:

```
SELECT DISTINCT GRANTEE, GRANTEETYPE, 'DATABASE' FROM SYSCAT.DBAUTH
UNION
SELECT DISTINCT GRANTEE, GRANTEETYPE, 'TABLE' FROM SYSCAT.TABAUTH
UNION
SELECT DISTINCT GRANTEE, GRANTEETYPE, 'PACKAGE' FROM
    SYSCAT.PACKAGEAUTH
UNION
SELECT DISTINCT GRANTEE, GRANTEETYPE, 'INDEX' FROM SYSCAT.INDEXAUTH
UNION
SELECT DISTINCT GRANTEE, GRANTEETYPE, 'COLUMN' FROM SYSCAT.COLAUTH
UNION
SELECT DISTINCT GRANTEE, GRANTEETYPE, 'SCHEMA' FROM SYSCAT.SCHEMAAUTH
UNION
SELECT DISTINCT GRANTEE, GRANTEETYPE, 'SERVER' FROM
    SYSCAT.PASSTHRUAUTH
ORDER BY GRANTEE, GRANTEETYPE, 3;
```

Periodically, the list retrieved by this statement should be compared with lists of user and group names defined in the operating system security facility. You can then identify those authorization names (userids) that are no longer valid and revoke their privileges.

To retrieve all authorization names that are directly authorized to access the table EMPLOYEE with the qualifier DSNOW:

```
SELECT DISTINCT GRANTEETYPE, GRANTEE FROM SYSCAT.TABAUTH
    WHERE TABNAME = 'EMPLOYEE' AND TABSCHEMA = 'DSNOW'
UNION
SELECT DISTINCT GRANTEETYPE, GRANTEE FROM SYSCAT.COLAUTH
    WHERE TABNAME = 'EMPLOYEE'AND TABSCHEMA = 'DSNOW';
```

To retrieve all authorization names that have been directly granted DBADM authority:

```
SELECT DISTINCT GRANTEE
  FROM SYSCAT.DBAUTH WHERE DBADMAUTH = 'Y';
```

To find out who can update the table EMPLOYEE with the qualifier DSNOW, issue the following statement:

```
SELECT DISTINCT GRANTEETYPE, GRANTEE FROM SYSCAT.TABAUTH
    WHERE TABNAME = 'EMPLOYEE' AND TABSCHEMA = 'DSNOW' AND
    (CONTROLAUTH = 'Y' OR UPDATEAUTH = 'Y' OR UPDATEAUTH = 'G')
UNION
SELECT DISTINCT GRANTEETYPE, GRANTEE FROM SYSCAT.DBAUTH
    WHERE DBADMAUTH = 'Y'
UNION
SELECT DISTINCT GRANTEETYPE, GRANTEE FROM SYSCAT.COLAUTH
    WHERE TABNAME = 'EMPLOYEE' AND TABSCHEMA = 'DSNOW'
    AND PRIVTYPE = 'U';
```

> **N O T E**   This retrieves any authorization names with DBADM authority, as well as those names to which CONTROL or UPDATE privileges have been directly granted. However, it will not return the authorization names of users who hold only SYSADM authority.

To retrieve a list of the database privileges that has been directly granted to an individual authorization name:

```
SELECT * FROM SYSCAT.DBAUTH
   WHERE GRANTEE = USER AND GRANTEETYPE = 'U';
```

To retrieve a list of the table privileges that were directly granted by a specific user: (The keyword USER in these statements is always equal to the value of a user's authorization name. USER is a read-only special register.)

```
SELECT * FROM SYSCAT.TABAUTH WHERE GRANTOR = USER;
```

The following statement retrieves a list of the individual column privileges that were directly granted by a specific user:

```
SELECT * FROM SYSCAT.COLAUTH WHERE GRANTOR = USER;
```

During database creation, SELECT privilege on the system catalog views is granted to PUBLIC. In most cases, this does not present any security problems. For very sensitive data, however, it may be inappropriate, because these tables describe every object in the database. If this is the case, consider revoking the SELECT privilege from PUBLIC, then grant the SELECT privilege as required to specific users. Granting and revoking SELECT on the system catalog views is done in the same way as for any view, but you must have either SYSADM or DBADM authority to do this.

To retrieve the owner and name of every table on which a user's authorization name has been directly granted SELECT privilege:

```
SELECT TABSCHEMA, TABNAME
   FROM SYSCAT.TABAUTH
   WHERE GRANTEETYPE = 'U' AND
   GRANTEE = USER AND
   SELECTAUTH = 'Y'
```

FIREWALL SUPPORT

A *firewall* is a set of programs and/or hardware, located at a network gateway server, that is used to prevent unauthorized access to a system or network. There are four types of firewalls:

1. Network level, packet-filter, or screening router firewalls
   - A screening router firewall works by screening incoming packets by protocol attributes.

- ○ The protocol attributes screened may include source or destination address, type of protocol, source or destination port, or some other protocol-specific attributes.
- ○ You need to ensure that all the ports used by DB2 are open for incoming and outgoing packets. DB2 uses port 523 for the DB2 Administration Server (DAS), which is used by the DB2 tools.
- ○ Determine the ports used by all your server instances by using the services file to map the service name in the server database manager configuration file to its port number.

2. Classic application level proxy firewalls
   - ○ A level proxy firewall is a technique that acts as an intermediary between a Web client and a Web server.
   - ○ A proxy firewall acts as a gateway for requests arriving from clients. When client requests are received at the firewall, the final server destination address is determined by the proxy software. The application proxy translates the address, performs additional access control checking and logging as necessary, and connects to the server on behalf of the client.
   - ○ The DB2 Connect product on a firewall machine can act as a proxy to the destination server.
   - ○ Also, a DB2 server on the firewall, acting as a hop server to the final destination server, acts like an application proxy.

3. Circuit level or transparent proxy firewalls
   - ○ A Circuit level firewall is a transparent proxy firewall that does not modify the request or response beyond what is required for proxy authentication and identification. An example of a transparent proxy firewall is SOCKS.
   - ○ DB2 supports SOCKS Version 4.

4. Stateful multi-layer inspection (SMLI) firewalls
   - ○ This is a sophisticated form of packet-filtering that examines all seven layers of the Open System Interconnection (OSI) model.
   - ○ Each packet is examined and compared against known states of friendly packets. Whereas screening router firewalls examine only the packet header, SMLI firewalls examine the entire packet, including the data.

WHAT IS LDAP?

Lightweight Directory Access Protocol (LDAP) is an industry standard access method to directory services. A directory service is a repository of resource information about multiple systems and services within a distributed environment, and it provides client and server access to these resources. Each database server instance will publish its existence to an LDAP server and provide database information to the LDAP directory when the databases are created. When a client connects to a database, the catalog information for the server can be retrieved from the LDAP directory. Each client is no longer required to store catalog information locally on each machine. Client applications search the LDAP directory for information required to connect to the database.

A caching mechanism exists so that the client searches the LDAP directory only once in its local directory catalogs. Once the information is retrieved, it is stored or cached on the local machine. Subsequent access to the same information is based on the values of the DIR_CACHE database manager configuration parameter and the DB2LDAPCACHE registry variable, as detailed in Table 4.6.

Table 4.6   Cached Information Available by Configuration Parameter and Registry Variable

DB2 Registry Variable (DB2LDAPCACHE)	DB2 Configuration (DIR_CACHE)	Cache Information
NO	NO	Read the information from LDAP
NO	YES	Read the information from LDAP once and insert it into the DB2 cache
YES	NO	If the required information is not found in the local cache, then the information is read from the LDAP directory and the local cache is refreshed
YES	YES	If the required information is not found in the local cache, then the information is read from the LDAP directory once and inserted into the DB2 cache

> **N O T E**   The DB2LDAPCACHE registry variable is applicable only to the database and node directories.

To ensure that you have the latest entries in the cache, do the following to update and remove incorrect entries from the database directory and node directory:

```
REFRESH LDAP DB DIR
REFRESH LDAP NODE DIR
```

Supported LDAP Client and Server Configurations

Table 4.7 summarizes the current supported LDAP client and server configurations:

- IBM SecureWay Directory Version 3.1 is an LDAP Version 3 server available for Windows NT, AIX, and Solaris.

Table 4.7   Supported LDAP Environments

LDAP-Supported Client	IBM SecureWay Directory	Microsoft Active Directory	Netscape LDAP Server
IBM LDAP Client	Supported	Not Supported	Supported
Microsoft LDAP/ADSI Client	Supported	Supported	Supported

- IBM SecureWay Directory is shipped as part of the base operating system on AIX and iSeries (AS/400), and with OS/390 Security Server.
- DB2 supports IBM LDAP client on AIX, Solaris, Windows NT, Windows 98, and Windows 2000.
- Microsoft Active Directory is an LDAP Version 3 server and is available as part of the Windows 2000 Server operating system.
- The Microsoft LDAP Client is included with the Windows operating system.

> **N O T E**   When running on Windows operating systems, DB2 supports using either the IBM LDAP client or the Microsoft LDAP client to access the IBM SecureWay Directory Server. If you want to explicitly select the IBM LDAP client, you must use the *db2set* command to set the DB2LDAP_CLIENT_PROVIDER registry variable to "IBM."
>
> ```
> db2set DB2LDAP_CLIENT_PROVIDER=IBM
> ```

Support for Windows Active Directory

DB2 exploits the Active Directory as follows:

1. The DB2 database servers are published in the Active Directory as the ibm_db2Node objects. The ibm_db2Node object class is a subclass of the ServiceConnectionPoint (SCP) object class. Each ibm_db2Node object contains protocol configuration information to allow client applications to connect to the DB2 database server. When a new database is created, the database is published in the Active Directory as the ibm_db2Database object under the ibm_db2Node object.
2. When connecting to a remote database, DB2 client queries the Active Directory, via the LDAP interface, for the ibm_db2Database object. The protocol communication to connect to the database server (binding information) is obtained from the ibm_db2Node object, under which the ibm_db2Database object is created.

Property pages for the ibm_db2Node and ibm_db2Database objects can be viewed or modified using the *Active Directory Users and Computer* Management Console at a domain controller. To setup the property page, run the *regsrv32* command to register the property pages for the DB2 objects, as follows:

```
regsvr32 %DB2PATH%\bin\db2ads.dll
```

You can view the objects by using the *Active Directory Users and Computer* Management Console at a domain controller. To get to the Administration Tool, select Start, Program, Administration Tools, Active Directory Users and Computer

> **N O T E**   You must select *Users, Groups, and Computers as containers* from the View menu to display the DB2 objects under the computer objects. If DB2 is not installed on the domain controller, you can still view the property pages of DB2 objects by copying the *db2ads.dll* file from %DB2PATH%*bin* and the resource DLL *db2adsr.dll* from %DB2PATH%*msg\locale-name* to a local directory on the domain controller. Then, you run the *regsrv32* command from the local directory to register the DLL.

Configuring DB2 to Use Microsoft Active Directory

To access Microsoft Active Directory, ensure that the following conditions are met:

1. The machine that runs DB2 must belong to a Windows 2000 domain.
2. The Microsoft LDAP client is installed. Microsoft LDAP client is part of the Windows 2000 operating system. For Windows 98, or Windows NT, you need to verify that the *wldap32.dll* exists under the system directory.
3. Enable the LDAP support. For Windows 2000, the LDAP support is enabled by the installation program. For Windows 98/NT, you must explicitly enable LDAP by setting the DB2_ENABLE_LDAP registry variable to YES, using the *db2set* command.

```
db2set  DB2_ENABLE_LDAP=YES
```

4. Log on to a domain user account when running DB2 to read information from the Active Directory.

Configuring DB2 in the IBM LDAP Environment

Before you can use DB2 in the IBM LDAP environment, you must configure the following on each machine:

1. Enable the LDAP support. For Windows 2000, the LDAP support is enabled by the installation program. For Windows 98/NT, you must explicitly enable LDAP by setting the DB2_ENABLE_LDAP registry variable to YES, using the *db2set* command.

```
db2set DB2_ENABLE_LDAP=YES
```

2. The LDAP server's TCP/IP host name and port number. These values can be entered during unattended installation using the DB2LDAPHOST response keyword, or you can manually set them later by using the *db2set* command:

```
db2set DB2LDAPHOST=<hostname[:port]>

  where hostname is the LDAP server's TCP/IP hostname
  and [:port] is the port number. If it is not specified, DB2 will
  use the default LDAP port (389).

db2set DB2LDAPHOST=newschemadirectory.service.dntteam.com:389
```

DB2 objects are located in the LDAP base distinguished name (baseDN). If you are using IBM SecureWay LDAP directory server Version 3.1, you do not have to configure the baseDN because DB2 can dynamically obtain this information from the server. However, if you are using IBM eNetwork Directory Server Version 2.1, you must configure the LDAP baseDN on each machine by using the *db2set* command:

```
db2set DB2LDAP_BASEDN=<baseDN>

  where baseDN is the name of the LDAP suffix that is defined at the
  LDAP server. This LDAP suffix is used to contain DB2 objects.

db2set DB2LDAP_BASEDN=o=phantom.com
```

3. The LDAP user's distinguished name and password. These are required only if you plan to use LDAP to store DB2 user-specific information.

Creating an LDAP User

DB2 supports setting DB2 registry variables and CLI configuration at the user level. (This is not available on the UNIX and Linux platforms.) User-level support provides user-specific settings in a multi-user environment. An example is Windows NT Terminal Server, where each logged on user can customize his or her own environment without interfering with the system environment or another user's environment.

When using the IBM LDAP directory, you must define an LDAP user before you can store user-level information in LDAP. You can create an LDAP user in one of the following ways:

* Create an LDIF file to contain all attributes for the user object, then run the LDIF import utility to import the object into the LDAP directory. The LDIF utility for the IBM LDAP server is LDIF2DB.

- Use the Directory Management Tool (DMT), available only for the IBM SecureWay LDAP Directory Server Version 3.1, to create the user object.

An LDIF file containing the attributes for a person object appears similar to the following:

```
File name: newuser.ldif
dn: cn=Jonathan Phan,ou=TestTeamI,ou=TESTTEAM,o=phantom.com,c=us
objectclass: ePerson
cn: Jonathan Phan
sn: phan
uid: jphan
userPassword: password
telephonenumber: 1-555-080-0096
facsimiletelephonenumber: 1-555-080-0099
title: TestTeamI
```

Following is an example of the LDIF command to import an LDIF file using the IBM LDIF import utility:

```
LDIF2DB -i newuser.ldif
```

> **N O T E** You must run the LDIF2DB command from the LDAP server machine. You must grant the required access (ACL) to the LDAP user object so that the LDAP user can add, delete, read, and write to its own object, using the LDAP Directory Server Web Administration tool.

Configuring the LDAP User for DB2 Applications

When using the Microsoft LDAP client, the LDAP user is the same as the operating system user account. However, when working with the IBM LDAP client and before using DB2, you must configure the LDAP user distinguished name and password for the current logged on user. This can be done using the *db2ldcfg* utility:

```
db2ldcfg - u <userDN> - w <password>  → set the user's DN and password
          - r                          → clear the user's DN and password
```

For example:

```
db2ldcfg -u "cn=Jonathan Phan,ou=TestTeamI,ou=TESTTEAM,o=phantom.com,
    c=us" -w password
```

Registration of DB2 Servers after Installation

Each DB2 server instance must be registered in LDAP to publish the protocol configuration information that is used by the client applications to connect to the DB2 server instance. When registering an instance of the database server, you need to specify an LDAP *node name*. The LDAP node name is used by client applications when they connect or attach to the server. You can catalog another alias name for the LDAP node by using the CATALOG LDAP NODE command.

> **N O T E** If you are working in a Windows 2000 domain environment, then during installation, the DB2 server instance is automatically registered in the Active Directory with the following information:
>
> ```
> nodename: TCP/IP hostname
> protocol type: TCP/IP
> ```

If the TCP/IP hostname is longer than 8 characters, it will be truncated to 8 characters.

The REGISTER command appears as follows:

```
db2 register db2 server in ldap as <ldap_node_name> protocol tcpip
```

The protocol clause specifies the communication protocol to use when connecting to this database server.

When creating an instance for DB2 Universal Database Enterprise Server Edition that includes multiple physical machines, the REGISTER command must be invoked once for each machine. Use the *rah* command to issue the REGISTER command on all machines.

> **N O T E** The same ldap_node_name cannot be used for each machine because the name must be unique in LDAP. You will want to substitute the hostname of each machine for the ldap_node_name in the REGISTER command. For example:
>
> ```
> rah ">DB2 REGISTER DB2 SERVER IN LDAP AS SANDIEGO
> PROTOCOL TCPIP"
> ```

The REGISTER command can be issued for a remote DB2 server. To do so, you must specify the remote computer name, instance name, and the protocol configuration parameters when registering a remote server. The command can be used as follows:

```
db2 register db2 server in ldap as <ldap_node_name>

    protocol tcpip
    hostname <host_name>
    svcename <tcpip_service_name>
    remote <remote_computer_name>
    instance <instance_name>
```

```
db2 register db2 server in ldap as SANDIEGO

    protocol tcpip
    hostname 192.168.1.51
    svcename 11001
    remote sunshine.dnt
    instance v8inst
```

The following convention is used for the computer name:

- If TCP/IP is configured, the computer name must be the same as the TCP/IP hostname.
- If APPN is configured, use the partner-LU name as the computer name.

When running in a high availability or failover environment and using TCP/IP as the communication protocol, the *cluster* IP address must be used.

Using the cluster IP address allows the client to connect to the server on either machine without having to catalog a separate TCP/IP node for each machine. The cluster IP address is specified using the hostname clause, shown as follows:

```
db2 register db2 server in ldap as <ldap_node_name> protocol tcpip
    hostname nnn.nnn.nnn.nnn svcename <tcpip_service_name>

where nnn.nnn.nnn.nnn is the cluster IP address.

db2 register db2 server in ldap as SANDIEGO protocol tcpip
    hostname 192.168.1.51 svcename 11001
```

Update the Protocol Information for the DB2 Server

The DB2 server information in LDAP must be kept current. For example, changes to the protocol configuration parameters or the server network address require an update to LDAP. To update the DB2 server in LDAP on the local machine, use the following command:

```
db2 update ldap ...
```

Examples of protocol configuration parameters that can be updated include:

- A TCP/IP hostname and service name or port number parameters.
- A NetBIOS workstation name.

To update a remote DB2 server protocol configuration parameters, use the UPDATE LDAP command with a node clause:

```
db2 update ldap node <node_name> hostname <host_name> svcename
<tcpip_service_name>


db2 update ldap node SANDIEGO hostname 192.168.1.101 svcename 11002
```

Catalog a Node Alias for ATTACH

A node name for the DB2 server must be specified when registering the server in LDAP. Applications use the node name to attach to the database server. If a different node name is required, such as when the node name is hard-coded in an application, use the CATALOG LDAP NODE command to make the change. The command would be similar to:

```
db2 catalog ldap node <ldap_node_name> as <new_alias_name>


db2 catalog ldap node SANDIEGO as SANDIEGO
```

To uncatalog an LDAP node, use the UNCATALOG LDAP NODE command. The command would appear similar to:

```
db2 uncatalog ldap node <ldap_node_name>


db2 uncatalog ldap node SANDIEGO
```

Deregistering the DB2 Server

Deregistration of an instance from LDAP also removes all the node, or alias, objects and the database objects referring to the instance. Deregistration of the DB2 server on either a local or a remote machine requires that the LDAP node name be specified for the server:

```
db2 deregister db2 server in ldap node <node_name>


db2 deregister db2 server in ldap node SANDIEGO
```

When the DB2 server is deregistered, any LDAP node entry and LDAP database entries referring to the same instance of the DB2 server are also uncataloged.

During the creation of a database within an instance, the database is automatically registered in LDAP if the server is registered. Registration allows remote client connection to the database without having to catalog the database and node on the client machine. When a client attempts to connect to a database, if the database does not exist in the database directory on the local machine, then the LDAP directory is searched.

If the name already exists in the LDAP directory, the database is still created on the local machine but a warning message is returned, stating the naming conflict in the LDAP directory. For this reason, you can manually catalog a database in the LDAP directory. The user can register databases on a remote server in LDAP by using the CATALOG LDAP DATABASE command. When registering a remote database, you specify the name of the LDAP node that represents the remote database server. You must register the remote database server in LDAP using the REGISTER DB2 SERVER IN LDAP command before registering the database.

To register a database manually in LDAP, use the CATALOG LDAP DATABASE command:

```
db2 catalog ldap database <dbname> at node <node_name> with "comment"

db2 catalog ldap database SAMPLE at node SANDIEGO with "My LDAP SAMPLE
database"
```

The following authentication levels are available when registering the database in LDAP:

CLIENT: Specifies that authentication takes place on the node from which the application is invoked.

SERVER: Specifies that authentication takes place on the node containing the target database.

SERVER_ENCRYPT: Specifies that authentication takes place on the node containing the target database, and passwords are encrypted at the source. Passwords are decrypted at the target, as specified by the authentication type cataloged at the source.

DCS_ENCRYPT: Specifies that authentication takes place on the node containing the target database, except when using DB2 Connect; in that case, authentication takes place at the DRDA application server (AS). Passwords are encrypted at the source, and decrypted at the target, as specified by the authentication type cataloged at the source.

DCS: Specifies that authentication takes place on the node containing the target database, except when using DB2 Connect; in that case, authentication takes place at the DRDA application server (AS).

KERBEROS: Specifies that authentication takes place using Kerberos Security Mechanism.

Attaching to a Remote Server in the LDAP Environment

In the LDAP environment, you can attach to a remote database server using the LDAP node name on the ATTACH command:

```
db2 attach to <ldap_node_name>
```

When a client application attaches to a node or connects to a database for the first time, because the node is not in the local node directory, DB2 searches the LDAP directory for the target node entry. If the entry is found in the LDAP directory, the protocol information of the remote server is retrieved. If you connect to the database and the entry is found in the LDAP directory, then the database information is also retrieved.

Using this information, DB2 automatically catalogs a database entry and a node entry on the local machine. The next time the client application attaches to the same node or database, the information in the local database directory is used without having to search the LDAP directory.

> **N O T E** The caching of LDAP information is not applicable to user-level CLI or DB2 profile registry variables. Also, there is an "in-memory" cache for the database, node, and DCS directories. However, there is no such cache for just the node directory.

Deregistering the Database from the LDAP Directory

The database is automatically deregistered from LDAP when:

- The database is dropped.
- The owning instance is deregistered from LDAP.

The database can be manually deregistered from LDAP using:

```
db2 uncatalog ldap database <dbname>

db2 uncatalog ldap database SANDIEGO
```

Refreshing LDAP Entries in Local Database and Node Directories

LDAP information is subject to change, so it is necessary to refresh the LDAP entries in the local and node directories. The local database and node directories are used to cache the entries in LDAP.

To refresh the database entries that refer to LDAP resources, use the following command:

```
db2 refresh ldap database directory
```

To refresh the node entries on the local machine that refer to LDAP resources, use the following command:

```
db2 refresh ldap node directory
```

As part of the refresh, all the LDAP entries that are saved in the local database and node directories are removed. The next time that the application accesses the database or node, it will read the information directly from LDAP and generate a new entry in the local database or node directory.

To ensure the refresh is done in a timely way, you may want to:

- Schedule a refresh that is run periodically.
- Run the REFRESH command during system bootup.
- Use an available administration package to invoke the REFRESH command on all client machines.
- Set DB2LDAPCACHE=NO to avoid LDAP information being cached in the database, node, and DCS directories.

Searching the LDAP Directory Partitions or Domains

DB2 searches the current LDAP directory partition or current Active Directory domain in the Windows 2000 environment. In an environment where there are multiple LDAP directory partitions or domains, you can set the search scope to improve performance.

For example, if the information is not found in the current partition or domain, automatic search of all other partitions or domains can be requested.

On the other hand, the search scope can be restricted to search only the local machine. The search scope is controlled through the DB2 profile registry variable, DB2LDAP_SEARCH_SCOPE. To set the search scope value at the global level in LDAP, use the *–gl* option, which means "global in LDAP," on the *db2set* command:

```
db2set -gl db2ldap_search_scope=<value>

db2set -gl db2ldap_search_scope=global
```

Possible values include *local*, *domain*, or *global*. The default value is *domain*, which limits the search scope to the current directory partition.

Setting the search scope in LDAP allows the setting of the default search scope for the entire enterprise. For example, you may want to initialize the search scope to *global* after a new database is created. This allows any client machine to search all other partitions or domains to find a database that is defined in a particular partition or domain. Once the entry has been recorded on each machine after the first connect or attach for each client, the search scope can be changed to *local*. Once changed to *local*, no client will scan any partition or domain.

> **NOTE** The DB2 profile registry variable DB2LDAP_SEARCH_SCOPE is the only registry variable that supports setting the variable at the global level in LDAP.

Setting DB2 Registry Variables at the User Level in the LDAP Environment

Under the LDAP environment, the DB2 profile registry variables can be set at the user level, which allows a user to customize their own DB2 environment.

To set the DB2 profile registry variables at the user level, use the *–ul* option:

```
db2set -ul <variable>=<value>
```

> **N O T E**   This is not supported on UNIX and Linux platforms.

DB2 has a caching mechanism. The DB2 profile registry variables at the user level are cached on the local machine. If the *–ul* parameter is specified, DB2 always reads from the cache for the DB2 registry variables. The cache is refreshed when:

- You update or reset a DB2 registry variable at the user level.
- The command to refresh the LDAP profile variables at the user level is:

```
db2set -ur

or to reset a registry variable:

db2set -r registry_variable_name
```

Enabling LDAP Support after Installation Is Complete

To enable LDAP support at some point following the completion of the installation process, use the following procedure on each machine:

- Install the LDAP support binary files. Run the setup program and select the LDAP Directory Exploitation support from Custom install. The setup program installs the binary files and sets the DB2 profile registry variable DB2_ENABLE_LDAP to YES.

> **N O T E**   For Windows 98/NT and UNIX platforms, you must explicitly enable LDAP by setting the DB2_ENABLE_LDAP registry variable to YES, using the *db2set* command.

- On UNIX platforms only, declare the LDAP server's TCP/IP hostname and (optional) port number using the following command:

```
db2set DB2LDAPHOST=<base_domain_name>[:port_number]

  where base_domain_name is the LDAP server's TCP/IP hostname, and
  [:port_number] is the port number. The default LDAP port is 389.
```

DB2 objects are located in the LDAP baseDN. If you are using IBM SecureWay LDAP directory server Version 3.1, you do not have to configure the base DN because DB2 can dynamically obtain this information from the server. However, if you are using IBM eNetwork Directory Server Version 2.1, you must configure the LDAP baseDN on each machine by using the DB2SET command:

```
db2setDB2LDAP_BASEDN=<baseDN>


where baseDN is the name of the LDAP suffix that is defined at the
LDAP server. This LDAP suffix is used to contain DB2 objects.
```

- Register the current instance of the DB2 server in LDAP by using the REGISTER LDAP AS command. For example:

```
db2 register ldap as <node-name> protocol tcpip
```

- Run the CATALOG LDAP DATABASE command if you have databases you would like to register in LDAP. For example:

```
db2 catalog ldap database <dbname> as <alias_dbname>
```

- Enter the LDAP user's distinguished name and password. These are required only if you plan to use LDAP to store DB2 user-specific information.

Removing/Disabling LDAP Support

To disable LDAP support, use the following procedure:

- For each instance of the DB2 server, deregister the DB2 server from LDAP:

```
db2 deregister db2 server in ldap node <nodename>

db2 deregister db2 server in ldap node SANDIEGO
```

- Set the DB2 profile registry variable DB2_ENABLE_LDAP to NO.

```
db2set DB2_ENABLE_LDAP=NO
```

> **NOTE** If LDAP support is available at the DB2 Connect gateway and the database is not found at the gateway database directory, then DB2 will look up LDAP and attempt to keep the found information.

Security Considerations in an LDAP Environment

Before accessing information in the LDAP directory, an application or user is authenticated by the LDAP server. The authentication process is called *binding* to the LDAP server.

It is important to apply access control on the information stored in the LDAP directory to prevent anonymous users from adding, deleting, or modifying the information.

Access control is inherited by default and can be applied at the container level. When a new object is created, it inherits the same security attribute as the parent object. An administration tool available for the LDAP server can be used to define access control for the container object.

By default, access control is defined as follows:

- For database and node entries in LDAP, everyone (or any anonymous user) has read access. Only the Directory Administrator and the owner or creator of the object has read/write access.
- For user profiles, the profile owner and the Directory Administrator have read/write access. One user cannot access the profile of another user if that user does not have Directory Administrator authority.

> **N O T E**   The authorization check is always performed by the LDAP server and not by DB2. The LDAP authorization check is not related to DB2 authorization. An account or auth ID that has SYSADM authority may not have access to the LDAP directory. When running the LDAP commands or APIs, if the bind distinguished name (bindDN) and password are not specified, DB2 binds to the LDAP server using the default credentials, which may not have sufficient authority to perform the requested commands, and an error will be returned.
>
> You can explicitly specify the user's bindDN and password using the USER and PASSWORD clauses for the DB2 commands or APIs.

Security Considerations for Windows 2000 Active Directory

The DB2 database and node objects are created under the computer object of the machine where the DB2 server is installed in the Active Directory. To register a database server or catalog a database in the Active Directory, you need to have sufficient access to create and/or update the objects under the computer object.

By default, objects under the computer object are readable by any authenticated users and updateable by administrators (users that belong to the Administrators, Domain Administrators, and Enterprise Administrators groups). To grant access for a specific user or a group, use the *Active Directory Users and Computer* Management Console as follows:

1. Start the Active Directory Users and Computer administration tool. Use Start, Program, Administration Tools, Active Directory Users and Computer.

2. Under View, select Advanced Features.

3. Select the Computers container.

4. Right-click on the computer object that represents the server machine where DB2 is installed and select Properties.

5. Select the Security tab, then add the required access to the specified user or group.

The DB2 registry variables and CLI settings at the user level are maintained in the DB2 property object under the user object. To set the DB2 registry variables or CLI settings at the user level, a user needs to have sufficient access to create objects under the User object.

By default, only administrators have access to create objects under the User object. To grant access to a user to set the DB2 registry variables or CLI settings at the user level, use the *Active Directory Users and Computer* Management Console as follows:

1. Start the Active Directory Users and Computer administration tool. Use Start, Program, Administration Tools, Active Directory Users and Computer.

2. Select the user object under the Users container.

3. Right-click on the user object and select Properties.

4. Select the Security tab.

5. Add the user name to the list by using the Add button.

6. Grant access to *Write* and *Create All Child Objects*.

7. Using the Advanced setting, set permissions to apply onto *This object and all child objects.*

8. Select the check box *Allow inheritable permissions from parent to propagate to this object.*

Extending the LDAP Directory Schema with DB2 Object Classes and Attributes

The LDAP Directory Schema defines object classes and attributes for the information stored in the LDAP directory entries. An object class consists of a set of mandatory and optional attributes. Every entry in the LDAP directory has an object class associated with it.

Before DB2 can store the information into LDAP, the Directory Schema for the LDAP server must include the object classes and attributes that DB2 uses. The process of adding new object classes and attributes to the base schema is called *extending the Directory Schema.*

> **N O T E**   If you are using IBM SecureWay LDAP Directory v3.1, all the object classes and attributes that are required by DB2 are included in the base schema. You do not have to extend the base schema with DB2 object classes and attributes.

Extending the Directory Schema for Windows 2000 Active Directory

Before DB2 can store information in the Windows 2000 Active Directory, the directory schema needs to be extended to include the new DB2 object classes and attributes. The process of adding new object classes and attributes to the directory schema is called *schema extension*.

You must extend the schema for Active Directory by running the DB2 Schema Installation program, *db2schex*, before the first installation of DB2 on any machine that is part of a Windows 2000 domain.

The *db2schex* program is found on the product CD-ROM. The location of this program on the CD-ROM is under the db2 directory and the common subdirectory. For example:

```
x:\db2\common

    where x: is the CD-ROM drive
```

The command is used as shown: *db2schex*.

There are other optional clauses associated with this command:

- To specify the user distinguished name: –b UserDN
- To specify the bind password: –w Password
- To uninstall the schema: –u
- To force uninstall to continue, ignoring errors: –k

> **NOTE**
>
> 1. If no user distinguished name and password are specified, *db2schex* binds as the currently logged user.
> 2. The user distinguished name clause can be specified as a Windows NT username.
> 3. To update the schema, you must be a member of the Schema Administrators group or have been delegated the rights to update the schema.

The DB2 Schema Installation program for Active Directory carries out the following tasks:

- Detects which server is the Schema Master.
- Binds to the Domain Controller that is the Schema Master.
- Ensures that the user has sufficient rights to add classes and attributes to the schema.
- Ensures that the schema master is writeable (that is, the safety interlock in the registry is removed).
- Creates all the new attributes.
- Creates all the new object classes.
- Detects errors, and if they occur, the program will roll back any changes to the schema.

DB2 Objects in the Windows 2000 Active Directory

DB2 creates objects in the Active Directory at two locations:

1. The DB2 database and node objects are created under the computer object of the machine where the DB2 Server is installed. For the DB2 server machine that does not belong to the Windows NT domain, the DB2 database and node objects are created under the *System* container.
2. The DB2 registry variables and CLI settings at the user level are stored in the DB2 property objects under the User object. These objects contain information that is specific to that user.

Netscape LDAP Directory Support and Attribute Definitions

The supported level for Netscape LDAP Server is v4.12 or later.

Within Netscape LDAP Server Version 4.12 or later, the Netscape Directory Server allows application to extend the schema by adding attribute and object class definitions into the following two files, slapd.user_oc.conf and slapd.user_at.conf.

These two files are located in the <Netscape_install path>\slapd-<machine_name>\config directory.

> **N O T E** If you are using iPlan Directory Server 5.0, you must review the documentation that accompanies that product for detailed instructions on how to extend the schema. After adding the DB2 schema definition, the Directory Server must be restarted for all changes to be active.

SECURITY IMPLEMENTATION AND USAGE

This section describes how to use new functions available in IBM DB2 Universal Database (for UNIX and Windows) to integrate data encryption easily into database applications.

For years, databases have been able to keep unauthorized persons from being able to see the data. This is generally covered by privileges and authorities within the database manager. In today's environments, there is an increasing need for privacy of stored data. This means that, even though a DBA may have complete access to the data in a table, there is information that the owner of the data would not want anyone else to see. This has surfaced in particular with Web-based applications where the user has entered data (such as credit card numbers) that is to be kept for subsequent uses of the application by the same user. People want assurance that nobody else can access this data.

This functionality allows the application to encrypt and decrypt data. When data is inserted into the database, it can be encrypted using an encryption password supplied by the user. When the data is retrieved, the same password must be supplied to decrypt the data. For situations where the same password is going to be used several times, the ENCRYPTION PASSWORD value can be set using an assignment statement and is valid for the length of a connection.

The following describes the SQL functions and gives some examples of how the encryption functions could be used. We also discuss the design and performance implications of having encrypted data in a relational database.

To ensure that you are using correct data types and lengths for encrypted data, be sure to read the "Table Column Definition" section under the ENCRYPT function in the SQL Reference.

- Encrypt (data-string-expression, password-string-expression, and hint-string-expression).
- Decrypt_Bin (encrypted-data, password-string-expression).
- Decrypt_Char (encrypted-data, password-string-expression).

The algorithm used to encrypt the data is an RC2 block cipher with padding. The 128-bit secret key is derived from the password using an MD2 message digest. The encryption password is not tied to DB2 authentication and is used for data encryption and decryption only.

An optional parameter, hint-password-expression, can be provided and is a string that would help a user remember the password-string-expression that is used to encrypt the data (for example, "Dwaine and Tom" as a hint to remember "DNTTEAM").

Column-Level Encryption (CLE)

CLE means that all values in a given column are encrypted with the same password. This type of encryption can be used in views and when one common password is used. When the same key is used for all of the rows in a table or tables, the ENCRYPTION PASSWORD special register can be quite useful.

Example 1 This example uses the ENCRYPTION PASSWORD value to hold the encryption password. An employee social security number is encrypted and stored in the EMP table in encrypted form.

```
-- Create emp table, set encryption password, and insert three rows:

create table emp (ssn varchar(124) for bit data);
set encryption password ='DNTTEAM';
insert into emp (ssn) values(encrypt('111-11-1111'));
insert into emp (ssn) values(encrypt('222-22-2222'));
insert into emp (ssn) values(encrypt('333-33-3333'));
```

```
-- Select data from emp table:

   select ssn from emp

      SSN
      ------------------------------------------------------------------
      x'0010F0FF0333D5A034E989260E4F99ED59070DD69B6E3C1B'
      x'005EA2FF0333D5A05F167D1BC1E9EAD33D7D4987B57D5670'
      x'00EE12FF0333D5A06174133D8E3A22756382F84B48F4DD05'

-- Set encryption password:

   set encryption password ='DNTTEAM';
   select decrypt_char(ssn) as ssn from emp;

      SSN
      -----------
      111-11-1111
      222-22-2222
      333-33-3333
```

Example 2   This example uses the ENCRYPTION PASSWORD value to hold the encryption password in combination with views. The following statement declares a view on the EMP table:

```
create view clear_ssn (ssn) as
    select decrypt_char(ssn) from emp;
```

In the application code, we set the ENCRYPTION PASSWORD to DNTTEAM and can now use the CLEAR_SSN view.

```
   select ssn from clear_ssn;

When there is no encryption password, the result encrypted
    x'0010F0FFE404A0D534E989260E4F99ED59070DD69B6E3C1B

   set encryption password ='DNTTEAM';
   select ssn from clear_ssn;

When encryption password is set, the result should be:  111-11-1111
```

Row-Column (Cell) or Set-Column Level Encryption (SCLE)

SCLE means that, within a column of encrypted data, many different passwords are used. For example, a Web site may need to keep customer credit card numbers (CCN). In this database, each customer could use his or her own password or phrase used to encrypt the CCN.

Example 1   The Web application collects user information about a customer. This information includes the customer name, which is stored in host variable V_NAME, the credit card number, which is stored in a host variable V_CCN, and the password, which is stored in a host variable V_USERPSWD. The application performs the insert of this customer information as follows:

```
create table customer (name char(20), ccn varchar(124) for bit data);

Application...

CREATE PROCEDURE insertCcn (IN v_cnn char(124), IN v_userpswd
char(128), v_name char(20))
   RESULT SETS 1
   LANGUAGE SQL
Insert_Ccn:
BEGIN NOT ATOMIC
   Declare SQLCODE Integer Default 0;
   Declare retCode Integer Default 0;
   BEGIN
      Insert into customer (ccn, name) values(encrypt(v_ccn,
      v_userpswd), v_name);
      If ( retCode <> 0 ) Then
      Return -200;
      END IF;
   END;
END Insert_Ccn
/

   call v8inst.inCcn('123456789','DNTTEAM','TPHAN');

or

   insert into customer (ccn, name)
   values(encrypt('123456789','DNTTEAM'),'TPHAN');
```

When the application needs to re-display the credit card information for a customer, the password is entered by the customer and again stored in host variable V_USERPSWD. The CCN can then be retrieved as follows:

```
Application...

CREATE PROCEDURE getCcn (IN v_userpswd char(128), v_name char(20))
   RESULT SETS 1
   LANGUAGE SQL
Get_Ccn:
BEGIN NOT ATOMIC
   Declare SQLCODE Integer Default 0;
   Declare retCode Integer Default 0;
   BEGIN
      DECLARE Cgetccn CURSOR WITH RETURN FOR
            Select decrypt_char(ccn, v_userpswd) from customer where name =
            v_name;
            Declare Continue Handler For SQLException, SQLWarning
```

```
                            Begin
                                Set retCode = SQLCODE;
                            End;
                OPEN Cgetccn;
                If ( retCode <> 0 ) Then
                                Return -200;
                END IF;
                Return 0;
        END;
END Get_Ccn
   /
```

```
...Application

    call v8inst.getCcn ('DNTTEAM','TPHAN');
```
or

If select without password decrypted:
```
    select * from customer;

            NAME            CCN
            -------------------------------------------------------------
            TPHAN       x'00DD23FF0333D5A2DCDE9395FDA51E4087C244BE694CABEE'
```

Result from select with decrypted password:
```
    select decrypt_char(ccn,'DNTTEAM') as ccn from customer where name ='TPHAN';

    CCN
    -------------
    123456789
```

If using the decrypt_char without the encrypted password, the query failed:
```
    select decrypt_char(ccn) from cust where name='DSNOW';
    SQL20145N  The decryption function failed. The password used for decryption
    does not match the password used to encrypt the data.  SQLSTATE=428FD
```

To correct the above, using the set encryption password before select statement:
```
    set encryption password='SANFRAN';
    select decrypt_char(ccn) as ccn from customer where name ='DSNOW';

    CCN
    -------------
    987654321
```

Example 2   This example uses the hint to help customers remember their passwords. Using the same application as example 3, the application stores the hint into the host variable V_PSWDHINT. Assume the values 'SANFRAN' for V_USERPSWD and 'MY_O' for V_PSWDHINT. The hint 'MY_O' is stored to help the user DSNOW remember the encryption password of SANFRAN.

```
Application...

  insert into customer (ccn, name) values(encrypt(v_ccn, v_userpswd,
  v_pswdhint), v_name);

...Application

  call v8inst.insertCcn ('987654321','SANFRAN','MY_O','DSNOW');

or

  insert into customer (ccn, name)
  values(encrypt('987654321','SANFRAN','MY_O'),'DSNOW');
```

If the customer requests a hint about the password used, the following query is used.

```
Application...
  select gethint(ccn) from customer where name = v_name;
  select decrypt_char(ccn, v_userpswd) from customer where name =
  v_name;
...Application

  call v8inst.getpwHint ('DSNOW');

or

  select gethint(ccn) as ccnhint from customer where name ='DSNOW';


    CCNHINT

    --------

    MY_O


The value for pswdhint is set to 'MY_O' to help the user about the
encryption of password SANFRAN:
  select decrypt_char(ccn,'SANFRAN') from customer where name
  ='DSNOW';


    CCN

    -------------

    987654321
```

Encrypting Non-Character Values (ENCV)

ENCV or the encryption of numeric and date/time data types is indirectly supported via casting. By casting non-character SQL types to varchar or char, they can be encrypted.

Example 1   Casting functions used when encrypting and decrypting TIMESTAMP data.

```
-- Create a table to store our encrypted value
   create table etemp (c1 varchar(124) for bit data);
   set encryption password='DNTTEAM';

-- Store encrypted timestamp
   insert into etemp values encrypt(char(CURRENT TIMESTAMP));

-- Select and decrypt timestamp
   select * from etemp;


   1

   --------------------------
   x'00F30DFF0333D5B1751BD041CD67DE921D711536B4A5E22FB36215BE9B05635
   499305'


   select timestamp(decrypt_char(c1)) from etemp;


   1

   --------------------------
   2003-01-10-12.34.51.933954
```

Example 2   Encrypt/decrypt double data.

```
   set encryption password='DNTTEAM';
   insert into etemp values encrypt(char(1.11111002E5));
   select double(decrypt_char(c1)) from etemp;


   1

   ----------------------------------
   +1.11111002000000E+005
```

Performance Considerations

Encryption can slow down SQL statements. Also, encrypted data will have a significant impact on your database design. In general, you want to encrypt a few very sensitive data elements in a schema, such as Social Security numbers, credit card numbers, patient names, account numbers, etc. Some data values are not very good candidates for encryption, for example, Booleans (true and false) or other small sets, such as the integers 1 through 10. These values, along with a column name, may be easy to guess, so you want to decide whether encryption is really useful. It is best to create indexes on encrypted data.

The following scenario illustrates our discussion. Consider a common master-detail schema where one programmer can work on many projects. We will implement column-level encryption on the employee's Social Security number (SSN). In the master table EMP and the detail table EMPPROJECT, the SSN will be stored in encrypted form.

```
-- Define Tables
  create table emp (ssn varchar(48) for bit data, name varchar(48));
  create table empProject( ssn varchar(48) for bit data, projectName
  varchar(48));

-- Create indexes
  create unique index idxEmp on emp (ssn) include (name);
  create index idxEmpPrj on empProject (ssn);

-- Add some data
  set encryption password='DNTTEAM';

  insert into emp values (encrypt('111-11-1111'),'Advanced Programmer');
  insert into emp values (encrypt('222-22-2222'),'Programmer');
  insert into empProject values (encrypt('111-11-1111'),'CLS Project');
  insert into empProject values (encrypt('222-22-2222'),'CLS Project');
  insert into empProject values (encrypt('111-11-1111'),'DB2 UDB Version
  8');

-- A. Find the programmers working on CLS Project
  select a.name, decrypt_char(a.ssn)
     from emp a, empProject b
     where a.ssn=b.ssn and b.projectname='CLS Project';


  NAME                          2
------------------------------------------
     Advanced Programmer        111-11-1111
     Programmer                 222-22-2222


-- B.  Build a list of the projects that the programmer with ssn='111-
11-1111' is working on

  select projectName from empProject where ssn=encrypt('111-11-1111');


  PROJECTNAME
  --------------------
  DB2 UDB Version 8
  CLS Project
```

The following is an example of how not to write the two queries on the EMP and EMPPROJECT table. Although these queries return the same answers as the above A and B, they also *decrypted* the SSN for all rows. *When the table gets very large the problem can be significant.*

```
select a.name, decrypt_char(a.ssn)
    from emp a, empProject b
    where decrypt_char(a.ssn)=decrypt_char(b.ssn) and b.project='CLS
    Project';


NAME                                           2
-------------------------------------------------
Programmer                              222-22-2222
Advanced Programmer                     111-11-1111
```

This would require decryption of every row of the EMP table and each 'CLS Project' row of the EMPPROJECT table to perform the join.

```
select projectName from empProject where decrypt_char(ssn)='111-11-
1111';


PROJECTNAME
----------------

DB2 UDB Version 8
CLS Project
```

This would require decryption of every row of the EMPPROJECT table.

In summary, using encryption functions in DB2 provides a simple way to encrypt sensitive data. These functions can be used to implement column- and row-column-level encryption. There are some important performance implications that developers should review during design and implementation. Data encryption adds a new tool to be used to hide private data, even from administrative staff.

> **N O T E** For additional information, refer to Appendix H—LDAP Integration in DB2 UDB Using Microsoft Active Directory—and Appendix I—Tuning DB2 UDB in the IBM LDAP Environment.

HOW DB2 FOR WINDOWS NT/2000 WORKS WITH WINDOWS NT/2000 SECURITY

Security is one of the most important features of any database management system. It is important to keep data safe and to limit data access to those with a need to know only. DB2 UDB has many security features of its own, but on Windows NT/2000, it also relies on the security features of the Windows NT/2000 operating system itself.

To understand security for DB2 UDB on Windows NT/2000, we must understand not only the many security features of DB2 UDB, but also the Windows NT/2000 security model and how it's used by DB2.

Terminology

Table 4.8 defines Windows NT/2000 and DB2 UDB terminology.

Table 4.8   Windows NT/2000 and DB2 UDB Terminology

Term	Description
Windows NT	Either Windows NT Workstation or Windows NT Server. Reference will be made to the common Windows NT features of the two products.
Windows NT Workstation	The Windows NT Workstation product. Cannot be a domain controller.
Windows NT Server	The Windows NT Server product. It is a superset of the NT Workstation product. A machine running Windows NT Server may be a Windows NT Workstation or a domain controller.
Workgroup	A collection of Windows Workstation. It can contain computers running any number of operating systems, including DOS, Windows 3.x, Windows for Workgroups, Windows 95/98, Windows NT Workstation, and Windows NT Server, and is identified by a unique name.
Domain	A domain is an arrangement of client and server computers, referenced by a specific (unique) name, that share a single user accounts database.
Domain Controller	Refers to the computer running Windows NT Server that manages all aspects of user-domain interactions and uses the information in the domain user accounts database to authenticate users logging onto domain accounts.
Primary Domain Controller	In a Windows NT server domain, the computer running the Windows NT server that authenticates domain logons and maintains the user accounts database for the domain. There can be only one per domain. It can also be referred to as the *primary domain controller* (PDC).
Trust Relationship	An administration and communications link between two domains. A trust relationship between two domains enables user accounts and global groups to be used in a domain other than the domain where these accounts are actually defined. Domains use established trust relationships to share account information and validate the rights and permissions of users and global groups residing in the trusted domain. Trusts, therefore, simplify administration by combining two or more domains into a single administrative unit.

Table 4.8   Windows NT/2000 and DB2 UDB Terminology (Continued)

Term	Description
Backup Domain Controller	These are servers that contain up-to-date and accurate copies of the user accounts database. These servers can also authenticate workstations in the absence of a primary domain controller (PDC). They can also be referred to as *BDCs*.
Server	A Windows NT Server that is part of a domain as a file, print, or application server but is not a domain controller.
Workstation	A machine running Windows NT Workstation or Windows NT Server in a domain that is not a domain controller or a file, print, or application server.
Right	The ability of a user or group of users to perform a Windows NT operation. Examples of rights are logging on to a server and performing backups. Rights apply to the computer as a whole, as opposed to permissions, which apply to specific objects. These can also be termed *user rights*.
Permission	Authority in Windows NT granted to a user or group of users to perform operations on specific objects, such as files, directories, printers, and other resources. Examples of permissions are read, change, full control, and no access. Permissions are applied on a user-by-user or group-by-group basis.
Instance	DB2 Administration unit. On a server, it represents an independent set of databases. A DB2 Server Instance runs as an NT Service.
Privilege	Within DB2 UDB, the right of a particular user or group of users to create, access, or modify an object.

A Windows NT domain is an arrangement of client and server computers referenced by a specific and unique name and sharing a single user accounts database called the *Security Access Manager* (SAM). One of the computers in the domain is the domain controller. The domain controller manages all aspects of user-domain interactions. The domain controller uses the information in the domain user accounts database to authenticate users logging onto domain accounts. For each domain, one domain controller is the primary domain controller (PDC). Within the domain, there may also be backup domain controllers (BDCs), which authenticate user accounts when there is no PDC or when the PDC is not available. Backup domain controllers hold a copy of the SAM database, which is regularly synchronized against the master copy on the PDC.

User accounts, user IDs, and passwords need to be defined only at the PDC to be able to access domain resources.

During the setup procedure, when a Windows NT server is installed, you may select to create:

- A PDC in a new domain.

- A BDC in a known domain.
- A stand-alone server in a known domain.

Selecting "controller" in a new domain makes that server the PDC.

The user may log on to the local machine or, when the machine is installed in a Windows NT domain, the user may log on to the domain. DB2 for Windows NT supports both of these options. To authenticate the user, DB2 checks the local machine first, then the domain controller for the current domain, and finally any trusted domains known to the domain controller.

Windows NT/2000 Authentication

We have discussed the concepts of Windows NT user accounts, local and global groups, and domains. The next logical topic is authentication. The actual process of user authentication is relatively simple. Authentication is verifying that a user is who they say they are.

Recall that user IDs and passwords are stored in the SAM database on Windows NT machines, but a user's user ID and password do not necessarily have to reside on the machine from which they log on. When Windows NT authenticates a user, it follows a simple hierarchy to look for a user ID and password. If you choose a workstation or local logon, Windows NT will look at only the local SAM. If the user is not in the local SAM, authentication will fail.

If you choose domain authentication, the domain controller that does the authentication can be either the PDC or a BDC. BDCs have a copy of the PDC's SAM database. To determine which domain controller will perform the authentication, a broadcast message is sent out from the user's machine, and the first domain controller to respond to the message will perform the authentication.

If the user is not known to the domain, (that is, the user ID is not in the SAM database of the PDC), then domain controllers of any trusted domains are queried. Either the PDC or a BDC can respond to an authentication request from a trusting domain.

Once the userid has been found and the password authenticated, any account or policy restrictions are determined, as well as a list of groups of which the user is a member.

Trust Relationships Between Domains

We have discussed the concept of a single domain; however, an enterprise may wish to establish more than one domain. These domains do not have to exist independently, nor do separate user accounts have to exist for each domain a given user wishes to log into. Interdependent multiple domains can be achieved through relationships between domains, called *trusts*.

Trusted Domains

Trust relationships between domains are established so that users from one domain can access resources in another domain without being re-authenticated.

There are two characteristics of a trust relationship:

1. One domain trusts another to authenticate users on its behalf and, therefore, grants access to resources in its domain without re-authenticating users.
2. An administrator from one domain trusts an administrator from another domain to administer resources in that domain.

The two domains in a trust relationship are called the *trusting* and the *trusted* domains. A trust relationship lets an administrator of one domain (the trusting domain) grant rights and permissions to global groups and users of another domain (the trusted domain). The administrator of the trusted domain must be, in turn, trusted because this administrator can control which users are members of global groups.

Trust relationships are not transitive. This means that explicit trust relationships need to be established in each direction between domains. There is no concept of an implicit or piggybacked trust relationship.

Models of Domain Trust

Choosing the right domain trust architecture for an enterprise can be an involved and complex task, with a number of considerations to be taken into account. To assist in this process, let's look at four common models of domain organization. They are:

1. The single domain model   All servers and workstations belong to one domain. There are no trust relationships to any other domain.

Advantages of this model include:

- It's easy to implement.
- It's a suitable design for a small to medium sized network.
- There are no trust relationships to establish or maintain.
- It has one set of administrators.

Disadvantages of this model include:

- The list of users and machines can grow to an undesirable size.
- Network and server performance problems may arise.

An example of a single domain model might be a small network with an independent domain. This could be a production environment, where it is desirable to keep the production data separate from the development environment. You might also have a number of small domains for an organization where the sharing or dividing of resources such as databases is not required. The ability to administer each domain separately is not an issue.

The most compelling reason not to implement this model, especially in a production environment, is generally the size of the domain, specifically the number of users and machines. These factors affect the size of the SAM database on the domain controllers.

2. The master domain model   This is the domain where all users are defined. All other domains trust the master domain. Domains other than the master domain have no users defined. The other domains are called *resource* or *slave domains*.

Advantages of this model include:

- Administration for the enterprise is centralized.
- It supports logical grouping of resources (such as divisions or departments).
- It supports geographical division of an enterprise.
- Global groups are defined only once.

Disadvantages of this model include:

- Performance may degrade on a WAN or with a large number of users.
- Local groups must be defined on each domain.
- Global administration can be cumbersome to establish.
- Master domain can be a single point of failure.

You might find the master domain model implemented where each department in an organization is on its own domain. However, all administration and authentication occurs in the master domain. The enterprise is split geographically, and resources are grouped accordingly. However, users are all defined and administered centrally. This model easily supports movement of personnel across domains.

3. The multiple master domain model   The master domains have trust relationships between each other and can each authenticate for the resource domains.

Advantages of this model include:

- It supports a large number of users with acceptable performance.
- Resources are grouped logically.
- Resource domains can be managed independently for security.

Disadvantages of this model include:

- Groups may need to be defined more than once for different domains.
- There are many trust relationships to manage.
- Maintenance of user accounts is more difficult because they are in multiple domains.

A multiple master domain may be established for the same reasons as a master domain. You may choose the multiple master model if you have too many users for one domain to handle all the authentication requests. To ease network traffic and speed user authentication requests, multiple master domains are created to service the resource domains.

4. The complete trust model   Domains exist with trust relationships to and from all other domains on the network. An example of a suitable environment where the complete trust model might be implemented is a development environment.

Advantages of this model include:

- It supports a large number of users.
- It does not require central administration.
- Resources and users are grouped logically into domains (from a browser perspective).
- Resources are managed independently for each domain.

Disadvantages of this model include:

- Lack of central administration can cause potentially severe network problems.
- There are a large number of trust relationships to manage.

To illustrate how this works, suppose that the DB2 instance requires Server authentication. The configuration is shown in Figure 4.1.

Each machine has a security database, Security Access Management, unless a client machine is running Windows 9x. Windows 9x machines do not have a SAM database. DC1 is the domain controller, in which the client machine, Ivan, and the DB2 for Windows NT server, Servr, are

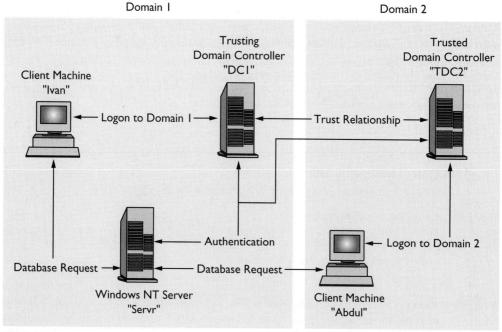

Figure 4.1
Server authentication configuration.

enrolled. TDC2 is a trusted domain controller for DC1, and the client machine, Abdul, is a member of TDC2's domain.

A DB2 for Windows NT Scenario with Server Authentication

1. Abdul logs on to the TDC2 domain (i.e., he is known in the TDC2 SAM database).

2. Abdul then connects to a DB2 database that is cataloged to reside on Servr:

```
db2 connect to remotedb user Abdul using xxxxxx
```

3. Servr determines where Abdul is known. The API that is used to find this information first searches the local machine (Servr), then the domain controller (DC1), before trying any trusted domains. Username Abdul is found on TDC2. This search order requires a single namespace for users and groups.

4. Servr then:
  a. Validates the username and password with TDC2.
  b. Finds out whether Abdul is an administrator by asking TDC2.
  c. Enumerates all Abdul's groups by asking TDC2.

A DB2 for Windows NT Scenario with
Client Authentication and a Windows NT Client Machine

1. Dale, the administrator, logs on to Servr and changes the authentication for the database instance to Client:

```
db2 update dbm cfg using authentication client
db2stop
db2start
```

2. Ivan, at a Windows client machine, logs on to the DC1 domain (i.e., he is known in the DC1 SAM database).

3. Ivan then connects to a DB2 database that is cataloged to reside on Servr:

```
db2 connect to remotedb user Ivan using yyyyyy
```

4. Ivan's machine validates the username and password. The API used to find this information first searches the local machine (Ivan), then the domain controller (DC1), before trying any trusted domains. Username Ivan is found on DC1.

5. Ivan's machine then validates the username and password with DC1.

6. Servr then:
  a. Determines where Ivan is known.
  b. Finds out whether Ivan is an administrator by asking DC1.
  c. Enumerates all Ivan's groups by asking DC1.

> **NOTE** Before attempting to connect to the DB2 database, ensure that DB2 Security Service has been started. The Security Service is installed as part of the Windows installation. To start the DB2 Security Service, enter the NET START DB2NTSECSERVER command.

A DB2 for Windows NT Scenario with Client Authentication and a Windows 9x Client Machine

1. Dale, the administrator, logs on to Servr and changes the authentication for the database instance to Client:

```
db2 update dbm cfg using authentication client
db2stop
db2start
```

2. Ivan, at a Windows 9x client machine, logs on to the DC1 domain (i.e., he is known in the DC1 SAM database).

3. Ivan then connects to a DB2 database that is cataloged to reside on Servr:

```
db2 connect to remotedb user Ivan using yyyyyy
```

4. Ivan's Windows 9x machine cannot validate the username and password. The username and password are, therefore, assumed to be valid.

5. Servr then:
  a. Determines where Ivan is known.
  b. Finds out whether Ivan is an administrator by asking DC1.
  c. Enumerates all Ivan's groups by asking DC1.

Support for Global Groups (on Windows)

DB2 also supports global groups. To use global groups, you must include global groups inside a local group. When DB2 enumerates all the groups that a person is a member of, it also lists the local groups the user is a member of indirectly (by the virtue of being in a global group that is itself a member of one or more local groups).

Global groups are used in two possible situations:

- Included inside a local group. Permission must be granted to this local group.
- Included on a domain controller. Permission must be granted to the global group.

Using a Backup Domain Controller with DB2

If the server you use for DB2 also acts as a backup domain controller (BDC), you can improve DB2 performance and reduce network traffic if you configure DB2 to use the BDC.

You specify the BDC to DB2 by setting the DB2DMNBCKCTLR registry variable.

If you know the name of the domain for which DB2 server is the BDC, use:

```
DB2DMNBCKCTLR=<domain_name>
```

where domain_name must be in uppercase.

To have DB2 determine the domain for which the local machine is a BDC, use:

```
DB2DMNBCKCTLR=?
```

> **NOTE** DB2 does not use an existing BDC by default because a BDC can get out of sync with the PDC, causing a security exposure. Domain controllers get out of sync when the PDC's security database is updated but the changes are not propagated to a BDC. This can happen if there are network latencies or if the computer browser service is not operational.

USER AUTHENTICATION WITH DB2 FOR WINDOWS NT

User authentication can cause problems for Windows NT users because of the way the operating system authenticates.

DB2 for Windows NT User Name and Group Name Restrictions

The following are the limitations in this environment:

- User names are limited to 30 characters within DB2. Group names are limited to 8 characters.
- User names under Windows NT are not case sensitive; however, passwords are case sensitive.
- User names and group names can be a combination of upper- and lowercase characters. However, they are usually converted to uppercase when used within DB2. For example, if you connect to the database and create the table schema1.table1, this table is stored as SCHEMA1.TABLE1 within the database. (If you wish to use lowercase object names, issue commands from the command line processor, enclosing the object names in quotation marks, or use third-party ODBC front-end tools.)
- A user cannot belong to more than 64 groups.

- DB2 supports a single namespace. That is, when running in a trusted domains environment, you should not have a user account of the same name that exists in multiple domains or that exists in the local SAM of the server machine and in another domain.

Groups and User Authentication on Windows NT

Users are defined on Windows NT by creating user accounts using the Windows NT administration tool called the *User Manager.* An account that contains other accounts, also called *members*, is a group.

Groups give Windows NT administrators the ability to grant rights and permissions to the users within the group at the same time, without having to maintain each user individually. Groups, like user accounts, are defined and maintained in the SAM database.

There are two types of groups: local and global.

- **Local groups.** A local group can include user accounts created in the local accounts database. If the local group is on a machine that is part of a domain, the local group can also contain domain accounts and groups from the Windows NT domain. If the local group is created on a workstation, it is specific to that workstation.
- **Global groups.** A global group exists only on a domain controller and contains user accounts from the domain's SAM database. That is, a global group can contain only user accounts from the domain on which it is created; it cannot contain any other groups as members. A global group can be used in servers and workstations of its own domain and in trusting domains.

The PDC holds the SAM for the domain. This SAM is replicated to any BDCs in the domain. Domain controllers do not have a local SAM database. They hold user and group data for the domain. In this sense, any groups created on the PDC, local or global, are domain groups.

Windows NT machines that are not domain controllers (NT Workstations and some NT servers) will each have their own SAM databases. User accounts and groups created on those machines are local to that machine. There is no Create Global Group option on machines that are not domain controllers.

Trust Relationships Between Domains on Windows NT

Trust relationships are an administration and communication link between two domains. A trust relationship between two domains enables user accounts and global groups to be used in a domain other than the domain where the accounts are defined. Account information is shared to validate the rights and permissions of user accounts and global groups residing in the trusted domain without being authenticated. Trust relationships simplify user administration by combining two or more domains into a single administrative unit.

There are two domains in a trust relationship:

- The trusting domain. This domain trusts another domain to authenticate users for them.
- The trusted domain. This domain authenticates users on behalf of (in trust for) another domain.

Trust relationships are not transitive. This means that explicit trust relationships need to be established in each direction between domains. For example, the trusting domain may not necessarily be a trusted domain.

DB2 for Windows NT Security Service

In DB2 UDB, we have integrated the authentication of user names and passwords into the DB2 System Controller. The Security Service is required only when a client is connected to a server that is configured for authentication CLIENT.

Installing DB2 on a Backup Domain Controller

In a Windows NT 4.0 environment, a user can be authenticated at either a primary or a backup controller. This feature is very important in large distributed LANs with one central PDC and one or more BDCs at each site. Users can then be authenticated on the BDC at their site instead of requiring a call to the PDC for authentication.

The advantage of having a backup domain controller, in this case, is that users are authenticated faster, and the LAN is not as congested as it would have been, had there been no BDC.

Authentication can occur at the BDC under the following conditions:

- The DB2 for Windows NT server is installed on the BDC.
- The DB2DMNBCKCTLR profile registry variable is set appropriately.

If the DB2DMNBCKCTLR profile registry variable is not set or is set to blank, DB2 for Windows NT performs authentication at the PDC.

The only valid declared settings for DB2DMNBCKCTLR are "?" or a domain name.

If the DB2DMNBCKCTLR profile registry variable is set to a question mark (DB2DMNBCKCTLR=?), then DB2 for Windows NT will perform its authentication on the BDC under the following conditions:

- The cachedPrimaryDomain is a registry value set to the name of the domain to which this machine belongs. (You can find this setting under HKEY_LOCAL_MACHINE, Software, Microsoft, Windows NT, Current Version, WinLogon.)
- The Server Manager shows the BDC as active and available.
- The registry for the DB2 Windows NT server indicates that the system is a BDC on the specified domain.

Under normal circumstances, the setting DB2DMNBCKCTLR=? will work; however, it will not work in all environments. The information supplied about the servers on the domain is dynamic, and Computer Browser must be running to keep this information accurate and current. Large LANs may not be running Computer Browser and, therefore, Server Manager's information may not be current. In this case, there is a second method to tell DB2 for Windows NT to authenticate at the BDC:

```
db2set DB2DMNBCKCTLR=xxx
```

where *xxx* is the Windows NT domain name for the DB2 server. With this setting, authentication will occur on the BDC, based on the following conditions:

- The machine is configured as a BDC for the specified domain. (If the machine is set up as a BDC for another domain, this setting will result in an error.)

DB2 for Windows NT Authentication with Groups and Domain Security

DB2 UDB allows you to specify either a local group or a global group when granting privileges or defining authority levels. A user is determined to be a member of a group if the user's account is defined explicitly in the local or global group, or implicitly by being a member of a global group defined to be a member of a local group.

DB2 for Windows NT supports the following types of groups:

- Local groups.
- Global groups.
- Global groups as members of local groups.

DB2 for Windows NT enumerates the local and global groups that the user is a member of, using the security database where the user was found. DB2 UDB provides an override that forces group enumeration to occur on the local Windows NT server where DB2 is installed, regardless of where the user account was found. This override can be achieved using the following commands:

```
For global settings:
db2set -g DB2_GRP_LOOKUP=local

For instance settings:
db2set -i <instance name> DB2_GRP_LOOKUP=local
```

After issuing this command, you must stop and start the DB2 instance for the change to take effect. Then create local groups and include domain accounts or global groups in the local group.

To view all DB2 profile registry variables that are set, type:

```
db2set -all
```

If the DB2_GRP_LOOKUP profile registry variable is set to local, then DB2 tries to find a user on the local machine only. If the user is not found on the local machine or is not defined as a member of a local or global group, then authentication fails. DB2 does not try to find the user on another machine in the domain or on the domain controllers.

If the DB2_GRP_LOOKUP profile registry variable is not set, then:

1. DB2 first tries to find the user on the same machine.
2. If the user name is defined locally, the user is authenticated locally.
3. If the user is not found locally, DB2 attempts to find the user name on its domain, then on trusted domains.

If DB2 is running on a machine that is a PDC or BDC in the resource domain, it is able to locate any domain controller in any trusted domain. This occurs because the names of the domains of BDCs in trusted domains are known only to a domain controller.

If DB2 is not running on a domain controller, you should issue:

```
db2set -g DB2_GRP_LOOKUP=DOMAIN
```

This command tells DB2 to use a domain controller in its own domain to find the name of a domain controller in the accounts domain. That is, when DB2 finds out that a particular user account is defined in domain x, rather than attempting to locate a domain controller for domain x, it sends that request to a domain controller in its own domain. The name of the domain controller in the account domain will be found and returned to the machine DB2 is running on. There are two advantages to this method:

1. A BDC is found when the PDC is unavailable.
2. A BDC is found that is close when the PDC is geographically remote.

SUMMARY

DB2 UDB Version 8 uses a combination of external security services and internal access control information to protect data and resources associated with a database server. Kerberos and LDAP have become the industry standard for the enterprise-class directory implementation and mechanism for secure network authentication and single sign-on. It is a good practice to define an adequate level of protection for your data, periodically audit the security setup, and make necessary changes to your security policy as needed.

Multi-Dimensional Clustering

Multi-dimensional clustering (MDC) enables a table to be physically clustered on more than one key, or dimension, simultaneously. Prior to Version 8, DB2 supported only single-dimensional clustering of data using clustering indexes. When a clustering index is defined on a table, DB2 attempts to maintain the physical order of the data on pages, based on the key order of the clustering index, as records are inserted into and updated in the table. This can significantly improve the performance of queries that have predicates containing the key(s) of the clustering index because, with good clustering, only a portion of the physical table needs to be accessed. In addition, when the pages are stored sequentially on disk, more efficient prefetching can be performed.

With MDC, these same benefits are extended to more than one dimension, or clustering key. In the case of query performance, range queries involving any one or combination of the specified dimensions of the table will benefit from the underlying clustering. These queries will need to access only those pages having records with the specified dimension values, and these qualifying pages will be grouped together in extents.

A table with a clustering index can become unclustered over time, as available space is filled in the table; however, an MDC table is able to maintain its clustering over the specified dimensions automatically and continuously, eliminating the need to reorganize the table in order to restore the physical order of the data.

MDC TERMINOLOGY

When an MDC table is created, the dimensional key (or keys) along which to cluster the table's data are specified. Each of the specified dimensions can be defined with one or more columns, the same as an index key. A dimension block index will be automatically created for each of the dimensions specified and will be used to access data quickly and efficiently along each of the specified dimensions. In addition, a block index will also be automatically created, containing all dimension key columns. The block index will be used to maintain the clustering of the data during insert and update activity, as well as for quick and efficient access to the data.

Every unique combination of the table's dimension values form a logical cell, which is physically comprised of blocks of pages, where a block is a set of consecutive pages on disk. The set of blocks that contain pages with data having the same key value of one of the dimension block indexes is called a *slice*. Every page of the table will be stored in only one block, and all blocks of the table will consist of the same number of pages, known as the *blocking factor*. The blocking factor is equal to the table space's extent size, so that the block boundaries line up with extent boundaries.

For the following table:

```
CREATE TABLE MDCTABLE (
Year INT,
Nation CHAR(25),
Color VARCHAR(10),
... )
ORGANIZE BY( Year, Nation, Color )
```

there will be three dimensions: YEAR, NATION, and COLOR. This would look like Figure 5.1.

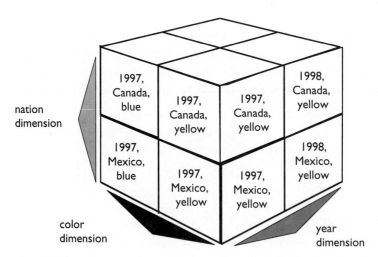

Figure 5.1
Dimensions.

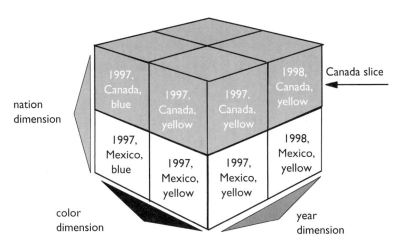

Figure 5.2
A slice of the table.

A slice contains all of the blocks of data with the same dimension value. In Figure 5.2, the CANADA slice contains all of the blocks where the NATION column contains the value CANADA.

In Figure 5.3, the YELLOW slice contains all of the blocks of data where the COLOR column contains the value YELLOW.

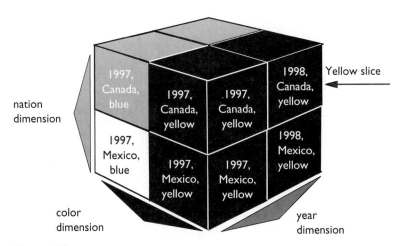

Figure 5.3
The yellow slice.

In Figure 5.4, the 1997 slice contains all of the blocks of data where the YEAR column contains the value 1997.

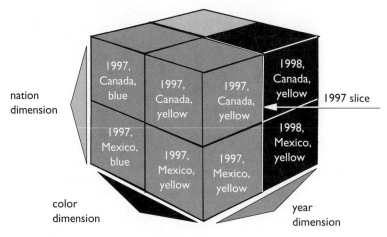

Figure 5.4
The 1997 slice.

All rows where the YEAR is 1997, the NATION is CANADA, and the color is YELLOW are stored in the same cell, as shown in Figure 5.5.

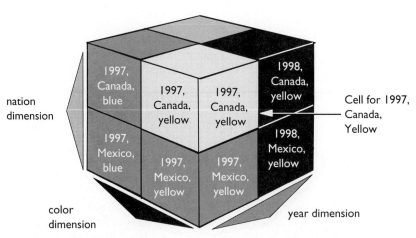

Figure 5.5
A cell.

For example, the PARTS table below is organized using two dimensions, SHIPPEDDATE and GENPART. GENPART is a generated column derived from the PARTNUM column, as shown below.

```
Create Table PARTS (
    partnum                integer,
    partname               char(30),
    shippeddate            date,
    quantity               float,
    price                  float,
    discount               float,
    shipmode               char(10),
    genpart                integer generated always as (partnum/100) )
ORGANIZE BY (shippeddate, genpart)
```

In this case, each block in the table will contain rows having the same value for the clustering attributes, SHIPPEDDATE and GENPART. A logical view of the physical clustering of this table is shown in Figure 5.6.

This figure shows the physical layout of the PARTS table in a logical two-dimensional view. Each unique attribute value combination of the two dimensions identifies a possible cell, for example, the combination of values of 2002-11-04 and 3 identifies the bottom right corner cell. Each cell

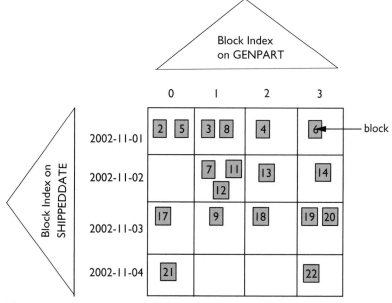

Figure 5.6
Logical view of an MDC table.

may have zero or more blocks of data. For example, the cell with the values 2002-11-04 and 3 has one block of data identified as block 22.

> **N O T E**   In Figure 5.6, there is no block number 1 because the first block of an MDC table is reserved.

A dimension block index is created for each of the dimension keys. The dimension block index identifies the list of blocks for a given key value. For example, for SHIPPEDDATE 2002-11-04, the list of blocks is 21 and 22. In addition, a composite block index will also be created automatically if the table has more than one dimension, and it points to individual cells with block entries.

DESIGN GUIDELINES FOR MDC TABLES

A crucial aspect when designing an MDC table is to choose the right set of dimensions for clustering the table and the right block size to minimize the space utilization. If the dimensions and block sizes are chosen appropriately, the benefits of the clustering can translate into significant performance and maintenance advantages. On the other hand, if the dimensions and/or block sizes are chosen incorrectly, performance can be degraded, and the space utilization could increase dramatically. Some alternatives that can be exploited to organize the table are:

- Varying the number of dimensions
- Varying the granularity of one or more dimensions
- Varying the block size
  - i.e., the extent size of the table space

One or more of the above techniques can be used in conjunction with detailed knowledge of the application and the data to identify the best organization for the MDC table. The following sections describe these aspects of the design of MDC tables in more detail.

Identify Candidate Dimension Attributes

The first step is to identify candidate dimension attributes for the table. The main criterion in choosing the candidates for the dimension column(s) is the need for clustering the data, based on a set of queries. The set of queries (either known or expected) should be examined for one or more of the following types of clauses or conditions that are good candidates for clustering:

- Range, equality, or IN-list predicates
  - For example:
    - SHIPPEDDATE > 2002-11-01
    - SHIPPEDDATE = 2002-11-04
- Roll in or Roll out of data
  - For example:
    - Load data for SHIPPEDDATE=2002-11-05
    - Delete data for SHIPPEDDATE=2002-11-01

- Group By clauses:
  - For example:
    - Group By SHIPPEDDATE
- Join clauses, especially in a star schema
  - For example:
    - ORDERS.PARTNUM = PARTS.PARTNUM and PARTS.PARTNUM < 2500
- Combinations of the above

A set of queries may have several candidate attributes that satisfy the criteria above. In this case, it is important to rank these attributes based on the workload characteristics to be able to choose an appropriate subset of the candidates for consideration. Once the number of candidates has been narrowed down, iterate through the following steps with variations of the set of dimension candidates before deciding on an appropriate selection.

Estimating the Number of Cells

Given a candidate dimension set, it is important to identify how many potential cells are likely to occur. The following query can be used to accurately determine the number of cells if a test table or an existing non-MDC table is available.

```
select distinct dimcol1, dimcol2,....dimcoln
from <table_name>
```

If the table does not exist, this can be accomplished by estimating the number of unique combinations of the dimension attributes. An estimate for the number of cells can be made by multiplying the cardinalities of the dimension columns. However, this estimate can be inaccurate if there are correlations between the dimension columns.

Let C represent the estimated number of cells and R represent the estimated number of rows in the table. The number of cells estimated by itself is not a crucial performance indicator. If disk usage is a concern, then when C is a relatively large fraction of R, this indicates that there may be a large amount of disk space being used and/or wasted.

Excessive Space May Be Used and/or Wasted If C/R Is Large

Each cell may have one partially filled block assigned to it, and these partially empty blocks can occupy a relatively large set of pages if C is large. One solution to this is to reduce the block size (table space extent size) so that less space is used and potentially wasted. Another solution is to reduce the number of cells by either reducing the number of dimensions or by using a generated expression to increase the granularity of the cells for one or more dimensions.

For example:

- The dimensions are SHIPPEDDATE and PARTNUM
- R = 1,000,000

- C = 100,000
  - the cardinality of SHIPPEDDATE = 1,000
  - the cardinality of PARTNUM = 100
- The block size (B) is 32 pages

In this case, there could potentially be up to 100,000 partially filled blocks or cells, using 3.2 million pages. This is a lot of disk space. If the extent size for the table space is instead set to four pages, the total space used would then be reduced to 400,000 pages.

The number of cells (C) could also be reduced to 10,000 (100,000 / 10 = 10,000) by using a generated column (GENSHIP) that is equal to SHIPPEDDATE/10, and the table could be organized using GENSHIP and PARTNUM.

> **N O T E** The above discusses dividing SHIPPEDDATE by 10 instead of 12, or 20, etc., in order to keep the generated column monotonic. Monotonicity will be discussed in detail later in this chapter.

The number of cells (C) could also be reduced by not using the column PARTNUM for the table's dimension. This would reduce the values of C to 1,000.

Estimating the Actual Space Usage per Cell

Assuming that there is no skew in the underlying data, the average number of rows per cell (RPC) can be estimated as:

```
RPC = R / C
```

> **N O T E** It is also possible to factor in the data skew and identify the average number of rows for the less frequent attribute values.

The space usage per cell (SPC) can be estimated as follows:

```
SPC = RPC * Average_Row_Size
```

Because the smallest page size supported by DB2 is 4 KB, having an SPC of less than 4,000 bytes times the extent size (or block size) will result in wasted space.

For a Low Value of SPC

Based on the example above, if C is reduced from 100,000 to 10,000 or even 1,000, this will increase the SPC to 10,000 or 100,000 bytes and allow for at least one reasonably sized block to be filled. If SPC is 100,000, an extent size of 16 and a page size of 4 KB will still utilize one full block.

Combining this with a relatively small value for C provides a good starting point for designing an MDC table.

For a High Value of SPC

When the value for SPC is high, each cell normally will require many blocks. In most situations, this will be acceptable from a performance perspective, as long as the choices of dimensions, granularity, and block size are appropriate. However, the performance may be further improved as follows:

- Increase the page size and extent size parameters.

> **N O T E**   This would require a new table space for the table.

- Add an additional dimension to increase the value of C.

For example:

- C = 10
- SPC = 10,000,000
- Page size = 4 KB
- Block size = 4 pages

This will require approximately 10,000,000/16,000, or 625 blocks per cell. Increasing the page size to 16 KB would decrease this to approximately 160 blocks per cell. Additionally, increasing the block size (table space extent size) to 32 can decrease this to 20 blocks per cell.

If the number of blocks per cell is too large, even after adjusting their sizes, then the number of cells (C) should be increased, if possible. This is best achieved by adding the next candidate dimension to the set.

The following sections describe the effect of the factors affecting MDC table layout in additional detail.

Varying the Number of Dimension Keys

The query workload analysis phase may identify a set of potential dimension keys. Note that a dimension key can be a composite set, i.e., (CITY, STATE) can be combined to form one dimension. In contrast, CITY, STATE implies that there are two dimensions. If city and state are always used together in the QUERY workload, using an aggregate dimension set is a good choice because this will automatically build the slices based on the combination of these values. However, if city or state is used independently, it is better to have two separate dimensions on CITY and STATE so that each slice can be examined independently.

Given a set of candidate dimension keys, the next step is to order them qualitatively, based on their priority. Next, identify the column cardinalities for each key by using the available statistics or by using a SELECT distinct query against a set of test data.

A method for choosing the table's dimensions is illustrated below:

> **1.** Estimate SPC for the highest priority dimension, assuming a reasonable block size.
> **2.** If SPC is too low:
>   ○ Change the granularity by adding a generated column or reduce the block size.
> **3.** If SPC is too high, add the next dimension candidate to the set and repeat.

Based on the example discussed previously:

If the SPC for SHIPPEDDATE is too large, add the PARTNUM column to the dimension. If the SPC is still too large, add the DISCOUNT column to the dimension.

If the SPC for SHIPPEDDATE is too low, a generated column can be built on the year and month of the SHIPPEDDATE, using the expression integer(SHIPPEDDATE) / 100. The function integer(DATE) returns the numeric form of the date as an integer data type, i.e., 2002-11-04 is returned as 20021104. Dividing this value by 100 yields an integer, 200211, that represents the date's year and month value.

Varying the Granularity of a Dimension Key

If one of the candidate dimension keys has too many possible unique values, a rollup technique can be used to decrease the granularity or cardinality of the dimension candidate in several cases. For example, the candidate dimension SHIPPEDDATE has a column cardinality that is quite high. A generated expression based on the YEARANDMONTH of the SHIPPEDDATE can be added to the table and used as a dimension for the table.

To add the column YEARANDMONTH to the table, add the following line to the create table statement:

```
YEARANDMONTH  integer generated always as integer(SHIPPEDDATE)/100
```

The YEARANDMONTH column can then be used as the table's dimension, as follows:

```
organize by (YEARANDMONTH)
```

This will reduce the value of C by a factor of roughly 30. If this is not sufficient, the data can be reduced to a YEAR by using the Year function or by using the function integer(SHIPPEDDATE)/10000.

There are two main points to remember when using granularity rollup.

- The rolled up granularity must remain useful as a dimension that helps the query workload. For example, if most queries on SHIPPEDDATE request ranges within a month, then rolling up to years might not be useful for improving the performance of these queries. The overhead of scanning an entire year to find a month will typically be too large.

- Attempt to use monotonicity-preserving expressions or functions to perform the rollup. For example, Yearandmonth and Year are monotonic functions. However, the function month(DATE) is not because it provides duplicate values for different years. Monotonic functions enable the DB2 optimizer to perform appropriate query rewrites to derive new predicates based on the rolled-up dimension columns. This subject is discussed in additional detail later in this chapter.

Varying the Block Size and Page Size Values

Given a value for SPC (the space occupied per cell), it is possible to adjust the page size and extent size for the table space to arrive at an optimal number of full blocks. In order to realize the full flexibility possible in the design of an MDC table, the table space's parameters may also need to be set accordingly, unlike regular tables. Consider the following scenario:

The value of SPC is relatively low and does not even fill a block, given the default values for the page size (4 KB) and extent size (16 or 32 pages). The extent size can be reduced to a lower number (i.e., 8 KB) and the SPC recalculated to verify whether this results in better block space occupancy. Although further reductions in the extent size could help, all the way to the smallest value of 2, it is important to consider the tradeoff of I/O overhead when using very small extent sizes. In these cases, any of the other techniques, such as varying the granularity or reducing the number of dimensions, should be considered, as well.

If the value of SPC is relatively large and can accommodate several blocks, consider increasing the page size and the block size parameters to arrive at an optimal value of blocks per cell. If the value of SPC is high, it might be possible to add another dimension to the table and obtain some additional performance benefits.

Using a Regular Table as a Baseline for the MDC Table Design

Because MDC is new in DB2 Version 8, regular tables in existing databases may be good candidates for organizing by dimensions. Therefore, a comparison can be made between an MDC table and a regular table while performing the conversion. While designing an MDC table, a regular table can provide a good indication of the lower bounds on the table's space utilization, especially if it has been reorganized or reloaded recently. In particular, the space utilization statistic FPAGES can be used to identify whether the clustering choices for an MDC table are reasonable.

Based on the example discussed previously, with the MDC version of the parts table named PART_MDC and the regular version of the table named PARTS, if the PARTS_MDC table is initially clustered based on the SHIPPEDDATE column, consider the following statistics after loading both tables with the same amount of data.

	PARTS_MDC	PARTS
FPAGES	200,000	100,000

In this case, space is being underutilized in the MDC table PARTS_MDC. Following the tuning guidelines described above, utilize a granularity rollup on the dates to YEARANDMONTH. After rebuilding the PARTS_MDC table with the dimension based on YEARANDMONTH, the statistics would look like:

	PARTS_MDC	PARTS
FPAGES	130,000	100,000

To save more space, the extent size for the table space can be reduced. After creating a new table space with a smaller extent size and recreating the table PARTS_MDC in the new table space, the statistics would look like:

	PARTS_MDC	PARTS
FPAGES	106,000	100,000

The exercise of rebuilding a table and loading data is time-consuming; therefore, it is more efficient and quicker to use the analytical techniques described above.

Summary of MDC Design Guidelines

The following list summarizes the design considerations for MDC tables:

- When identifying candidate dimensions, search for attributes that are not too granular, thereby enabling more rows to be stored in each cell. This approach will make better use of block-level indexes.
- Higher data volumes may improve population density.
- It may be useful to load the data first as non-MDC tables for analysis only.
- The table space extent size is a critical parameter for efficient space utilization.
- Although an MDC table may require a greater initial understanding of the data, the payback is that query times will likely improve.
- Some data may be unsuitable for MDC tables and would be better implemented using a standard clustering index.
- Although a smaller extent size will provide the most efficient use of disk space, the I/O for the queries should also be considered.

- A larger extent will normally reduce I/O cost, because more data will be read at a time, all other things being equal.
  - This, in turn, makes for smaller dimension block indexes, because each dimension value will need fewer blocks.
  - In addition, inserts will be quicker, because new blocks will be needed less often.

MDC PERFORMANCE GUIDELINES

The following section will describe tips and techniques for understanding the performance characteristics of workloads using MDC tables that are different from regular table design choices. These performance aspects consist of the following:

- Query processing and validating query plans
- Choosing RID indexes to complement the dimension block indexes
- Performance tuning parameters for queries, inserts, and load
- Limitations and troubleshooting tips

Query Processing Overview

In general, the query workload should take advantage of the multi-dimensional clustering by using block indexes effectively. Block indexes can be used for index scans, index ANDing, index ORing, nested loop joins, star joins, hash joins, and group by clauses.

Block Index Scans

If the table PARTS is created with the dimensions SHIPPEDDATE and GENPART, consider queries with predicates in the WHERE clause of the form:

- SHIPPEDDATE = '2002-11-11'
- SHIPPEDDATE > '2002-11-11'
- SHIPPEDDATE < '2002-11-11'
- SHIPPEDDATE BETWEEN '2002-11-01' and '2002-11-30'

All of these predicates are perfect candidates for using the block index defined on the SHIPPEDDATE column. The block index scans should provide performance benefits because the units of I/O and processing are in blocks, or extents, and the size of these indexes is usually much more compact than corresponding RID indexes. In addition, only the first page of the block will need to be checked for valid data, not the entire block.

For the statement:

```
select SHIPPEDDATE from parts where SHIPPEDDATE < '2002-11-05'
```

the access plan looks like the following:

```
Access Plan:
-----------
Total Cost:    438.915
Query Degree:  1

                Rows
               RETURN
               (   1)
                Cost
                 I/O
                  |
                 14
               FETCH
               (   2)
               438.915
                112
             /----+----\
          3.5              16
        IXSCAN       TABLE: USER1
        (   3)         PARTS
       0.0061235
            0
            |
           16
      INDEX: SYSIBM
    SQL0211171657071
```

In this example, the block index is scanned to determine the block(s) that contain the qualifying rows, then the blocks of the table are scanned to read the qualifying rows of data.

> **N O T E**   Notice that the index name above is SQL0211171657071 because it was system generated when the table was created. For ease of examining EXPLAIN information, etc., it is normally a good idea to rename these indexes to make the name more easily understood/remembered.

Block Index ANDing

For an MDC table that contains two or more dimensions, the query workload should contain query predicates that are selective on two or more attributes. For example, the PARTS table has dimensions on SHIPPEDDATE, GENPART, and DISCOUNT. If a query contains predicates of the form:

- SHIPPEDDATE > '2002-11-01' AND DISCOUNT > 0.3

or

- PARTNUM between 100 and 200 AND DISCOUNT = 0.4

then access plans can combine the block indexes, using index ANDing.

> **N O T E** It is possible for an index scan on one dimension to be selected as well.

Block Index ORing

For the PARTS table defined with three dimensions on SHIPPEDDATE, GENPART, and DISCOUNT, queries containing predicates of the form shown below are candidates for Block Index ORing:

- SHIPPEDDATE > '2002-11-01' OR DISCOUNT = 0.3

or

- DISCOUNT IN (0.1, 0.2, 0.3)

Combining Dimension Block Indexes and Record Indexes

MDC tables also allow all of the flexibilities available to regular tables. Regular indexes (RID indexes) can also be created on MDC tables to complement the dimension block indexes. These indexes can be combined with block indexes to perform index ANDing and ORing. For example, if the PARTS table has dimensions on SHIPPEDDATE and DISCOUNT, and a RID index on PARTNUM, then predicates such as the following can use index ANDing and ORing techniques combining block and RID indexes:

- SHIPPEDDATE > '2002-11-01' AND PARTNUM=101
- DISCOUNT < 0.1 OR PARTNUM between 100 and 200

The following are some guidelines for defining RID indexes to complement block indexes:

- Define RID indexes on attributes or sets of attributes that have not been chosen as dimensions.
- If the dimension for the PARTS table had been defined on only the SHIPPEDDATE column, then PARTNUM and DISCOUNT are candidates for defining RID indexes.
- RID indexes can be defined on attributes with large column cardinalities that appear in equality predicates.
- If the SHIPMODE column on the PARTS table has a small number of distinct values, it would not be a good candidate for a dimension. However, if many queries use the SHIPMODE as a predicate (i.e., SHIPMODE='Ground'), then a RID index would be useful.

- In some cases, a RID index on a rolled-up dimension column can also benefit the query workload. For example, if the PARTNUM column is rolled up to GENPART, as above, a RID index can be defined on PARTNUM for queries with equality predicates such as 'PARTNUM = 1200', whereas queries with range predicates such as 'PARTNUM > 1000' can use the dimension index.

Index-Only Access Restrictions on Block Indexes

Because dimension block indexes can occasionally point to empty blocks, it is not possible to just look at the index key entries for clauses such as EXISTS, MIN, MAX, or DISTINCT. The query plan for these types of clauses on an MDC table case will read the data in the block to verify the presence of a row before proceeding. This can result in degradation in the query performance.

If such queries are likely to occur in the query workload, then RID indexes should be created on the referenced columns to take advantage of index-only access.

Monotonicity

The derivation of block-level range predicates from column-level range predicates can only be done for columns that have been generated using a monotonic expression.

The MONTH function is not monotonic because the range of dates between Sept 2002 and Mar 2003, although increasing, correspond to the month values between 09 and 03, which is decreasing. However, the expression integer(DATE)/100 generates values 200209 and 200303, which increase as the date increases; therefore, this expression is monotonic.

If the optimizer determines that the expression involved in a generated column is not monotonic, it will not be able to generate corresponding predicates on the generated column for range predicates on the base column, but it will still be able to generate predicates on the generated column for equality and IN predicates.

> **N O T E**   *Monotonic* means that an increasing range of values on the base column corresponds to a range of values on the generated column that is never decreasing.

> **N O T E**   In some cases, the optimizer will not be able to determine definitively whether an expression is monotonic, and in these cases, it will have to assume that the expression is not monotonic.

SPACE USAGE WITH MDC TABLES

The following section will use the table space MDCTS, defined as:

```
create tablespace mdcts pagesize 4k
   managed by database using (file 'd:\mdcts' 10000) extentsize 32
```

and the table T1, defined as:

```
create table t1(c1 varchar(30), c2 int, c3 int) organize by (c1, c2)
in mdcts
```

for the basis of discussion.

Before creating the table, there will be four extents used for the container tag and three extents of table space overhead. The LIST TABLESPACES command does not show the pages used by the container tag, so the output of the command would show three extents used as follows:

```
Tablespace ID                                = 3
   Name                                      = MDCTS
   Type                                      = Database managed space
   Contents                                  = Any data
   State                                     = 0x0000
      Detailed explanation:
         Normal
   Total pages                               = 10000
   Useable pages                             = 9952
   Used pages                                = 96
   Free pages                                = 9856
   High water mark (pages)                   = 96
   Page size (bytes)                         = 4096
   Extent size (pages)                       = 32
   Prefetch size (pages)                     = 32
   Number of containers                      = 1
```

Creating a table will use two extents for the data object and its extent map, two extents for the index object and its extent map, and two extents for the MDC table's block map and its extent map.

> **N O T E**   The first block or extent (Extent 0) of an MDC data object cannot hold any rows.

A block map is used to determine quickly and efficiently whether there are blocks in the table that have been emptied and disassociated from any existing cells and are therefore available for reuse. If there are no blocks available, a new block (extent) will need to be created in the table, and the block map will be extended to account for the new block. Therefore, creating the above

table will require six additional extents in the table space. The output of the LIST
TABLESPACES command after the table has been created would look like the following:

```
Tablespace ID                                  = 3
   Name                                        = MDCTS
   Type                                        = Database managed space
   Contents                                    = Any data
   State                                       = 0x0000
      Detailed explanation:
         Normal
   Total pages                                 = 10000
   Useable pages                               = 9952
   Used pages                                  = 288
   Free pages                                  = 9664
   High water mark (pages)                     = 288
   Page size (bytes)                           = 4096
   Extent size (pages)                         = 32
   Prefetch size (pages)                       = 32
Number of containers                           = 1
```

When an MDC table is created, DB2 will automatically build at least one index, the block
dimension index. Additional dimension indexes may also be created.

For the above table, there will be a block dimension index created on C2, C1. In addition, there
will be two dimension indexes created, one on C1 and one on C2. To examine the indexes that
are created, use the following statement:

```
select indname, colnames, indextype from syscat.indexes where tabname ='T1'
```

This statement would produce the following output:

```
INDNAME                         COLNAMES              INDEXTYPE
------------------              ---------             ---------
SQL021118211811590              +C2+C1                BLOK
SQL021118211811770              +C2                   DIM
SQL021118211811780              +C1                   DIM
```

As illustrated above, a dimension block index has a type of BLOK, and a dimension index has a
type of DIM.

N O T E   A normal RID index will have a type of REG.

Given the following delimited ASCII file, named file.del:

```
aaaaaaa,              11,                    9
bbb,                  22,                    10
cccccc,               33,                    11
bbb,                  22,                    7
dddd,                 44,                    5
```

If the data is loaded into the MDC table t1 as follows:

```
load from file.del of del insert into t1
```

the data is selected from the table t1 as follows:

```
select * from t1
```

and the data is returned as follows:

```
C1                    C2                     C3
-------               -------                -------
aaaaaaa               11                     9
bbb                   22                     10
bbb                   22                     7
cccccc                33                     11
dddd                  44                     5
```

The sequence of rows returned is different from the sequence in which they were entered. The fourth row (bbb, 22, 7) in the input file is the third row in the output of the SELECT statement. The rows are retuned in this order because an MDC table places the rows with the same dimension keys, which are the values on dimension columns, in the same block. Therefore, the rows (bbb, 22, 10) and (bbb, 22, 7) are in the same block in the table and will therefore be read at the same time, and returned before the blocks containing (cccccc, 33, 11) and (dddd, 44, 5).

N O T E   No special options are required to load into an MDC table.

In the above example, when the first row from the file is loaded, a new extent will be created, and the row will be placed in Extent 1 for the table. Therefore, the table would logically look like:

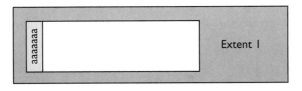

When the second row from the file is loaded, a new extent will be created, and the row will be placed in Extent 2 of the table. The table now logically looks like:

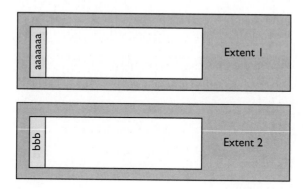

When the third row from the file is loaded, a new extent will be created, and the row will be placed in Extent 3 of the table. The table would logically look like:

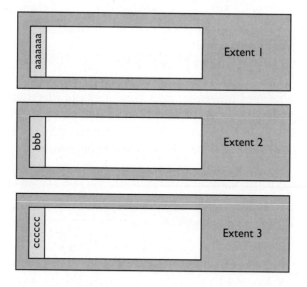

When the fourth row from the file is loaded, the data in the dimension columns is the same as in row 2; therefore, the row will be placed in the same extent as row 2 (Extent 2). The table now logically looks like:

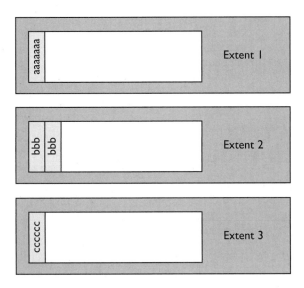

When the fifth row from the file is loaded, a new extent will be created, and the row will be placed in Extent 4 of the table. The table now logically looks like:

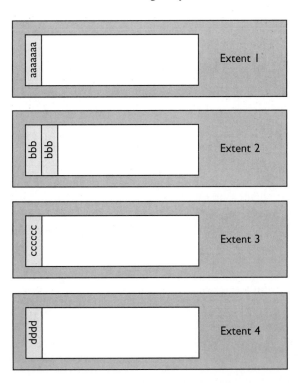

Therefore, an additional four extents of data are created when inserting the data into the table. In total, there would be 10 extents used for this data, the block map, and the indexes for this table.

The next example uses the following table:

```
create table city(name char(30), zipcode char(10), state char(2))
organize by (state)
```

with the following data inserted into the table:

Phoenix,	85001,	AZ
Los Angeles	90001,	CA
Tempe,	85820,	AZ
San Francisco,	94101,	CA
Boston,	02101,	MA
San Diego,	92126,	CA
Tiburon,	94920,	CA
Buffalo,	14201,	NY
Albany,	12202,	NY
Chicago,	60601,	IL
Kansas City,	64101,	MO
Kansas City,	66101,	KS

This will require seven new extents in the table's data object because there are seven distinct values for the dimension column, STATE.

When the data is selected from the table CITY, as follows:

```
select * from city
```

the data is returned as follows:

NAME	ZIPCODE	STATE
Phoenix	85001	AZ
Tempe	85280	AZ
Los Angeles	90001	CA
San Francisco	94101	CA
San Diego	92126	CA
Tiburon	94920	CA
Boston	02101	MA
Buffalo	14201	NY
Albany	12201	NY
Chicago	60601	IL
Kansas City	64101	MO
Kansas City	66101	KS

The table would logically look like Figure 5.7.

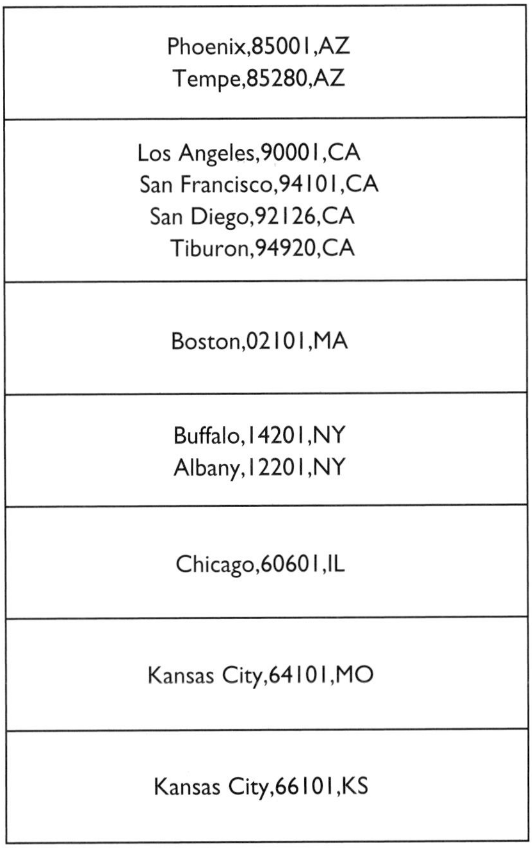

```
┌─────────────────────────────────┐
│        Phoenix,85001,AZ         │
│        Tempe,85280,AZ           │
├─────────────────────────────────┤
│                                 │
│      Los Angeles,90001,CA       │
│      San Francisco,94101,CA     │
│      San Diego,92126,CA         │
│      Tiburon,94920,CA           │
├─────────────────────────────────┤
│                                 │
│        Boston,02101,MA          │
│                                 │
├─────────────────────────────────┤
│                                 │
│        Buffalo,14201,NY         │
│        Albany,12201,NY          │
├─────────────────────────────────┤
│                                 │
│        Chicago,60601,IL         │
│                                 │
├─────────────────────────────────┤
│                                 │
│      Kansas City,64101,MO       │
│                                 │
├─────────────────────────────────┤
│                                 │
│      Kansas City,66101,KS       │
│                                 │
└─────────────────────────────────┘
```

Figure 5.7
Logical view of the MDC table.

MDC INDEXES

When an MDC table is created, DB2 will automatically create the block dimension and regular dimension indexes, if needed.

> **N O T E**   In the initial release of DB2 Version 8, the index is being created in the reverse order from what is described in the documentation, when there are composite dimensions. It is important to note that this will change in FixPack 1.

The following examples will show the current index definition, as well as how the index will be defined once FixPack 1 is installed. It is also important to note that existing block indexes will not be dropped and recreated when FixPack 1 is installed.

```
create table city(name char(30), zipcode char(10), state char(2))
organize by (state)
```

The relevant information from the SYSCAT.INDEXES view is below:

```
COLNAMES                            INDEXTYPE
-------------                       -----------
+STATE                              DIM
```

In this case, because there is only one dimension column, there will be a dimension index on the column STATE, and no block dimension index because block dimension indexes are required only when there is more than one dimension. This will not change in FixPack 1.

For the following table:

```
create table city(name char(30), zipcode char(10), state char(2))
organize by (state,name)
```

the relevant information from the SYSCAT.INDEXES view is below:

```
COLNAMES                            INDEXTYPE
-------------                       -----------
+NAME+STATE                         BLOK
+STATE                              DIM
+NAME                               DIM
```

In this case, there will be three indexes created, a block dimension index on NAME and STATE, a dimension index on STATE, and a dimension index on NAME. The block dimension index will change to STATE and NAME in FixPack 1. After the FixPack, the relevant information from the SYSCAT.INDEXES view is below:

```
COLNAMES                            INDEXTYPE
-------------                       -----------
+STATE+NAME                         BLOK
+STATE                              DIM
+NAME                               DIM
```

For the following table:

```
create table city(name char(30), zipcode char(10), state char(2))
organize by (state,(state,name))
```

the relevant information from the SYSCAT.INDEXES view is below:

```
COLNAMES                          INDEXTYPE
------------                      -----------
+STATE+NAME                       BLOK
+STATE                            DIM
+NAME                             DIM
```

In this case, there will be three indexes created, a block dimension index on STATE and NAME, a dimension index on STATE, and a dimension index on NAME. This will not change in FixPack 1.

For the following table:

```
create table mdcex1 (c1 int,c2 int,c3 int,c4 int)
organize by dimensions (c1,c4,(c3,c1),c2)
```

the relevant information from the SYSCAT.INDEXES view is below:

```
COLNAMES                          INDEXTYPE
-------------                     -----------
+C2+C3+C1+C4                      BLOK
+C2                               DIM
+C3+C1                            DIM
+C4                               DIM
+C1                               DIM
```

With FixPack1, the block dimension index information will change to:

```
COLNAMES                          INDEXTYPE
--------------                    -----------
+C4+C3+C1+C2                      BLOK
```

For the following table:

```
create table mdcex2 (c1 int,c2 int,c3 int,c4 int)
organize by dimensions (c1,c2,(c3,c1),c4)
```

the relevant information from the SYSCAT.INDEXES view is below:

```
COLNAMES                          INDEXTYPE
--------------                    -----------
+C4+C3+C1+C2                      BLOK
+C4                               DIM
+C3+C1                            DIM
+C2                               DIM
+C1                               DIM
```

With FixPack1, the block dimension index information will change to:

COLNAMES	INDEXTYPE
+C2+C3+C1+C4	BLOK

For the following table:

```
create table mdcex3 (c1 int,c2 int,c3 int,c4 int)
organize by dimensions (c1,(c2,c3),(c2,c1),c4)
```

the relevant information from the SYSCAT.INDEXES view is below:

COLNAMES	INDEXTYPE
+C4+C2+C1+C3	BLOK
+C4	DIM
+C2+C1	DIM
+C2+C3	DIM
+C1	DIM

With FixPack1, the block dimension index information will change to:

COLNAMES	INDEXTYPE
+C2+C3+C1+C4	BLOK

SUMMARY

An MDC table is just like any other table; it can be partitioned with a partitioning key, and that partitioning key may or may not also be one of the table's dimensions. An MDC table can have views, MQTs, referential integrity, triggers, RID indexes, replication, etc., defined upon it.

In an environment with referential integrity relationships, either or both of the parent and child tables may benefit from block-level clustering, depending on the query workload against these tables and the nature of the data contained in them. Similarly, in a star-schema environment, the fact table may benefit from block-level clustering, as may one or more of the dimension tables. Each table should be evaluated separately, and the dimensions should be chosen based on the query workload, data distribution, and expected cell density.

With the correct choice of dimensions for the MDC tables, the unique and powerful performance enhancements that multi-dimensional clustering provides can be leveraged.

The DB2 Optimizer

This chapter discusses the different strategies that the DB2 optimizer takes when a query is presented to it and how we should analyze and interpret the choices that the DB2 optimizer makes.

JOINING IN DB2 UDB

In the previous version of DB2, the DB2 optimizer would normally choose between two different join methods: a nested loop join and a merge join. However, in DB2 Version 7, when the DB2_HASH_JOIN registry variable was set to YES, the optimizer was also able to consider using a hash join when optimizing the access plan. Because hash joins can significantly improve the performance of certain queries, especially in DSS environments where the queries are normally quite large and complex, hash joins are always available in DB2 UDB Version 8 but are considered only when the optimization level is five or higher.

> **NOTE** To disable the optimizer from considering hash joins, set the DB2_HASH_JOIN registry variable to NO.

Join Methods

When joining two tables, no matter which join method is being used, one table will be selected to be the outer table, and the other table will be the inner table. The optimizer decides which will be the outer table and which will be the inner table based on the calculated cost and the join method selected. The outer table will be accessed first and will be scanned only once. The inner table may be scanned multiple times, depending on the type of join and the indexes that are present on the tables. It is also important to remember that, even though an SQL statement may join more than two tables, the optimizer will join only two tables at a time and keep the intermediate results if necessary.

Nested Loop Join

When performing a nested loop join, for each qualifying row in the outer table, there are two methods that can be used to find the matching rows in the inner table (Figure 6.1).

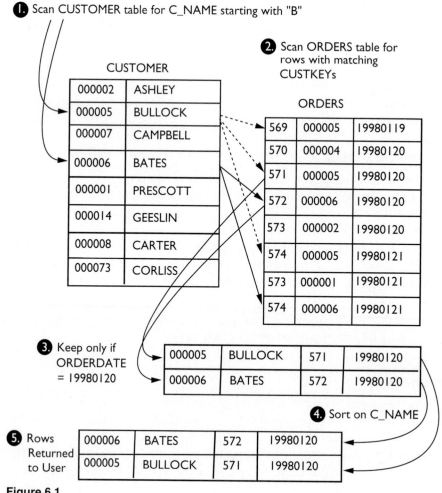

Figure 6.1
Nested loop join.

1. Scan the entire inner table.

  ○ Read every row in the inner table, and for each row determine whether it should be joined with the row from the outer table.

2. Perform an index lookup of the joined column(s) on the inner table.

  ○ This is possible when the predicate used for the join includes a column that is contained in an index on the inner table and can dramatically reduce the number of rows accessed in the inner table.

In nested loop joins, the decision of which is the outer table and which is the inner table is very important because the outer table is scanned only once, and the inner table is accessed once for every qualifying row in the outer table. The optimizer uses a cost-based model to decide which table will play which role in the join. Some of the factors taken into account by the optimizer when making this decision include:

- Table size
- Buffer pool size
- Predicates
- Ordering requirements
- Presence of indexes

> **N O T E**   The joined columns cannot be Long Varchar or LOB columns.

Merge Join

Merge joins (Figure 6.2) require that the SQL statement contain an equality join predicate (i.e., a predicate of the form table1.column = table2.column). A merge scan join also requires that the input tables be sorted on the joined columns. This can be achieved by scanning an existing index or by sorting the tables before proceeding with the join.

With a merge join, both of the joined tables will be scanned at the same time, looking for matching rows. In a merge join, both the outer and inner tables will be scanned only once unless there are duplicate values in the outer table, in which case, some parts of the inner table may be scanned again for each duplicated value. Because the tables are generally scanned only once, the decision on which is the outer and which is the inner table is somewhat less important than with a nested loop join; however, because of the possibility of duplicate values, the optimizer will attempt to choose the table with fewer duplicate values as the outer table.

> **N O T E**   The joined columns cannot be Long Varchar or LOB columns.

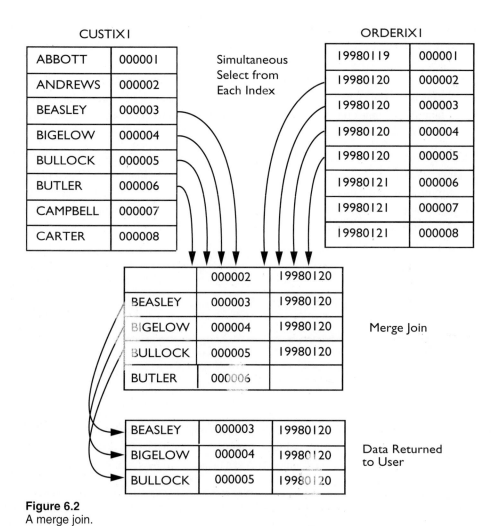

Figure 6.2
A merge join.

Hash Join

Hash joins require one or more equality join predicates between the joined tables, in which the data types for each of the joined columns must be the same. In the case of CHAR data types, even the length of the column must be the same. In the case of DECIMAL data types, the precision and scale must be the same. The fact that hash joins can handle more than one equality predicate between the joined tables is a distinct advantage over merge joins, which can handle only one equality predicate.

For hash joins, the inner table (also known as the *build table*) is scanned first, and the qualifying rows are copied into memory buffers. These buffers are divided into partitions based on a hash code computed from the column(s) in the join predicate(s). If there is not enough space in memory to hold the entire build table, some partitions will be written into temporary tables. Then the outer table (also known as the *probe table*) is scanned. For each row in the probe table, the same hashing algorithm is applied to the join column(s). If the hash code obtained matches the hash code of a row in the build table, the actual values in the join columns will be compared. If the partition that matches the probe table row is in memory, the comparison can take place immediately. If the partition was written to a temporary table, the probe row will also be written into a temporary table. Finally, the temporary tables containing rows from the same partitions are processed to match the rows. Because of the advantages of keeping the build table in memory, the optimizer will normally choose the smaller table as the build table to avoid having to create a temporary table.

If intra-partition parallelism is enabled, the hash join may be executed in parallel. When a hash join is executed in parallel, the build table is dynamically partitioned into multiple parallel tuple streams, and each stream is processed by a separate task to enter the build tuples into memory. At the end of processing the build table streams, the hash join process adjusts the contents of memory and performs any needed movement of partitions into or out of memory. Next, multiple parallel tuple streams of the probe table are processed against the in-memory partitions and may be spilled for any tuples from hash join partitions that were spilled to temporary tables. Finally, the spilled partitions are processed in parallel, with each task processing one or more of the spilled partitions.

Which Join Method to Use?

The previous sections have described the different join methods available in DB2 UDB, and based on these discussions, it appears that certain join methods seem to be a better choice than others. For example, merge joins have the advantage of scanning the tables only once when compared with nested loop joins that scan the inner table for every row of the outer table. At first glance, a merge join seems to be a better choice; however, if the correct index exists on the outer table, a nested loop join can end up being a better choice.

Similarly, at first glance, a hash join seems to be a better choice than a merge scan join because it does not need to sort the input tables before executing. If the order of the rows in the outer table needs to be preserved, a merge join or nested loop join might be a better choice because a hash join cannot guarantee ordering of the output; it may need to spill to disk, which would disrupt the ordering of the rows.

The $10,000 question then is, How does the DB2 UDB optimizer decide which join method to use for a particular join? First, the optimizer must take into account the types of the predicates in the SQL query. After examining the join predicates and the current optimization level, one or more of the join methods may be eliminated. Once the optimizer has determined which of the join methods are possible, it will decide which join method to use based on the calculated costs of the available join methods.

The optimization level is a database configuration parameter that specifies the amount of optimization to be done for any given SQL statement. The higher the optimization level, the more potential access plans that will be examined in search of the best (i.e., lowest cost) access plan. In DB2 UDB Version 8, the optimization level can be: 0, 1, 2, 3, 5, 7, or 9. Not all join methods are available at all optimization levels.

- A nested loop join is available to the optimizer for all optimization levels.
- A merge join is available to the optimizer at optimization level 1 or higher.
- A hash join is available to the optimizer at optimization level 5 or higher.

How to Tune and Monitor Hash Joins

Hash joins can significantly improve the performance of certain queries, especially in Decision Support Systems (DSS) that have complex queries. One of the performance advantages that hash join has over merge join is that it does not require any sorts beforehand, which could be very costly. The key for hash join is to be able to fit all (or as many as possible) rows of the build table into memory without having to spill to disk. The memory used for these buffers comes from the database sort heap, so the tuning of the SORTHEAP, SHEAPTHRES, and SHEAPTHRES_SHR configuration parameters is very important.

As discussed previously, SORTHEAP is a database configurable parameter that defines the maximum amount of memory that could be used for a sort or for a hash join. Each sort or hash join has a separate SORTHEAP that is allocated as needed by the database manager. Not necessarily all sorts and hash joins allocate this amount of memory; a smaller SORTHEAP could be allocated if not all the memory is needed. SORTHEAP can be allocated from shared or private memory, depending on the requirements of the operation. A shared SORTHEAP is used only for intra-parallel queries where degree > 1; a private SORTHEAP is used when only one agent will perform the sort or hash join and there is no need to share the memory with other agents. A single query might have more than one hash join, and/or sort and multiple SORTHEAPs may be required and allocated at the same time, depending on the nature of the plan.

For private sorts or hash joins, SHEAPTHRES acts as an instance-wide soft limit on the total amount of memory that all concurrent private sorts can consume. When this consumption reaches the limit, the memory allocated for additional incoming SORTHEAP requests will be reduced significantly.

For shared sorts or hash joins, SHEAPTHRES_SHR acts as an instance-wide hard limit on the total amount of memory that all shared sorts can consume. When this consumption gets close to the limit, the memory allocated for additional incoming SORTHEAP requests will be reduced significantly, and eventually no more shared sort memory requests will be allowed.

In uniprocessor systems, hash join uses only private SORTHEAPs. In SMP systems (with intra-parallel = ON and dft_degree > 1), hash join uses shared SORTHEAPs for the first part of the operation and private SORTHEAPs for the last phase. For more information on these parameters, see the *Administration Guide: Performance* that comes with DB2 UDB.

How do we tune these parameters? As in most tuning exercises, you need to have a starting point: a baseline benchmark, by defining a workload to test and using the appropriate tools to measure the test results. After that, it is an iterative process of changing one parameter at a time and measuring again. In most cases, you would already have values set for SORTHEAP and SHEAPTHRES in your existing system, so we suggest that you start with what your current settings are. If you have a brand new installation, you can follow the rules of thumb for DSS systems, which are to allocate 50% of the usable memory to buffer pools and the other 50% for SHEAPTHRES. Then make your SORTHEAP equal to the SHEAPTHRES divided by the number of complex concurrent queries that would be executing at one time, multiplied by the maximum number of concurrent sorts and hash joins that your average query has. (A good starting number for this is 5 or 6.) In summary:

```
SORTHEAP = SHEAPTHRES / (complex concurrent queries * max number of
concurrent sorts and hash joins in your average query)
```

The number of "complex concurrent queries" is not equal to the number of "concurrent users" in a DB2 database. There are usually many more users than complex concurrent queries executing at a time. In most DSS TPC-H benchmarks, which try to push the databases to their limits, no more than 8 or 9 is used as the number of complex concurrent queries (a.k.a. *streams*) for databases up to 10 TB, so start conservatively and move up as necessary.

After determining the starting SORTHEAP, SHEAPTHRES, and SHEAPTHRES_SHR values, run an average workload and collect database and database manager snapshots. DB2 offers a number of monitor elements to be able to monitor hash joins. All hash join monitor elements are collected by default, so there is no need to enable any monitor switches. For details on enabling, capturing, and examining DB2 snapshots, refer to the *System Monitor and Reference Guide*. Below is a description of the database monitor elements that are related to hash joins.

Total hash joins   This monitor element counts the total number of hash joins executed. This value can be collected with a database or application snapshot.

Hash join overflows   This monitor element counts the total number of times that hash joins exceeded the available SORTHEAP while trying to put the rows of the build table in memory. This value can be collected with a database or application snapshot.

Hash joins small overflows   This monitor element counts the total number of times that hash joins exceeded the available SORTHEAP by less than 10% while trying to put the rows of the build table in memory. The presence of a small number of overflows suggests that increasing the database SORTHEAP may help performance. This value can be collected with a database or application snapshot.

Total hash loops   This monitor element counts the total number of times that a single partition of a hash join was larger than the available SORTHEAP. This value can be collected with a database or application snapshot.

If DB2 cannot fit all of the rows of the build table in memory, certain partitions are spilled into temporary tables for later processing. When processing these temporary tables, DB2 attempts to load each of the build partitions into a SORTHEAP. Then the corresponding probe rows are read, and DB2 tries to match them with the build table. If DB2 cannot load some build partitions into a SORTHEAP, DB2 must resort to the hash loop algorithm. It is very important to monitor hash loops because hash loops indicate inefficient execution of hash joins and might be the cause of severe performance degradation. It might indicate that the SORTHEAP size is too small for the workload or, more likely, the SHEAPTHRES or SHEAPTHRES_SHR are too small, and the request for SORTHEAP memory could not be obtained.

Hash join threshold   This monitor element counts the total number of times that a hash join SORTHEAP request was limited due to concurrent use of shared or private memory heap space. This means that hash join requested a certain amount of SORTHEAP but got less than the amount requested. It might indicate that the SHEAPTHRES or SHEAPTHRES_SHR are too small for the workload. This value can be collected with a database manager snapshot.

Hash joins can provide a significant performance improvement with a small amount of tuning. Simply by following some basic rules of thumb, significant improvements can be obtained in typical DSS workloads when using hash joins. Hash joins can also improve the scalability when having many concurrently sorting applications.

The main parameters that affect hash joins are SORTHEAP, SHEAPTHRES, and SHEAPTHRES_SHR, with the SORTHEAP having the largest impact. Increasing the size of the SORTHEAP can potentially avoid having hash loops and overflows, which are the biggest cause of poor performance in hash joins.

The optimal method for tuning hash joins is to determine how much memory is available for the SHEAPTHRES and SHEAPTHRES_SHR, then to tune the SORTHEAP accordingly.

The key for tuning hash join is: *Make the SORTHEAP as large as possible to avoid overflows and hash loops, but not so large as to hit SHEAPTHRES or SHEAPTHRES_SHR.*

> **N O T E**   However, if the SORTHEAP is too large, it may result in paging and an increase in the number of POST_THRESHOLD_SORTs, which will take up a lot of CPU cycles. The optimizer takes into consideration the SORTHEAP size in determining the access plan. After the SORTHEAP is changed, rebind all static packages. In addition, setting the registry variable DB2_BIN_SORT to YES will enable a new sort algorithm that can reduce the CPU time and elapsed time of sorts under many circumstances.

Joining in a Partitioned Database

When two tables are joined together in a partitioned database, the data being joined must be physically located in the same database partition. If the data is not physically located in the same database partition, DB2 must move the data to a database partition by shipping the data from one partition to another. The movement of data between database partitions can be costly when the database is very large. Therefore, it is important to examine the largest and most frequently joined tables in the database and to choose a partitioning key to minimize the amount of data movement. Once the appropriate data is available in the database partition, DB2 can then determine the optimal join technique to execute the SQL statement.

In general, the best join strategy is to have all of the large, frequently accessed tables partitioned in such a way as to resolve the most frequent join requests on their database partitions with minimal data movement. The worst join strategy is to have the large, frequently accessed tables partitioned in such a way as to force the movement of the data to the appropriate partitions for the majority of the joins.

Collocated Table Joins

A collocated join is the best performing partitioned database join strategy. For a collocated join to be possible, all the data to perform the join must be located in each of the local database partitions. With a collocated join, no data needs to be shipped to another database partition except to return the answer set to the coordinator partition. The coordinator database partition assembles the answer set for final presentation to the application.

DB2 will perform a collocated join if the following conditions are true:

- For tables residing in a nonpartitioned database partition group
  - If all the tables reside within a nonpartitioned database partition group, then any join may be resolved on that partition group; therefore, all the tables will be collocated.
- For tables residing in a partitioned database partition group
  - The joined tables must be defined in the same partition group.
- The partitioning key for each of the joined tables must match, i.e., have the same number and sequence of columns.
  - For example, assume that the CUSTOMER table is partitioned on C_CUSTKEY, and the ORDERS table is partitioned on O_CUSTKEY. Each table is partitioned on one column, and the column types are compatible; therefore, a collocated join can occur.
  - If instead the CUSTOMER is partitioned on C_CUSTKEY, but the ORDERS table is partitioned on O_CUSTKEY, O_ORDERKEY, the CUSTOMER and ORDERS table will no longer have the ability to participate in a collocated join. Once the ORDERS table added an additional column to the partitioning key, the value that the partitioning key will hash to is now different than when it was just O_CUSTKEY. Therefore, there is no guarantee that the rows in the CUSTOMER table on any given partition will directly map to those in the ORDERS table on the same partition.

- For each column in the partitioning key of the joined tables, an equijoin predicate must exist.
  - If the ORDERS table is partitioned on O_ORDERKEY, and the LINEITEM table is partitioned on L_ORDERKEY, for these two tables to be eligible for a collocated join, the SQL request must specify that the join columns are equal, such as: ORDERS.O_ORDERKEY=LINEITEM.L_ORDERKEY.
- Corresponding partitioning key columns must be partition compatible.
  - If the O_ORDERKEY column is defined as SMALLINT in the ORDERS table and L_ORDERKEY is defined as INTEGER in the LINEITEM table, even though they are defined as different integer types, they are still compatible and may be used to join the two tables in a collocated join.

Ultimately, the data to complete the join must be found in the local database partition for DB2 to resolve the join. The collocated table join is the best performing type of join because the data already resides on the local database partition. DB2's goal in all the other join strategies is to relocate the data to the appropriate partition so that it may perform a join on each participating database partition.

Figure 6.3 is a diagram of the process flow of a collocated table join. The initial request is sent to the coordinator partition. From the coordinator partition, the request is split across all appropriate database partitions. Each partition scans the ORDERS table, applies the ORDERS predicates, scans the LINEITEM table, applies the LINEITEM predicates, performs the join locally, and inserts the answer set into a table queue. The table queue is then sent to the coordinator partition, where it is read and processed. The final answer set is then returned to the originating application.

The next sections will examine the access plan chosen for the following SQL statement:

```
Select O_ORDERPRIORITY, COUNT(DISTINCT O_ORDERKEY)
From ORDERS, LINEITEM
   where  L_ORDERKEY = O_ORDERKEY
     and  L_COMMITDATE < L_RECEIPTDATE
   group by O_ORDERPRIORITY
```

> **N O T E**   The output of the explain tool does not explicitly state the type of partitioned join strategy that was chosen by the DB2 optimizer.

In this statement, the two tables involved in the join are ORDERS and LINEITEM. Both tables are defined in the same database partition group, and the partitioning keys for each of these tables is listed below:

Table Name	Partitioning Key	Data Type
Orders	O_ORDERKEY	Integer
Lineitem	L_ORDERKEY	Integer

The optimizer is able to choose a collocated join in this case because all of the requirements for a collocated join have been met.

- The tables reside in the same database partition group.
- The partitioning keys for both LINEITEM and ORDERS contain the same number of columns.

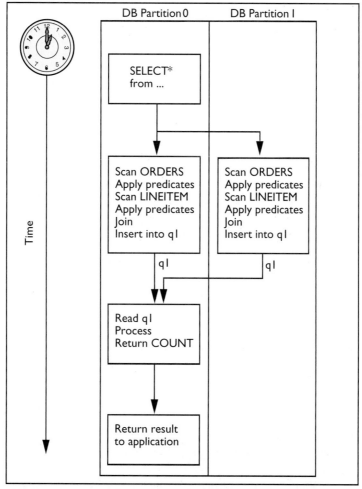

Figure 6.3
The flow of a collocated join.

- The partitioning key for each table is defined as INTEGER; therefore, they are collocatable.
- The two tables are joined based on the equijoin of L_ORDERKEY = O_ORDERKEY.

Once the collocated join of the tables on each database partition completes, the answer sets will be returned to the coordinator partition for final assembly and to be returned to the application. The coordinator subsection of the explain information for this statement looks like Figure 6.4.

```
Coordinator Subsection:
    Distribute Subsection #1                           ◄──── (A)
    |   Broadcast to Node List
    |   |   Nodes = 1, 2
    Access Table Queue  ID = q1  #Columns = 3
    |   Output Sorted #Key Columns = 2
    Final Aggregation
    |   Group By
    |   Column Function(s)
    Return Data to Application
    |   #Columns = 2
```

Figure 6.4
Coordinator subsection explain output.

For an SQL statement executed in a partitioned database environment, the first subsection of each DB2 UDB explain output is the coordinator subsection. The coordinator subsection explains steps that the optimizer intends to take to execute the plan that it has decided will be the most efficient. This subsection is the key to the process flow to resolve the request.

> **N O T E**   The term *node* is used in place of *database partition* in the explain snapshot in Figure 6.4. Node was the old term for database partition and is still used in some utilities, error messages, etc.

From the coordinator subsection of the above explain snapshot, the first step (designated as *A* in the explain output in Figure 6.4) is to distribute subsection #1 to database partitions 1 and 2. Subsection #1 may be found in Figure 6.5. The activities in subsection #1 will occur on each partition.

1. In subsection #1, DB2 will perform a relation scan (also known as a *table scan* or *full table scan*) of the ORDERS table.
2. The output from the scan will be placed in a temporary table referred to as *t1*.
3. The temporary table t1 will then be merge joined with the LINEITEM table on each database partition. The temporary table t1 will be the outer table, and the LINEITEM table will be the inner table of the collocated join. Because the join can be directly resolved within each database partition, it is safe to conclude that the optimizer has chosen a collocated join strategy.

```
Subsection #1:
   Access Table Name = DB2INST1.ORDERS  ID = 9          ◄─────────── ①
   |  #Columns = 2
   |  Relation Scan
   |  |  Prefetch: Eligible
   |  Lock Intents
   |  |  Table: Intent Share
   |  |  Row  : Next Key Share
   |  Insert Into Sorted Temp Table  ID = t1
   |  |  #Columns = 2
   |  |  #Sort Key Columns = 1
   |  |  Sortheap Allocation Parameters:
   |  |  |  #Rows      = 75201
   |  |  |  Row Width = 24
   |  |  Piped
   Sorted Temp Table Completion  ID = t1
   Access Temp Table  ID = t1                           ◄─────────── ②
   |  #Columns = 2
   |  Relation Scan
   |  |  Prefetch: Eligible
   Merge Join                                           ◄─────────── ③
   |  Access Table Name = DB2INST1.LINEITEM  ID = 2
   |  |  #Columns = 3
   |  |  Relation Scan
   |  |  |  Prefetch: Eligible
   |  |  Lock Intents
|  |  |  Table: Intent Share
   |  |  |  Row  : Next Key Share
   |  |  Sargable Predicate(s)
   |  |  |  #Predicates = 1
   |  |  Insert Into Sorted Temp Table  ID = t2
   |  |  |  #Columns = 1
   |  |  |  #Sort Key Columns = 1
   |  |  |  Sortheap Allocation Parameters:
   |  |  |  |  #Rows      = 10023
   |  |  |  |  Row Width = 8
   |  |  |  Piped
   |  Sorted Temp Table Completion  ID = t2             ◄─────────── ④
   |  Access Temp Table  ID = t2
   |  |  #Columns = 1
   |  |  Relation Scan
   |  |  |  Prefetch: Eligible
   Insert Into Sorted Temp Table  ID = t3              ◄─────────── ⑤
   |  #Columns = 2
   |  #Sort Key Columns = 2
   |  Sortheap Allocation Parameters:
   |  |  #Rows      = 10023
   |  |  Row Width = 24
   |  Piped
   Access Temp Table  ID = t3
   |  #Columns = 2
   |  Relation Scan
   |  |  Prefetch: Eligible
   |  Partial Predicate Aggregation
   |  |  Group By
   |  |  Column Function(s)
```

Figure 6.5
Subsection #1 of the explain output.

4. The output from the merge join of the temporary table t1 and the LINEITEM table will be a new, sorted temporary table, t2.

5. The temporary table t2 will be further processed to resolve any predicates that may be resolved at the partition level. The DISTINCT processing will be performed at the partition level, and duplicate rows will be eliminated, with the final partition level answer set placed in the temporary table t3.

6. The rows in the temporary table t3 will then be inserted into table queue q1 (Figure 6.6). Table queue q1 will then be sent back to the coordinator partition, where the processing is returned to the coordinator subsection. In the second step, B, the coordinator partition reads from the table queue, q1, performs the final aggregation of the result set received, and returns the final version of the data to the application requestor.

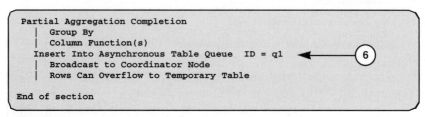

```
Partial Aggregation Completion
    |   Group By
    |   Column Function(s)
   Insert Into Asynchronous Table Queue   ID = q1
    |   Broadcast to Coordinator Node
    |   Rows Can Overflow to Temporary Table

End of section
```

Figure 6.6
Rows in temporary table t3 inserted into table queue q1.

Directed Outer Table Joins

A directed outer table join can be selected between two partitioned tables only when there are equijoin predicates on all partitioning key columns. With a directed outer table join chosen by the optimizer, rows of the outer table are directed to a set of database partitions, based on the hashed values of the joining columns. Once the rows are relocated on the target database partitions, the join between the two tables will occur on these database partitions.

Figure 6.7 is a diagram of the process flow for a directed outer table join strategy.

- The initial request is sent to the coordinator partition from the originating application.
- The coordinator partition dispatches the request to all relevant partitions.
- The partitions scan the table that DB2 has chosen as the outer table and apply any predicates to the interim result set.
- The partitions hash the join columns of the outer table that correspond to the inner table's partitioning key.
- Based on the hashing values, the rows are then sent via table queue to the relevant target partitions.
- The target partitions receive outer table rows via a table queue.

- The receiving partitions scan the inner table and apply any predicates.
- The partitions then perform a join of the received outer table rows and inner table.
- The partitions then send the results of the join back to the coordinator partition.
- The coordinator partition performs any final aggregation or other necessary processing and returns the final result set to the originating application.

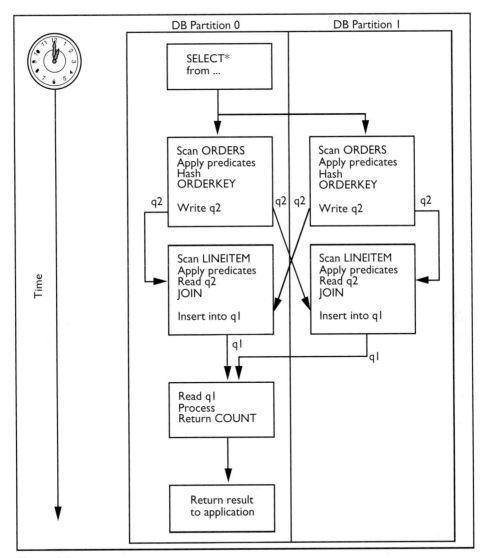

Figure 6.7
Flow of a directed outer table join.

For a directed outer table join, the explain will always show the inner table as a temporary table and the outer table as a table queue that has been hashed to the target database partitions. As noted in the collocated table join strategy section, the explain output no longer explicitly states what type of partitioned join strategy is being employed to resolve the request.

Directed Inner Table Join

With the directed inner join strategy, rows of the inner table are directed to a set of database partitions, based on the hashed values of the joining columns. Once the rows are relocated on the target database partitions, the join between the two tables occurs on these database partitions. As with directed outer join, the directed inner table join may be chosen as the join strategy only when there are equijoin predicates on all partitioning key columns of the two partitioned tables.

The flow of processing for a directed inner table join is identical to the process flow for the directed outer table join, except that the table that was directed to the target database partitions based on the hashed value of the joining columns is taken by DB2 as the inner table of the join on the database partition.

In the directed inner table join strategy, the explain will always show the outer table as a temporary table and the inner table as a table queue that has been hashed to the target partitions. As noted previously, the explain output no longer explicitly states which join strategy has been chosen by the optimizer.

The next section will examine the explain snapshot for a directed inner table join strategy. The following SQL statement was used to generate the explain snapshot.

```
Select C_NAME, COUNT(DISTINCT O_ORDERKEY)
  from CUSTOMER, ORDERS
  where C_CUSTKEY = O_CUSTKEY
    and C_ACCTBAL> 0
    and YEAR(O_ORDERDATE) = 1998
  group by C_NAME
```

The two tables involved in this statement are the CUSTOMER table and the ORDERS table. The partitioning keys for each of these tables are:

Table Name	Partitioning Key	Data Type
Orders	O_ORDERKEY	Integer
Customer	C_CUSTKEY	Integer

The CUSTOMER and ORDERS tables are not joined on their partitioning keys; therefore, this join *cannot* be collocated. The CUSTOMER and ORDERS join predicate from the above SQL statement is C_CUSTKEY = O_CUSTKEY. An equijoin predicate is required for a directed inner or directed outer table join; therefore, this statement is eligible for a directed table join.

The next section will examine the explain output (Figure 6.8) generated for the SQL statement above.

The coordinator subsection explains the steps that the optimizer intends to take to obtain the requested results. The first task (found in the explain output, Figure 6.8, *A*) is to distribute subsection #2 to database partitions 1 and 2. Subsection #2 may be found on the following pages.

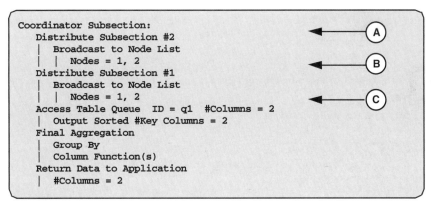

```
Coordinator Subsection:
   Distribute Subsection #2                              ◄─────  A
   |   Broadcast to Node List
   |   |   Nodes = 1, 2                                  ◄─────  B
   Distribute Subsection #1
   |   Broadcast to Node List
   |   |   Nodes = 1, 2                                  ◄─────  C
   Access Table Queue   ID = q1   #Columns = 2
   |   Output Sorted #Key Columns = 2
   Final Aggregation
   |   Group By
   |   Column Function(s)
   Return Data to Application
   |   #Columns = 2
```

Figure 6.8
Coordinator subsection explain snapshot.

The activities that occur in subsection #2 (Figure 6.9) are described below and occur on both database partition 1 and 2 simultaneously.

1. In subsection #2, DB2 will perform a relation scan (table scan) of the ORDERS table and apply any predicates.
2. The output from the scan and the application of the predicates will be placed in a temporary table, t3.
3. The temporary table t3 will then be read. Rows from temporary table t3 will be inserted into table queue q2 and distributed to the appropriate target partitions, based on the hash value of the O_CUSTKEY column that will be used to join to the CUSTOMER table.

In task *B* (Figure 6.8) in the coordinator subsection, the coordinator passes control to subsection #1, where the request is distributed to partitions 1 and 2 (Figure 6.10).

4. In subsection #1, DB2 will perform a relation scan (table scan) of the CUSTOMER table and apply any predicates.

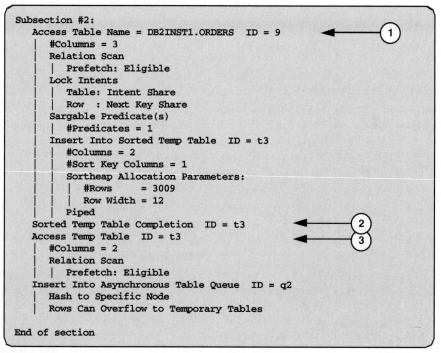

```
Subsection #2:
   Access Table Name = DB2INST1.ORDERS   ID = 9
   |  #Columns = 3
   |  Relation Scan
   |  |  Prefetch: Eligible
   |  Lock Intents
   |  |  Table: Intent Share
   |  |  Row  : Next Key Share
   |  Sargable Predicate(s)
   |  |  #Predicates = 1
   |  Insert Into Sorted Temp Table   ID = t3
   |  |  #Columns = 2
   |  |  #Sort Key Columns = 1
   |  |  Sortheap Allocation Parameters:
   |  |  |  #Rows      = 3009
   |  |  |  Row Width = 12
   |  |  Piped
   Sorted Temp Table Completion   ID = t3
   Access Temp Table   ID = t3
   |  #Columns = 2
   |  Relation Scan
   |  |  Prefetch: Eligible
   Insert Into Asynchronous Table Queue   ID = q2
   |  Hash to Specific Node
   |  Rows Can Overflow to Temporary Tables

End of section
```

Figure 6.9
Subsection #2 activity.

5. The output from the scan and the application of the predicates will be placed in a temporary table, t1.

6. The temporary table t1 will be merge joined to the rows that were hashed to the database partition via the table queue, q2. In this example, the temporary table based on the CUSTOMER table is the outer table of the join, and the hashed rows from ORDERS in table queue, q2, is the inner table of the join. Based on the information in the explain, the optimizer has chosen a directed inner table join.
   ○ Once the merge join is complete, the result set will be further processed to apply any additional predicates and any possible aggregations.

7. The result set is then written to the table queue q1 and broadcast back to the coordinator partition.

In task *C* (Figure 6.8) in the coordinator subsection, the table queue q1 that has been sent from each participating partition is read by the coordinator partition, final aggregation is performed, and the final result set is returned to the originating application.

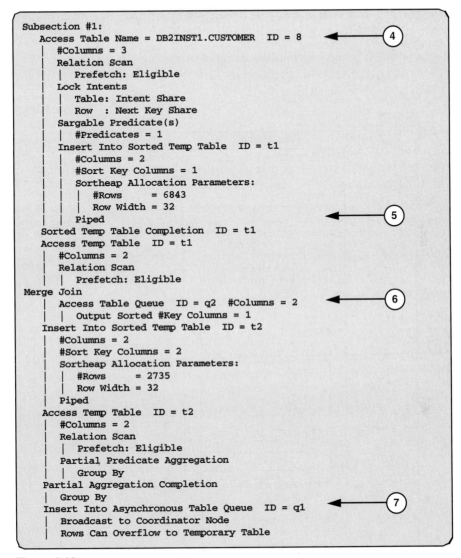

Figure 6.10
Subsection #1 activity.

Directed Inner and Outer Table Joins

The directed inner and outer table join is basically a combination of a directed inner table join and a directed outer table join. With this technique, rows of the outer and inner tables are directed to a set of database partitions, based on the values of the joining columns, where the join will occur.

A directed inner and outer table join may be chosen by the optimizer when the following situation occurs:

- The partitioning keys of both tables are different from the join columns.
- At least one equijoin predicate must exist between the tables being joined in the query.
- Both tables are relatively large.

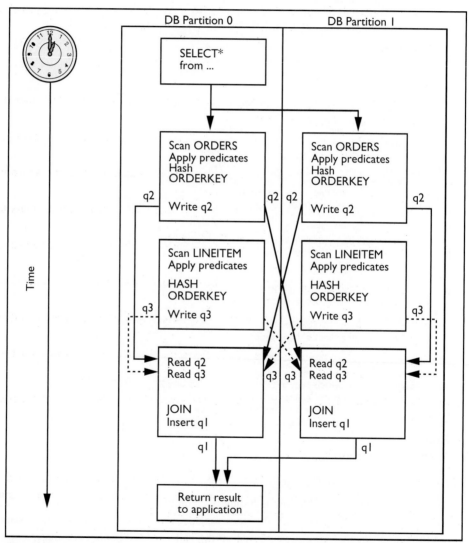

Figure 6.11
Flow of a directed inner and outer join.

Figure 6.11 is a diagram of the processing of a directed inner and outer join strategy. The process flow is explained below. Please note that these activities are being executed simultaneously across multiple database partitions during each step.

- The initial request is sent to the coordinator database partition from the originating application.
- The coordinator database partition dispatches the request to all relevant nodes.
- The outer table will be scanned on all nodes that contain the table that DB2 has chosen as the outer table of the join. Predicates will be applied where appropriate.
- The inner table will be scanned on all database partitions that contain the table that DB2 has chosen as the inner table of the join. Predicates will be applied where appropriate.
- The outer table database partitions will hash each selected row from the outer table, using the join columns specified in the query.
- The inner table database partitions will hash each selected row from the inner table, using the join columns specified in the query.
- Each participating database partition will send the hashed rows to the appropriate database partition via hashed table queues.
- The selected database partitions will receive the hashed table queues for the outer table rows.
- The selected database partitions will receive the hashed table queues for the inner table rows.
- The nodes perform the join of the received outer table rows to the received inner table rows. Predicates will be applied where appropriate.
- The results of the join are then sent from the database partitions to the coordinator partition.
- The coordinator partition performs any additional processing and returns the final result to the originating application.

The directed inner and outer table join strategy is characterized by the local join of two hashed table queues.

Broadcast Table Joins

A broadcast join is always an option for the DB2 optimizer. A broadcast table join will be chosen when the join is not eligible for any of the other join strategies or in the case where the optimizer determines that a broadcast table join is the most economical solution.

A broadcast join may be chosen in the following situations:

- If there are no equijoin predicates between the joined tables.
- If the optimizer determines that it is the most cost-effective join method.

- When there is one very large table and one very small table, of which neither is partitioned on the join predicate columns.
  - Rather than relocate the data in both tables, it may be more efficient to broadcast the smaller table to all the database partitions where the larger table resides.
- If the result set from applying the predicates to a large table results in a very small table.

Figure 6.12 is a diagram of the process flow of an outer table broadcast join. The process flow is explained below. Note that these activities are being executed simultaneously across multiple database partitions during each step.

- The initial request is sent to the coordinator partition from the originating application.
- The coordinator partition dispatches the request to all relevant nodes.
- The database partitions scan the table that DB2 has chosen as the outer table and apply any appropriate predicates to the interim result set.
- The database partitions transmit the full resultant outer table to all relevant database partitions via table queues.
- The database partitions receive the full resultant outer table via table queue.
- The receiving database partitions scan the inner table and apply any predicates. The output from this step is placed in a temporary table.
- The database partitions then perform a join of the received outer table and the local temporary inner table.
- The database partitions then send the results of the join back to the coordinator partition.
- The coordinator partition performs any final aggregation or other necessary processing and returns the final result set to the originating application.

With a broadcast outer table join, the rows from the outer table are broadcast to the database partitions where the inner table has rows. With a broadcast inner table join, the rows from the inner table are broadcast to the database partitions where the outer table has rows. Essentially, the two broadcast join strategies are equivalent with the inner and outer tables reversed.

When optimizing the following SQL statement:

```
Select C_NAME, C_ACCTBAL
  from   CUSTOMER, NATION
  where C_NATIONKEY > N_NATIONKEY and C_ACCTBAL > 0
  order by C_NAME
```

the DB2 optimizer selected a broadcast inner table join, as shown in the statement's explain snapshot (Figure 6.13). The two tables involved in this request are CUSTOMER and NATION, and the partitioning keys for these tables are:

Table Name	Partitioning Key	Data Type
Nation	N_NATIONKEY	Integer
Customer	C_CUSTKEY	Integer

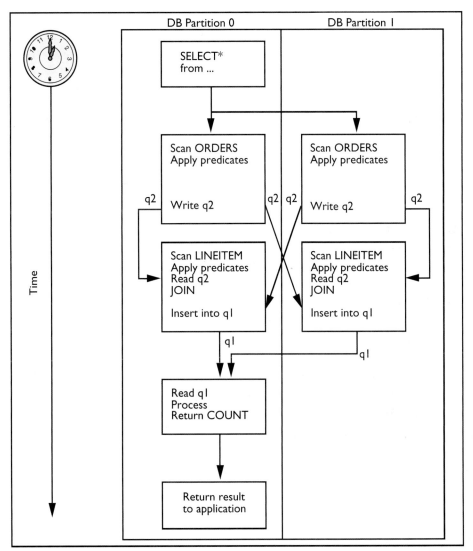

Figure 6.12
Broadcast join processing flow.

The CUSTOMER and NATION tables are not partitioned on the same key; therefore, this join is not eligible for a collocated join. In addition, the two tables are not joined with an equijoin statement (C_NATIONKEY > N_NATIONKEY); therefore, this join is not eligible for any of the directed joins. The only option left to the optimizer is a broadcast join.

When examining the explain snapshot, first start with the coordinator subsection.

    1. The first step (Figure 6.13, step 1) in the coordinator subsection is to distribute subsection #2 to partitions 1 and 2. Subsection #2 may be found on the following pages. The

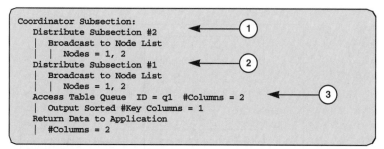

Figure 6.13
Explain output for coordinator subsection.

steps in subsection #2 and subsection #1 occur simultaneously across all specified partitions in the explain snapshot.

- In subsection #2, DB2 will perform a relation scan (table scan) of the NATION table.
- The output from the scan will be placed in table queue q1 and broadcast to all partitions named in subsection #1.

2. In Figure 6.13, step 2 in the coordinator subsection, subsection #1 is distributed to database partitions 1 and 2.

- In subsection #1, DB2 will perform a relation scan (table scan) of the CUSTOMER table (step 1, Figure 6.14). Any predicates that may be applied are applied at this time.
- The output from the scan is placed in temporary table t1 (step 2, Figure 6.14).
- The temporary table t1 is then nested loop joined to the received broadcast table queue (step 3, Figure 6.14). Any appropriate predicates are applied at this time.
- The result set is inserted into table queue q1 and broadcast back to the coordinator partition (step 4, Figure 6.14).

3. In Figure 6.13, step 3 in the coordinator subsection, the coordinator partition receives the q1 table queues sent from database partitions 1 and 2. The data is then sorted and returned to the originating application.

Partitioned Join Strategies and Performance

Based on the detailed descriptions of the various partitioned join strategies above, the following table is a summary of the characteristics of the various partitioned database join strategies mentioned above.

Join Strategy	Inner Table	Outer Table
Collocated Join	Temporary Table	Temporary Table
Directed Inner Join	Temporary Table	Hashed Table Queue
Directed Outer Join	Hashed Table Queue	Temporary Table
Directed Inner and Outer Join	Hashed Table Queue	Hashed Table Queue
Broadcast Inner Join	Temporary Table	Broadcast Table Queue
Broadcast Outer Join	Broadcast Table Queue	Temporary Table

```
Subsection #1:
    Access Table Name = DB2INST1.CUSTOMER   ID = 8        ◄————— ①
    |   #Columns = 3
    |   Relation Scan
    |   |   Prefetch: Eligible
    |   Lock Intents
    |   |   Table: Intent Share
    |   |   Row  : Next Key Share
    |   Sargable Predicate(s)
    |   |   #Predicates = 1
    |   Insert Into Sorted Temp Table   ID = t1
    |   |   #Columns = 3
    |   |   #Sort Key Columns = 1
    |   |   Sortheap Allocation Parameters:
    |   |   |   #Rows      = 6843
    |   |   |   Row Width = 40
    |   |   Piped
    Sorted Temp Table Completion   ID = t1        ◄————— ②
    Access Temp Table   ID = t1
    |   #Columns = 3
    |   Relation Scan
    |   |   Prefetch: Eligible
    Nested Loop Join                              ◄————— ③
    |   Data Stream 1: Evaluate at Open
    |   |   Not Piped
    |   |   Access Table Queue   ID = q2   #Columns = 1
    |   Insert Into Temp Table   ID = t2
    |   |   |   #Columns = 1
    |   End of Data Stream 1
    |   Access Temp Table   ID = t2
    |   |   #Columns = 1
    |   |   Relation Scan
    |   |   |   Prefetch: Eligible
    |   |   Sargable Predicate(s)
    |   |   |   #Predicates = 1
    Insert Into Asynchronous Table Queue   ID = q1
    |   Broadcast to Coordinator Node
    |   Rows Can Overflow to Temporary Table      ◄————— ④
```

Figure 6.14
Subsection #1 activity.

Performance

From a performance point of view, the type of partitioned database join strategy that the optimizer chooses can impact performance. With the exception of a collocated join, all of the parallel join strategies require relocation of data across database partitions before the request may be resolved at the partition level. If the larger tables in the database are frequently being broadcast across database partitions, the current partition keys may need to be reevaluated to ensure they are correct for the given workload. The larger amount of data that is moved between database partitions, the larger the impact on the performance of the query.

Broadcasting small tables to the database partition where they may be joined with your largest tables is desirable. Placing small tables in a single-partition database partition group is often desirable and will force DB2 to perform a broadcast of the table to the database partitions of the larger tables. The goal in a multi-partition database is to perform as much work as possible at the partition level, not at the coordinator partition level.

MATERIALIZED QUERY TABLES

A materialized query table (MQT) is a table that is defined based on the result of a query of one or more base tables. Prior to v8.1, MQTs required an aggregation operator in their defining SQL and, thus, were called *Automatic Summary Tables*. The next section describes how MQTs can provide effective performance improvements in a database.

Avoiding Repetitious Calculations

Materialized query tables can help to avoid having to repeat calculations, such as SUMs, for a number of queries that reference the same base table. For a CUSTOMER_ORDER table that stores customer orders for a number of years, the table will grow very large. If the applications run multiple queries on orders for only the year 2002, and only three columns from the table are used in these queries, such as:

```
select SUM(AMOUNT), trans_dt
from db2inst2.CUSTOMER_ORDER
where trans_dt between '1/1/2002' and '12/31/2002'
group by trans_dt
```

or

```
select SUM(AMOUNT), status
from db2inst2.CUSTOMER_ORDER
where trans_dt between '1/1/2002' and '12/31/2002'
group by status
```

the queries can be executed using index scans, assuming that the table is indexed appropriately. The explain plan below is an excerpt from the first statement above, and it shows that the query has an execution cost of 152455 timerons, to retrieve only 378 rows.

```
-------------------- SECTION -----------------------------------------
Section = 1

SQL Statement:

  select SUM(AMOUNT), trans_dt
  from db2inst2.CUSTOMER_ORDER
  where trans_dt between '1/1/2002' and '12/31/2002'
  group by trans_dt

Estimated Cost                          = 152455
Estimated Cardinality                   = 378
```

Creating an MQT that contains the columns being selected and precomputes the sum can lead to a substantial savings in execution time. For this example, the MQT should be created as follows:

```
CREATE TABLE DB2INST2.SUMMARY_CUSTOMER_ORDER_2002 AS
(SELECT SUM(AMOUNT) AS TOTAL_SUM, TRANS_DT, STATUS
    FROM DB2INST2.CUSTOMER_ORDER
    WHERE TRANS_DT BETWEEN '1/1/2002' AND '12/31/2002'
    GROUP BY TRANS_DT, STATUS)
    DATA INITIALLY DEFERRED REFRESH DEFERRED;
```

The clause DATA INITIALLY DEFERRED instructs DB2 not to insert the data into the MQT as part of the CREATE TABLE statement. Instead, the DBA will have to perform a REFRESH TABLE statement to populate the MQT. The clause REFRESH DEFERRED indicates that the data in the table reflects the result of the query as a snapshot only at the time the REFRESH TABLE statement was issued. For more information on creating MQTs, see the SQL Reference.

To populate the MQT created above, issue the following statement:

```
REFRESH TABLE DB2INST2.SUMMARY_CUSTOMER_ORDER_2002;
```

Once the MQT has been populated, queries run against the MQT can run much faster than queries run against the base table, because the MQT contains many fewer rows, and the SUM has already been precomputed. An excerpt from the execution once the MQT has been created and populated shows a dramatic performance improvement, with an estimated cost of 101 timerons versus the original cost of 152455 timerons.

```
-------------------- SECTION ------------------------------------------
Section = 1

SQL Statement:

    select sum(total_sum), trans_dt
    from db2inst2.summary_customer_order_2002
    where trans_dt between '1/1/2002' and '12/31/2002'
    group by trans_dt

Estimated Cost                      = 101
Estimated Cardinality               = 25
```

NOTE If the data in the CUSTOMER_ORDER table for the year 2002 gets updated after the MQT was refreshed, the MQT may need to be refreshed again.

For an MQT based on a table that changes frequently, it may be best to use the REFRESH IMMEDIATE option when creating the MQT to enable DB2 to update the MQT automatically as the base table is being updated.

Avoiding Resource-Intensive Scans

Assume a set of frequently executed reports that query up-to-date totals for the year 2002. The reports, which used to run very quickly in January, are now running more and more slowly as the amount of data for the year increases. Assume also that the table is indexed appropriately and the queries are being executed using index scans.

MQTs can be used to help improve performance in this case, as well. However, because the data is being updated all the time and the reports need current data, the MQT cannot be defined using the REFRESH DEFERRED option, because the MQT will get out of sync with the base table the next time the base table is updated. For an MQT based on a table that changes frequently, the REFRESH IMMEDIATE option should be used when creating the MQT to enable DB2 to update the MQT automatically as the base table is being updated. The MQT can be created as follows:

```
CREATE TABLE DB2INST2.SUMMARY_CUSTOMER_ORDER_2002 AS(
SELECT TRANS_DT, STATUS, COUNT(*) AS COUNT_ALL,
SUM(AMOUNT) AS SUM_AMOUNT, COUNT(AMOUNT) AS COUNT_AMOUNT
    FROM DB2INST2.CUSTOMER_ORDER
    GROUP BY TRANS_DT, STATUS)
    DATA INITIALLY DEFERRED
    REFRESH IMMEDIATE
    ENABLE QUERY OPTIMIZATION
```

> **N O T E**   Although the statement above is interested only in SUM(AMOUNT), it is best to include the COUNT(*) and COUNT(AMOUNT) in the full select. This helps to optimize the maintenance of the MQT. An example follows.

To enable the optimizer to choose the MQT automatically, even when it is not explicitly referenced in the query, as we did in the example above, the ENABLE QUERY OPTIMIZATION must be in effect. This option is the default.

If all of the records for a given date are being deleted from the base table, as in the statement:

```
DELETE FROM DB2INST2.CUSTOMER_ORDER WHERE TRANS_DT = '4/21/2002'
```

DB2 must detect that all of the records for a particular date are now deleted and delete all of the corresponding records in the MQT. Having the COUNT field allows DB2 to do this quickly, without having to scan either the table or its index. The COUNT(AMOUNT) is required only when the AMOUNT column is nullable.

Because this table was created with the REFRESH DEFERRED option, the MQT must be populated manually, as follows:

```
REFRESH TABLE DB2INST2.SUMMARY_CUSTOMER_ORDER_2002;
```

Because the table (MQT) has been enabled for optimization, it is also good practice to gather statistics on the table, as follows:

```
RUNSTATS ON TABLE DB2INST2.SUMMARY_CUSTOMER_ORDER_2002
  WITH DISTRIBUTION
```

The query above can now be routed to the MQT in the query rewrite phase of the optimization, and its new access plan would look like the following:

```
-------------------- SECTION ----------------------------------------
Section = 1

SQL Statement:

   select SUM(AMOUNT), trans_dt
   from db2inst2.customer_order
   where trans_dt >= '1/1/2002'
   group by trans_dt

Estimated Cost                       = 392
Estimated Cardinality                = 268
```

The detailed access plan shows that the optimizer is using the MQT (Summary Table) to resolve this query, even though the query is selected from the CUSTOMER_ORDER table, not the MQT:

```
Subsection #1:
   Access Summary Table Name = DB2INST2.SUMMARY_CUSTOMER_ORDER_2002
   ID = 2,46
   |   #Columns = 2
   |   Relation Scan
```

Whenever the CUSTOMER_ORDER table is modified, an exclusive table lock may be obtained and held on the MQT SUMMARY_CUSTOMER_ORDER_2002 until the end of the transaction. That is true only for MQTs with aggregate functions created with the REFRESH IMMEDIATE option. Therefore, transactions modifying relevant fields in the CUSTOMER_ORDER table (including all inserts, updates, and deletes) must be kept very short to reduce lock contention. This issue does not apply to MQTs created with the REFRESH DEFERRED option, nor to replicated MQTs (described in the next section).

Enabling Collocated Joins Using Replicated MQTs

In a partitioned database, the performance of joins can be greatly enhanced through collocation of rows of the different tables involved in the join. Figure 6.15 describes such an environment, where the STORE and TRANS tables have both been partitioned on the STOREID column. An SQL query that requires a join on the STOREID column will see significant performance benefits from this partitioning scheme because of the greater parallelism achieved through collocated joins.

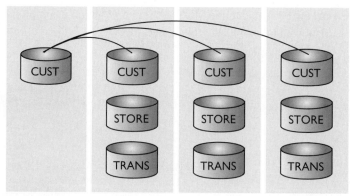

Figure 6.15
Replicating tables for collocation.

However, when the CUST table is also involved in the join, then a collocated join is not possible, because the CUST table does not have a STOREID column and, therefore, cannot be partitioned by STOREID. Although DB2 UDB can choose to perform a directed join in this particular case, the performance would be less efficient than that of a collocated join, because the movement of data rows occurs during the query execution.

A materialized query table can be used to replicate tables to other database partitions to enable collocated joins, even when not all of the tables are joined on the partitioned key. In Figure 6.15, the CUST table is replicated to the other database partitions using the materialized query table infrastructure in order to enable collocated joins for superior performance.

For another example, the table CUSTOMER_ADDRESS has a reference to another table, ZIP_CODE, but the CUSTOMER_ADDRESS and ZIP_CODE tables are not collocated. However, these two tables are very frequently joined. Without a replicated MQT, the access plan would look like the following. In this case, every time a query is issued that causes the join, it is necessary to broadcast the entire ZIP_CODE table to every database partition.

> **N O T E**   Access plans will be discussed in more detail later in this chapter, so this section will examine only the relevant pieces of the explain plan.

```
------------------- SECTION ----------------------------------------
Section = 1

SQL Statement:

  select c.*, z.zip, z.state_name, z.country_name
  from db2inst2.customer_address c join db2inst2.zip_code z on
                              c.zip_cd = z.zip_cd


Estimated Cost        = 100975
Estimated Cardinality = 255819


Coordinator Subsection:
  Distribute Subsection #2
  |  Broadcast to Node List
  |  |  Nodes = 0, 1
  Distribute Subsection #1
  |  Broadcast to Node List
  |  |  Nodes = 0, 1
  Access Table Queue  ID = q1   #Columns = 38
  Return Data to Application
  |  #Columns = 38


Subsection #1:
  Access Table Queue  ID = q2   #Columns = 4
  |  Output Sorted
  |  |  #Key Columns = 1
  |  |  |  Key 1: (Ascending)
  Nested Loop Join
.
  .
    .

  Insert Into Asynchronous Table Queue Completion  ID = q1
```

```
Subsection #2:
  Access Table Name =
  DB2INST2.ZIP_CODE   ID = 2,590
  |  #Columns = 4
  |  Relation Scan
  |  |  Prefetch: Eligible
  .

  .

  .

  |  |  Broadcast to All Nodes of Subsection 1
  |  |  Rows Can Overflow to Temporary Table
  Insert Into Asynchronous Table Queue Completion   ID = q2

End of section
```

This may be a good situation in which to use a replicated MQT. A replicated MQT should be created based on a table in a single-partition database partition group, which would allow collocated joins if replicated to other database partitions. To create the replicated MQT, use the CREATE TABLE statement with the REPLICATED option, as below:

```
CREATE TABLE DB2INST2.SUMMARY_ZIP_CODE
AS (SELECT * FROM DB2INST2.ZIP_CODE)
DATA INITIALLY DEFERRED REFRESH IMMEDIATE
ENABLE QUERY OPTIMIZATION
REPLICATED
```

By default, the first column will be hashed, and since no table space is defined, USERSPACE1 is used.

> **N O T E**   Aggregates are not allowed in the definition of a replicated MQT.

If the table ZIP_CODE table has a unique index on ZIP_CD, this index should be created on the MQT, as well, to let the optimizer know that this column is unique and to allow it to choose an access plan based on this knowledge. To populate the MQT, create an index on it and update the table's and index's statistics, using the following commands:

```
REFRESH TABLE DB2INST2.SUMMARY_ZIP_CODE

CREATE UNIQUE INDEX CU_ZIP_CD
ON DB2INST2.SUMMARY_ZIP_CODE(ZIP_CD)

RUNSTATS ON TABLE DB2INST2.SUMMARY_ZIP_CODE
WITH DISTRIBUTION AND DETAILED INDEXES ALL
```

This will allow the optimizer's query rewrite facility to reroute the query to the MQT, eliminating the need to broadcast the ZIP_CODE table to all database partitions every time the query is run. The new access plan would look like the following:

```
------------------- SECTION -----------------------------------
Section = 1

SQL Statement:

  select c.*, z.zip, z.state_name, z.country_name
  from db2inst2.customer_address c join db2inst2.zip_code z on
                              c.zip_cd = z.zip_cd


Estimated Cost        = 54176
Estimated Cardinality = 255819


Coordinator Subsection:
  Distribute Subsection #1
  |  Broadcast to Node List
  |  |  Nodes = 0, 1
  Access Table Queue   ID = q1
  #Columns = 38
  Return Data to Application
  |  #Columns = 38


Subsection #1:
  Access Summary Table Name = DB2INST2.SUMMARY_ZIP_CODE   ID = 2,47
  |  #Columns = 4
  |  Relation Scan

   .

   .

   .

  Nested Loop Join
  |  Access Table Name = DB2INST2.CUSTOMER_ADDRESS   ID = 2,591
  |  |  #Columns = 35
  |  |  Index Scan:  Name = DB2INST2.CU_ZIP_CD   ID = 2

   .

   .

   .

  |  |  Insert Into Asynchronous Table Queue   ID = q1
  |  |  |  Broadcast to Coordinator Node
  |  |  |  Rows Can Overflow to Temporary Table
  Insert Into Asynchronous Table Queue Completion   ID = q1


End of section
```

In this case, the cost is lower when the optimizer uses the MQT to allow a collocated join; however, if there were more partitions, and the partitions were placed on more than one server, the difference in costs between these access plans would be much greater.

Using replicated MQTs may yield significant performance advantages when the table that is being replicated to the other partitions:

- is very frequently joined
- is not heavily updated
- is not too large

However, it may still make sense for infrequently updated larger tables to be replicated if the one-time cost of replication can be offset by the performance benefits of collocation.

> **N O T E**   The locking issues described previously for REFRESH IMMEDIATE tables do not occur for replicated MQTs.

REFRESH IMMEDIATE vs. REFRESH DEFERRED

REFRESH IMMEDIATE MQTs affect performance of queries in the same manner that indexes do. They:

- Speed up the performance of relevant select statements, while returning current data
- Are automatically chosen by the optimizer whenever it makes sense
- Can degrade the performance of insert, update, and delete statements
- Cannot be updated directly
- May occupy considerable disk space
- May have exclusive locks held during updates of their base tables

To examine the performance impact of MQTs on updates, first examine the explain plan for an INSERT statement shown below:

```
-------------------- SECTION ----------------------------------------
Section = 1


SQL Statement:

  insert into db2inst2.zip_code(zip_cd, zip, state_cd, state_name,
    country_name) values (60606, '60606', 'IL', 'Illinois',
    'United States')


Estimated Cost        = 25
Estimated Cardinality = 1
```

Next, examine the explain plan for the same statement, but with a REFRESH IMMEDIATE MQT based on the table, as below:

```
-------------------- SECTION ----------------------------------------
Section = 1


SQL Statement:

  insert into db2inst2.zip_code(zip_cd, zip, state_cd, state_name,
    country_name) values (60606, '60606', 'IL', 'Illinois',
    'United States')


Estimated Cost                     = 50
Estimated Cardinality              = 1
```

In this example, the estimated cost of inserting a record into the base table is doubled when a REFRESH IMMEDIATE MQT is defined on the table. On the other hand, REFRESH DEFERRED MQTs have no effect on the performance of insert, update, and delete statements.

As a rule of thumb, use REFRESH IMMEDIATE MQTs in moderation, to optimize frequently run queries in which current data is important.

> **N O T E**   Some MQTs are not eligible for immediate refreshes. The exact rules defining when they can and cannot be defined as REFRESH IMMEDIATE are described in the SQL Reference.

Let the Optimizer Decide

The optimizer may choose to reroute a query to an MQT defined with the REFRESH IMMEDIATE option instead of its base table, depending on:

- The current statistics on the base table, the MQT, and their indexes
- The value of the CURRENT QUERY OPTIMIZATION setting

The optimizer may choose to reroute a query to an MQT defined with the REFRESH DEFERRED option if CURRENT REFRESH AGE setting is set to ANY.

> **N O T E**   The CURRENT QUERY OPTIMIZATION and CURRENT REFRESH AGE options are described in detail in the SQL Reference.

The best practices for using MQTs are as follows:

- Create an appropriate MQT for the queries being executed.
- Create appropriate indexes on the base table and MQT.
- Keep the statistics current.
- Let the optimizer choose whether to use the base table or the MQT; do not explicitly reference the MQT in the SQL.

In some cases, the optimizer may choose not to use the MQT in place of the base table. In these cases, the SQL statement can be rewritten to reference the MQT directly. And the optimizer will use the MQT in the access plan, regardless of whether it was defined as REFRESH DEFERRED or REFRESH IMMEDIATE, and regardless of the values of CURRENT REFRESH AGE and CURRENT QUERY OPTIMIZATION.

MQTs are very useful in various situations and can have a significant performance impact. The above examples illustrated how applying MQTs could significantly improve query performance but can also negatively impact update performance if performed frequently. Although MQTs are very convenient and effective, they do come at a price of additional disk space.

MQTs created with the REFRESH DEFERRED option do not impact the performance of inserts, updates, and deletes on the base tables but may not be used by the optimizer as often as MQTs created with the REFRESH IMMEDIATE option.

UNDERSTANDING DB2 QUERY ACCESS PLANS

The previous sections used the explain tool to examine DB2 access plans. The next sections will introduce the db2exfmt tool and discuss how to interpret its output. The db2exfmt tool reads the explain tables and builds an ASCII report with the explain information, as well as a graphical representation of the access plan.

The output of the db2exfmt tool includes the following information:

- Overview
  - DB2 version and release level
  - Basic database configuration parameters
- Original SQL statement text
  - The SQL statement as it was presented to the DB2 engine
- "Optimized" SQL statement text
  - SQL-like representation of the query after it has been rewritten, views merged, constraints and triggers added
  - Triggers are not shown
- Access plan
  - An overview graph of the query access plan
  - Details of the LOw LEvel Plan OPerators (LOLEPOPs)

Overview Area

As shown below, the main information in the overview area is the version and release level of
DB2, as well as the date and time when the tool was run.

```
DB2 Universal Database Version 8.1, 5622-044 (c) Copyright IBM Corp.
1991, 2002
Licensed Material - Program Property of IBM
IBM DATABASE 2 Explain Table Format Tool


*********************** EXPLAIN INSTANCE **************************


DB2_VERSION:                        08.01.0
SOURCE_NAME:                        SQLC2E03
SOURCE_SCHEMA:                      NULLID
SOURCE_VERSION:
EXPLAIN_TIME:                       2002-11-03-16.57.30.133000
EXPLAIN_REQUESTER:                  DWAINE
```

Database Context Area

The database context area lists the configuration parameters that have the biggest impact on the
performance of the database and its applications, including:

- CPU speed
- Communication speed
- Buffer pool size
- Sort heap size
- Average number of applications

```
Database Context:
----------------
Parallelism:                        None
CPU Speed:                          1.094264e-006
Comm Speed:                         1
Buffer Pool size:                   80000
Sort Heap size:                     4096
Database Heap size:                 1200
Lock List size:                     40
Maximum Lock List:                  22
Average Applications:               1
Locks Available:                    903
```

Package Context Area

The package context indicates whether the SQL was dynamic or static, as well as the optimization level, isolation level, and degree of intra-partition parallelism used for the statement.

```
Package Context:
----------------
SQL Type:                          Dynamic
Optimization Level:                5
Blocking:                          Block All Cursors
Isolation Level:                   Cursor Stability


-------------------- STATEMENT 1   SECTION 203 ----------------------
QUERYNO:                           1
QUERYTAG:
Statement Type:                    Select
Updatable:                         No
Deletable:                         No
Query Degree:                      1
```

Original Statement

The original statement contains the SQL statement as it was originally run by the application.

```
Original Statement:
-------------------
select l_returnflag, l_linestatus, sum(l_quantity) as sum_qty,
sum(l_extendedprice) as sum_base_price, sum(l_extendedprice * (1 -
l_discount)) as sum_disc_price, sum(l_extendedprice * (1 - l_discount)
* (1 + l_tax)) as sum_charge, avg(l_quantity) as avg_qty,
avg(l_extendedprice) as avg_price, avg(l_discount) as avg_disc,
count(*) as count_order
from tpcd.lineitem
where l_shipdate <= date ('2002-12-01') - 90 day
group by l_returnflag, l_linestatus
order by l_returnflag, l_linestatus
```

Optimized Statement

The optimized statement contains the SQL statement as it was rewritten by the query rewrite facility of the DB2 optimizer. The internal names (Q1, Q2, Q3) represent the table's position in the select list.

The query rewrite facility can also perform the following functions if applicable:

- Automatically redirect the query to a materialized query table if one can be used to satisfy the query
- Precompute constant expressions
- Optimize aggregates
- Remove/replace subselects

```
Optimized Statement:
--------------------
SELECT Q3.$C7 AS "L_RETURNFLAG",
   Q3.$C6 AS "L_LINESTATUS", Q3.$C5 AS "SUM_QTY",
   Q3.$C4 AS "SUM_BASE_PRICE", Q3.$C3 AS "SUM_DISC_PRICE",
   Q3.$C2 AS "SUM_CHARGE",(Q3.$C5 / Q3.$C0) AS "AVG_QTY", (Q3.$C4 /
   Q3.$C0) AS "AVG_PRICE", (Q3.$C1 / Q3.$C0) AS "AVG_DISC",
   INTEGER(Q3.$C0) AS "COUNT_ORDER"
FROM
   (SELECT SUM(Q2.$C2), SUM(Q2.$C3), SUM(Q2.$C4),
   SUM(Q2.$C5),SUM(Q2.$C6),SUM(Q2.$C7), Q2.$C0, Q2.$C1
FROM
   (SELECT Q1.L_LINESTATUS, Q1.L_RETURNFLAG, Q1.COUNT,
   Q1.S5, Q1.S4, Q1.S3, Q1.S2, Q1.S1
   FROM TPCD.L_SUMMARY AS Q1
   WHERE (Q1.L_SHIPDATE <= '09/02/2002')) AS Q2
   GROUP BY Q2.$C1, Q2.$C0) AS Q3
ORDER BY Q3.$C7, Q3.$C6
```

Access Plan

Access Plan Example 1

```
Access Plan:
-----------
Total Cost:    23296.9
Query Degree:  1

        Rows
        RETURN
        (   1)
        Cost
         I/O
          |
          6
        GRPBY
        (   2)
        23296.9
         12728
          |
          24
        MDTQ
        (   3)
        23296.9
         12728
          |
          6
        GRPBY
        (   4)
        23296.7
         12728
          |
          6
        TBSCAN
        (   5)
        23296.7
         12728
          |
          6
        SORT
        (   6)
        23296.7
         12728
```

```
             |
          478775
          TBSCAN
          (    7)
          22453.8
           12728
             |
          496100
     TABLE: TPCD.L_SUMMARY
```

The db2exfmt tool builds an ASCII/text graph of the access plan as above. The elements of the access plan are read from the bottom up.

Starting at the bottom of the access plan, we see that the base table accessed for this query is the L_SUMMARY table, and it has a cardinality of 496100 rows. The table is accessed via a table scan (relation scan) and the data then sorted. The output of the sort is then scanned, the data grouped on the specified column, and then directed to the coordinator partition, using a merge directed table queue. On the coordinator partition, the data is again grouped before being returned to the application.

The operators that can be encountered in the db2exfmt output can be broken into the following categories:

- Table operators
  - TBSCAN—Table Scan
  - IXSCAN—Index Scan
  - FETCH—Fetch from table
- Joins
  - MSJOIN—Merge Scan Join
  - NLJOIN—Nested Loop Join
  - HSJOIN—Hash Join
- Aggregation
  - GRPBY—Group By
  - SUM—Sum
  - AVG—Average
  - MIN—Minimum
  - MAX—Maximum
  - Etc.
- Temp/Sort
  - TEMP—Insert into temp table
  - SORT—Sort
- Special Operations
  - IXAND—Index ANDing

    o RIDSCA—Index ORing or List Prefetch

    o IXA—Star Schema Bitmap Indexing

    o BTQ—Broadcast Table Queue

    o DTQ—Directed Table Queue

    o MDTQ—Merge Directed Table Queue

    o MBTQ—Merge Broadcast Table Queue

    o LTQ—Local Table Queue, for intra-partition parallelism

Access Plan Example 2

In the following access plan example, the path of execution is read from the bottom up, and from left to right.

Each row that is found by the index scan (IXSCAN) in step 14 is passed to the nested loop join (NLJOIN) in step 13. The nested loop join (NLJOIN) then accesses the inner table, based on the join predicates and local predicates (if any) returned by the fetch (FETCH) in step 15, based on the index scan (IXSCAN) in step 16. Each joined row is returned from the nested loop join (NLJOIN) to the next operator in the access plan. Execution continues until the entire outer stream is exhausted.

```
                                    |
                                3.87404
                                NLJOIN
                                (  13)
                                125.206
                                   5
                        /-------+------\
              0.968511                    4
              IXSCAN                    FETCH
              (  14)                    (  15)
              75.0966                   100.118
                 3                         4
                 |                  /----+---\
          4.99966e+06        4            1.99987e+07
        INDEX: TPCD      IXSCAN      TABLE: TPCD
        UXP_NMPK         (  16)      PARTSUPP
                         75.1018
                            3
                            |
                       1.99987e+07
                INDEX: TPCD.UXPS_PK2KSC
```

However, the graph does not give all of the details. It is important to know why the fetch is required on the inner table and what columns are the tables being joined on. This information can be found in the access plan details.

For example, for the nested loop join in step 13, the detailed information is below. The cost information in the detailed information contains:

- Total cost in units of timerons
  - Not the elapsed time in a serial environment
  - Based on the elapsed time in a parallel environment
- Cost model is based on resource consumption
  - Total CPU and I/O resources consumed
- Communication costs are considered in a parallel environment
- Elapsed time could be different because of parallel I/O and overlap between CPU and I/O operations in a serial environment
- Plan costs are cumulative
  - In general, each plan operator adds cost to the plan

Based on the detailed information below, the total cumulative cost is 125.206 timerons. The Re-Total Cost is the estimated cost to reexecute this sub plan. The Cumulative First Row Cost is the estimated cost to return the first row of the result set. The Estimated Bufferpool Buffers is the expected number of buffer pool pages required by this operator.

```
13) NLJOIN: (Nested Loop Join)
    Cumulative Total Cost:          125.206
    Cumulative CPU Cost:            164264
    Cumulative I/O Cost:            5
    Cumulative Re-Total Cost:       0.062461
    Cumulative Re-CPU Cost:         49744
    Cumulative Re-I/O Cost:         0
    Cumulative First Row Cost:      125.204
    Estimated Bufferpool Buffers:   6
Arguments:
---------
    EARLYOUT: (Early Out flag)
    FALSE
    FETCHMAX: (Override for FETCH MAXPAGES)
    IGNORE
    ISCANMAX: (Override for ISCAN MAXPAGES)
    IGNORE
```

The arguments for the nested loop join indicate the following:

EARLYOUT   Indicates whether the optimizer will get the next outer row after finding the first match on the inner row. This guarantees one match on the inner.

FETCHMAX   Specifies the maximum number of pages to prefetch for a fetch or index scan.

ISCANMAX   A nested loop join can override the original settings if it is an ordered nested loop join.

```
13) NLJOIN: (Nested Loop Join)
Predicates:
-----------
16) Predicate used in Join
Relational Operator:                Equal (=)
Subquery Input Required:            No
Filter Factor:                      5.00034e-08


Predicate Text:
--------------
(Q1.PS_PARTKEY = Q2.P_PARTKEY)
```

The predicate information includes the estimated selectivity of the predicate, based on the table and column statistics, as well as the predicate being applied by the operator. In this case, the columns being joined are the PARTKEY columns in table Q1 and Q2.

The join will then have two input streams, one for the inner table and one for the outer table.

```
13) NLJOIN: (Nested Loop Join)
Input Streams:
-------------
  5) From Operator #14
  Estimated number of rows:         0.968511
    Partition Map ID                1
    Partitioning:                   (MULT )
                                    Multiple Partitions

    Number of columns:              3
    Subquery predicate ID:          Not Applicable


    Column Names:
    ------------
    +$RID$+P_PARTKEY+P_NAME


    Partition Column Names:
    ----------------------
    +1: PS_PARTKEY
```

The estimated stream cardinality from operator 14 in this case is .968511, and it is returning three columns. In this case, the operation is occurring on multiple partitions in the database. The partitioning key is PS_PARTKEY.

The estimated stream cardinality from operator 15, as seen below, is 4, and it is returning four columns. This operation is also occurring on multiple partitions, and the partitioning key is PS_PARTKEY.

```
13) NLJOIN: (Nested Loop Join)
Input Streams:
-------------
   9) From Operator #15
   Estimated number of rows:          4
   Partition Map ID:                  1
   Partitioning:                      (MULT )
                                      Multiple Partitions
   Number of columns:                 4
   Subquery predicate ID:             Not Applicable


   Column Names:
   ------------

      +PS_PARTKEY(A)+PS_SUPPKEY(A)+$RID$+PS_AVAILQTY


   Partition Column Names:
   ----------------------

   +1: PS_PARTKEY
```

The detailed information for the fetch operation shows that the columns PS_PARTKEY and PS_SUPPKEY are being passed to the fetch from the index scan in operation 16, and the fetch is then retrieving the PS_AVAILQTY column from the table PARTSUPP. The PS_AVAILQTY column must be retrieved from the table because it is not contained in the index used in operator 16.

```
15) FETCH :
(Fetch)
    Arguments:
    ---------

    ...

    Input Streams:
    -------------
                     7) From Operator #16
                        Column Names:
                        ------------

                        +PS_PARTKEY(A)+PS_SUPPKEY(A)+$RID$
```

```
    8) From Object TPCD.PARTSUPP
                   Column Names:
                   ------------
                   +PS_AVAILQTY
```

In the index scan in step 16, the optimizer is applying a start and stop predicate to the index scan. The scan will read only the index leaf pages where Q1.PS_PARTKEY = Q2.P_PARTKEY; it does not need to scan the entire index. From step 16, the estimated number of rows returned by the index scan is four.

```
16) IXSCAN: (Index Scan)
    Predicates:
    ----------
    16) Start Key Predicate
       Relational Operator:          Equal (=)
       Subquery Input Required:      No
       Filter Factor:                5.00034e-08


       Predicate Text:
       ---------------
       (Q1.PS_PARTKEY = Q2.P_PARTKEY)


    16) Stop Key Predicate
       Relational Operator:          Equal (=)
       Subquery Input Required:      No
       Filter Factor:                5.00034e-08


       Predicate Text:
       ---------------
       (Q1.PS_PARTKEY = Q2.P_PARTKEY)
```

The details for the sort operation in step 16 of the explain plan below indicate that I/O occurred during the sort. Therefore, the sort must have overflowed and could not be accomplished within the sort heap.

```
3.65665e+07
  TBSCAN
  (  15)
  6.87408e+06
  1.45951e+06
     |
```

```
   3.65665e+07
   SORT
   ( 16)
   6.14826e+06
   1.30119e+06
      |
   3.65665e+07
   TBSCAN
   ( 17)
   2.00653e+06
   1.14286e+06
      |
   3.74999e+07
 TABLE: TPCD
 ORDERS
```

The detailed information about the table scan following the sort (i.e., step 15 above) will list the estimated number of buffer pool buffers, which gives an estimate for the size of the overflowed temporary table. Based on the following piece of the explain graph, the estimated size of the overflowed sort table will be 163976 pages.

```
15) TBSCAN: (Table Scan)
    .
    .
    .
    Estimated Bufferpool Buffers:   163976
```

Recognizing List Prefetch

The following explain graph shows an example of list prefetch. In step 12, the index scan is applying the predicates and returning the row identifiers (RIDs) to the sort operation in step 11. The RIDs are then sorted based on the page number, and passed to the RID Scan (RIDSCN) operation in step 10. The RID scan will build a list of the pages and call the prefetchers to retrieve the pages into the buffer pool. The fetch operation in step 9 can then fetch and process the pages because they should already be in the buffer pool, due to the work of the prefetchers.

```
            455.385
            FETCH
            (  9)
            308.619
            61.2878
         /----+---\
    455.385           15009
    RIDSCN      TABLE: TPCD
    ( 10)      L_SUMMARY2
    219.093
    17.4697
       |
```

```
       455.385
       SORT
       (  11)
       219.091
       17.4697
         |
       455.385
       IXSCAN
       (  12)
       218.559
       17.4697
         |
        15009
   INDEX: TPCD
 L_SUMMARY2_IDX
```

Recognizing Index ORing

The following explain graph shows an example of index ORing. In steps 6, 8, and 10, the index scan is applying the predicates and returning the RIDs to the sort operations above. The RIDs are then sorted based on the page number, any duplicates are eliminated, and the results are then passed to the RID Scan (RIDSCN) operation in step 4. The RID scan will build a list of the pages and call the prefetchers to retrieve the pages into the buffer pool. The fetch operation in step 3 can then fetch and process the pages because they should already be in the buffer pool, due to the work of the prefetchers. In this case, the fetch operation must reapply the predicates due to the OR predicates.

```
                    59537.2
                    FETCH
                    (   3)
                    62819.1
                    37361.7
                  /----+---\
          59537.2        1.50002e+08
          RIDSCN         TABLE: TPCD
          (   4)            LINEITEM
          803.781
          82.2908
            |
```

```
            +------------------+------------------+
    59383.3              150.002            4.00006
    SORT                 SORT               SORT
    (    5)              (    7)            (    9)
    653.127              75.5534            75.1057
    76.2908              3                  3
       |                    |                  |
    59383.3              150.002            4.00006
    IXSCAN               IXSCAN             IXSCAN
    (    6)              (    8)            (   10)
    510.773              75.4177            75.1022
    76.2908              3                  3
       |                    |                  |
  1.50002e+08          1.50002e+08        1.50002e+08
    INDEX:               INDEX:             INDEX:
    TPCD.L_SD            TPCD.L_SK_PK       TPCD.L_OK
```

Recognizing Index ANDing

The following explain graph shows an example of index ANDing. In steps 7 and 8, the index scan is applying the predicates and returning the RIDs from the index. The index ANDing (IXAND) operation then hashes the RIDs into the dynamic bitmap and starts returning the RIDs as it works on the last index. The RIDs are then sorted based on the page number, any duplicates are eliminated, and the results are then passed to the RIDSCN operation in step 4. The RID scan will build a list of the pages and call the prefetchers to retrieve the pages into the buffer pool. The fetch operation in step 3 can then fetch and process the pages because they should already be in the buffer pool, due to the work of the prefetchers. In this case, the fetch operation must reapply the predicates because the bitmap used is a reducing bitmap, and not all "qualified" rows are truly qualified.

As shown by the access plan graph below, index ANDing is considered when there is a large number of rows to process, but the expected result set is relatively small. In this case, the indexes scanned had approximately 250000 rows and 500000 rows, respectively, but the expected number of rows returned by the fetch is only four.

```
                  |
               4.4314
               FETCH
               (    3)
               5475.6
               1952.4
```

```
                    /----+---\
             886.281       1.50002e+08
             RIDSCN          TABLE: TPCD
              (   4)           LINEITEM
             4027.9
             1100.96
                |
             886.281
              SORT
              (   5)
             4027.9
             1100.96
                |
             886.281
             IXAND
              (   6)
             4026.01
             1100.96
           /------+-----\
      248752              534445
      IXSCAN              IXSCAN
       (   7)              (   8)
      1480.95             2509.07
      430.024             670.935
         |                   |
     1.50002e+08         1.50002e+08
   INDEX: TPCD         INDEX: TPCD
   L_OK                L_SD
```

Handling Predicates

Query predicates can be handled in two different manners within DB2:

1. When data is being fetched, the most straightforward approach is to return one row at a time and wait for the next request to fetch another one. Each returned row is then evaluated to determine whether it matches the given predicate(s). After evaluating the row against the given predicates, the next row is returned, and the same cycle is executed until reaching the end of the table being scanned. Although this approach might be the simplest, it causes a large number of round trips, which can turn into a performance penalty.

2. An alternative is when a record is fetched, to reference it in memory and directly evaluate the predicate to determine whether the row qualifies. If the row does qualify, it is returned at the end of the predicate evaluation. If the row does not qualify, the next row is fetched immediately.

Definitions and Terminology

A predicate that can be processed using method 2, described above, is known as a *sargable predicate* (SARG). There are three types of sargable predicates:

- BLOCK—These predicates are resolved while scanning the block index scan for a multi-dimensional clustering (MDC) table.
- INDEX—These predicates are resolved while performing a conventional index scan.
- DATA (Database Managed Space, or DMS)—These predicates are resolved while scanning the data pages.

All predicates for which method 2, described above, cannot be applied are referred to as *residual predicates* (RES). In this case, the rows must be returned one at a time and evaluated, as described in method 1.

Sargable Predicates vs. Residual Predicates

Based on the definitions and descriptions given above, it is evident that residual predicates are systematically more expensive in their processing than are sargable predicates. However, it is sometimes impossible to "push down" the evaluation of a predicate to make it sargable, and there are two main reasons for this:

- LOB and Long Varchar data types cannot be evaluated directly without retrieving the row because, when fetching LOBs and Long Varchars, only a locator is returned, not the actual data.
- The evaluation of a predicate requires that more than one page of data be fixed in the buffer pool.
  - As an example, consider a predicate comparing two columns from two different tables: The first row would need to be fetched from the first data page, and the second row would need to be fetched simultaneously from a different data page before the comparison can be made.

Analyzing Problem SQL Statements

Performance problems in a database can be a result of:

- The instance and database configuration parameter settings
- The physical layout of the database
- Inefficient SQL, normally due to incorrect/inefficient indexing

The next section will focus on analyzing SQL statements to determine what, if any, indexes should be created to help optimize problem SQL statements.

There are numerous methods that can be used to analyze the executing SQL statements to determine which statements, if any, need to be investigated. These include:

- Statement event monitor
- Dynamic SQL snapshot
- SQL snapshot table function

The event monitor tracks each execution of an SQL statement, whereas the snapshot monitor and table function provide one entry for each unique statement, along with information such as the number of times the statement was executed, the total execution time, the number of sorts performed, etc.

To obtain an SQL snapshot or get valid information from the dynamic SQL table function, the STATEMENT snapshot monitor switch must be turned on. If the switch is turned on at the session level, the get snapshot or table function must be run in the same session. If the switch is set at the DB2 instance level, the get snapshot or table function can be run from any session with a connection to the database.

To set the STATEMENT monitor switch at the instance level, first run the following command, then stop and restart the DB2 instance.

```
update dbm cfg using dft_mon_stmt on
```

Analyzing the output of the SQL statement snapshot or table function can take a good deal of time, especially if a large number of statements have been run. A spreadsheet can be used to aid in the analysis of this information; however, the output of the SQL snapshot must be parsed and converted to a format that is readable by a spreadsheet first. Appendix B, parseSQL.pl, is a Perl program that will parse the output of the SQL snapshot and convert the information to comma-delimited format so it can be imported into a spreadsheet.

The output of the SQL snapshot table function can be either exported directly to ASCII delimited format to be analyzed using the same spreadsheet or inserted into a table and analyzed using SQL statements. To make the insertion into a table easiest, export the table in IXF format, so that the table to store the data does not need to exist. For example:

```
export to try.ixf of ixf
SELECT * FROM TABLE(SNAPSHOT_DYN_SQL('SAMPLE',-1 ))
as SNAPSHOT_DYN_SQL
```

To import this into a table to be analyzed, the table need not exist because the IXF file contains the table definition. The command to create a new table and import the data is as follows:

```
import from try.ixf of ixf
create into sqlsnap
```

To capture the SQL snapshot using the table function and create an ASCII delimited file for analysis using a spreadsheet, use the following command:

```
export to try.del of del
SELECT * FROM TABLE(SNAPSHOT_DYN_SQL('SAMPLE',-1 ))
as SNAPSHOT_DYN_SQL
```

The information reported by the SQL snapshot or table function that is important when looking for poorly performing SQL is:

- Number of executions
- Rows read
- Rows written
- Statement sorts
- Total execution time
- Statement text

A statement that is run once a day and takes 10 seconds is much less important than one that runs 1,000 times a day and takes 10 seconds to run each time.

The Rows read gives an indication of the efficiency of the statement. A large number of rows read normally indicates that a table scan is being performed to resolve the query. Even if the query runs quickly, performing table scans is not efficient, and the query should be analyzed to determine whether it is indexed correctly.

The rows written and statement sorts elements of the snapshot are normally examined together. Overflowed sorts cause rows to be written to temporary tables in the database; therefore, if the statement is causing sorts to occur and there are no rows written, the sort is occurring within the sort heap. If there are rows written, the sort very likely overflowed. Regardless of whether or not the sort overflowed, all statements with sorts should be examined. Another item to examine is the average number of sorts per execution. To calculate this, divide the statement sorts by the number of executions, as follows:

```
Sorts per execution = (Statement sorts / Number of executions)
```

> **NOTE** Any statement with more than one sort per execution should be examined immediately.

The total execution time is for all executions of the statement. Even though a statement may have a total execution time of 5,000 seconds, if it was run 20,000 times, this is not excessive. However, if it was run only once, this is very excessive. Therefore, it is important to examine the average execution time as follows:

```
Avg execution time = (Total execution time / Number of executions)
```

For example, in the following SQL snapshot entry, the total execution time is 2.25 seconds, which seems like a lot for a simple statement like this. However, the statement was executed over 15,000 times, so the average execution time is very low. There are no sorts happening when this statement is run, so in this case everything appears to be fine.

```
Number of executions                    = 15616
Number of compilations                  = 1
Worst preparation time (ms)             = 11
Best preparation time (ms)              = 11
Internal rows deleted                   = 0
Internal rows inserted                  = 0
Rows read                               = 0
Internal rows updated                   = 0
Rows written                            = 0
Statement sorts                         = 0
Total execution time (sec.ms)           = 2.254846
Total user cpu time (sec.ms)            = 0.980000
Total system cpu time (sec.ms)          = 0.100000
Statement text                          = SELECT SUM(B.DEDUCTION) …
```

For the following statement, the total execution time is 23.35 seconds for 29 executions. Although each execution is under one second, the most interesting piece of information in this snapshot is the fact that the 29 executions are causing 6604 sorts to occur. Although the statement may not be taking an excessive amount of time to run, it is using a great deal of resources to perform this many sorts and should be examined to determine whether the underlying tables are indexed correctly.

```
Number of executions                    = 29
Number of compilations                  = 1
Worst preparation time (ms)             = 35
Best preparation time (ms)              = 35
Internal rows deleted                   = 0
Internal rows inserted                  = 0
Rows read                               = 4
Internal rows updated                   = 0
Rows written                            = 0
Statement sorts                         = 6604
Total execution time (sec.ms)           = 23.352040
Total user cpu time (sec.ms)            = 23.590000
Total system cpu time (sec.ms)          = 0.000000
Statement text                          = SELECT PAGE_NUM …
```

Steps in Analyzing a Poorly Performing Query

When a poorly performing SQL statement is found, the following steps can be used to help determine the cause of the problem and find a solution:

- Ensure that all tables in the query (and their indexes) have current statistics.
  - Distribution table statistics and detailed index statistics should be gathered.
- Determine whether new/changed indexes will help.
  - Looking at the query sometimes is enough to determine a good index.
  - For complex queries, use the index advisor.
- Determine whether an MQT will help.
  - Especially for a query that is executed many times

Determining Good Indexes

An indicator that the current indexes on a table may not be defined correctly (or that more indexes are needed) is when the SQL statement is performing one or more sorts per execution.

Indexing Example 1

For the piece of the SQL snapshot shown below, a sort is required each time the statement is executed.

```
Number of executions               = 378
  .
  .
  .
Statement sorts                    = 378
Statement text                     = SELECT custkey,
custname FROM user1.customer ORDER BY custkey DESC
```

To determine whether the table has current statistics, execute the following statement:

```
select stats_time from syscat.tables where tabname='CUSTOMER'
```

If the output of the above statement is as follows:

```
STATS_TIME
--------------------------
2002-10-06-09.45.13.468000

1 record(s) selected.
```

and the current date is October 6, unless there has been a large number of inserts or deletes since 9:45 A.M., the statistics are current. The next step is to examine the current indexes defined on the CUSTOMER table, as follows:

```
describe indexes for table user1.customer
```

View the output of the above statement, as follows:

```
Index             Index             Unique          Number of
schema            name              rule            columns
-------------     ----------------  --------------  --------------


0 record(s) selected.


SQL0100W No row was found for FETCH, UPDATE or DELETE; or the result
of a query is an empty table. SQLSTATE=02000
```

In this case, there are no indexes that can be used by the optimizer to retrieve the data columns or to help order the data. Therefore, a good first step is to examine the statement to determine what indexes may help.

In this example, there are two columns being selected from the table; therefore, an index can be created on these two columns. The ORDER BY clause in the statement is descending (DESC); therefore, the index should be created either with the CUSTKEY column in descending order or using the ALLOW REVERSE SCANS option.

The order of the key columns in the index is also important. The key column with the highest cardinality (i.e., most unique values) should be the first key in the index because it is the most selective and will narrow down the search must faster.

To determine the cardinality of the key columns for the above select statement, use the following:

```
select colname, colcard from syscat.columns where tabname='CUSTOMER'
```

The output of the above statement looks like:

```
COLNAME                           COLCARD
-------                           -------
CUSTKEY                           1709
CUSTNAME                          203
ADDRESS                           609

3 record(s) selected.
```

In this case, the customer key column (CUSTKEY) has the highest cardinality and, therefore, should be the first column in the index. The CUSTKEY column is also a unique identifier within this table. Thus, there are two options in this case:

- Create a non-unique index with CUSTKEY and CUSTNAME.
- Create a unique index on CUSTKEY and include the CUSTNAME column.

Therefore, any of the following four indexes would help improve the performance of this statement:

```
create index cust_ix on customer (custkey desc, custname)
create index cust_ix on customer (custkey, custname) allow reverse scans
create unique index cust_ix on customer (custkey desc) include (custname)
create unique index cust_ix on customer (custkey) include (custname) allow reverse scans
```

The fact that the CUSTKEY column is unique also helps the optimizer choose better access plans; therefore, if a unique index can be used, this is preferable.

Because the table has current statistics, when the index is created, collect the index statistics at the same time, as follows:

```
create unique index cust_ix on customer (custkey) include (custname)
allow reverse scans
collect detailed statistics
```

After creating the index and rerunning the application, the SQL snapshot information for this statement looks like the following:

```
Number of executions               = 378
    .
    .
    .
  Statement sorts                   = 0
  Statement text                    = SELECT custkey,
    custname FROM user1.customer ORDER BY custkey DESC
```

Indexing Example 2

The following statement has been found to be running slowly:

```
select empid, empname
from employees
order by empid
```

If there are no indexes on the table, the first step should be to create one or more indexes to help select the EMPID and EMPNAME columns and sort the EMPID column. Before adding the index, the access plan for the statement looks like the following:

```
Access Plan:
-----------
  Total Cost:                       4709.851
  Query Degree:                     1
```

```
        Rows
       RETURN
       (   1)
        Cost
         I/O
          |
        9600
       TBSCAN
       (   2)
       470.851
         109
          |
        9600
        SORT
       (   3)
       470.849
         109
          |
        9600
       TBSCAN
       (   4)
       454.206
         109
          |
        9600
   TABLE: USER1
 EMPLOYEES
```

Because the EMPID column is unique in this table, create an index and capture index statistics at the same time, as follows:

```
create unique index emp_ix on employees (empid) collect detailed statistics
```

```
Access Plan:
-----------
  Total Cost:                     650.384
  Query Degree:                   1

             Rows
            RETURN
            (   1)
             Cost
              I/O
               |
```

```
                    109
                   FETCH
                   (   2)
                  650.384
                    2
               /----+---\
         109              109
       IXSCAN      TABLE: USER1
       (   3)      EMPLOYEES
      0.248997
          0
          |
         109
    INDEX: USER1
 EMP_IX
```

The new index has eliminated the sort from the access plan and has greatly reduced the query's cost; however, the query can still be improved. Because the query is accessing only two columns, drop the index above and create a new index with both columns to eliminate the need to FETCH the rows from the table, as follows:

```
create unique index emp_ix on employees (empid) include (empname)
collect detailed statistics
```

In this case, the index contains all of the columns being selected, so the entire query should be able to be handled by the index, without needing to read data from the table. This is known as *index-only access* and is the fastest type of data access. The new access plan is shown below:

```
Access Plan:
-----------
  Total Cost:              50.2709
  Query Degree:           1

      Rows
    RETURN
    (   1)
     Cost
      I/O
       |
      109
    IXSCAN
    (   2)
    50.2709
      2
      |
     109
   INDEX: USER1
 EMP_IX
```

In an index-only access plan, the index is scanned (IXSCAN) and the data returned either to the application or to another database operation other than a fetch from the base table, as shown previously.

Writing Better SQL Statements

When the DB2 optimizer compiles SQL statements, it can rewrite them into a form that can be optimized more easily. The optimizer then generates a number of alternative execution plans for satisfying the SQL statement. It estimates the execution cost of each alternative plan, using the statistics for tables, indexes, columns, and functions, and chooses the plan with the lowest estimated execution cost.

The optimizer must choose an access plan that will produce the result set for the query that was submitted. Therefore, as noted in the following guidelines, the query should be written to retrieve only the data that is required. This helps to ensure that the optimizer can choose the best access plan.

Some guidelines for writing efficient SELECT statements are:

- Specify only the required columns.
  - Do not use select * unless all columns are needed.
- Limit the number of rows returned.
- Specify the FOR UPDATE clause if applicable.
- Specify the OPTIMIZED FOR n ROWS clause.
- Specify the FETCH FIRST n ROWS ONLY clause if applicable.
- Specify the FOR FETCH ONLY clause if applicable.
- Avoid data type conversions if possible.
  - Particularly numeric data type conversions.

Specify Only Needed Columns in the Select List

Specify only those columns that are needed in the select list. Although it may be simpler to specify all columns with an asterisk (*), needless processing and returning of unwanted columns can result in slower response time.

Limit the Number of Rows Returned by Using Predicates

Limit the number of rows selected by using predicates to restrict the answer set to only those rows that you require. There are four types of predicates, each with its own distinct method of processing and associated cost. The type of predicate is determined by how and when that predicate is used in the evaluation process. These predicate types are listed below, ordered in terms of performance, starting with the most favorable:

1. Range delimiting predicates
2. Index SARGable predicates
3. Data SARGable predicates
4. Residual predicates

Range delimiting predicates are those used to define the start key and/or stop key for an index search.

Index SARGable predicates are not used to define the start/stop key for an index search but can be evaluated from the index because the columns involved in the predicate are part of the index key. For example, assume a table named STAFF and an index defined on the columns NAME, DEPT, and SVC_YEARS in the table. For the following SQL statement:

```
SELECT name, job, salary FROM staff
WHERE name = 'John' and
dept = 10 and
svc_years > 5
```

The predicates name='John' and dept=10 would be range delimiting predicates, whereas svc_years > 5 would be evaluated as an index SARGable predicate, because the start key value for the index search cannot be determined by this information only. The start key value may be 6, 10, or even higher.

If the statement were written as follows:

```
SELECT name, job, salary FROM staff
WHERE name = 'John' and
dept = 10 and
svc_years >=5
```

the svc_years >=5 clause can now be evaluated using a range delimiting predicate, because the index search can start from the key value 5.

> **N O T E** SARGable refers to something that can be used as a search argument.

DB2 will make use of the index in evaluating these predicates, rather than reading the base table. These range delimiting predicates and index SARGable predicates reduce the number of data pages that must be accessed by reducing the set of rows that need to be read from the table. Index SARGable predicates do not affect the number of index pages that are accessed.

Data SARGable predicates are predicates that cannot be evaluated using the index and must be evaluated by reading the data. Typically, these predicates require the access of individual rows from a base table. DB2 will retrieve the columns needed to evaluate the predicate, as well as any others to satisfy the columns in the SELECT list that could not be obtained from the index.

For example, assume that a table named PROJECT has an index defined on the PROJNUM column. For the following query:

```
SELECT projnum, projname, repemp FROM project
WHERE dept='D11'
ORDER BY projnum
```

The predicate dept='D11' will be processed as data SARGable, because there are no indexes defined on the DEPT column, and the base table must be accessed to evaluate that predicate.

Residual predicates, typically, are those that require I/O beyond the simple accessing of a base table. Examples of residual predicates include those using quantified subqueries (subqueries with ANY, ALL, SOME, or IN) or those that require reading Long Varchar or LOB data.

Residual predicates are the most expensive of the four types of predicates. Because residual predicates and data SARGable predicates require more resources and cost more than range delimiting predicates and index SARGable predicates, limit the number of rows qualified by range delimiting predicates and index SARGable predicates whenever possible.

Specify the FOR UPDATE Clause

If an application will update fetched data, specify the FOR UPDATE clause in the SELECT statement of the cursor definition. By doing this, DB2 can choose appropriate locking levels [i.e., a U (update) lock instead of an S (shared) lock] to save the cost to perform lock conversion when the UPDATE is performed.

Specify the OPTIMIZE FOR n ROWS Clause

Specify the OPTIMIZE FOR n ROWS clause in the SELECT statement when the number of rows required is less than the total number of rows that could be returned. Using the OPTIMIZE FOR clause influences query optimization based on the assumption that the first *n* rows should be retrieved quickly, whereas the application can wait for the remaining rows.

Row blocking is a technique that reduces overhead by retrieving a number of rows in a single operation. These rows are stored in a cache, and each FETCH request in the application gets the next row from the cache. The OPTIMIZE FOR n ROWS clause will determine the number of records to be blocked. For example, if OPTIMIZE FOR 10 ROWS is specified, the block of rows returned to the client will contain ten rows.

```
SELECT projno,projname,repemp FROM project
WHERE deptno='D11' OPTIMIZE FOR 10 ROWS
```

Specify the FETCH FIRST n ROWS ONLY Clause

Specify the FETCH FIRST n ROWS ONLY clause if the application should not retrieve more than *n* rows, regardless of how many rows there might be in the result set when this clause is not specified. This clause cannot be specified with the FOR UPDATE clause.

For example, the following statement will retrieve the first five rows from the result set, not the entire result set:

```
SELECT projno,projname,repemp FROM project
WHERE deptno='D11' FETCH FIRST 5 ROWS ONLY
```

The FETCH FIRST n ROWS ONLY clause also determines the number of rows that are blocked in the communication buffer. If the FETCH FIRST n ROWS ONLY and OPTIMIZE FOR n ROWS clauses are both specified, the lower of the two values is used to determine the number of rows to be blocked.

> **NOTE** The OPTIMIZE FOR n ROWS clause does not limit the number of rows that can be fetched or affect the result in any way, other than performance. Using OPTIMIZE FOR n ROWS can improve the performance if no more than *n* rows are retrieved but may degrade performance if more than *n* rows are retrieved.

Specify the FOR FETCH ONLY Clause

When fetching rows, if the application will not update the rows retrieved, specify the FOR FETCH ONLY clause in the SELECT statement. This can improve performance by allowing the query to take advantage of record blocking. This can also improve concurrency because exclusive locks will never be obtained when this clause is specified.

> **NOTE** The FOR READ ONLY clause is equivalent to the FOR FETCH ONLY clause.

Avoid Data Type Conversions

Data type conversions (particularly numeric data type conversions) should be avoided whenever possible. When two values are compared, it is more efficient to compare rows with the same data type. For example, TableA and TableB are being joined using col1 in Table1 and col2 in Table2. If the columns col1 and col2 are the same data type, no data type conversion is required. If they are not the same data type, a data type conversion occurs to compare values at run time, and this will affect the performance of the query.

Additional Ways to Help the Optimizer

Marking Tables as Volatile

In some situations, scratch tables are used during processing that can grow from being empty to thousands (or even hundreds of thousands) of rows and shrink back to no rows in a very short period of time. It is impossible in this case to keep the statistics current, which can make it difficult for the optimizer to choose optimal access plans.

To account for a table that grows and shrinks rapidly during processing, the table can be marked as VOLATILE. If the table is marked as VOLATILE, the optimizer will use an index to scan the table (if one exists), regardless of the current statistics, if the index can provide index-only access or can apply a predicate during the index scan.

Use the Selectivity Clause

The DB2 optimizer uses the statistics to estimate the selectivity of each clause in an SQL statement. In most cases, when given current statistics, the optimizer is able to estimate the selectivity accurately. However, when a host variable is used in the predicate, the estimate of the clause selectivity can be wrong, and the optimizer can choose inefficient access plans.

The selectivity clause can be specified in the SQL statement when:

- The predicate is a basic predicate where at least one expression contains host variables
- The predicate is a LIKE predicate where the match expression, predicate expression, or escape expression contains host variables

In order for the optimizer to consider the selectivity clause, the registry variable SELECTIVITY must be set to YES.

Below is an example of how the selectivity clause can be used:

```
SELECT c1, c2 FROM t1 WHERE c1 = :hv1 SELECTIVITY 1
```

SUMMARY

The DB2 optimizer is an advanced, cost-based optimizer and normally chooses very efficient access plans. However, to enable the optimizer to choose an efficient plan, ensure that:

- The tables are indexed correctly for the workload
- The table and index statistics are current
- The optimization level is set correctly based on the workload
- Parallelism is enabled only if the workload will benefit from it

Federated Database Access

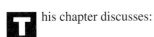 his chapter discusses:

- Federated System features, concepts, terminology, and usage.
- How to plan, configure, and administer a federated system.
- How to interface with a federated system.

Depending on the data sources that you want to access, you might need to install and configure:

- DB2 Relational Connect, a separately orderable IBM product that is used with DB2 for UNIX and Windows, Enterprise Server Edition. Relational Connect feature contains wrappers for the non-IBM relational databases.
  - It is required if you want to access data stored in Oracle, Sybase, Microsoft SQL Server, and ODBC data sources.
  - You can access and join data from different data sources with a single SQL statement and a single interface.
  - It provides fast and robust connectivity to IBM mainframe databases for e-business and other applications running under UNIX and Windows operating systems.
- DB2 Life Sciences Data Connect enables a DB2 federated system to integrate genetic, chemical, biological, and other research data from distributed sources. DB2 Life Sciences Data Connect supports the following data sources:
  - A table-structured file has a regular structure consisting of a series of records, where each record contains the same number of fields, separated by an arbitrary delimiter. A null value is represented by two consecutive delimiters. Table-structured files can be sorted or unsorted.

- ○ Documentum is document management software that provides management of document content and attributes, such as check-in, check-out, workflow, and version management. The Documentum product is a three-tier, client-server system built on top of a relational database. A Docbase is a Documentum repository that stores document content, attributes, relationships, versions, renditions, formats, work flow, and security. Documentum Query Language (DQL), an extended SQL dialect, is used to query Documentum data.
- ○ An Excel spreadsheet or workbook is a file created using the Microsoft Excel application and has a file extension of xls.
- ○ Basic Local Alignment Search Tool (BLAST) is a utility that is maintained by the National Center for Biotechnology Information (NCBI). BLAST is used to scan a nucleotide or amino acid sequence database for *hits*. A BLAST hit contains one or more high-scoring segment pairs (HSPs). A HSP is a pair of sequence fragments whose alignment is locally maximal and whose similarity score exceeds some threshold value. NCBI provides an executable, blastall, that is used to perform BLAST searches on BLAST-able data sources.
- ○ The Extensible Markup Language (XML) is a universal format for structured documents and data. XML files have a file extension of xml. Like HTML, XML makes use of tags for structuring data in the document.

> **NOTE** Customers accessing federated data sources, using DB2 Relational Connect Version 7 to connect to non-IBM data sources, or DB2 Life Sciences Data Connect Version 7 should wait to upgrade to DB2 Version 8 until this functionality is available.

DB2 Version 8 supports federation among the IBM family of database products, including:

- DB2 Universal Database (UDB) for Linux, UNIX, and Windows
- DB2 for z/OS
- DB2 for iSeries
- IBM Informix IDS
- IBM Informix XPS

WHAT IS A FEDERATED SYSTEM?

A federated system consists of:

- A DB2 instance that operates as a federated server
- One or more data sources
- A database that acts as the federated database
- Clients (users and applications) that access the federated database and data sources

With a federated system, you can send distributed requests to multiple data sources within a single SQL statement. For example, you can join data that is located in a DB2 UDB table, an Oracle table, and a Sybase view in a single SQL statement.

Federated Server

The federated server is a database manager instance to which application processes connect and submit requests. Any number of DB2 instances can be configured to function as federated servers. You can use existing DB2 instances as your federated server, or you can create new ones specifically for the federated system. The DB2 federated instance that manages the federated system is called a *server* because it responds to requests from end users and client applications.

The federated server often sends parts of the requests it receives to the data sources for processing. A pushdown operation is an operation that is processed remotely. The federated instance is referred to as the *federated server*, even though it acts as a client when it pushes down requests to the data sources.

There are two main features distinguishing a federated server from other application servers:

- A federated server is configured to receive requests that might be partially or entirely intended for data sources. The federated server distributes these requests to the data sources.
- A federated server uses DRDA communication protocols (such as SNA and TCP/IP) to communicate with DB2 family instances. However, unlike other application servers, a federated server uses other protocols to communicate with non-DB2 family instances.

Data Sources

Typically, a federated system data source is a relational DBMS instance (such as Oracle, Informix, Microsoft SQL Server, or Sybase) and one or more databases that are supported by the instance. However, there are other types of data sources (such as life sciences data sources and search algorithms) that you can include in your federated system.

Data sources are semi-autonomous:

- Local operations can continue simultaneously.
- Data sources can join or leave the federation.
- Data sources cooperate to support two-phase commit.

For example, the federated server can send queries to Oracle data sources at the same time that Oracle applications can access these data sources. A DB2 federated system does not monopolize or restrict access to the other data sources, beyond integrity and locking constraints.

Federated Database

Users and applications interface with the federated database managed by the federated server. The federated database contains catalog entries that identify data sources and their characteristics. The federated server consults the information stored in the federated database system catalog and the data source wrapper to determine the best plan for processing SQL statements.

The federated database system catalog contains:

- Information about objects at the data sources.
- Information about the objects in the federated database.
  - The catalog in a federated database is called the *global catalog* because it contains information about the entire federated system.
  - DB2 query optimizer uses the information in the global catalog and the data source wrapper to plan the best way to process SQL statements.
  - The information stored in the global catalog includes remote and local information, such as column names, column data types, column default values, and index information.
  - Remote catalog information is the information or name used by the data source.
  - Local catalog information is the information or name used by the federated database.
  - The global catalog also includes other information about the data sources. For example, it includes information the federated server uses to connect to the data source and map the federated user authorizations to the data source user authorizations.

> **N O T E**   For relational data sources, the information stored in the global catalog includes both remote and local information. For non-relational data sources, the information stored in the global catalog varies from data source to data source.

To see the data source table information that is stored in the global catalog, query the federated SYSCAT.TABLES, SYSCAT.TABOPTIONS, SYSCAT.COLUMNS, and SYSCAT.COLOPTIONS catalog views.

The SQL Compiler and the Query Optimizer

To obtain data from data sources, users and applications submit queries in DB2 SQL to the federated database. When a query is submitted, the DB2 SQL Compiler uses information in the global catalog and the data source wrapper to help it process the query. This includes information about connecting to the data source, server attributes, mappings, index information, and processing statistics.

As part of the SQL Compiler process, the query optimizer analyzes a query. The Compiler develops alternative strategies, called *access plans*, for processing the query. Access plans might call for the query to be:

- Processed by the data sources
- Processed by the federated server
- Processed partly by the data sources and partly by the federated server

DB2 evaluates the access plans primarily on the basis of information about the data source capabilities and the data. The wrapper and the global catalog contain this information. DB2 decomposes the query into segments that are called *query fragments*. Typically, it is more efficient to push down a query fragment to a data source if the data source can process the fragment.

> **N O T E** The processing of segments of a query at a data source instead of at the federated server is called *push-down processing*.

However, the query optimizer takes into account other factors, such as:

- The amount of data that needs to be processed
- The processing speed of the data source
- The amount of data that the fragment will return
- The communication bandwidth

The query optimizer generates local and remote access plans for processing a query fragment, based on resource cost. DB2 then chooses the plan it believes will process the query with the least resource cost.

If any of the fragments are to be processed by data sources, DB2 submits these fragments to the data sources. After the data sources process the fragments, the results are retrieved and returned to DB2. If DB2 performed any part of the processing, it combines its results with the results retrieved from the data source. DB2 then returns all results to the client.

Compensation

DB2 Federated Server does not push down a query fragment if the data source cannot process it or if the federated server can process it faster than the data source can process it. The ability by DB2 to process SQL that is not supported by a data source is called *compensation*. A federated server compensates for the loss of functionality at the data source either by simulating the data source function or by returning the set of data to the federated server and performing the function locally.

The federated server compensates for lack of functionality at the data source in two ways:

- It can ask the data source to use one or more operations that are equivalent to the DB2 function stated in the query.
- It can return the set of data to the federated server and perform the function locally.

With compensation, the federated server can support the full DB2 SQL dialect for queries against data sources, even data sources with weak SQL support or no SQL support. You must use the DB2 SQL dialect with a federated system, except in a pass-through session.

Pass-Through Sessions

In a federated system, a special DB2 session submits SQL statements directly to data sources, using the SQL dialect associated with that data source. You use a pass-through session to perform an operation that is not possible with DB2 SQL/API or to perform actions not supported by SQL. You can use both static and dynamic SQL in a pass-through session.

For example, use a pass-through session to create a procedure, create an index, or perform queries in the native dialect of the data source.

```
CREATE USER MAPPING FOR USER SERVER SYBSERVER
  OPTIONS (REMOTE_AUTHID 'xxxxxxxx', REMOTE_PASSWORD 'yyyyyyyy');

SET PASSTHRU SYBSERVER;

SELECT count(*) FROM dbo.sysobjects;

SET PASSTHRU RESET;
```

The following restrictions apply to pass-through sessions:

- You must use the SQL dialect or language commands of the data source. As a result, you do not query a nickname, but instead query the data source objects directly.
- When performing UPDATE or DELETE operations in a pass-through session, you cannot use the WHERE CURRENT OF CURSOR condition.

Wrappers and Wrapper Options

Wrappers are mechanisms by which the federated server interacts with data sources. The federated server uses routines stored in a library called a *wrapper module* to implement a wrapper. These routines allow the federated server to perform operations such as connecting to a data source and retrieving data from it iteratively. Typically, the DB2 federated instance owner uses the CREATE WRAPPER statement to register a wrapper in the federated system.

```
create WRAPPER sqlnet;
```

There are wrappers for each supported data source. Some wrappers have default wrapper names. When you use the default name (Table 7.1) to create the wrapper, the federated server automatically picks up the data source library associated with the wrapper.

Table 7.1   Federated Server Default Wrapper Names

Data Source	Default Wrapper Name(s)
DB2 UDB for Linux, UNIX, and Windows	DRDA
DB2 UDB for z/OS and OS/390	DRDA
DB2 UDB for iSeries	DRDA
DB2 UDB for VM and VSE	DRDA
Informix	INFORMIX
Oracle	SQLNet or Net8
Microsoft SQL Server	no default
ODBC	OLEDB
Sybase	CTLIB, DBLIB
BLAST	no default
Documentum	no default
Microsoft Excel	no default
Table-structured files	no default
XML	no default

There is one wrapper for each type of data source. For example, suppose that you:

- Want to access data in three DB2 for z/OS database tables, one DB2 for iSeries table, two Informix tables, and one Informix view.
- Need to create only two wrappers: one for the DB2 data source objects (DRDA wrapper) and one for the Informix data source objects (INFORMIX wrapper). After these wrappers are registered in the federated database, you can use these wrappers to access other objects from these data sources.

You use the server definitions and nicknames to identify the specifics (name, location, and so forth) of each data source object. A wrapper can:

- Connect to the data source using the standard connection API of that data source.
- Submit queries to the data source.
- For data sources that do not support SQL, one of two actions will occur:
  - For data sources that support SQL, the query is submitted in SQL.
  - For data sources that do not support SQL, the query is translated into the native query language of the source or into a series of source API calls.
- Receive results sets from the data source using the data source standard API of that data source.

- Respond to the federated server queries about the default data type mappings for a data source.
- Respond to the federated server queries about the default function mappings for a data source.

Wrapper options are used to configure the wrapper or to define how DB2 uses the wrapper. Currently, there is only one wrapper option, DB2_FENCED. The DB2_FENCED wrapper option indicates whether the wrapper is fenced or trusted by DB2. A fenced wrapper operates under some restrictions.

The current default setting for DB2_FENCED is N. The following example sets the DB2_FENCED option on for wrapper SQLNET:

```
alter WRAPPER sqlnet OPTIONS(set DB2_FENCED 'Y');
```

Server Definitions

After wrappers are created for the data sources, the federated instance owner defines the data sources to the federated database. The instance owner supplies a name to identify the data source and other information that pertains to the data source. If the data source is an RDBMS, this information includes:

- The type and version of the RDBMS
- The database name for the data source on the RDBMS
- Metadata that is specific to the RDBMS

For example, a DB2 family data source can have multiple databases. The definition must specify which database the federated server can connect to. In contrast, an Oracle data source has one database, and the federated server can connect to the database without knowing its name. The database name is not included in the federated server definition of an Oracle data source.

The name and other information that the instance owner supplies to the federated server are collectively called a *server definition*. Data sources answer requests for data and are servers in their own right.

The CREATE SERVER and ALTER SERVER statements are used to create and modify a server definition.

```
create server HOST390 type
  DB2/390 version 7.1
  wrapper drda
  authorization TST1TXP password xxxxxxxx
  OPTIONS (node 'HDB1NODE', dbname 'HDB1', password 'Y');
```

When you create server definitions, it is important to understand the options that you can specify about the server. Server options specify data integrity, location, security, and performance information. Some server options are specific to data sources. Some server options configure the wrapper, and some affect the way DB2 uses the wrapper. Server options are specified as parameters in the CREATE SERVER and ALTER SERVER statements.

The federated server options:

- Compatibility options: COLLATING_SEQUENCE, IGNORE_UDT
- Data integrity options: IUD_APP_SVPT_ENFORCE
- Location options: CONNECTSTRING, DBNAME, IFILE
- Security options: FOLD_ID, FOLD_PW, PASSWORD
- Performance options: COMM_RATE, CPU_RATIO, IO_RATIO, LOGIN_TIMEOUT, PACKET_SIZE, PLAN_HINTS, PUSHDOWN, TIMEOUT, VARCHAR_NO_TRAILING_BLANKS

To set a server option value temporarily, use the SET SERVER OPTION statement. This statement overrides the value for the duration of a single connection to the federated database. The overriding value does not get stored in the global catalog.

An example statement to set the passwords that will not need to be validated at the data source when the server option PASSWORD is set to N follows:

```
set server option password to 'N' for server HOST390;
```

The CPU_RATIO option indicates:

- The processing capacity of the data source compared with the federated server.
- The data source is faster or the federated server is slower if the value is less than 1.
- The data source is slower or the federated server is faster if the value is greater than 1.
- The federated server and the data source have the same processing capacity if the value is set to 1. It is the default value.

This is an example of setting the CPU_RATIO to indicate that the data source SUNSERV is 2 times faster than the federated server. Setting this value low influences the optimizer indicating that if an element of an SQL statement can be pushed down to the data source, it can be performed faster by the data source. Therefore, the optimizer tends to give more work to the data-source and to push down to the data source the more complex SQL to perform.

```
ALTER SERVER SUNSERV OPTIONS (ADD CPU_RATIO '0.5');
```

Here is an example to ensure that when authorization IDs are sent to your server HOST390, the case of the IDs will remain unchanged. Let's assume that this data source has started to run on an upgraded CPU that's only half as fast as your local CPU. You will need to inform the optimizer of this statistic:

```
ALTER SERVER HOST390 OPTIONS (ADD FOLD_ID 'N', SET CPU_RATIO '2.0');
```

The IO_RATIO option indicates:

- The disk I/O rate of the data source compared with the federated server.
- The data source is faster or the federated server is slower if the value is less than 1.
- The data source is slower or the federated server is faster if the value is greater than 1.
- The federated server and the data source have the same disk I/O rate if the value is set to 1. It is the default value.

This is an example of setting the CPU_RATIO to indicate that the federated server runs twice as fast as the CPU that supports HPSERV and the I/O devices at the federated server process data one and one-half times as fast as the I/O devices at HPSERV server.

```
ALTER SERVER HPSERV OPTIONS (ADD CPU_RATIO '2', IO_RATIO '1.5');
```

The COMM_RATE option indicates:

- The communications data rate between the federated server and the data source.
- Default value is 2, meaning 2,000,000 bytes/second.
- Values can be set only in whole numbers, with each whole number meaning 1,000,000 bytes/second.
  - 1 means 1,000,000 bytes/second
  - 3 means 3,000,000 bytes/second

Setting a lower value influences the federated server's cost-based optimizer by indicating it should send more SQL, and SQL of greater complexity, to the data source to reduce the volume of data that has to cross the network between the data source and the federated server.

This is an example of setting COMM_RATE to indicate the network communications data rate to data source SUNSERV is 1,000,000 bytes/second.

```
ALTER SERVER SUNSERV OPTIONS (ADD COMM_RATE '1');
```

User Mappings and User Options

When a federated server needs to push down a request to a data source, the server must first establish a connection to the data source. The server does this by using a valid user ID and password to that data source. By default, the federated server attempts to access the data source with the user ID and password that are used to connect to DB2. If the user ID and password are the same between the federated server and the data source, the connection is established. If the user ID and password to access the federated server differ from the user ID and password to access a data source, you must define an association between the two authorizations. Once you define the association, distributed requests can be sent to the data source. This association is called a *user mapping*.

You use the CREATE USER MAPPING statement and the user option REMOTE_PASSWORD to map the passwords. Use the ALTER USER MAPPING statement to modify an existing user mapping.

```
create user mapping for TPHAN server HOST390
  OPTIONS (remote_authid 'TST1TXP', remote_password 'xxxxxxxx');
```

User options provide authorization and accounting string information for user mappings between the federated server and a data source. These options can be used with any data source that supports user ID and password authorization. For example, suppose that a user has the same ID but different passwords for the federated database and a data source. For the user to access the data source, it is necessary to map the passwords to one another.

These options are used with the CREATE USER MAPPING statement:

- ACCOUNTING_STRING is used to specify a DRDA accounting string. Valid settings include any string of length 255 or less. This option is required only if accounting information is needed. The default setting is none.
- REMOTE_AUTHID indicates the authorization ID used at the data source. Valid settings include any string of length 255 or less. If this option is not specified, the ID used to connect to database is used. The default setting is none.
- REMOTE_DOMAIN indicates the Windows NT domain used to authenticate users connecting to this data source. Valid settings include any valid Windows NT domain name. If this option is not specified, the data source will authenticate using the default authentication domain for that database. The default setting is none.
- REMOTE_PASSWORD indicates the authorization password used at the data source. Valid settings include any string of length 32 or less. If this option is not specified, the password used to connect to the database is used. The default setting is none.

This is an example of a user, TPHAN, who uses a federated database to connect to a DB2 UDB for OS/390 and z/OS data source called HOST390. He uses one authorization ID to access DB2 and another authorization ID to access HOST390, and he has created a mapping between these two IDs. He has been using the same password with both IDs, but now he decides to use a separate password, pw390, with the ID for HOST390. Accordingly, he needs to map his federated database password to pw390.

```
alter user mapping for TPHAN server HOST390
  OPTIONS (ADD REMOTE_PASSWORD 'pw390');
```

Another example is where Tom uses a local database to connect to an Oracle data source called MYORA. He accesses the local database under the authorization ID TPHAN; TPHAN maps to ORAID, the authorization ID under which he accesses MYORA. Tom is going to start accessing MYORA under a new ID, PHANTOM. So TPHAN now needs to map to PHANTOM.

```
alter user mapping for TPHAN server MYORA
  options ( SET  REMOTE_AUTHID 'PHANTOM' );
```

Nicknames and Data Source Objects

After you create the server definitions and user mappings, the federated instance owner creates the nicknames. A nickname is an identifier that is used to reference the object located at the data sources that you want to access. The objects that nicknames identify are referred to as *data source objects*.

Table 7.2 shows the data source objects you can reference when you create a nickname.

Table 7.2   Data Source Objects

Data Source	Reference Objects
DB2 UDB for Linux, UNIX, and Windows	Nicknames, summary tables, tables, views
DB2 UDB for z/OS and OS/390	Tables, views
DB2 UDB for iSeries	Tables, views
DB2 UDB for VM and VSE	Tables, views
Informix	Tables, views, synonyms
Oracle	Tables, views
Microsoft SQL Server	Tables, views
ODBC	Tables, views
Sybase	Tables, views
BLAST	FASTA files indexed for BLAST search algorithms
Documentum	Objects and registered tables in a Documentum Docbase
Microsoft Excel	.xls files (only the first sheet in the workbook is accessed)
Table-structured files	.txt files (text files that meet a verify specific format)
XML	Sets of items in an XML document

Nicknames are not alternative names for data source objects in the same way that aliases are alternative names. They are pointers by which the federated server references these objects. Nicknames are typically defined with the CREATE NICKNAME statement.

When an end user or a client application submits a distributed request to the federated server, the request does not need to specify the data sources. Instead, it references the data source objects by their nicknames. The nicknames are mapped to specific objects at the data source. The mappings eliminate the need to qualify the nicknames by data source names. The location of the data source objects is transparent to the end user or the client application.

When you create a nickname for a data source object, metadata about the object is added to the global catalog. The query optimizer uses this metadata, and the information in the wrapper, to facilitate access to the data source object. For example, if the nickname is for a table that has an index, the global catalog contains information about the index. The wrapper contains the mappings between the DB2 data types and the data source data types.

```
create nickname DEPT for HOST390.DB2TTEST.DEPT;
```

> **N O T E**   With the current version, you cannot execute DB2 utility operations (LOAD, REORG, REORGCHK, IMPORT, RUNSTATS, and so on) on nicknames.

Column Options

You can supply the global catalog with additional metadata information about the nicknamed object. This metadata describes values in certain columns of the data source object. You assign this metadata to parameters that are called *column options*. The column options tell the wrapper to handle the data in a column differently than it normally would.

Column options are used to provide other information to the wrapper, as well. For example, for XML data sources, a column option is used to tell the wrapper the Xpath expression to use when the wrapper parses the column out of the XML document. The SQL compiler and query optimizer use the metadata to develop better plans for accessing the data.

The primary purpose of column options is to provide information about nickname columns to the SQL compiler. Setting column options for one or more columns to Y allows the SQL compiler to consider additional pushdown possibilities for predicates that perform the evaluation operation. This assists the SQL compiler in reaching global optimization.

These columns options are:

- NUMERIC_STRING
- VARCHAR_NO_TRAILING_BLANKS

You can define column options in the CREATE NICKNAME and ALTER NICKNAME statements. For example, a column with the data type of VARCHAR doesn't have trailing blanks. The nickname for the table is NCKTAB1, and the local name for the column is COL1:

```
alter nickname NCKTAB1 alter column COL1
  OPTIONS ( ADD VARCHAR_NO_TRAILING_BLANKS 'Y')
```

Data Type Mappings

The data types at the data source must map to corresponding DB2 data types so that the federated server can retrieve data from data sources. For most data sources, the default type mappings are in the wrappers. The default type mappings for DB2 data sources are in the DRDA wrapper. The default type mappings for Informix are in the INFORMIX wrapper, and so forth.

For some nonrelational data sources, you must specify data type information in the CREATE NICKNAME statement. The corresponding DB2 for Linux, UNIX, and Windows data types must be specified for each column of the data source object when the nickname is created. Each column must be mapped to a particular field or column in the data source object.

For example:

- The Oracle type FLOAT maps by default to the DB2 type DOUBLE.
- The Oracle type DATE maps to the DB2 type TIMESTAMP.
- The DB2 for z/OS type DATE maps by default to the DB2 type DATE.

When values from a data source column are returned to the federated database, the values conform fully to the DB2 data type to which the data source column is mapped. If this is a default mapping, the values also conform fully to the data source type in the mapping. For example, suppose an Oracle table with a FLOAT column is defined to the federated database. The default mapping of Oracle FLOAT to DB2 DOUBLE automatically applies to that column. Consequently, the values that are returned from the column will conform fully to both FLOAT and DOUBLE.

For some wrappers, you can change the format or length of values that are returned. You do this by changing the DB2 data type to which the values must conform. For example, the Oracle data type DATE is used as a timestamp; the Oracle DATE data type contains century, year, month, day, hour, minute, and second. It is the default; the Oracle DATE data type maps to the DB2 TIMESTAMP data type. Suppose that several Oracle table columns have a data type of DATE. You want queries of these columns to return only the hour, minute, and second. You can override the default data type mapping so that the Oracle DATE data type maps to the DB2 TIME data type. When Oracle DATE columns are queried, only the time portion of the timestamp values is returned to DB2.

```
create type mapping MY_ORACLE_DATE from SYSIBM.TIME
  to SERVER TYPE ORACLE TYPE DATE;
```

> **N O T E** If you change a type mapping, nicknames created before the type mapping change do not reflect the new mapping.

Unsupported data types   DB2 federated servers do not support:

- LONG VARCHAR
- LONG VARGRAPHIC
- DATALINK
- User-defined data types (UDTs) created at the data source

You cannot create a user-defined mapping for these data types. However, you can create a nickname for a view at the data source that is identical to the table that contains the user-defined data types. The view must *cast* the user-defined type column to the built-in, or system, type.

A nickname can be created for a remote table that contains LONG VARCHAR columns. However, the results will be mapped to a local DB2 data type that is not LONG VARCHAR.

Function Mappings and Function Templates

For the federated server to recognize a data source function, the function must be mapped against an existing DB2 function. DB2 supplies default mappings between existing built-in data source functions and built-in DB2 functions. For most data sources, the default function mappings are in the wrappers. The default function mappings from DB2 for Linux, UNIX, and Windows functions to DB2 for z/OS functions are in the DRDA wrapper. The default function mappings from DB2 for Linux, UNIX, and Windows functions to Sybase functions are in the CTLIB and DBLIB wrappers, and so forth.

To use a data source function that the federated server does not recognize, you must create a function mapping. The mapping you create is between the data source function and a counterpart function at the federated database.

Function mappings are typically used when a new built-in function and a new user-defined function become available at the data source. Function mappings are also used when a DB2 counterpart function does not exist; you must create one on the DB2 federated server that meets the following requirements:

- If the data source function has input parameters:
  - The DB2 counterpart function must have the same number of input parameters that the data source function has.
  - The data types of the input parameters for the DB2 counterpart function must be compatible with the corresponding data types of the input parameters for data source function.
- If the data source function has no input parameters:
  - The DB2 counterpart function cannot have any input parameters.

The DB2 counterpart function can be either a complete function or a function template. A function template is a DB2 function that you create to invoke a function on a data source. The federated server recognizes a data source function when there is a mapping between the data source function and a counterpart function at the federated database. You can create a function template to act as the counterpart when no counterpart exists.

> **NOTE**   When you create a function mapping, it is possible that the return values from a function evaluated at the data source will be different than the return values from a compatible function evaluated at the DB2 federated database. DB2 will use the function mapping, but it might result in an SQL syntax error or unexpected results.

However, unlike a regular function, a function template has no executable code. After you create a function template, you must then create the function mapping between the template and the data source function. You create a function template with the CREATE FUNCTION statement, using the AS TEMPLATE parameter. You create a function mapping by using the CREATE FUNCTION MAPPING statement. When the federated server receives queries specifying the function template, the federated server will invoke the data source function.

Function Mappings Options

The CREATE FUNCTION MAPPING statement includes parameters called *function mapping options*. You can assign values that pertain to the mapping or to the data source function within the mapping. For example, you can include estimated statistics on the overhead that will be consumed when the data source function is invoked. The query optimizer uses these estimates to decide whether the function should be invoked by the data source or by the DB2 federated database.

Index Specifications

When you create a nickname for a data source table, information about any indexes that the data source table has is added to the global catalog. The query optimizer uses this information to expedite the processing of distributed requests. The catalog information about a data source index is a set of metadata and is called an *index specification*. A federated server does not create an index specification when you create a nickname for:

- A table that has no indexes
- A view, which typically does not have any index information stored in the remote catalog
- A data source object that does not have a remote catalog from which the federated server can obtain the index information

> **NOTE**   You cannot create an index specification for an Informix view.

Suppose that a nickname is created for a table that has no index, but the table acquires an index later. Suppose that a table acquires a new index, in addition to the ones it had when the nickname was created. Because index information is supplied to the global catalog at the time the nickname is created, the federated server is unaware of the new indexes.

Similarly, when a nickname is created for a view, the federated server is unaware of the underlying table (and its indexes) from which the view was generated. In these circumstances, you can supply the necessary index information to the global catalog. You can create an index specification for tables that have no indexes. The index specification tells the query optimizer which column or columns in the table to search on to find data quickly.

In a federated system, you use the CREATE INDEX statement against a nickname to supply index specification information to the global catalog. If a table acquires a new index, the CREATE INDEX statement that you create will reference the nickname for the table and contain the information about the index of the data source table. If a nickname is created for a view, the CREATE INDEX statement that you create will reference the nickname for the view and contain information about the index of the underlying table for the view.

```
create unique index IDEPT
   on EMPLOYEE (WORKDEPT, JOB) SPECIFICATION ONLY;
```

OVERVIEW OF THE TASKS TO SET UP A FEDERATED SYSTEM

This section describes the tasks required to establish and use a federated system. Although the tasks identify the types of users who typically execute the tasks, other types of users can also perform these tasks. To establish and use a DB2 federated system:

System Administrator:

1. Determines and designates a server as a DB2 federated server
2. Installs and configures the data source client software and links DB2 to the client software
3. Installs DB2 and creates the DB2 instance
4. Installs DB2 Relational Connect (if necessary)

Database Administrator:

5. Creates a wrapper for each category of data source that is to be included in the federated system
6. Supplies the federated server with a server definition for each data source and might supply server options to assist in optimizing distributed requests
7. Defines an association between the authorization IDs that are used to access the federated database and the authorization IDs that are used to access a data source
8. Creates nicknames for the data source objects that are to be accessed

Application Programmers/End Users:

9. Retrieves information from data sources:

- Using the DB2 SQL dialect, application programmers and end users submit queries using the nicknames associated with the data source objects.
- Application programmers and end users occasionally use a pass-through session to submit queries, DML statements, and DDL statements directly to data sources. In a pass-through session, you use the SQL dialect of the data source, rather than the SQL dialect of DB2.

Optional tasks are often performed by the Database Administrators and Application Programmers:

- Modifying the mapping between a DB2 data type and a data source data type to override the default data type mapping
- Modifying the mapping between a DB2 function and a data source function to override the default function mapping
- Providing the federated server with the index specification information if a data source table has an index that the federated server is unaware of

After a federated system is set up, the information in data sources can be accessed as though it is in one large database. Users and applications send queries to one federated database, which retrieves data from multiple data sources. Applications work with the federated database just like with any other DB2 database.

How Do You Interact with a Federated System?

You interface with a federated server exactly the same as you do with any other DB2 UDB. Typically, you interact with the federated system using one of these methods:

- Application programs
- The DB2 command line processor (CLP)
- The DB2 Command Center
- The DB2 Control Center
- Reporting tools

> **N O T E**   The federated examples assume you are using the DB2 command line processor (CLP) or the DB2 Command Center to issue DB2 commands, unless otherwise noted.

The steps in the federated documentation specify which tasks can be performed through the Control Center. These steps provide the corresponding commands and SQL statements that can be entered in the DB2 CLP or the DB2 Command Center.

DB2 Command Line Processor (CLP)

You can perform all of the tasks necessary to set up, configure, tune, and maintain the federated system through the CLP. In some cases, the only way to perform certain tasks is to use either the DB2 CLP or the DB2 Command Center. For example:

- Modify wrapper options
- Create, alter, or drop user-defined data type mappings
- Create, alter, or drop user-defined function mappings

DB2 Command Center

Through the Command Center, you can create and run distributed requests without having to manually type out lengthy SQL statements. Use the Command Center when you are tuning the performance of the federated system. The Command Center is a convenient way to use the DB2 Explain functionality to look at the access plans for distributed requests. The Command Center can also be used to work with the SQL Assistant tool.

DB2 Control Center

The Control Center allows you to perform most of the tasks necessary to set up, configure, and modify the federated system. The Control Center uses panels—dialog boxes and wizards—to guide you through a task. These panels contain interactive help when your mouse hovers over a control such as a list box or command button. Additionally, each panel has a help button that provides information about the panel task and links to related concepts and reference information.

The Control Center is the easiest way to perform the essential data source configurations:

- Connect to the DB2 federated instance
- Create the wrappers
- Create the server definitions and server options
- Create the user mappings
- Create the nicknames

You can also use the Control Center to modify the data source configuration. You can alter or drop wrappers, server definitions, server options, user mappings, and nicknames.

Application Programs

Applications do not require any special coding to work with federated data. Applications access the system just like any other DB2 client application. Applications interface with the federated database that is within the federated server. To obtain data from data sources, they submit queries in DB2 SQL to the federated database. DB2 then distributes the queries to the appropriate data sources, collects the requested data, and returns this data to the applications. However, because DB2 interacts with the data sources through nicknames, you need to be aware of the following:

- The SQL restrictions when working with nicknames. For additional information, refer to the SQL Reference Guide.
- How to perform operations on nicknamed objects.

SETTING UP THE FEDERATED SERVER AND DATABASE

This section discusses all the steps required to set up the federated server and database. Subsequent sections discuss the steps to configure access to specific data sources.

A federated server and database are simply a DB2 server and database that you set up and configure to access data sources. To set up your federated system, you need to:

- Set up the server and database
- Configure access to the server and database

To set up the server and database, you need to install the required software on the server, create the DB2 instance, and create the database. To configure access to the server and database, you need to provide the server and database with information about the data sources that you want to access.

The edition of DB2 server software you install depends on the data sources you want to access. You must consult the installation documentation to determine the specific software you are installing and the disk spaced required.

Setting Up the Server

There are basic steps to set up the federated server:

A. Setting Up the Server to Access Data Source

1. Install and configure the client configuration software.
2. Install the DB2 server software on the server that will act as the federated server. This includes:
   - Creating a DB2 instance on the federated server
   - Specifying the user authorities information for the instance
3. Install and configure any additional required software on the federated server. This might include DB2 Relational Connect and DB2 Life Sciences Data Connect.

B. Verify Federated Server Setup and Data Source Environment Variables

4. Verify the server setup:
   - Confirming the link between the client libraries and DB2
   - Ensuring the proper permissions defined on the wrapper library files
5. Check the data source environment variables.
   - Verifying that the FEDERATED parameter is set to YES.

C. Create a DB2 Database on the Federated Server Instance that Will Act as the Federated Database

The DB2 instance owner then proceeds with the steps to configure access to specific data sources.

Because the setup steps vary from data source to data source, the specific steps are provided in separate topics. Before you start the setup, ensure that your system meets installation, memory, and disk requirements. Additionally, you must have the right authority to perform the installation.

- On UNIX, log on under a user ID that has root authority.
- On Windows, log on with the Administrator account that you have defined for DB2 installation.

Setting Up the Server to Access DB2 Family Data Sources

To set up the federated server for DB2 family data sources, you need to install the proper DB2 server software on the server that will act as the federated server. The DB2 server software that you install depends on the data sources that you want to access. You install the DB2 server software by using the DB2 Setup Wizard.

To install the DB2 server software:

1. Log on to the system.
2. Close all open programs so that the DB2 installation program can update files as required.
3. Insert the DB2 CD and start the setup program to install the DB2 server software.

```
On UNIX, change the directory where the CD-ROM is mounted and enter
   the ./db2setup command to start the setup program.

On Windows, the autorun starts the DB2 Setup Wizard.
```

4. The DB2 Setup Launchpad opens. From this window, review the installation prerequisites and release notes for the setup information.
5. Proceed through the DB2 Setup Wizard installation panels and make your selections. As part of the installation:
   ○ Create a DB2 instance on the federated server.
   ○ Specify the user authorities information for the instance.
6. Click **Finish** on the last DB2 Setup Wizard installation panel to copy the DB2 files to your system. When you complete the installation, DB2 is installed in the one of the following directories, depending on your operating system:

```
On AIX:  /usr/opt/db2_08_01
On HP-UX, Linux, Solaris:  /opt/IBM/db2/V8.1
On Windows:  \Program Files\IBM\SQLLIB
```

7. To enable the DB2 server to access data sources, set the FEDERATED parameter to YES, by issuing this DB2 command:

```
db2 update dbm cfg using federated YES
```

8. After the DB2 server software is installed, a user with SYSADM authority should check the setup.

9. Create the federated database.

10. The DB2 instance owner then configures the server to access the DB2 family data sources.

Setting Up the Server to Access Informix Data Sources

To set up the federated server for DB2 family data sources, you need to install the proper DB2 server software on the server that will perform as the federated server. You install the DB2 server software by using the DB2 Setup Wizard.

The steps to set up the federated server for Informix data sources are:

1. Log on to the system.

2. Close all open programs so that the DB2 installation program can update files as required.

3. Install and configure the Informix Client SDK software on the server that will perform as the DB2 federated server.

> **N O T E**   Refer to the installation procedures in the documentation that comes with the Informix database software for specific details on how to install the client software.

4. To ensure that the client software is able to connect to the Informix server, run the Informix demo program to test the connection.

5. Insert the DB2 CD and start the setup program to install the DB2 server software.

```
On UNIX, change the directory where the CD-ROM is mounted and enter
   the ./db2setup command to start the setup program.

On Windows, the autorun starts the DB2 Setup Wizard.
```

6. The DB2 Setup Launchpad opens. From this window, review the installation prerequisites and release notes for the setup information.

7. Select the Custom installation option. You must use the Custom installation to set up support for Informix data sources.

8. Proceed through the DB2 Setup Wizard installation panels and choose **Set up Informix data source support**. The setup will require you to identify:

- The local path where you installed the Informix client software
- The name of the default Informix server

> **N O T E**   The Custom installation will update the
> sqllib/cfg/db2dj.ini file to set several data source environment variables:
> INFORMIXDIR and INFORMIXSERVER. If you need to set the
> INFORMIXSQLHOSTS environment variable, you will need to set it
> manually. On UNIX, the installation will also link DB2 to the Informix
> client software. If you do not install the Informix client software before
> you run the DB2 Custom installation, you will have to set the
> environment variables manually and link DB2 to the client software.

9. Proceed through the DB2 Setup Wizard installation panels and make your selections. As part of the installation:
   - Create a DB2 instance on the federated server.
   - Specify the user authorities information for the instance.
10. Click **Finish** on the last DB2 Setup Wizard installation panel to copy the DB2 files to your system. When you complete the installation, DB2 is installed in the one of the following directories, depending on your operating system:

```
On AIX:  /usr/opt/db2_08_01
On HP-UX, Linux, Solaris:  /opt/IBM/db2/V8.1
On Windows:  \Program Files\IBM\SQLLIB
```

11. To enable the DB2 server to access data sources if required, set the FEDERATED parameter to YES, by issuing this DB2 command:

```
db2 update dbm cfg using federated YES
```

12. After the DB2 server software is installed, a user with SYSADM authority should check the setup.
13. Create the federated database.
14. The DB2 instance owner then configures the server to access the Informix data sources.

Checking the Federated Server Setup

After the federated server is set up, you can avoid potential problems by checking several key settings:

- Check the data source environment variables (UNIX and Windows for Informix data sources).
- Confirm the link between DB2 and the data source client libraries (UNIX only).
- Check the wrapper library file permissions (UNIX only).
- Ensure that the FEDERATED parameter is set to YES (UNIX and Windows).

Checking the Data Source Environment Variables

When you set up the federated server, the installation process attempts to set the environment variables for the Informix, Oracle, Sybase, and Microsoft SQL Server data sources.

- For Oracle, Sybase, and Microsoft SQL Server data sources, you need to check the environment variables only if your federated server uses a UNIX operating system.
- For Informix data sources, you need to check the environment variables on both UNIX and Windows operating systems.

Check to make certain that the environment variables for the data sources you want access are set in the sqllib/cfg/db2dj.ini file.

The data source environment variables will not be set in the sqllib/cfg/db2dj.ini file if you:

- Install the data source client software after the DB2 federated server is set up
- Have not installed the data source client software

To set the environment variables:

1. Install the client software (if necessary).
2. Set the environment variables. You can also manually set the environment variables. The quickest way to set the data source environment variables is:
   - For Informix data sources, run the DB2 server Custom installation again.
   - For Oracle, Microsoft SQL Server, and Sybase data sources, run the DB2 Relational Connect installation again.

Creating the Federated Database

After you set up the federated server, the DB2 instance owner creates a DB2 database on the federated server instance that will act as the federated database. You can create the database two ways:

- Through the DB2 Control Center
- Through the DB2 Command Center or DB2 CLP

The advantage of using the DB2 Control Center is that you do not have to key in each statement and command. It is the easiest way to create a database quickly.

A federated server that is properly set up to access your data sources includes the installation and configuration of any required software, such as the client software, DB2 Relational Connect, or DB2 Life Sciences Data Connect.

You need SYSADM or SYSCTRL authority to create a DB2 database. Create a DB2 database on the federated server instance that will act as the federated database. For example:

```
db2 create database sample
```

This command:

- Initializes a new database
- Creates the three initial table spaces
- Creates the system tables
- Allocates the recovery log

In a multiple database partitions environment, this command affects all database partitions that are listed in the db2nodes.cfg file. The database partition from which this command is issued becomes the catalog partition for the new database.

Configuring Access to Data Sources

This section shows how to configure a federated server and database to access your data sources:

- It contains information about the basic steps needed to perform the configuration steps quickly.
- It outlines several optional steps, if you need them, to fine-tune the data source configuration.
- To help you avoid problems, the end of this chapter contains configuration troubleshooting advice.

The basic steps and recommended interface are:

1. Prepare the federated server for the data source.
2. Create the wrappers.
3. Create the server definitions.
4. Create the user mappings.
5. Test the connection to the data source server.
6. Create the nicknames.

However, before you can configure access to a data source, you must make sure that the federated server has been set up properly. It is especially important that you:

- Link DB2 to the client software. This creates the data source wrapper libraries on the federated server.
- Set up the data source environment variables.

Prepare the Federated Database

Configuring access to a data source involves supplying the federated database with information about the data source.

For DB2 family data sources   There are two steps that are required to prepare the federated database to access DB2 family data sources:

- Cataloging a node entry in the federated node directory
- Cataloging the remote database in the federated system database directory

For example, if TCP/IP is your communication protocol, you must issue the CATALOG TCP/IP NODE command:

```
CATALOG TCPIP NODE DB2NODE
  REMOTE HOST390 SERVER 1300;

where:
DB2NODE is a name that you assign to the node that you are cataloging.
HOST390 is the host name of the system where the data source resides.
1300 is the service name or primary port number of the server database
manager instance. If a service name is used, it is case sensitive.
```

An example of cataloging the remote database using the CATALOG DATABASE command is:

```
catalog database DB2DB390 AS CLNTS390
  AT NODE DB2NODE
  AUTHENTICATION SERVER;

where:
DB2DB390 is a name of the database you are cataloging.
CLNTS390 is an alias for the database being cataloged.
DB2NODE is the name of the node you specified when cataloging the node
entry in the node directory.
SERVER is the authentication that takes place on the DB2 data source node.
```

Create the Wrapper

It is recommended that you use the default wrapper name. A wrapper can:

- Connect to the data source using the standard connection API of that data source
- Submit queries to the data source. For data sources that do not support SQL, one of two actions will occur:
  - For data sources that support SQL, the query is submitted in SQL.
  - For data sources that do not support SQL, the query is translated into the native query language of the source or into a series of source API calls.
- Receive results sets from the data source using the data source standard API of that data source
- Respond to the federated server queries about the default data type mappings for a data source

- Respond to the federated server queries about the default function mappings for a data source

The following example shows a CREATE WRAPPER statement:

```
CREATE WRAPPER DRDA;
```

Supply the Server Definition

After you create the wrapper, you need to identify each data source server that you want to access. To create a server definition, use the DB2 Control Center. You can also issue the CREATE SERVER statement in the DB2 Command Center or the CLP. The parameters and options required with the CREATE SERVER statement depend on the data source you want to access.

For DB2 family data sources   Suppose that you have two DB2 for OS/390 databases:

- The MYDB database is on the HOST390 server and contains a client table and an employee table.
- The MYDB2 database is on the HOST2390 server and contains a sales table.
- You will need to create two server definitions: one for the HOST390 server and one for the HOST2390 server.
- You will then need to create three nicknames, one for each of the tables.

An example of the server definition for the HOST390 server is:

```
CREATE SERVER HOST390
   TYPE DB2/390
   VERSION 7.1
   WRAPPER DRDA
   AUTHORIZATION 'DSNOW' PASSWORD 'yyyyyyyy'
   OPTIONS (DBNAME 'MYDB');

where:
HOST390 is a name that you assign to the data source server. This name
must be unique.
DB2/390 is type of data source to which you are configuring access.
7.1 is the version of data source server software that you want to
access.
DRDA is the wrapper name that you specified in the CREATE WRAPPER
statement.
'DSNOW' is the authorization ID at the data source. This value is case
sensitive.
'yyyyyyyy' is the password associated with the authorization ID at the
data source. This value is case sensitive.
'MYDB' is the name of the database that you want to access. This value
is case sensitive.
The AUTHORIZATION parameter, the PASSWORD parameter, and the DBNAME
option are required.
```

Additional server options   When you create the server definition, you can specify additional server options in the CREATE SERVER statement. There are general server options and data source-specific server options.

For example, when connecting to a data source, the federated server tries to connect using all possible combinations of upper- and lowercase for the user ID and password. This means that the server might make up to nine connect attempts before successfully connecting to the data source server. These attempts can slow down connect times. You can prevent this by specifying values for the FOLD_ID and FOLD_PW server options.

```
CREATE SERVER HOST390
   type DB2/390 version 7.1
   WRAPPER DRDA
   AUTHORIZATION 'DSNOW' PASSWORD 'yyyyyyyy'
   OPTIONS ( NODE 'MYNODE', DBNAME 'MYDB', FOLD_ID 'U',
      FOLD_PW 'U', COLLATING_SEQUENCE 'Y' );
```

This specifies whether the data source uses the same collating sequence as DB2 for Linux, UNIX, and Windows.

Valid values are Y (the same collating sequence is used) and N (a different collating sequence is used). If the COLLATING_SEQUENCE option is not specified, it is assumed that the data source has a different collating sequence than the DB2 collating sequence.

A simple test to compare collating sequences   You can use an API to display the collating sequence of the federated database and a data source. Below is a simple way to find out the basics about the collating sequence by seeing the results of its use using an ORDER BY operation simply by creating a table with a character column, inserting a few values, then doing SELECT from the column with an ORDER BY clause.

Here is the example of DDL to create such a table and insert numbers, uppercase letters, and lowercase letters:

```
CREATE TABLE MYTAB (COL1  CHAR(1));

INSERT INTO MYTAB VALUES ('1');
INSERT INTO MYTAB VALUES ('2');
INSERT INTO MYTAB VALUES ('jonathan');
INSERT INTO MYTAB VALUES ('JONATHAN');
INSERT INTO MYTAB VALUES ('michael');
INSERT INTO MYTAB VALUES ('MICHAEL');
INSERT INTO MYTAB VALUES ('tiffany');
INSERT INTO MYTAB VALUES ('TIFFANY');

SELECT COL1 FROM MYTAB ORDER BY 1;
```

```
The result from DB2 UDB ESE on UNIX:
  COL1
  -------
  1
  2
  jonathan
  JONATHAN
  michael
  MICHAEL
  tiffany
  TIFFANY

  8 record(s) selected.
```

```
The result from Oracle server:
  COL1
  -------
  1
  2
  JONATHAN
  MICHAEL
  TIFFANY
  jonathan
  michael
  tiffany

  8 record(s) selected.
```

Note: Oracle does not have the same collating sequence as the DB2 federated server.

```
In a similar test for DB2/400, the result is:
  COL1
  -------
  jonathan
  michael
  tiffany
  JONATHAN
  MICHAEL
  TIFFANY
  1
  2

  8 record(s) selected.
```

Note: The collating sequence on DB2/400 is different from that in the DB2 ESE on UNIX federated database.

With DB2 data sources, a useful option to set is PUSHDOWN. If you set PUSHDOWN to Y, the federated server will consider letting the DB2 data source evaluate operations. This is the default setting. If you set PUSHDOWN to N, the federated server will retrieve only columns from the remote data source and will not let the data source evaluate other operations, such as joins.

Once the server definition is created, use the ALTER SERVER statement to apply additional server options.

```
ALTER SERVER HOST390 TYPE DB2/390 VERSION 7.1 OPTIONS ( ADD PUSHDOWN 'N' );
```

Create the User Mappings

When you request access to a DB2 server, access is granted if the authorization IDs are the same between the federated database and the DB2 server. If a user's authorization ID to access the federated database differs from the user's authorization ID to access a data source, you need to define an association—a user mapping—between the two authorizations IDs so that distributed requests can be sent to the data source.

> **N O T E**   The REMOTE_AUTHID is the connect authorization ID, not the bind authorization ID. Use the CREATE USER MAPPING statement to map the local user ID to the DB2 server user ID and password.

For example:

```
CREATE USER MAPPING FOR DB2ADMIN
    SERVER HOST390
    OPTIONS (REMOTE_AUTHID 'db2admin',
      REMOTE_PASSWORD 'admin');

where:
DB2ADMIN is the local user ID that you are mapping to a user ID
defined at a DB2 family data source server.
HOST390 is the name of the DB2 family data source server that you
defined in the CREATE SERVER statement.
'db2admin' is the connect authorization user ID at the DB2 family data
source server to which you are mapping DB2USER. This value is case
sensitive unless you set the FOLD_ID server option to 'U' or 'L' in
the CREATE SERVER statement.
'admin' is the password associated with 'db2admin'. This value is case
sensitive unless you set the FOLD_PW server option to 'U' or 'L' in
the CREATE SERVER statement.

You can use the DB2 special register USER to map the authorization ID
of the person issuing the CREATE USER MAPPING statement to the data
source authorization ID specified in the REMOTE_AUTHID user option.
```

The following is an example of the CREATE USER MAPPING statement, which includes the USER special register:

```
CREATE USER MAPPING FOR USER
  SERVER HOST390
  OPTIONS (REMOTE_AUTHID 'db2admin',
    REMOTE_PASSWORD 'admin');
```

Test the Connection to the Data Source Server

Test the connection to the DB2 server to ensure that you can establish a connection, using the server definition and user mappings you defined. Open a pass-through session, and for DB2 for z/OS and OS/390, issue a SELECT statement against the DB2 system tables.

For example:

```
SET PASSTHRU HOST390;

SELECT count(*) FROM sysibm.systables;

SET PASSTHRU RESET;
```

If the SELECT returns a count, your server definition and user mapping are set up properly. If the SELECT returns an error, you may have to:

- Check the remote server to make sure it is started.
- Check the listener on the remote server to make sure that it is configured for incoming connections.
- Check your user mapping to make sure that the settings for the remote_authid and remote_password options are valid for connections to the DB2 server.
- Check the DB2 catalog entries for node and database.
- Check your DB2 federated variables to make sure that they are correct for working with the remote DB2 server. This includes the system environment variables, db2dj.ini variables, and DB2 Profile Registry (db2set) DB2COMM variable.
- Check your server definition and possibly drop it and create it again.
- Check your user mapping and possibly alter it or create another, if necessary.

Create the Nicknames for the Tables and Views

The federated database relies on catalog statistics for nicknamed objects to optimize query processing. These statistics are gathered when you create a nickname for a data source object using the CREATE NICKNAME statement.

The federated database verifies the presence of the object at the data source, then attempts to gather existing data source statistical data. Information useful to the optimizer is read from the data source catalogs and put into the global catalog on the federated server. Because some or all of the data source catalog information might be used by the optimizer, it is advisable to update statistics (using the data source command equivalent to RUNSTATS) at the data source before you create a nickname.

Use the CREATE NICKNAME statement to assign a nickname to a view or table located at your DB2 family data source. You will use these nicknames, instead of the names of the data source objects, when you query the DB2 family data source. Nicknames can be up to 128 characters in length. The following example shows a CREATE NICKNAME statement:

```
CREATE NICKNAME STAFF390 FOR HOST390.DBTTEST.STAFF;

where:
   STAFF390 is a unique nickname used to identify the DB2 table or
   view.
   HOST390.DBTTEST.STAFF is a three-part identifier for the remote
   object.
     • HOST390 is the name you assigned to the DB2 database server in
       the CREATE SERVER statement.
     • DBTTEST is the name of the remote schema to which the table or
       view belongs. This value is case sensitive.
     • STAFF is the name of the remote table or view that you want to
       access.
```

> **NOTE**   The nickname is a two-part name: the schema and the nickname. If you omit the schema when creating the nickname, the schema of the nickname will be the authid of the user creating the nickname.

Repeat this step for each DB2 table or view for which you want to create a nickname. When you create the nickname, the federated server will use the connection to query the data source catalog. This query tests your connection to the data source using the nickname. If the connection does not work, you will receive an error message.

Improving Performance by Setting the DB2_DJ_COMM Environment Variable (UNIX)

If you find that it takes an inordinate amount of time to access the DB2 data source server, you can improve the performance by setting the DB2_DJ_COMM environment variable to load the wrapper when the federated server initializes, rather than when you attempt to access the data source.

```
db2set DB2_DJ_COMM= 'libdb2drda.a'
```

WORKING WITH THE FEDERATED DATA

This section describes how to access and update data at the data sources:

- Working with nicknames
- Transaction support in a federated system
- Selecting data in a federated system
- Modifying data in a federated system

Working with Nicknames

When you want to select or modify data source data, you query the nicknames using the SELECT, INSERT, UPDATE, and DELETE statements. You submit queries in DB2 SQL to the federated database. You can join data from local tables and remote data sources using a single SQL statement, as though all the data were local. For example, you can join data that is located in:

- A local DB2 for Windows table in the federated database, an Oracle table, and a Sybase view
- A DB2 for z/OS table on one server, a DB2 for z/OS table on another server, and an Excel spreadsheet

By processing SQL statements as though the data sources were ordinary relational tables or views within the federated database, the federated system can join relational data with data in nonrelational formats.

Tables and views that reside in the federated database are local objects. You do not create nicknames for these objects. You use the actual object name in your queries.

Remote objects are objects not located in the federated database. For example:

1. Tables and views in another DB2 database instance on the federated server: You need to create nicknames for these objects.
2. Data source objects that reside in another data source, such as: Oracle, Sybase, Documentum, and ODBC. You need to create nicknames for these objects.

Before you query the data sources, make sure that you understand how to leverage the capabilities of the federated system effectively:

1. SQL statements you can use with nicknames
2. Accessing new data source objects
3. Accessing data sources using PASSTHRU
4. Accessing heterogeneous data through federated views

The SQL Statements You Can Use with Nicknames

A federated system is designed to make it easy to access data, regardless of where it is actually stored. This is accomplished by creating nicknames for all the data source objects (such as tables and views) that you want to access.

For example, if the nickname DEPT is created to represent the remote table HOST390.DBTTEST.DEPT, you would use the statement SELECT * FROM DEPT to query information in the remote table. You are querying the nickname instead of having to remember the underlying data source information. When you create a query, you do not have to be concerned with issues such as:

1. The name of the table at the data source
2. The server on which it resides
3. The type of DBMS on which the table resides, such as Informix or Oracle
4. The query language or SQL dialect that the DBMS uses
5. The data type mappings between the data source and DB2

All the underlying metadata stored in the federated database catalog as part of the federated system setup and configuration provide the federated server with the information it needs to process your queries. After the federated system is set up, you can use the nicknames to query the data sources or further enhance the federated system configuration.

Accessing New Data Source Objects

Periodically, you will want to access data source objects that do not have nicknames. These might be new objects added to a data source, such as a newly created view, or existing objects that were not registered with the federated server when it was initially set up. In either case, these objects are new to the federated server. To access these new objects, you need to create nicknames for them, using the CREATE NICKNAME statement.

The federated system needs to be configured to access the data source. A server definition for the data source server on which the object resides needs to exist in the federated database. You create a server definition using the CREATE SERVER statement.

You must have one of the following authorizations to issue the CREATE NICKNAME statement:

- SYSADM or DBADM
- IMPLICIT_SCHEMA authority on the federated database, if the implicit or explicit schema name of the nickname does not exist
- CREATEIN privilege on the schema, if the schema name of the nickname exists
- The remote user ID in your user mapping must have SELECT privilege at the data source

Accessing Data Sources Using Pass-Through Session

You can submit SQL statements directly to data sources by using a special mode called *pass-through*. You submit SQL statements in the SQL dialect used by the data source. Use a pass-through session when you want to perform an operation that is not possible with the DB2 SQL/API.

Similarly, you can use a pass-through session to perform actions that are not supported by SQL, such as certain administrative tasks. However, you cannot use a pass-through session to perform all administrative tasks.

For example, you can run the statistics utility used by the data source, but you cannot start or stop the remote database. You can query only one data source at a time in a pass-through session. Use the SET PASSTHRU command to open a session. When you use the SET PASSTHRU RESET command, it closes the pass-through session. If you use the SET PASSTHRU command instead of SET PASSTHRU RESET, the current pass-through session is closed and a new pass-through session is opened.

> **N O T E**   Pass-through sessions do not support non-relational data sources.

Accessing Heterogeneous Data through Federated Views

A federated view is a view in the federated database whose base tables are located at remote data sources. The base tables are referenced in the federated view by nicknames, instead of by the data source table names. When you query from a federated view, data is retrieved from the remote data source.

The action of creating a federated database view of data source data is sometimes referred to as *creating a view on a nickname*. This is because you reference the nicknames instead of the data sources when you create the view.

These views offer a high degree of data independence for a globally integrated database, just as views defined on multiple local tables do for centralized relational database managers.

Use the CREATE FEDERATED VIEW statement to create a federated view. You must have one of the following authorizations to issue the CREATE FEDERATED VIEW statement:

- SYSADM or DBADM

Or, for each nickname in any full select:

- CONTROL or SELECT privilege on the underlying table or view and at least one of the following:
  - IMPLICIT_SCHEMA authority on the federated database, if the implicit or explicit schema name of the view does not exist.

○ CREATEIN privilege on the schema, if the schema name of the view refers to an existing schema.

Privileges for the underlying objects are not considered when defining a view on a federated database nickname. Authorization requirements of the data source for the table or view referenced by the nickname are applied when the query is processed. The authorization ID of the statement may be mapped to a different remote authorization ID by a user mapping.

A federated view that is:

- Created from more than one nicknamed data source object is read-only view.
- Created from only one nicknamed data source object may or may not be read-only view.
- Created from one non-relational data source is read only.
- Created from a relational data source might allow updates, depending on what is included in the CREATE FEDERATED VIEW statement.

Transaction Support in a Federated System

Before you submit transactions to the federated database, it is important that you understand the type of transactions supported in a federated system.

Single-Site Update and Two-Phase Commit

A transaction is commonly referred to in DB2 as a *unit of work*. A unit of work is a recoverable sequence of operations within an application process. A unit of work is used by the database manager to ensure that a database is in a consistent state. Any reading from or writing to the database is done within a unit of work. A point of consistency (or commit point) is a time when all recoverable data that an application accesses is consistent with related data.

A unit of work is implicitly begun when any data in the database is read from or written to. An application must end a unit of work by issuing either a COMMIT or a ROLLBACK statement. The COMMIT statement makes permanent all changes made within a unit of work. The ROLLBACK statement removes these changes from the database.

Changes made by the unit of work become visible to other applications after a successful COMMIT. If the application ends normally without either of these statements being explicitly issued, the unit of work is automatically committed.

Recommendation   Your applications should always explicitly commit or roll back units of work. If an application ends abnormally in the middle of a unit of work, the unit of work is automatically rolled back.

A transaction can involve one or more databases. A transaction that involves two or more databases is a distributed unit of work (DUOW). In a DUOW that involves reading from one or more databases to update another database, or in a non-distributed unit of work, each COMMIT is processed in one operation. Accordingly, the operation is called a one-phase commit.

In a DUOW involving updates of multiple databases, data consistency is important. The two-phase commit protocol is commonly used to ensure data consistency across multiple databases within a DUOW. Two-phase commit will be supported on federated systems in a future release.

Considerations with Transparent DDL

COMMIT or ROLLBACK statements need to be issued before and after transparent DDL transactions. Transparent DDL creates a table on a remote data source and creates a nickname in the local federated database for the remote table. Because transparent DDL is updating both local and remote objects at the same time, each transparent DDL statement has to be the only update within the transaction. If there is any update prior to the transparent DDL transaction, a COMMIT or ROLLBACK statement has to be issued before the transparent DDL transaction. Likewise, a COMMIT or ROLLBACK statement has to be issued after the transparent DDL transaction before any other update can occur.

Considerations with Pass-Through Session

All statements sent through PASSTHRU sessions are treated as updates by the federated server. The purpose of this is to ensure data integrity. If a statement set through a PASSTHRU session is successful, it is recorded as an update, regardless of the type of statement. This includes SELECT statements. If a statement is not successful, it is not recorded. Likewise, if a PASSTHRU session is empty, a statement following the empty PASSTHRU session will not be blocked.

Considerations with the Autocommit Option in the DB2 CLP

By default, the DB2 CLP will automatically commit each SQL statement executed. If you elect to turn the autocommit command option OFF, make certain you explicitly issue COMMIT and ROLLBACK statements at the end of each transaction.

Recommendation   Set the autocommit command option ON for distributed units of work whenever applicable. If you have set this command option OFF, you can turn it on by issuing this command:

```
UPDATE COMMAND OPTIONS USING c ON;
```

INSERT, UPDATE, and DELETE Privileges

The privileges required to issue INSERT, UPDATE, and DELETE statements on nicknames are similar to the privileges required to issue these statements on tables:

- You can grant or revoke SELECT, INSERT, UPDATE, and DELETE privileges on a nickname.

- You must hold adequate privileges on the data source to perform SELECT, INSERT, UPDATE, or DELETE operations on the underlying object.

When a query is submitted to the federated database, the authorization privileges on the nickname in the query are checked. The authorization requirements of the data source object referenced by the nickname are applied only when the query is actually processed. If you do not have SELECT privilege on the nickname, you cannot select from the object to which the nickname refers. Likewise, just because you have a privilege on the nickname, such as UPDATE, this does not mean you will automatically be authorized to update the object that the nickname represents. Passing the privileges checking at the federated server does not imply you will pass the privilege checking at the remote data source. Through user mappings, a federated server user ID is mapped to the data source user ID. The privilege restrictions will be enforced at the data source.

Restrictions   You cannot perform INSERT, UPDATE, or DELETE operations on a nickname that uses the following wrapper: Sybase DBLIB, ODBC, DB2 Life Sciences Data Connect wrapper. Update of nicknames has the following restrictions:

- A nicknamed object whose data source does not permit update cannot be updated.
- A federated view with UNION ALL statements for multiple nicknamed objects is a read-only view. It cannot be updated.

Referential Integrity

You cannot define a constraint on a nickname. In the federated environment, DB2 does not compensate for referential integrity differences between data sources. DB2 does not interfere with referential integrity enforcement at the data sources. However, referential integrity constraints at a data source can affect nickname updates.

For example, suppose an insert into a table at a data source violates a referential integrity constraint at that data source. DB2 maps the resulting error to a DB2 error. Referential integrity between data sources is the responsibility of the applications.

LOBs

There are three types of LOBs:

- character large objects (CLOBs)
- double-byte character large objects (DBCLOBs)
- binary large objects (BLOBs)

Using DB2 UDB ESE Version 8 for Linux, UNIX, and Windows, you can perform read operations against LOBs located in all the relational data sources. Additionally, you can perform write operations against LOBs located in Oracle (Version 7.3 or higher) data sources using the NET8 wrapper.

N O T E   Non-relational data sources do not support LOBs.

Application Savepoint

To protect statement-level atomicity for INSERT, UPDATE, or DELETE against a nickname, enhancement is made in the federated system to guard against potential data inconsistency. Application savepoints at the data sources are incorporated in the global design.

If a data source does not support application savepoints, the federated system is unable to ensure statement-level atomicity at run time in the event of an error. A new SQL error code, SQLCODE-20190, is returned to the users when the federated system detects potential exposure of data inconsistency on any INSERT, UPDATE, or DELETE operation against nicknames residing in this data source.

To open up insert, update, or delete against nicknames on such a data source, the user may turn off the blocking logic via ALTER SERVER command to set server option IUD_APP_SVPT_ENFORCE to N. Some data sources, such as Informix, do not support application savepoints. If you are accessing data sources that do not support cursor application savepoints, you need to change your server definitions. Add the IUD_APP_SVPT_ENFORCE server option and set the option to N. This will enable you to update the data source using nicknames. Use the ALTER SERVER statement to add this option to the server definition.

N O T E   You cannot define a trigger on a nickname.

Selecting Data in a Federated System

Use the SELECT statement to select data from data sources.

To select data using a nickname, the privileges held by the authorization ID of the statement must include SELECT privilege on the nickname (for the federated database to accept the request) and the SELECT privilege on the underlying table object (for the data source to accept the request).

Some of the types of distributed requests used with a federated system are requests that query:

- A single remote data source
- A local data source and a remote data source
- Multiple remote data sources

The federated database is a local data source. Tables and views in the federated database are local objects. You do not create nicknames for these objects; you use the actual object name in your SELECT statement.

Remote data sources include: another DB2 for the Linux, UNIX, and Windows database instance on the federated server; another DB2 for the Linux, UNIX, and Windows database instance on another server; and data sources other than DB2 for Linux, UNIX, and Windows.

Modifying Data in a Federated System

With a federated system, you can perform INSERT, UPDATE, and DELETE operations on nick-named objects. The following sections include examples for performing these operations.

Inserting/Updating/Deleting Data into/to/from Data Source Objects

There are two types of data source objects:

- Local data source objects are objects that reside in the federated database. You do not create nicknames for these objects; you use the actual object name in your INSERT, UPDATE, and DELETE statements.
- Remote data source objects are any objects that do not reside in the federated database, including objects that reside on the federated server.

To insert, update, delete using a nickname, the privileges held by the authorization ID of the statement must include INSERT, UPDATE, DELETE privilege on the nickname (for the federated database to accept the request) and the INSERT, UPDATE, DELETE privilege on the underlying table object (for the data source to accept the request).

Restrictions   INSERT, UPDATE, DELETE is not available through the ODBC wrapper, the DBLIB wrapper, or the wrappers that are provided from DB2 Life Sciences Data Connect. Suppose you have an Informix table that has been created as follows:

```
CREATE TABLE infx_table (c1 INTEGER, c2 VARCHAR(20));
```

You can use the following SQL to configure the federated server to access this table:

```
CREATE WRAPPER informix;

CREATE SERVER infx_server
  TYPE Informix
  VERSION 9.3
  WRAPPER Informix
  OPTIONS(ADD NODE 'inf93',
    ADD DBNAME 'inf_db',
    ADD IUD_APP_SVPT_ENFORCE 'N');

CREATE USER MAPPING FOR USER SERVER infx_server
  OPTIONS(ADD REMOTE_AUTHID 'infx_authid',
    ADD REMOTE_PASSWORD 'infx_pswd');
```

```
CREATE NICKNAME infx_table_nn FOR
  infx_server."infx_authid"."infx_table;
```

You can issue INSERT, UPDATE, and DELETE statements using the infx_table_nn nickname. For example:

```
INSERT INTO infx_table_nn VALUES(1,'Heather');
INSERT INTO infx_table_nn VALUES(2,'Jenny');
UPDATE infx_table_nn SET c2='JENNIFER' WHERE c1=2;
DELETE FROM infx_table_nn WHERE c1=1;
```

SAMPLE CONFIGURATION FEDERATED BETWEEN DB2 ON OS/390 AND DB2 ON SUN SOLARIS

This section describes the high-level design of the federated system. The environment requirements for accessing a host DB2 on OS/390 data from a DB2 UDB ESE on Sun Solaris are shown in Table 7.3.

Table 7.3 Federated System Environment Requirements

Requirement	Data Source Database	Federated Database
Environment	OS/390 DB2 V6	Sun Solaris 8 DB2 UDB Enterprise Server EditionV8.1
Hostname	HOST390	s4500db
IP Address	210.100.100.210	192.168.10.100
User ID (SYSADM)	tst1sys	dsnow
Instance Owner ID		dsnow
Database	HDB1	sample
Communication Port	1300	50000
User ID (DBADM)	tst1txp	tphan
User ID		user_n (where n is sequence start at 1, i.e., user_1)
Data Source	DB2 OS/390	DB2 UDB for Linux, UNIX, and Windows
Wrapper	DRDA	DRDA
Table	list of tables	list of tables
View	list of views	list of views
Nickname	list of nicknames	list of nicknames

Table 7.3   Federated System Environment Requirements (Continued)

Requirement	Data Source Database	Federated Database
Catalog Node		HDB1NODE
DCS Database Alias	HDB1	
DB2 Subsystem Name	HDB1	
Protocol	TCPIP	TCPIP
Contact	Responsible DBA	Responsible DBA

Worksheet: For Windows Clients Connecting to DB2 for OS/390 Database via DB2 Connect Gateway

Table 7.4 lists the communication information for the Windows clients accessing the federated system via a DB2 Connect Gateway.

  DNS Suffix: phantom.com
  Subnet Mask: 255.255.255.0
  Default Gateway: 10.2.200.1

Table 7.4   Windows Client Communication Information

Windows Client	Hostname	IP Address	User ID
User_1	Phantom_1	10.2.200.150	user_1
User_2	Phantom_2	10.2.200.151	user_2
User_3	Phantom_3	10.2.200.152	user_3
User_4	Phantom_4	10.2.200.153	user_4

Federated Database System Test Scenarios

The following describes different scenarios for a distributed join to be performed against DB2 tables or views on the OS/390 environment (remote) and DB2 UDB tables or views on the Sun Solaris environment (local).

- A distributed join of one local table (DB2 for Sun Solaris) with a nickname that references a remote table (DB2 for OS/390)
- A distributed join of one local table with a nickname that references a remote view
- A distributed join of one local view with a nickname that references a remote table
- A distributed join of one local view with a nickname that references a remote view

- A combination of the above, a distributed join of one local table with a local view, a nickname that references a remote table, and a nickname that references a remote view
- A federated view based on the combination of the above, a distributed join of one local table with a local view, a nickname that references a remote table, and a nickname that references a remote view

Using DB2 Connect (Optional)

DB2 Connect has several connection solutions. DB2 Connect Personal Edition provides direct connectivity to host and iSeries database series, whereas DB2 Connect Enterprise Edition provides indirect connectivity that allows clients to access host and iSeries database servers through the DB2 Connect server. DB2 Connect Unlimited Edition provides a unique packaging solution that makes product selection and licensing easier.

DB2 Connect Enterprise Edition is a connectivity server that concentrates and manages connections from multiple desktop clients and Web applications to DB2 database servers running on host or iSeries systems. IBM's DB2 UDB for iSeries, DB2 for OS/390 and z/OS, and DB2 for VSE and VM databases continue to be the systems of choice for managing most critical data for the world's largest organizations. Although these host and iSeries databases manage the data, there is a great demand to integrate this data with applications running on Windows and UNIX workstations.

DB2 Connect Enterprise Edition is most appropriate for environments where:

- Host and iSeries database servers do not support native TCP/IP connectivity and direct connectivity from desktop workstations via SNA is not desirable.
- Web servers run Web-based applications.
- Web servers run Web-based applications using data-aware Java applications.
- A middle-tier application server is used.
- TP monitors, such as CICS, Encina, Microsoft Transaction Server (MTS), Tuxedo, Component Broker, and MQSeries, are used.

DB2 Connect Personal Edition provides access from a single workstation to DB2 databases residing on servers such as OS/390, z/OS, OS/400, VM, and VSE, as well as to DB2 UDB servers on UNIX and Windows operating systems. DB2 Connect Personal Edition provides the same rich set of APIs as DB2 Connect Enterprise Edition.

DB2 Connect Personal Edition is used to connect a single Windows operating system or Linux workstation to a host or iSeries database. DB2 Connect Personal Edition is best suited for environments where native TCP/IP support is provided by the database servers, and the application being deployed is a traditional two-tier client-server application.

DB2 Connect Unlimited Edition is a unique package offering that allows complete flexibility of DB2 Connect deployment and simplifies product selection and licensing. This product contains both DB2 Connect Personal Edition and DB2 Connect Enterprise Edition with license terms and conditions that allow the unlimited deployment of any DB2 Connect product. License charges are based on the size of the S/390 or zSeries server that DB2 Connect users will be working with.

CONFIGURATION OF A FEDERATED DATABASE SYSTEM

This section explains how to configure a federated server to access data stored in DB2 family databases.

Enabling Federated Database Functionality

To take advantage of federated database functionality:

On UNIX Systems

During the installation of DB2 UDB, you must select the Distributed Join for DB2 Data Sources option and optionally create an instance to use with this option. If you choose to create an instance, the FEDERATED parameter will be set to YES by default. If you choose to create an instance at a later date, you must manually set the FEDERATED parameter to YES for that instance.

This is necessary only if you are creating an instance using db2icrt. If you go back to using db2setup to either create or set up an existing instance, the FEDERATED parameter will be set to YES again.

On Windows Systems

Federated database functionality is enabled by default as part of the DB2 installation.

Adding a DB2 Data Source to a Federated System

This section explains how to add a DB2 Data Source to a federated system.

Step 1

The first step is to configure network communications. Configuring your federated server to access DB2 family data sources is similar to configuring a client to communicate with a DB2 server. Refer to the Configuration Client-to-Server Communication Using the Client Configuration Assistance section in the IBM DB2 Quick Beginnings for DB2 Client.

> **N O T E**   Bind the utilities and the applications to the host database server. You need BINDADD authority to bind.

```
db2 "connect to HDB1 user TST1TXP using xxxxxxxx"

Database Connection Information
Database server       = DB2 OS/390 6.1.1
SQL authorization ID  = TST1TXP
Local database alias  = HDB1

cd ~dsnow/sqllib/bnd

db2 "bind @ddcsmvs.1st blocking all sqlerror continue messages
  ddcsmvs.msg grant public"
```

Step 2

Catalog an entry in the federated server's node directory that points to the location of the DB2 data source. The federated server determines the access method to use, based on the type of node being cataloged and the type of DB2 family database being accessed.

```
db2 "catalog tcpip node HDB1NODE remote 210.100.100.210 server 1300"
db2 "catalog database HDB1 as HDB1 at node HDB1NODE
  authentication dcs"
db2 "catalog dcs database HDB1 as HDB1"

Check catalog:
db2 list node directory

Node Directory
Number of entries in the directory = 1

Node 1 entry:
Node name                          = HDB1NODE
Comment                            =
Protocol                           = TCPIP
Hostname                           = 210.100.100.210
Service name                       = 1300

db2 list db directory
System Database Directory
Number of entries in the directory = 1

Database 1 entry:
Database alias                     = HDB1
Database name                      = HDB1
Node name                          = HDB1NODE
Database release level             = 9.00
```

```
Comment                           =
Directory entry type              = Remote
Authentication                    = DCS
Catalog node number               = -1


db2 list dcs directory
Database Connection Services (DCS) Directory
Number of entries in the directory = 1


DCS 1 entry:
Local database name               = HDB1
Target database name              = HDB1
Application requestor name        =
DCS parameters                    =
Comment                           =
DCS directory release level       = 0x0100
```

Step 3

Use the CREATE WRAPPER statement to define the wrapper module that will be used to access DB2 data sources. Wrappers are the mechanism that federated servers use to communicate with and retrieve data from data sources.

```
db2sampl


db2 "connect to SAMPLE user dsnow using yyyyyyyy"
Database Connection Information


Database server        = DB2/SUN 8.1.0
SQL authorization ID   = DSNOW
Local database alias   = SAMPLE


db2 "create wrapper drda"
DB20000I  The SQL command completed successfully.


Check wrapper:
db2 "select substr(wrapname,1,8) as wrapname, wraptype,
     substr(library,1,18) as library
  from syscat.wrappers"


WRAPNAME                  WRAPTYPE              LIBRARY
--------                  --------              -------

DRDA                      R                     libdrda.so


1 record(s) selected.
```

Step 4

Set the DB2_DJ_COMM environment variable to include the wrapper library that corresponds to the wrapper module that you created in the previous step (optional).

```
db2set  DB2_DJ_COMM='libdb2drda.a'
```

Step 5

Use the CREATE SERVER statement to define each DB2 server to which communications are configured.

```
db2 "create server HOST390
  type DB2/390
  version 7.1 wrapper drda
  authorization 'TST1TXP'
  password 'xxxxxxxx'
  options(node 'HDB1NODE', dbname 'HDB1')"

Check Federated Server:
db2 "select substr(servername,1,8) as servername,
  substr(setting,1,18) as setting,
    substr(option,1,18) as option from syscat.serveroptions"

SERVERNAME               SETTING              OPTION
----------               ---------            ------
HOST390                  HDB1NODE             NODE
HOST390                  HDB1                 DBNAME

2 record(s) selected.
```

Step 6

If a user ID or password at the federated server is different from a user ID or password at a DB2 family data source, use the CREATE USER MAPPING statement to map the local user ID to the user ID and password defined at the DB2 family data source.

```
User name:       DSNOW

  db2 "create user mapping for DSNOW server HOST390
    options(remote_authid 'TST1TXP', remote_password 'xxxxxxxx')"

User name:       TPHAN
  db2 "create user mapping for TPHAN server HOST390
    options(remote_authid 'TST1TXP', remote_password 'xxxxxxxx')"
```

```
Check user mapping:
db2 "select substr(authid,1,8) as authid,
   substr(servername,1,8) as servername,
   substr(option,1,18) as option,
   substr(setting,1,18) as setting
   from syscat.useroptions"
```

AUTHID	SERVERNAME	OPTION	SETTING
DSNOW	HOST390	REMOTE_AUTHID	TST1TXP
DSNOW	HOST390	REMOTE_PASSWORD	n…Ã|'†Q•_xÈAM˜_ø
TPHAN	HOST390	REMOTE_AUTHID	TST1TXP
TPHAN	HOST390	REMOTE_PASSWORD	_¶{Z_»_¥_K_àß«>À

```
4 record(s) selected.
```

Step 7

Use the CREATE NICKNAME statement to assign a nickname to a view or table located at your DB2 family data source. You will use this nickname when you query the DB2 family data source.

```
db2 "drop nickname DNTNCK.ACCOUNT_XREF"

DB21034E  The command was processed as an SQL statement because it was
not a valid Command Line Processor command. During SQL processing it
returned:
SQL0204N  "DNTNCK.ACCOUNT_XREF" is an undefined name. SQLSTATE=42704

db2 "create nickname DNTNCK.ACCOUNT_XREF for
   HOST390.DB2TTEST.ACCOUNT_XREF"
DB20000I  The SQL command completed successfully.

Check nicknames:
db2 "select substr(tabname,1,18) as tabname,
     substr(tabschema,1,18) as tabschema,
     substr(tbspace,1,18) as tbspace, type
     from syscat.tables where type='N'"
```

TABNAME	TABSCHEMA	TBSPACE	TYPE
ACCOUNT_XREF	DNTNCK	–	N

```
1 record(s) selected.
```

```
db2 "select substr(d.tabschema,1,8) as schema_name,
    substr(d.tabname,1,30) as table_name,
    substr(a.setting,1,8)||'.'||substr(b.setting,1,8)||'.'||
    substr(c.setting,1,30) as three_parts_nickname
  from syscat.taboptions a, syscat.taboptions b,
    syscat.taboptions c, syscat.tables d
  where d.type='N' and d.tabname=a.tabname and
    d.tabname=b.tabname and d.tabname=c.tabname and
    a.option='SERVER' and b.option='REMOTE_SCHEMA' and
    c.option='REMOTE_TABLE'
  union select substr(d.tabschema,1,8) as schema_name,
    substr(d.tabname,1,30) as table_name,
    substr(a.setting,1,8)||'.'||substr(b.setting,1,8)||'.'||
    substr(c.setting,1,30) as three_parts_nickname
  from syscat.taboptions a, syscat.taboptions b,
    syscat.taboptions c, syscat.tables d
  where d.type='N' and d.tabname=a.tabname and
    d.tabname=c.tabname and
    d.tabname=b.tabname and a.option='SERVER' and
    b.option='REMOTE_SCHEMA' and
    c.option='REMOTE_TABLE'
  order by 1"


SCHEMA_NAME          TABLE_NAME           THREE_PARTS_NICKNAME
-----------          -----------          --------------------
DNTNCK               ACCOUNT_XREF         HOST390 .DB2TTEST .ACCOUNT_XREF

1 record(s) selected.
```

Step 8

Repeat the previous step for all database objects for which you want to create nicknames.

Step 9

Use the CREATE ALIAS statement to define an alias for a nickname (optional).

```
db2 "create alias dnt.account_xref for DNTNCK.ACCOUNT_XREF"

db2 "select substr(tabname,1,18) as tabname,
  substr(tabschema,1,18) as tabschema,
  type, substr(base_tabname,1,18) as basename,
  substr(base_tabschema,1,8) as baseschema
  from syscat.tables where type='A'"
```

```
TABNAME          TABSCHEMA      TYPE          BASENAME          BASESCHEMA
-------------    -------------  -------------  -------------     -------------
ACCOUNT_XREF     DNT            A             ACCOUNT_XREF      DNTNCK

1 record(s) selected.
```

Step 10

Grant permission:

```
db2 "grant all on DNTNCK.ACCOUNT_XREF to user DSNOW"
DB20000I  The SQL command completed successfully.

db2 "grant all on DNTNCK.ACCOUNT_XREF to user TPHAN"
DB20000I  The SQL command completed successfully.
```

Verifying Connections to a DB2 Data Source

This section explains how to verify that you have correctly configured your federated system to access a DB2 Data Source.

```
db2 "connect to SAMPLE user tphan using zzzzzzzz"
Database Connection Information

Database server          = DB2/SUN 8.1.0
SQL authorization ID     = TPHAN
Local database alias     = SAMPLE

db2 "select * from dntnck.account_xref"

ACCT_NUM                          ACCT_OFFICE
------------------                -----------
00000000000001001                 111
00000000000001011                 111
00000000000001101                 111
00000000000001111                 111
00000000000002001                 222
00000000000002011                 222
00000000000002101                 222
00000000000002111                 222

8 record(s) selected.
```

SQL Statements Summary

Table 7.5 presents descriptions for SQL statements.

Table 7.5   SQL Statements Used in the Federated System

SQL Statement	Description
create wrapper	registers a wrapper in a particular DB2 UDB database
drop wrapper	drops a wrapper and all servers, nicknames, and user mappings depending on it
create server	registers a data source in a particular DB2 UDB database as a federated server
alter server	changes OPTIONS of a federated server
set server option	temporarily creates a server option or temporarily resets its value
drop server	drops a server and all nicknames and user mappings depending on it
create user mapping	creates a mapping from a DB2 user to user/login at a data source
alter user mapping	changes a user mapping
drop user mapping	drops a user mapping
create nickname	registers a data source table or view in the DB2 UDB catalog
alter nickname	alters the nickname characteristics
create alias	defines an alias for a nickname
drop alias	drops an alias
drop nickname	drops the nickname
create type mapping	overrides or adds to the Default Type Mappings used when nicknames are created
create function mapping	overrides or adds to the Default Function Mappings
drop function mapping	drops function mappings
set passthru	sends all statements that follow to a data source "as is"
set passthru reset	ends all pass-through sessions

Federated Database Considerations

The following section describes additional considerations in a federated database system. It also provides recommendations for improving federated database query performance.

Federated Database Object Naming Rules

- Nicknames, mappings, index specifications, servers, and wrapper names cannot exceed 128 bytes.

- Server and nickname options and option settings are limited to 255 bytes.
- Names for federated database objects can also include:
  - ○ Valid accented letters
  - ○ Multi-byte characters, except multi-byte spaces (for multi-byte environments)

Pushdown Analysis

Pushdown analysis tells the DB2 optimizer whether an operation can be performed at a remote data source. An operation can be a function, such as relational operator, system, or user functions, or an SQL operator (GROUP BY, ORDER BY, and so on).

Functions that cannot be pushed down can significantly impact query performance. Consider the effect of forcing a selective predicate to be evaluated locally instead of at the data source. This approach could require DB2 to retrieve the entire table from the remote data source, then filter it locally against the predicate. If your network is constrained and the table is large, query performance could suffer.

> **NOTE** Pushdown analysis is performed only on relational data sources. Pushdown analysis does not determine how a query can be pushed down for non-relational data sources.

Connection to the Data Source

CONNECTSTRING specifies additional connection-relevant information for certain types of data sources. CONNECTSTRING server options are:

- IFILE—full path to the interfaces or sql.ini file that contains the connection details used by Sybase Open Client to access the Sybase server. This is particularly useful if you don't want to copy the interfaces or sql.ini file into the DB2 instance owner's \SQLLIB subdirectory but would rather use the interfaces or sql.ini file within the Sybase Open Client directory. For instance, on Windows systems, the sql.ini file is usually in the C:\Sybase\ini subdirectory.
- TIMEOUT—specifies the time, in seconds, that Federated Server should wait for results from Sybase server. If there are no problems on Sybase server or the user is willing to wait indefinitely for Sybase to provide results to SQL that is sent to it from the federated server, this CONNECTSTRING parameter does not need to be specified. But if there are problems, Sybase Open Client will wait indefinitely, and so will Federated Server. If you were in a DB2 CLP window, you need to issue Ctrl+C to stop the wait. Any other application would just *hang*.
- LOGIN_TIMEOUT—specifies the time, in seconds, that Federated Server should wait for Sybase server to respond to connections. If the Sybase server is running and there are no problems connecting to it, this parameter does not need to be specified. Otherwise, Sybase Open Client and DB2 Federated Server will wait indefinitely.

- PACKET_SIZE—size of data packets between Federated Server and Sybase. Large results sets from Sybase will perform better with a larger PACKET_SIZE.

Here is an example of specifying CONNECTSTRING on the initial create server statement to Sybase:

```
CREATE SERVER SYBS1000 TYPE SYBASE
  VERSION 11.9 WRAPPER CTLIB
  OPTIONS (NODE 'sybn1000', DBNAME 'testdb');
```

Here is an example of setting server option CONNECTSTRING with values for IFILE, LOGIN_TIMEOUT, and TIME_OUT:

```
ALTER SERVER SYBS1000
  OPTIONS (ADD CONNECTSTRING 'IFILE="c:\Sybase\ini\sql.ini",
    TIMEOUT=20, LOGIN_TIMEOUT=5');
```

The ability of a data source to process the SQL sent to it by the federated server will have a major impact on the time it takes for Federated Server to provide results to the users of the federated database. The SQL statement that will be sent to a data source can be determined by using Federated Server's explain facilities (dynexpln). Input to the Federated Server explain facility is the SQL statement that the user or application will give to the federated database. The output of the explain facility will include the whole plan that Federated Server will use to execute the statement, including showing the SQL statement(s) to be sent to each of the data sources.

> **N O T E**   The dynexpln tool is still available for backward compatibility. It is recommended to use the dynamic-options of db2expln to perform all of the functions of dynexpln.

If the plan to execute the SQL involves the creation of temporary tables in the federated database, availability of buffers to hold the pages of the temporary table will improve performance by avoiding the disk I/O involved if the pages of the temporary table have to be written out to disk. Also, if the plan involves a sort to be done in the federated database, for instance, if there is an ORDER BY clause that is not pushed down to a data source, the availability of sort resources in the federated database will affect performance.

For a sample, view the following SQL statement:

```
select count(*) from DNTNCK.ACCOUNT_XREF
    WHERE ACCT_NUM>'000000000000001001';
```

- Does the data source have adequate CPU capacity to process the statement?
- Is this index accessible?
- Does the data source support *Plan_Hints*?

- Is there enough sort space if sort is needed?
- How large is the temporary space?

Additional DB2 Federated Server options that could make the federated server send more *efficient* SQL to the data source, particularly for a specific data sources, are contained in the Plan_Hints server option. It is supported by only certain data sources and, even there, they need to be enabled. So the default setting for server option Plan_Hints is N. But if the data source does support Plan_Hints and the support is enabled, Federated Server can send the data source plan hints if the server option Plan_Hints is specified with a setting of Y.

```
ALTER SERVER ORASERV OPTIONS (ADD PLAN_HINTS 'Y');
```

Temporary Tables

Though the temporary table will be created in the federated database's table space for temporary tables, there will no disk I/O involved if all the pages of this temporary table will fit into available page buffers for this table space.

If the default temporary table space TEMPSPACE was created when the federated database was created, the pages of the table space will be kept in memory in the IBMDEFAULTBP buffer pool, and the database configuration parameter BUFFPAGE of the federated database determines the maximum number of pages that can be kept in memory.

Sort Allocation

If the execution plan indicates that a temporary table is created and used, and that ORDER BY has not been pushed down to a data source, it very likely that the ORDER BY will be executed in the federated database on the temporary table. This is particularly likely to happen if the federated database and the data source have different collating sequence, as indicated by the server option COLLATING_SEQUENCE whose default setting, if not explicitly specified, is N.

If a sort will be done in the federated database, the database configuration parameter SORTHEAP for the federated database and the Database Manager Configuration parameter SHEAPTHRES for the DB2 instance containing the federated database could have an impact.

Database configuration parameter SORTHEAP indicates the maximum memory allocated for a sort. The parameter is specified in number of pages. If a sort cannot fit into this allocation, it overflows into temporary table space tables. As discussion earlier, if the temporary table can't fit into the available memory buffers for the table space, there will be disk I/O. It is better, if possible, if the sort can be done using the memory pages allocated for sorts, so a larger value for SORTHEAP can improve performance.

Database Manager Configuration parameter SHEAPTHRES indicates the maximum memory allocated for sorts by users of all databases within the DB2 instance containing the federated database. Logically, it should be a multiple of the largest SORTHEAP value in the database configurations of the databases within the DB2 instance.

For example, we set the SORTHEAP for the federated database to 50,000 pages. So SHEAPTHRES in the Database Manager Configuration for the instance containing this federated database should be a multiple of 50,000.

Network Considerations

The network speed and number of hops between the federated server and a data source can have a big impact on how long it takes to give the federated user the result from an SQL statement when it:

- Returns a large result set from the data source
- Processes a large number of SQL statements at the data source

It is generally recommended that:

- The federated server and data source be collocated on the same system if possible
- As minimal a number of network hops as possible are used between the federated server and the data source

The DB2 Federated Server's Database Manager Configuration parameter RQRIOBLK can have an impact on performance if large blocks of data are transferred between the data source and the federated server. RQRIOBLK determines the maximum size of blocks of records that can be transferred at once between a DB2 server and its network clients; it also determines the size of the blocks that the federated server can receive from data sources. The default value is 32,767 bytes, which is already quite large. But a value as high as 65,535 bytes can be specified.

So if RQRIOBLK = 32,767 (the default value) and the result from the data source is 10,000 records with row length of 100, then ((10,000 records * 100 bytes) / 32,767 bytes per block) = 31 is the number of blocks needed to send the result from the data source to the federated server.

If the update of the Database Manager Configuration RQRIOBLK = 65,535, the result of 10,000 100-byte records would require ((10,000 records * 100 bytes) / 65,535 bytes per block) = 16 as the number of blocks needed to send the result from the data source to the federated server.

To find out the current value of RQRIOBLK, look at the Database Manager Configuration of the DB2 instance that has the federated database:

```
GET DATABASE MANAGER CONFIGURATION | grep -i rqrioblk
```

To set RQRIOBLK to the maximum value:

```
UPDATE DBM CFG USING RQRIOBLK 65535
```

The parameter RQRIOBLK size might improve performance of queries with large results from data sources, but it might not resolve the real issue with network performance if the data rate of the network between the federated server and the data source is slow. If there are lots of routers to be traversed between the data source and the federated server, performance on selects from nicknames will be slow.

NICKNAME CHARACTERISTICS AFFECTING GLOBAL OPTIMIZATION

The following sections contain nickname-specific factors that can affect global optimization.

Index Considerations

DB2 can use information about indexes at data sources to optimize queries. For this reason, it is important that the index information available to DB2 be current. The index information for nicknames is initially acquired at the time the nickname is created. Index information is not gathered for nickname on objects that do not have indexes such as views.

Creating Index Specifications on Nicknames

You can create an index specification for a nickname. Index specifications build an index definition (not an actual index) in the catalog for use by the DB2 optimizer. Use the CREATE INDEX SPECIFICATION ONLY statement to create index specifications.

Consider creating index specifications when:

- DB2 is unable to retrieve any index information from a data source during nickname creation
- You want an index for a nickname on a view
- You want to encourage the DB2 optimizer to use a specific nickname as the inner table of a nested loop join. The user can create an index on the joining column if none exists.

Consider your needs before issuing CREATE INDEX statements against a nickname for a view. In one case, if the view is a simple SELECT on a table with an index, creating indexes on the nickname (locally) that match the indexes on the table at the data source can significantly improve query performance. However, if indexes are created locally over views that are not simple select statements (for example, a view created by joining two tables), query performance may suffer. For example, if an index is created over a view that is a join of two tables, the optimizer may choose that view as the inner element in a nested loop join. The query will have poor performance because the join will be evaluated several times. An alternative is to create nicknames for each of the tables referenced in the data source view and create a local view at DB2 that references both nicknames.

Catalog Statistics Considerations

Catalog statistics describe the overall size of nicknames and the range of values in associated columns. They are used by the optimizer when calculating the least-cost path for processing queries containing nicknames. Nickname statistics are stored in the same catalog views as table statistics. Although DB2 can retrieve the statistical data held at a data source, it cannot automatically detect updates to existing statistical data at data sources.

Furthermore, DB2 has no mechanism for handling object definition or structural changes (adding a column) to objects at data sources. If the statistical data or structural data for an object has changed, you have two choices:

- Manually update the statistics in the SYSSTAT.TABLES view. This approach requires fewer steps, but it will not work if structural information has changed.
- Run the equivalent of RUNSTATS at the data source. Then drop the current nickname. Re-create the nickname. Use this approach if structural information has changed.

By doing this, you will ensure that Federated System knows about all indexes on remote objects.

To check nickname statistics in SYSSTAT.COLUMNS:

```
select char(colname,20) as colname, colcard,
    char(high2key, 15) as high,
    char(low2key, 15) as low
  from sysstat.columns
  where tabschema = 'DNTNCK' and
    tabname = 'ACCOUNT_XREF';
```

The results may be blank; if so, you can supply values based on knowledge or remote source statistics.

```
update sysstat.columns set colcard=1000,
    high2key = '1999-12-31',
    low2key  = '1995-01-01'
  where colname = 'ACCT_NUM' and
    tabname = 'ACCOUNT_XREF' and
    tabschema in ('DNTNCK');
```

Distributed Queries Using Materialized Query Tables (MQTs) on Nicknames

If your distributed query matches one of the following:

- The data underneath the nickname is infrequently updated
- The nickname is frequently joined with local data
- The nickname to a remote table is frequently queried (i.e., code or lookup tables)

you can speed up the distributed query by using MQTs on nickname:

- Make a local copy of the nickname using a MQT:

```
create table tphan.mqt_account as
   (select a.acct_num, a.acct_office, b.acct_cd, b.acct_desc
   from dntnck.account_xref a, tphan.account b
   where a.acct_num=b.acct_num)
   data initially deferred refresh deferred maintained by user;


refresh table tphan.mqt_account;
```

The following should be noted:

- DATA INITIALLY DEFERRED—data is not inserted into the table as part of the CREATE TABLE statement. A REFRESH TABLE statement specifying the *table-name* is used to insert data into the table.
- REFRESH DEFERRED—data in the table can be refreshed at any time using the REFRESH TABLE statement. The data in the table reflects the result of the query only as a snapshot at the time the REFRESH TABLE statement is processed. System-maintained MQTs defined with this attribute do not allow INSERT, UPDATE, or DELETE statements (SQLSTATE 42807). User-maintained MQTs defined with this attribute do allow INSERT, UPDATE, or DELETE statements.
- MAINTAINED BY USER—indicates that the data in the MQT is maintained by the user. The user is allowed to perform UPDATE, DELETE, or INSERT operations against user-maintained MQTs. The REFRESH TABLE statement, used for system-maintained MQTs, cannot be invoked against user-maintained MQTs. Only a REFRESH DEFERRED MQT can be defined as MAINTAINED BY USER.

Analyzing Query Optimization

There are two utilities provided with DB2 that show global access plans:

- Visual explain. Start it with the db2cc command. Use it to view the query access plan graph. The execution location for each operator is included in the detailed display of an operator. You can also find the remote SQL statement generated for each data source in the RQUERY (select operation) operator. By examining the details of each operator, you can see the number of rows estimated by the DB2 optimizer as input to and output from each operator. You can also see the estimated cost to execute each operator, including the communications cost.
- SQL explain. Start it with the db2expln command. Use it to view the access plan strategy as text. SQL explain does not provide cost information; however, you can get the access plan generated by the remote optimizer for those data sources supported by the remote explain function.

> **N O T E** For additional information, refer to Appendix F: Explain Tools.

SUMMARY

With a federated system you can send distributed requests to multiple data sources within a single SQL statement. The power of a DB2 federated system is in its ability to:

- Join data from local tables and remote data sources, as if all the data are local.
- Take advantage of the data source processing strengths by sending distributed requests to the data sources for processing.
- Compensate for SQL limitations at the data source by processing parts of a distributed request at the federated server.

Performance Tuning

Performance is one of the most important keys in any type of database system. This chapter focuses on a number of performance tuning tips with DB2 Universal Database (UDB). Although some tuning tips are the same regardless of the database workload, there are differences between OLTP and DSS type workloads, and these differences will be noted where applicable.

An OLTP workload typically consists of many applications concurrently running short transactions that include not only selects but also inserts, updates, and deletes. In contrast, DSS workloads are generally read-only transactions, but the transactions are much more complex and normally read much more data.

Performance of a database and the applications that access it are influenced by many factors. This chapter first discusses some fundamentals of performance tuning as it relates to DB2. It then concentrates on how to configure DB2 for optimal performance, using database and database manager configuration parameters, as well as DB2 registry variables. In the database configuration parameter monitoring and tuning section, this chapter will present a list of database manager and database configuration parameters in their order of importance and make recommendations for setting and monitoring these parameters.

PERFORMANCE FUNDAMENTALS

The Magic Triangle of Performance

When considering performance and tuning, it is important to understand the performance triangle. The sides of the performance represent: CPU, memory, and I/O (Figure 8.1).

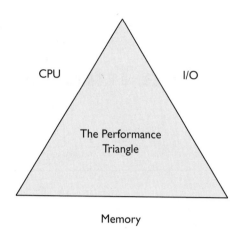

Figure 8.1
The Magic Triangle of Performance.

In an ideal world, the triangle would be an equilateral triangle and would be in perfect balance. While performance tuning on a DB2 UDB server, it is important to consider the trade-offs when making tuning decisions. For example, when tuning sorting within a database, if tuning only for memory and, therefore, reducing the sort heap, we would see an increase in both CPU usage and I/O for the sorting of the data using temporary tables. To attempt to minimize the I/O involved in sorting, the amount of memory assigned to the sort heaps would need to be increased, and this would also lead to increased CPU usage. These three things (CPU, I/O, and memory) must be balanced in order to tune for optimal performance on the database.

Ensure Enough Available Memory

An OLTP workload is much more dependent on memory for performance than a DSS workload; however, both workloads require sufficient memory in order to perform optimally. For OLTP workloads, the memory is normally used for database buffer pools, whereas a DSS workload normally requires much more memory for sorting.

In DB2 UDB Version 8 with full 64-bit support, there are no longer limits on the maximum size of the buffer pools. For an OLTP workload, a good starting point for the initial size of the buffer pool is 75% of the usable memory installed on the database server. For a DSS workload, a starting point for the size of the buffer pools is 50% of the usable memory installed on the server to leave enough memory for application sorting.

In many of today's database servers, a process or thread is dedicated to each client that connects to a database. For a typical OLTP workload that handles large numbers of connected users who perform relatively short-lived transactions with some delay between subsequent transactions, this puts a heavy load on the database server because system resources are being tied up by client connections that are not performing any work. DB2 UDB Version 8 has implemented a connection-multiplexing architecture, the Connection Concentrator, that will allow users to move from a configuration where the number of connected users is constrained by the physical limitations of the underlying hardware to a scenario where the limiting factor will be solely based on the transaction load and the machine's ability to handle such a load.

Ensure Sufficient I/O Handling Capability

No matter what type of disk subsystem is used on the database server, there must be enough physical disks to support a high volume of concurrent transactions for an OLTP system or the large amount of data read for a DSS system. As a general rule of thumb, there should be at least six to ten physical disks per CPU on the database server to ensure adequate throughput and to ensure that there are no bottlenecks.

The best way to estimate the I/O handling capability needed to ensure good performance for the database is to prototype the actual transactions and database to determine the number of I/O requests required per transaction and the number of transactions that will be processed per second. Then the I/O rate for the disk controllers and the disk subsystem can be used to determine how many controllers and disks are required to achieve the desired level of performance.

Use the DB2 Configuration Advisor for an Initial Set of Database Configuration Parameters

The Configuration Advisor will ask a series of questions about the database server, nature of the workload, transactions, priority, connections, and isolation level to determine a starting set of database configuration parameter values. These parameters can later be modified to suit the production workload and for additional fine-tuning.

To configure a database for performance using the Configuration Advisor:

1. Open the DB2 Control Center.
2. Select/right-click the database to be configured.
3. Choose Configuration Advisor.
4. Complete each of the applicable wizard pages.
5. Each page is discussed below.
6. The Finish button is available once enough information has been supplied for the Advisor to configure performance parameters for the database.
7. Click Finish to get a list of suggested configuration parameters for the database.

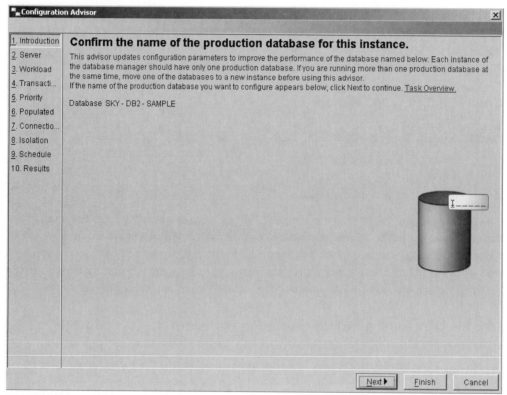

Figure 8.2
The Configuration Advisor introduction page.

Introduction

The introduction page shown in Figure 8.2 lists the database that is currently being examined to recommend the configure performance parameters. Verify that the correct database is shown.

Server

Use the server page shown in Figure 8.3 to specify what percentage of the server's memory is to be used by the database manager. For a dedicated DB2 server, choose 100%; if other applications are also running on the server, set the value to less than 100%.

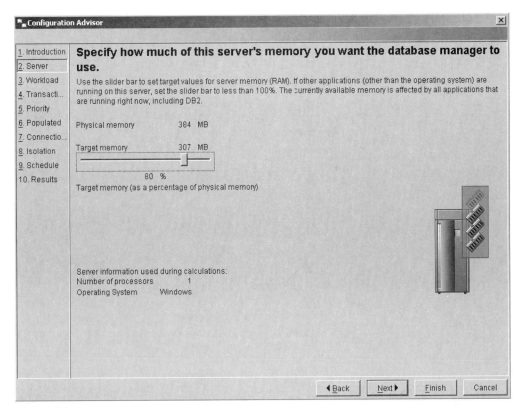

Figure 8.3
The Configuration Advisor server page.

Workload

On the workload page shown in Figure 8.4, indicate the type of workload for which the database will be used. Indicate whether the database is used mainly for queries (such as in a data warehousing environment), for transactions (such as order entry), or for a mixed workload (for a combination of queries and transactions).

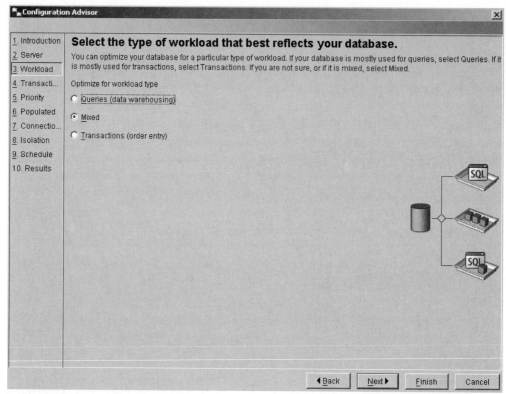

Figure 8.4
The Configuration Advisor workload.

Transactions

Use the transaction page shown in Figure 8.5 to describe a typical SQL transaction for the database. Indicate whether the average number of SQL statements per transaction is typically less than 10 or more than 10. It is also important to give an indication of the transaction rate for the database.

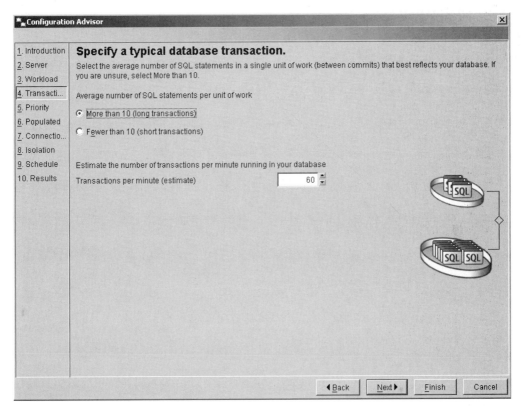

Figure 8.5
The Configuration Advisor transactions page.

Priority

Specify the priority for the selected database on the priority page shown in Figure 8.6. If the database is optimized for fast transaction processing, the database may take longer to recover in the event of an error. If the database is optimized for fast recovery time, transaction performance normally will be slower. If it is equally important to optimize both, choose to balance the optimization of the two.

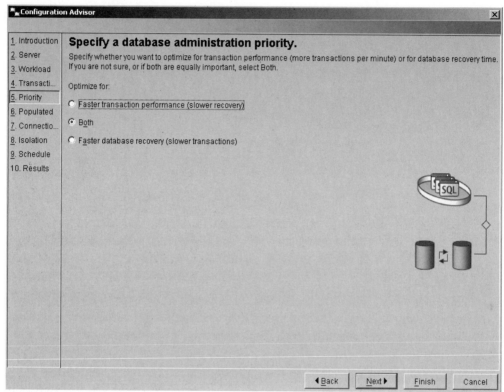

Figure 8.6
The Configuration Advisor priority page.

> **N O T E**   Use the Performance Monitor and/or Snapshot Monitor
> to get an accurate measurement of the number of transactions per
> minute if the database is already operational.

Populated

Indicate whether the database has been populated with data on the populated page, shown in Figure 8.7.

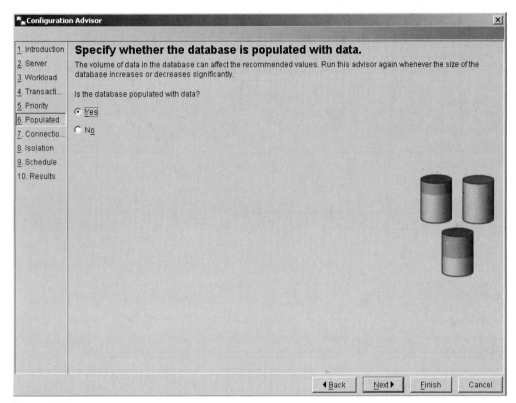

Figure 8.7
The Configuration Advisor populated page.

Connections

Indicate the average number of local applications and the average number of remote applications that will connect to the database on the Configuration Advisor connections page, shown in Figure 8.8. If these numbers are not available and a good estimate is not available, use the default values.

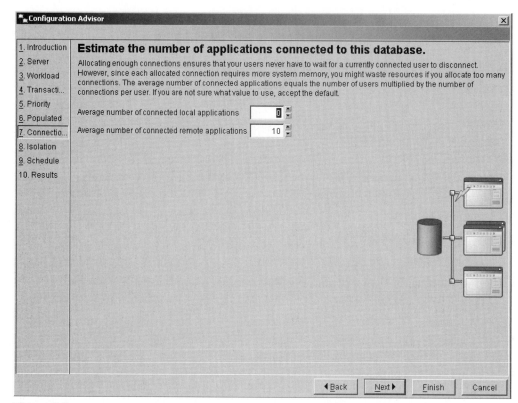

Figure 8.8
The Configuration Advisor connections page.

> **N O T E**   Use the Performance Monitor to get an accurate
> measurement of the number of remote and local applications that
> connect to the database.

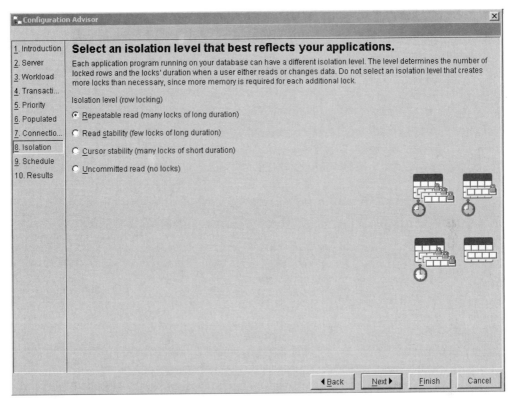

Figure 8.9
The Configuration Advisor isolation page.

Isolation

Specify the isolation level that the applications will use to access the database on the isolation page, shown in Figure 8.9. If multiple isolation levels are used, specify the one that is used most frequently in the applications or the one used by the most important application.

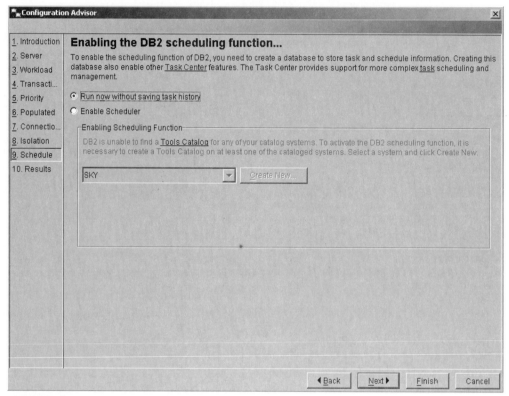

Figure 8.10
The Configuration Advisor schedule page.

Schedule

On the Configuration Advisor schedule page (Figure 8.10), specify whether a tools database should be created to store information about scheduled tasks.

Results

The results page (Figure 8.11) will display the Configuration Advisor's recommended configuration parameter settings, based on the information provided. These settings can be applied immediately or can be saved to a script to be applied at a later time.

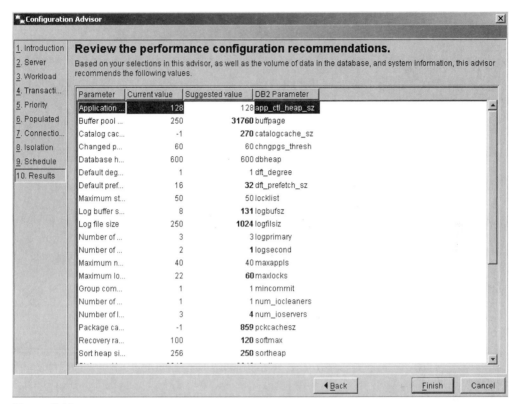

Figure 8.11
The Configuration Advisor results page.

Use Proper Indexes

To allow the optimizer to choose efficient access plans that will perform well, it is important to ensure that columns that are frequently accessed with SQL statements containing joins, group by's, or order by's be properly indexed. Columns that are foreign keys for referential constraints should also be indexed. In addition, any column that is accessed frequently should also be indexed, either in a separate index or as an include column on a unique index.

For example, a table (t1) contains columns c1, c2, c3, c4, and c5. If column c1 is unique, but the queries typically always access columns c1 and c2 together, create a unique index (inx1) on column c1 and include column c2. This can be done as follows:

```
create unique index inx1 on t1 (c1) include (c2)
```

The Index Advisor (also known as Index wizard from the DB2 Control Center) is a utility that will analyze an SQL statement, or a group of statements, and make suggestions for indexes that could improve the performance of the specified query or queries. If no indexes are currently defined for the table or tables, this would be a good starting set of indexes to use. If there are already existing indexes on the table or tables, the indexes suggested by the Index Advisor should not be blindly added. It is important first to examine existing indexes to determine whether they can be modified (i.e., dropped and re-created with different columns or a different order of the columns), then to create the index if this is not possible.

For an OLTP workload, it is important not to have too many indexes defined because each index adds extra overhead for insert, update, and delete processing. This is not the case in a query-only workload and is the reason that many data warehouses/data marts have much more space used by indexes than by the actual data so that the indexes are available to support any type of query on the system.

Type II indexes provide much better concurrency than type I indexes and should be used wherever possible. Any new tables created with DB2 UDB Version 8 will use type II indexes by default. For a database that was created on a previous version of DB2 and migrated to Version 8, all existing indexes will be type I indexes; however, they can be converted to type II indexes when a table is reorganized. If an existing table already has indexes defined, any new indexes will be created as type I indexes.

Do Not Hold Locks Longer than Absolutely Necessary

Locks should be held only as long as absolutely required. Applications should not be written with a lot of application logic or user interaction required between SQL statements. When an application involves multiple interactions with the database, each database interaction should have its own transaction to commit and should free up all locks before returning activity to the application. Keep the duration of a transaction as short as possible. In addition, because type II indexes allow much better concurrency and help reduce locking, as compared to type I indexes, they should be used whenever possible.

Use Stored Procedures or Compound SQL
Whenever Possible for OLTP Systems

Generally, stored procedures should be used when an OLTP transaction has more than four or five statements within a transaction. This helps to minimize the number of network trips required for the transaction and will result in the application holding onto locks and other resources for a shorter period of time.

Use Efficient SQL

In general, don't use multiple SQL statements where one SQL statement will provide the same results. In addition, providing detailed search conditions by specifying more predicates in a query will help the optimizer choose more optimal access plans.

It is also important that the application use queries that do not return more rows and/or columns than necessary. For example, ensure that the SQL statements filter the rows that are needed in the database and do not return every row in the table(s), then expect the application to do the filtering.

Use Parallelism Only When the Workload Requires

For a large, complex query, intra-partition parallelism is good, and the result set can normally be returned much quicker. However, an insert of a single row does not require nine (eight subagents plus the coordinating agent) agents. In a typical OLTP environment, there are normally hundreds (if not more) of applications running in parallel. If each of them were assigned nine agent processes to handle their simple tasks, there would be far too many agent processes running on the system, causing a great deal more system overhead than is required.

Ensure Current Catalog Statistics

The DB2 UDB optimizer relies heavily on the table and index statistics stored in the database catalogs to estimate the costs for potential access plans and determine the best plan. If these statistics are incorrect or out of date, the optimizer cannot choose an optimal access plan. In extreme cases, we have seen SQL statements that have been optimized and executed with out-of-date statistics take over 45 minutes to complete. After updating the table and index statistics, and reoptimizing the SQL statement, it was able to finish in less than a second. This is a tremendous difference and may not be true for all SQL statements, but it does give an example of how important it really is to ensure that the table and index statistics are current.

Statistics for objects are updated in the system catalog tables only when explicitly requested. There are several ways to update some or all of the statistics:

- Using the RUNSTATS (run statistics) utility
- Using LOAD, with the statistics collection option specified
- Coding SQL UPDATE statements against a set of predefined catalog views
- Using the REORGCHK UPDATE STATISTICS command

The RUNSTATS utility analyzes the specified tables and indexes, and calculates statistical information that is then stored in the system catalog tables to be used when optimizing SQL statements. The RUNSTATS utility should be run to calculate and capture new statistics under the following conditions:

- When a table is loaded with data, and the appropriate indexes have been defined
- When a table has been reorganized using the REORG utility
- When there have been extensive updates, deletions, or insertions that affect a table and its indexes
  - ◦ "Extensive" typically means that 10–20% of the data in the table has changed
- When the prefetch size for a table space is changed
- When the REDISTRIBUTE DATABASE PARTITION GROUP command is run

When optimizing SQL queries, the decisions made by the SQL compiler are heavily influenced by the optimizer's model of the tables and indexes referenced in the statement. This model is used by the optimizer to estimate the cost of a set of potential access paths that can be used to resolve the particular query. A key element in the data model is the set of statistics gathered about the data contained in the database and stored in the system catalog tables. This includes statistics for tables, nicknames, indexes, columns, and user-defined functions (UDFs). A change in the data statistics can result in a change in the access plan selected as the most efficient method of accessing the desired data.

Examples of the statistics available that help define the data model to the optimizer include:

- The number of pages in a table and the number of pages that contain data
- The number of rows in a table
- Statistics about individual columns, such as the number of distinct values in a column
- The degree to which rows have been moved from their original page to other pages (known as *overflow records*)
- The degree of clustering between the data and the index, i.e., the extent to which the physical sequence of rows in the table follows the indexes defined on the table
- Statistics about the index, such as the number of index levels and the number of leaf pages in each index
- The number of occurrences of frequently used column values
- The distribution of column values across the range of values present in the column
- Cost estimates for UDFs

An easy way to determine whether the RUNSTATS utility has been run is to query the system catalog tables. For example:

```
select stats_time, tbname, nleaf, nlevels, stats_time from
   syscat.indexes
```

If the RUNSTATS utility has not been run, the value of "-1" will be stored for the columns nleaf and nlevels in the SYSIBM.SYSINDEXES table. After runstats is run, there will be a value other than "-1" stored for the nleaf and nlevels columns, and the timestamp when the RUNSTATS command was run will be stored for the stats_time column. If the time of the last statistics update is not current, it may be a good idea to run the RUNSTATS command for the tables and indexes.

CONFIGURATION PARAMETER TUNING

Every database and every set of applications are unique in many aspects, and these differences have a profound impact on the performance of the database system. To get the most from the database and the server, it is important that the database manager and database be properly tuned for the specific environment.

The Performance Configuration wizard or the AUTOCONFIGURE command will provide a very good starter set for the configuration of the system. Although this configuration likely will not provide the absolute best performance, it is a much better starting point than the default configuration parameters.

Different types of applications and users have different response time requirements and expectations. Applications could range from simple data entry screens to strategic applications involving dozens of complex SQL statements accessing dozens of tables per unit of work. For example, response time requirements could vary considerably in a telephone customer service application versus a batch report generation application.

Some configuration parameters can also be set to automatic. If the parameter is set to automatic, DB2 will automatically adjust these parameters to reflect the current resources required by the applications and available on the server.

The changes to many configuration parameters can now take place immediately (i.e., online). This means that the instance need not be stopped and restarted or the database need not be reactivated for the parameter change to take effect. In order for these changes to take effect immediately, the IMMEDIATE option must be specified when the configuration parameter change is made. Otherwise, the change will be deferred until DB2 is stopped and restarted or the database is reactivated.

Database Manager Configuration Parameter Tuning and Monitoring

The database manager (or instance) configuration parameters have an effect on the overall system and all databases in the instance. The parameters listed in Table 8.1 have the most significant impact on overall system and database performance.

Application Support Layer Heap Size (ASLHEAPSZ)

Background

The application support layer heap is a communication buffer between an application and its associated DB2 agent. This buffer is allocated in shared memory by each agent process for a particular DB2 instance. If the application request or the output from DB2 cannot fit into this buffer, they will be split into multiple send-and-receive pairs.

The size of the application support layer heap should be set so that it can handle the majority of requests using a single send-and-receive pair. The size of the send-and-receive request is based on the storage required to hold:

- The input SQLDA
- All of the associated data in the SQLVARs
- The output SQLDA
- Other fields that do not generally exceed 250 bytes

Table 8.1   Configuration Parameter Performance Impact

Parameter	Description
ASLHEAPSZ	Application support layer heap size
RQRIOBLK	Maximum requester I/O block size
SHEAPTHRES	Sort heap threshold
INTRA_PARALLEL	Enable intra-partition parallelism
MAX_QUERYDEGREE	Maximum query degree of parallelism
MAXTOTFILOP	Maximum total of files open
QUERY_HEAP_SZ	Query heap size
FCM_NUM_BUFFERS	No. of inter-partition communication buffers
NUM_POOLAGENTS	Agent pool size
NUM_INITAGENTS	Initial number of agents in pool
AGENTPRI	Priority of agents

In addition to being the communication buffer between the application and its associated DB2 agent, this parameter is also used for two other purposes.

1. The application support layer heap determines the I/O block size when a cursor defined with blocking is opened. The memory required for blocked cursors is allocated out of the application's private address space, and if the database client cannot allocate the memory for a blocking cursor out of its private memory, a nonblocking cursor will be used.
2. The application support layer heap is also used to determine the communication size between the db2 agents and the processes used to support UDFs and fenced stored procedures. The size of the application support layer heap is allocated from shared memory for each UDF and stored procedure process or thread that is active on the system.

Configuring

The following formula should be used to calculate a minimum number of pages for the application support layer heap.

```
aslheapsz >=(sizeof(input SQLDA) + sizeof(each input SQLVAR) +
  sizeof(output SQLDA) + 250) / 4096
```

To set the application support layer heap size, use the following command:

```
update dbm cfg using aslheapsz 20
```

Once the database is operational, monitor the system to determine whether blocked cursor requests are being rejected and increase this parameter until this condition is eliminated.

Monitoring

DB2 does not monitor the usage of the application support layer heap; however, it does monitor the number of block cursor requests that are rejected. The number of rejected block cursor requests can be determined by using a database manager snapshot, as follows:

```
get snapshot for all on <database_name> |
grep -i "Rejected Block Remote Cursor requests"
```

This will capture a snapshot for the specified database and extract the monitor element concerned with the number of rejected block cursor requests. This will produce output like the following:

```
Rejected Block Remote Cursor requests      =  2283
```

In this case, a number of requests for blocked cursors were unable to be handled, and a non-blocked cursor was used. A nonblocked cursor requires more network round trips and is much less efficient than a blocked cursor. It is good practice to eliminate the "Rejected Remote Block Cursor requests" completely by monitoring the database and increasing the ASLHEAPSZ parameter until the "Rejected Remote Block Cursor requests" element is zero.

Automatic: No

Online: No

Maximum Requester I/O Block Size (RQRIOBLK)

Background

The maximum requester I/O block size is the maximum amount of data that can be sent back and forth between a DB2 client and server. The communication block is allocated in agent private memory by each agent process for a DB2 instance; however, DB2 uses only what it needs up to this maximum size. If the application request or the output from DB2 is larger than the block size, the data will be split into multiple pieces and sent in multiple communication packets.

The default maximum requester I/O block size is 32 KB, and the maximum size is 64 KB. The default value is sufficient for most workloads; however, if the size of the application requests and/or result sets generated is greater than 32 KB, increasing the maximum requester I/O block size will result in fewer communication packets being sent back and forth across the network and can result in result sets being returned to the application quicker.

Configuring

Because DB2 allocates only as much memory as needed, setting the maximum requester I/O block size to 64 KB will not hurt performance but in many cases will help improve performance. To set this parameter to a value of 64 KB, use the command:

```
update dbm cfg using rqrioblk 64
```

Monitoring

The effectiveness of the setting for the maximum requester I/O block size cannot be monitored by DB2; it can be examined only by using network monitoring tools to count the number of communication packets sent between the DB2 client and server. Therefore, it is recommended that the maximum requester I/O block size be set to 64 KB to minimize network traffic.

Automatic: No

Online: No

Sort Heap Threshold (SHEAPTHRES)

Background

When an SQL query requires that the data be returned in specified order, the result set may or may not require sorting. DB2 will attempt to perform the ordering of the data using an index; however, if an index cannot be used, a sort will take place. For example, consider the following SQL statement:

```
select projno from project order by projno desc
```

With no indexes defined on the table, the access plan would need to sort the PROJNO column from the table to return the data in descending order. The access plan would look like the following:

```
Access Plan:
-----------
    Total Cost:             3589.463
    Query Degree:           1

                       Rows
                      RETURN
                      (   1)
                       Cost
                       I/O
                        |
```

```
                          46
                        TBSCAN
                        (    2)
                        25.1692
                           1
                           |
                          46
                         SORT
                        (    3)
                        25.1678
                           1
                           |
                          46
                        TBSCAN
                        (    4)
                        25.1396
                           1
                           |
                          46
                  TABLE: DWAINE
                  PROJECT
```

Notice that the access plan requires that the entire table be scanned and the data sorted in order to return the project number in descending order.

The following statement creates an index on the PROJNO column that is either in descending order or is defined to allow reverse scans:

```
create index projx on project (projno) allow reverse scans collect
   detailed statistics
```

As long as index statistics are gathered after the index is created or during the index creation, as specified above, the access plan would look like the following.

```
Access Plan:
-----------
Total Cost:        341.134
Query Degree:      1

        Rows
       RETURN
       (    1)
        Cost
        I/O
          |
```

```
        22680
      IXSCAN
      (    2)
      341.134
         37
         |
        22680
   INDEX: DWAINE
 PROJX
```

In this case, the index can be used to retrieve the data and ensure the order of the project numbers without needing to sort the data. This resulted in significant cost savings for the query because the cost went from 3589.463 to 341.134 timerons.

If at all possible, sorts should be minimized, if not completely eliminated. However, if sorts cannot be eliminated, it is important to tune the sorts to work as efficiently as possible. To do this, it is important to understand how DB2 handles sort operations.

A sort operation typically occurs in two steps:

1. The sort phase
2. The return of the result of the sort phase

The manner in which DB2 performs these two steps results in different ways in which to describe the sort operation. When describing the sort phase, the sort is categorized as either overflowed or non-overflowed. When describing the return of the results from the sort phase, the sort is categorized as either piped or non-piped.

Overflowed vs. Non-Overflowed

If the table data that is being sorted cannot fit entirely within the configured sort heap, it will overflow into a temporary table in the system temporary table space. The sort heap is a piece of memory that is allocated when a sort is being performed. The size of the sort heap is limited by the database configuration parameter SORTHEAP, discussed later in this chapter. Non-overflowed sorts perform better than overflowed sorts because the entire operation happens in memory, and no disk I/O is required for a temporary table.

Piped vs. Non-Piped

If the information that has been sorted can be returned directly to the next operation in the access plan without requiring a temporary table to store a final, sorted list of data, it is referred to as a *piped sort*. If the information that has been sorted requires a temporary table to be returned to the next operation in the access plan, it is referred to as a *non-piped sort*.

A piped sort performs better than a non-piped sort because the entire operation happens in memory, and no disk I/O is required for a temporary table. The DB2 optimizer will determine whether a non-overflowed sort can be performed and whether a piped sort can be calculating the size of the expected result set with the value of the SORTHEAP database configuration parameter.

The sort heap threshold parameter (SHEAPTHRES) sets the maximum number of memory pages that can be used for private sorts. In DB2 UDB Version 8, a new database configuration parameter, SHEAPTHRES_SHR, is used to limit the maximum number of memory pages that can be used for shared sorts within the database.

If intra-partition parallelism is disabled, DB2 can use only private sorts. If intra-partition parallelism is enabled, DB2 can choose between private and shared sorts to determine which will be more efficient. Each individual sort will have a separate sort heap allocated where the data will be sorted. The optimizer will attempt to calculate the size of the sort heap that will be needed, based on the table statistics, to know whether it requires more space than the configured SORTHEAP to complete. If it requires more than SORTHEAP, the sort will be overflowed; otherwise, DB2 will attempt to allocate an entire SORTHEAP for the sort.

The sort heap threshold parameter controls the sum of all private and shared SORTHEAPs allocated by all applications for all databases in the DB2 instance. When the value set for SHEAPTHRES is reached for private sorts, DB2 will begin reducing the allocation of additional SORTHEAPs to the applications so that applications will still be given space for sorts. If this reduced amount of SORTHEAP is sufficient for the sort, it will not overflow; if it is insufficient, the sort will overflow.

When intra-partition parallelism is enabled, DB2 will allocate a piece of shared memory equal in size to the SHEAPTHRES_SHR, in case a shared sort is performed. This shared memory size is a hard limit and cannot be exceeded. Therefore, when the value set for SHEAPTHRES_SHR is reached for shared sorts, DB2 will stop allocating additional shared SORTHEAPs to the applications, and all shared sorts will be overflowed.

Configuring

The default value for SHEAPTHRES is quite low, especially for decision support databases. It is good practice to increase the value for SHEAPTHRES significantly because it can have a very dramatic effect on performance. However, increasing the SHEAPTHRES blindly can mask a real problem in the system or applications.

When determining an appropriate value for the SHEAPTHRES parameter, consider the following:

- Hash joins and dynamic bitmaps used for index ANDing and star joins use sort heap memory. Increase the size of the SORTHEAP and SHEAPTHRES when these techniques are used.
- Increase the SHEAPTHRES when large sorts are frequently required.

- The value of SHEAPTHRES needs to be based on the value of the SORTHEAP, as well as on the average number of applications executing in the database.
  - For example, if database monitoring shows that, on average, there are 12 applications concurrently executing in DB2, setting the SHEAPTHRES to 12–15 times the SORTHEAP would be a good starting point.
- Also important is the number of concurrent sorts per query.

To set the SHEAPTHRES configuration parameter, use the following command:

```
update dbm cfg using sheapthres 80000
```

Once the database is operational, monitor the system to determine whether the sort heap threshold is being reached.

Monitoring

Due to the impact of sorting on database performance, DB2 monitors a number of things in relation to sort activity. Sorts that are started after the sort heap threshold has been reached may not get an entire SORTHEAP allocated and, therefore, have a much higher chance of overflowing. The number of sorts stated after the SHEAPTHRES has been reached is reported in the post threshold sorts database monitor element.

In addition, the number of piped sorts requested and accepted and the number of overflowed sorts are also available in the snapshot information. These are related to the sort heap, as well as to the sort heap threshold and will be discussed in more detail when the sort heap is discussed later in this chapter.

To determine whether the sort heap threshold is being reached, take a database manager snapshot, using the following command:

```
get snapshot for database manager | grep -i "Post threshold sorts"
```

This will capture a snapshot for the specified database and extract the monitor element concerned with the number of post threshold sorts. This would produce output like the following:

```
Post threshold sorts                 =  16
```

This information can also be captured using an SQL statement, as follows:

```
SELECT post_threshold_sorts FROM TABLE(SNAPSHOT_DBM(-1 )) as
    SNAPSHOT_DBM
```

This would produce output like the following:

```
POST_THRESHOLD_SORTS
--------------------
                  16
```

If this value is excessive, the size of the sort heap and/or sort heap thresholds should be examined to determine whether they are sufficient. In addition, the applications should be examined to ensure they are using appropriate indexes.

If the allocation of one more sort heaps equals or exceeds the sort heap threshold, a piped sort cannot be performed, and any request for a piped sort will get rejected. A sort heap will be allocated to handle the sorting of the data, but it will be a reduced size.

The percentage of piped sort requests that have been serviced by the database manager can be calculated using the formula:

```
Percent Piped Sorts = (piped_sorts_accepted / piped_sorts_requested) * 100%
```

If this percentage of piped sorts is low, the sort performance could be improved by increasing the sort heap threshold.

The number of piped sort requests that have been rejected by DB2 can be calculated using the following formula:

```
Piped Sorts Rejected = piped_sorts_requested - piped_sorts_accepted
```

A high number of rejected pipe sort requests may indicate that the value of either the sort heap or the sort heap threshold is too small to support the current workload.

Another indicator of sort performance is the percentage of post threshold sorts. DB2 allocates sort heaps at the beginning of sorts and at the beginning of any sort merge phase. If at any time during a sort a request to allocate a sort heap would exceed the SHEAPTHRES, the sort would be classified as a post threshold sort. The percentage of post threshold sorts is calculated using the following formula:

```
Percent Post Threshold Sorts = (post_threshold_sorts / sum of total_sorts) * 100%
```

The total amount of private sort heap that is currently allocated can be monitored using the following:

```
get snapshot for database manager | grep -i "Private Sort heap
allocated"

or

SELECT sort_heap_allocated FROM TABLE(SNAPSHOT_DBM(-1 )) as
SNAPSHOT_DBM
```

Automatic: No

Online: No

Enable Intra-Partition Parallelism (INTRA_PARALLEL)

Background

Intra-partition parallelism refers to the ability to break up a query into multiple parts within a single database partition and to execute these parts at the same time. This type of parallelism subdivides what is usually considered a single database operation, such as index creation, database load, or SQL queries into multiple parts, many or all of which can be executed in parallel within a single database partition. Intra-partition parallelism can be used to take advantage of multiple processors of a symmetric multiprocessor (SMP) server.

Intra-partition parallelism can take advantage of either data parallelism or pipeline parallelism. Data parallelism is normally used when scanning large indexes or tables. When data parallelism is used as part of the access plan for an SQL statement, the index or data will be dynamically partitioned, and each of the executing parts of the query (known as *package parts*) is assigned a range of data to act on. For an index scan, the data will be partitioned based on the key values, whereas for a table scan, the data will be partitioned based on the actual data pages.

Configuring

Intra-partition parallelism in DB2 UDB is enabled or disabled using the database manager configuration parameter INTRA_PARALLEL. Intra-partition parallelism should be enabled only if the server has more than one processor (CPU). To enable intra-partition parallelism in DB2 UDB, the INTRA_PARALLEL configuration must be set to YES. This can be done using the following command:

```
update dbm cfg using intra_parallel yes
```

The degree of parallelism can then be controlled at the instance level, the database level, the application level, or the statement level.

Monitoring

If intra-partition parallelism is enabled, DB2 will invoke multiple db2 agents to process the request. The number of agents that are handling each request is returned by the command:

```
list applications show detail
```

If the number of agents is greater than one, intra-partition parallelism is being used, and the degree of parallelism is one less than the number of agents, because there is a coordinating agent associated with the operation.

Automatic: No

Online: No

Maximum Query Degree of Parallelism (MAX_QUERYDEGREE)

Background

The maximum degree of intra-partition parallelism specifies the maximum number of subagent processes that any SQL statement can use within the database instance (or database partition, if the database is partitioned). This parameter is effective only if intra-partition parallelism is enabled by setting the INTRA_PARALLEL configuration parameter to YES.

The default value for the maximum degree of intra-partition parallelism is -1, or ANY. This value allows the DB2 optimizer to set the degree of parallelism based on the number of CPUs in the server and the current workload on the server. If a value greater than one is specified, this value will limit the degree of parallelism for all SQL statements executed within the database instance or database partition.

Configuring

For a non-partitioned database running on a server with more than one CPU, the maximum degree of intra-partition parallelism should normally be set to ANY (-1) to allow DB2 to determine dynamically the degree of intra-partition parallelism for individual SQL queries. This can be done using the command:

```
UPDATE DBM CFG USING MAX_QUERYDEGREE -1 IMMEDIATE
```

For a multi-partitioned database on a large SMP server, the maximum degree of parallelism for each partition should be limited so that no partition attempts to use all of the CPUs on the server. This can be done using the MAX_QUERYDEGREE instance configuration parameter. For a 32-way SMP server with eight database partitions, the maximum degree of parallelism for each partition could be limited to four, as follows:

```
UPDATE DBM CFG USING MAX_QUERYDEGREE 4 IMMEDIATE
```

For an SMP server with 16 CPUs, running two separate DB2 instances, the maximum degree of parallelism for each partition could be limited to eight, as follows:

```
UPDATE DBM CFG USING MAX_QUERYDEGREE 8 IMMEDIATE
```

Monitoring

If intra-partition parallelism is enabled, DB2 will invoke multiple db2 agents to process the request. The number of agents that are handling each request is returned by the command:

```
list applications show detail
```

If the number of agents is greater than one, intra-partition parallelism is being used, and the degree of parallelism is one less than the number of agents, because there is a coordinating agent associated with the operation.

Automatic: No

Online: Yes

Query Heap Size (QUERY_HEAP_SZ)

Background

A query heap is used to store each SQL statement in the private memory for the db2 agent executing the statement. The information that is stored in the query heap for an SQL statement includes the following:

- the input SQLDA
- the output SQLDA
- the statement text
- the SQLCA
- the package name
- the package creator
- the section number
- a consistency token
- the cursor control block for any blocking cursors

The query heap size specifies the maximum amount of memory that can be allocated for the query heap and allows the DBA to ensure that an application does not consume an excessive amount of memory within a DB2 agent. When an application connects to DB2, the initial size of the query heap that is allocated will be the minimum of two pages, or the size of the application support layer heap (ASLHEAPSZ). If the currently allocated query heap is not large enough to handle the request, the query heap will be reallocated with a larger size that will handle the request, as long as it does not exceed the query heap size. If the amount of query heap required is more than 1.5 times larger than the application support layer heap, the query heap will be reallocated to the size of the application support layer heap when the query completes.

Configuring

The query heap size should be set to a minimum of five times the size of the application support layer heap to allow for queries that are larger than the application support layer heap and to allow for enough memory to support three to four concurrent blocking cursors, as well.

In most cases, the default value will be sufficient; however, if the applications are accessing large LOBs, the query heap size may need to be increased to be able to accommodate the LOBs. To increase the size of the query heap size, use the following command:

```
update dbm cfg using query_heap_sz 10000
```

Monitoring

The currently allocated size of the query heap cannot be monitored.

Automatic: No

Online: No

Number of FCM Buffers (FCM_NUM_BUFFERS)

Background

Fast communications manager (FCM) is used to communicate between database partitions in a multi-partitioned database or between subagents working on behalf of the same application if intra-partition parallelism is enabled. FCM is responsible for sending data back and forth between the database partitions or subagent processes.

The number of FCM buffers specifies the number of 4-KB buffers that are used for:

- Communication between database partitions in a multi-partitioned database
- Communication within a database partition or instance if intra-partition parallelism is enabled

The implementation of FCM is slightly different in AIX than on other platforms. For AIX, if there is enough room in the general database manager memory area, the FCM buffer heap will be allocated there. In this situation, each database partition server will have its own dedicated FCM buffers. In this case, each database partition will have FCM_NUM_BUFFERS buffers allocated.

If there is not enough room in the general database manager memory, the FCM buffer heap will be allocated from a separate memory area that is shared by all database partitions on the server. In this case, there will be a total of FCM_NUM_BUFFERS buffers allocated for the whole server.

For all platforms except AIX, if there are multiple database partitions created on a single server, one pool of FCM buffers will be shared by all database partitions on the same server. The number of buffers is specified by the FCM_NUM_BUFFERS database manager configuration parameter.

The DB2_FORCE_FCM_BP registry variable can be used to allow DB2 to communicate between database partitions on the same server entirely through shared memory, instead of using the high-speed interconnect. If the DB2_FORCE_FCM_BP registry variable is set to YES, the FCM buffers are always created in a separate memory segment so that communication between the FCM daemons for the different database partitions on the same server will occur through shared memory. Otherwise, FCM daemons on the same server must communicate through UNIX sockets using the high-speed interconnect, even if they are on the same server. Communicating through shared memory is faster, but if DB2 is installed in 32-bit mode, there will be less shared memory available for other uses, particularly for database buffer pools.

Configuring

Normally, the default value of the number of FCM buffers is sufficient. However, if there are multiple database partitions within the same server, it may be necessary to increase the value of this parameter. It may also be necessary to increase the value of this parameter if DB2 runs out of message buffers, due to:

- The number of users on the server
- The number of database partitions on the server
- The complexity of the applications accessing the database

It is important to consider how many FCM buffers in total will be allocated on the servers where the database partitions reside. To increase the size of the query heap size, use the following command:

```
update dbm cfg using fcm_num_buffers 4096 immediate
```

Monitoring

DB2 UDB provides monitors solely for the purpose of monitoring the FCM and its efficiency. To gather the snapshot for all database partitions in the database, use the following command:

```
get snapshot for FCM for all dbpartitionnums
```

To gather the snapshot for a specific database partition, use the following command:

```
get snapshot for FCM for dbpartitionnum <x>
```

The output of the get snapshot command would look like the following for each database partition:

```
Node FCM information corresponds to          = 0
Free FCM buffers                             = 2172
Free FCM buffers low water mark              = 1682
Free FCM message anchors                     = 384
Free FCM message anchors low water mark      = 156
Free FCM connection entries                  = 384
Free FCM connection entries low water mark   = 308
Free FCM request blocks                      = 506
Free FCM request blocks low water mark       = 218
```

The snapshot information above is for database partition zero (0). If the database has multiple partitions, there will be a snapshot report generated for each database partition. To analyze the number of FCM buffers, it is important to look at the current allocation of the FCM buffers, as well as the maximum number of FCM buffers that have been allocated, i.e., the low water mark for the free FCM buffers. These numbers can then be compared with the configured number of FCM buffers from the database manager configuration.

The above information can also be obtained using the following SQL statement:

```
SELECT * FROM TABLE(SNAPSHOT_FCM(-1 )) as SNAPSHOT_FCM
```

The output of this statement would look like the following:

```
SNAPSHOT_TIMESTAMP          BUFF_FREE BUFF_FREE_BOTTOM MA_FREE MA_FREE_BOTTOM CE_FREE CE_FREE_BOTTOM RB_FREE RB_FREE_BOTTOM PARTITION_NUMBER
--------------------------- --------- ---------------- ------- -------------- ------- -------------- ------- -------------- ----------------
2002-10-05-21.06.18.693011       2174             1682     384            156     384            308     506            218                0

1 record(s) selected.
```

If the percentage of free FCM buffers (PFFCMBuf) drops below 10%, there is a potential that
DB2 may run out of available buffers, and this would indicate that the number of FCM buffers
should be increased. The PFFCMBuf is calculated from the snapshot and the database manager
configuration, using the following formula:

```
PFFCMBuf = (Free_FCM_buffers_low_water_mark / FCM_NUM_BUFFERS) * 100%
```

If the number of FCM buffers were set to 4096 as above, based on the above snapshot, the
PFFCMBuf would be:

```
PFFCMBuf = (1682 / 4096) * 100%


PFFCMBuf = 41%
```

In this case, there seems to be plenty of FCM buffers available for future requests. However, this
should be monitored over time, as well, because the low water mark would show the smallest
number of available FCM buffers available for the entire time that DB2 UDB was running.

The low water mark for the free message anchors, free connection entries, and free request
blocks should also be monitored. If the low water mark for any of these snapshot elements is less
than 10% of the corresponding configured parameter value, increase the value of the corresponding parameter.

Automatic: No

Online: Yes

Agent Pool Size (NUM_POOLAGENTS)

Background

When an application connects to a DB2 database, it is assigned one or more DB2 agent processes to handle the connection and perform the work on behalf of the application. When an
application disconnects from the database, the agent process could be terminated; however, this
is not very efficient. The overhead of continually terminating the agent processes and starting
new agent processes when needed can be quite high, and DB2 can avoid this by keeping the idle
agent in a "pool" to be reused by other applications.

The agent pool is the place where idle agents are held by DB2 so that they can be reused. When the connection concentrator is not enabled (i.e., the setting of the maximum number of connections {MAX_CONNECTIONS} is equal to the maximum number of coordinating agents {MAX_COORDAGENTS}), this configuration parameter specifies the maximum size of the idle agent pool. All idle agents, regardless of whether they are coordinating agents or subagents, count toward this limit. If the workload causes more agents to be created than specified by the size of the agent pool, the agents will be terminated when they finish executing their current request.

When the connection concentrator is enabled (i.e., the setting of the maximum number of connections {MAX_CONNECTIONS} is greater than the number of coordinating agents {MAX_COORDAGENTS}), this configuration parameter will be used as a guideline for how large the agent pool will be when the system workload is low. A database agent will always be returned to the pool, no matter what the value of this parameter is.

The DB2 Connection Concentrator

The DB2 connection concentrator allows DB2 UDB servers to provide support for thousands of users simultaneously executing business transactions, while drastically reducing the resources required on the database server. It accomplishes this goal by concentrating the workload from all of the applications in a much smaller number of database server connections.

The DB2 connection concentrator uses logical agents (LAs) to handle the application context while database agents (DAs) handle the actual DB2 connections. When a new application connects to a database, it is assigned an LA. Because a DA is needed to pass the SQL to the DB2 server, one is assigned to perform the work for the LA as soon as a new transaction is initiated. The key to this architecture is the fact that the DA is disassociated from the LA and is returned to the agent pool when a transaction completes.

The connection concentrator is activated when the number of maximum logical agents is set higher than the number of database agents.

Although connection concentration is similar in concept to connection pooling, there are some main differences. Connection pooling saves the cost of establishing a new database connection when one is no longer needed by a terminating application. In other words, one application has to disconnect before another application can reuse a pooled connection. Connection concentration, on the other hand, allows DB2 to make a connection available to an application as soon as another application has finished a transaction and does not require that the other application disconnect from the database. With connection concentration, a database connection and its resources are used by an application only while it has an active transaction. As soon as the transaction completes, the connection and associated resources are available for use by any other application that is ready to have a transaction executed.

In previous versions of DB2, every application connected to a database had an agent process assigned to it to manage the database connection, as well as any application requests. In the above architecture, there is a one-to-one relationship between connections and db2 agents. The connection concentrator permits a many-to-one relationship between connections and agents.

The logical agents represent an application but without reference to a particular database agent. The logical agent contains all of the information and control blocks required by an application (i.e., the application's context). If there are N applications connected to the DB2 server, there will be N logical agents on the server. The database agents are the processes that execute the application's requests but which have no permanent attachment to any given application. The database agents are associated with logical agents to perform transactions, and at the end of the transaction, end the association and return to the available pool. An overview of connection concentration is shown in Figure 8.12.

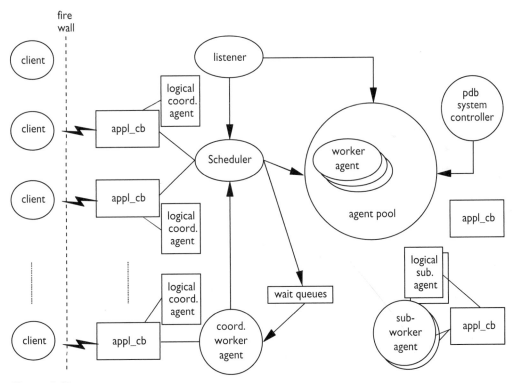

Figure 8.12
Connection concentrator overview.

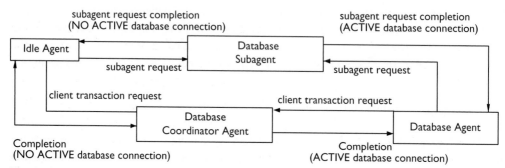

Figure 8.13
Database agent transition diagram.

When a transaction request is initiated by an application, the scheduler will detect activity on the client connection and associate a database agent (worker agent in Figure 8.12) to service the logical agent. When a transaction completes, the database agent servicing it will be returned to the pool to service another logical agent. Only when additional work has been detected by the scheduler for this connection would a worker agent be again associated with its logical agent.

Figure 8.13 shows the various states and transitions that database agents can undergo while servicing applications. An idle agent is a physical agent that currently does not have a database connection or an application attachment. Any physical agent that has a database connection but no application attachment is considered a database agent. When a client transaction is started, a logical agent is associated with that transaction request (see Figure 8.14). DB2 will then attempt to find a database agent (or an idle agent, if no database agent is available) to service the logical agent request. Once identified, the agent will become a database coordinator agent.

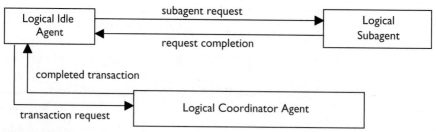

Figure 8.14
Logical agent transition diagram.

During the processing of the transaction a number of subagent requests, known as *logical sub-agents*, may be created in order to complete the transaction. The system will then try to find either a database agent or an idle agent to service these logical subagents. Once an agent is found, it becomes a database subagent. At the end of the transaction, the database coordinator agent could possibly disassociate from the logical coordinator agent and return to a database agent state. If the application terminates its database connection, the database agent will return to an idle state.

Any information in the database agent's private memory will be lost when a database agent (or an idle agent) is associated with a different logical agent. Database connection information is modified only when the database agent disconnects from one database and connects to another. Logical coordinator agents will return to their initial state (logical idle agent) at the end of the client connection.

The association of applications to logical agents is controlled by the logical agent scheduler. When activity on the client connection is detected, the logical agent scheduler attempts to find a database agent to service the logical agent. If there currently are no available database agents, the scheduler will place the logical agent into a queue of logical agents that are to be serviced when a database (or idle) agent becomes available.

During the course of processing a transaction and its many requests, certain information (both shared and private) is required by the DB2 components. Depending on whether this information is relevant across transaction or request boundaries determines whether the information will be stored at either the:

- shared application level—application-level information, also sometimes called *application-persistent data*
- shared database level—database-level information, or *database-persistent data*
- private agent level—agent-level information

Any agent-level information is considered to be nonpersistent and relevant only to the current transaction. Transaction information that needs to be shared among database agents or needs to span transactional boundaries (i.e., cursors defined WITH HOLD) will be stored in the transaction information area. In systems where shared transaction information is required, this information will be allocated from shared memory; otherwise, it will be allocated from private memory. As a result, when a database agent is disassociated from either a logical coordinator agent or a logical subagent, this agent-level information is no longer associated to either a database or application, and it will be lost. When the database agent (or idle agent) is associated to another logical coordinator or logical subagent, the agent level information will be reinitialized based on information stored at the application level. Also contained in each component's information is a pointer to the shared database-level information (Figure 8.15).

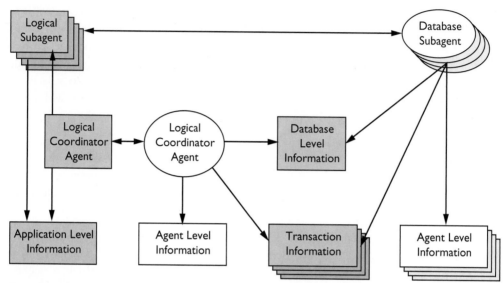

Figure 8.15
The agent memory model.

Information that normally resides in the agent's private memory that needs to be preserved beyond the end of a transaction will need to be moved into shared memory space. The amount of additional shared memory required is offset by the reduction in the amount of duplicate information that is being stored across components. The cost of associating and disassociating agents will be reduced because private memory areas will be refreshed, rather than de-allocating and allocating memory, as is done in DB2 Version 7.1.

Activating the connection concentrator   The connection concentrator will be activated when the value of MAX_CONNECTIONS is greater than the value of MAX_COORDAGENTS, as follows:

```
update dbm cfg using max_coordagents 80
update dbm cfg using max_connections 1200
```

Table 8.2 defines the key parameters related to connection concentration.

Table 8.2   Key Parameters Related to Connection Concentration

Configuration Parameter	Meaning When Concentrator Is		Range of Values
	Not Enabled	**Enabled**	
max_connections (This parameter was referred to as maxagents in Version 7)	This is the maximum number of client connections allowed per partition. Concentrator is not enabled when MAX_CONNECTIONS equals MAX_COORDAGENTS.	Concentrator is enabled when MAX_CONNECTIONS is greater than MAX_COORDAGENTS.	1 to 64,000
maxagents	This is the maximum number of database agents, whether coordinator agents or subagents, available at any given time. This parameter can be used in a memory-constrained server to limit the total number of agents on the server.		1 to 64,000
max_coordagents	This parameter determines the maximum number of coordinator agents that can exist at one time on a server in a partitioned or nonpartitioned database environment. One coordinator agent is acquired for each local or remote application that connects to a database or attaches to an instance. Therefore, when the concentrator is not enabled, the total number of coordinator agents will always be greater than or equal to the number of connections.	When the concentrator is enabled, there may be more connections than coordinator agents to service them. An application is in an active state only if there is a coordinator agent servicing it. Otherwise, the application is in an inactive state. Requests from an active application will be served by the database coordinator agent and the subagents. Requests from an inactive application will be queued until a database coordinator agent is assigned to service the application, when the application becomes active. This parameter can also be used to control the load on the system.	0 to MAXAGENTS

Table 8.2   Key Parameters Related to Connection Concentration (Continued)

Configuration Parameter	Meaning When Concentrator Is		Range of Values
	Not Enabled	**Enabled**	
num_initagents	This parameter determines the initial number of idle agents that are created in the agent pool when the instance is started.		0 to NUM_POOLAGENTS
num_poolagents	This parameter determines the maximum size of the idle agent pool. If more agents are created than indicated by this parameter, agents will be terminated when they finish executing their current request, rather than be returned to the pool.	When the concentrator is enabled, this parameter will be used as a guideline for how large the agent pool will be when the system workload is low. A database agent will always be returned to pool, no matter what the value of this parameter is. Based on the system load and the time agents remain idle in the pool, the logical agent scheduler may terminate as many of them as to bring down the size of the idle pool back to this parameter (see note below).	0 to MAXAGENTS
appl_group_mem_sz	This parameter determines the maximum size for the application group shared memory segment. Application control group heap is allocated from shared memory. All applications attached to the same segment share one application shared workspace.		1 to 64,000
appl_ctl_heap_sz	This parameter determines the maximum size for the application control shared memory set. Application control heaps are allocated from this shared memory. For parallel systems, space is also required for the application control heap, which is shared between the agents that are working on behalf of the same application on one database partition.		1 to 64,000
appl_group_share_heap_ratio	Specifies the percentage of memory devoted to the shared heap.		1 to 99

Table 8.2   Key Parameters Related to Connection Concentration (Continued)

Configuration Parameter	Meaning When Concentrator Is		Range of Values
	Not Enabled	**Enabled**	
appl_trans_heap_sz	NOT USED	This parameter determines the maximum size of the application transaction heap for each application. This heap is used by DB2 to work on the active transaction. In a parallel configuration, space is required to hold information shared between the agents that are working on behalf of the same transaction.	1 to 64,000
applheapsz	This parameter defines the number of private memory pages available to be used by the database manager on behalf of a specific agent or subagent. The heap is allocated when an agent or subagent is initialized for an application. The amount allocated will be the minimum amount needed to process the request given to the agent or subagent. As the agent or subagent requires more heap space to process larger SQL statements, the database manager will allocate memory as needed, up to the maximum specified by this parameter. The application heap (applheapsz) is allocated out of agent private memory.		1 to 64,000

N O T E   When the workload is high and the connection concentrator is enabled, there are likely far more connections to be serviced than available database agents to service them. A subagent will return to the agent pool after servicing a request, so that it can be used for other requests. A coordinator agent will return to pool if there is no application waiting to be served at the time the agent finishes the transaction and checks for waiting applications, but there could be clients available immediately. An agent will terminate only after it has been idle and waiting in the pool for an amount of time determined by the logical agents scheduler, which indicates that the workload on the system has gone down.

Based on the system load and the length of time that agents remain idle in the pool, the logical agent scheduler may terminate as many agents as necessary to reduce the size of the idle agent pool to the specified value. If the value for this configuration parameter is zero (0), agents will be created as needed, and may be terminated when they finish executing their current request. If the value of this configuration parameter is equal to MAXAGENTS and the agent pool is full of associated subagents, the server cannot be used as a coordinator node, because no new coordinator agents can be created.

Setting the appropriate value for this parameter can reduce the cost of continually creating and terminating DB2 agent processes. However, setting this value too high will leave idle DB2 agent processes on the system and will, therefore, not release the memory allocated by the agent processes.

Configuring

For a decision support workload characterized by relatively few concurrent applications, the size of the agent pool should be relatively small to avoid having an agent pool that is full of idle DB2 agents. For a transaction-processing workload characterized by many concurrent applications, the size of the agent pool should be increased to avoid the cost of constant creation and termination of the DB2 agents.

To specify the size of the agent pool, use the following command:

```
update dbm cfg using num_poolagents 256
```

Monitoring

There are a number of different aspects of the agent pool that can be examined using the database manager snapshot. To capture a database manager snapshot and extract the information related to the agent pool, use the following command:

```
get snapshot for database manager | grep  'Agents'
```

The output of this command would look like the following:

```
High water mark for agents registered                  = 43
High water mark for agents waiting for a token         = 0
Agents registered                                      = 43
Agents waiting for a token                             = 0
Idle agents                                            = 21
Agents assigned from pool                              = 328
Agents created from empty pool                         = 35
Agents stolen from another application                 = 12
High water mark for coordinating agents                = 20
Max agents overflow                                    = 0
Gateway connection pool agents stolen                  = 0
```

The same information can be captured using an SQL statement, as follows:

```
SELECT AGENTS_REGISTERED, AGENTS_REGISTERED_TOP, AGENTS_WAITING_TOP,
   IDLE_AGENTS, AGENTS_FROM_POOL, AGENTS_CREATED_EMPTY_POOL,
   COORD_AGENTS_TOP, MAX_AGENT_OVERFLOWS, AGENTS_STOLEN,
   NUM_GW_CONN_SWITCHES
FROM TABLE(SNAPSHOT_DBM(-1 )) as SNAPSHOT_DBM;
```

The output of the SQL statement would look like the following:

AGENTS_ REGISTERED	AGENTS_ REGISTERED_ TOP	AGENTS_ WAITING_TOP	IDLE_AGENTS	AGENTS_FROM_ POOL	AGENTS_ CREATED_ EMPTY_POOL	COORD_AGENTS _TOP	MAX_AGENT_ OVERFLOWS	AGENTS_STOLEN	NUM_GW_CONN_ SWITCHES
43	43	0	21	328	35	12	20	0	0

```
1 record(s) selected.
```

Based on the above snapshot information, there were:

- 328 times that an application requested a new agent process and an agent was available in the agent pool
- 35 times that an application requested a new agent process and there were no agents available in the agent pool, so a new agent process was created
- 12 times that an application requested a new agent process and there were no unassociated idle agents available in the agent pool, so an agent that was idle but associated with an other coordinating agent was "stolen"

The snapshot information also shows that:

- There are currently 43 agent processes in the DB2 instance.
- There are currently 21 idle agent processes in the DB2 instance.
- The maximum number of agent processes in the DB2 instance has been 43.
- The maximum number of coordinating agent processes in the DB2 instance has been 20.

It is important that agent processes be available in the agent pool when needed so that they do not need to be created. The percentage of times that an agent process needs to be created (percentage of agents created [PAC]) is calculated using the following formula:

```
PAC = ((Agents created from empty pool) / (Agents assigned from pool +
   Agents stolen from another application)) * 100%

PAC = ((35) / (328 + 12)) * 100%

PAC = 10.3%
```

The PAC can also be determined using the following SQL statement:

```
select (INT((FLOAT(AGENTS_CREATED_EMPTY_POOL)) /
  (FLOAT(AGENTS_FROM_POOL + AGENTS_STOLEN)) * 100))
  AS "PercentAgentsCreated"
FROM TABLE(SNAPSHOT_DBM(-1 )) as SNAPSHOT_DBM;
```

This statement would result in the following output:

```
PercentAgentsCreated
--------------------
                  23
1 record(s) selected.
```

Based on the above snapshot, a new agent process had to be created 23% of the time. For a small number of creations like those shown in this snapshot (i.e., 35) this is not excessive; however, if this ratio stays constant over time, this will cause a significant load on the server. To improve this ratio, the size of the agent pool can be increased so that there is a higher probability that when an agent is needed, there will be one available in the agent pool. To ensure that there are agents available for application requests when DB2 is started, the initial size of the agent pool (NUMINITAGENTS) can be set to a value greater than zero(0).

Automatic: No

Online: No

Initial Number of Agents in the Agent Pool (NUM_INITAGENTS)

Background

Regardless of the size of the DB2 agent pool as discussed above, the first few applications will need to create new agent processes unless DB2 pre-creates some agent processes when the instance is started. The initial number of agents in the agent pool (NUM_INITAGENTS) specifies the number of DB2 agents for DB2 to pre-create when the instance is started so that the first applications will not have to wait for processes to be created. This pre-allocates DB2 agents in the agent pool for use by subsequent applications.

Configuring

For a decision support workload characterized by relatively few concurrent applications, the initial number of agents in the agent pool should be relatively small. For a transaction-processing workload characterized by many concurrent applications, the initial number of agents in the agent pool should be increased to avoid the cost of agent creation when the applications work with the database.

To specify the size of the agent pool, use the following command:

```
update dbm cfg using num_initagents 100
```

Monitoring

Monitor to determine whether the initial size of the DB2 agent pool is the same as discussed above for the size of the agent pool. The agent pool can be examined using the database manager snapshot, as follows:

```
get snapshot for database manager | grep 'Agents'
```

The output of this command would look like the following:

```
High water mark for agents registered          = 43
High water mark for agents waiting for a token  = 0
Agents registered                               = 43
Agents waiting for a token                      = 0
Idle agents                                     = 21
Agents assigned from pool                       = 328
Agents created from empty pool                  = 35
Agents stolen from another application          = 12
High water mark for coordinating agents         = 20
Max agents overflow                             = 0
Gateway connection pool agents stolen           = 0
```

The same information can be captured using an SQL statement, as follows:

```
SELECT AGENTS_REGISTERED, AGENTS_REGISTERED_TOP, AGENTS_WAITING_TOP,
    IDLE_AGENTS, AGENTS_FROM_POOL, AGENTS_CREATED_EMPTY_POOL,
    COORD_AGENTS_TOP, MAX_AGENT_OVERFLOWS, AGENTS_STOLEN,
    NUM_GW_CONN_SWITCHES
FROM TABLE(SNAPSHOT_DBM(-1 )) as SNAPSHOT_DBM;
```

The output of the SQL statement would look like the following:

AGENTS_ REGISTERED	AGENTS_ REGISTERED_ TOP	AGENTS_ WAITING_TOP	IDLE_AGENTS	AGENTS_FROM_ POOL	AGENTS_ CREATED_ EMPTY_POOL	COORD_AGENTS _TOP	MAX_AGENT_ OVERFLOWS	AGENTS_STOLEN	NUM_GW_CONN_ SWITCHES
43	43	0	21	328	35	12	20	0	0

1 record(s) selected.

Based on the above snapshot information, there were:

- 328 times that an application requested a new agent process and an agent was available in the agent pool
- 35 times that an application requested a new agent process and there were no agents available in the agent pool, so a new agent process was created
- 12 times that an application requested a new agent process and there were no unassociated idle agents available in the agent pool, so an agent that was idle but associated to another coordinating agent was *stolen*

The snapshot information also shows that:

- There are currently 43 agent processes in the DB2 instance.
- There are currently 21 idle agent processes in the DB2 instance.
- The maximum number of agent processes in the DB2 instance has been 43.
- The maximum number of coordinating agent processes in the DB2 instance has been 20.

If the initial size of the agent pool is set to zero (0), having 35 DB2 agent processes created is not an excessive amount. However, if the initial size of the agent pool is 100, as defined above, there should be very few, if any, agents created.

For a DB2 instance with the initial size of the agent pool greater than zero, it is important that agent processes be available in the agent pool when needed so that they do not need to be created. The percentage of times that an agent process needs to be created is calculated using the following formula:

```
PAC = ((Agents created from empty pool) / (Agents assigned from pool +
   Agents stolen from another application)) * 100%


PAC = ((35) / (328 + 12)) * 100%


PAC = 10.3%
```

The PAC can also be determined using the following SQL statement:

```
select (INT((FLOAT(AGENTS_CREATED_EMPTY_POOL)) /
   (FLOAT(AGENTS_FROM_POOL + AGENTS_STOLEN)) * 100))
   AS "PercentAgentsCreated"
FROM TABLE(SNAPSHOT_DBM(-1 )) as SNAPSHOT_DBM;
```

This statement would result in the following output:

```
PercentAgentsCreated
--------------------
                  23
1 record(s) selected.
```

Based on the above snapshot, a new agent process had to be created 23% of the time. For a small number of creations like shown in this snapshot (i.e., 35), this is not excessive; however, if this ratio stays constant over time, this will cause a significant load on the server. To improve this ratio, the size of the agent pool can be increased so that there is a higher probability that when an agent is needed, there will be one available in the agent pool. To ensure that there are agents available for application requests when DB2 is started, the initial size of the agent pool (NUMINITAGENTS) can be set to a value greater than zero(0).

Automatic: No

Online: No

Priority of Agents (AGENTPRI)

Background

When processes or threads are created within DB2, they are created without any special priority setting and, therefore, will be handled the same as any other process or thread on the server. The agent priority parameter (AGENTPRI) controls the priority given by the operating system to all DB2 agents, as well as other database manager instance processes or threads. This priority determines how processing time (i.e., the number of CPU time slices) is given to the various DB2 processes or threads, relative to the other processes or threads running on the server.

> **N O T E** This also includes coordinating agents and subagents, the parallel system controllers, and the FCM daemons if intra-partition parallelism is enabled and/or the database is partitioned.

When the agent priority is set to -1, the DB2 processes/threads are not given any special priority on the server, and they are scheduled in the normal way that the operating system schedules all processes/threads. When the agent priority is set to a value other than -1, DB2 will create its processes and threads with a priority specified by this parameter. This parameter provides a mechanism to control the priority that DB2 will execute on the server.

This parameter can be used to increase throughput, especially if the server is not a dedicated DB2 server (i.e., there are other applications running on the server). The valid values for this configuration parameter are dependent on the operating system on the DB2 server. For a UNIX server, lower values mean a higher system priority, whereas on Windows, a higher value means a higher system priority. On UNIX, when the agent priority is set to a value between 41 and 125, DB2 will create the agent processes with a static priority set to the value of the agent priority parameter.

Configuring

The default agent priority is normally good for most situations because it provides a good compromise between response time to the users/applications and DB2 throughput. If the server is shared between DB2 and other applications and it is important not to impact the database performance, this parameter can be changed to provide priority to DB2. However, it is important to benchmark both DB2 and the applications at different AGENTPRI settings to determine the optimal value for this parameter. Take care when increasing the priority of the DB2 processes/threads because the performance of other applications can be severely degraded.

> **N O T E** If this parameter is set to a nondefault value on UNIX, the governor cannot be used to alter agent priorities.

The agent priority can be increased as follows:

```
UNIX:
update dbm cfg using agentpri 75

Windows:
update dbm cfg using agentpri 5
```

To reset the agent priority back to the default setting so that no special priority is given to the DB2 processes/threads, use the following command:

```
update dbm cfg using agentpri -1
```

Monitoring

DB2 does not directly monitor the priority of its processes or threads; therefore, operating system tools must be used. The availability of these tools and the quantity/quality of the information available from these tools are much better on UNIX and Linux than on Windows. The main tools available to monitor the process/thread priority are:

- vmstat
- mpstat
- sar
- top

When examining the output of these tools it is important to:

- Ensure that DB2 is getting all the CPU time that it needs. Any non-DB2 processes/threads using a significant amount of CPU time should be investigated.
- Average CPU usage should be less than 80% to allow for "spikes" in system activity.
- Ensure that there are no "sustained" spikes, i.e., where CPU usage > 95% for more than a few seconds.
- The ratio of user to system CPU usage should be 3:1 or more.
- Ensure that the workload is being distributed among the available CPUs on the server.
- The run queue should remain at zero or less, and it should not increase over time.

When using these system tools to monitor a DB2 server, take the snapshots during both an average workload and a peak workload. Also make sure to take the snapshots over a long enough period of time, not just over a 1- to 2-minute period. The snapshots should be taken at intervals of 5 minutes (300 seconds) for at least 12 intervals, as follows:

```
vmstat 300 12 > vmstat.out
```

Giving the following output from vmstat:

procs			memory			page						disk				faults			cpu		
r	b	w	swap	free	re	mf	pi	po	fr	de	sr	f0	m0	m1	m4	in	sy	cs	us	sy	id
0	0	12	19128	6008	2	66	203	120	242	0	33	0	0	0	1	573	927	523	6	3	91
0	0	20	2733560	45008	0	2	10	0	0	0	0	0	0	0	0	301	116	142	5	2	93
0	0	20	2733400	42648	1	0	83	0	0	0	0	0	1	0	0	804	220	291	11	4	85
0	0	20	2733392	37992	0	0	18	0	0	0	0	0	0	0	0	719	418	536	29	11	60
0	0	20	2733384	36632	0	10	2	0	0	0	0	0	0	0	0	439	373	337	18	5	77
0	0	20	2733320	34232	0	21	28	0	0	0	0	0	0	0	1	803	5285	5248	32	9	58
0	0	20	2733288	33472	3	0	7	65	65	0	0	0	0	0	0	517	654	729	21	6	73
0	0	20	2733264	33456	8	6	15	182	182	0	0	0	0	0	0	727	521	660	27	9	64
0	0	20	2724504	32016	11	35	21	284	356	0	13	0	0	0	0	909	711	823	34	10	56
0	0	20	2724128	32392	12	9	14	239	260	0	3	0	0	0	0	737	449	579	23	8	68
0	0	20	2717624	32272	3	107	21	94	240	0	23	0	0	0	0	397	421	255	8	4	88
0	0	20	2683008	31840	2	94	14	82	207	0	21	0	0	0	1	375	377	215	6	3	91
0	0	20	2677624	31888	1	0	1	40	40	0	0	0	0	0	0	268	149	127	4	2	94
0	0	20	2688680	33040	2	1	16	70	83	0	1	0	0	0	0	382	293	211	9	4	87
0	0	20	2698344	33344	5	15	16	184	184	0	0	0	0	0	0	563	558	373	18	6	76
0	0	20	2685208	32376	6	93	15	148	198	0	8	0	0	0	0	506	586	344	15	6	79
0	0	20	2677560	31888	3	0	12	103	112	0	1	0	0	0	0	413	290	205	8	4	88
0	0	20	2688536	33280	0	18	0	0	0	0	0	0	0	0	1	185	109	54	0	1	99
0	1	20	2695360	33384	13	42	79	465	575	0	18	0	0	0	0	1534	788	702	14	6	81

In the above series of vmstat snapshots, the system is mostly idle. The server never has less than 56% of idle, available CPU cycles; and the run queue is never more than zero. But these snapshots also show that the CPU usage can change in a matter of seconds from 44% CPU usage to 1% CPU usage; therefore, although it is important to look at the individual values, it is important to look at the average values, as well.

For the following line from the information above:

0	0	20	2733288	33472	3	0	7	65	65	0	0	0	0	0	0	517	654	729	21	6	73

the server is 73% idle; the run queue is 0; the user to system CPU usage is 21 / 6, or 3.5 to 1; and there are no sustained CPU spikes. Therefore, the system is working within recommended guidelines.

Another command tool that should be used to examine the processes with the highest CPU usage is **ps aux**. When this command is run, the output will be a list of all processes on the server, along with the percentage of the server CPU time that it is consuming. If any non-DB2 process is consuming a significant amount of CPU time, it should be examined to determine what the process is and whether it should be running on the server.

Automatic: No

Online: No

Keep Fenced Process (KEEPFENCED)

Background

The built-in functions supplied by DB2 UDB are quite rich and cover most applications, but using UDFs can extend these capabilities. UDFs can be written in Visual Basic, C/C++, and Java to perform operations within any SQL statement that returns a single, scalar value or a table. UDFs also provide a way to standardize applications by implementing a common set of UDFs. Duplication of code is avoided, and many applications can process data in the same way, thus ensuring consistent results.

A stored procedure resides on a database server, executing and accessing the database locally to return information to client applications. Using stored procedures allow a client application to pass control to a stored procedure on the database server. This allows the stored procedure to perform intermediate processing on the database server without transmitting unnecessary data across the network. Only those records that are actually required at the client need to be transmitted. This can result in reduced network traffic and better overall performance.

A stored procedure also saves the overhead of having a remote application pass multiple SQL commands to a database on a server. With a single statement, a client application can call the stored procedure, which then performs the database work and returns the results to the client application. The more SQL statements that are grouped together for execution in the stored procedure, the larger the savings will result from avoiding the overhead associated with network flows for each SQL statement when issued from the client.

UDFs and stored procedures can be run in two modes in DB2 UDB—fenced and unfenced. Fenced mode UDFs and stored procedures run in a DB2 agent on the DB2 server and use normal client-server communications. Unfenced mode UDFs and stored procedures run within the DB2 server process. To optimize fenced UDFs and stored procedures, the KEEPFENCED configuration parameter can be used to keep the agent associated with the fenced mode UDF/stored procedure after the call is complete.

If KEEPFENCED is set to NO and the routine being executed is not thread safe, a new fenced mode process is created and destroyed for each fenced mode UDF or stored procedure invoked. If KEEPFENCED is set to NO and the routine being executed is thread safe, the fenced mode process will be kept running, but the thread created for the call is terminated. If KEEPFENCED is set to YES, the fenced mode process or thread will be reused for subsequent fenced mode UDF or stored procedure calls. When the DB2 instance is stopped, all outstanding fenced mode processes and threads will be terminated.

Setting the KEEPFENCED parameter to YES will typically result in the consumption of additional system resources (i.e., memory) for each active fenced mode process, up to the value specified by the FENCED_POOL configuration parameter.

Configuring

In an environment in which the number of fenced mode requests is large, relative to the number of nonfenced mode requests, setting KEEPFENCED to YES can improve the fenced mode process performance by avoiding the initial fenced mode process creation overhead because an existing fenced mode process will be used to process the call. This is particularly true for Java routines because it eliminates the need to start the Java Virtual Machine (JVM). However, when KEEPFENCED is set to YES, additional resources will be used on the DB2 UDB server.

To set the KEEPFENCED parameter to YES, use the following command:

```
update dbm cfg using keepfenced YES
```

Automatic: No

Online: No

Maximum Total of Files Open (MAXFILOP)

Background

As applications are accessing tables, DB2 may need to retrieve data from disk. To be able to read the data quickly and efficiently from disk, DB2 keeps the files for the database objects open so that it does not need to open and close the file each time, saving time to retrieve the data for the application. If the value for MAXFILOP is too small, DB2 may use up an excessive amount of CPU time opening and closing files, and this time cannot be used to process the SQL statements.

With DB2, it is important to be aware of when a file is accessed by an SQL statement. For tables and indexes stored in SMS table spaces, all objects are stored in their own files. In DMS table spaces, each container is a file, and the table and index objects are read from within the file by DB2. Therefore, the setting for MAXFILOP will likely need to be higher if the databases in the instance are using a significant number of SMS table spaces.

Configuring

The default value for MAXFILOP is too low for most databases. It is good practice to increase the value for MAXFILOP significantly because it uses a negligible amount of resources on the database server and can have a significant impact on performance, especially for OLTP type systems. This parameter specifies the number of files that can be open at any given time for a database. If DB2 attempts to open a file and the MAXFILOP has been reached, one of the files must be closed.

For most systems, a value of 2000 for MAXFILOP is a good starting point. However for large databases with a number of tables and indexes using SMS table spaces, a higher value may be required. To set the parameter to a value of 2000, use the command:

```
update dbm cfg using maxfilop 2000
```

Once the database is operational, monitor the system to determine whether files are being opened and closed. If database files are being opened and closed as a result of the workload, increase this parameter until this condition is eliminated.

Monitoring

DB2 does not monitor the number of database files opened, just the number that were closed. To determine whether database files are being opened and closed, take a database manager snapshot, using the following:

```
get snapshot for database on <database_name> | grep -i "Database
files closed"
```
or
```
SELECT files_closed FROM TABLE(SNAPSHOT_DATABASE('SAMPLE',-1 )) as
SNAPSHOT_DATABASE
```

This will capture a snapshot for the specified database and extract the monitor element concerned with the number of database files closed. This would produce output like the following:

```
Database files closed           =   389

or

FILES_CLOSED
------------
         389
```

In this case, there were 389 cases where a database file was needed, but the maximum number of open database files has been reached, and a file had to be closed in order to open the required file. This number may or may not be excessive, depending on how long the database has been active. If the database has been active for hours or days, this number would not be alarming. However, if the database has been active for only a couple minutes, this number may be excessive. It is good practice to completely eliminate all "Database files closed" by monitoring the database and increasing the MAXFILOP parameter until the "Database files closed" element is zero.

Automatic: No

Online: No

DATABASE CONFIGURATION PARAMETER TUNING AND MONITORING

The database configuration parameters have an effect on the database, as well as on all applications that access the database. The parameters listed in Table 8.3 have the most significant impact on the performance of the database and its applications.

Table 8.3   Database Configuration Parameter Descriptions

Parameter	Description
BUFFPAGE	Default Buffer Pool Size
LOGBUFSZ	Log Buffer Size
APPLHEAPSZ	Application Heap Size
SORTHEAP	Sorting
SHEAPTHRES_SHR	Sorting
LOCKLIST	Locking
MAXLOCKS	Locking
NUM_IOCLEANERS	Number of Asynchronous Page Cleaners
NUM_IOSERVERSW	Number of I/O Servers
MINCOMMIT	Number of Commits to Group
CATALOGCACHE_SZ	Catalog Cache Size
CHNGPGS_THRESH	Changed Pages Threshold
AVG_APPLS	Average Number of Concurrent Applications

Default Buffer Pool Size (BUFFPAGE)

Background

As discussed previously, a DB2 buffer pool is an area in memory into which database pages containing table rows or index keys are read and manipulated. The purpose of the buffer pool is to improve database system performance by caching frequently accessed pages in memory to eliminate the need for I/O to retrieve the pages because data can be accessed much faster from memory than from a disk. Therefore, the fewer times the database manager needs to read from or write to a disk, the better will be the performance. The configuration of the buffer pool (or buffer pools) is one of the most important tuning areas because it is here that most of the data manipulation takes place for applications connected to the database.

When a buffer pool is created or altered, its size can be explicitly specified or it can be set to use the default buffer pool size. To use the default buffer pool size, as specified by the BUFFPAGE database configuration parameter, the size of the buffer pool must be set to -1 when the buffer pool is created or altered.

If the database has a single large buffer pool, the default buffer pool size can be used. For a database with multiple buffer pools, the buffer pools will need to be sized independently, and attempting to use one size for all of the buffer pools will normally lead to suboptimal performance.

Configuring

To change the default buffer pool size and to increase the default buffer pool size, use the following commands:

```
update db cfg for <dbname> using BUFFPAGE bigger_value
alter bufferpool IBMDEFAULTBP size -1
```

Monitoring

Monitoring of the effectiveness of the database buffer pool or buffer pools is covered in detail in the Monitoring Buffer Pool Activity section of Chapter 2, Data Manipulation, so it will not be repeated here.

Automatic: No

Online: Yes

Log Buffer Size (LOGBUFSZ)

Background

Just as buffer pools help to improve database performance, the log buffer is used to improve logging performance by providing an area of memory for the DB2 engine to write log records to instead of writing directly to disk. DB2 uses a dual buffering technique so that, as it is asynchronously writing a log buffer to disk, DB2 can continue logging to the other log buffer. The log buffers are written to disk when any of the following conditions occur:

- A transaction commits (or MINCOMMIT transactions commit).
- The log buffer is full.
- One second has elapsed since the last log buffer flush.

Configuring

Buffering of the log records results in more efficient log file I/O because the log records are written to disk less frequently, and multiple log records can be written with each write request. The default size of the log buffer is normally too small for most update workloads. When increasing the value of the log buffer, it is also important to consider the size of the database heap (DBHEAP) because the log buffer area is allocated from within the database heap.

Typically, the log buffer should be increased to a minimum value of 256 pages, as follows

```
update database cfg for <dbname> using LOGBUFSZ 256
```

to help improve overall performance, especially for online workloads.

Monitoring

The database logging activity and I/O effectiveness can be examined using a database snapshot. To capture a database snapshot and extract the information related to the logging activity, use the following:

```
get snapshot for database on <database_name> | grep -i "Log space"
```
or
```
SELECT sec_log_used_top, tot_log_used_top, total_log_used,
total_log_available
FROM TABLE(SNAPSHOT_DATABASE('SAMPLE',-1 )) as SNAPSHOT_DATABASE
```

The output of the get snapshot command would look like the following:

```
Log space available to the database (Bytes)    = 4549916
Log space used by the database (Bytes)          = 550084
Maximum secondary log space used (Bytes)        = 0
Maximum total log space used (Bytes)            = 550084
```

The SQL statement above would produce the following output:

```
SEC_LOG_USED_TOP  TOT_LOG_USED_TOP  TOTAL_LOG_USED  TOTAL_LOG_AVAILABLE
----------------  ----------------  --------------  -------------------
               0            550084          550084              4549916
```

However, when examining the log space, it is important to ensure that there are enough primary log files configured to handle normal processing. Secondary logs should be used for exceptions only in cases where the amount of logging is expected to be heavier than normal, i.e., nightly batch processing. It is also important that there be sufficient log space available at all times to ensure that there is no danger of encountering a log full condition.

To determine the current amount of log space available (CLSA), use the following formula:

```
CLSA = Log space available to the database - Log space used by the database
```

or the following SQL statement:

```
SELECT total_log_available - total_log_used as "CurrentLogSpaceAvail"
  FROM TABLE(SNAPSHOT_DATABASE('SAMPLE',-1 ))
  as SNAPSHOT_DATABASE
```

To determine the minimum amount of log space available, use the following formula:

```
CLSA = Log space available to the database - Maximum total log space used
```

or the following SQL statement:

```
SELECT total_log_available - tot_log_used_top as
  "CurrentLogSpaceAvail"
  FROM TABLE(SNAPSHOT_DATABASE('SAMPLE',-1 ))
  as SNAPSHOT_DATABASE
```

To capture a database snapshot and extract the information related to the I/O effectiveness of the database logging, use the following:

```
  get snapshot for database on <database_name> | grep -i "Log pages"
or

  SELECT log_reads, log_writes FROM
  TABLE(SNAPSHOT_DATABASE('SAMPLE',-1 )) as SNAPSHOT_DATABASE
```

We can use the database snapshot to determine whether the LOGBUFSZ parameter is optimal by looking at the lines shown in the following example:

```
Log pages read        = 0
Log pages written     = 12644
```

The ratio between the number of log pages read to the number of log pages written should be as small as possible. Ideally, there should not be any log pages read, and the number of log pages written will depend on the insert/update/delete workload on the database server. When there are a significant number of log pages read, it is an indication that the size of the log buffer should be increased.

Automatic: No

Online: No

Application Heap Size (APPLHEAPSZ)

Background

The application heap size (APPLHEAPSZ) defines the number of private memory pages available to be used by a DB2 UDB instance on behalf of each DB2 agent and/or subagent. This heap is used to store a copy of the currently executing sections of the access plan for the application associated with the DB2 agent or subagent.

> **N O T E**   If the database is partitioned, the executing sections of the SQL statements for the agents and subagents will be stored in the application control heap (APP_CTL_HEAP_SZ), not in the application heap.

The application heap is allocated when an agent or subagent is initialized for an application. The amount of memory allocated will be only what is needed to process the request that has been given to the DB2 agent or subagent. When a DB2 agent or subagent requires additional application heap to be able to process larger SQL statements, DB2 will allocate additional memory, up to the maximum specified by the application heap size.

Configuring

For a database with small, relatively simple SQL, the default application heap size is normally adequate. However, for large, complex SQL, the default may not be large enough, and applications may run out of application heap and encounter errors. In DB2 UDB Version 7, the default value of the application heap was normally too low. However, in DB2 UDB Version 8, the default value has been increased to 256 pages.

If an application does encounter errors running out of application heap, the size of the application heap can be increased as follows:

```
update database cfg for <database_name> using applheapsz 1024
```

Monitoring

It is not possible to monitor the size of the application heap allocated within each DB2 agent or subagent directly. Therefore, in most cases, it is best to increase the application heap size, as above, and when an application receives an error indicating that there is not enough storage in the application heap to increase the value of this parameter. Because DB2 allocates only what is required, do not increase the size of the database heap by small amounts. If an error is encountered, double the size of the database heap and test to see whether the error has been eliminated.

Automatic: No

Online: No

Sorting (SORTHEAP, SHEAPTHRES_SHR)

Background

The sort heap (SORTHEAP) size specifies the maximum number of private memory pages to be used for private sorts or the maximum number of shared memory pages to be used for shared sorts. If the DB2 optimizer chooses to perform a private sort, the sort heap size affects agent private memory. If the DB2 optimizer chooses to perform a shared sort, the sort heap size affects the database-level shared memory. Each sort operation will have a separate sort heap that will be allocated as needed by DB2 where the underlying data will be sorted. Normally, DB2 will allocate a full sort heap. However, if directed by the optimizer, a smaller amount of memory than specified by the sort heap size may be allocated, using the information provided by the optimizer and the database statistics.

The sort heap threshold is an instance-level configuration parameter, as described previously. Private and shared sorts use memory from two different memory areas at the operating system level. The total size of the shared sort memory area is allocated and statically predetermined at the time of the first connection to (or activation of) a database based on the value of the shared sort heap threshold (SHEAPTHRES_SHR) parameter. The total size of the private sort memory area is allocated as needed and is not restricted in size. Because of the fundamental differences between shared and private memory, the sort heap threshold (SHEAPTHRES and SHEAPTHRES_SHR) parameters are applied differently for private and shared sorts:

- For private sorts, the sort heap threshold parameter is an instance-wide soft limit on the total amount of memory that can be used by private sorts at any given time. When the total usage of private sort memory for a DB2 instance reaches this limit, the memory allocated for new private sort requests will be reduced by a factor of one half.
- For shared sorts, the sort heap threshold parameter is a database-wide hard limit on the total amount of memory that can be used by shared sorts at any given time. When the total usage of shared sort memory for a DB2 instance reaches this limit, no further shared sort memory requests will be allowed until one of the currently executing shared sorts completes.

Configuring

The default value for SHEAPTHRES is quite low, especially for decision support databases. It is good practice to increase the value for SHEAPTHRES significantly because it can have a very dramatic effect on performance. However, increasing the SHEAPTHRES blindly can mask a real problem in the system or applications.

> **N O T E**   By default, SHEAPTHRES_SHR is equal to SHEAPTHRES.

When determining an appropriate value for the SHEAPTHRES and SHEAPTHRES_SHR parameters, consider the following:

- Hash joins and dynamic bitmaps used for index ANDing and star joins use sort heap memory. Increase the size of the SORTHEAP, SHEAPTHRES, and SHEAPTHRES_SHR when these techniques are used.
- Increase the SHEAPTHRES when large private sorts are frequently required.
- Increase the SHEAPTHRES_SHR when large shared sorts are frequently required.
- The values of SHEAPTHRES and SHEAPTHRES_SHR need to be based on the value of the SORTHEAP, as well as on the average number of applications executing in the database.
  - For example, if database monitoring shows that, on average, there are 12 applications concurrently executing in DB2, setting the SHEAPTHRES to 12–15 times the SORTHEAP would be a good starting point.

- Because shared sorts are less common than private sorts, setting the SHEAPTHRES_SHR to 5 times the SORTHEAP would be a good starting point.

To set the SHEAPTHRES configuration parameter, use the following command:

```
update dbm cfg using sheapthres 80000
```

To set the SHEAPTHRES_SHR configuration parameter, use the following command:

```
update db cfg for <database_name> using sheapthres_shr 30000
```

Once the database is operational, monitor the system to determine whether the sort heap threshold is being reached. However, sorts may also be overflowed without hitting the sort heap threshold if they require more memory than the configured sort heap size. These sort overflows may be eliminated by increasing the size of the sort heap, as follows:

```
update database cfg for <database_name> using sortheap 6000
```

Monitoring

Due to the impact of sorting on database performance, DB2 monitors a number of things in relation to sort activity.

Sorts that are started after the sort heap threshold has been reached may not get an entire SORTHEAP allocated and, therefore, have a much higher chance of overflowing. The number of sorts stated after the SHEAPTHRES has been reached is reported in the post threshold sorts database monitor element.

In addition to the number of piped sorts requested and accepted, the number of overflowed sorts is also available in the snapshot information. These are related to the sort heap, as well as the sort heap threshold, and they will be discussed in more detail when the sort heap is discussed later in this chapter.

To determine whether the sort heap threshold is being reached, take a database manager snapshot, using the following command:

```
get snapshot for database manager | grep -i "Post threshold sorts"
```

This will capture a snapshot for the specified database and extract the monitor element concerned with the number of database files closed. This would produce output like the following:

```
Post threshold sorts                    =  16
```

This information can also be captured using an SQL statement, as follows:

```
SELECT post_threshold_sorts FROM TABLE(SNAPSHOT_DBM(-1 )) as
   SNAPSHOT_DBM
```

This would produce output like the following:

```
POST_THRESHOLD_SORTS
--------------------
                  16
```

If this value is excessive, the size of the sort heaps and/or sort heap threshold should be examined to determine whether they are sufficient. In addition, the applications should be examined to ensure that they are using appropriate indexes.

If the allocation of one more sort heap equals or exceeds the sort heap threshold, a piped sort cannot be performed, and any request for a piped sort will get rejected. A sort heap will be allocated to handle the sorting of the data, but it will be a reduced size.

The percentage of piped sorts requests that have been serviced by the database manager can be calculated by using the formula:

```
Percent Piped Sorts = (piped_sorts_accepted / piped_sorts_requested) * 100%
```

If this percentage of piped sorts is low, the sort performance could be improved by increasing the sort heap threshold. The number of piped sort requests that have been rejected by DB2 can be calculated using the following formula:

```
Piped Sorts Rejected = piped_sorts_requested - piped_sorts_accepted
```

A high number of rejected pipe sort requests may indicate that either the value of sort heap or sort heap threshold is too small to support the current workload.

Another indicator of sort performance is the percentage of post threshold sorts. DB2 allocates sort heaps at the beginning of sorts and at the beginning of any sort merge phase. If at any time during a sort a request to allocate a sort heap would exceed the SHEAPTHRES, the sort would be classified as a post threshold sort. The percentage of post threshold sorts is calculated using the following formula:

```
Percent Post Threshold Sorts = (post_threshold_sorts / sum of total_sorts ) * 100%
```

The total amount of private sort heap that is currently allocated can be monitored using the following:

```
   get snapshot for database manager | grep -i "Private Sort heap
   allocated"

or

   SELECT sort_heap_allocated FROM TABLE(SNAPSHOT_DBM(-1 )) as
   SNAPSHOT_DBM
```

For an online database, it is also important to examine the number of sort operations per transaction (SPT), as well as the percentage of overflowed sorts (POS), as follows:

```
SPT = (Total Sorts) / (Commit statements attempted + Rollback
    statements attempted)

POS = (Sort overflows * 100 ) / (Total sorts)
```

Because online databases need to provide instantaneous results, the number of sort operations per transaction should be as low as possible. If the average number of sorts per transaction is three or more, this indicates that there are far too many sorts per transaction. If the percentage of overflowed sorts is greater than 3%, there may be serious and unexpected large sorts occurring. When this happens, increasing the SORTHEAP and/or SHEAPTHRES will likely only mask the underlying performance problem, not fix it. The best action to help correct these sorting issues is to capture dynamic SQL snapshots, look for poorly performing SQL statements, and add proper indexes as required.

See Appendix B for a sample script to parse the output of a dynamic SQL snapshot and output the information in ASCII-delimited format so that it can be read into a spreadsheet to be examined.

Automatic: No

Online: Yes

Locking (LOCKLIST, MAXLOCKS, LOCKTIMEOUT, DLCHKTIME)

Background

The lock list is an area of memory used to store all locks that are currently active within a database. The maximum storage for lock list database configuration parameter (LOCKLIST) indicates the amount of storage that is allocated to the lock list for each database. Each database has its own lock list that contains information about the locks held by all applications concurrently connected to the database. Locking is the mechanism that DB2 UDB uses to control concurrent access to data in the database by multiple applications. Within a DB2 database, locks can be obtained on both rows and tables but not on pages.

The amount of space required for a lock depends on whether DB2 is installed in 32-bit mode or 64-bit mode and on whether it is the first lock on a database object or a subsequent lock on a database object.

When DB2 is installed in 32-bit mode, each lock will require either 36 or 72 bytes of space in the database lock list, depending on whether other locks are held on the object:

- 72 bytes are required to hold a lock on an object that has no other locks held on it.
- 36 bytes are required to record a lock on an object that has an existing lock held on it.

When DB2 is installed in 64-bit mode, each lock will require either 56 or 112 bytes of space in the database lock list, depending on whether other locks are held on the object:

- 112 bytes are required to hold a lock on an object that has no other locks held on it.
- 56 bytes are required to record a lock on an object that has an existing lock held on it.

The maximum percentage of the lock list before escalation database configuration parameter (MAXLOCKS) parameter defines the percentage of the lock list that can be held by an application before DB2 UDB will perform lock escalation for the application. Lock escalation is the process of replacing a number of row locks with a single table lock, therefore reducing the number of locks in the database's lock list and making space available for new locks to be obtained. When the number of locks held by any one application reaches this percentage of the total lock list size, DB2 will perform lock escalation as follows:

1. Examine the lock list for the identified application to determine which object has the most row-level locks.
2. Request an equivalent table-level lock.
3. Release the row-level locks once the table lock is granted.

If, after replacing the row locks with a single table lock, the MAXLOCKS value is no longer exceeded for the application, lock escalation will stop. If not, lock escalation will continue on other database tables until the percentage of the lock list held by the application is below the MAXLOCKS configuration parameter.

> **N O T E**   The MAXLOCKS configuration parameter multiplied by the MAXAPPLS configuration parameter cannot be less than 100.

Lock escalation will also occur if the lock list becomes full for any reason. When the lock list is full, DB2 will perform lock escalation as follows:

1. Examine the lock list to determine which application has the most locks.
2. Examine the lock list for the identified applications to determine which object has the most row-level locks.
3. Request an equivalent table-level lock.
4. Release the row-level locks once the table lock is granted.

If, after replacing the row locks with a single table lock, the lock list is still full (because other applications can still obtain locks while the escalation is occurring), lock escalation will continue following the same procedure as above. If the lock escalation causes space to become available in the lock list, lock escalation will stop.

Although the escalation process itself does not take much time, locking entire tables (versus locking individual rows) can cause a decrease in concurrency, and overall database performance may be impacted for subsequent accesses against the affected tables. Lock escalation can also cause deadlocks as the row locks are being converted to the table lock.

Deadlocks

When multiple applications are working with data in the same database, there are opportunities for a deadlock to occur between two or more applications, especially if lock escalations are occurring. A deadlock is created when one application is waiting for a lock that is held by another application, and that application is waiting for a lock held by the first application. Each of the waiting applications is locking data needed by another application, while also holding a lock held by the waiting application. Mutual waiting for other applications to release locks on the data leads to a deadlock condition. In this case, the applications could potentially wait forever until one of the other applications releases a lock on the held data.

Because applications do not voluntarily release locks on data that they need, DB2 UDB uses a deadlock detector process to detect and break deadlocks to allow application processing to continue. As its name suggests, the deadlock detector is started every period of time defined by the deadlock check time (DLCHKTIME), when it reads the database lock list and examines the information about the DB2 agents that are waiting on locks. If a deadlock condition is detected, the deadlock detector arbitrarily selects one of the applications involved in the deadlock as the victim. The victim application will be rolled back by DB2, and its locks will be released so that the other applications can continue. The victim application will receive an SQL 911 error code with a reason code of 2.

In Version 8, DB2 has enhanced the diagnostics available when a deadlock occurs, and the deadlock can now be debugged without the need to reproduce the condition with event monitors or snapshot monitoring turned on. When the diagnostic level is set to 4, a record will be written to the diagnostic log, indicating which application caused the deadlock condition, as well as the SQL statement it was executing. An example of the diagnostic record is below:

```
Request for lock "REC: (2, 13) RID 0000000B" in mode "..U" failed due
  to deadlock
Application caused the lock wait is "*LOCAL.DB2.00F888145716"
Statement: 7570 6461 7465 2074 3120 7365 7420 6331    update t1 set c1
3d32 3120 7768 6572 6520 6332 3d39                    =21 where c2=9
```

Based on the above diagnostic entry, we can determine that:

- DB2 was attempting to acquire a record lock (REC) to execute this statement.
- The lock mode requested was Update (U).

- The application that caused the error had an application ID of "LOCAL.DB2.00F888145716".
- The statement that caused the error was "update t1 set c1=21 where c2=9".

The LOCKTIMEOUT configuration parameter can be used to prevent applications from waiting indefinitely for locks. By default, the lock timeout is set to -1, which tells DB2 to wait indefinitely for locks. To time out the locks after a set period of time, the lock timeout parameter can be set to a specific value.

Configuring

The size of the lock list can be estimated as follows:

The minimum lock list size would occur if all (or almost all) of the locks exist on objects that already have locks. The maximum lock list size would occur if all locks are unique and exist on objects without any other locks. Therefore, the lower bound for the lock list would be calculated as follows:

```
MinLockList = (ALA * LS1 * MAXAPPLS) / 4096

Where:                  ALA = Average # of locks per application
                        LS1 = Lock Size (either 36 or 56 bytes, depending
                        on whether DB2 is running in 32-bit or 64-bit
                        mode)
```

The upper bound for the lock list would be calculated as follows:

```
MaxLockList = (ALA * LS2 * MAXAPPLS) / 4096

Where:                  ALA = Average # of locks per application
                        LS2 = Lock Size (either 72 or 112 bytes, depending
                        on whether DB2 is running in 32-bit or 64-bit
                        mode)
```

Then attempt to estimate the percentage of unique locks versus subsequent locks on the same object and use this percentage to choose a value between these extremes as the initial size of the lock list.

The default value for MAXLOCKS is 10%. This is normally too small and can cause unnecessary lock escalation. A value of 25–30% is normally a better balance between overall concurrency and minimizing lock escalations.

To configure the size of the lock list to be 500 pages and increase the MAXLOCKS to 30%, use the following commands:

```
update db cfg for <database_name> using LOCKLIST 500
update db cfg for <database_name> using MAXLOCKS 30
```

The default deadlock check time is 10 seconds (10,000 milliseconds), and the default lock time-out is indefinite (-1). To increase the deadlock check time to 30 seconds and enable locks to time out after waiting for 5 seconds, use the following commands:

```
update db cfg for <database_name> using DLCHKTIME 30000
update db cfg for <database_name> using LOCKTIMEOUT 5
```

Monitoring

Lock escalation will cause more table locks and fewer row-level locks, thus reducing concurrency within the database. In addition to reduced concurrency, lock escalation can also cause deadlocks to occur, which will result in transactions being rolled back. Due to the importance of locking on overall database performance, there is a database monitor specifically for locking. It is important to note that, because the lock snapshots capture timestamp information within the monitor elements, they are the most expensive (i.e., they have the largest overhead) of the database monitors.

As with other monitor information, the data can be captured using a database monitor snapshot or an SQL statement. However, it is important to note that the SQL snapshot acquires a lock while capturing the lock snapshot information, so in reality, the number of "real" locks on the system is one less than the number reported by the SQL statement. The following command will capture a database snapshot and return only the locking-related information for the database:

```
get snapshot for database on <database_name> | grep -i 'Lock'
```

The following SQL statement will provide the same information as the above command:

```
SELECT LOCKS_HELD, LOCK_WAITS, LOCK_WAIT_TIME,
LOCK_LIST_IN_USE, DEADLOCKS, LOCK_ESCALS, X_LOCK_ESCALS,
LOCKS_WAITING,  LOCK_TIMEOUTS, INT_DEADLOCK_ROLLBACKS
FROM TABLE(SNAPSHOT_DATABASE('SAMPLE',-1 )) as SNAPSHOT_DATABASE;
```

If the above command and SQL statement were executed at the same time, the output of the command would look like the following:

```
Locks held currently                        = 12
Lock waits                                  = 0
Time database waited on locks (ms)          = 0
Lock list memory in use (Bytes)             = 2080
Deadlocks detected                          = 1
Lock escalations                            = 0
Exclusive lock escalations                  = 0
Agents currently waiting on locks           = 0
Lock Timeouts                               = 0
Internal rollbacks due to deadlock          = 1
```

The output of the SQL statement would look like the following:

```
LOCKS_HELD            LOCK_WAITS       LOCK_WAIT_TIME
LOCK_LIST_IN_USE      DEADLOCKS        LOCK_ESCALS
LOCKS_WAITING         LOCK_TIMEOUTS    INT_DEADLOCK_ROLLBACKS    X_LOCK_ESCALS
-----------------     -------------    ----------------------    -------------
13                    0                0                         1
2116                  1                0
0                     0                0

1 record(s) selected.
```

Notice that there is an extra lock reported in the output of the SQL statement, as well as 36 extra bytes of lock list usage. This information was captured on a 32-bit DB2 instance where a lock will use 36 bytes of the lock list for a lock if there are already other locks on the same object.

Locks Held

In general, the number of locks held should be as low as possible because applications holding locks for long periods of time will hurt application concurrency. For a database with a large number of applications, there will normally be some locks held at any give time, especially for an online system with inserts, updates, or deletions.

When examining the number of locks held, it is important also to examine the number of currently connected applications. For a system with 100 connected users, 100 locks is not excessive. However, if there are only five applications connected to the database, each application is holding 20 locks on average, which can be excessive.

The average number of locks per applications (ALA) is calculated using:

```
ALA = Locks held currently / Applications connected currently
```

or

```
SELECT  (real (real(APPLS_CUR_CONS)) / (real(LOCK_WAIT_TIME)))
   as AverageLocksPerApp
   FROM TABLE(SNAPSHOT_DATABASE('SAMPLE',-1 )) as SNAPSHOT_DATABASE;
```

Lock wait time: The time that the database has waited on locks should be as low as possible because when DB2 is waiting for the lock, the applications are also waiting. A single lock wait may not seem too bad if we look only at the number of lock waits. However, if the lock waited for 5 minutes, it is very important to examine the reason for this and attempt to eliminate the source of the lock wait.

Lock list memory in use: If the amount of lock list in use is approaching the size of the lock list, this is an indication that lock escalation may be imminent. For normal operations, the lock list should not be more than 60% used. This leaves the remaining 40% of the lock list for exception processing. The percentage of the lock list used (PLU) is calculated using the following formula:

```
PLU = (Lock list memory in use / LOCKLIST) * 100%
```

Deadlocks detected: As discussed previously, when a deadlock is encountered, one of the applications involved in the deadlock will be rolled back and will need to redo the entire transaction. All deadlocks should be investigated and eliminated, if possible.

Lock escalations/exclusive lock escalations: Lock escalations cause decreased application concurrency and in many cases, the application may encounter lock waits and/or deadlocks while performing the lock escalation. These locking issues are even more likely with exclusive lock escalations because a number of exclusive row locks are converted to an exclusive table lock, and no other applications can access any row in the entire table.

Lock timeouts: The number of lock timeouts needs to be analyzed in conjunction with the setting for the LOCKTIMEOUT database configuration parameter. If the LOCKTIMEOUT parameter were configured to a low value to cause locks to time out quickly, the number of lock timeouts would normally be higher. If the LOCKTIMEOUT parameter is configured to a relatively high value, lock timeouts should not occur frequently, and when a lock timeout is encountered, it should be examined.

In Version 8, DB2 has enhanced the diagnostics available when a lock timeout occurs, and the lock timeout can now be debugged without the need to reproduce the condition with event monitors or snapshot monitoring turned on. When the diagnostic level is set to 4, a record will be written to the diagnostic log, indicating which application caused the lock timeout condition, as well as the SQL statement it was executing. An example of the diagnostic record is below:

```
Request for lock "TAB: (2, 13)" in mode ".IX" timed out
Application caused the lock wait is "*LOCAL.DB2.007340152709"
Statement: 7570 6461 7465 2074 3120 7365 7420 6331 update t1 set c1
3d63 312b 3531 3231 30                                      =c1+51210
```

Based on the above diagnostic entry, we can determine that:

- DB2 was attempting to acquire a table lock (TAB) to execute this statement.
- The lock mode requested was Intent-eXclusive (IX).
- The application that caused the error had an application ID of "LOCAL.DB2.007340152709".
- The statement that caused the error was "update t1 set c1=c1+51210".

Automatic: No

Online: Yes

Number of Asynchronous Page Cleaners (NUM_IOCLEANERS)

Background

When a DB2 agent, acting on behalf of an application, needs to access table or index pages it will first look for the pages in the database buffer pool area. If the page cannot be found in the buffer pool area, it will be read from disk into the buffer pool. If the buffer pool is full, DB2 must select a "victim" page to be overwritten in the buffer pool. If the victim page is dirty (i.e., it was changed since it was read into the buffer pool and has not been written to disk), it must first be written to disk before it can be over written. During the write operation, the application must wait. To reduce the likelihood that the victim page will be dirty, DB2 uses page cleaners to asynchronously write dirty pages to disk before they are chosen as victims.

> **N O T E**   An additional benefit of the page cleaners writing the dirty pages to disk is the reduction in the amount of work required in the event that there is a problem with DB2 and a database restart/recovery is required.

The number of asynchronous page cleaners database configuration parameter (NUM_IOCLEANERS) specifies the number of asynchronous page cleaner processes that can be run for the database. If this parameter is set to zero (0), there will be no page cleaners available for the database and as a result, the database agents will perform all of the page writes from the buffer pool to disk synchronously.

If the applications for a database consist primarily of transactions that update data, an increase in the number of cleaners will help improve the performance and will also reduce the recovery time from soft failures, such as power outages, because the contents of the database on disk will be more up to date at any given time.

How the Page Cleaners Are Triggered

The page cleaners can be triggered in three different ways.

Dirty page threshold: When a page in the buffer pool is changed, it is added to the buffer pool's dirty list. At this time, DB2 checks to see whether this addition to the dirty list exceeds the changed page threshold (aka. dirty page threshold) for the buffer pool. If the changed page threshold is exceeded, the page cleaners will be triggered.

The changed page threshold database configuration parameter (CHNGPGS_THRESH) represents the percentage of the buffer pool that can be dirty before the page cleaners are triggered.

LSN gap: When transactions are occurring against the database, they will be logged. To reduce the amount of work required in the event of a problem, DB2 will trigger the page cleaners as it writes to the log file(s).

The percentage of the log file reclaimed before the soft checkpoint database configuration parameter SOFTMAX represents the percentage of a log file that is written before the page cleaners are triggered.

Dirty page steals: When an agent requests a page that must be read from disk and DB2 chooses the victim page, if the page is dirty, the page must first be written to disk before it can be used to read the new page that the agent has requested. After a number of dirty victim pages have been selected, DB2 will automatically trigger the page cleaners to write the dirty pages to disk.

How the Page Cleaners Work

When the page cleaners are triggered, all of the page cleaners are triggered at the same time. They will each gather up to 400 pages from the dirty lists for the database buffer pools. The pages from the dirty list will then be written to disk, one page at a time, until the page cleaner has processed its assigned dirty pages. Once it has written all of the pages, it will check to see whether there are more pages to be written or whether there have been any new triggers. If so, it will gather a new list of pages to process; if not, it will wait for the next page cleaner trigger.

Configuring

Because all page cleaners are started whenever a page cleaner trigger is hit, having too many page cleaners can overwhelm the run queue on the server and cause a significant performance impact on the system. Therefore, as a rule of thumb, set the number of page cleaners equal to the number of CPUs in the database server.

For example, for a server with 16 CPUs, the following command will set the number of asynchronous page cleaners to 16:

```
update db cfg for <database_name> using NUM_IOCLEANERS 16
```

Monitoring

When examining the effectiveness of the asynchronous page cleaners, it is important to examine the ratio of asynchronous data and index page writes. The percentage of asynchronous data (PADW) and index page writes (PAIX) can be calculated using the following formulas:

```
PADW =   (Asynchronous pool data page writes / Buffer pool data writes) * 100%

PAIX =   (Asynchronous pool index page writes / Buffer pool index writes) * 100%
```

The number of page cleaners could potentially be reduced if:

- PADW is close to 100%
- PAIX is close to 100%

It is also important to understand which of the three I/O cleaner triggers is causing the page cleaners to be activated and to write the dirty pages from the buffer pools to disk. This information is available in the database snapshot information or through an SQL table function. To take a database snapshot and extract the entries that describe the page cleaner triggers in the database snapshot, use the following command:

```
get snapshot for database on <database_name> | grep -i 'cleaner triggers'
```

The SQL table function that will return the page cleaner triggers would look like the following:

```
SELECT DB_NAME,
    POOL_LSN_GAP_CLNS,
    POOL_DRTY_PG_STEAL_CLNS,
    POOL_DRTY_PG_THRSH_CLNS
    FROM TABLE(SNAPSHOT_DATABASE('SAMPLE',-1 ))
    as SNAPSHOT_DATABASE
```

The output of the get snapshot command would look like the following:

```
LSN Gap cleaner triggers                     = 142
Dirty page steal cleaner triggers            = 2
Dirty page threshold cleaner triggers        = 396
```

The output of the SQL function would look like the following:

```
DB_NAME   POOL_LSN_GAP_CLNS   POOL_DRTY_PG_STEAL_CLNS   POOL_DRTY_PG_THRSH_CLNS
-------   -----------------   -----------------------   -----------------------
SAMPLE                  142                         2                       396

1 record(s) selected.
```

In this case, the page cleaners were triggered by the "good" triggers (changed page threshold and/ or LSN gap) well over 99% of the time. As was explained earlier, a dirty page steal trigger is done only after a number of pages have been synchronously written to disk and their associated clients forced to wait. If the number of "bad" page cleaner triggers (i.e., dirty page steal triggers) is more than a couple of percentage points of the total number of triggers, the values set for changed page threshold and soft max, as well as the number of page cleaners, should be examined.

The percentage of bad page cleaner triggers (PBPCT) is calculated as follows:

```
PBPCT = ((LSN gap cleaner triggers) / (Dirty page steal cleaner
    triggers + Dirty page threshold cleaner triggers + LSN gap cleaner
    triggers)) * 100%
```

Based on the snapshot information above, the PBPCT equals:

```
PBPCT = ((2) / (142 + 396 + 2)) * 100%

PBPCT = 0.37%
```

This ratio is very good and indicates that the system is primarily writing dirty pages to disk using the asynchronous page cleaners, and applications are not waiting for synchronous page writes. However, based on the following snapshot information for the page cleaner triggers, the PBPCT is much higher.

```
DB_NAME   POOL_LSN_GAP_CLNS    POOL_DRTY_PG_STEAL_CLNS    POOL_DRTY_PG_THRSH_CLNS
-------   -----------------    ----------------------    -----------------------
SAMPLE                   17                      2034                       1192

1 record(s) selected.
```

The PBPCT equals:

```
PBPCT = ((2034) / (17 + 1192 + 2034)) * 100%

PBPCT = 62.7%
```

In this case, the asynchronous page cleaners are rarely being triggered by the pool LSN gap trigger. This indicates that the database configuration parameter SOFTMAX may be set too high. To determine the value of the SOFTMAX configuration variable, use the command:

```
get db cfg for sample | grep -i softmax
```

This returns the following:

```
Percent log file reclaimed before soft chckpt (SOFTMAX) = 100
```

In this case, the page cleaners are being triggered each time a log file is filled. Because this value is not abnormally high, next examine the log file size by using the command:

```
get db cfg for sample | grep -i logfilsiz
```

This returns the following:

```
Log file size (4KB)                          (LOGFILSIZ) = 250000
```

The log file size for this database is 250,000 4-KB pages, or 1 GB. Therefore, the page cleaners are being triggered only after 1 GB of log information has been written. If the log file size cannot be reduced, the SOFTMAX configuration parameter can be reduced to cause the page cleaners to be triggered more frequently. To update the SOFTMAX configuration parameter to cause the page cleaners to trigger after 10% of a log has been written, use the following command:

```
update db cfg for sample using softmax 10
```

If the log files do not need to be this large and can be reduced, the log file size can be changed to 250 4K pages or 1 MB using the following command:

```
update db cfg for sample using logfilsiz 250
```

Asynchronous Pages per Write

When the page cleaners are triggered, it is important that they be writing to disk as efficiently as possible. Having the page cleaners triggered too infrequently and writing a large number of pages to disk will cause the system to slow down. Likewise, having the page cleaners triggered frequently but writing a small number of pages to disk is also inefficient.

The number of pages written per page cleaner trigger is not captured in any of the DB2 snapshots. However, the average number of pages written per asynchronous write request can be calculated, using the database base and buffer pool snapshot information. The average pages per asynchronous write (APPAW) can be calculated using the formula:

```
APPAW = ((Asynchronous pool data page writes + Asynchronous pool index
   page writes) / (Dirty page steal cleaner triggers +  Dirty page
   threshold cleaner triggers + LSN gap cleaner triggers))
```

Based on the following information from the database and buffer pool snapshots:

```
LSN Gap cleaner triggers                            = 142
Dirty page steal cleaner triggers                   = 2
Dirty page threshold cleaner triggers               = 396

Asynchronous pool data page writes                  = 167660
Asynchronous pool index page writes                 = 178944
```

the APPAW would be:

```
APPAW = (167660 + 178944) / (142 + 2 + 396)


APPAW = 641.9
```

In this case, the page cleaners wrote an average of 641.9 pages, or 2.5 MB, each time they were triggered. This value needs to be examined in the context of the size of the buffer pool that is being examined. For a 1-GB buffer pool, this is a small value, and perhaps the page cleaners are being triggered too aggressively. For a 100-MB buffer pool, this value is much more reasonable.

Automatic: No

Online: No

Number of I/O Servers (NUM_IOSERVERS)

Background

When a DB2 agent acting on behalf of an application needs to access table or index pages, it will first look for the pages in the database buffer pool area. If the page cannot be found in the buffer pool area, it will be read from disk into the buffer pool. I/O is very expensive and in this case, the agent cannot do anything but wait for the read request to finish before it can access the page.

These page reads are typically done one page at a time and if the application also needs to access subsequent pages within the table or index, this is not an efficient method for reading the pages into the buffer pool.

In many situations, DB2 UDB can anticipate the pages that will be requested by an application and read them into the buffer pool before the agent actually attempts to access them. This is referred to as *prefetching*. Prefetching can improve the database performance because the pages will be found in the buffer pool when the agent accesses them, reducing or eliminating the time the application must wait for the page to be read from disk into the buffer pool. This is more relevant to DSS-type workloads that scan large indexes and tables than it is for OLTP-type workloads that involve less scanning and more random insert/update/delete activity.

Prefetching can be enabled by the DB2 optimizer when it is building the access plan for a statement and determines that it will be scanning a large portion of a table or index. It can also be enabled or triggered when DB2 is executing an access plan and detects that it has read a number of pages in sequence and will likely continue to do so. This is known as *sequential detection* and can be enabled or disabled using the database configuration parameter SEQDETECT.

Configuring

If the prefetch size is set as a multiple of the table space extent size (i.e., prefetch size = extent size × number of containers) for all of the table spaces in the database and all of the table spaces are being scanned at the same time, the number of prefetchers should be equal to the number of disks belonging to the database. However, if one or more of the table spaces has been set up using more aggressive prefetching (i.e., the prefetch size is a multiple of this value) and/or some of the table spaces are not being scanned at the same time as the others, the calculation becomes more complicated. To determine the number of prefetchers required in this case:

- Determine the table spaces that will potentially be scanned at the same time.
- For each of these table spaces, determine the number of prefetchers required to service a scan of it (based on the formulas above).
- Sum these values to determine the total number of prefetchers required.

The number of prefetchers for the database can be set using the following command:

```
update db cfg for <database_name> using NUM_IOSERVERS 64
```

Monitoring

An important aspect of the prefetching performance that can be analyzed using the snapshot information is the amount of synchronous versus asynchronous I/O. The percentage of asynchronous read requests (or asynchronous read ratio, ARR) is calculated using the following formula:

```
ARR = ((Asynchronous data reads + Asynchronous index reads) / (Data
   logical reads + Index logical reads)) * 100%
```

The ARR can also be calculated by using the SQL table function as follows:

```
select BP_NAME,
  (INT(((FLOAT(pool_Async_data_Reads + pool_async_index_Reads)) /
  (FLOAT(Pool_Index_L_Reads + Pool_data_L_Reads))) * 100))
  AS Asynch_Read_Ratio
  FROM TABLE(SNAPSHOT_BP('SAMPLE',-1 ))
  as SNAPSHOT_BP;
```

For the following buffer pool snapshot:

```
                          Bufferpool Snapshot

Bufferpool name                            = IBMDEFAULTBP
Database name                              = SAMPLE
Database path                              = /v1/db2/NODE0000/SQL00001/
Input database alias                       = SAMPLE
Buffer pool data logical reads             = 523956
Buffer pool data physical reads            = 33542
Buffer pool data writes                    = 288
Buffer pool index logical reads            = 257949
Buffer pool index physical reads           = 11323
Total buffer pool read time (ms)           = 12012
Total buffer pool write time (ms)          = 720
Asynchronous pool data page reads          = 5227
Asynchronous pool data page writes         = 276
Buffer pool index writes                   = 255
Asynchronous pool index page reads         = 451
Asynchronous pool index page writes        = 239
Total elapsed asynchronous read time       = 819
Total elapsed asynchronous write time      = 663
Asynchronous read requests                 = 3553
Direct reads                               = 69664
Direct writes                              = 16902
Direct read requests                       = 2780
Direct write requests                      = 411
Direct reads elapsed time (ms)             = 4830
Direct write elapsed time (ms)             = 979
Database files closed                      = 17
Data pages copied to extended storage      = 0
Index pages copied to extended storage     = 0
Data pages copied from extended storage    = 0
Index pages copied from extended
  storage                                  = 0
Unread prefetch pages                      = 0
```

```
Vectored IOs                        = 0
Pages from vectored IOs             = 0
Block IOs                           = 0
Pages from block IOs                = 0
Physical page maps                  = 0
```

the ARR would be:

```
ARR = ((5227 + 451) / (523956 + 257949)) * 100%
ARR = 0.73 %
```

This is a very small value and would indicate that there is very little prefetch activity occurring for this database. This could be due to a number of reasons, such as:

1. The workload is reading and writing single rows, so it cannot take advantage of prefetching.
2. There are too few prefetchers configured for the database.
3. The table spaces in the database are set up with only one container each, so that prefetching cannot take place.

For a system with multiple buffer pools, it is normally a good idea to separate tables with a high percentage of asynchronous reads from those with a low percentage of asynchronous reads. The ARR can also be examined for each table space to help separate the table spaces with high and low ARRs. For the following table space snapshot information, we see that there are four table spaces with different access patterns:

```
Tablespace name                     = TSPC1
   Buffer pool data logical reads   = 1200
   Asynchronous pool data page reads = 32
   Buffer pool index logical reads  = 3400
   Asynchronous pool index page reads = 128

Tablespace name                     = TSPC2
   Buffer pool data logical reads   = 15000
   Asynchronous pool data page reads = 14000
   Buffer pool index logical reads  = 90000
   Asynchronous pool index page reads = 86000

Tablespace name                     = TSPC3
   Buffer pool data logical reads   = 9000
   Asynchronous pool data page reads = 8600
   Buffer pool index logical reads  = 6250
   Asynchronous pool index page reads = 5975
```

```
Tablespace name                                = TSPC4
   Buffer pool data logical reads              = 7200
   Asynchronous pool data page reads           = 1400
   Buffer pool index logical reads             = 800
   Asynchronous pool index page reads          = 770
```

In this case, the ARRs would be:

```
TBSPC1                  3.5%
TBSPC2                  95.2%
TBSCP3                  95.6%
TBSPC4                  27.1%
```

Because the table spaces TBSPC1 and TBSPC4 both have low ARRs, they should not be placed in the same buffer pool as table space TBSPC2 or TBSPC3. Because the table spaces TBSPC2 and TBSPC3 both have a high ARR, they could be placed in the same buffer pool. However, DB2 places a limit on the number of pages that can be prefetched into a buffer pool before they are accessed by a db2 agent, so having two table spaces with a high ARR in the same buffer pool may have an adverse effect. It may be more optimal to place the table spaces TBSPC2 and TBSPC3 in their own buffer pools.

Physical Read Rate

It is also important to examine the rate at which DB2 is reading pages from disk. This should be calculated for all table spaces and when compared, will show whether the I/O is spread evenly across all table spaces or whether the workload on certain table spaces is causing more I/O than in other table spaces.

The rate at which pages are read from disk (or page read rate, PRR) is calculated using the following formula:

```
PRR = (Data physical reads + Index physical reads) / (Time since
   monitor switches reset or activated)
```

Based on the above buffer pool snapshot, the PRR would be:

```
PRR = (33542 + 11323) / (23.53 seconds)


PRR = 1906.7 reads per second
```

Examining the table space snapshot for the table spaces using the identified buffer pool may provide additional information to help determine which table space(s) are being read most often. Any table space(s) with a significantly higher I/O rate than the other table spaces can be examined to determine whether the performance could be improved by assigning the table space to its own buffer pool or by adding containers to the table space to improve the I/O bandwidth.

Read Time

For every millisecond that a db2 agent spends waiting for a page to be read into the buffer pool, the application is also waiting. The database snapshots do not provide information on the amount of time taken by each read request. However, they do provide enough information to calculate the average time taken per read request. The average read time (ART) is calculated using the following formula:

```
ART = (Total buffer pool read time) / (Data physical reads + Index
   physical reads)
```

The ART can also be calculated using the SQL table function, as follows:

```
select BP_NAME,
   (INT(((FLOAT(pool_read_time)) / (FLOAT(Pool_Index_p_Reads +
   Pool_data_p_Reads))) * 100))
   AS Avg_Read_Time_in_ms
   FROM TABLE(SNAPSHOT_BP('SAMPLE',-1 ))
   as SNAPSHOT_BP;
```

The SQL table function can also be used to calculate the buffer pool, data, and index hit ratios, as well as the ARR and ART in one SQL statement. This can be done using the following statement:

```
select BP_NAME,
(INT((1 - ((FLOAT(pool_Index_P_Reads + pool_data_P_Reads)) /
(FLOAT(Pool_Index_L_Reads + Pool_data_L_Reads)))) * 100))
AS BPool_Hit_Ratio,
(INT((1 - ((FLOAT(pool_Data_P_Reads)) / (FLOAT(Pool_Data_L_Reads)))) * 100))
AS Data_Hit_Ratio,
(INT((1 - ((FLOAT(pool_Index_P_Reads)) / (FLOAT(Pool_Index_L_Reads)))) * 100))
AS Index_Hit_Ratio,
(INT(((FLOAT(pool_Async_data_Reads + pool_async_index_Reads)) /
(FLOAT(Pool_Index_L_Reads + Pool_data_L_Reads))) * 100))
AS Asynch_Read_Ratio,
(INT(((FLOAT(pool_read_time)) / (FLOAT(Pool_Index_p_Reads +
Pool_data_p_Reads))) * 100))
AS Avg_Read_Time_in_ms
FROM TABLE(SNAPSHOT_BP('SAMPLE',-1 ))
as SNAPSHOT_BP;
```

The output of this statement looks like the following:

```
BP_NAME       BPOOL_HIT_RATIO DATA_HIT_RATIO  INDEX_HIT_RATIO ASYNCH_READ_RATIO  AVG_READ_TIME_IN_MS
------------- --------------- --------------  --------------- -----------------  -------------------
IBMDEFAULTBP  69              78              63              0                  362
1 record(s) selected.
```

Automatic: No

Online: No

Number of Commits to Group (MINCOMMIT)

Background

The number of commits to group database configuration parameter (MINCOMMIT) allows the writing of the database log buffer to disk until a minimum number of commits have been performed. This delay can help reduce the database manager overhead associated with the writing of log buffers to disk. This can result in improved performance when there are multiple applications running against a database and many commits are requested by the applications within a very short time frame.

> **NOTE** The grouping of commits will occur only when the value of this parameter is greater than one and when the number of applications connected to the database is greater than or equal to the value of this parameter.

When commit grouping is being performed, application commit requests are held until either the number of commit requests equals the value of this parameter or one second has elapsed.

Configuring

The MINCOMMIT value can have a significant impact on performance, both positive and negative, and must be set correctly. The default value for MINCOMMIT is 1, and for online applications with many short transactions this should not be changed unless there is a large number of applications executing in the database at the same time; otherwise, very short transactions may be dramatically increased.

When there is a large number of concurrent applications with short transactions and the log buffer is being flushed too frequently by the application commits, the MINCOMMIT parameter can be adjusted if there is a large number of commits per second. The number of transactions per second can be determined using the database snapshots and the MINCOMMIT parameter adjusted accordingly. The number of commits to group can be increased by using the following command:

```
update db cfg for <database_name> using MINCOMMIT 5
```

If the MINCOMMIT database configuration parameter is increased, the log buffer (LOGBUFSZ) may also need to be increased to avoid having a full log buffer force a flush to disk during these heavy load periods. In this case, the size of the log buffer can be calculated by using the following formula:

```
LOGBUFSZ = MINCOMMIT * (log space used, on average, by a transaction)
```

In a decision support/data warehousing system, leave MINCOMMIT set to 1. Setting MINCOMMIT greater than 1 can greatly increase processing time if there are not enough concurrent transactions per second to warrant it.

Monitoring

The database monitor can be used to determine the average number of transactions that have been performed over a period of time, as follows:

```
get snapshot for database on <database_name>
```

The important elements of the snapshot that should be analyzed are below:

```
Last reset timestamp                    = 09-12-2002 14:51:43.786876
Snapshot timestamp                      = 09-12-2002 14:56:27.787088
Commit statements attempted             = 1011
Rollback statements attempted           = 10
Log space used by the database (Bytes)  = 3990
Log pages written                       = 23
```

The number of transactions per second can be calculated by using the following formula:

```
TPS = ((Commit statements attempted + Rollback statements attempted) /
(Last reset timestamp - Snapshot timestamp))
```

An estimation of the number of log buffer flushes can be made using the database snapshot information. If the log buffer is being flushed every second, the number of log flushes would equal:

```
NumLF = Last reset timestamp - Snapshot timestamp
```

If the log buffer is being flushed only once it is filled, the number of log flushes would equal:

```
NumLF = Log pages written / LOGBUFSZ
```

The actual number of log buffer flushes will have been between these two calculated values. The log space used per transaction can then be calculated using the following formula:

```
LSPT = (Log space used by the database / (Last reset timestamp -
   Snapshot timestamp))
```

Automatic: No

Online: Yes

Catalog Cache Size (CATALOGCACHE_SZ)

Background

The catalog cache is allocated out of the database shared memory and is used to cache system catalog information. In DB2 UDB Version 7, the catalog cache existed only on the catalog partition, so that application needing information from the database system catalog always had to make a call to the catalog partition to retrieve the information. In a partitioned database in DB2 UDB Version 8, there is one catalog cache for each database partition. Caching catalog information at individual partitions allows the database manager to reduce its internal overhead by eliminating the need to access the system catalogs (and/or the catalog node in a partitioned database environment) to obtain information that has previously been retrieved. The catalog cache is used to store:

- SYSTABLES information (including packed descriptors)
- Authorization information, including SYSDBAUTH information and execute privileges for routines
- SYSROUTINES information

The use of the catalog cache can help improve the overall performance of:

- Binding packages and compiling SQL statements
- Operations that involve checking database-level privileges
- Operations that involve checking execute privileges for routines
- Applications that are connected to noncatalog partitions in a partitioned database environment

Configuring

If the size of the catalog cache is set to the default value of -1 in a partitioned database, the value used to calculate the size of the catalog cache will be four times the value specified for the MAXAPPLS configuration parameter, with a minimum value of eight.

For a database with a large number of objects and/or users, the default size of the catalog cache may not be sufficient, especially in a partitioned database. The size of the catalog cache can be configured using the following command:

```
update db cfg for <database_name> using CATALOGCACHE_SZ 32
```

Monitoring

When preparing execution strategies for SQL statements, DB2 first checks the catalog cache to learn about the definition of the database, table spaces, tables, indexes, and views. If all the required information is available in the cache, DB2 can avoid disk I/Os and access to the catalog partition and, therefore, shorten plan preparation times. Having a high package cache hit ratio (95% or better) is key for online database applications.

Keep increasing the CATALOGCACHE_SZ until you reach 95%. Issue the command db2 get snapshot for database on DBNAME and compute the hit ratio using the following formula:

```
(1 - (Catalog cache inserts / Catalog cache lookups)) * 100
```

You should also increase the CATALOGCACHE_SZ if the value of catalog cache overflows is greater than zero. In addition, if the value of catalog cache heap full is greater than zero, both DBHEAP and CATALOGCACHE_SZ should be proportionally increased.

Automatic: No

Online: Yes

Changed Pages Threshold (CHNGPGS_THRESH)

Background

As discussed previously, the changed pages threshold is one of the triggers of the asynchronous page cleaners within a database. The changed pages threshold specifies the level (percentage) of changed pages within the database buffer pool(s) at which the asynchronous page cleaners will be started, if they are not currently active. When the page cleaners are triggered, all of the page cleaners are triggered at the same time. They will each gather up to 400 pages from the dirty lists for the database buffer pools. The pages from the dirty list will then be written to disk one page at a time until the page cleaner has processed its assigned dirty pages. Once it has written all of the pages, it will check to see whether there are more pages to be written or whether there have been any new triggers. If so, it will gather a new list of pages to process; if not, it will wait for the next page cleaner trigger.

Configuring

The default setting for the changed pages threshold is too high for most online databases. When set to 60%, it is typically never the trigger for the page cleaners and when it is the page cleaner trigger, the amount of data to be written to disk can be quite high. This can cause a significant slowdown of the system as the I/O cleaners are triggered and flush the dirty pages. With the changed pages threshold set to 20% or 30%, the amount of data to be written to disk is much less, and the impact on the system is much less. In addition, there is a much higher possibility that the changed pages threshold will trigger the page cleaners.

To update the database configuration to set the changed pages threshold to 25%, use the following command:

```
update db cfg for <database_name> using CHNGPGS_THRESH 25
```

Monitoring

When analyzing the page cleaner activity, it is important to understand which of the three I/O cleaner triggers is causing the page cleaners to be activated and write the dirty pages from the buffer pools to disk. This information is available in the database snapshot information or through an SQL table function. To take a database snapshot and extract the entries that describe the page cleaner triggers in the database snapshot, use the following command:

```
get snapshot for database on <database_name> | grep -i 'cleaner
    triggers'
```

The SQL table function that will return the page cleaner triggers would look like the following:

```
SELECT DB_NAME,
    POOL_LSN_GAP_CLNS,
    POOL_DRTY_PG_STEAL_CLNS,
    POOL_DRTY_PG_THRSH_CLNS
    FROM TABLE(SNAPSHOT_DATABASE('SAMPLE',-1 ))
    as SNAPSHOT_DATABASE
```

The output of the get snapshot command would look like the following:

```
LSN Gap cleaner triggers                              = 142
Dirty page steal cleaner triggers                     = 2
Dirty page threshold cleaner triggers                 = 396
```

The output of the SQL function would look like the following:

```
DB_NAME  POOL_LSN_GAP_CLNS  POOL_DRTY_PG_STEAL_CLNS  POOL_DRTY_PG_THRSH_CLNS
-------  -----------------  -----------------------  -----------------------
SAMPLE                 142                        2                      396

1 record(s) selected.
```

In this case, the page cleaners were triggered by the "good" triggers (changed page threshold and/ or LSN gap) well over 99% of the time. As was explained earlier, a dirty page steal trigger is done only after a number of pages have been synchronously written to disk and their associated clients forced to wait. If the number of "bad" page cleaner triggers (i.e., dirty page steal triggers) is more than a couple of percentage points of the total number of triggers, the values set for changed page threshold and softmax, as well as the number of page cleaners, should be examined.

The percentage of bad page cleaner triggers (PBPCT) is calculated as follows:

```
PBPCT = ((LSN Gap Cleaner Triggers) / (Dirty page steal cleaner
    triggers + Dirty page threshold cleaner triggers + LSN gap cleaner
    triggers)) * 100%
```

Based on the snapshot information above, the PBPCT equals:

```
PBPCT = ((2) / (142 + 396 + 2)) * 100%
PBPCT = 0.37%
```

This ratio is very good and indicates that the system is primarily writing dirty pages to disk using the asynchronous page cleaners, and applications are not waiting for synchronous page writes. However, based on the following snapshot information for the page cleaner triggers, the PBPCT is much higher.

```
DB_NAME  POOL_LSN_GAP_CLNS  POOL_DRTY_PG_STEAL_CLNS  POOL_DRTY_PG_THRSH_CLNS
-------  -----------------  ----------------------- -----------------------

SAMPLE                  17                     2034                    1192


1 record(s) selected.
```

The PBPCT equals:

```
PBPCT = ((2034) / (17 + 1192 + 2034)) * 100%
PBPCT = 62.7%
```

Automatic: No

Online: No

Average Number of Active Applications (AVG_APPLS)

Background

The average number of active applications is used by the DB2 optimizer to estimate the amount of resources, particularly buffer pool space, that will be available to run the access plan for the statement being optimized.

Configuring

When setting this parameter, use the database monitor to capture the average number of concurrently executing applications over a period of time and, using a sampling technique, calculate an average. To update the database configuration to set the average number of active applications based on the snapshot information, use the following command:

```
update db cfg for <database_name> using AVG_APPLS 16
```

Monitoring

To take a database snapshot and extract the entry that gives the number of concurrently executing applications, use the following command:

```
get snapshot for database on <database_name> |
grep -i 'Appls. executing in db manager currently'
```

The SQL table function that will also return the number of concurrently executing applications would look like the following:

```
SELECT APPLS_IN_DB2
FROM TABLE(SNAPSHOT_DATABASE('SAMPLE',-1 ))as SNAPSHOT_DATABASE
```

The output of the get snapshot command would look like the following:

```
Appls. executing in db manager currently   = 12
```

The output of the SQL function would look like the following:

```
APPLS_IN_DB2
------------
          12

1 record(s) selected.
```

This information should be captured over a period of time, at average as well as peak workloads, and averaged to determine an optimal value for this parameter.

Automatic: No

Online: Yes

REGISTRY VARIABLE TUNING

The DB2 registry variables have an effect on the entire DB2 instance and all databases within the instance, as well as on all applications that access any of the databases. The following registry variables have the biggest effect on performance of the instance, databases, and applications:

- DB2_USE_PAGE_CONTAINER_TAG
- DB2_HASH_JOIN
- DB2_PARALLEL_IO
- DB2_NO_PKG_LOCK
- DB2_NT_NOCACHE
- DB2_SPIN_LATCHES

DB2_USE_PAGE_CONTAINER_TAG

Background

When a DMS table space is created, the file or raw device containers will be pre-allocated by DB2. Within the first extent of each container, DB2 will create the container tag as it does with SMS table spaces.

In previous versions of DB2 UDB, the container tag was stored in a single page to minimize the space requirements. Large Storage Area Networks (SANs) and disk arrays using Redundant Array of Independent Disks (RAID) technology have become more popular, and many databases are being created on RAID-protected disks. When using a one-page container, the beginning and end of an extent could not be made to line up with the beginning and end of a stripe on the disks and normally would cause suboptimal I/O because each I/O would need to access more than one disk. If the extent size is set to be equal to or an integer multiple of the RAID stripe size, by making the container a full extent in size, the I/Os would always line up with the underlying disk stripes. In DB2 UDB Version 7, the container tag could be made a full extent using the DB2_STRIPED_CONTAINERS registry variable.

Now, in DB2 UDB Version 8, the tag is created as a full extent in size by default for DMS table spaces. To force DB2 to create the tag on a single page, the new registry variable DB2_USE_PAGE_CONTAINER_TAG should be set to ON. To activate changes to this registry variable, the DB2 instance must be stopped and restarted.

Platforms: All

Default: On for DMS table spaces, off for SMS table spaces

Values: ON, OFF

DB2_HASH_JOIN

Background

In previous versions of DB2, the DB2 optimizer would normally choose between two different join methods: a nested loop join or a merge join. When the DB2_HASH_JOIN registry variable was set to YES, the optimizer was also able to consider using a hash join when optimizing the access plan if the optimization level was 5 or higher. Because hash joins can significantly improve the performance of certain queries, especially in DSS environments where the queries are normally quite large and complex, hash joins are always available in DB2 UDB Version 8 but are still considered only when the optimization level is 5 or higher. Because hash joins require more resources than a nested loop join or a merge scan join, they can be disabled if needed.

> **NOTE** To disable hash joins, set the DB2_HASH_JOIN registry variable to NO.

Hash joins are discussed in more detail in Chapter 6, The DB2 Optimizer.

Platforms: All

Default: On

Values: ON, OFF

DB2_ANTIJOIN

Background

DB2 can examine incoming SQL statements to determine whether a NOT EXISTS subquery can be converted to an anti-join that DB2 is able to process more efficiently. In a nonpartitioned database, the default is for DB2 to search for these opportunities. In a partitioned database, the DB2_ANTIJOIN registry variable must be set to YES before DB2 will attempt to replace NOT EXISTS subqueries with an anti-join.

Platforms: All

Default: Yes for nonpartitioned databases; No for partitioned databases

Values: Yes, No

DB2_INLIST_TO_NLJN

Background

Under certain conditions, the query rewrite facility of the optimizer can rewrite an IN list to a join, which can provide better performance if there is an index on the column with the IN list. In this case, the list of values would be accessed first and joined to the base table with a nested loop join, using the index to apply the join predicate.

If the IN list contains parameter markers or host variables, the optimizer does not have accurate information to determine the best join method for the rewritten version of the query. In this case, this registry variable causes the optimizer to favor nested loop joins to join the list of values, using the table that contributes the IN list as the inner table in the join.

For example, the following query:

```
SELECT * FROM EMPLOYEE
   WHERE DEPTNO IN ('D11 ','D21 ','E21 ')
```

could be rewritten as:

```
SELECT * FROM EMPLOYEE
   (VALUES 'D11 ','D21 ','E21)AS V(DNO)
   WHERE DEPTNO =V.DNO
```

Platforms: All

Default: No

Values: Yes, No

DB2_CORRELATED_PREDICATES

Background

When this registry variable is set to YES, the optimizer uses the KEYCARD statistical information about the unique indexes in an attempt to detect cases of correlation between join predicates. If correlation is detected, the optimizer will dynamically adjust the combined selectiveness of the correlated predicates, obtaining a more accurate estimate of the join size and total query cost.

Adjustment can also be done for correlation of simple equality predicates if there is an index on the columns in the predicates. In this case, the index does not need to be unique, but the columns in the equality predicates of the SQL statements must include all columns in the index. In this example:

```
WHERE C1=5 AND C2=10
```

if there is an index on C1 and C2, the optimizer will look for correlation between the columns.

Platforms: All

Default: Yes

Values: Yes, No

DB2_REDUCED_OPTIMIZATION

Background

The DB2_REDUCED_OPTIMIZATION registry variable tells the DB2 UDB optimizer to reduce the available optimization features at the specified optimization level. By reducing the number of optimization techniques used, the time and resource use during optimization are also reduced.

> **NOTE**   Although optimization time and resource use might be reduced, the risk of producing a less-than-optimal data access plan is increased.

When the registry variable is set to NO, the optimizer does not change its optimization techniques. However, when the registry variable is set to YES:

- If the optimization level is 5 (the default) or lower, the optimizer disables some optimization techniques that might consume significant preparation time and resources but do not usually produce a better access plan.

- If the optimization level is exactly 5, the optimizer scales back or disables some additional techniques, which might further reduce optimization time and resource use but also further increases the risk of a less-than-optimal access plan.
- For optimization levels lower than 5, some of these techniques might not be in effect in any case. If they are, however, they remain in effect.

If the registry variable is set to any integer value, the effect is the same as though it were set to YES. However, in addition, when dynamically prepared queries are optimized at level 5:

- If the total number of joins in any query block exceeds the setting of the DB2_REDUCED_OPTIMIZATION registry variable, the optimizer will switch to greedy join enumeration instead of disabling the additional optimization techniques, as described above.

When the optimization level is set to 5, the optimizer can dynamically reduce the optimization for dynamically executed queries. If the DB2_REDUCED_OPTIMIZATION registry variable is set to DISABLE, the optimization level cannot be reduced at level 5, and the optimizer will perform full level 5 optimization.

> **N O T E** The dynamic optimization reduction at optimization level 5 takes precedence over the behavior described for optimization level of exactly 5 when DB2_REDUCED_OPTIMIZATION is set to YES, as well as the behavior described for the integer setting.

Platforms: All

Default: No

Values: Yes, No, Disable, any integer value

DB2_OVERRIDE_BPF

Background

When a database is activated or started (i.e., during the first connection to the database), DB2 automatically creates four hidden buffer pools for the database, in addition to the IBMDEFAULTBP and any user-created buffer pools. These buffer pools are hidden and do not have entries in the system catalog tables. In addition, these buffer pools cannot be used directly by assigning table spaces to them and cannot be altered.

There will be one hidden buffer pool per page size (i.e., 4 KB, 8 KB, 16 KB, and 32 KB) to ensure that there is a buffer pool available under all circumstances. DB2 UDB will use these buffer pools under the following conditions:

- When the CREATE BUFFERPOOL statement is executed and the IMMEDIATE option is specified but there is not enough memory available to allocate the buffer pool
  - If this occurs, a message is written to the administration notification log.
  - Any table spaces that are using the buffer pool will be remapped to the hidden buffer pool with the same page size.
- When the IBMDEFAULTBP and/or any of the user-created buffer pools cannot be allocated when the database is activated or started
  - If this occurs, a message is written to the administration notification log.
  - Any table space that is using a buffer pool that was not allocated will be remapped to the hidden buffer pool with the same page size.
  - DB2 will be fully functional because of the hidden buffer pools, but performance will be drastically reduced.
- When a table space is created and its page size does not correspond to the page size of any of the user-created buffer pools
- During a roll forward operation if a buffer pool is created and the DEFERRED option is specified
  - Any table spaces that are created and assigned to this buffer pool will be remapped to the hidden buffer pool with the same page size for the duration of the roll forward operation.

By default, the hidden buffer pools will be created with a size of 16 pages. This can be changed using the DB2_OVERRIDE_BPF registry variable.

Platforms: All

Default: Not set

Values: Any positive integer

DB2_PINNED_BP

Background

The buffer pools are the work area for the database, and all searching for and manipulation of the data and indexes must take place within the buffer pools. In order for DB2 to scan a table or an index, the pages of the table or index must be in the database's buffer pool (or buffer pools). In a constrained system, the operating system may potentially swap/page the buffer pool out of the server's real memory. If the buffer pool is swapped/paged out of real memory, it must be first read from disk before it can be manipulated. Keeping the buffer pool(s) in the server's real memory allows database performance to be more consistent.

The DB2_PINNED_BP registry variable is used to ensure that the buffer pools for all databases in the DB2 instance are kept in the server's real memory. This registry variable is used on both

AIX and HP/UX; however, when used for a 64-bit DB2 instance in HP/UX, the DB2 instance group must also be given the MLOCK privilege.

To do this, a user with root access rights must perform the following actions:

   1. Add the DB2 instance group to the /etc/privgroup file.
   2. Issue the command setprivgrp -f /etc/privgroup.

For example, if the DB2 instance group belongs to db2inst1 group, the following line must be added to the /etc/privgroup file:

```
db2inst1 MLOCK
```

Platforms: AIX, HP/UX

Default: No

Values: Yes, No

DB2_FORCE_FCM_BP

Background

For a multi-partitioned database on AIX, when the DB2 instance is started, the FCM buffers used for inter-partition communication are allocated from either the database global memory or from a separate shared memory segment, if there is not enough global memory available. If the DB2_FORCE_FCM_BP registry variable is set to YES, the FCM buffers are created in a shared memory segment. Otherwise, the database partitions on the same server node will communicate through UNIX sockets.

Communicating through shared memory is faster than UNIX sockets. However, if the DB2 instance is created as a 32-bit instance, this will use a whole segment of shared memory and, therefore, reduce the number of shared memory segments available for other uses, particularly for database buffer pools.

Platforms: AIX

Default: No

Values: Yes, No

DB2_AWE

Background

Address Windowing Extensions (AWE), allows the allocation of up to 64 GB of shared memory on 32-bit Windows 2000 and Windows XP servers. To use this registry variable, Windows must be configured correctly to support AWE, and the DB2 instance owner must also be assigned the "lock pages in memory" right.

> **N O T E** If AWE support is enabled, extended storage cannot be used for any of the buffer pools in the database. Also, buffer pools referenced with this registry variable must already exist.

Platforms: Windows 2000, Windows XP

Default: NULL

Values: X, Y where X = buffer pool ID and Y = number of pages for the buffer pool

DB2_BINSORT

Background

The DB2_BINSORT registry variable enables a new binary sort algorithm that reduces the CPU usage and overall elapsed time of sorts. This new algorithm extends the extremely efficient binary sorting technique for integer data types to all data types, such as BIGINT, CHAR, VARCHAR, FLOAT, and DECIMAL, as well as combinations of these data types.

Platforms: All

Default: Yes

Values: Yes, No

DB2_AVOID_PREFETCH

Background

The DB2_AVOID_PREFETCH registry variable specifies whether prefetching should be used during restart recovery of a database. By default, prefetching will be used; however, if DB2_AVOID_PREFETCH is set to YES, DB2 will not perform prefetching during restart recovery.

Platforms: All

Default: Off

Values: On, Off

DB2TCPCONNMGRS

Background

TCP/IP connection managers are processes or threads that are running in a DB2 instance to accept incoming connection requests from clients using the TCP/IP protocol. If the DB2TCPCONNMGRS registry variable is not set, the default number of connection manager processes or threads is created. If the DB2TCPCONNMGRS registry variable is set to a value between 1 and 8, the specified number of connection manager processes or threads is created. If the DB2TCPCONNMGRS registry variable is set to a value less than 1, one connection manager process or thread is created.

> **N O T E**   Having the number of connection managers set to 1 can limit performance for remote connections in databases with a lot of users, frequent connects and disconnects, or both.

Platforms: All

Default: The square root of the number of CPUs in the server, rounded up to a maximum of 8 on an SMP server.

Values: 1, 2, 3, 4, 5, 6, 7, 8

DB2MAXFSCRSEARCH

Background

To insert a record, DB2 must find enough contiguous free space on a page for the record. Inserts can occur in three modes:

- Scan mode
- Append mode
- Base on clustering index

When the insert is operating in scan mode, DB2 must scan the free space maps in the object for a page with enough contiguous free space. To speed up the searching for free space, DB2 stores a free space control record (FSCR) on the first page of an object and on every 500th page of the object. Then, when DB2 is scanning for free space, it needs to read only every 500th page and examine the FSCR to determine whether any of the next 500 pages contains enough free space to hold the record.

The DB2MAXFSCRSEARCH registry variable applies to the scan mode only. When in scan mode, the DB2MAXFSCRSEARCH registry variable specifies how many FSCRs to search for free space before switching to append mode. To optimize insert performance, DB2 will switch to append mode after searching for free space in five FSCRs. Larger values for the DB2MAXFSCRSEARCH registry variable will optimize space reuse, and smaller values will optimize for insert speed. Setting the DB2MAXFSCRSEARCH registry variable to -1 forces DB2 to search all FSCRs before switching to append mode for the insert.

The first insert into a table after the database is activated will start at the beginning of the object. For example, when inserting a record into a table, DB2 will scan the FSCR on page 0; if space is available on pages 0–499 for the record, it will be inserted. If no space is available, it will check the FSCR on page 500. If space is available on pages 500–999 for the record, it will be inserted. If no space is available, it will check the FSCR on page 1000. If space is available on pages 1000–1499 for the record, it will be inserted. If no space is available, it will check the FSCR on page 1500.

In this case, the FSCR on page 1000 indicated there was enough contiguous free space on page 1002 for the record to be inserted, so DB2 will read page 1002 into the buffer pool and insert the record.

To optimize subsequent insert performance, DB2 will keep an FSPR pointer (FSCR Ptr) on page 1000 because DB2 knows there was insufficient space on any page prior to this, so there is no sense in rescanning these pages unless a record is deleted. If a record on pages 0 through 999 is deleted, the FSCR Ptr will be moved to the FSCR for the page where the record was deleted.

For example, if a record is deleted from page 833, the FSCR Ptr will be moved to the FSCR for page 833, page 500 in this case, as shown in Figure 8.16.

In this case, the next scan for free space will start at page 500, not at the beginning of the object. This is a relatively simple example, but if the FSCR Ptr is on page 25500 and a delete occurs on page 23328, the FSCR Ptr will be moved to page 23000, not back to the beginning of the table.

Platforms: All

Default: 5

Values: −1, 1–33554

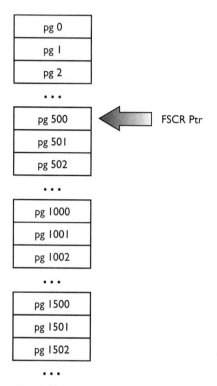

Figure 8.16
Free space control record pointer.

DB2_SELECTIVITY

Background

The DB2 optimizer uses the catalog statistics to estimate the selectivity of the predicates in the SQL statement when determining the optimal access plan for the statement. In some cases, the estimates can be significantly different from the real data, especially if the SQL statement uses host variables and can, therefore, produce inefficient access plans. If the selectivity of a particular predicate is known, it can be specified in the SQL statement as follows:

```
|--+-----+--+-predicate--+---------------------------------+-+---->
   '-NOT-' |                  '-SELECTIVITY--numeric-constant-' |
           '-(search-condition)---------------------------'


     .-----------------------------------------------------------.
     V                                                           |
>----+-----------------------------------------------------------+-
+--|
      '-+-AND-+--+-----+--+-predicate--+---------------------------+-+-'
        '-OR--'  '-NOT-' |                  '-SELECTIVITY--numeric-constant-' |
                         '-(search-condition)---------------------------'
```

The selectivity clause requires that the DB2_SELECTIVITY registry variable be set to YES and that:

- The predicate be a basic predicate where at least one expression contains host variables
- The predicate is a LIKE predicate where the match expression, predicate expression, or escape expression contain host variables

Platforms: All

Default: No

Values: Yes, No

DB2_PRED_FACTORIZE

Background

The DB2 optimizer can rewrite SQL queries to make them more efficient by adding additional predicates from disjuncts in the query. In some circumstances, these additional predicates can alter the estimated cardinality of the intermediate and final result sets and produce better access plans. The DB2_PRED_FACTORIZE registry variable specifies whether the query rewrite facility can look for opportunities to add these additional predicates. If the DB2_PRED_FACTORIZE registry variable is set to YES, the following query:

```
SELECT n1.empno, n1.lastname
  FROM employee n1, employee n2
WHERE   ((n1.lastname='SNOW '
  AND n2.lastname='PHAN ')
  OR (n1.lastname='PHAN '
  AND n2.lastname='SNOW '))
```

could be rewritten by the optimizer to include the following additional predicates:

```
SELECT n1.empno, n1.lastname
  FROM employee n1, employee n2
WHERE n1.lastname IN ('SNOW ','PHAN ')
  AND n2.lastname IN ('SNOW ','PHAN ')
  AND ((n1.lastname='SNOW '
  AND n2.lastname='PHAN ')
  OR (n1.lastname='PHAN '
  AND n2.lastname='SNOW '))
```

Platforms: All

Default: No

Values: Yes, No

DB2MEMDISCLAIM

Background

On AIX, memory used by DB2 agent processes may retain some associated paging space. This paging space may remain reserved, even when the associated memory is freed by the DB2 agent process. Whether this paging space is released depends on the AIX system's virtual memory management allocation policy. The DB2MEMDISCLAIM registry variable controls whether DB2 agents can explicitly request that AIX de-allocate the reserved paging space when the memory is freed.

The DB2MEMDISCLAIM registry variable, when set to YES, can result in smaller paging space requirements and possibly less disk activity from paging. On a DB2 server where paging space is plentiful and there is enough real memory so that paging never occurs, setting the DB2MEMDISCLAIM registry variable to NO can provide a minor performance improvement.

The DB2MEMDISCLAIM registry variable should be used in conjunction with the DB2MEMMAXFREE registry variable.

Platforms: AIX

Default: Yes

Values: Yes, No

DB2MEMMAXFREE

Background

This registry variable specifies the maximum number of bytes of unused private memory that is retained by DB2 agent processes before the unused paging space is returned to the operating system. The DB2MEMMAXFREE registry variable should be used in conjunction with the DB2MEMDISCLAIM registry variable.

Platforms: AIX

Default: 8388608

Values: Any positive integer value

DB2_MMAP_READ

Background

DB2_MMAP_READ is used in conjunction with DB2_MMAP_WRITE to allow DB2 to use memory-mapped I/O, which can be more efficient. In most environments, memory-mapped I/O should be used to avoid operating system locks when multiple processes are reading from and writing to different sections of the same file. However, when memory-mapped I/O is enabled, DB2 cannot read from JFS file system cache.

Platforms: AIX

Default: On

Values: Off, On

DB2_MMAP_WRITE

Background

This registry variable is used in conjunction with DB2_MMAP_READ, above, to allow DB2 to use memory-mapped I/O, which can be more efficient. In most environments, memory-mapped I/O should be used to avoid operating system locks when multiple processes are reading from and writing to different sections of the same file. However, when memory-mapped I/O is enabled, DB2 cannot read from JFS file system cache.

Platforms: AIX

Default: On

Values: Off, On

OTHER IMPORTANT CONFIGURATION PARAMETERS

CPUSPEED

The CPUSPEED is used by the optimizer when modeling the SQL statement to help determine the lowest cost access plan. Some operations are very CPU intensive and may not be good choices for slower processors.

When setting up DB2, the CPUSPEED should be set to -1 so that the first time DB2 is started, it will run a program to calculate the CPUSPEED, then update the database manager configuration. Do not set the CPUSPEED to a specific value unless you are modeling what access plan the optimizer would choose on newer/faster CPUs.

DIAGLEVEL/NOTIFYLEVEL

The default diagnostic level is 3, which specifies that all errors and warnings should be written to the db2diag.log file. In most cases, this is sufficient and will not cause any significant performance impact.

Setting the DIAGLEVEL or NOTIFYLEVEL to 4 will also log informational messages that can help debug problems if they occur; however, this can contribute to a significant degradation in system performance.

SUMMARY

As this chapter has explained, the performance of a database and the applications that access it are influenced by many factors, including the database and database manager configuration, as well as DB2 registry variables. This chapter discussed how to configure DB2 for optimal performance, using database and database manager configuration parameters and DB2 registry variables, as well as how to monitor the database to ensure that the configuration parameters are configured correctly.

This chapter also introduced and discussed the performance tuning commandments:

- Understand the Magic Triangle of Performance
- Ensure enough available memory
- Ensure sufficient I/O handling capability
- Use proper indexes
- Do not hold locks longer than absolutely necessary
- Use efficient SQL
- Use parallelism only when workload requires it
- Ensure that the catalog statistics are current

Database Communications

T his chapter discusses the following concepts related to communications between DB2 clients and servers, as well as between database partitions. These topics include:

1. Ability to configure a partitioned database on multiple servers
2. Ability to configure connections to hosts systems
3. Ability to troubleshoot connection problems

DB2 Enterprise Server Edition is a multi-user version of DB2 designed for use in partitioned or non-partitioned database environments. Partitioned database systems can manage high volumes of data and provide benefits such as increased performance, high availability, and failover support.

DATABASE PARTITION CONFIGURATION FILE (db2nodes.cfg)

The database partition configuration file contains configuration information that tells DB2 which database partition on which server participates in an instance. There is a db2nodes.cfg file for each instance in a partitioned database environment.

- On Linux and UNIX: $HOME/sqlllib/db2nodes.cfg
- On Windows: <install_path>\sqllib\db2\db2nodes.cfg

The db2nodes.cfg file must contain one entry for each database partition on a particular server that will participate in the instance. When you create an instance, the db2nodes.cfg file is automatically created, and an entry for the instance-owning database partition is added.

On Linux and UNIX, the database partition configuration file (db2nodes.cfg) uses the following format:

dbpartitionnum	hostname	port_number	netname
0	host1	0	net1
1	host1	1	net1
2	host2	0	net2

where:

dbpartitionnum is the number DB2 uses to identify a database partition. Database partition numbers must be:

- Unique
- In ascending order (gaps can exist in the sequence)
- In the range between 0 and 999

hostname is the network interface DB2 uses to communicate between database partitions.

- It is defined in the /etc/hosts file

port_number is the logical port DB2 uses to distinguish between multiple database partitions on a server. The logical port field must satisfy the following:

- Unique per entry per server
- If not specified, the default is 0
- If using multiple database partitions on a single server, the logical port number must start at 0 and continue with an increment of one, i.e., next port would be 1, 2, 3, and so on
- A range of ports must be defined in the /etc/services
- Reserves one port for each database partition

netname is the switch network interface DB2 uses to improve performance, specific on RS/6000 SP, using the switch technology (optional).

- If not specified, the default is host name

On Windows, the database partition configuration file (db2nodes.cfg) uses the following format:

dbpartitionnum	hostname	machinename	port_number	netname
0	host1	machine1	0	net1
1	host1	machine1	1	net1
2	host2	machine2	0	net2

where:

dbpartitionnum is the number DB2 uses to identify a database partition. Database partition number must be:

- Unique
- In ascending order (gaps can exist in the sequence)
- In the range between 0 and 999

hostname is the TCP/IP host name.

- It is defined in the c:\winnt\system32\drivers\etc\hosts

machinename is the workstation name if the database partition is created on a remote machine.

port_number is the logical port DB2 uses to distinguish between multiple database partitions on a server. The logical port field must satisfy the following:

- Unique per entry per server
- If not specified, the default is 0
- If using multiple database partition on a single server, the logical port number must start at 0 and continue with an increment of one, i.e., next port would be 1, 2, 3, and so on
- A range of ports must be defined in c:\winnt\system32\drivers\etc\services
- Reserves one port for each database partition

netname is the network name or IP address (optional).

Windows Considerations

For DB2 on Windows, the database partition configuration file is created for you when you create an instance.

- Use the *db2nlist* command to list all database partitions in a database partition server.
- Use the *db2ncrt* command to add a database partition server to an instance.
- Use the *db2ndrop* command to drop a database partition server to an instance.
- Use the *db2nchg* command to modify a database partition server configuration, including moving the database partition server from one machine to another, changing the TCP/IP host name, or selecting a different logical port or network name.
- *Do not attempt to create or modify the database partition configuration file manually.*

DEFAULT PORT RANGE

To enable Fast Communications Manager (FCM), a port or port range must be reserved in the services file on each server in the partitioned database system. At a minimum, the services file must contain one entry for each database partition within a particular server. The services file is located as follows:

- On Linux and UNIX: /etc/services
- On Windows: c:\winnt\system32\drivers\etc\services

You can define DB2 port entries using one of the following formats; however, format #2 is recommended:

Format #1: Define a group of port names with a port range:

```
port_name                          port_number
---------                          -----------
DB2_v8inst                         60000/tcp
DB2_v8inst_END                     60003/tcp
```

Format #2: Define a specific port name and port range to a database partition:

```
port_name                          port_number
---------                          -----------
DB2_v8inst                         60000/tcp
DB2_v8inst_1                       60001/tcp
DB2_v8inst_2                       60002/tcp
DB2_v8inst_END                     60003/tcp
```

where:

port_name is the name of the partitioned instance. For the first port entry, the port name must be the name of the instance (v8inst), preceded by DB2_. In this example, the first port name is DB2_v8inst. For the second port entry or subsequence port entry, the port name must be the name of the instance, preceded by DB2_ and suffixed by _n, where *n* is incremented by 1. In this example, the second port name is DB2_v8inst_1, and the third port name is DB2_v8inst_2. For the last port entry, the port name must be the name of the instance, preceded by DB2_ and suffixed by _END. In this example, the last port entry is DB2_v8inst_END.

port_number is the port number that you reserve for database partition server communications. For best practices, reserve one port number for each database partition per server (host name).

- Same port must be reserved on all servers
- Must be followed by /tcp

> **N O T E** To avoid conflict with other applications, it is recommended to use high values for DB2 port numbers and reserve a few extra ports for future growth.

Sample db2nodes.cfg and /etc/services Configuration

Let's look at some following db2nodes.cfg files, using the rules described above.

Scenario 1

Two servers, one database partition per server, two ports have been reserved:

```
cat db2nodes.cfg
0                        server1                   0
1                        server2                   0


cat /etc/services | grep db2inst1
DB2_db2inst1            60000/tcp
DB2_db2inst1_END       60001/tcp
```

Scenario 2

Two servers, two database partitions per server, four ports have been reserved. Because there are multiple database partitions on the same server, the first port number must start at 0 and continue by 1 for each server:

```
cat db2nodes.cfg
0                        server1                   0
1                        server1                   1
2                        server2                   0
3                        server2                   1


cat /etc/services | grep db2inst1
DB2_db2inst1            60000/tcp
DB2_db2inst1_1         60001/tcp
DB2_db2inst1_2         60002/tcp
DB2_db2inst1_END       60003/tcp
```

Scenario 3

Three servers, two database partitions on server1, two database partitions on server2, and one database partition on server3, five ports have been reserved:

```
cat db2nodes.cfg
0                        server1                   0
1                        server1                   1
2                        server2                   0
3                        server2                   1
4                        server3                   0
```

```
cat /etc/services | grep db2inst1
DB2_db2inst1           60000/tcp
DB2_db2inst1_1         60001/tcp
DB2_db2inst1_2         60002/tcp
DB2_db2inst1_3         60003/tcp
DB2_db2inst1_END       60004/tcp
```

Scenario 4

Single Windows server name IBM-N2VQMD9FCEA, four database partitions, four ports have been reserved.

```
cat c:\sqllib\db2\db2nodes.cfg
0               IBM-N2VQMD9FCEA   IBM-N2VQMD9FCEA   0
1               IBM-N2VQMD9FCEA   IBM-N2VQMD9FCEA   1
2               IBM-N2VQMD9FCEA   IBM-N2VQMD9FCEA   2
3               IBM-N2VQMD9FCEA   IBM-N2VQMD9FCEA   3


more c:\winnt\system32\drivers\etc\services\db2nodes.cfg | grep -i db2
DB2_DB2         60000/tcp
DB2_DB2_1       60001/tcp
DB2_DB2_2       60002/tcp
DB2_DB2_END     60003/tcp
```

Scenario 5

Two Windows servers, four database partitions on server IBM-N2VQMD9FCEA and two database partitions on server IBM-Y2KQMD9FCEB, six ports have been reserved.

```
cat c:\sqllib\db2\db2nodes.cfg
0               IBM-N2VQMD9FCEA   IBM-N2VQMD9FCEA   0
1               IBM-N2VQMD9FCEA   IBM-N2VQMD9FCEA   1
2               IBM-N2VQMD9FCEA   IBM-N2VQMD9FCEA   2
3               IBM-N2VQMD9FCEA   IBM-N2VQMD9FCEA   3
4               IBM-Y2KQMD9FCEB   IBM-Y2KQMD9FCEB   0
5               IBM-Y2KQMD9FCEB   IBM-Y2KQMD9FCEB   1


more c:\winnt\system32\drivers\etc\services\db2nodes.cfg | grep -i db2
DB2_DB2         60000/tcp
DB2_DB2_1       60001/tcp
DB2_DB2_2       60002/tcp
DB2_DB2_3       60003/tcp
DB2_DB2_4       60004/tcp
DB2_DB2_END     60005/tcp
```

NON-PARTITIONED DATABASE ENVIRONMENT

When installing DB2 ESE in a non-partitioned database environment you need to make the following preparation.

Preparing the Environment for Installation

Before performing the DB2 installation, you need to verify that the server:

- meets the necessary installation requirements (i.e., software level, etc.)
- has the correct operating system version and fix level
- has enough memory to run DB2
- has enough disk space for DB2 product installation
- has the necessary user accounts for installation and setup

For UNIX and Linux:

- You must update kernel parameters to the recommended values for HP-UX, Linux, and Solaris.
  - Use *db2osconf* for Solaris.
- A system restart is required.
- For Solaris, set the following network parameters:
  - Set the TCP network parameters:

```
ndd -set /dev/tcp tcp_xmit_hiwat 65536
ndd -set /dev/tcp tcp_recv_hiwat 65536
```

- *tcp_xmit_hiwat* is the send buffer window size, in bytes. The default value for *tcp_xmit_hiwat* is 16,384 bytes.
- *tcp_recv_hiwat* is the receive window size, in bytes. The default value for *tcp_recv_hiwat* is 24,576 bytes.
- *tcp_max_buf* is the maximum buffer size, in bytes. It controls how large the send and receive buffers are set to by an application using setsockopt(3SOCKET). The default value for tcp_max_buf is 1,048,576 bytes. If TCP connections are being made in a high-speed network environment, increase the value to match the network link speed.
  - Set the UDP network parameters:

```
ndd -set /dev/udp udp_xmit_hiwat 65536
ndd -set /dev/udp udp_recv_hiwat 65536
```

- *udp_xmit_hiwat* is the maximum UDP socket datagram size, in bytes. The default value for udp_xmit_hiwat is 8,192 bytes.
- *udp_recv_hiwat* is the maximum UDP socket receive buffer size, in bytes. The default value for udp_recv_hiwat is 8,192 bytes.

- *udp_max_buf* is the maximum buffer size, in bytes. It controls how large the send and receive buffers, in bytes, are set to by an application using UDP or setsockopt(3SOCKET). The default value for udp_max_buf is 262,144 bytes. Do not change the value. If this parameter is set to a very large value, UDP socket applications can consume too much memory.
   o To list the current network settings:

```
no -get /dev/tcp <network_parm>
no -get /dev/udp <network_parm>
```

- For AIX, set the following network parameters:
   o Set the maximum number of processes to a higher value. The default value for maxuproc is 500.

```
chdev -l sys0 -a maxuproc='4096'
```

   o List the current TCP/IP network setting:

```
no -a | pg
```

   o Set the TCP/IP network parameters:

```
no -o thewall=1048576
no -o rfc1323=1
no -o tcp_sendspace=655360
no -o tcp_recvspace=655360
no -o udp_sendspace=65536
no -o udp_recvspace=655360
no -o sb_max=1310720
```

- *thewall* controls the maximum amount of RAM, in KB, that the mbuf management facility can allocate. The default value for thewall is 131,024.
- *rfc1323*—if the value of this variable is nonzero, it allows the TCP window size to be the maximum of 32 bits instead of 16 bits. What this means is that you can set tcp_recvspace and tcp_sendspace to be greater than 64 KB. The default value for rfc1323 is 0.
- *tcp_sendspace* sets the default socket send buffer. It keeps an application from overflowing the socket send buffer and limits the number of mbufs by an application. The default value for tcp_sendspace is 16,384.
- *tcp_recvspace* is used as the default socket receive buffer size when an application opens a TCP socket. The default value for tcp_recvspace is 16,384.
- *udp_sendspace* sets the limit for the amount of memory that can be used by a single UDP socket for buffering outgoing data. If a UDP application fills this buffer space, it must sleep until some of the data has passed on to the next layer of the protocol stack. The default value for udp_sendspace is 9,216.

- *udp_recvspace* sets the size limit of the receive space buffer for any single UDP socket. The default value for udp_recvspace is 41,920.
- *sb_max* controls the upper limit for any buffer. The default value for sb_max is 1,048,576.
- Create a DB2 home file system and other necessary file systems and/or raw devices to store database file structure, log files, backup images, table space containers, etc.

> **N O T E** For recommended kernel parameters, refer to the DB2 ESE Quick Beginnings Guide.

INSTALLING THE DB2 SERVER

After preparing the environment, you will install the DB2 product, using the DB2 Setup Wizard. The installation includes the following:

- Install the DB2 product.
- Set up DB2 Administration Server.
- Set up Administration contact and health monitor notification.
- Set up DB2 instance and configuration.
  - The DB2COMM registry variable determines which protocols will be enabled when the database manager is started. You can use the *db2set –all* command to verify or to set the DB2COMM registry to TCPIP protocol, using:

```
db2set DB2COMM=TCPIP
```

  - You can use the db2 get dbm cfg command to verify the service name or to update SVCENAME in the database manager configuration file using:

```
db2 update dbm cfg using SVCENAME db2c_db2inst1
```

- You can use the *db2licm –l* command to verify the existing license product

Verifying the Installation

After you have successfully installed DB2, it is recommended that you verify the installation. To verify the installation, you will:

- Log on to the DB2 server.
- Start the database manager by entering the *db2start* command.
- Verify the correct service name (TCP/IP) that the database manager listens to:

```
db2 get dbm cfg | grep -i svcename
```

- Start the DB2 Administration Server by entering the *db2admin start* command.

- Verify listener port:

```
netstat -a | grep db2inst
```

- Create a sample database using *db2sampl*.
- Once the sample database has been created successfully, you will run SQL commands to retrieve sample data:

```
db2 connect to sample
db2 "select * from staff"
db2 terminate
```

PARTITIONED DATABASE ENVIRONMENT

Let's take a look at the DB2 ESE configuration with four database partitions, four servers, and one database partition per server. The following setup instructions are based on this configuration but can easily be adjusted for partitioned configurations with a fewer or greater number of servers and database partitions. For example, server_1 is the primary or instance-owning database partition server; server_2, server_3, and server_4 are the participating database partition servers.

When you install DB2 ESE with multiple-partition database environment, you need to follow similar considerations as described in the single-partition database environment.

Preparing the Environment for Installation

Before performing the DB2 installation, you need to verify that each server:

- meets the necessary installation requirements
- has the correct operating system version and fix level
- has enough memory to run DB2
- has enough disk space for DB2 product installation
- belongs to the same network
- has the necessary user accounts for installation and setup
- can communicate with each other via TCP/IP
- has consistent time and date settings

For UNIX:

- You must update kernel parameters to the recommended values for HP-UX, Linux, and Solaris.
  - Use *db2osconf* for Solaris.
- A system restart is required.
- For Solaris, set the following network parameters:
  - Set the TCP network parameters:

```
ndd -set /dev/tcp tcp_xmit_hiwat 65536
ndd -set /dev/tcp tcp_recv_hiwat 65536
```

      ○ Set the UDP network parameters:

```
ndd -set /dev/udp udp_xmit_hiwat 65536
ndd -set /dev/udp udp_recv_hiwat 65536
```

      ○ To list the current network settings:

```
no -get /dev/tcp <network_parm>
no -get /dev/udp <network_parm>
```

- For AIX, set the following network parameters:
  ○ Set the maximum number of processes to a higher value. The default value for maxuproc is 500.

```
chdev -l sys0 -a maxuproc='4096'
```

      ○ To list the current TCP/IP network setting:

```
no -a | pg
```

      ○ To set the TCP/IP network parameters:

```
no -o thewall=1048576
no -o rfc1323=1
no -o tcp_sendspace=655360
no -o tcp_recvspace=655360
no -o udp_sendspace=65536
no -o udp_recvspace=655360
no -o sb_max=1310720
```

- Create a DB2 home file system on the primary server (server_1) and share this home directory to the participating servers (server_2, server_3, and server_4). This will be the instance home directory. You also need to create necessary file systems and/or raw devices to store database file structure, log files, backup images, table space containers, etc.

> **N O T E** For additional kernel parameters, refer to the DB2 ESE Quick Beginnings Guide.

Installing the DB2 Server

After preparing the environment, you will install the DB2 product using the DB2 Setup Wizard. The installation includes the following:

- It is recommended to install an instance-owning database partition server for the primary server (server_1) first:

```
./db2setup
```

- Set up DB2 Administration Server (for the primary server, then the remaining participating servers).
  - Create DAS instance:

```
./dasicrt db2as
```

> **NOTE**   The db2icrt and dasicrt commands must be run from the
> DB2 installation directory as root:
>
> On AIX: /usr/opt/db2_08_01/instance
> On HP-UX, Linux, Solaris: /opt/IBM/db2/V8.1/instance
> On Windows: \Program Files\IBM\SQLLIB\bin

  - Start Administration Server:

```
db2admin start
```

- It is recommended in setup to create a local administration contact list on the instance-
  owning database partition. When the DB2 Administration Server is installed and configured on the other participating database partition servers, it will be configured to use
  the contact list on the instance-owning database partition server.

> **NOTE**   After installation, the instance-owning database partition
> on the server_1, the db2nodes.cfg file was updated as follows:
>
> 0 server_1 0

- Set up DB2 instance and configuration.
  - Create DB2 instance:

```
./db2icrt -a SERVER -u db2fenc1 db2inst1
```

  - Modify *.profile* to include db2profile as needed:

```
# The following three lines have been added by UDB DB2.
if [ -f $HOME/db2inst1/sqllib/db2profile ]; then
. $HOME/db2inst1/sqllib/db2profile
fi
```

  - The DB2COMM registry variable determines which protocols will be enabled when
    the database manager is started. You can use the *db2set –all* command to verify or to
    set the DB2COMM registry to TCPIP protocol using:

```
db2set DB2COMM=TCPIP
```

○ You can use the db2 get dbm cfg command to verify the service name or to update SVCENAME in the database manager configuration file using:

```
db2 update dbm cfg using SVCENAME db2c_db2inst1
```

○ For communication between the DB2 server and remote clients, you need to add two entries in the /etc/services file on all servers:

```
db2c_db2inst1              50000/tcp               # remote client's port
```

○ To enable the Control Center to manage partitioned databases, you must have a Control Center listener daemon running on each server. This daemon is called *dd2cclst*, and it is used by all instances that are created on a given server. On all servers, you must reserve a port called *db2ccmsrv* in the /etc/services for use by the db2cclst daemon:

```
db2ccmsrv                 50100/tcp               # Control Center Listener
```

- You can use the *db2licm –l* command to verify the existing license product.
- Verify the port range that DB2 has reserved for database partitions communication. Before you create a DB2 instance, you must decide (as a minimum) how many database partitions will be defined per server.
- Verify that the port range is available on each participating database partition server.
- During the installation process, you specify a location and name for two response files. The first response file is for installing a replica of the primary server. The second response file is for installing database partition servers on participating computers (i.e., /dbhome/db2inst1/AddPartitionResponse.file).
- For each participating database partition server, server_2, server_3, and server_4, you will install a database partition server using the response file created from the previous step. This ensures that the same components are installed and configured the same way:

```
db2setup -r /dbhome/db2inst1/AddPartitionResponse.file
```

> **N O T E**   You must log on to each participating server and perform a response file installation.

- Verify and update the database partition configuration file (db2nodes.cfg) as needed. Based on the current configuration, with four servers and a database partition per server, update db2nodes.cfg to appear similar to the following:

```
0                         server_1                0
1                         server_2                0
2                         server_3                0
3                         server_4                0
```

- Verify and enable communication between database partitions as needed. Communication between database partitions is handled by the FCM. To enable FCM, a port or port range must be reserved in the /etc/systems file on each computer in your partitioned database system. This task must perform on the participating server only.
- Verify and enable the execution of remote commands. In a partitioned database environment, each database partition must have the authority to perform remote commands on all other database partition servers participating in an instance. This can be done by updating the .rhosts file in the home directory for the instance.

   ○ Add entries to the /dbhome/db2inst1/.rhosts file for each server, including the primary server. The .rhosts file has the following format:

```
hostname                                instance_owner_ID
--------                                -----------------
server_1.dntteam.com                    db2inst1
server_2.dntteam.com                    db2inst1
server_3.dntteam.com                    db2inst1
server_4.dntteam.com                    db2inst1
```

> **NOTE** This is a preferred approach for the .rhosts file.

   - Instead of specifying each host name individually, you may specify the following entry in the .rhosts file, but this may pose a security risk and should be done only in a test environment. The following entry in the .rhosts allows this "trusted" user db2inst1 to execute remote commands from any hosts that are defined in the /etc/hosts file:

```
+  db2inst1
```

> **NOTE** For information on errors encountered during installation, on Windows, see the db2.log file. This db2.log file stores general information and error messages resulting from the install and uninstall activities. On Linux and UNIX, see the /tmp/db2setup.log.

POST-INSTALLATION SETUP

Once DB2 has been successfully installed on all servers, there are a number of post-installation setup tasks. To set up/verify DB2 after installation:

- Review/update the database partition configuration file (db2nodes.cfg). On Windows, do not attempt to create or modify the database partition configuration file manually.

```
0                        server_1                        0
1                        server_2                        0
2                        server_3                        0
3                        server_4                        0
```

- Review/enable communications between the database partitions. This requires that you update the /etc/services file on each server:

```
db2c_db2inst1      50000/tcp          # remote client port
db2ccmsrv          50100/tcp          # used by Control Center Listener
DB2_db2inst1       60000/tcp          # instance owning port
DB2_db2inst1_1     60001/tcp          # database partition port
DB2_db2inst1_2     60002/tcp          # database partition port
DB2_db2inst1_END   60003/tcp          # database partition port
```

- Review/enable the execution of remote commands. This allows each database partition to perform remote commands on the other database partitions. This task must be performed on each server. View the $HOME/.rhosts file:

```
+ db2inst1
```

Verifying the Installation

After you have successfully installed DB2 on all servers, it is recommended that you verify the installation. To verify the installation, you will:

- Log on to the DB2 server.
- Start the database manager by entering the *db2start* command.
- Verify the correct service name (TCP/IP) that the database manager listens to:

```
db2 get dbm cfg | grep -i svcename
```

- Start the DB2 Administration Server by entering the *db2admin start* command.
- Verify listener port:

```
netstat -a | grep db2inst
```

- Create a sample database using *db2sampl*.

> **N O T E**   The sample database will be created with four database
> partitions, based on the db2nodes.cfg, defined in the previous step.

- Once the sample database has been created successfully, you will run SQL commands to retrieve sample data:

```
db2 connect to sample
db2 "select * from staff"

1
-----------
        35

db2 terminate
```

- Verify that data has been evenly distributed across database partitions. The output will list the database partitions used by the employee table. The specific output will depend on the number of partitions in the database and the number of partitions in the partition groups that is used by the table space where the employee table was created.

```
db2 "select distinct dbpartitionnum(id) from staff"

1
-----------
          0
          1
          2
          3
```

N O T E There are four database partitions (0, 1, 2, and 3).

The following output displays the row count for each database partition:

```
db2 "select count(*) from staff where dbpartitionnum(id)=0"

1
-----------
          8

db2 "select count(*) from staff where dbpartitionnum(id)=1"

1
-----------
         11

db2 "select count(*) from staff where dbpartitionnum(id)=2"

1
-----------
          6

db2 "select count(*) from staff where dbpartitionnum(id)=3"

1
-----------
         10

db2 terminate
```

INSTALLING AND CONFIGURING DB2 CLIENT TO DB2 SERVER COMMUNICATIONS

There are three types of DB2 clients: run time client, administration client, and application development client. To install and configure DB2 client to DB2 server connections, you must do the following:

- The client machine must meet the necessary installation requirements (operating system, CPU, memory, and disk space for DB2 product installation).
- The client machine has the necessary user accounts for installation and setup.
- The client machine can communicate to the DB2 server.

Then you're ready to install the DB2 product, using the DB2 Setup Wizard (or execute the *db2setup* command at the UNIX command prompt), assuming that the server has been set up, the instance has been started, and the sample database has been created.

After DB2 client successfully installed, you should configure it to access the remote DB2 server using the Configuration Assistant or using the command line processor:

- Log on to the system with a valid DB2 user ID.
- Start the Configuration Assistant using the *db2ca* command.
- Search for servers.
- Test the connection using the Configuration Assistant.

or

- Catalog the TCP/IP node on the DB2 client:

```
db2 catalog tcpip node node_name remote hostname
   server service_name

db2 catalog tcpip node nphantom remote 192.168.1.51
   server 50000
```

- Catalog the database on the DB2 client:

```
db2 catalog database database_name as database_alias
   at node node_name authentication auth_value

db2 catalog database sample as rsample
   at node nphantom authentication server
```

- Test the client-server connection:

```
db2 connect to rsample user v8inst
db2 "select tabname from syscat.tables"
db2 terminate
```

INSTALLING AND CONFIGURING DB2 CLIENT TO DB2 HOST COMMUNICATIONS

In this section, we describe the possible alternatives and the steps during the implementation of the connectivity configuration and the OS/390 functions. The environment consists of two workstations connected in a LAN remotely connected to the OS/390. One of the workstations has been also used as a gateway.

Preparing the DB2 for OS/390 for DB2 Connect

To prepare DB2 UDB for OS/390 to receive connection requests from DB2 Connect, you must complete the following steps at the OS/390 host:

- Prepare OS/390 for DB2 Connect.
  This step consists of making sure that DB2 is at the right maintenance level and that TCP/IP is active on the host system.

  ○ Verify the DB2 for OS/390 maintenance (i.e., PTFs).
  ○ Verify the TCP/IP on OS/390 (i.e., started tasks TCPIPMVS and TCIPOE).

- Configure TCP/IP for DB2 UDB for OS/390.
  This step consists of configuring TCP/IP communications between your DB2 Connect workstation and the DRDA Application Servers running DB2 for OS/390.

  ○ Prepare the LE/370 run-time library in the DDF startup JCL procedure.
  ○ Enable DDF for MVS OpenEdition in RACF.
  ○ Customize the TCP/IP data sets or files.

- Configure DB2 UDB for OS/390.
  Before you can use DB2 Connect, your DB2 for OS/390 Administrator must configure DB2 for OS/390 to permit connections from the DB2 Connect workstation. This step highlights the minimum updates required to permit the DB2 Connect application requester to make a connection to DB2 for OS/390.

  ○ Set up DDF as an application server (i.e., update table SYSIBM.IPNAMES).
  ○ Define a VTAM LU for DB2 UDB for OS/390.
  ○ Update the BSDS data set.
  ○ Change DSNZPARM parameters for activating DDF. The DDF parameter must be set to something other than NO to have DDF work at all. The EXTSEC parameter, which defaults to NO, should be set to YES, because it will provide clients the actual reason why their connection failed due to a security violation.
  ○ Start DDF.

INSTALLING DB2 CONNECT PERSONAL EDITION

To install and configure DB2 Connect Personal Edition to DB2 for OS/390 communications, you must do the following:

- The client machine must meet the necessary installation requirements (operating system, CPU, memory, and disk space for DB2 product installation).
- The client machine must have the necessary user accounts for installation and setup.
- The client machine must be able to communicate to the OS/390.

Then you're ready to install the DB2 product, using the DB2 Setup Wizard.

CONFIGURING DB2 CLIENTS IN A TWO-TIER ENVIRONMENT

Before you start configuring your workstation, identify the TCP/IP name or the IP address from the OS/390 host, its port, and the DB2 subsystem you want to connect to.

After the DB2 client successfully installed, you should configure it to access the remote DB2 server, using the Configuration Assistant or the command line processor:

- Log on to the system with a valid DB2 user ID.
- Start the Configuration Assistant using the *db2ca* command.
- Search for servers.
- Test the connection using Configuration Assistant.

or

- Catalog the TCP/IP node on the DB2 client:

```
db2 catalog tcpip node node_name remote hostname
  server service_name

db2 catalog tcpip node nhost390 remote 210.100.100.210
  server 1300
```

- Catalog the database on the DB2 client:

```
db2 catalog database database_name as database_alias
  at node node_name authentication auth_value

db2 catalog database db2t as db2t
  at node nhost130 authentication dcs
```

- Catalog the DCS database:

```
db2 catalog DCS database dcs_name as dcs_aliast

db2 catalog DCS database db2t as db2t
```

- Test the client-server connection:

```
db2 connect to db2t user os390id
db2 "select * from sysibm.sysdummy1"
db2 terminate
```

CONFIGURING DB2 CLIENTS IN A THREE-TIER ENVIRONMENT

In this environment, the clients connect to a gateway with DB2 Connect Enterprise Edition installed. The gateway serves as a DRDA application requester to the host. In our example, we used the workstation of CLIENT1, with only the client application enabler installed, to connect to the host via the DB2 connect gateway of SERVER1.

Configure the Host

Refer to the Configure TCP/IP for DB2 UDB for OS/390 from the above section.

Configure DB2 Connect Gateway to Accept Incoming Clients

To accept incoming clients, the necessary protocols have to be started first. Normally, you configure these protocols with the installation of DB2 Connect. The most common protocol used is TCP/IP, so we document only the usage of TCP/IP between the client and the server. Protocols are started during the start of DB2. The following are *automatically* configured (if, during installation of DB2 Connect, you configured TCP/IP) for you to accept incoming clients.

You can always configure TCP/IP *after installation* of DB2 Connect by doing the following:

- Update the DB2COMM registry value to include TCP/IP:

```
db2set DB2COMM=TCPIP
```

   ○ You can check your DB2COMM value with:

```
db2set -all
```

- Update the services file on c:\winnt\system32\drivers\etc. The following port should be there. You can choose any available port number and name. The default port is 50000.

```
db2cDB2 50000/tcp          #connection port for the DB2 instance DB2
```

- Update the service name (SVCENAME) parameter in the database manager configuration file:

```
db2 update dbm cfg using svcename db2cDB2
```

> **N O T E**   The service name is case-sensitive.

- Stop and restart the database instance.

Configure the DB2 Client

From the DB2 client, you can use the Client Configuration Assistant or the command line processor to configure your access to the DB2 host subsystem:

- Log on to the system with a valid DB2 user ID.
- Start the Configuration Assistant using the db2ca command.
- Search for servers.
- Test the connection using Configuration Assistant.

or

- Catalog the TCP/IP node on the DB2 client:

```
db2 catalog tcpip node node_name remote hostname
  server service_name

db2 catalog tcpip node nserver1 remote 192.168.1.51
  server 50000
```

- Catalog the database on the DB2 client:

```
db2 catalog database database_name as database_alias
  at node node_name

db2 catalog database db2t as db2t at node nserver1
```

- Test the client-server connection:

```
db2 connect to db2t user os390id
db2 "select * from sysibm.sysdummy1"
db2 terminate
```

FCM COMMUNICATION BUFFERS CONSIDERATIONS

The FCM memory requirements are allocated either from the Database Manager Shared Memory (DMSM) or from both the DMSM and the FCM Buffer Shared Memory, depending on whether the partitioned database system uses multiple database partitions on the same server.

- If you have a partitioned database system that does not have multiple database partitions on the same server, then for each database partition or each server, the FCM memory requirements are allocated from the DMSM:

```
DMSM = (FCM Connection Retries +
        FCM Message Anchors +
        FCM Request Blocks +
        FCM Buffers)
```

- If you have a partitioned database system that does have multiple database partitions on the same server, then for each database partition, the FCM memory requirements are allocated from the DMSM:

```
DMSM = (FCM Connection Retries +
        FCM Message Anchors +
        FCM Request Blocks)
```

For each server or for all database partitions on the same server, one pool of FCM buffers is allocated from the FCM Buffer Shared Memory.

> **N O T E**   By default, the FCM Request Blocks is set to 2048; the FCM Connection Retries and the FCM Message Anchors are 0.75 × FCM Request Blocks.

For example, using the default values, the FCM memory required per database partition is:

```
 (2048 + 1536 + 1536) * 4096 = 5120 * 4096 = 20 MB
```

The DB2_FORCE_FCM_BP registry variable can be used to allow DB2 to communicate between database partitions on the same server entirely through shared memory, instead of using the high-speed interconnect. If the DB2_FORCE_FCM_BP registry variable is set to YES, the FCM communication buffers are created in a separate memory segment so that communication between the FCM daemons for the different database partitions on the same server will occur through shared memory. Otherwise, FCM daemons on the same server must communicate through UNIX sockets using the high-speed interconnect, even if they are on the same server. Communicating through shared memory is faster, but if DB2 is installed in 32-bit mode, there will be less shared memory available for other uses, particularly for database buffer pools.

To analyze the number of FCM buffers (FCM_NUM_BUFFERS), it is important to look at the current allocation of the number of FCM buffers, as well as the maximum number of FCM buffers that have been allocated, i.e., the low water mark for the free FCM buffers. These numbers can then be compared with the configured number of FCM buffers from the database manager configuration. If the percentage of free FCM buffers drops below 10%, there is a potential that DB2 may run out of available buffers, and this would indicate that the number of FCM buffers should be increased.

Example of Overallocated FCM Communication Buffers

The system is running four database partitions on a single DB2 server with a total of 2 GB of available memory. The DBA decided to add another four database partitions to this server (a total of eight database partitions), and db2 failed to start. Assume that the FCM_NUM_BUFFERS was set to 30,000, due to the high number of concurrent applications.

Observation

For this particular DB2 server, the FCM memory is taken up by FCM communication buffers on a server that has a 256-MB shared segment on AIX and a registry variable DB2_FORCE_FCM_BP set to YES, which means the FCM communication buffer is shared among the database partitions on this server.

When there were only four database partitions, DB2 started successfully. Because the FCM_NUM_BUFFERS was set to 30,000, the FCM memory requirements reserved a total of only $30,000 \times 4$ KB $= 117$ MB on this server.

After the DBA added another four database partitions, DB2 failed to start or would hang. The DBA had to reduce the FCM_NUM_BUFFERS down to 24,000 in order to get all eight database partitions to start.

Resolution

Based on the FCM memory structures, the FCM Connection Entries, FCM Message Anchors, and FCM Request Blocks are allocated on a per-partition basis in the same shared memory segment as the FCM communication buffers.

The total of FCM memory for four database partitions on the same server when the FCM_NUM_BUFFERS is set at 30,000 is: $117 + (20 \times 4) = 197$ MB, and DB2 started successfully.

With the same value for the FCM_NUM_BUFFERS, four additional database partitions were added, requiring the FCM memory to handle a total of eight database partitions on the same server, $117 + (20 \times 8) = 277$ MB, which is more than the shared memory segment (256 MB), resulting in a failure of DB2 to start.

Therefore, when FCM_NUM_BUFFERS was reduced to 24,000, all eight database partitions started successfully. Because the total of the FCM memory for eight database partitions on the same server is less than the shared memory segment (256 MB):

```
(24,000 * 4 KB) + (20 * 8) = 253 MB
```

SUMMARY

As this chapter has explained, for partitioned database systems, the FCM requires substantial memory space, especially if the value of FCM_NUM_BUFFERS is large. For configuring the FCM, start with the default value for the number of FCM buffers (FCM_NUM_BUFFERS) and use the database system monitor to monitor the low water mark for the free buffers, tuning this parameter as needed.

Performance Tuning Examples

T his chapter will present some examples of typical performance tuning problems and the steps taken to resolve the problems. These examples are based on experiences at real customer locations. This chapter will first present the problem, then discuss the steps that were taken to determine the cause of the problem and to develop a solution to the problem.

EXAMPLE 1: CREATE INDEX TAKING TOO LONG

Problem Description

CustomerA was creating indexes for a large table in its database, but the time required to create the index appeared to be excessive. The following is the db2batch output, which shows the time required to create the index:

```
-----------------------------------------------
Statement number: 1

create index x1 on staff (id)

Elapsed Time is:             1068.922    seconds
-----------------------------------------------
```

Problem Analysis and Resolution

Step 1: Examine the Database and Database Manager Configuration Parameters

Database manager configuration   The three parameters in the database manager configuration that typically have a big impact on the create index operation are the SHEAPTHRES,

MAX_QUERYDEGREE, and INTRA_PARALLEL, and these parameters are highlighted in bold below. In this case, intra-partition parallelism was disabled; therefore, the index creation could not take advantage of the multiple CPUs in the server. If intra-partition parallelism is enabled, there will be sort heap used during the index creation in all subagent processes; therefore, the sort heap threshold (SHEAPTHRES) may also need to be increased.

```
Node type = Database Server with local clients

Database manager configuration release level              = 0x0a00

CPU speed (millisec/instruction)            (CPUSPEED) = 4.000000e-05

Max number of concurrently active databases      (NUMDB) = 8
Data Links support                          (DATALINKS) = NO
Federated Database System Support           (FEDERATED) = NO
Transaction processor monitor name        (TP_MON_NAME) =

Default charge-back account            (DFT_ACCOUNT_STR) =

Java Development Kit installation path        (JDK_PATH) = /wsdb/v81/
   bldsupp/AIX/jdk1.3.0

Diagnostic error capture level               (DIAGLEVEL) = 3
Notify Level                               (NOTIFYLEVEL) = 3
Diagnostic data directory path               (DIAGPATH) =

Default database monitor switches
   Buffer pool                        (DFT_MON_BUFPOOL) = OFF
   Lock                                  (DFT_MON_LOCK) = OFF
   Sort                                  (DFT_MON_SORT) = OFF
   Statement                             (DFT_MON_STMT) = OFF
   Table                                (DFT_MON_TABLE) = OFF
   Timestamp                        (DFT_MON_TIMESTAMP) = ON
   Unit of work                          (DFT_MON_UOW) = OFF
Monitor health of instance and databases    (HEALTH_MON) = OFF

SYSADM group name                        (SYSADM_GROUP) = BUILD
SYSCTRL group name                      (SYSCTRL_GROUP) =
SYSMAINT group name                    (SYSMAINT_GROUP) =

Database manager authentication          (AUTHENTICATION) = SERVER
Cataloging allowed without authority    (CATALOG_NOAUTH) = YES
Trust all clients                       (TRUST_ALLCLNTS) = YES
Trusted client authentication           (TRUST_CLNTAUTH) = CLIENT
```

```
Use SNA authentication                    (USE_SNA_AUTH) = NO
Bypass federated authentication            (FED_NOAUTH) = NO


Default database path                       (DFTDBPATH) = /home/dsnow


Database monitor heap size (4KB)           (MON_HEAP_SZ) = 90
Java Virtual Machine heap size (4KB)      (JAVA_HEAP_SZ) = 1024
Audit buffer size (4KB)                    (AUDIT_BUF_SZ) = 0
Size of instance shared memory (4KB)   (INSTANCE_MEMORY) = AUTOMATIC
Backup buffer default size (4KB)            (BACKBUFSZ) = 1024
Restore buffer default size (4KB)           (RESTBUFSZ) = 1024

Sort heap threshold (4KB)                  (SHEAPTHRES) = 20000

Directory cache support                      (DIR_CACHE) = YES

Application support layer heap size (4KB)    (ASLHEAPSZ) = 15
Max requester I/O block size (bytes)         (RQRIOBLK) = 32767
Query heap size (4KB)                    (QUERY_HEAP_SZ) = 1000
DRDA services heap size (4KB)             (DRDA_HEAP_SZ) = 128


Priority of agents                            (AGENTPRI) = SYSTEM
Max number of existing agents                (MAXAGENTS) = 200
Agent pool size                          (NUM_POOLAGENTS) = 100(calculated)
Initial number of agents in pool         (NUM_INITAGENTS) = 0
Max number of coordinating agents       (MAX_COORDAGENTS) = MAXAGENTS
Max no. of concurrent coordinating agents  (MAXCAGENTS) = MAX_COORDAGENTS
Max number of client connections        (MAX_CONNECTIONS) = MAX_COORDAGENTS

Keep fenced process                         (KEEPFENCED) = YES
Number of pooled fenced processes          (FENCED_POOL) = MAX_COORDAGENTS
Initialize fenced process with JVM       (INITFENCED_JVM) = NO
Initial number of fenced processes       (NUM_INITFENCED) = 0


Index re-creation time                        (INDEXREC) = RESTART


Transaction manager database name          (TM_DATABASE) = 1ST_CONN
Transaction resync interval (sec)       (RESYNC_INTERVAL) = 180
```

```
SPM name                          (SPM_NAME) =
SPM log size               (SPM_LOG_FILE_SZ) = 256
SPM resync agent limit       (SPM_MAX_RESYNC) = 20
SPM log path                  (SPM_LOG_PATH) =

TCP/IP Service name               (SVCENAME) =
Discovery mode                    (DISCOVER) = SEARCH
Discovery communication protocols  (DISCOVER_COMM) =
Discover server instance      (DISCOVER_INST) = ENABLE

Maximum query degree of parallelism    (MAX_QUERYDEGREE) = ANY
Enable intra-partition parallelism      (INTRA_PARALLEL) = NO

No. of int. communication buffers(4KB)(FCM_NUM_BUFFERS) = 512
```

Database configuration for database sample   The three parameters in the database manager configuration that typically have a big impact on the create index operation are the LOGBUFSZ, SORTHEAP, and BUFFPAGE, and these parameters are highlighted in bold below.

- The log buffer size (LOGBUFSZ) is important because the create index operation will cause log records to be created. In this case, the log buffer was very small and had to be increased.
- The sort list heap (SORTHEAP) is used to sort the index keys while creating an index. Because the table was large, the sort heap was also increased so that the sorting need not spill to a temp table.
  - On AIX, also verify the ulimit for the instance owner to ensure it is not too small, causing sort overflows. In this case, the operating system was not AIX, so this was not the cause.
- In this case, the default buffer pool size (BUFFPAGE) is 1,000 4-KB pages. To determine the real size of the buffer pool, use the following statement:

```
select * from syscat.bufferpools
```

  - In this case, there was only one buffer pool (IBMDEFAULTBP), and it had a size of 300,000 4-KB pages.
  - This was done on a 32-bit instance of DB2, so the size of the buffer pool could not have been increased much higher without hitting the operating system limitations.

```
Database configuration release level              = 0x0a00
Database release level                            = 0x0a00

Database territory                                = US
Database code page                                = 819
Database code set                                 = ISO8859-1
Database country/region code                      = 1
```

```
Dynamic SQL Query management              (DYN_QUERY_MGMT) = DISABLE

Discovery support for this database        (DISCOVER_DB) = ENABLE

Default query optimization class          (DFT_QUERYOPT) = 5
Degree of parallelism                       (DFT_DEGREE) = 1
Continue upon arithmetic exceptions     (DFT_SQLMATHWARN) = NO
Default refresh age                     (DFT_REFRESH_AGE) = 0
Number of frequent values retained       (NUM_FREQVALUES) = 10
Number of quantiles retained             (NUM_QUANTILES) = 20


Backup pending                                           = NO

Database is consistent                                   = NO
Rollforward pending                                      = NO
Restore pending                                          = NO

Multi-page file allocation enabled                       = NO

Log retain for recovery status                           = NO
User exit for logging status                             = NO

Data Links Token Expiry Interval (sec)       (DL_EXPINT) = 60
Data Links Write Token Init Expiry Intvl(DL_WT_IEXPINT) = 60
Data Links Number of Copies            (DL_NUM_COPIES) = 1
Data Links Time after Drop (days)        (DL_TIME_DROP) = 1
Data Links Token in Uppercase               (DL_UPPER) = NO
Data Links Token Algorithm                  (DL_TOKEN) = MAC0

Database heap (4KB)                            (DBHEAP) = 1200
Size of database shared memory (4KB)  (DATABASE_MEMORY) = AUTOMATIC
Catalog cache size (4KB)           (CATALOGCACHE_SZ) = (MAXAPPLS*4)
Log buffer size (4KB)                       (LOGBUFSZ) = 8
Utilities heap size (4KB)               (UTIL_HEAP_SZ) = 5000
Buffer pool size (pages)                    (BUFFPAGE) = 1000
Extended storage segments size (4KB)     (ESTORE_SEG_SZ) = 16000
Number of extended storage segments    (NUM_ESTORE_SEGS) = 0
Max storage for lock list (4KB)             (LOCKLIST) = 100

Max size of appl. group mem set (4KB)  (APPGROUP_MEM_SZ) = 20000
Percent of mem for appl. group heap   (GROUPHEAP_RATIO) = 70
Max appl. control heap size (4KB)      (APP_CTL_HEAP_SZ) = 128
```

```
Sort heap thres for shared sorts (4KB) (SHEAPTHRES_SHR) = (SHEAPTHRES)
Sort list heap (4KB)                           (SORTHEAP) = 256
SQL statement heap (4KB)                       (STMTHEAP) = 4096
Default application heap (4KB)               (APPLHEAPSZ) = 256
Package cache size (4KB)                      (PCKCACHESZ) = (MAXAPPLS*8)
Statistics heap size (4KB)                 (STAT_HEAP_SZ) = 4384

Interval for checking deadlock (ms)          (DLCHKTIME) = 10000
Percent. of lock lists per application        (MAXLOCKS) = 10
Lock timeout (sec)                          (LOCKTIMEOUT) = -1

Changed pages threshold                 (CHNGPGS_THRESH) = 60
Number of asynchronous page cleaners    (NUM_IOCLEANERS) = 1
Number of I/O servers                    (NUM_IOSERVERS) = 1
Index sort flag                              (INDEXSORT) = YES
Sequential detect flag                       (SEQDETECT) = YES
Default prefetch size (pages)           (DFT_PREFETCH_SZ) = 32

Track modified pages                          (TRACKMOD) = OFF

Default number of containers                            = 1
Default tablespace extentsize (pages)     (DFT_EXTENT_SZ) = 32

Max number of active applications             (MAXAPPLS) = AUTOMATIC
Average number of active applications        (AVG_APPLS) = 1
Max DB files open per application             (MAXFILOP) = 64

Log file size (4KB)                          (LOGFILSIZ) = 1000
Number of primary log files                 (LOGPRIMARY) = 3
Number of secondary log files                (LOGSECOND) = 2
Changed path to log files                   (NEWLOGPATH) =
Path to log files                                        = /home/dsnow/
   dsnow/NODE0000/SQL00001/SQLOGDIR/
Overflow log path                      (OVERFLOWLOGPATH) =
Mirror log path                          (MIRRORLOGPATH) =
First active log file                                    =
Block log on disk full                  (BLK_LOG_DSK_FUL) = NO
Percent of max active log space by transaction(MAX_LOG) = 0
Num. of active log files for 1 active UOW(NUM_LOG_SPAN) = 0

Group commit count                           (MINCOMMIT) = 1
Percent log file reclaimed before soft chckpt (SOFTMAX) = 100
Log retain for recovery enabled              (LOGRETAIN) = OFF
User exit for logging enabled                 (USEREXIT) = OFF
```

```
Auto restart enabled                    (AUTORESTART) = ON
Index re-creation time                    (INDEXREC) = SYSTEM
                                                        (RESTART)
Default number of loadrec sessions  (DFT_LOADREC_SES) = 1
Number of database backups to retain  (NUM_DB_BACKUPS) = 12
Recovery history retention (days)   (REC_HIS_RETENTN) = 366

TSM management class                   (TSM_MGMTCLASS) =
TSM node name                          (TSM_NODENAME) =
TSM owner                                (TSM_OWNER) =
TSM password                          (TSM_PASSWORD) =
```

Step 2: Adjust Relevant Parameters and Determine Values for the Task Being Optimized

The relevant database manager and database configuration parameters were adjusted, based on the analysis of their currently set values, and the appropriate values for the task being organized were determined. The configurations were updated as follows:

```
update dbm cfg using intra_parallel on
update dbm cfg using sheapthres 60000
update db cfg for sample using logbufsz 256
update db cfg for sample using sortheap 1000
```

The instance was stopped and restarted.

Step 3: Rerun the CREATE INDEX Statement

The db2batch output showing the timing of the create index is below. Although the create index time was improved, it was still higher than expected.

```
-----------------------------------------------
Statement number: 1

create index x1 on staff (id)

Elapsed Time is:            897.214   seconds
-----------------------------------------------
```

Step 4: Check the System for I/O Bottlenecks, Excess Paging, or Other Processes/Applications Using Excessive System Resources

This required operating system tools such as vmstat, iostat, and/or top to capture the memory, I/O, and process level information.

N O T E It is important to capture the snapshots from these tools over a period of time, not taking just one snapshot, especially because the first line of the output of the vmstat and iostat tools contains average information since the server was started and is not really useful in analyzing a problem.

While the create index statement is running, capture vmstat output, as follows:

```
vmstat 5 > vmstat.out
```

This will capture a vmstat snapshot every 5 seconds and write the output to the file vmstat.out. This command will run until a Ctrl-C is issued on the terminal where the command was run. After this, examine the vmstat.out file.

Below is the vmstat.out file that was captured while the create index statement was running:

kthr		memory		page						faults			cpu			
r	b	avm	fre	re	pi	po	fr	sr	cy	in	sy	cs	us	sy	id	wa
1	1	16243	29168	0	0	0	0	0	0	305	2890	870	14	6	80	0
2	1	16243	29165	0	0	0	0	0	0	212	2010	550	25	7	68	0
0	1	16243	29165	0	0	0	0	0	0	217	1175	584	24	2	74	0
0	1	16243	29165	0	0	0	0	0	0	224	1970	563	25	6	63	2
2	1	16243	29165	0	0	0	0	0	0	217	1171	583	23	2	75	0
2	1	16243	29165	0	0	0	0	0	0	211	1968	550	25	7	68	0
0	1	16243	29165	0	0	0	0	0	0	217	1175	584	24	1	75	0
2	1	16328	29072	0	0	0	0	0	0	217	1202	584	23	3	74	0

The analysis of the vmstat output above did not indicate any problems. The run queue was small and did not grow over time. There was no paging occurring at any time during the run (as indicated by pi = 0). The CPUs were not waiting for I/O (as indicated by the wa column).

While the create index statement was running, the iostat information was captured, as follows:

```
iostat 5 > iostat.out
```

The iostat.out file was created as follows:

Disks:	% tm_act	Kbps	tps	Kb_read	Kb_wrtn
Hdisk0	12.6	13.2	7.3	46	0
hdisk1	8.8	9.6	6.4	28	0
cd0	0.0	0.0	0.0	0	0
Disks:	% tm_act	Kbps	tps	Kb_read	Kb_wrtn
Hdisk0	10.6	11.3	6.9	37	0
hdisk1	9.8	10.9	6.8	33	0
cd0	0.0	0.0	0.0	0	0

Disks:	% tm_act	Kbps	tps	Kb_read	Kb_wrtn
Hdisk0	12.9	13.7	7.8	49	0
hdisk1	8.4	9.3	6.2	30	0
cd0	0.0	0.0	0.0	0	0

The iostat showed that the disks were relatively inactive. The most active disk was busy only 12.9% of the time. In addition, the amount of data read (Kb_read) for the disks was quite low.

In this case each of the Hdisks was actually a disk array that could support much higher throughput. Disk arrays make the disk volume look like one disk to the OS tools; therefore, it was important to understand the physical disk implementation when examining the output of these tools.

In reexamining the database and database manager configurations, the NUM_IOSERVERS configuration parameter warranted further investigation. The parameter was set as follows:

```
Number of I/O servers              (NUM_IOSERVERS) = 1
```

DB2 was not taking advantage of I/O parallelism and was not reading from the disks in parallel. In addition, because the containers were on a RAID-5 disk, we checked the DB2_PARALLEL_IO registry variable to determine whether it was set for the table space(s) where the table was created. In this, case it was not enabled.

The number of prefetchers (I/O servers) was increased as follows:

```
update db cfg for sample using num_ioservers 6
```

In this case, the number of prefetchers was set to six because the disk volume is using RAID-5 technology with six data disks and one parity disk per array. Therefore, there were six disks servicing the table space for the data.

Parallel I/O was enabled as follows:

```
db2set DB2_PARALLEL_IO=*
```

The DB2 instance was stopped and restarted to enable the registry variable.

Step 5: Rerun the CREATE INDEX Statement

The db2batch output showing the timing of the create index is below. Although the create index time was improved, it was still higher than expected.

```
-------------------------------------------------
Statement number: 1

create index x1 on staff (id)

Elapsed Time is:              437.391    seconds
-------------------------------------------------
```

Step 6: Recheck the System Resource Usage

In this case, two sessions were opened, and the vmstat and iostat were captured for the entire time the index was being created.

Some of the entries from the beginning and end of the vmstat.out and iostat.out files are below:

kthr		memory		page						faults			cpu			
r	b	avm	fre	re	pi	po	fr	sr	cy	in	sy	cs	us	sy	id	wa
1	1	16243	29168	0	0	0	0	0	0	305	2890	870	14	6	80	0
2	1	16243	29165	0	0	0	0	0	0	212	2010	550	35	7	58	0
0	1	16243	29165	0	0	0	0	0	0	217	1175	584	34	2	64	0
0	1	16243	29165	0	0	0	0	0	0	224	1970	563	35	6	53	2
.																
.																
.																
2	1	16243	29165	0	0	0	0	0	0	211	1968	550	25	7	61	7
0	1	16243	29165	0	0	0	0	0	0	217	1175	584	24	1	66	9
2	1	16328	29072	0	0	0	0	0	0	217	1202	584	23	3	67	7

Disks:	% tm_act	Kbps	tps	Kb_read	Kb_wrtn
Hdisk0	12.6	13.2	7.3	46	0
hdisk1	8.8	9.6	6.4	28	0
cd0	0.0	0.0	0.0	0	0

Disks:	% tm_act	Kbps	tps	Kb_read	Kb_wrtn
Hdisk0	10.6	11.3	6.9	37	0
hdisk1	9.8	10.9	6.8	33	0
cd0	0.0	0.0	0.0	0	0

Disks:	% tm_act	Kbps	tps	Kb_read	Kb_wrtn
Hdisk0	12.9	13.7	7.8	49	0
hdisk1	8.4	9.3	6.2	30	0
cd0	0.0	0.0	0.0	0	0
.					
.					
.					

Disks:	% tm_act	Kbps	tps	Kb_read	Kb_wrtn
Hdisk0	24.7	36.1	16.3	1	317
Hdisk1	24.5	36.0	16.1	2	311
cd0	0.0	0.0	0.0	0	0

Disks:	% tm_act	Kbps	tps	Kb_read	Kb_wrtn
Hdisk0	24.6	36.1	16.3	1	315
Hdisk1	24.9	36.9	16.4	2	321
cd0	0.0	0.0	0.0	0	0
Disks:	% tm_act	Kbps	tps	Kb_read	Kb_wrtn
Hdisk0	24.5	36.0	16.2	1	315
Hdisk1	24.6	36.4	16.5	2	323
cd0	0.0	0.0	0.0	0	0

An analysis of this information shows differences in the processing between the beginning and end of the create index processing. At the beginning of the processing, all of the I/O activity was shown to be reading the data file. At the end of the create index processing, all of the activity is write activity. This was due to the manner in which DB2 creates indexes.

Because DB2 logs only the creation of index pages and not the creation of every index key value, it must flush all of the new log pages to disk at the end of the index creation. With a CHNGPGS_THRESH setting of 60% and a 1.2-GB buffer pool, at the end of the index creation, there can be up to 720 MB of pages in the buffer pool that needs to be flushed to disk. By decreasing the value of the CHNGPGS_THRESH configuration parameter to 20%, there will be a maximum of only 240 MB of pages in the buffer pool to be flushed to disk. This can result in greatly improved index creation times.

Step 7: Adjust Relevant Parameters and Determine Values for the Task Being Optimized

The relevant database manager and database configuration parameters were adjusted, based on the analysis of their currently set values, and the appropriate values for the task being organized were determined. The changed pages threshold was updated as follows:

```
update db cfg for sample using chngpgs_thresh 20
```

Step 8: Rerun the CREATE INDEX Statement

The db2batch output showing the timing of the create index improved dramatically.

```
-------------------------------------------------
Statement number: 1

create index x1 on staff (id)

Elapsed Time is:          38.451    seconds
-------------------------------------------------
```

EXAMPLE 2: UNABLE TO GET DESIRED THROUGHPUT

Problem Description

CustomerB was in the midst of implementing a new application, performing stress tests before going into production. While performing the stress test, the database server could not ramp up to the desired number of client applications while achieving the required response times.

Problem Analysis and Resolution

Step 1: Examine the Database and Database Manager Configuration Parameters

Database manager configuration   The three parameters in the database manager configuration that stand out are highlighted in bold below. In this case, the application is mainly an online application; therefore, intra-partition parallelism should be disabled. Because there will be a large number of concurrent applications, the sort heap threshold (SHEAPTHRES) will need to be high; however, the existing value is sufficient.

```
Node type = Database Server with local and remote clients

Database manager configuration release level            = 0x0900

CPU speed (millisec/instruction)            (CPUSPEED) = 8.580921e-07

Max number of concurrently active databases     (NUMDB) = 8
Data Links support                         (DATALINKS) = NO
Federated Database System Support          (FEDERATED) = YES
Transaction processor monitor name        (TP_MON_NAME) =

Default charge-back account            (DFT_ACCOUNT_STR) =

Java Development Kit 1.1 installation path    (JDK_PATH) =

Diagnostic error capture level             (DIAGLEVEL) = 3
Notify Level                              (NOTIFYLEVEL) = 3
Diagnostic data directory path               (DIAGPATH) = /products/db2/
   fsprdi/sqllib/db2dump

Default database monitor switches
   Buffer pool                        (DFT_MON_BUFPOOL) = OFF
   Lock                                  (DFT_MON_LOCK) = OFF
   Sort                                  (DFT_MON_SORT) = OFF
   Statement                             (DFT_MON_STMT) = OFF
   Table                                (DFT_MON_TABLE) = OFF
```

```
   Unit of work                               (DFT_MON_UOW) = OFF
Monitor health of instance and databases    (HEALTH_MON) = OFF

SYSADM group name                           (SYSADM_GROUP) = DBA
SYSCTRL group name                          (SYSCTRL_GROUP) = DBASCTL
SYSMAINT group name                         (SYSMAINT_GROUP) = DBAMNT

Database manager authentication             (AUTHENTICATION) = SERVER
Cataloging allowed without authority        (CATALOG_NOAUTH) = NO
Trust all clients                           (TRUST_ALLCLNTS) = YES
Trusted client authentication               (TRUST_CLNTAUTH) = CLIENT
Use SNA authentication                      (USE_SNA_AUTH) = NO
Bypass federated authentication             (FED_NOAUTH) = NO

Default database path                       (DFTDBPATH) = /products/db2/
   fsprdi

Database monitor heap size (4KB)            (MON_HEAP_SZ) = 56
UDF shared memory set size (4KB)            (UDF_MEM_SZ) = 256
Java Virtual Machine heap size (4KB)        (JAVA_HEAP_SZ) = 2048
Audit buffer size (4KB)                     (AUDIT_BUF_SZ) = 0
Backup buffer default size (4KB)            (BACKBUFSZ) = 1024
Restore buffer default size (4KB)           (RESTBUFSZ) = 1024

Sort heap threshold (4KB)                   (SHEAPTHRES) = 100000

Directory cache support                     (DIR_CACHE) = YES

Application support layer heap size (4KB)   (ASLHEAPSZ) = 15
Max requester I/O block size (bytes)        (RQRIOBLK) = 32767
Query heap size (4KB)                       (QUERY_HEAP_SZ) = 16000
DRDA services heap size (4KB)               (DRDA_HEAP_SZ) = 128

Priority of agents                          (AGENTPRI) = SYSTEM
Max number of existing agents               (MAXAGENTS) = 200
Agent pool size                             (NUM_POOLAGENTS) = 4 (calculated)
Initial number of agents in pool            (NUM_INITAGENTS) = 0
Max number of coordinating agents           (MAX_COORDAGENTS) = MAXAGENTS
Max no. of concurrent coordinating agents   (MAXCAGENTS) = MAX_COORDAGENTS
Max number of logical agents                (MAX_LOGICAGENTS) = MAX_COORDAGENTS

Keep fenced process                         (KEEPFENCED) = YES
Number of pooled fenced processes           (FENCED_POOL) = MAX_COORDAGENTS
Initialize DARI process with JVM            (INITFENCED_JVM) = NO
Initial number of fenced DARI process       (NUM_INITFENCED) = 0
```

```
Index re-creation time                              (INDEXREC) = RESTART


Transaction manager database name              (TM_DATABASE) = 1ST_CONN
Transaction resync interval (sec)          (RESYNC_INTERVAL) = 180


SPM name                                        (SPM_NAME) = it_ibm60
SPM log size                            (SPM_LOG_FILE_SZ) = 256
SPM resync agent limit                   (SPM_MAX_RESYNC) = 20
SPM log path                              (SPM_LOG_PATH) =


TCP/IP Service name                             (SVCENAME) = 50000
Discovery mode                                  (DISCOVER) = SEARCH
Discovery communication protocols          (DISCOVER_COMM) = TCPIP
Discover server instance                   (DISCOVER_INST) = ENABLE
```

Maximum query degree of parallelism   (MAX_QUERYDEGREE) = ANY
Enable intra-partition parallelism   (INTRA_PARALLEL) = NO

```
No. of int. communication buffers(4KB)(FCM_NUM_BUFFERS) = 1024
Node connection elapse time (sec)           (CONN_ELAPSE) = 10
Max number of node connection retries (MAX_CONNRETRIES) = 5
Max time difference between nodes (min) (MAX_TIME_DIFF) = 60


db2start/db2stop timeout (min)             (START_STOP_TIME) = 10
```

Database configuration for database sample   The three parameters in the database manager configuration that stand out are highlighted in bold below.

- Because the applications will be performing a lot of inserts/updates/deletes, the log
  buffer size (LOGBUFSZ) will be important. However, the log buffer is sized adequately for this workload.
- Because this is an online application, the sort list heap (SORTHEAP) should not be too
  large. When it is too large, the DB2 optimizer will tend to favor sorts over index scans, and
  with a large number of concurrent applications, sorting will be detrimental to performance.
- In this case, the default buffer pool size (BUFFPAGE) is 1,000 4-KB pages. To determine the real size of the buffer pool, use the following statement:

```
select * from syscat.bufferpools
```

- In this case, there is only one buffer pool (IBMDEFAULTBP), and it has a size of
  5,000 4-KB pages.
- This is a rather small buffer pool; therefore, increasing the size of the buffer pool
  likely will help performance.

```
Database configuration release level                            = 0x0a00
Database release level                                          = 0x0a00

Database territory                                             = US
Database code page                                            = 819
Database code set                                             = ISO8859-1
Database country/region code                                  = 1

Dynamic SQL Query management            (DYN_QUERY_MGMT) = DISABLE

Discovery support for this database      (DISCOVER_DB) = ENABLE

Default query optimization class         (DFT_QUERYOPT) = 5
Degree of parallelism                     (DFT_DEGREE) = 1
Continue upon arithmetic exceptions  (DFT_SQLMATHWARN) = NO
Default refresh age                   (DFT_REFRESH_AGE) = 0
Number of frequent values retained    (NUM_FREQVALUES) = 10
Number of quantiles retained           (NUM_QUANTILES) = 20

Backup pending                                               = NO

Database is consistent                                        = NO
Rollforward pending                                           = NO
Restore pending                                               = NO

Multi-page file allocation enabled                            = NO

Log retain for recovery status                               = NO
User exit for logging status                                 = NO

Data Links Token Expiry Interval (sec)       (DL_EXPINT) = 60
Data Links Write Token Init Expiry Intvl(DL_WT_IEXPINT) = 60
Data Links Number of Copies             (DL_NUM_COPIES) = 1
Data Links Time after Drop (days)        (DL_TIME_DROP) = 1
Data Links Token in Uppercase                (DL_UPPER) = NO
Data Links Token Algorithm                   (DL_TOKEN) = MAC0

Database heap (4KB)                            (DBHEAP) = 1200
Size of database shared memory (4KB) (DATABASE_MEMORY) = AUTOMATIC
```

```
Catalog cache size (4KB)                 (CATALOGCACHE_SZ) = (MAXAPPLS*4)
Log buffer size (4KB)                           (LOGBUFSZ) = 256
Utilities heap size (4KB)                   (UTIL_HEAP_SZ) = 5000
Buffer pool size (pages)                        (BUFFPAGE) = 1000
Extended storage segments size (4KB)      (ESTORE_SEG_SZ) = 16000
Number of extended storage segments     (NUM_ESTORE_SEGS) = 0
Max storage for lock list (4KB)                 (LOCKLIST) = 100

Max size of appl. group mem set (4KB)   (APPGROUP_MEM_SZ) = 20000
Percent of mem for appl. group heap     (GROUPHEAP_RATIO) = 70
Max appl. control heap size (4KB)        (APP_CTL_HEAP_SZ) = 128

Sort heap thres for shared sorts (4KB) (SHEAPTHRES_SHR) = (SHEAPTHRES)
Sort list heap (4KB)                            (SORTHEAP) = 1024
SQL statement heap (4KB)                        (STMTHEAP) = 4096
Default application heap (4KB)                 (APPLHEAPSZ) = 256
Package cache size (4KB)                       (PCKCACHESZ) = (MAXAPPLS*8)
Statistics heap size (4KB)                   (STAT_HEAP_SZ) = 4384

Interval for checking deadlock (ms)            (DLCHKTIME) = 10000
Percent. of lock lists per application          (MAXLOCKS) = 10
Lock timeout (sec)                           (LOCKTIMEOUT) = -1

Changed pages threshold                    (CHNGPGS_THRESH) = 60
Number of asynchronous page cleaners       (NUM_IOCLEANERS) = 10
Number of I/O servers                      (NUM_IOSERVERS) = 10
Index sort flag                               (INDEXSORT) = YES
Sequential detect flag                        (SEQDETECT) = YES
Default prefetch size (pages)            (DFT_PREFETCH_SZ) = 32

Track modified pages                           (TRACKMOD) = OFF

Default number of containers                             = 1
Default tablespace extentsize (pages)      (DFT_EXTENT_SZ) = 32

Max number of active applications               (MAXAPPLS) = AUTOMATIC
Average number of active applications          (AVG_APPLS) = 1
Max DB files open per application               (MAXFILOP) = 64

Log file size (4KB)                            (LOGFILSIZ) = 1000
Number of primary log files                   (LOGPRIMARY) = 3
Number of secondary log files                  (LOGSECOND) = 2
Changed path to log files                     (NEWLOGPATH) =
```

```
Path to log files                                          = /databases/
  sample/logs
Overflow log path                    (OVERFLOWLOGPATH) =
Mirror log path                        (MIRRORLOGPATH) =
First active log file                                  =
Block log on disk full                (BLK_LOG_DSK_FUL) = NO
Percent of max active log space by transaction(MAX_LOG) = 0
Num. of active log files for 1 active UOW(NUM_LOG_SPAN) = 0

Group commit count                          (MINCOMMIT) = 1
Percent log file reclaimed before soft chckpt (SOFTMAX) = 100
Log retain for recovery enabled             (LOGRETAIN) = OFF
User exit for logging enabled                (USEREXIT) = OFF

Auto restart enabled                      (AUTORESTART) = ON
Index re-creation time                       (INDEXREC) = SYSTEM
                                                          (RESTART)
Default number of loadrec sessions      (DFT_LOADREC_SES) = 1
Number of database backups to retain     (NUM_DB_BACKUPS) = 12
Recovery history retention (days)        (REC_HIS_RETENTN) = 366

TSM management class                      (TSM_MGMTCLASS) =
TSM node name                              (TSM_NODENAME) =
TSM owner                                     (TSM_OWNER) =
TSM password                               (TSM_PASSWORD) =
```

Step 2: Make Changes Based on the Examination of Configuration Information

The size of the buffer pool was increased as follows:

```
alter bufferpool IBMDEFAULTBP immediate size 500000
```

Step 3: Retest

After increasing the size of the buffer pool, the response time improved, and more concurrent users were able to connect to the database and run the applications; however, the system was still unable to attain the required number of applications.

Step 4: Check System for I/O Bottlenecks, Excess Paging, or Other Processes/Applications Using Excess System Resources

This requires operating system tools such as vmstat, iostat, and/or top to capture the memory, I/O, and process level information. It is important to capture the snapshots from these tools over a period of time, not taking just one snapshot, especially because the first line of the output of the vmstat and iostat tools contains average information since the server was started and is not really useful in analyzing a problem.

While the applications are running, and particularly when the system begins to stop responding, capture iostat output, as follows:

```
iostat 5 > iostat.out
```

Next, examine the iostat.out file, below:

Disks:	% tm_act	Kbps	tps	Kb_read	Kb_wrtn
Hdisk0	2.6	13.2	7.3	19	0
Hdisk1	1.8	9.2	7.3	19	0
Hdisk2	1.8	9.2	7.3	19	0
Hdisk3	1.8	9.2	7.3	19	0
Hdisk4	1.8	9.2	7.3	19	0
Hdisk5	42.8	213.2	107.3	237	286
Hdisk6	1.8	9.2	7.3	19	0
Hdisk7	1.8	9.2	7.3	19	0
Hdisk8	1.8	9.2	7.3	19	0
Hdisk9	1.8	9.2	7.3	19	0
cd0	0.0	0.0	0.0	0	0

Disks:	% tm_act	Kbps	tps	Kb_read	Kb_wrtn
Hdisk0	2.6	13.2	7.3	19	0
Hdisk1	1.8	9.2	7.3	19	0
Hdisk2	1.8	9.2	7.3	19	0
Hdisk3	1.8	9.2	7.3	19	0
Hdisk4	1.8	9.2	7.3	19	0
Hdisk5	47.1	234.7	111.3	261	292
Hdisk6	1.8	9.2	7.3	19	0
Hdisk7	1.8	9.2	7.3	19	0
Hdisk8	1.8	9.2	7.3	19	0
Hdisk9	1.8	9.2	7.3	19	0
cd0	0.0	0.0	0.0	0	0

Disks:	% tm_act	Kbps	tps	Kb_read	Kb_wrtn
Hdisk0	2.6	13.2	7.3	19	0
Hdisk1	1.8	9.2	7.3	19	0
Hdisk2	1.8	9.2	7.3	19	0
Hdisk3	1.8	9.2	7.3	19	0
Hdisk4	1.8	9.2	7.3	19	0
Hdisk5	43.3	214.6	109.8	283	239
Hdisk6	1.8	9.2	7.3	19	0
Hdisk7	1.8	9.2	7.3	19	0
Hdisk8	1.8	9.2	7.3	19	0
Hdisk9	1.8	9.2	7.3	19	0
cd0	0.0	0.0	0.0	0	0

The iostat output shows that one disk is much busier than all of the other disks; therefore, it is important to understand what part of the database is physically stored on Hdisk5.

In this case, the disks are not striped volumes, they are just a bunch of disks (JBOD); therefore, use the operation system tools to determine what file system was created on Hdisk5, then analyze the database to determine what part of the database is stored on that file system.

Step 5: Determine What Is on Hdisk5

The operating system tools indicate that the file system /tablespaces/sample/temp was created on Hdisk5. Based on the name of the file system, it appears to be where the temporary table space was created. This can be verified as follows:

Determine the table space ID for the temporary table space:

```
select tbspaceid, tbspace from syscat.tablespaces where datatype='T'
```

The output of the statement above is:

```
TBSPACEID    TBSPACE
-----------  -----------
          1  TEMPSPACE1

1 record(s) selected.
```

Determine the container definitions for the temporary table space as follows:

```
list tablespace containers for 1
```

The output of the statement above is:

```
Tablespace Containers for Tablespace 1

  Container ID                         = 0
  Name                                 = /tablespaces/sample/temp
  Type                                 = Path
```

Therefore, the disk with the most activity is the disk where the temporary table space has been placed.

Step 6: Determine and Implement a More Optimal Database Layout

Based on the iostat output, there are 10 physical disks in the server. To eliminate the I/O bottleneck and spread the I/O across as many disks as possible, the physical design of the database needed to be changed. Instead of isolating each of the table spaces to its own physical disk, each table space would be created with eight containers, with one container on each of the disks Hdisk2 through Hdisk9. In this case, because it was an online system, one disk was set aside for the database logs and another for the operating system paging space.

To change the physical layout of the database, an offline backup was taken, the database was dropped, and a redirected restore was performed. During the redirected restore, the table space definitions were changed.

Step 7: Retest

After changing the table space definitions, the response time improved even more, and the desired number of concurrent applications were able to run successfully.

Step 8: Check the System to Ensure Elimination of the I/O Bottleneck

While the applications are running, capture iostat output as follows:

```
iostat 5 > iostat.out
```

Next examine the iostat.out file, below:

Disks:	% tm_act	Kbps	tps	Kb_read	Kb_wrtn
Hdisk0	2.6	13.2	7.3	19	0
Hdisk1	4.8	12.2	17.3	0	78
Hdisk2	12.1	29.2	27.2	109	134
Hdisk3	12.5	29.4	27.1	127	125
Hdisk4	12.2	29.1	27.5	113	130
Hdisk5	12.3	29.3	27.4	116	124
Hdisk6	12.4	29.3	27.4	124	126
Hdisk7	12.3	29.1	27.2	103	131
Hdisk8	12.4	29.4	27.3	108	132
Hdisk9	12.2	29.1	27.1	110	130
cd0	0.0	0.0	0.0	0	0

The iostat output now shows that the I/O is spread evenly across the data disks, and none of the disks is busy more than 15% of the time. This leaves room for the I/O subsystem to handle additional requests if needed.

EXAMPLE 3: QUERY1 TAKING TOO LONG TO RUN

Problem Description

CustomerC is running an application and has identified a particular query that is taking over 45 minutes to complete, returning only one row.

Problem Analysis and Resolution

Step 1: Identified the Query

The customer was able to determine the problem query, using the application snapshot and dynamic SQL snapshot. The problem query was identified as:

```
select a.c2, b.c2, c.c3 from a,b,c
  where a.c1=b.c1 and
  b.c2=c.c2 and
  c.c3=a.c3 and
  c.c1=50193
```

Step 2: Run Explain for the SQL Statement

The explain plan for the SQL statement indicated the following:

```
Estimated Cost = 2968724
Estimated Cardinality = 99996
```

The DBA knew that, because the column C1 in the table C is a primary key, there can be a maximum of only one row returned by the SQL statement. Therefore, the estimated cardinality in the access plan is not correct. A difference in the expected cardinality and the optimizer's estimated cardinality this large is normally due to old or nonexistent statistics.

Step 3: Check to Determine Whether the Tables' Statistics Are Current

To determine when the last time statistics were gathered for these three tables, use the following statement:

```
select stats_time from syscat.tables where tabname in ('A','B','C')
```

The output of the above statement was:

```
STATS_TIME
----------------------------
   -
   -
   -

3 record(s) selected.
```

Therefore, the tables do not have current statistics.

Step 4: Gather Statistics for the Tables

To gather statistics, use the RUNSTATS command as follows:

```
runstats on table user.a with distribution and detailed indexes all
runstats on table user.b with distribution and detailed indexes all
runstats on table user.c with distribution and detailed indexes all
```

Step 5: Retest

After running the RUNSTATS command for all of the tables in the statement, it was able to complete in less than two seconds, and the explain plan indicated the following:

```
Estimated Cost = 183
Estimated Cardinality = 1
```

EXAMPLE 4: QUERY2 TAKING TOO LONG TO RUN

Problem Description

After fixing the problem above and running RUNSTATS for all tables in the database, CustomerC found another statement that was taking too long to complete.

Problem Analysis and Resolution

Step 1: Identify the Query

The customer was able to determine the problem query, using the application snapshot and dynamic SQL snapshot. The problem query was identified as:

```
select c1,c2 from f
  where c1=67 and
  c2='NS'
```

Step 2: Run Explain for the SQL Statement

The explain plan for the identified statement, as shown below, indicated that the optimizer had chosen an index-only access plan.

```
Estimated Cost = 5814.739
Estimated Cardinality = 1

Access Plan:
-----------
        Total Cost:            5814.739
        Query Degree:          1

     Rows
    RETURN
    (   1)
     Cost
      I/O
      |
    888.548
    IXSCAN
    (   2)
    5814.739
       2
       |
     955343
  INDEX: USER1
  FX1
```

Step 3: Check the Indexes

An index-only access plan normally provides good performance, and because the query is returning only one row, there appears to be something wrong with the table or indexes. The indexes for the table can be examined using the DESCRIBE TABLE command. The SHOW DETAIL option is required to get a listing of the key columns for the index.

```
describe indexes for table f show detail
```

The output of the above statement was:

Index schema	Index name	Unique rule	Number of columns	Column names
USER1	FX1	D	2	+C2+C1

Therefore, there is one index named *FX1* on the table, and the index keys are C2 and C1. Because there is a + sign before each column name, the index keys are in ascending order.

Step 4: Examine the Key Cardinality

To examine the cardinality of the index keys, there are two options, assuming that RUNSTATS was run recently:

1. Select the CARD column from the SYSCAT.COLUMNS view.
2. Select the FIRSTKEYCARD and FIRST2KEYCARD columns from the SYSCAT.INDEXES view.

The following statement will query the SYSCAT.INDEXES view to examine the key cardinality:

```
select firstkeycard, first2keycard from syscat.indexes
  where indname='FX1'
```

The output of this statement is:

```
FIRSTKEYCARD          FIRST2KEYCARD
-------------------- --------------------
                   4                34816

1 record(s) selected.
```

Therefore, there are only four distinct values for C2 and 34,816/4, or 8,704 distinct values for C1. Therefore, if the order of the keys were reversed, the selectivity of the query would be improved, and the index would be able to find the result much quicker with an index defined as C1,C2.

Step 5: Create the New Index

Create the new index and capture the index statistics as follows:

```
create index fx2 on f (c1,c2) collect statistics
```

Step 6: Retest

After creating the new index, the query was able to complete in less than a second. The new access plan is again using index-only access, but it is now using the new index. The new access plan looked like the following:

```
Estimated Cost = 42.6512
Estimated Cardinality = 1


Access Plan:
-----------
          Total Cost:              42.6512
          Query Degree:            1


        Rows
      RETURN
      (    1)
        Cost
        I/O
         |
       888.548
       IXSCAN
      (    2)
      5814.739
          2
         |
       955343
    INDEX: USER1
  FX2
```

EXAMPLE 5: PERIODIC NOTICEABLE SLOWDOWN OF DATABASE RESPONSE TIME

Problem Description

CustomerC is running an eCommerce site with the backed data store on DB2. At various times throughout the day, the database response time for application requests becomes very long.

Problem Analysis and Resolution

Step 1: Examine the Database and Database Manager Configuration Parameters

Database manager configuration   The three parameters in the database manager configuration that stand out are highlighted in bold below. In this case, the application is mainly an online application; therefore, intra-partition parallelism should be disabled. Because there will be a large number of concurrent applications, the sort heap threshold (SHEAPTHRES) will need to be high; however, the existing value is sufficient.

```
Node type = Database Server with local clients

Database manager configuration release level         = 0x0a00
CPU speed (millisec/instruction)           (CPUSPEED) = 4.000000e-05

Max number of concurrently active databases     (NUMDB) = 8
Data Links support                          (DATALINKS) = NO
Federated Database System Support           (FEDERATED) = NO
Transaction processor monitor name        (TP_MON_NAME) =

Default charge-back account            (DFT_ACCOUNT_STR) =

Java Development Kit installation path      (JDK_PATH) = /wsdb/v81/
   bldsupp/AIX/jdk1.3.0

Diagnostic error capture level             (DIAGLEVEL) = 3
Notify Level                             (NOTIFYLEVEL) = 3
Diagnostic data directory path              (DIAGPATH) =

Default database monitor switches
   Buffer pool                      (DFT_MON_BUFPOOL) = OFF
   Lock                                (DFT_MON_LOCK) = OFF
   Sort                                (DFT_MON_SORT) = OFF
   Statement                           (DFT_MON_STMT) = OFF
   Table                              (DFT_MON_TABLE) = OFF
   Timestamp                      (DFT_MON_TIMESTAMP) = ON
   Unit of work                         (DFT_MON_UOW) = OFF
Monitor health of instance and databases  (HEALTH_MON) = OFF

SYSADM group name                        (SYSADM_GROUP) = BUILD
SYSCTRL group name                      (SYSCTRL_GROUP) =
SYSMAINT group name                    (SYSMAINT_GROUP) =

Database manager authentication         (AUTHENTICATION) = SERVER
```

```
Cataloging allowed without authority   (CATALOG_NOAUTH) = YES
Trust all clients                      (TRUST_ALLCLNTS) = YES
Trusted client authentication          (TRUST_CLNTAUTH) = CLIENT
Use SNA authentication                  (USE_SNA_AUTH) = NO
Bypass federated authentication          (FED_NOAUTH) = NO


Default database path                      (DFTDBPATH) = /home/dsnow


Database monitor heap size (4KB)         (MON_HEAP_SZ) = 90
Java Virtual Machine heap size (4KB)    (JAVA_HEAP_SZ) = 1024
Audit buffer size (4KB)                 (AUDIT_BUF_SZ) = 0
Size of instance shared memory (4KB)  (INSTANCE_MEMORY) = AUTOMATIC
Backup buffer default size (4KB)           (BACKBUFSZ) = 1024
Restore buffer default size (4KB)          (RESTBUFSZ) = 1024
```

Sort heap threshold (4KB)   (SHEAPTHRES) = 80000

```
Directory cache support                    (DIR_CACHE) = YES

Application support layer heap size (4KB)    (ASLHEAPSZ) = 15
Max requester I/O block size (bytes)        (RQRIOBLK) = 32767
Query heap size (4KB)                    (QUERY_HEAP_SZ) = 1000
DRDA services heap size (4KB)            (DRDA_HEAP_SZ) = 128


Priority of agents                          (AGENTPRI) = SYSTEM
Max number of existing agents             (MAXAGENTS) = 200
Agent pool size                       (NUM_POOLAGENTS) = 100(calculated)
Initial number of agents in pool       (NUM_INITAGENTS) = 0
Max number of coordinating agents    (MAX_COORDAGENTS) = MAXAGENTS
Max no. of concurrent coordinating agents  (MAXCAGENTS) = MAX_COORDAGENTS
Max number of client connections       (MAX_CONNECTIONS) = MAX_COORDAGENTS


Keep fenced process                       (KEEPFENCED) = YES
Number of pooled fenced processes        (FENCED_POOL) = MAX_COORDAGENTS
Initialize fenced process with JVM    (INITFENCED_JVM) = NO
Initial number of fenced processes     (NUM_INITFENCED) = 0


 Index re-creation time                       (INDEXREC) = RESTART


Transaction manager database name         (TM_DATABASE) = 1ST_CONN
Transaction resync interval (sec)     (RESYNC_INTERVAL) = 180
```

```
SPM name                           (SPM_NAME) =
SPM log size                (SPM_LOG_FILE_SZ) = 256
SPM resync agent limit        (SPM_MAX_RESYNC) = 20
SPM log path                    (SPM_LOG_PATH) =

TCP/IP Service name               (SVCENAME) =
Discovery mode                    (DISCOVER) = SEARCH
Discovery communication protocols  (DISCOVER_COMM) =
Discover server instance          (DISCOVER_INST) = ENABLE

Maximum query degree of parallelism  (MAX_QUERYDEGREE) = ANY
Enable intra-partition parallelism    (INTRA_PARALLEL) = NO

No. of int. communication buffers(4KB)(FCM_NUM_BUFFERS) = 512
```

Database configuration for database sample   The three parameters in the database manager configuration that stand out are highlighted in bold below.

- Since the applications will be performing a lot of inserts/updates/deletes, the log buffer size (LOGBUFSZ) will be important. However, the log buffer is sized adequately for this workload.
- Because this is an online application, the sort list heap (SORTHEAP) should not be too large. When it is too large, the DB2 optimizer will tend to favor sorts over index scans, and with a large number of concurrent applications, sorting will be detrimental to performance.
- In this case, the default buffer pool size (BUFFPAGE) is 1,000 4-KB pages. To determine the real size of the buffer pool, use the following statement:

```
select * from syscat.bufferpools
```

- In this case, there is only one buffer pool (IBMDEFAULTBP), and it has a size of 675,000 4-KB pages.
- This is adequately sized for this workload.

```
Database configuration release level              = 0x0a00
Database release level                            = 0x0a00

Database territory                                = US
Database code page                                = 819
Database code set                                 = ISO8859-1
Database country/region code                      = 1

Dynamic SQL Query management         (DYN_QUERY_MGMT) = DISABLE

Discovery support for this database     (DISCOVER_DB) = ENABLE
```

```
Default query optimization class        (DFT_QUERYOPT) = 5
Degree of parallelism                     (DFT_DEGREE) = 1
Continue upon arithmetic exceptions    (DFT_SQLMATHWARN) = NO
Default refresh age                   (DFT_REFRESH_AGE) = 0
Number of frequent values retained     (NUM_FREQVALUES) = 10
Number of quantiles retained            (NUM_QUANTILES) = 20


Backup pending                                         = NO

Database is consistent                                 = NO
Rollforward pending                                    = NO
Restore pending                                        = NO
```

Multi-page file allocation enabled   = NO

```
Log retain for recovery status                         = NO
User exit for logging status                           = NO


Data Links Token Expiry Interval (sec)     (DL_EXPINT) = 60
Data Links Write Token Init Expiry Intvl(DL_WT_IEXPINT) = 60
Data Links Number of Copies            (DL_NUM_COPIES) = 1
Data Links Time after Drop (days)       (DL_TIME_DROP) = 1
Data Links Token in Uppercase              (DL_UPPER) = NO
Data Links Token Algorithm                 (DL_TOKEN) = MAC0


Database heap (4KB)                           (DBHEAP) = 1200
Size of database shared memory (4KB)  (DATABASE_MEMORY) = AUTOMATIC
Catalog cache size (4KB)              (CATALOGCACHE_SZ) = (MAXAPPLS*4)
```
Log buffer size (4KB)   (LOGBUFSZ) = 256
```
Utilities heap size (4KB)              (UTIL_HEAP_SZ) = 5000
```
Buffer pool size (pages)   (BUFFPAGE) = 1000
```
Extended storage segments size (4KB)    (ESTORE_SEG_SZ) = 16000
Number of extended storage segments   (NUM_ESTORE_SEGS) = 0
Max storage for lock list (4KB)             (LOCKLIST) = 100


Max size of appl. group mem set (4KB) (APPGROUP_MEM_SZ) = 20000
Percent of mem for appl. group heap   (GROUPHEAP_RATIO) = 70
Max appl. control heap size (4KB)      (APP_CTL_HEAP_SZ) = 128


Sort heap thres for shared sorts (4KB) (SHEAPTHRES_SHR) = (SHEAPTHRES)
```
Sort list heap (4KB)   (SORTHEAP) = 4096
```
SQL statement heap (4KB)                    (STMTHEAP) = 4096
Default application heap (4KB)             (APPLHEAPSZ) = 256
Package cache size (4KB)                   (PCKCACHESZ) = (MAXAPPLS*8)
Statistics heap size (4KB)               (STAT_HEAP_SZ) = 4384
```

```
Interval for checking deadlock (ms)           (DLCHKTIME) = 10000
Percent. of lock lists per application        (MAXLOCKS) = 10
Lock timeout (sec)                            (LOCKTIMEOUT) = -1

Changed pages threshold                   (CHNGPGS_THRESH) = 60
Number of asynchronous page cleaners      (NUM_IOCLEANERS) = 10
Number of I/O servers                     (NUM_IOSERVERS) = 40
Index sort flag                               (INDEXSORT) = YES
Sequential detect flag                        (SEQDETECT) = YES
Default prefetch size (pages)            (DFT_PREFETCH_SZ) = 32

Track modified pages                          (TRACKMOD) = OFF

Default number of containers                            = 1
Default tablespace extentsize (pages)    (DFT_EXTENT_SZ) = 32

Max number of active applications             (MAXAPPLS) = AUTOMATIC
Average number of active applications         (AVG_APPLS) = 1
Max DB files open per application             (MAXFILOP) = 64

Log file size (4KB)                           (LOGFILSIZ) = 100000
Number of primary log files                  (LOGPRIMARY) = 32
Number of secondary log files                (LOGSECOND) = 8
Changed path to log files                    (NEWLOGPATH) =
Path to log files                                       = /databases/sample
  /logs
Overflow log path                        (OVERFLOWLOGPATH) =
Mirror log path                            (MIRRORLOGPATH) =
First active log file                                   =
Block log on disk full                   (BLK_LOG_DSK_FUL) = NO
Percent of max active log space by transaction(MAX_LOG) = 0
Num. of active log files for 1 active UOW(NUM_LOG_SPAN) = 0

Group commit count                            (MINCOMMIT) = 1
Percent log file reclaimed before soft chckpt (SOFTMAX) = 100
Log retain for recovery enabled              (LOGRETAIN) = OFF
User exit for logging enabled                 (USEREXIT) = OFF

Auto restart enabled                        (AUTORESTART) = ON
Index re-creation time                        (INDEXREC) = SYSTEM (RESTART)
Default number of loadrec sessions       (DFT_LOADREC_SES) = 1
Number of database backups to retain     (NUM_DB_BACKUPS) = 12
Recovery history retention (days)        (REC_HIS_RETENTN) = 366
```

```
TSM management class                          (TSM_MGMTCLASS) =
TSM node name                                 (TSM_NODENAME) =
TSM owner                                        (TSM_OWNER) =
TSM password                                  (TSM_PASSWORD) =
```

Step 2: Check the System for I/O Bottlenecks, Excess Paging, or Other Processes/Applications Using Excess System Resources

This requires operating system tools such as vmstat, iostat, ps, and/or top to capture the memory, I/O, and process level information. It is important to capture the snapshots from these tools over a period of time, not taking just one snapshot, especially because the first line of the output of the vmstat and iostat tools contains average information since the server was started and is not really useful in analyzing a problem.

Step 3: Make Changes Based on Examination of Configuration Information

While the system is experiencing the slowdown, capture iostat output as follows:

```
iostat 5 > iostat.out
```

Next, examine the iostat.out file. Below is an entry from the iostat.out file.

Disks:	% tm_act	Kbps	tps	Kb_read	Kb_wrtn
hdisk0	2.6	13.2	7.3	19	21
hdisk1	8.3	99.2	37.3	3	208
hdisk2	8.3	99.2	37.3	3	208
hdisk3	8.3	99.2	37.3	3	208
hdisk4	8.3	99.2	37.3	3	208
hdisk5	8.3	99.2	37.3	3	208
hdisk6	8.3	99.2	37.3	3	208
hdisk7	8.3	99.2	37.3	3	208
cd0	0.0	0.0	0.0	0	0

The other entries were very similar to the above, so they are not shown here. In this case, the I/O activity is all writes and is spread across all of the disks on which the database resides, i.e., hdisk1 through hdisk7.

Next, run the top or ps aux command to determine which processes are currently executing that could be causing the I/O. The output of the ps aux command is below:

USER	PID	%CPU	%MEM	SZ	RSS	TTY STAT	STIME	TIME COMMAND
inst1	40970	10.0	2.0	40	23888	- A	Oct 03	572:36 db2pclnr
inst1	32776	10.0	2.0	40	23888	- A	Oct 03	570:33 db2pclnr
inst1	24582	10.0	2.0	40	23888	- A	Oct 03	576:07 db2pclnr
inst1	16388	10.0	2.0	40	23888	- A	Oct 03	538:13 db2pclnr
inst1	122974	10.0	0.0	320	324	- A	Oct 03	548:32 db2pclnr

```
inst1      294988 10.0  0.0  700    720    - A    Oct 03 513:02 db2pclnr
inst1       23109 10.0  2.0   52  23900    - A    Oct 03 522:04 db2pclnr
inst1      401514 10.0  2.0  184  24032    - A    Oct 03 509:06 db2pclnr
inst1       81940 10.0  2.0  116  23964    - A    Oct 03 511:07 db2pclnr
inst1      262242 10.0  0.0  936    940    - A    Oct 03 511:01 db2pclnr
```

The ps aux command shows that there are 10 db2pclnr processes running, using all of the available CPU cycles. The db2pclnr process is the I/O cleaner or page cleaner process that asynchronously flushes dirty pages from the buffer pools to disk.

> **N O T E**   The ps aux command gives more information than just db2pclnr processes; however, only the relevant information is shown above.

Step 4: Determine Which I/O Cleaner Triggers Caused the Buffer Pool Flush

To determine which of the triggers for the page cleaners actually caused the I/O cleaners to start, a database snapshot is required. To capture the database snapshot, use the following command:

```
get snapshot for database on sample > sample.db.snap
```

To take a snapshot and extract just the lines with the page cleaner trigger information, use the following command:

```
get snapshot for database on sample | grep -i 'triggers'
```

The output from the above command looks like the following:

```
LSN Gap cleaner triggers            = 0
Dirty page steal cleaner triggers   = 0
Dirty page threshold cleaner triggers = 1
```

Therefore, the I/O cleaners were triggered by the changed pages threshold (CHNGPGS_THRESH) database configuration parameter. Looking back at the database configuration information above, the CHNGPGS_THRESH configuration parameter is set to 60, as shown below:

```
Changed pages threshold              (CHNGPGS_THRESH) = 60
```

As discussed previously, there is only one buffer pool (IBMDEFAULTBP), and it has a size of 675,000 4-KB pages. Therefore, when the CHNGPGS_THRESH triggers the I/O cleaners, there are $675,000 \times .6$, or 405,000 dirty pages that need to be flushed to disk. When the I/O cleaners are triggered, all of the configured page cleaners (10, in this case) are started at the same time. Therefore, there will be 10 db2pclnr processes working to write 1.6 GB of data to disk.

Step 5: Reduce the Changed Pages Threshold Parameter Setting

To reduce the impact of the page cleaners when they are triggered, they need to be triggered more often but with fewer dirty pages to write to disk. This can be done by:

- Reducing the changed pages threshold (CHNGPGS_THRESH)
- Reducing the percent log file reclaimed before soft checkpoint (SOFTMAX)

Update the database configuration to reduce the CHNGPGS_THRESH and SOFTMAX, as follows:

```
update db cfg for sample using chngpgs_thresh 20
update db cfg for sample using softmax 50
```

This will cause the I/O cleaners to be triggered when half a log file is filled or when 20% of the buffer pool is occupied by dirty pages. This will trigger the I/O cleaners more frequently but with less work to perform when they are triggered.

Step 6: Retest

After reducing the CHNGPGS_THRESH and SOFTMAX, the Web servers were reconnected to the database, and the performance slowdown did not reoccur.

The page cleaner trigger information from the snapshots was recaptured and looked like the following:

```
LSN Gap cleaner triggers              = 0
Dirty page steal cleaner triggers     = 0
Dirty page threshold cleaner triggers = 4
```

Useful DB2 Commands

This section provides information about the system commands that can be entered at an operating system command prompt, or in a shell script, to access and maintain the database manager. Appendix A also explains how to invoke and use the command line processor (CLP) and describes CLP options. The CLP is used to execute database utilities, SQL statements, and online help. The CLP offers a variety of command options and can be started in:

- Interactive input mode, characterized by the *db2 =>* input prompt
- Command mode, where each command must be prefixed by *db2*
- Batch mode, which uses the –f file input option.

SYSTEM COMMANDS

db2adutl—Work with TSM Archived Images

This utility allows users to query, extract, verify, and delete backup images, logs, and load copy images saved using Tivoli Storage Manager (formerly ADSM). On UNIX-based operating systems, this utility is located in the sqllib/adsm directory. On Windows, it is located in sqllib\bin.

Usage:

- Anyone can access the utility.
- No connection to the database is required.
- Command parameters:

    QUERY: Queries the TSM server for DB2 objects

EXTRACT: Copies DB2 objects from the TSM server to the current directory on the local machine

DELETE: Either deactivates backup objects or deletes log archives on the TSM server

VERIFY: Performs consistency checking on the backup copy that is on the server. This parameter causes the entire backup image to be transferred over the network.

TABLESPACE: Includes only table space backup images

FULL: Includes only full database backup images

NONINCREMENTAL: Includes only non-incremental backup images

INCREMENTAL: Includes only incremental backup images

DELTA: Includes only incremental delta backup images

LOADCOPY: Includes only load copy images

LOGS: Includes only log archive images

BETWEEN sn1 AND sn2: Specifies that the logs between log sequence number 1 and log sequence number 2 are to be used

SHOW INACTIVE: Includes backup objects that have been deactivated

TAKEN AT timestamp: Specifies a backup image by its timestamp

KEEP n: Deactivates all objects of the specified type except for the most recent *n* by timestamp

OLDER THAN timestamp or n days: Specifies that objects with a timestamp earlier than timestamp or *n* days will be deactivated

DATABASE database_name: Considers only those objects associated with the specified database name.

DBPARTITIONNUM db-partition-number: Considers only those objects created by the specified database partition number

PASSWORD password: Specifies the TSM client password for this server, if required. If a database is specified and the password is not provided, the value specified for the tsm_password database configuration parameter is passed to TSM; otherwise, no password is used.

NODENAME node_name: Considers only those images associated with a specific TSM node name

WITHOUT PROMPTING: The user is not prompted for verification before objects are deleted

OWNER owner: Considers only those objects created by the specified owner

VERBOSE: Displays additional file information

Notes: One parameter from each group below can be used to restrict what backup images types are included in the operation:

- Granularity
  - ○ FULL—include only database backup images.
  - ○ TABLESPACE—include only table space backup images.
- Cumulativeness
  - ○ NONINCREMENTAL—include only non-incremental backup images.
  - ○ INCREMENTAL—include only incremental backup images.
  - ○ DELTA—include only incremental delta backup images.
- Compatibilities
  - ○ For compatibility with versions earlier than Version 8, the key word NODE can be substituted for DBPARTITIONNUM.

Take a database backup using TSM:

```
$ db2 backup database sample use tsm

Backup successful. The timestamp for this backup is : 20020811130942
```

Output from db2adutl:

```
$ db2adutl query

Query for database SAMPLE
Retrieving full database backup information.
full database backup image: 1, Time: 20020811130942,
Oldest log: S0000028.LOG, Sessions used: 1
full database backup image: 2, Time: 20020811142241,
Oldest log: S0000029.LOG, Sessions used: 1
Retrieving table space backup information.
table space backup image: 1, Time: 20020811094003,
Oldest log: S0000026.LOG, Sessions used: 1
table space backup image: 2, Time: 20020811093043,
Oldest log: S0000025.LOG, Sessions used: 1
table space backup image: 3, Time: 20020811105905,
Oldest log: S0000027.LOG, Sessions used: 1
Retrieving log archive information.
Log file: S0000025.LOG
Log file: S0000026.LOG
Log file: S0000027.LOG
Log file: S0000028.LOG
Log file: S0000029.LOG
Log file: S0000030.LOG
```

```
$ db2adutl delete full taken at 20020811093043 db sample

Query for database SAMPLE
Retrieving full database backup information. Please wait.
full database backup image:
SAMPLE.0.v8inst.NODE0000.CATN0000.20020811093043.001
Do you want to deactivate this backup image (Y/N)? y
Are you sure (Y/N)? y

$ db2adutl query

Query for database SAMPLE
Retrieving full database backup information.
full database backup image: 1, Time: 20020811130942,
Oldest log: S0000028.LOG, Sessions used: 1
full database backup image: 2, Time: 20020811142241,
Oldest log: S0000029.LOG, Sessions used: 1
Retrieving table space backup information.
table space backup image: 1, Time: 20020811094003,
Oldest log: S0000026.LOG, Sessions used: 1
table space backup image: 3, Time: 20020811105905,
Oldest log: S0000027.LOG, Sessions used: 1
Retrieving log archive information.
Log file: S0000026.LOG
Log file: S0000027.LOG
Log file: S0000028.LOG
Log file: S0000029.LOG
Log file: S0000030.LOG
```

db2ckbkp—Check Backup

This utility can be used to test the integrity of a backup image or multiple parts of a backup image and to determine whether the image can be restored. It can also be used to display the metadata stored in the backup header.

Usage:

- Anyone can access the utility, but users must have read permissions on image backups in order to execute this utility against them.
- No connection to the database is required.
- Command parameters:

  –a: Displays all available information

  –c: Displays results of checkbits and checksums

  –d: Displays information from the headers of DMS table space data pages

–h: Displays media header information, including the name and path of the image expected by the restore utility

–H: Displays the same information as –h but reads only the 4-KB media header information from the beginning of the image. It does not validate the image. This option is not valid in combination with any other option.

–l: Displays log file header data

–n: Prompts for tape mount; assume one tape per device

–o: Displays detailed information from the object headers

–p: Displays the number of pages of each object type

image_name: The name of the backup image file. One or more files can be checked at a time.

Notes:

- If the complete backup consists of multiple objects, the validation will succeed only if *db2ckbkp* is used to validate all of the objects at the same time.
- If a backup image was created using multiple sessions, db2ckbkp can examine all of the files at the same time. Users are responsible for ensuring that the session with sequence number 001 is the first file specified.
- This utility can also verify backup images that are stored on tape (except images that were created with a variable block size). This is done by preparing the tape as for a restore operation, then invoking the utility, specifying the tape device name.

  For example, on UNIX: db2ckbkp –h /dev/rmt0

  Or on Windows: db2ckbkp –d \\.\tape1

- If the image is on a tape device, specify the tape device path. You will be prompted to ensure it is mounted, unless option '–n' is given. If there are multiple tapes, the first tape must be mounted on the first device path given. (That is the tape with sequence 001 in the header.)

Take a database backup:

```
$ db2 backup database sample to /data/dbbackup

Backup successful. The timestamp for this backup image is : 20020828231900
```

The following is sample output from db2ckbkp:

```
$ db2ckbkp  /data/dbbackup/SAMPLE.0.v8inst.NODE0000.CATN0000.001

[1] Buffers processed:  #####
Image Verification Complete - successful.

$ db2ckbkp —h /data/dbbackup/SAMPLE.0.v8inst.NODE0000.CATN0000.001
```

```
======================
MEDIA HEADER REACHED:
======================
        Server Database Name               -- SAMPLE
        Server Database Alias              -- SAMPLE
        Client Database Alias              -- SAMPLE
        Timestamp                          -- 20020828231900
        Database Partition Number          -- 0
        Instance                           -- v8inst
        Sequence Number                    -- 1
        Release ID                         -- A00
        Database Seed                      -- 719E1F66
        DB Comment's Codepage (Volume)     -- 0
        DB Comment (Volume)                --
        DB Comment's Codepage (System)     -- 0
        DB Comment (System)                --
        Authentication Value               -- 255
        Backup Mode                        -- 0
        Backup Type                        -- 0
        Backup Gran.                       -- 0
        Status Flags                       -- 1
        System Cats inc                    -- 1
        Catalog Partition Number           -- 0
        DB Codeset                         -- ISO8859-1
        DB Territory                       --
        Backup Buffer Size                 -- 4194304
        Number of Sessions                 -- 1
        Platform                           -- 4

The proper image file name would be:
SAMPLE.0.v8inst.NODE0000.CATN0000.20020828231900.001
[1] Buffers processed:  #####
Image Verification Complete - successful.
```

db2ckrst—Check Incremental Restore Image Sequence

This utility allows the user to query the database history in order to generate a suggested sequence of backup image timestamps. It also gives a simplified restore syntax needed for a manual restore.

Usage:

- Anyone can access the utility.
- No connection to the database is required.

- Command parameters:

  –d database name /alias: Specifies the alias name for the database that will be restored

  –t timestamp: Specifies the timestamp for a backup image that will be incrementally restored

  –r: Specifies the type of restore that will be executed. The default is database.

  –n tablespace name: Specifies the name of one or more table spaces that will be restored

  –h/–u/–?: Displays help information. When this option is specified, all other options are ignored, and only the help information is displayed.

Notes:

- The database history must exist in order for this utility to be used. If the database history does not exist, specify the HISTORY FILE option in the RESTORE command before using this utility.
- If the FORCE option of the PRUNE HISTORY command is used, you will be able to delete entries that are required for recovery from the most recent, full database backup image. The default operation of the PRUNE HISTORY command prevents required entries from being deleted. It is recommended that you do not use the FORCE option of the PRUNE HISTORY command.
- This utility should not be used as a replacement for keeping records of your backups.

The following is sample output from db2ckrst:

```
$ db2ckrst —d sample —t 20020828233730 —r database

Suggested restore order of images using timestamp 20020828233730 for
database sample.
================================
restore db sample incremental taken at 20020828233730
restore db sample incremental taken at 20020828233647
restore db sample incremental taken at 20020828233730
================================


$ db2ckrst —d sample —t 20020828233730 —r  tablespace —n userspace1

Suggested restore order of images using timestamp 20020828233730 for
database sample.
================================
restore db sample tablespace ( USERSPACE1 ) incremental taken at
   20020828233730
restore db sample tablespace ( USERSPACE1 ) incremental taken at
   20020828233647
restore db sample tablespace ( USERSPACE1 ) incremental taken at
   20020828233730
================================
```

db2flsn—Find Log Sequence Number

This utility returns the log file name that contains the log record identified by the given log sequence number (LSN). The input LSN must be a string of length 12 or 16 representing the LSN in hex.

Usage:

- Anyone can access the utility.
- No connection to the database is required.
- Command parameters:

    −q: Specifies that only the log file name be printed. No error or warning messages will be printed, and status can be determined only through the return code. Valid error codes are:

    ○ 100 Invalid input
    ○ 101 Cannot open LFH file
    ○ 102 Failed to read LFH file
    ○ 103 Invalid LFH
    ○ 104 Database is not recoverable
    ○ 105 LSN too big
    ○ 500 Logical error

    Other valid return codes are:

    ○ 0 Successful execution
    ○ 99 Warning: the result is based on the last known log file size.

Notes:

- The log header control file SQLOGCTL.LFH must reside in the current directory.
- Since this file is located in the database directory, the tool can be run from the database directory, or the control file can be copied to the directory from which the tool will be run.
- The tool uses the LOGFILSIZ database configuration parameter. DB2 records the three most recent values for this parameter and the first log file that is created with each LOGFILSIZ value; this enables the tool to work correctly when LOGFILSIZ changes. If the specified LSN predates the earliest recorded value of LOGFILSIZ, the tool uses this value and returns a warning. This tool can be used only with recoverable databases. A database is recoverable if it is configured with LOGRETAIN set to ON or USEREXIT set to ON.

The following is sample output from these commands:

```
$ db2flsn 000000BF0030
Given LSN is contained in log file S0000002.LOG
```

```
$ db2flsn -q 000000BF0030
S0000002.LOG

$ db2flsn 000000BE0030
Warning: the result is based on the last known log file size.
The last known log file size is 23 4K pages starting from log extent 2.
Given LSN is contained in log file S0000001.LOG

$ db2flsn -q 000000BE0030
S0000001.LOG
```

db2inidb—Initialize a Mirrored Database

This utility initializes a mirrored database in a split mirror environment. The mirrored database can be initialized as a clone of the primary database, placed in rollforward pending state, or used as a backup image to restore the primary database.

Usage:

- User must have one of the following: sysadm, sysctrl, or sysmaint.
- No connection to the database is required.
- Command parameters:

   database_alias: Specifies the alias of the database to be initialized

   SNAPSHOT: Specifies that the mirrored database will be initialized as a clone of the primary database

   STANDBY: Specifies that the database will be placed in rollforward pending state. New logs from the primary database can be fetched and applied to the standby database. The standby database can then be used in place of the primary database if it goes down.

   MIRROR: Specifies that the mirrored database is to be used as a backup image, which can be used to restore the primary database

   RELOCATE USING config_file: Specifies that the database files are to be relocated, based on the information listed in the configuration file

Sample command from db2inidb:

```
$ db2inidb <database_alias> as < snapshot | standby |mirror >
  [ relocate using <config_file> ]

$ db2initdb sample as snapshot
```

CLP COMMANDS

ARCHIVE LOG

This utility closes and truncates the active log file for a recoverable database. If user exit is enabled, an archive request is issued.

Usage:

- The user must be one of the following: sysadm, sysctrl, sysmaint, or dbadm.
- No connection to the database is required.
- Command parameters:

    DATABASE database-alias: Specifies the alias of the database whose active log is to be archived

    USER username: Identifies the user name under which a connection will be attempted

    USING password: Specifies the password to authenticate the user name

    ON ALL DBPARTITIONNUMS: Specifies that the command should be issued on all database partitions in the db2nodes.cfg file. This is the default if a database partition number clause is not specified

    EXCEPT: Specifies that the command should be issued on all database partitions in the db2nodes.cfg file, except those specified in the database partition number list

    ON DBPARTITIONNUM/ON DBPARTITIONNUMS: Specifies that the logs should be archived for the specified database on a set of database partitions

    db-partition-number: Specifies a database partition number in the database partition number list

    TO db-partition-number: Used when specifying a range of database partitions for which the logs should be archived. All database partitions from the first database partition number specified, up to and including the second database partition number specified, are included in the database partition number list.

Notes:

- This command can be used to collect a complete set of log files up to a known point. The log files can then be used to update a standby database.
- This command can be executed only when the invoking application or shell does not have a database connection to the specified database. This prevents a user from executing the command with uncommitted transactions. As such, the ARCHIVE LOG command will not forcibly commit the user's incomplete transactions. If the invoking application or shell already has a database connection to the specified database, the command will terminate and return an error. If another application has transactions in progress with the specified database when this command is executed, there will be a

slight performance degradation because the command flushes the log buffer to disk. Any other transactions attempting to write log records to the buffer will have to wait until the flush is complete.

- If used in a partitioned database environment, a subset of database partitions may be specified by using a database partition number clause. If the database partition number clause is not specified, the default behavior for this command is to close and archive the active log on all database partitions.
- Using this command will use up a portion of the active log space, due to the truncation of the active log file. The active log space will resume its previous size when the truncated log becomes inactive. Frequent use of this command may drastically reduce the amount of the active log space available for transactions.

For compatibility with versions earlier than Version 8:

- The keyword NODE can be substituted for DBPARTITIONNUM.

Sample output from db2 archive log:

```
$ db2 archive log for database SAMPLE


DB20000I  The ARCHIVE LOG command completed successfully.
```

LIST HISTORY

This command lists entries in the history file. The history file contains a record of recovery and administrative events. Recovery events include full database and table space level backup, incremental backup, restore, and rollforward operations. Additional logged events include create, alter, drop, or rename table space, reorganize table, drop table, and load.

Usage:

- Anyone can access the utility.
- An explicit instance attachment is not required. If the database is listed as remote, an instance attachment to the remote server is established for the duration of the command.
- Command parameters:

  HISTORY: Lists all events that are currently logged in the history file

  BACKUP: Lists backup and restore operations

  ROLLFORWARD: Lists rollforward operations

  DROPPED TABLE: Lists dropped table records

  LOAD: Lists load operations

  CREATE TABLESPACE: Lists table space create and drop operations

RENAME TABLESPACE: Lists table space renaming operations

REORG: Lists reorganization operations

ALTER TABLESPACE: Lists alter table space operations

ALL: Lists all entries of the specified type in the history file

SINCE timestamp: A complete timestamp (format yyyymmddhhmmss) or an initial prefix (minimum yyyy) can be specified. All entries with timestamps equal to or greater than the timestamp provided are listed.

CONTAINING schema.object_name: This qualified name uniquely identifies a table.

CONTAINING object_name: This unqualified name uniquely identifies a table space.

FOR DATABASE database-alias: Used to identify the database whose recovery history file is to be listed

Notes:

The report generated by this command contains the operation symbols listed in Table A.1 and operation types listed in Table A.2.

Table A.1 Operation Symbols

Operation	Description
A	Create table space
B	Backup
C	Load copy
D	Dropped table
F	Rollforward
G	Reorganize table
L	Load
N	Rename table space
O	Drop table space
Q	Quiesce
R	Restore
T	Alter table space
U	Unload

Table A.2 Operation Types

Backup Types	Description
F	Offline
N	Online
I	Incremental offline
O	Incremental online
D	Delta offline
E	Delta online
Rollforward Types	**Description**
E	End of logs
P	Point in time
Load Types	**Description**
I	Insert
R	Replace
Alter Tablespace Types	**Description**
C	Add containers
R	Rebalance
Quiesce Types	**Description**
S	Quiesce share
U	Quiesce update
X	Quiesce exclusive
Z	Quiesce reset

PRUNE HISTORY/LOGFILE

This command is used to delete entries from the recovery history file or to delete log files from the active log file path. Deleting entries from the recovery history file may be necessary if the file becomes excessively large and the retention period is high. Deleting log files from the active log file path may be necessary if logs are being archived manually (rather than through a user exit program).

Usage:

- The user must be one of the following: sysadm, sysctrl, sysmaint, or dbadm.
- Connection to the database is required.

- Command parameters:

HISTORY timestamp: Identifies a range of entries in the recovery history file that will be deleted. A complete timestamp (in the form yyyymmddhhmmss) or an initial prefix (minimum yyyy) can be specified. All entries with timestamps equal to or less than the timestamp provided are deleted from the recovery history file.

WITH FORCE OPTION: Specifies that the entries will be pruned according to the timestamp specified, even if some entries from the most recent restore set are deleted from the file. A restore set is the most recent full database backup, including any restores of that backup image. If this parameter is not specified, all entries from the backup image forward will be maintained in the history.

LOGFILE PRIOR TO log-file-name: Specifies a string for a log file name, for example, S0000100.LOG. All log files prior to (but not including) the specified log file will be deleted. The LOGRETAIN database configuration parameter must be set to RECOVERY or CAPTURE.

UPDATE HISTORY FILE

This command updates the location, device type, or comment in a history file entry.

Usage:

- The user must be one of the following: sysadm, sysctrl, sysmaint, or dbadm.
- Connection to the database is required.
- Command parameters:

FOR object-part: Specifies the identifier for the backup or copy image. It is a timestamp with an optional sequence number from 001 to 999.

LOCATION new-location: Specifies the new physical location of a backup image. The interpretation of this parameter depends on the device type.

DEVICE TYPE new-device-type: Specifies a new device type for storing the backup image. Valid device types are:

- **D**—Disk
- **K**—Diskette
- **T**—Tape
- **A**—TSM
- **U**—User exit
- **P**—Pipe
- **N**—Null device
- **X**—XBSA
- **Q**—SQL statement
- **O**—Other

> **COMMENT new-comment:** Specifies a new comment to describe the entry

Note: The history file is used by database administrators for record keeping. It is used internally by DB2 for the automatic recovery of incremental backups.

ONLINE UTILITY

INSPECT

This utility inspects the database for architectural integrity, checking the pages of the database for page consistency. The inspection checks whether the structures of table objects and table spaces are valid.

In a single-partition system, the scope is that of a single partition only. In a partitioned database system, it is the collection of all logical partitions defined in db2nodes.cfg.

Usage:

- The user must be one of the following: sysadm, sysctrl, sysmaint, dbadm, or control privilege, if dealing with a single table.
- Connection to the database is required.
- Command parameters for the db2inspf utility:

   data-file: The unformatted inspection results file to format

   out-file: The output file for the formatted output

   –tsi n: Table space ID. Format out only for tables in this table space.

   –ti: n Table ID. Format out only for table with this ID; table space ID must also be provided.

   –e: Format out errors only

   –s: Summary only

Sample output from db2 inspect and db2inspf:

```
$ db2 connect to sample

$ db2  inspect  check  database  results  inspect_sample.err
```

The online inspect check processing will write out unformatted inspection data results to the results file specified. The file will be written out to the diagnostic data directory path. If there is no error found by the check processing, this result output file will be erased at the end of INSPECT operation. If there are errors found by the check processing, this result output file will not be erased at the end of INSPECT operation. After check processing completes, to see inspection details, the inspection result data must be formatted out with the utility *db2inspf*. The results file will have a file extension of the database partition number.

In a partitioned database environment, each database partition will generate its own results output file with an extension corresponding to its database partition number. The output location for the results output file will be the database manager diagnostic data directory path. If the name of a file that already exists is specified, the operation will not be processed; the file will have to be removed before that file name can be specified.

You can use the option KEEP to always keep the result output file.

```
$ db2 inspect   check   database   results   keep   inspect_sample.err

$ db2inspf  inspect_sample.err   inspect_sample.fmt
```

parseSQL.pl

T he following PERL program will parse the output of the SQL snapshot and convert the information to comma-delimited format so that it can be imported into a spreadsheet.

```perl
#!/usr/local/bin/perl -w
#!/usr/bin/perl -w
#use English;

#=================================================================
#
# parseSQL.pl
#
# Parses a Dynamic SQL snapshot, outputs the report lines in delimited
# ascii format so that is can be read into a spread sheet
# for analysis and sorting of the output.
#
# USAGE:
# parseSQL.pl input-file "string to start a new row in the output file"
# match_character output-file
#
# e.g. parseSQL.pl dynsql.out "^ Number of executions" = > temp.out
# The above commands will open and parse the file dynsql.out
# and write the information on the right side of the '='
# and write a new line each time it finds "^ Number of executions"
#
# example command
# perl parseSQL.pl sql.snap "^ Number of executions" = > temp.txt
#
#=================================================================
```

```perl
if ( $#ARGV < 2 )
   {
     die "For usage info - Read the comments at the top of the source
         file\n\n";
   }

my $file = $ARGV[0];
my $filetmp = $file . ".temp-file1";
open (FILE,$file) || die "Cannot read from $file";
open (TMP, ">$filetmp") || die "Cannot write to $filetmp\n";
my $counter = 0;

#print $ARGV[1];

$title = "";
$count=0;
while (<FILE>) {
   #$counter++ if s/=/x/gi;
   chomp;
   if ( m/$ARGV[1]/gi )
   {
      $count = $count + 1;
      if ($count > 0 )
         {print TMP "\n";}
   }
   $temppos = index($_, $ARGV[2]);
   #print  TMP "\n$_\n";
   @words = split(/$ARGV[2]/, $_);
   #if ($#words >= 1)
   if ($temppos >= 1)
   {
      if ($count == 1)
      {
          grep(s/ *$|\t|\n//, $words[0]);
          grep(s/^ *|\t|\n//, $words[0]);
          $title = $title . $words[0] . "\t";
      }
      #print TMP "$words[1]\t";
      #print  TMP "\n$_\n";
      $temps = substr($_, $temppos+1);
      print TMP "$temps\t";
   }
   else
   {
      #print "\nstart\n" ;
   }
}
```

```perl
print "$title\n";

close TMP;

open (TMP, "<$filetmp") || die "Cannot read from $filetmp\n";
while (<TMP>)
{
   print $_;
}
```

C

exfmtDIF.pl

T he following PERL program will parse the output of the SQL snapshot and convert the information to comma-delimited format so that it can be imported into a spreadsheet.

```perl
#!/usr/bin/perl
#
#  exfmtDIF.pl - Find differences between access plans obtained by
#  the db2exfmt utility
#
#  Description:
#  exfmtDIF will identify differences in two
#  access plans obtained using the db2exfmt tool with -g option.
#
#  Details:
#  For each statement that is the same in the two plans,
#  retreive the access plan and compare them.
#
#  - If the second file contains a query not found in the first,
#    the difference will not be revealed.
#

use English;

if (scalar(@ARGV) != 2) {

  print "$PROGRAM_NAME requires 2 plans to compare\n";
  exit;

}
```

```perl
$filename1 = @ARGV[0];
$filename2 = @ARGV[1];

open(FILE1, "<$filename1");
open(FILE2, "<$filename2");
@file1 = <FILE1>;
@file2 = <FILE2>;
close(FILE1);
close(FILE2);

main();

#
# Main body of program.  Gets the statements and plans for each
# file and compares queries and plans to find differences
#
sub main2
{
  my(@queries1) = get_statements(@file1);
  my(@queries2) = get_statements(@file2);
  my(@plans1) = get_plans(@file1);
  my(@plans2) = get_plans(@file2);
  my($querycount1) = $#queries1+1;
  my($querycount2) = $#queries2+1;

  my($index1) = 0;
  my($found) = 0;

  #  For each query from the first file
  while ($index1 < $querycount1)
  {
    my($index2) = 0;

    # Compare to every query in the second file
    while ($index2 < $querycount2)
    {

      # If the queries are the same, compare the associated access
      # plans
      if (@queries1[$index1] eq @queries2[$index2])
      {
        my($i) = $index1 + 1;
        my($j) = $index2 + 1;
        print "$filename1, plan \#$i  vs.  $filename2, plan \#$j: ";
        if (compare_plans(@plans1[$index1], @plans2[$index2]))
        {
          print "same\n";
```

```perl
        }
        else
        {
          print "**DIFFERENT**\n";

          print "$filename1, plan \#$i:\n";
          my($fmtplan) = fmt_plan(@plans1[$index1]);
          print "$fmtplan\n";

          print "$filename2, plan \#$j:\n";
          $fmtplan = fmt_plan(@plans2[$index2]);
          print "$fmtplan\n";
        }
        $index2 = $querycount2;
        $found = 1;
      }
      $index2++;
    }
    if ($found == 0)
    {
      print "QUERY:\n@queries1[$index1]\n\n not found in $filename2";
    }
    $index1++;
  }
}


#
# Get all the 'Original Statement' queries from the
# given array of text
#
sub get_statements
{
  my(@data) = @_;
  my(@stmts) = ();

  while (@data)
  {
    if (shift(@data) =~ /^Original Statement:/)
    {
      shift(@data);
      my($line) = shift(@data);

      # Get the original statement block
      my(@stmt) = ();
      while ($line !~ /^\s*$/)
      {
        push(@stmt, $line);
        $line = shift(@data);
```

```perl
        }
        push(@stmt, "\n");
        push(@stmts,join(' ',@stmt));
      }
    }
  }
  return @stmts;
}


#
# Get all the access plans from the inputted text array
#
sub get_plans
{
  my(@data) = @_;
  my(@plans) = ();

  while (@data)
  {
    if (shift(@data) =~ /^Access Plan:/)
    {
      shift(@data);
      shift(@data);
      shift(@data);
      shift(@data);

      my($line) = shift(@data);

      # Get the access plan block
      my(@plan) = ();
      while ($line !~ /^\s*$/)
      {
        push(@plan, $line);
        $line = shift(@data);
      }
      push(@plan, "\n");
      push(@plans,join(' ',@plan));
    }
  }
  return @plans;
}


#
# Compares the two access plan strings
# Returns 1 if they are the same, otherwise, returns 0
#
sub compare_plans
{
  my($plan1,$plan2) = @_;
```

```perl
   $plan1 = fmt_plan($plan1);
   $plan2 = fmt_plan($plan2);
   if ($plan1 eq $plan2)
   {
     return 1;
   }
   else
   {
     return 0;
   }
}

#
# Formats an access plan string to discard information
# that we do not care about when comparing access plans
#
sub fmt_plan
{
  my($plan) = @_;
  $plan =~ s/\d*e\+\d*//g;      # take out exponent
  $plan =~ s/[^a-zA-Z]\d/ /g;# replace numbers not beside a letter with blanks
  $plan =~ s/[^a-zA-Z]\d/ /g;# replace numbers not beside a letter with blanks
  $plan =~ s/\./ /g;            # replace periods with blanks
  $plan =~ s/\(/ /g;            # replace brackets with blanks
  $plan =~ s/\)/ /g;
  $plan =~ s/\n\s+\n/\n/g;      # take out blank lines
  return $plan;
}
```

Comparing Index Advisor Recommended Indexes with Existing Indexes

B elow is a Korn shell script to compare the indexes recommended by the index advisor with the existing indexes.

> **NOTE** In this script, please change the following:
>
> dbname: to the name of the database
> SCHEMA: to the table schema
>
> And if the Index Advisor does not recommend any indexes, there will be no output.

```
#!/usr/bin/ksh
#
#Passed name of file containing SQL
FN=${1%.sql}
STMT="db2advis -d dbname  -i ${FN}.sql -t 0  -o ${FN}.inx >
${FN}.advis"
#echo $STMT
eval $STMT
db2  connect to dbname
echo " " > ${FN}.sug
grep CREATE ${FN}.inx | grep -v ET | cut -d"\"" -f4 | while read TN
do
#echo $TN
STMT="db2  \"export to temp of del messages /dev/null select
substr(tabname,1,20),substr(colnames,1,30) from syscat.indexes where
tabschema='SCHEMA' and tabname='$TN' \""
```

```
#echo $STMT
eval $STMT
echo "     " >> ${FN}.sug
echo "Current Existing indexes" >> ${FN}.sug
cat temp >> ${FN}.sug
echo "DB2ADVIS Recommended indexes"  >> ${FN}.sug
grep CREATE ${FN}.inx | grep -v ET  | grep $TN  >> ${FN}.sug
done
```

Configuration Parameters That Can Be Changed Online

onfigurable online configuration parameters take immediate effect without the need to stop and start the instance or deactivate and activate the database. You no longer have to disconnect users when you fine-tune your system, giving you more flexibility for deciding when to change the configuration.

Key database and database manager configuration parameters can be set online. For example, memory heaps such as CATALOGCACHE_SZ, PCKCACHE_SZ, STMTHEAP, SORTHEAP, and UTIL_HEAP_SZ are dynamic, allowing you to adjust memory usage as workloads vary over time. Other parameters, such as LOCKLIST, MAXLOCKS, and DLCHKTIME, will allow you to adjust the locking characteristics of your database system, which can improve performance.

You can choose to defer a change to a configurable online configuration parameter so that the configuration change will be made at the next instance start or database activation. A SHOW DETAILS option has been added to the GET DATABASE and GET DATABASE MANAGER CONFIGURATION commands that will list both the current value and the value that will be used at the next instance start or database activation.

In a few cases, you can set the parameter you are configuring to automatic, and DB2 will then adjust its value automatically as workload on the system changes. For example, setting MAXAPPLS to automatic says there is no limit to the maximum number of applications, except when memory is exhausted. The GET DATABASE and GET DATABASE MANAGER CONFIGURATION commands have been changed to indicate the configuration values set to automatic and their current values.

For some database manager configuration parameters, the database manager must be stopped (*db2stop*) and restarted (*db2start*) for the new parameter values to take effect.

For some database parameters, changes will take effect only when the database is reactivated. In these cases, all applications must first disconnect from the database. (If the database was activated, it must be deactivated and reactivated.) Then, at the first new connect to the database, the changes will take effect.

Other parameters can be changed online; these are called *configurable online configuration parameters.*

If you change the setting of a configurable online database manager configuration parameter while you are attached to an instance, the default behavior of the UPDATE DBM CFG command will be to apply the change immediately. If you do not want the change applied immediately, use the DEFERRED option on the UPDATE DBM CFG command.

For clients, changes to the database manager configuration parameters take effect the next time the client connects to a server.

If you change a configurable online database configuration parameter while connected, the default behavior is to apply the change online, wherever possible. You should note that some parameter changes may take a noticeable amount of time to take effect, due to the overhead associated with allocating space. To change configuration parameters online from the command line processor, a connection to the database is required.

Each configurable online configuration parameter has a propagation class associated with it. The propagation class indicates when you can expect a change to the configuration parameter to take effect. There are three propagation classes:

- **Immediate**: Parameters that change immediately upon command or API invocation. For example, DIAGLEVEL has a propagation class of immediate.
- **Statement boundary**: Parameters that change on statement and statement-like boundaries. For example, if you change the value of SORTHEAP, all new SQL requests will start using the new value.
- **Transaction boundary**: Parameters that change on transaction boundaries. For example, a new value for DL_EXPINT is updated after a COMMIT statement.

Changing some database configuration parameters can influence the access plan chosen by the SQL optimizer. After changing any of these parameters, you should consider rebinding your applications to ensure the best access plan is being used for your SQL statements. Any parameters that were modified online (for example, by using the UPDATE DATABASE CONFIGURATION USING <parm> IMMEDIATE command) will cause the SQL optimizer to choose new access plans for new SQL statements. However, the SQL statement cache will not be purged of existing entries. To clear the contents of the SQL cache, use the FLUSH PACKAGE CACHE statement.

Although new parameter values may not be immediately effective, viewing the parameter settings (using GET DATABASE MANAGER CONFIGURATION or GET DATABASE CONFIGURATION commands) will always show the latest updates. Viewing the parameter settings using the SHOW DETAIL clause on these commands will show both the latest updates and the values in memory.

```
$ db2 attach to v8inst
```

```
$ db2 get dbm cfg show detail
```

The "Automatic" column in Tables E.1–E.3 indicates whether the parameter supports the AUTOMATIC keyword on the UPDATE DBM CFG or UPDATE DB CFG FOR <dbname> command. If you set a parameter to automatic, DB2 will automatically adjust the parameter to reflect current resource requirements for the instance or the database.

Table E.1   Configurable Database Manager Configuration Parameters

Parameter	Configurable Online	Automatic
catalog_noauth	Yes	No
comm_bandwidth	Yes	No
conn_elapse	Yes	No
cpuspeed	Yes	No
dft_account_str	Yes	No
dft_monswitches - dft_mon_bufpool - dft_mon_lock - dft_mon_sort - dft_mon_stmt - dft_mon_table - dft_mon_timestamp - dft_mon_uow	Yes	No
dftdbpath	Yes	No
diaglevel	Yes	No
diagpath	Yes	No
discover_inst	Yes	No
fcm_num_buffers	Yes	No
fed_noauth	Yes	No
health_mon	Yes	No
indexrec	Yes	No
instance_memory	No	Yes

Table E.1   Configurable Database Manager Configuration Parameters (Continued)

Parameter	Configurable Online	Automatic
max_connretries	Yes	No
max_querydegree	Yes	No
notifylevel	Yes	No
start_stop_time	Yes	No
use_sna_auth	Yes	No

Table E.2   Configurable Database Configuration Parameters

Parameter	Configurable Online	Automatic
autorestart	Yes	No
avg_appls	Yes	No
blk_log_dsk_ful	Yes	No
catalogcache_sz	Yes	No
database_memory	No	Yes
dbheap	Yes	No
dft_degree	Yes	No
dft_extent_sz	Yes	No
dft_loadrec_ses	Yes	No
dft_prefetch_sz	Yes	No
dft_queryopt	Yes	No
discover_db	Yes	No
dlchktime	Yes	No
dl_expint	Yes	No
dl_num_copies	Yes	No
dl_time_drop	Yes	No
dl_token	Yes	No
dl_upper	Yes	No
dl_wt_iexpint	Yes	No
indexrec	Yes	No

Table E.2   Configurable Database Configuration Parameters (Continued)

Parameter	Configurable Online	Automatic
locklist	Yes	No
logsecond	Yes	No
maxappls	Yes	Yes
maxfilop	Yes	No
maxlocks	Yes	No
mincommit	Yes	No
num_db_backups	Yes	No
num_freqvalues	Yes	No
num_quantiles	Yes	No
pckcachesz	Yes	No
seqdetect	Yes	No
sortheap	Yes	No
stmtheap	Yes	No
tsm_mgmtclass	Yes	No
tsm_nodename	Yes	No
tsm_owner	Yes	No
tsm_password	Yes	No
util_heap_sz	Yes	No

Table E.3   DAS Configuration Parameters

Parameter	Configurable Online	Automatic
contact_host	Yes	No
das_codepage	Yes	No
das_territory	Yes	No
db2system	Yes	No
discover	Yes	No
jdk_path	Yes	No
smtp_server	Yes	No

Explain Tools

For SQL tuning, it is often necessary to determine the access path chosen by the optimizer for the query. Under the federated database architecture, the best performance is achieved when the query is passed through to the remote database and all of the steps of the access plan are executed on the remote database.

EXPLAIN on the DB2 ESE server will show which operations are performed locally and which are performed on the remote server. To see the "real" access plan, it will be necessary to run EXPLAIN on the remote database.

> **N O T E**   Without a minimum of DB2 on OS/390 experience, the easiest way to get DB2 on OS/390 EXPLAIN results is to use Visual EXPLAIN for DB2 on OS/390.

For example, if the query is embedded in a stored procedure, it will be necessary to copy the query out of the stored procedures and replace parameter markers with hard-coded values to run EXPLAIN on the query.

The sections below describe how to create the EXPLAIN tables, how to run EXPLAIN from the command line, how to interpret the output of EXPLAIN, and how to use Visual EXPLAIN on a federated system.

EXPLAIN TABLES

DB2 ESE uses explain tables to store access plan information so that users can see the decision that the optimizer has made. These tables are:

- EXPLAIN_ARGUMENT

- EXPLAIN_INSTANCE
- EXPLAIN_OBJECT
- EXPLAIN_OPERATOR
- EXPLAIN_PREDICATE
- EXPLAIN_STATEMENT
- EXPLAIN_STREAM

The EXPLAIN tables must be created for each user ID that will run EXPLAIN (on each database). The tables can be created using Visual EXPLAIN (see below) or by a script run from the DB2 command line:

```
$ db2 -tvf  $HOME/sqllib/misc/EXPLAIN.DDL


  where $HOME is the DB2 ESE instance owner's directory
```

For DB2 on OS/390, a slightly different procedure is required: For a user to be able to create his or her own explain tables on OS/390, the user must be granted CREATE TABLESPACE authority in the particular database in which the EXPLAIN tables will be created.

> **N O T E**   Check with the DB2 on OS/390 SYSADM to get the appropriate authority granted or have the SYSADM person create the explain tables for your user ID.

There are two ways to create explain tables for DB2 on OS/390 host390:

1. From a TSO session via SPUFI, execute explain DDL
2. From a UNIX command line, connect to host390 using OS/390 user ID and password (i.e., tst1txp), and execute EXPLAIN.DDL

EXPLAIN COMMANDS

There are two explain tools available that can be run from the command line. In addition, you can use the db2exfmt to format the contents of the explain tables into a legible, organized output.

db2exfmt

- This command is used to format the contents of the explain tables into a legible, organized output.
- It is located in the instance owner /sqllib/bin directory.

To use the tool, read access for the explain tables being formatted is required.

```
$ db2exfmt -d sample -e % -n % -s % -g TIC -w -1 -# 0
```

To get the syntax and help on db2exfmt:

```
$ db2exfmt -h
```

db2expln

- This command is used to explain SQL statements contained in packages. These include packages generated as part of the stored procedure build process.
- The statements in the packages are static SQL where the access path has already been selected and prepared through the BIND process.
- The program connects and binds itself to a database using the db2expln.bnd file the first time the database is accessed. The db2expln.bnd file is in the ../sqllib/bnd directory.
- To run db2expln, you must have SELECT privilege to the system catalog views, as well as EXECUTE authority for the db2expln package.
- When you use the dynamic options of db2expln, the statement is prepared as true dynamic SQL, and the generated plan is explained from the SQL cache.

To use db2expln, you need to specify the package name that corresponds to a given stored procedure. You can use following query to get the package name.

```
$ db2 "select substr(procschema,1,8),
    substr(procname,1,32),
    substr(implementation,1,8)
  from syscat.procedures"
```

You can then invoke db2expln on package P7597614 as follows:

```
$ db2expln -d SAMPLE -c tphan -p P7597614 -s 0 -o db2expln_P7597614.rpt
```

Alternatively, to explain all the packages of schema tphan, you can use the wild card character %:

```
$ db2expln -d SAMPLE -c tphan -p % -s 0 -o db2expln_all_packages.rpt
```

To explain a dynamic statement contained in the file stmt1.sql:

```
$ db2expln -d SAMPLE -stmtfile stmt1.sql -terminator @
  -o db2expln_stmt1.rpt
```

To get the syntax and help on db2expln:

```
$ db2expln -h
```

dynexpln

- The dynexpln tool is still available for backward compatibility. It is recommended to use the dynamic options of db2expln to perform all of the functions of dynexpln.
- It is used to explain SQL statements that are not embedded and bound into packages. The access path is being determined dynamically during execution time.

- The statements are dynamic SQL.
- To run dynexpln, you must have BINDADD authority for the database, as well as any privileges needed for the SQL statements being explained.

To use dynexpln, the preferred approach is to create a file and code the SQL statements, which need to be explained in the file. Assuming the file is stmt1.sql, the dynexpln can then be invoked as follows:

```
$ dynexpln -d SAMPLE -f stmt1.sql -o dynexpln_stmt1.out
```

As an alternative, an SQL statement can be explained inline:

```
$ dynexpln -d SAMPLE -o dynexpln_stmt1.out
          -q "select acct_type from dnpnck.account_xref"
```

You can also invoke dynexpln interactively where you will be prompted to supply required parameters:

```
$ dynexpln
```

To get the syntax and help on db2expln:

```
$ dynexpln -h
```

EXPLAIN OUTPUT

An example of EXPLAIN output on DB2 ESE Solaris is shown below:

```
SQL Statement:
  select acct_type
  from dntnck.account_xref

Estimated Cost        = 3
Estimated Cardinality = 1000

Distributed Subquery #1
|   #Columns = 1
Return Data to Application
|   #Columns = 1

Distributed Subquery #1:
Server: HOST390   (DB2/390 7.1)
Subquery SQL Statement:

     SELECT A0."ACCT_TYPE"
     FROM "TST1TXP"."ACCOUNT_XREF" A0

Nicknames Referenced:
   DNTNCK.ACCOUNT_XREF   ID = 165   Base = TST1TXP.ACCOUNT_XREF
```

The output shows the Federated Database translation of the nickname into the target table residing on the OS/390. To see the access path from the HOST390 server, you must use the Visual Explain for the OS/390.

A few differences between the Visual Explain implemented on UNIX (i.e., Solaris) and on OS/390 are listed below.

On UNIX:

- It is part of the Control Center.
- It automatically creates the Plan Tables as needed.
- It provides timeron values for each operation (join, lookup, sort, etc.), which gives an indication of how costly certain operations are.

On OS/390:

- It is a stand-alone product that can be downloaded from the IBM Web site.
- It requires the Plan Tables to be available under your TSO user ID.
- It provides an easy way to check whether statistics information for tables and indexes is current.

Under the current federated database system, both UNIX and OS/390 EXPLAIN will be required to get a complete picture of query performance. On UNIX, we will expect to see a very simple plan consisting ideally of a fetch from a remote query. To see which indexes and join paths, etc., are used, we will need to look at the DB2 for OS/390 EXPLAIN.

Starting and Stopping
a DB2 Instance

his appendix describes the necessary steps to stop and start a DB2 instance. There are many ways to stop and start a DB2 instance, but the following steps will guide you to stop a DB2 instance to ensure that any defunct DB2 processes, interprocess communications, and defunct DARI processes have been removed successfully.

Current configuration:

Instance: db2inst1
Database: sample
Server: phantom

1. Stop the DB2 instance.

- Check existing applications that are currently connected to the database by logging on to phantom server as DB2 instance owner db2inst1:

```
$ db2 list applications

Auth Id   Appl. Name   Appl. Handle   Appl. Id                          DB       # of
                                                                        Name     Agents

-------   ----------   ------------   ------------------------          -----    ------
DB2INST1  db2bp        207            *LOCAL.db2inst1.010824003917       SAMPLE   1
DB2INST1  java         276            CCF21FFC.E5D8.010829004049         SAMPLE   1
DB2INST1  java         51             CCF21FFC.E5D9.010829004051         SAMPLE   1
```

- If there is any application connected to the database, you can tell who is currently connected and from which location they are connected. In this case, there is one local connection from db2inst1 user ID, and there are two remote connections from IP address: 204.242.31.252 converted from hex to decimal: CCF21FFC.

- For remote connections, after you get the IP address, you can get the hostname by issuing the nslookup command:

```
$ /usr/sbin/nslookup 204.242.31.252

Server:   charter.phantom.com
Address:   204.242.31.83

Name:      phantom.phantom.com
Address:   204.242.31.252
```

- If there are any applications connected to the database, verify that they are not currently executing:

```
$ db2 list applications show detail | egrep -i "executing|pending"
```

- If there are applications executing or pending, you can now force them off. Then verify to make sure there is no application connected to the database. If you see the following message, you're ready to stop the DB2 instance:

```
$ db2 force application all

DB20000I  The FORCE APPLICATION command completed successfully.
DB21024I  This command is asynchronous and may not be effective
immediately.

$ db2 list applications

SQL1611W  No data was returned by Database System Monitor.
SQLSTATE=00000
```

- Now you can stop the DB2 instance. When you get the message "SQL1064N DB2STOP processing was successful" you're ready to do the next step. If you get the message below, you must start this step again:

```
$ db2stop

SQL1025N  The database manager was not stopped because databases are
still active.
```

- LAST RESORT. If for some reason you cannot stop the DB2 instance or DB2 commands are hung, you must run this utility to remove the DB2 engine and client's IPC resources for that instance. This is your lifesaver:

```
$ ipclean

ipclean: Removing DB2 engine and client's IPC resources for db2inst1.
```

2. Stop the DB2 Administration Server instance.

- Skip this step if DB2 Admin instance is not running; otherwise, execute this command:

```
$ db2admin stop
```

3. Remove defunct DARI processes, DB2 background processes, or other defunct threads.

- List all DB2 processes for this instance:

```
$ ps —ef | grep db2

db2as 23797 23796  0   Aug 28 ?        0:00 db2sysc
db2as 23800 23798  0   Aug 28 ?        0:00 db2sysc
db2inst1 22229     1  0 13:08:01 pts/5    0:00 /db2/dbhome/db2inst1/
   sqllib/bin/db2bp 20580 5
db2as 23802 23797  0   Aug 28 ?        0:00 db2sysc
db2as 23801 23797  0   Aug 28 ?        0:00 db2sysc
db2as 23799 23797  0   Aug 28 ?        0:00 db2sysc
```

- From the list above, we notice that there are processes belonging to the DB2 Admin services instance, so you must leave them alone. There is only one process that belongs to db2inst1, and that is a DB2 background process that did not get cleaned up after executing ipclean. Get the PID number and kill that process:

```
$ kill —9 22229
```

- Most of the time, you will see many defunct processes, and to save time, you should execute the following command instead of executing the kill -9 ${PID} command many times:

```
$ ps —ef | grep db2inst1 | awk '{print "kill —9 "$2}' > /tmp/kpid
$ chmod +x /tmp/kpid
$ /tmp/kpid
```

- Verify that no defunct processes are left. Repeat this step if necessary:

```
$ ps —ef | grep db2inst1
```

4. Remove defunct interprocess communication segments.

- List all memory segments:

```
$ ipcs —am | grep db2inst1

IPC status from <running system> as of Thu Aug 30 13:16:55 2001
T     ID            KEY           MODE          OWNER         GROUP
Shared Memory:
m     9910          0x74006380    --rw-rw-rw-   db2inst1      db2grp
m     59714         0x61006380    --rw-------   db2inst1      db2grp
```

- From the list above, you notice that there are two memory segments that were not removed when executing ipclean. You must remove them manually:

```
$ ipcrm —m 9910
$ ipcrm —m 59714
```

- List all semaphore segments:

```
$ ipcs —as | grep db2inst1

IPC status from <running system> as of Thu Aug 30 13:16:55 2001
T     ID            KEY           MODE          OWNER         GROUP
Shared Memory:
s     1900549       0x74006380    --ra-ra-ra-   db2inst1      db2grp     1
s     1310727       00000000      --ra-ra----   db2inst1      db2grp     1
s     2031624       0x73006380    --ra-ra-ra-   db2inst1      db2grp     1
```

- From the list above, notice that there are three semaphore segments that were not removed after executing ipclean. You must remove them manually:

```
$ ipcrm —s 1900549
$ ipcrm —s 1310727
$ ipcrm —s 2031624
```

- List all message queue segments:

```
$ ipcs —aq | grep db2inst1

IPC status from <running system> as of Thu Aug 30 13:16:55 2001
T     ID            KEY           MODE          OWNER         GROUP
Shared Memory:
q     1572868       0x01dadd16    -Rrw-------   db2inst1      db2grp 65535
q     901125        0x01eba5ed    --rw-------   db2inst1      db2grp 65535
q     1609739       00000000      --rw-------   db2inst1      db2grp 65535
q     659468        00000000      -Rrw-------   db2inst1      db2grp 65535
```

- From the list above, notice that there are four message queue segments that were not removed after executing ipclean. You must remove them manually:

```
$ ipcrm —q 1572868
$ ipcrm —q 901125
$ ipcrm —q 1609739
$ ipcrm —q 659468
```

- Verify that there are no defunct interprocess communications left. Repeat this step if necessary:

```
$ ipcs —a | grep db2inst1
```

5. Before you start the DB2 instance, it is best practice to back up the previous db2diag.log, any event logs, notification log, and the associated trap files, and start with a fresh copy.

- Move the current db2diag.log to the backup directory:

```
$ mkdir —p /db2/backup/db2inst1/diaglogSep12
$ cd /db2/dbhome/db2inst1/sqllib/db2dump
$ mv db2diag.log /db2/backup/db2inst1/diaglogSep12/
$ mv db2eventlog* /db2/backup/db2inst1/diaglogSep12/
$ mv db2inst1.nfy /db2/backup/db2inst1/diaglogSep12/
$ touch db2diag.log db2inst1.nfy db2eventlog.nnn
  where nnn is the database partition number
$ chmod 666 db2diag.log db2inst1.nfy db2eventlog.*
```

- If there are any trap files, group them together:

```
$ cd /db2/dbhome/db2inst1/sqllib/db2dump
$ tar —cvf /db2/backup/db2inst1/diaglog/trapAug292001.tar t* c* l* [0-9]*
```

- Or execute this keepDiagLog.sh script:

```
#!/bin/ksh
#
# Clean up db2diag.log, trap files, dump files, etc
#
# Usage:  keepDiagLog.sh
#
# Execute as DB2 instance owner
#
LOGTIME=`date '+%y%m%d%H%M%S'`
DIAGDIR=${HOME}/sqllib/db2dump
typeset instname=${1-db2inst1}
typeset ROOTDIR=${2-/dbbackup}
typeset dbname=${3-sample}
typeset OLDDIR=${4-${ROOTDIR}/${instname}/${dbname}/db2diag${LOGTIME}}
mkdir —p ${OLDDIR}
cd ${DIAGDIR}
cp —r * ${OLDDIR}/
```

```
for j in `ls`
do
  if  [ -d "${j}" ]; then
    rm —r ${j}
  else
    rm ${j}
  fi
done
touch db2diag.log ${instname}.nfy
chmod 666 db2diag.log ${instname}.nfy
exit 0
# You need to add the steps for the event log files based on the
# number of database partitions defined on your server.
```

6. Now you're ready to start the DB2 instance.

- Start the DB2 instance:

```
$ db2start

SQL1063N  DB2START processing was successful.
```

7. And you're ready to start the DB2 Admin instance.

- Start the DB2 Admin instance:

```
$ db2admin start
```

8. Verify the database connection.

- Connect to the sample database:

```
$ db2 connect to sample

   Database Connection Information
 Database server        = DB2/SUN 8.1.0
 SQL authorization ID   = DB2INST1
 Local database alias   = SAMPLE
```

- Disconnect from the sample database:

```
$ db2 terminate
```

9. Reactivate the database to improve performance.

- Activate the sample database:

```
$ db2 activate database sample

DB20000I  The ACTIVATE DATABASE command completed successfully.
```

LDAP Integration in DB2 UDB Using Microsoft Active Directory

This appendix describes a scenario where a customer wants to utilize the LDAP capabilities of DB2 ESE using Microsoft Active Directory. The OS environments were Windows 95 clients and AIX or Solaris servers.

To access Microsoft Active Directory, ensure that the following conditions are met:

- The machine that runs DB2 must belong to a Windows 2000 domain.
- The Microsoft LDAP client is installed (it is part of the Windows 2000 operating system). For Windows 98 or Windows NT, you need to verify that the wldap32.dll exists under the system directory.
- Enable the LDAP support (it is enabled under Windows 2000 installation program). For Windows 98/NT, you must explicitly enable LDAP by setting the DB2_ENABLE_LDAP registry variable to YES, using the db2set command.
- Log on to a domain user account when running DB2 to read information from the Active Directory.

> **N O T E** If DB2 UDB is installed on a Solaris system, the necessary IBM SecureWay Directory Client software is installed with DB2's LDAP Exploitation component. On other platforms, the IBM SecureWay Directory Client needs to be installed separately.

IMPLEMENTATION GUIDELINES

LDAP Directory Server

- Extend the schema to support classes and attributes needed by DB2 UDB.
- Obtain the LDAP server TCP/IP hostname and connection port number.
- Obtain the LDAP base distinguished name (baseDN).
- Create a user distinguished name (DN) and password for DB2 directory updates.
- Create eApplicationSystem object with systemName=DB2.

DB2 UDB Server

- Install DB2 UDB ESE on AIX.
- Install IBM LDAP Client Software on same box as DB2 server.
- Configure DB2 to use the LDAP server.
- Register the DB2 server instance with the LDAP directory.
- Create a test database (SAMPLE) and verify that it is automatically registered in the LDAP directory.
- Catalog an existing database and verify that it is added to the LDAP directory.

DB2 UDB Client

- Install IBM LDAP Client code on the workstation.
- Make sure that DB2 UDB LDAP Directory Exploitation is installed.
- Configure the DB2 client to use the LDAP server.
- Test database connections.
  - An LDAP registered database
  - A non-LDAP database (catalog database and node on the client are without LDAP)

Test Scenarios

Perform the following test scenarios and observe differences in behavior:

- Change DB2LDAPCACHE variable setting from YES to NO.
- Catalog the same database with more than one database alias.
- Issue the refresh LDAP database and node directory commands after making changes to the LDAP directory.
- Catalog different databases on different servers with the same alias.
- Locally catalog a database (on the client) with an alias that is already in LDAP but not yet cached to the client.

Step #1 Before you can use DB2 in the IBM LDAP environment, you must select the IBM LDAP client on Windows client systems; use the db2set command to set the DB2LDAP_CLIENT_PROVIDER registry variable to IBM:

```
$ db2set DB2LDAP_CLIENT_PROVIDER=IBM
```

On each DB2 UDB machine (client and server):

Step #2 Enable LDAP support:

```
$ db2set DB2_ENABLE_LDAP=YES
```

Step #3 Specify LDAP server's TCP/IP hostname and port number:

```
$ db2set DB2LDAPHOST=newschemadirectory.service.dntteam.com:389
```

Step #4 Specify the LDAP baseDN:

```
$ db2set DB2LDAP_BASEDN=o=phantom.com
```

Step #5 Specify the LDAP user's DN and password for the DB2 instance owner to use LDAP to store DB2 user-specific information. Log in as DB2 instance owner and run the db2ldcfg utility:

```
$ db2ldcfg -u "cn=Jonathan Phan,
    ou=TestTeamI,
    o=phantom.com, c=us"
    -w password
```

Step #6 Each DB2 server instance must be registered in LDAP to publish the protocol configuration information that is used by the client applications to connect to it:

```
$ db2 register db2 server in ldap as SANDIEGO protocol tcpip
    hostname 192.168.1.51 svcename 11001
    remote sunshine_dnt instance v8inst
```

This creates a node directory entry equivalent to that resulting from the following:

```
catalog tcpip node <node_name>
    remote <hostname>
    server <port>
    remote_instance <instance>
```

Step #7 A remote DB2 database server can also be registered using this form of the register command:

```
$ db2 register db2 server in ldap as <ldap_node_name>
    protocol tcpip
    hostname <host_name>
    svcename <tcpip_service_name>
    remote <remote_computer_name>
    instance <instance_name>
```

Step #8 (optional)   To change the DB2 database server information in LDAP, run the following update LDAP command:

```
$ db2 update ldap node SANDIEGO hostname 192.168.1.101 svcename 11002
```

Step #9   Create the sample database:

```
$ db2sampl
```

Step #10   The database is automatically registered in LDAP during the creation of a database within an instance. If the name already exists in the LDAP directory, the database is still created on the local machine but a warning message is returned, stating the naming conflict in the LDAP directory. In this case, the user can manually register the database:

```
$ db2 catalog ldap node SANDIEGO as SANDIEGO

$ db2 catalog ldap database SAMPLE at node SANDIEGO
      with "My LDAP SAMPLE database"
```

Step #11   You can also manually refresh the database and node entries that refer to LDAP resources:

```
$ db2 refresh ldap database directory

$ db2 refresh ldap node directory
```

Tuning DB2 UDB in the IBM LDAP Environment

This appendix describes some performance and tuning tips for DB2 UDB ESE in the IBM LDAP environment.

- On a multi-processor AIX machine set MALLOCMULTIHEAP to the number of processor before starting LDAP. For example, to set the heap on a machine with eight processors:

```
$ export MALLOCMULTIHEAP=heaps:8
```

- Adjust the value of SHEAPTHRES parameter. This would help only if you are using fuzzy searches, search filters with Boolean operators, etc. Use database monitor to see whether your sort heap is exceeding its limit.
- Adjust the value of BUFFPAGE parameter.
- Adjust the value of DBHEAP parameter.
- Adjust the value of SORTHEAP parameter.
- Adjust the value of MAXLOCKS parameter.
- Create index all attributes that you want to use in a search. Indexes are defined in LDAP schema files.
- Perform REORGCHK, REORT, RUNSTATS, or REBIND as necessary after a large number of update, insert, or delete activities.
- Enable LDAP concurrent read/write (by default, the current read/write is disabled).

```
For version 3.1 or earlier:
$ set LDAP_CONCURRENTRW=ON

For version 3.2 or later:
$ set LDAP_CONCURRENTRW=TRUE
```

- Increase the entry cache size. The effectiveness of your LDAP cache depends on your workload. If your workload makes multiple requests for the same entry within a short period of time, bigger cache size might help. By default, the entry cache size is 1,000 (meaning it will cache 1,000 entries). To set the size to a different value, set RDBM_CACHE_SIZE to that value.
- Disable the access control cache if and only if the clients bind as the LDAP administrator. If your application binds to the LDAP server as the LDAP administrator (which frequently is the case), the access control cache is not used. To turn off the access control cache, set ACLCACHE to NO; default is YES.

```
$ set ACLCACHE=NO
```

- If clients bind as individual users, do not turn the access control cache off. You may change its size by setting ACLCACHESIZE (default is RDBM_CACHE_SIZE).

DB2 Support Information

DB2 Support Resources

If you have a technical problem, you can call the IBM Customer Support if you have already purchased a support license. The following describes various DB2 resources available for technical support:

Software Defect Resolution—problems related to bugs in the DB2 software or error messages from the DB2 software that indicate calling technical support. Contact IBM Customer Support and open a PMR (Problem Monitoring Record).

Consult Line—technical guidance and assistance on how-to, implementation, installation, and configuration. Product specialists will be available offsite or onsite on a contractual consulting basis. Contact the local IBM representative for details.

Web-based online technical support for FixPaks, download, online documentation, technical notes, white papers, newsgroups, etc. For detailed information, refer to the following sites:

> **http://www.ibm.com/software/data/**
>
> The DB2 World Wide Web pages provide current DB2 information about news, product descriptions, education schedules, and more.
>
> **http://www.ibm.com/software/data/db2/library/**
>
> The DB2 Product and Service Technical Library provide access to frequently asked questions, fixes, books, and up-to-date DB2 technical information.
>
> **http://www.ibm.com/software/data/db2/udb/ad/**
>
> For updated information on developing applications.

http://www.redbooks.ibm.com

For information related to how-to, research, reference, and cookbook manuals available in PDF, HTML, and hard copy

http://www.elink.ibmlink.ibm.com/pbl/pbl/

The International Publications ordering Web site provides information on how to order books.

ftp.software.ibm.com

Log on as anonymous. In the directory /ps/products/db2, you can find demos, fixes, information, and tools relating to DB2 and many other products.

comp.databases.ibm-db2 or bit.listserv.db2-l

These most popular Internet newsgroups are available for users to discuss their experiences with DB2 products.

Opening a PMR

Getting technical support involves opening a problem ticket called *PMR*, which is used to store details and keep track of the progress and status of the problem. Prior to making the initial call, you need to collect the following basic information:

- **Customer ID**—an IBM-assigned customer number.
- **Authorized Contact Name(s)**—only registered names are authorized to open a PMR.
- **Severity Level**—This is based on the level of impact to production. Level 1 means the production environment is down and would need immediate response. Level 2 means production environment is not down but would still need immediate response. Level 3 means production environment is not down and no immediate response needed.
- **Operating System Level**—The operating system version, release, and maintenance level. You also need to specify the hardware configuration, such as machine type, model, etc.
- **DB2 Level**—The DB2 product software version, FixPak level. Use the db2level command to get this information.
- **Problem Description**—You must state a brief synopsis of the problem, describing its symptoms, error messages, and procedure that re-created the error.

Once a PMR is opened, it will be queued and assigned to a DB2 Level 2 Specialist, who will be contacting you to assess and analyze the problem. At that point, the DB2 Level 2 Specialist will be requesting detailed diagnostic and other related information.

COLLECTING DIAGNOSTIC INFORMATION

The following list details instructions on how to gather diagnostic information needed by IBM Customer Support.

1. Operating System Information

For AIX

```
#!/usr/bin/ksh
#
# Get AIX system information
# USAGE:  getos.sh 0
#
today=`date +"%Y%m%d_%H%M%S"`
typeset dbpartnum=${1-0}
typeset outfs=${2-/db2wkarea/${dbpartnum}/output}
mkdir -p ${outfs}
lscfg > ${outfs}/lscfg_${today}.txt
no -a > ${outfs}/no_${today}.txt
df -k > ${outfs}/df_k_${today}.txt
lsfs > ${outfs}/lsfs_${today}.txt
cat /etc/services > ${outfs}/services_${today}.txt
cat /etc/host > ${outfs}/hosts_${today}.txt
exit
```

For Solaris

```
#!/bin/ksh
#
# Get Sun Solaris information
# Usage: getOS.sh
#
today=`date +"%Y%m%d_%H%M%S"`
/bin/showrev > ${outdir}/showrev_${today}.txt
/etc/sysdef -i > ${outdir}/sysdef_${today}.txt
/bin/dmesg > ${outdir}/dmesg_${today}.txt
df -k > ${outdir}/df_${today}.txt
/usr/platform/`uname -m`/sbin/prtdiag > ${outdir}/prtdiag_${today}.txt
cat /var/adm/messages > ${outdir}/messages_${today}.txt
cat /etc/vfstab > ${outdir}/vfstab_${today}.txt
cat /etc/passwd > ${outdir}/passwd_${today}.txt
cat /etc/group > ${outdir}/group_${today}.txt
cat /etc/system > ${outdir}/system_${today}.txt
cat /etc/services > ${outdir}/services_${today}.txt
exit
```

2. DB2 Information

```ksh
#!/usr/bin/ksh -x
#
# USAGE:  getdb.sh dbname dbpartnum instname
#
today=`date +"%Y%m%d_%H%M%S"`
typeset dbname=${1-sample}
typeset dbpartnum=${2-0}
typeset instname=${3-db2inst1}
typeset outfs=${4-/tmp/${dbpartnum}/${instname}}
mkdir -p ${outfs}
db2level > ${outfs}/dblevel_${today}.txt
db2 get dbm cfg > ${outfs}/dbmcfg_${today}.txt
db2set -all > ${outfs}/dbreg_${today}.txt
db2 list node directory > ${outfs}/dbnode_${today}.txt
db2 list db directory > ${outfs}/dbdir_${today}.txt
db2 get db cfg for ${dbname} > ${outfs}/${dbname}_dbcfg_${today}.txt
db2look -d ${dbname} -a -x -l -f -e -p\
  > ${outfs}/${dbname}_${today}.ddl
db2 connect to ${dbname}
db2 "select * from syscat.bufferpools"\
  > ${outfs}/${dbname}_buff_${today}.txt
db2 "list tablespaces show detail"\
  > ${outfs}/${dbname}_ts_${today}.txt
for tsid in `awk '$0 ~ /Tablespace ID/ {print $4}' ${outfs}/
${dbname}_ts_${today}.txt`
do
db2 "list tablespace containers for $tsid show detail"\
  >> ${outfs}/${dbname}_container_${today}.txt
done
db2 terminate
exit
```

3. Copy of the db2diag.log, Any trap and dump Files

4. Details of the Errors

Describe the origin and symptoms of the problem. Explain how the error can be recreated by supplying applicable code fragment of the program, SQL, and stored procedures. If possible, describe the difference in results between executing the stored procedure or SQL in the command line and executing from within an application. Indicate whether the problem is an abend (abnormal termination), suspension, looping, or slow response time.

5. DB2 Trace

DB2 Customer Support may request a trace if the information you already sent is not enough to diagnose a problem. When it is being collected, the information is recorded in chronological order.

The following is a step-by-step instruction on how to run a db2 trace. Tracing to memory is the preferred method of tracing. However, if the server-client DB2 crashes before the trace is dumped into a file, tracing to a file has to be used.

a. Log in as db2inst1.
b. Start DB2 UDB trace; enter:

```
db2trc   on   -l 8000000
```

c. Recreate the problem.
d. Dump the trace output:

```
db2trc   dump   nov19trc.dmp
```

e. Stop DB2 UDB trace; enter:

```
db2trc   off
```

f. Format DB2 UDB trace output; enter:

```
db2trc   fmt   nov19trc.dmp   nov19trc.txt
db2trc   flw   nov19trc.dmp   nov19trc.flw
```

g. View DB2 UDB trace output file; enter:

```
pg   nov19trc.txt
```

6. DB2 DRDA Trace

DB2 Customer Support may request a DRDA trace if the information you already sent is not enough to diagnose a problem. The db2drdat command traces DRDA dataflow exchanged between DRDA Application Requesters and DRDA Application Servers.

a. Turn on DRDA trace.

```
db2drdat   on   -i   -r   -s   -c
```

b. Recreate the problem.
c. Turn off DRDA trace; enter:

```
db2drdat   off
```

d. View DRDA trace file; enter:

```
pg   db2drdat.dmp
```

7. DB2 CLI Trace

DB2 Customer Support may request a CLI trace. This file can be found in the ../sqllib/cfg directory.

a. Take a backup of the CLI trace file; enter:

```
cp  db2cli.ini  db2cli.bak
```

b. Add trace parameters:

```
[COMMON]
Trace=1
TracePathName=C:\TRACE\cli
TraceFlush=1
TraceComm=1
jdbctrace=1
jdbctraceflush=1
jdbctracepathname=c:\trace\jcbc
```

where TracePathName must be an existing directory. Do not specify a file, only a path.

SENDING DIAGNOSTIC INFORMATION

Collect all the diagnostic information and files listed in the previous section and move or copy them to a separate directory, i.e.,

```
mkdir  pmr123456
```

where 123456 is the pmr number.

```
cp  <files>  pmr123456/
```

Tar all files and compress the resulting file; enter:

```
cd  pmr123456
tar  —cvf  pmr123456.tar  *
compress  pmr123456.tar
```

Send the file to a destination specified by DB2 Customer Support using the ftp site:

FTP Server:	testcase.boulder.ibm.com
Username:	anonymous
Password:	<your email ID>
Directory:	ps/toibm/db2
Filename:	pmr123456.tar.Z

DB2 Connect Implementation

DB2 Connect Enterprise Edition (CEE) is a connectivity server that concentrates and manages connections from multiple desktop clients and Web applications to DB2 database servers running on host or iSeries systems. IBM's DB2 Universal Database (UDB) for iSeries, DB2 for OS/390 and z/OS, and DB2 for VSE and VM databases continue to be the systems for managing most critical data for the world's largest organizations. Although these host and iSeries databases manage the data, there is a great demand to integrate this data with applications running on Windows and UNIX workstations.

DB2 Connect Enterprise Edition enables local and remote client applications to create, update, control, and manage DB2 databases and host systems using Structured Query Language (SQL), DB2 APIs (Application Programming Interfaces), ODBC (Open Database Connectivity), JDBC (Java Database Connectivity), SQLJ (Embedded Java), or DB2 CLI (Call Level Interface).

You can use the Configuration Assistant to manage your database connections to remote servers. This is the preferred method to set up any client-server communications. With the Configuration Assistant, you can:

- Catalog and uncatalog databases
- Export and import client profiles that contain database and configuration information for a client
- Test connections to local or remote databases identified
- Bind applications to a database by selecting utilities or bind files from a list
- Add, change, delete CLI/ODBC data sources, and configure CLI/ODBC configuration settings
- Tune the client configuration parameters
- Update the database server password

INSTALLING DB2 CONNECT ENTERPRISE EDITION

The typical steps to install and configure DB2 CEE are as follows:

1. Determine how you want to use DB2 Connect in your network.
2. Verify that you have the correct hardware and software prerequisites on both your workstation and the host database server.
3. Verify that your host or iSeries database server is configured to accept connections from DB2 Connect servers.
4. Install your DB2 Connect software. You will use this workstation to configure and verify your host and iSeries connections.

   - Log on to the system as a user with administrator authority.
   - Enter the ./db2setup command to start the DB2 Setup wizard.

5. After installation, establish the connection between DB2 Connect and your host or iSeries database system. You can use the Configuration Assistant to configure host or iSeries databases.
6. Bind the programs and utilities provided with DB2 Connect to your host or iSeries database.
7. Test the connection.
8. Install and configure a DB2 client. Use this workstation to test connectivity from the DB2 client to host and iSeries database servers, as well as to test applications that use this connectivity.
9. Use the Configuration Assistant to connect the client to the host or iSeries system through DB2 Connect.
10. Install DB2 clients on all end-user workstations that will use applications that connect to host and iSeries database servers.
11. You are now ready to use DB2 Connect with all your applications. Workstations that will be used for application development should have the DB2 Application Development Client installed.
12. If you want to use your workstation to administer DB2 UDB for OS/390 and z/OS or DB2 UDB for UNIX, Windows NT, Windows 2000, Windows XP, and Windows .NET servers, install the DB2 Administration Client.

Sample Questions

This appendix contains sample certification exam questions that help verify your understanding of the topics discussed in this book.

Q01. SYSADM privileges are:

    A. Highest set of privileges available in DB2 ESE

    B. Lowest set of privileges available in DB2 ESE

    C. Set of privileges at the DBADM level

    D. None of the above

Q02. Given the following users:

User appusr1 belongs to group usr1grp and user appusr2 belongs to group db2grp. User appusr1 is the owner of the instance db2inst1 and has updated the database manger configuration set the SYSADM_GROUP to usr1grp.

If user appusr2 wants to drop db2inst1 instance and create a new instance db2inst2, user appusr2 needs:

    A. User appusr1 to grant DBADM privilege to user appusr2

    B. User appusr1 to grant SYSADM privilege to user appusr2

    C. System Administrator (root) to grant SYSADM and DBADM to user appusr2

    D. System Administrator (root) to add user appusr2 to the group usr1grp

    E. System Administrator (root) to add user appusr1 to the group db2grp

Q03. If you set TRUST_ALLCLNTS=YES and TRUST_CLNTAUTH=SERVER, then authentication for Trusted non-DRDA Client Authentication with password is at:

    A. CLIENT

    B. SERVER

    C. CLIENT and SERVER

    D. None of the above

Q04. Kerberos authentication is supported only for clients and servers running Windows 2000, Windows XP, and Windows 2003 operating systems. In addition, both the client and server machines must:

    A. Belong to the same Windows workgroup

    B. Belong to the same Windows domain

    C. Belong to the different Windows workgroup

    D. Belong to the different Windows domain

Q05. With an authentication type of KRB_SERVER_ENCRYPT at the server, if the clients do not support the Kerberos security system, then the effective system authentication type is equivalent to:

    A. CLIENT

    B. SERVER

    C. CLIENT_ENCRYPT

    D. SERVER_ENCRYPT

Q06. During database creation, SELECT privilege on the system catalog views is granted to the PUBLIC group. To prevent non-privileged viewers from viewing the catalog, you must:

    A. Revoke the SELECT privilege from PUBLIC.

    B. Grant the SELECT privilege as required to specific users.

    C. Revoke the SELECT privilege from PUBLIC; grant the SELECT privilege as required to specific users.

    D. Revoke the CONTROL privilege from PUBLIC.

Q07. A caching mechanism exists so that the client searches the LDAP directory only once in its local directory catalogs. Once the information is retrieved, it is cached on the local machine. Subsequent access to the same information is based on the value of the DIR_CACHE Database Manager Configuration parameter and the DB2LDAPCACHE registry variable. Which one of the following statements is correct?

    A. If DB2LDAPCACHE=NO and DIR_CACHE=NO, then always read the information from LDAP.

    B. If DB2LDAPCACHE=NO and DIR_CACHE=YES, then always read the information from LDAP once and insert it into the DB2 cache.

    C. If DB2LDAPCACHE=YES and DIR_CACHE=NO, then always read the information from LDAP.

    D. If DB2LDAPCACHE=YES and DIR_CACHE=YES, then always read the information from LDAP once and insert it into the DB2 cache.

    E. A and B

    F. C and D

Q08. When running on Windows operating systems, DB2 supports using either IBM LDAP client or the Microsoft LDAP client to access the IBM SecureWay Directory Server. If you want to select the IBM LDAP client explicitly, you must use:

    A. db2set DB2_ENABLE_LDAP=YES

    B. db2set DB2LDAP_CLIENT_PROVIDER=IBM

    C. db2 update dbm cfg DB2_ENABLE_LDAP=YES

    D. db2 update dbm cfg DB2LDAP_CLIENT_PROVIDER=IBM

Q09. To enable LDAP explicitly, execute the following command:

    A. db2set DB2_LDAP=YES

    B. db2set DB2_ENABLE_LDAP=YES

    C. db2 update dbm cfg using DB2_LDAP YES

    D. db2 update dbm cfg using DB2_ENABLE_LDAP YES

Q10. To avoid LDAP information being cached in the database, node, and DCS directories, which one of the following is correct?

    A. db2set DB2LDAPCACHE=NO

    B. db2set DB2LDAPCACHE=YES

    C. db2set DB2LDAPREFRESH=NO

    D. db2set DB2LDAPREFRESH=YES

Q11. Before accessing information in the LDAP directory, an application or user is authenticated by:

    A. The DB2 server

    B. The LDAP server

    C. The distinguished name

    D. The operating system

Q12. In a multi-partition database, with four database partitions created for each server, there are four identical DB2 servers with a cluster. How many entries will be required in the /etc/services file?

    A. 4

    B. 8

    C. 16

    D. 32

Q13. In a partitioned database environment, if there are four DB2 servers and two database partitions for each DB2 server, then how many db2nodes.cfg files will be required?

    A. 1

    B. 2

    C. 4

    D. 8

Q14. Which of the following statements is true about Federated Database support in DB2?

    A. Any number of DB2 instances can be configured to function as federated servers.

    B. Federated Server uses DRDA communication protocols to communicate with DB2 family instances.

    C. Federated servers use only a single protocol to communicate with non-DB2 family instances.

    D. A and B

    E. A and C

Q15. What is the processing of a query fragment at a data source instead of at the federated server known as?

    A. LOCAL

    B. REMOTE

    C. PASSTHRU

    D. PUSHDOWN

Q16. In a federated system, the query optimizer generates local and remote access plans for processing a query fragment, based on resource cost. Which of the following statements is true?

    A. DB2 chooses the plan it believes will process the query with the most resource cost.

    B. DB2 chooses the plan it believes will process the query with the least resource cost.

    C. DB2 queries the federated server statistics and submits the query fragment to the data source.

    D. DB2 queries the data source statistics and submits the query fragment to the federated server.

Q17. Select the correct answer based on following statement:

```
alter server MYSERV options (ADD CPU_RATIO '0.2');
```

    A. The optimizer models the CPU at the federated server as two times faster than the CPU at the MYSERV server.

    B. The optimizer models the CPU at the federated server as two times slower than the CPU at the MYSERV server.

    C. The optimizer models the CPU at the MYSERV server as five times faster than the CPU at the federated server.

    D. The optimizer models the CPU at the MYSERV server as five times slower than the CPU at the federated server.

Q18. Select the correct answer based on following statement:

```
alter server MYSERV options (SET CPU_RATIO '2.0');
```

    A. The optimizer models the CPU at the federated server as two times faster than the CPU at the MYSERV server.

    B. The optimizer models the CPU at the federated server as two times slower than the CPU at the MYSERV server.

    C. The optimizer models the CPU at the MYSERV server as five times faster than the CPU at the federated server.

    D. The optimizer models the CPU at the MYSERV server as five times slower than the CPU at the federated server.

Q19.   Select the correct answer based on following statement:

```
alter server MYSERV options (SET IO_RATIO '2.0');
```

    A. The I/O devices at the federated server process data are two times faster than the I/O devices at the MYSERV server.

    B. The I/O devices at the federated server process data are two times slower than the I/O at the MYSERV server.

    C. The I/O devices at the MYSERV server process data are 20 times faster than the I/O at the federated server.

    D. The I/O devices at the MYSERV server process data are 20 times slower than the I/O at the federated server.

    E. None of the above

Q20.   Select the correct answer based on following statement:

```
alter server MYSERV options (ADD COMM_RATE '2');
```

    A. The network communications data rate to the federated server is at 2,000,000 bytes per second.

    B. The network communications data rate to the data source MYSERV is at 2,000,000 bytes per second.

    C. The network communications data rate at the data source MYSERV is two times faster than the network communications data rate at the federated server.

    D. The network communications data rate at the federated server is two times faster than the network communications data rate at the data source MYSERV.

Q21.   How many blocks will be required to receive a result set from the data source MYSERV of 10,000 records with a row length of 100 if the RQRIOBLK is set to 65,535?

    A. 100

    B. 50

    C. 31

    D. 16

Q22. Given the following statement:

```
create table mqt_account as
          (select a.c1, a.c2, b.c1
            from taba a, tabb b
          where a.c1=b.c2)
data initially DEFERRED refresh <REFRESH OPTION>;
```

Which of the refresh options below should be used to allow the user to perform INSERT, UPDATE, and DELETE operations against the materialized query table?

    A. refresh DEFERRED MAINTAINED BY USER

    B. refresh IMMEDIATE MAINTAINED BY USER

    C. refresh DEFERRED MAINTAINED BY SYSTEM

    D. refresh IMMEDIATE MAINTAINED BY SYSTEM

Q23. Which of the following sets of configuration parameters allow the database to use infinite active log space?

    A. Set LOGBUFSZ=8, LOGPRIMARY=10, and LOGSECOND=4

    B. Set LOGBUFSZ=8, LOGPRIMARY=10, and LOGSECOND=–1

    C. Set LOGBUFSZ=8, LOGPRIMARY=–1, and LOGSECOND=–1

    D. Set LOGBUFSZ=8, LOGPRIMARY=–1, and LOGSECOND=4

Q24. At the database level, mirroring log files helps protect the database SAMPLE from accidental deletion of an active log. In order to achieve this, which of the following is required?

    A. db2set DB2_NEW_LOGPATH2=YES

    B. Update db cfg for SAMPLE using NEWLOGPATH2 /dblogm/SAMPLE

    C. db2set DB2_MIRROR_LOGPATH=YES

    D. Update db cfg for SAMPLE using MIRRORLOGPATH /dblogm/SAMPLE

Q25. Which of the following statements is incorrect when referring to the Declared Global Temporary tables?

    A. Defines a temporary table for the current session

    B. Does not appear in the system catalog

    C. When the session terminates, the rows of the table are deleted, and the description of the temporary table is dropped.

    D. Changes to the table are not logged.

    E. All of the above

Q26. A transaction that receives a log disk full error (SQL0968C) will fail and be rolled back. In addition, DB2 will stop processing. To prevent disk full errors from causing DB2 to stop processing when it cannot create a new log file in the active log path, you should:

    A. Increase space for the active log directory.

    B. Reduce the LOGPRIMARY, LOGSECOND, and LOGFILSIZ.

    C. Set BLK_LOG_DSK_FUL to YES.

    D. A and B

    E. A and C

    F. B and C

Q27. Which of the following commands will collect a complete set of log files up to a known point in time?

    A. db2 connect to SAMPLE; db2 archive log for database SAMPLE

    B. db2 terminate; db2 archive log for database SAMPLE

    C. db2 connect to SAMPLE; db2 truncate log for database SAMPLE

    D. db2 terminate; db2 truncate log for database SAMPLE

Q28. For some reason, the user exit did not work properly for the SAMPLE database, and the DIAGLEVEL is set 2. You need to determine the cause of the problem. Which of the information (files) will you need to analyze to help you to identify the problem and determine the solution to resolve it?

    A. View the db2diag.log and verify USEREXIT database configuration parameter is set to ON.

    B. View the ARCHIVE.LOG and USEREXIT.ERR.

    C. Increase space for the active log directory.

    D. View the notification log.

Q29. Which of the following statements best describe incremental delta backup image?

    A. A copy of all database data that has changed since the most recent, successful, full backup operation

    B. A copy of all database data that has changed since the last successful backup (full, incremental, or incremental delta) operation

    C. A copy of all database data that has changed since the last successful incremental backup

    D. A copy of all database data that has changed since the last successful incremental delta backup

    E. None of the above

Q30. Which of the following options is required to enable online and incremental backups?

    A. LOGRETAIN=YES, USEREXIT=YES
    B. TRACKMOD=YES, LOGRETAIN=YES
    C. USEREXIT=YES, TRACKMOD=NO
    D. TRACKMOD=NO, LOGRETAIN=YES

Q31. The database SAMPLE is defined on all four partitions numbered 0 through 3. Database partition 0 is the catalog partition. What is the correct way to perform an offline backup of this database?

```
1.  db2 terminate
2.  db2 force application all
3.  db2stop
4.  db2start
5.  db2_all '<<+0< db2 backup database SAMPLE to /dbbackup/SAMPLE'
6.  db2_all '<<-0< db2 backup database SAMPLE to /dbbackup/SAMPLE'
```

    A. Step 3, 4, 5, and 6
    B. Step 3, 4, 6, and 5
    C. Step 1, 2, 5, and 6
    D. Step 1, 2, 6, and 5

Q32. The database SAMPLE is defined on all four partitions numbered 0 through 3. Database partition 0 is the catalog partition. What is the correct way to restore this database from the recent full offline backup images below?

```
SAMPLE.0.v8inst.NODE0000.CATN0000.20020829013314.001
SAMPLE.0.v8inst.NODE0001.CATN0000.20020829013401.001
SAMPLE.0.v8inst.NODE0002.CATN0000.20020829013012.001
SAMPLE.0.v8inst.NODE0003.CATN0000.20020829013028.001
```

1. `db2 terminate`

2. `db2 force application all`

3. `db2_all '<<+0< db2 restore database SAMPLE from /dbbackup/SAMPLE'`

4. `db2_all '<<+0< db2 restore database SAMPLE from /dbbackup/SAMPLE taken at 20020829013314'`

5. `db2_all '<<-0< db2 restore database SAMPLE from /dbbackup/SAMPLE'`

6. `db2_all '<<+1< db2 restore database SAMPLE from /dbbackup/SAMPLE taken at 20020829013401'`

7. `db2_all '<<+2< db2 restore database SAMPLE from /dbbackup/SAMPLE taken at 20020829013012'`

8. `db2_all '<<+3< db2 restore database SAMPLE from /dbbackup/SAMPLE taken at 20020829013028'`

    A. Step 1, 2, 3, and 5

    B. Step 1, 2, 4, 6, 7, and 8

    C. Step 1, 2, 3, 6, 7, and 8

    D. Step 1, 2, 4, and 5

Q33. Which of the following statements will roll forward a table space backup to the end of logs on database partition number 2?

    A. db2 rollforward database SAMPLE to end of logs on tablespace(ts1)

    B. db2 rollforward database SAMPLE to end of logs on partitionnum(2)

    C. db2 rollforward database SAMPLE to end of logs on dbpartitionnum(2) tablespace(TS1)

    D. db2 rollforward tablespace for database SAMPLE to end of logs on dbpartitionnum(2)

Q34. Which of the following statements is true about db2inidb utility?

    A. The snapshot option clones the primary database to offload work from the source database, such as running reports, analysis, or populate target system.

    B. The standby option continues rolling the log files forward; even new log files that are created by the source database are constantly fetched from the source system.

    C. The mirror option uses the mirrored system as a backup image to restore over the source system.

    D. The relocate option allows the split mirror to be relocated in terms of the database name, database directory path, container path, log path, and the instance name associated with the database.

    E. All of the above

    F. None of the above

Q35. Given the following sequences:

    1. The full offline database backup image is copied from the primary server to the standby server.

    2. The database on the standby server restores from the recent full offline database backup image received from the primary server.

    3. The archived log files are copied from the primary server to the standby server.

    4. The database on the standby server rolls forward to the end of logs and stops.

    5. The clients reconnect to the standby database and resume operations.

Which of the following availability methods is being used in this scenario?

    A. Split mirror

    B. Split mirror and suspended I/O

    C. Split, standby, and mirror

    D. Log shipping

Q36. In a partitioned database environment, you do not have to suspend I/O writes on all partitions simultaneously. Which of the following statements is true?

    A. You can suspend a subset of one or more partitions to create split mirror for performing offline backups.

    B. If the catalog partition is included in the subset, it must be the first partition to be suspended.

    C. If the catalog partition is included in the subset, it must be the last partition to be suspended.

    D. A and B

    E. A and C

Q37. In this example, database partition number 0 is running on server1 configured for automatic failover. After the server1 failed over to the server2, database partition number 0 and database partition number 1 are both running on server2. Which of the following db2nodes.cfg files would exist on server2?

    A. The contents of the db2nodes.cfg file:

```
0 server1 0
1 server2 0
```

    B. The contents of the db2nodes.cfg file:

```
0 server1 0
1 server2 1
```

    C. The contents of the db2nodes.cfg file:

```
0 server2 0
1 server2 1
```

    D. The contents of the db2nodes.cfg file:

```
0 server1 0
1 server1 0
```

Q38. There are two logical database partitions (0 and 1) defined on server1 and two logical database partitions (2 and 3) defined on server2, and the servers are configured for automatic failover. After the failover, database partition 2 and 3 also are running on server1. Which of the following db2nodes.cfg files would exist on server2?

A. The contents of the db2nodes.cfg file:

```
0 server1 0
1 server1 1
2 server1 0
3 server1 1
```

B. The contents of the db2nodes.cfg file:

```
0 server1 0
1 server1 1
2 server2 2
3 server2 3
```

C. The contents of the db2nodes.cfg file:

```
0 server1 0
1 server1 1
2 server1 2
3 server1 3
```

D. The contents of the db2nodes.cfg file:

```
0 server1 0
1 server1 1
2 server2 0
3 server2 1
```

Q39. When loading data into a table, which statement is true for the target table in share lock mode? Which of the following LOAD options will allow existing data in the table to be selected?

A. ALLOW NO ACCESS
B. ALLOW READ ACCESS
C. ALLOW INCLUSIVE ACCESS
D. ALLOW SHARE ACCESS

Q40. Which of the following LOAD options will prevent existing data in the table to be selected?

    A. ALLOW NO ACCESS

    B. ALLOW READ ACCESS

    C. ALLOW INCLUSIVE ACCESS

    D. ALLOW SHARE ACCESS

Q41. In a partition databases environment, when you issue the db2start command, you will get the following output:

```
11-20-2002 15:14:05 1 0 SQL6048N A communication error occurred during
START or STOP DATABASE MANAGER processing.
11-20-2002 15:14:05 2 0 SQL6048N A communication error occurred during
START or STOP DATABASE MANAGER processing.
11-20-2002 15:14:05 3 0 SQL6048N A communication error occurred during
START or STOP DATABASE MANAGER processing.
11-20-2002 15:14:05 4 0 SQL6048N A communication error occurred during
START or STOP DATABASE MANAGER processing.
```

To resolve this communication error, you must:

    A. Set DB2 registry DB2COMM=tcpip.

    B. Create $HOME/.rhosts.

    C. Change permission to $HOME/.rhosts.

    D. Update dbm cfg using SVCENAME db2cdb2inst1.

Q42. In a partition database environment, when you issue the db2start command, you will get the following output:

```
SQL6031N Error in the db2nodes.cfg file at the line number "2".
Reason code "9".
```

The content of the db2nodes.cfg is:

```
0 server1 1
1 server1 1
2 server2 0
3 server3 0
```

Based on the db2nodes.cfg file above, which of the following db2nodes.cfg files will fix this problem?

A. The hostname at line "2" is not valid.

```
0 server1 1
1 server2 1
2 server2 0
3 server3 0
```

B. The hostname/port at line "2" is not unique.

```
0 server1 0
1 server1 1
2 server2 0
3 server3 0
```

C. A syntax error exists at line "2".

```
0 server1 1
1 server1 X
2 server2 0
3 server3 0
```

D. The dbpartitionnum value at line "2" is not valid.

```
0 server1 1
4 server1 1
2 server2 0
3 server3 0
```

Q43. If you issue a db2start restart command, you will get the following error:

```
db2start dbpartitionnum 3 restart hostname server3 port 3 netname
netserv3


11-20-2002 15:14:05 3 0 SQL6031N Error in the db2nodes.cfg file at
line "5".  Reason code "12".
```

The content of the /etc/services file is:

```
DB2_db2inst1         50501/tcp
DB2_db2inst1_END     50502/tcp
```

The content of the db2nodes.cfg file is:

```
0 server1 0 netserv1
1 server2 0 netserv2
2 server3 0 netserv3
```

Based on the db2nodes.cfg and /etc/services files above, how many entries will be required in the /etc/services file?

    A. 1

    B. 2

    C. 3

    D. 4

Q44. How many buffer pools are created when a database is created?

    A. 1

    B. 2

    C. 3

    D. 4

Q45. How many table spaces are created when a database is created?

    A. 1

    B. 2

    C. 3

    D. 4

Q46. How many database partition groups are created when a database is created?

    A. 1

    B. 2

    C. 3

    D. 4

Q47. For a database with the following table spaces defined:

    Tablespace1 with a page size of 4 KB

    Tablespace2 with a page size of 4 KB

    Tablespace3 with a page size of 4 KB

What is the minimum number of buffer pools required?

    A. 1

    B. 2

    C. 3

    D. 4

Q48. For a database with the following table spaces defined:

    Tablespace1 with a page size of 4 KB

    Tablespace2 with a page size of 8 KB

    Tablespace3 with a page size of 4 KB

What is the minimum number of buffer pools required?

    A. 1

    B. 2

    C. 3

    D. 4

Q49. To create a user table space with a page size of 32 KB, which of the following must already exist?

    A. A buffer pool with a page size of 32 KB

    B. A system temporary table space with a page size of 32 KB

    C. A user temporary table space with a page size of 32 KB

Q50. In which of the following table spaces can the table below be created?

```
Create table T1(c1 int,c2 char (200), c2 varchar(10000))
```

     A. Tablespace1 with a page size of 4 KB
     B. Tablespace2 with a page size of 8 KB
     C. Tablespace3 with a page size of 16 KB
     D. Tablespace4 with a page size of 32 KB

Q51. What is the minimum page size for table space TS1, given the following statement?

```
Create table T1(c1 int,c2 char (200), c2 varchar(3800))
   in TS1 long in TSLONG
```

     A. 4 KB
     B. 8 KB
     C. 16 KB
     D. 32 KB

Q52. What is the minimum size of a DMS table space, given an extent size of 64 4-KB pages?

     A. 1 MB or 4 extents
     B. 1.5 MB or 6 extents
     C. 2 MB or 8 extents
     D. 3 MB or 12 extents

Q53. If a table space contains a single table with a row size of 700 bytes, including overhead, what is the minimum page size for the table space in order for the table to contain 100 million rows?

     A. 4 KB
     B. 8 KB
     C. 16 KB
     D. 32 KB

Q54. If the following table is created in a DMS table space:

```
Create table table1 (c1 int not null primary key,
   c2 char(30),
   c3 char(10),
   c4 int)
```

How many table space extents will be used for the table?

     A. 1
     B. 2
     C. 3
     D. 4

Q55. Which tool can be used to enable an SMS table space to allocate space an extent at a time, rather than a page at a time?

    A. db2alloc

    B. db2empfa

    C. db2extal

    D. db2mulpg

Q56. For a database created using a single-byte code page containing the following tables:

```
TableA
--------------------
C1A Char(250)
C2A Char(250)
C3A Char(250)
C4A Int
C5A VarChar(2000)


TableB
---------------------
C1B VarChar(2000)
C2B Int
C3B Int
C4B Int
```

Given the following SQL statement:

```
Select A.C5A, A.C2A, B.C1B, B.C2B, B.C3B, B.C4B
  from TableA A, TableB B
  where A.C4A = B.C4B
  and B.C4B > 100
```

What is the minimum page size for the table space where the temporary table will be created?

    A. 4 KB

    B. 8 KB

    C. 16 KB

    D. 32 KB

Q57. What type of table space can contain both INDEXes and LOBs for a table?

    A. SMALL

    B. MEDIUM

    C. LARGE

    D. EXTRA LARGE

Q58. What option will insert the database partition number to each container name in a create table space statement?

    A. #N

    B. $N

    C. %N

    D. @N

Q59. Which of the following is *not* a valid option for the ALTER TABLESPACE command?

    A. resize

    B. drop

    C. remove

    D. extend

Q60. What is the page size for the catalog table space?

    A. 4 KB

    B. 8 KB

    C. 16 KB

    D. 32 KB

Q61. Table space TS1 was created using the following SQL statement:

```
CREATE TABLESPACE TS1 MANAGED BY DATABASE
   USING (FILE 'CONT1' 2000, FILE 'CONT2' 2000)
```

Which of the following SQL statements cannot be used to change the size of all of the containers in TS1 to 5,000 pages each?

    A. ALTER TABLESPACE TS1 RESIZE (ALL CONTAINERS 5000)

    B. ALTER TABLESPACE TS1 EXTEND (ALL 3000)

    C. ALTER TABLESPACE TS1 RESIZE (FILE 'CONT1' 5000, FILE 'CONT2' 5000)

    D. ALTER TABLESPACE TS1 INCREASE (ALL CONTAINERS 3000)

Q62. To set aside an area of the buffer pool for block-based prefetching, which of the following options must be set?

    A. NUMBLOCKPAGES

    B. BLOCKAREA

    C. RESERVEDAREA

    D. PAGESIZE

Q63. Which privilege level is the minimum necessary to alter a buffer pool?

    A. SYSCTRL

    B. DBADM

    C. SYSMAINT

    D. DBCONTROL

Q64. If insufficient memory is available to create a new buffer pool, which of the following will occur?

    A. An error is returned, and the buffer pool is not created.

    B. A warning is returned, and the buffer pool is created as large as the available memory.

    C. A warning is returned, and the buffer pool will not be created until the database is reactivated.

    D. The database is automatically reactivated.

Q65. Given a database in a 32-bit instance of DB2 with an existing 250,000 4-KB pages buffer pool, to create a new buffer pool automatically with a size of 50,000 4-KB pages, to which of the following values must the DATABASE_MEMORY configuration parameter be set?

    A. Automatic

    B. 50,000

    C. 200,000

    D. 300,000

Q66. Given the following user-defined table spaces and associated page sizes:

Table Space Name	Page Size
Userspace1	16K
Tempspace1	16K
Tempspace2	8K
tbspc1	8K
tbspc2	16K

What is the minimum number of buffer pools that must exist in this database?

    A. 1

    B. 2

    C. 3

    D. 4

Q67. Given the following statements:

```
CREATE BUFFERPOOL bp1 SIZE 100000;
ALTER TABLESPACE tbspc1 BUFFERPOOL bp1;
```

Which of the following statements will fail?

  A. Alter bufferpool bp1 size 50000

  B. Alter bufferpool bp1 size -1

  C. Alter bufferpool bp1 size 150000

  D. Drop bufferpool bp1

Q68. Given the following statements:

```
CREATE BUFFERPOOL bp1 SIZE 100000;
ALTER TABLESPACE tbspc1 BUFFERPOOL bp1;
CREATE BUFFERPOOL bp2 SIZE 200000;
DROP BUFFERPOOL bp1;
```

When will the memory for buffer pool BP1 be freed back to the operating system?

  A. Immediately

  B. When another buffer pool is created

  C. When the database is reactivated

  D. When the table space tbspc1 is dropped

Q69. Given the following instance and database configuration information:

```
INTRA_PARALLEL = YES
MAX_QUERYDEGREE = 4
DFT_DEGREE = 8
```

How many total agent/subagent processes will be used to process the select * from table1 statement?

  A. 4

  B. 5

  C. 8

  D. 9

Q70. Given the following statement:

```
CREATE TABLE T1
  ( c1 int, c2 int, c3 char(10), c4 char(10))
    organize by ( (c1,c3), c2)
```

How many indexes will be automatically created by DB2?

    A. 1

    B. 2

    C. 3

    D. 4

Q71. For the table:

```
create table t1(c1 varchar(30), c2 int, c3 int) organize by (c1, c2)
```

and the following file loaded into the table:

```
aaaaaaa,11,9
bbb,22,10
cccccc,33,11
bbb,22,7
dddd,44,5
bbb,44,7
dddd,44,23
dddd,22,5
```

With an empty table, how many extents will the above data cause to be used in the table?

    A. 1

    B. 5

    C. 6

    D. 7

    E. 8

Q72. Which two of the following generated columns are monotonic?

    A. int (current date / 10)

    B. int (current date / 100)

    C. int (current date / 1000)

    D. int (current date / 10000)

    E. int (current date / 100000)

Q73. When tuning a database for an OLTP workload, which of the following memory areas will provide the biggest impact for performance?

    A. Sorting

    B. Buffer pools

    C. Inter-partition communications

    D. Lock list

Q74. Given the following output from the SYSIBM.INDEXES view:

TBNAME	INDNAME	NLEAF	NLEVELS
MYTAB	X1	-1	-1
MYTAB	X2	-1	-1

What action should be taken?

    A. Drop and recreate index X1.

    B. Perform REORG on table MYTAB.

    C. Perform RUNSTATS on table MYTAB.

    D. Drop and recreate index X2.

Q75. Assuming a LOCKLIST of 20,000 pages with each user wanting to insert 30,000 rows into a table (assuming also that all inserted rows will be unique), how many concurrent users effectively perform the work?

    A. 70

    B. 37

    C. 15

    D. 5

Q76. Given 50 concurrent batch jobs inserting 30,000 rows, which of the following is the minimum size for the LOCKLIST that would allow the jobs to complete successfully?

    A. 20,000

    B. 30,000

    C. 40,000

    D. 50,000

Q77. To allow the optimizer to choose efficient access plans that will perform well, it is important to ensure that columns that are frequently accessed with SQL statements containing joins, group by's, or order by's be properly:

    A. Dropped

    B. Indexed

    C. Clustered

    D. Reorganized

Q78. Given the following table:

```
create tab1 (c1 int, c2 int, c3 int, c4 int, c5 int);
```

If column c1 is unique and the queries typically access columns c1 and c2 together, which of the following indexes will improve the query performance?

    A. create unique index xtab1 on tab1 (c1, c2)

    B. create unique index xtab1 on tab1 (c1) include (c2)

    C. create unique index xtab1 on tab1 (c1); create index xtab2 on tab1 (c2)

    D. create unique index xtab1 on tab1 (c2, c1)

    E. create unique index xtab1 on tab1 (c2) include (c1)

Q79. A database was created under DB2 UDB Version 7.x and migrated to Version 8.x. What is the type of all indexes created for this database?

    A. UNIQUE

    B. Type I

    C. Type II

    D. NON UNIQUE

Q80. For a database that was created on a previous version of DB2 and migrated to Version 8, all existing indexes will be Type I indexes; however, they can be converted to Type II indexes when:

    A. A table is clustered.

    B. A table is rebound with new package lists.

    C. A table is dropped and recreated.

    D. A table is reorganized.

Q81. Which of the following methods cannot be used to update index and/or table statistics in the system catalog tables?

    A. Using UPDATE statements that operate against a set of predefined catalog views

    B. Using the LOAD utility

    C. Using the REORG utility

    D. Using the REORGCHK command

    E. Using the RUNSTATS utility

Q82. Which of the following SQL statements can be used to determine whether RUNSTATS has been executed for a given table?

    A. select tabname, nleaf, nlevels, stats_time from syscat.tables
    B. select tabname, card, stats_time from syscat.indexes
    C. select tabname, card, stats_time from syscat.tables
    D. select tabname, nleaf, nlevels, stats_time from syscat.indexes

Q83. Given the following element from a database snapshot:

```
Rejected Block Remote Cursor requests          = 2283
```

and the following configuration parameter settings:

```
RQRIOBLK                         = 32767
QUERY_HEAP_SZ                    = 1000
ASLHEAPSZ                        = 15
DOS_RQRIOBLK                     = 4096
```

Which of the following actions would improve query performance?

    A. Increase RQRIOBLK.
    B. Increase QUERY_HEAP_SZ.
    C. Increase ASLHEAPSZ.
    D. Increase DOS_RQRIOBLK.

Q84. Which of the following configuration parameters can be used to limit the maximum number of memory pages that can be used for shared sorts within a database?

    A. SORTHEAP
    B. SHEAPTHRES
    C. SHEAPTHRES_SHR
    D. SHEAPTHRES_PRIVATE

Q85. Which of the following configuration parameter settings will allow DB2 to use shared sorts?

    A. SHEAPTHRES=ON
    B. SHEAPTHRES_SHR=ON
    C. INTRA_PARALLEL=ON
    D. FEDERATED=ON

Q86.   Given the following piece of snapshot output:

```
Post threshold sorts              = 32
Piped sorts rejected              = 25
```

and the following configuration parameter settings:

```
DFT_MON_SORT                      = ON
SHEAPTHRES                        = 10000
SHEAPTHRES_SHR                    = 5000
SORTHEAP                          = 256
INDEXSORT                         = YES
```

Which actions will improve query performance?

      A. Set SHEAPTHRES=5000 and DFT_MON_SORT=OFF.

      B. Set SHEAPTHRES=5000 and INDEXSORT=NO.

      C. Set SHEAPTHRES=20000, SHEAPTHRES_SHR=20000 and SORTHEAP=512.

      D. Set SHEAPTHRES=5000, SHEAPTHRES_SHR=5000 and SORTHEAP=128.

Q87.   On an SMP server with 32 CPUs running four separate DB2 instances: db2inst1, db2inst2, db2inst2, and db2inst4, which of the following will divide the available CPUs evenly between all instances?

      A. For each instance run update dbm cfg using max_querydegree 4 immediate.

      B. For each instance run update dbm cfg using max_querydegree 8 immediate.

      C. For each instance run update dbm cfg using max_querydegree 16 immediate.

      D. For each instance run update dbm cfg using max_querydegree 32 immediate.

Q88.   Which of the following configuration parameter settings will activate the connection concentrator?

      A. MAX_CONNECTIONS= MAX_COORDAGENTS

      B. MAX_CONNECTIONS> MAX_COORDAGENTS

      C. MAX_CONNECTIONS< MAX_COORDAGENTS

Answers to Sample Questions

This appendix contains the answers to the sample certification exam questions in Appendix L.

A01. A   SYSADM privileges are the highest set of privileges available in DB2 ESE.

A02. D   To drop DB2 instance db2inst1, appusr2 must have SYSADM privileges. Therefore, the System Administrator must add the user appusr2 to the group usr1grp.

A03. B   If you set TRUST_ALLCLNTS=YES and TRUST_CLNTAUTH=SERVER, then authentication for Trusted non-DRDA Client Authentication with be performed at the SERVER.

A04. B   Kerberos authentication types are supported only on clients and servers running Windows 2000, Windows XP, and Windows .NET operating systems. In addition, both the client and server machines must belong to the same Windows domain.

A05. D   With an authentication type of KRB_SERVER_ENCRYPT at the server and clients that support the Kerberos security system, the effective system authentication type is KERBEROS. If the clients do not support the Kerberos security system, then the effective system authentication type is equivalent to SERVER_ENCRYPT.

A06. C   For sensitive data, consider revoking the SELECT privilege from PUBLIC, then granting the SELECT privilege as required to specific users.

A07. E   If DB2LDAPCACHE=NO and DIR_CACHE=NO, always read the information from LDAP. If DB2LDAPCACHE=NO and DIR_CACHE=YES, always read the information from LDAP once and insert it into the DB2 cache.

A08. B   When running on Windows operating systems, DB2 supports using either IBM LDAP client or the Microsoft LDAP client to access the IBM SecureWay Directory Server. If you want to select the IBM LDAP client explicitly, you must use the db2set command to set the DB2LDAP_CLIENT_PROVIDER registry variable to IBM.

A09. A   To enable LDAP explicitly by setting the DB2_ENABLE_LDAP registry variable to YES using the db2set command.

A10. A   Set DB2LDAPCACHE=NO to avoid LDAP information being cached in the database, node, and DCS directories.

A11. B   The authorization check is always performed by the LDAP server, not by DB2 or the operating system. The LDAP authorization check is not related to DB2 authorization.

A12. C   Answer A is correct because there are four DB2 servers, one entry per server. At the minimum, you will need to reserve four entries in the /etc/services file. Using the best practices, however, you will need to add an additional entry for each database partition for a particular server within the partitioned database environment. Therefore, you will need a total of 16 entries reserved in the /etc/services file.

A13. A   There is one and only one db2nodes.cfg file for each instance in a partitioned database environment.

A14. D   Any number of DB2 instances can be configured to function as federated servers. Federated servers use DRDA communication protocols to communicate with DB2 family instances. Federated servers use other protocols to communicate with non-DB2 family instances (not a single protocol).

A15. D   The processing of segments of a query at a data source instead of at the federated server is called *function pushdown*.

A16. B   The query optimizer generates local and remote access plans for processing a query fragment, based on resource cost. DB2 then chooses the plan it believes will process the query with the least resource cost.

A17. C   The CPU at the MYSERV server is five times faster than the CPU at the federated server.

A18. B   The data source has started to run on an upgraded CPU that's only half as fast as the federated server.

A19. A   The data source has started to run on an upgraded CPU that's only half as fast (or two times slower) as the federated server.

A20. B   The network communications data rate to the data source MYSERV is at 2,000,000 bytes per second.

A21. D A result set of 10,000 records with row length of 100 bytes, then number of blocks it will be required to send is: $10,000 \times 100 / 65,535$ or approximately 16 blocks.

A22. A Only a REFRESH DEFERRED materialized query table can be defined as MAINTAINED BY USER. Only insert, update, and delete are valid actions for materialized query table using the MAINTAINED BY USER option.

A23. B If the LOGSECOND is set to -1, the database is configured with infinite active log space. LOGPRIMARY cannot be set to -1

A24. D The MIRRORLOGPATH database configuration parameter allows the database to write an identical copy of log files to a different path.

A25. D Changes to the table are not logged if you created the Declared Global Temporary table with NOT LOGGED option. The Declared Global Temporary table is logged, and LOGGED is the default option.

A26. E If the BLK_LOG_DSK_FUL is set to YES, the applications will hang when DB2 encounters a log disk full error. You are then able to resolve the error, and the transaction can continue because the DB2 will attempt to create a log file every five minutes until it succeeds and will write a message to the administration log.

A27. B To collect a complete set of log files up to a known point in time you can initiate on demand log archiving by invoking the ARCHIVE LOG command. The issuer of this command cannot have a connection to the specific database, although other users may be connected.

A28. B Other tasks can be used for additional information related to this problem. The ARCHIVE.LOG and USEREXIT.ERR are the most critical files that you will need to verify why the user exit failed.

A29. B This is the best answer to describe the incremental delta function. Delta or incremental delta backup image is a copy of all database data that has changed since the last successful backup (full, incremental, or delta) operation.

A30. B To enable online full backup, you must set LOGRETAIN to YES and set TRACKMOD to YES to allow incremental backup.

A31. C To perform an offline backup of all database partitions for SAMPLE database, you must ensure that no connection exists to the database, back up the catalog partition first, then back up the remaining of the database partitions. The backup command will fail if you stop the DB2 instance.

A32. B To perform a restore from the recent offline backup of all database partitions for SAMPLE database, you must restore the catalog partition first, then all other database partitions of the SAMPLE database. Using TAKEN AT is required because there are multiple database backup images residing in the /dbbackup/SAMPLE directory.

A33. C   To roll forward a table space that resides on a database partition number 2 to the end of log, you must specify the database partition number associated with the given table space name, TS1.

A34. E   All of these above options are valid under db2inidb tool. In addition to these options, the usage for each option is also correct described.

A35. D   Log shipping is the process of copying whole log files to a standby server, either from an archive device or through a user exit program running against the database on the primary server. The database on the standby server is continuously rolling forward through the log files produced by primary server.

A36. E   You can suspend a subset of one or more partitions to create a split mirror for performing offline backups. If the catalog partition is included in the subset, it must be the last partition to be suspended.

A37. C   After the failover, the database partitions 0 and 1 are running on server2.

A38. C   After the failover, the database partitions that were executing on server2, which is defined as database partitions 2 and 3, start up on server1. Because server1 is already running database partitions 0 and 1, database partitions 2 and 3 will be started as logical database partitions 2 and 3 with the logical ports 2 and 3.

A39. B   The ALLOW READ ACCESS option prevents all write access to the table by other applications, but it allows read access to preloaded data.

A40. A   The ALLOW NO ACCESS option locks the table exclusively and allows no access to the table data while the table is being loaded. This is the default option.

A41. B and C   When you receive SQL6048 from db2start, the cause of this is that you don't have the $HOME/.rhosts file for communication among hosts, and the file permission may not be corrected.

A42. B   The statement cannot be processed because of a problem with the db2nodes.cfg file. The main reason for this is that the hostname/port couple at line "2" of the db2nodes.cfg file is not unique. The port number at line "2" is the same as the port number at line "1" for the same hostname. To correct this problem, set port number for server1 at line "1" to 0.

A43. C   You have only two ports defined in /etc/services on server1 and server2. Now you try to failover database partition 3, and you are not allowed to use the third port. Ensure that the DB2 port range defined in the /etc/services file is large enough to handle all possible partitions to be started. To correct the problem, increase the value for DB2_db2inst1_END in /etc/services to at least 50503.

A44. A   There is one buffer pool, the IBMDEFAULTBP, created when a database is created.

A45. C   There are three table spaces created when a database is created: SYSCATSPACE, TEMPSPACE1, and USERSPACE1.

A46. C   There are three database partition groups created when a database is created, regardless of whether or not the database is partitioned: IBMCATGROUP, IBMDEFAULTGROUP, and IBMTEMPGROUP.

A47. A   Because all of the table spaces have a 4-KB page size and the default page size for a database is 4 KB, only one buffer pool is REQUIRED.

A48. B   Because the table spaces have a 4-KB and 8-KB page size and the default page size for a database is 4 KB, a minimum of two buffer pools are REQUIRED.

A49. A   To create a table space, a buffer pool with the same page size must already exist.

A50. C or D   Because the row size is > 8 KB, the table must be created in a table space with either a 16-KB or a 32-KB page size.

A51. B   The row has a length of

Bytes	Column Name and Overhead
3800	C3
200	C2
4	C1
4	row overhead
16	length of LONG VARCHAR pointer

The total is larger than the max length (4005) for a 4-KB page and, therefore, requires a minimum 8-KB page size.

A52. B   Each DMS table space has three extents of overhead, plus a tag of one extent in size, plus there must be two extents available to create an object; this is a total of six extents.

A53. B   For a 4-KB page size, only 5 rows could fit on a page; this would require 20,000,000 pages, which would be larger than allowed.

For an 8-KB page size, 11 rows could fit on a page; this would require 9,090,909 pages, which is allowed.

A54. D   The table would use one object for the object map and one for the data object, as well as one object for the index's object map and one index object because the table has a primary key that would cause DB2 to create an index, for a total of four.

A55. B   The db2empfa tool enables multipage allocation, or allocation of an extent at a time. This can have a significant effect for bulk inserts.

A56. B   Adding up the size of the columns gives:

$2000 + 250 + 2000 + 4 + 4 + 4$

Even without the overhead, this is over 4005, so would require a minimum page size of 8 KB.

A57. C   Large table spaces can now contain indexes, as well as LOBs and Long Varchars.

A58. B   The $N parameter can append the database partition number to a container name in the create tablespace statement.

A59. C   Remove is not a valid option; a container can be dropped using the DROP option.

A60. A   The size of the catalog table space cannot be changed, and it is the default page size, i.e., 4 KB.

A61. D   Because both containers are 2,000 pages, increasing all containers by an additional 3,000 pages will make them both 5,000 pages.

A62. A   The NUMBLOCKPAGES defines the number of pages that should exist in the block-based area of the buffer pool for block-based prefetching.

A63. A   SYSCTRL is the lowest authority/privilege from the list that can alter a buffer pool.

A64. C   If there is not enough memory available to create a new buffer pool, an error message will be returned to the user, and the buffer pool will be allocated after the database is stopped and restarted.

A65. D   The value AUTOMATIC tells DB2 to allocate what is needed when it starts. By setting DATABASE_MEMORY to a real value, the specified amount of memory is reserved for future use.

In this case, $200,000 + 50,000 = 250,000$. Therefore, the lowest value given greater than 250,000 is 300,000.

A66. C   There must be a minimum of one buffer pool for every page size. In the list, we see 8-KB and 16-KB page sizes. However, the catalog table space uses a 4-KB page size; therefore, there are three page sizes, so three buffer pools are required.

A67. D   A buffer pool cannot be dropped while a table space is associated with it.

A68. C   The memory can be re-allocated within DB2 to other buffer pools, etc., but will still be held by DB2 until the database is stopped and restarted.

A69. B   Because MAXDEGREE = 4, the select will use a degree of parallelism of 4. Therefore, there will be 4 subagents, plus the coordinating agent, for a total of 5.

A70. C   There will be a block index on (C2,C1,C3) and two dimension indexes on C3, and (C1,C2).

A71. C　The data will then use six extents, as follows:

Extent 1	aaaaaaa	11
Extent 2	bbb	22
Extent 3	ccccc	33
Extent 4	dddd	44
Extent 5	bbb	44
Extent 6	dddd	22

A72. B and D　Both (current date / 100) and (current date / 10000) increase as the value of current date increases, so they are monotonic. Dividing by 100 will remove the day part of the date; dividing by 10000 will remove the day and month part of the date. In both cases, the result will not decrease as the date increases.

A73. B　To maintain optimal performance in an OLTP workload, the data pages need to be in the buffer pools, so I/O can be avoided. Sorting should be avoided because it is costly and degrades performance.

A74. C　There are no current statistics for the table MYTAB and its indexes; therefore, the optimizer may be choosing sub-optimal access plans. To allow the optimizer to choose the best access plans, statistics should be gathered for the table and its indexes.

A75. B　Because each lock requires 72 bytes of lock list, each user will require approximately 527.5 pages of the lock list. Therefore with 20,000 pages of the lock list, the maximum number of users would be 37.

A76. B　Because each lock requires 72 bytes of lock list, each user will require approximately 527.5 pages of the lock list. Therefore, for 50 concurrent users, there would need to be approximately 26,400 pages of the lock list. The value of 30,000 is the minimum value in the list that is greater than this value.

A77. B　Although clustered columns will help in the retrieval of data, sorting, joining, and ordering can be done most efficiently using indexes so that sorts are not required.

A78. B　The unique index on column c1 that includes the column c2 will allow index-only access when columns c1 and c2 are queried in the same SQL statement. All other indexes would require either a sort or access to the data object to retrieve the values from column c2.

A79. B　DB2 UDB Version 7.x supported only Type I indexes. When a Version 7 databases is migrated to Version 8, the indexes are not changed to Type II indexes during the migration process. To convert Type I indexes to Type II indexes, the tables need to be reorged.

A80. D　The REORG command has an option (CONVERT) to convert Type I indexes to Type II indexes. By default, they will not be converted. For example:

```
Reorg indexes all for table user.table1 convert
```

A81. C   The REORG command cannot gather statistics for a table as the table is being operated on.

A82. C   CARD is not a column in the SYSCAT.INDEXES view, and NLEAF and NLEVELS are not valid columns in the SYSCAT.TABLES view, so these would not work. A table may not have indexes but may still have statistics, so the SYSCAT.TABLES view must be queried. If the STATS_TIME column is '-', then statistics have not been run for the table.

A83. A   Increasing the requestor I/O block size (RQRIOBLK) will allow DB2 to send and receive larger blocks of data, thereby reducing the number of blocked cursor requests.

A84. C   The SHEAPTHRES_SHR parameter is new in Version 8 and limits the maximum amount of memory that can be used for shared sorts within a database. Be aware that this is a HARD limit, unlike the SHEAPTHRES configuration parameter.

A85. C   Enabling intra-partition parallelism using the INTRA_PARALLEL parameter allows the DB2 optimizer to consider shared sorts when optimizing statements.

A86. C   Increasing the sort heaps and the associated sort heap thresholds can help improve performance; however, this may cause other implications. Therefore, these changes should be made with caution.

A87. A   Setting the maximum degree of parallelism for each instance to 8 will allow each application within an instance to use up to eight subagents to process an SQL request. If each instance has a number of applications, this may overwhelm the server. Therefore, for this configuration, using a maximum degree of parallelism of 4 will allow multiple applications to run concurrently within each instance.

A88. B   The connection concentrator is activated when the maximum number of connections is set higher than the maximum number of coordinating agents.

Index

A

Active Directory Users and Computer Management
Console, 314, 325, 326
Active logs, 152, 171
ADD DATABASE PARTITION GROUP option, ALTER
BUFFERPOOL statement, 90
ADD DBPARTITIONNUM, 59
ADD option, ALTER TABLESPACE command, 30–36
ADD TO STRIPE SET option, 53
Address Windowing Extensions (AWE), 80, 87
Administrative authority, 306
AGENTPRI, 545–547
background, 545
configuring, 545–546
monitoring, 546–547
AIX, operating system information, 707
ALL CONTAINERS clause, 35
ALL DBPARTITIONNUMS option, CREATE
BUFFERPOOL statement, 79
ALTER BUFFERPOOL statement, 82, 89–90
ADD DATABASE PARTITION GROUP option, 90
BLOCKSIZE option, 90
bufferpool-name option, 89–90
DBPARTITIONNUM option, 89
DEFERRED option, 89
NUMBLOCKPAGES option, 90
SIZE option, 89–90
ALTER DATABASE PARTITION GROUP statement,
60–61
ALTER SERVER statement, 470, 479
ALTER TABLESPACE command, 8, 11, 30, 33, 40, 43,
46, 48–49, 53, 78, 96, 98
ADD option, 30–36
BEGIN NEW STRIPE SET option, 30–31, 34–37,
52–53
DROP option, 35–36
EXTEND option, 35–36
options, 30–36
REDUCE option, 35–36
RESIZE option, 35–36
ALTER TABLESPACE parameter, LIST HISTORY utility,
664
Altering buffer pools, 89–91
Altering table spaces, 30–53
adding containers to a table space, 36–38
ALTER TABLESPACE command, 8, 11, 30, 33, 40,
43, 46, 48–49, 53
options, 30–36
dropping containers from a table space, 38–43
extending/enlarging containers in a table space, 43–46

reducing/shrinking containers in a table space,
46–48
table space high water mark, 40–41
lowering, 41–43
table space rebalance, 48–49
monitoring, 49–53
and/or top (tool), 637, 650
APPLHEAPSZ, 554–555
background, 554–555
configuring, 555
monitoring, 555
Application level proxy firewalls, 311
Application packages, 277
Application programmer, 307
Application savepoint, 479
Application support layer heap size (ASLHEAPSZ),
517–519
background, 517–518
configuring, 518–519
monitoring, 519
ARCHIVE LOG utility, 662–663
command parameters, 662
DATABASE database-alias parameter, 662
db-partition-number parameter, 662
ON ALL DBPARTITIONNUMS parameter, 662
ON DBPARTITIONNUM/ON DBPARTITIONNUMS
parameter, 662
Archive logging, 138
Archived log, 152
Associated subagents, 117
Asynchronous pages per write, 111–112
Asynchronous read ratio, 106–108
ATTACH, cataloging a node alias for, 319
Authentication methods, 300–306
authentication types, 301–302
Kerberos authentication, 303–305
authentication types, 303
client, 303
Kerberos server, 303
Key Distribution Center (KDC), 303
KRB_SERVER_ENCRYPT, 304
server, 303
service ticket (ST), 303–304
ticket-granting ticket (TGT), 303–304
in a Windows environment, 304
partitioned database authentication considerations, 306
Authentication types, 301–302, 303
CLIENT, 301–302
TRUST_ALLCLNTS, 301–302
TRUST_CLNTAUTH, 305
SERVER, 301, 305
SERVER_ENCRYPT, 301, 305

LICENSE AGREEMENT AND LIMITED WARRANTY

READ THE FOLLOWING TERMS AND CONDITIONS CAREFULLY BEFORE OPENING THIS DISK PACKAGE. THIS LEGAL DOCUMENT IS AN AGREEMENT BETWEEN YOU AND PRENTICE-HALL, INC. (THE "COMPANY"). BY OPENING THIS SEALED DISK PACKAGE, YOU ARE AGREEING TO BE BOUND BY THESE TERMS AND CONDITIONS. IF YOU DO NOT AGREE WITH THESE TERMS AND CONDITIONS, DO NOT OPEN THE DISK PACKAGE. PROMPTLY RETURN THE UNOPENED DISK PACKAGE AND ALL ACCOMPANYING ITEMS TO THE PLACE YOU OBTAINED THEM FOR A FULL REFUND OF ANY SUMS YOU HAVE PAID.

1. **GRANT OF LICENSE:** In consideration of your payment of the license fee, which is part of the price you paid for this product, and your agreement to abide by the terms and conditions of this Agreement, the Company grants to you a nonexclusive right to use and display the copy of the enclosed software program (hereinafter the "SOFTWARE") on a single computer (i.e., with a single CPU) at a single location so long as you comply with the terms of this Agreement. The Company reserves all rights not expressly granted to you under this Agreement.

2. **OWNERSHIP OF SOFTWARE:** You own only the magnetic or physical media (the enclosed disks) on which the SOFTWARE is recorded or fixed, but the Company retains all the rights, title, and ownership to the SOFTWARE recorded on the original disk copy(ies) and all subsequent copies of the SOFTWARE, regardless of the form or media on which the original or other copies may exist. This license is not a sale of the original SOFTWARE or any copy to you.

3. **COPY RESTRICTIONS:** This SOFTWARE and the accompanying printed materials and user manual (the "Documentation") are the subject of copyright. You may not copy the Documentation or the SOFTWARE, except that you may make a single copy of the SOFTWARE for backup or archival purposes only. You may be held legally responsible for any copying or copyright infringement which is caused or encouraged by your failure to abide by the terms of this restriction.

4. **USE RESTRICTIONS:** You may not network the SOFTWARE or otherwise use it on more than one computer or computer terminal at the same time. You may physically transfer the SOFTWARE from one computer to another provided that the SOFTWARE is used on only one computer at a time. You may not distribute copies of the SOFTWARE or Documentation to others. You may not reverse engineer, disassemble, decompile, modify, adapt, translate, or create derivative works based on the SOFTWARE or the Documentation without the prior written consent of the Company.

5. **TRANSFER RESTRICTIONS:** The enclosed SOFTWARE is licensed only to you and may not be transferred to any one else without the prior written consent of the Company. Any unauthorized transfer of the SOFTWARE shall result in the immediate termination of this Agreement.

6. **TERMINATION:** This license is effective until terminated. This license will terminate automatically without notice from the Company and become null and void if you fail to comply with any provisions or limitations of this license. Upon termination, you shall destroy the Documentation and all copies of the SOFTWARE. All provisions of this Agreement as to warranties, limitation of liability, remedies or damages, and our ownership rights shall survive termination.

7. **MISCELLANEOUS:** This Agreement shall be construed in accordance with the laws of the United States of America and the State of New York and shall benefit the Company, its affiliates, and assignees.

8. **LIMITED WARRANTY AND DISCLAIMER OF WARRANTY:** The Company warrants that the SOFTWARE, when properly used in accordance with the Documentation, will operate in substantial conformity with the description of the SOFTWARE set forth in the Documentation. The Company does not warrant that the SOFTWARE will meet your requirements or that the operation of the SOFTWARE will be uninterrupted or error-free. The Company warrants that the media on which the SOFTWARE is delivered shall be free from defects in materials and workmanship under normal use for a period of thirty (30) days from the date of your purchase. Your only remedy and the Company's only obligation under these limited warranties is, at the Company's option, return of the warranted item for a refund of any amounts paid by you or replacement of the item. Any replacement of SOFTWARE or media under the warranties shall not extend the original warranty period. The limited warranty set forth above shall not apply to any SOFTWARE which the Company determines in good faith has been subject to misuse, neglect, improper installation, repair, alteration, or damage by you. EXCEPT FOR THE EXPRESSED WARRANTIES SET FORTH ABOVE, THE COMPANY DISCLAIMS ALL WARRANTIES, EXPRESS OR IMPLIED, INCLUDING WITHOUT LIMITATION, THE IMPLIED WARRANTIES OF MERCHANTABILITY AND FITNESS FOR A PARTICULAR PURPOSE. EXCEPT FOR THE EXPRESS WARRANTY SET FORTH ABOVE, THE COMPANY DOES NOT WARRANT, GUARANTEE, OR MAKE ANY REPRESENTATION REGARDING THE USE OR THE RESULTS OF THE USE OF THE SOFTWARE IN TERMS OF ITS CORRECTNESS, ACCURACY, RELIABILITY, CURRENTNESS, OR OTHERWISE.

IN NO EVENT, SHALL THE COMPANY OR ITS EMPLOYEES, AGENTS, SUPPLIERS, OR CONTRACTORS BE LIABLE FOR ANY INCIDENTAL, INDIRECT, SPECIAL, OR CONSEQUENTIAL DAMAGES ARISING OUT OF OR IN CONNECTION WITH THE LICENSE GRANTED UNDER THIS AGREEMENT, OR FOR LOSS OF USE, LOSS OF DATA, LOSS OF INCOME OR PROFIT, OR OTHER LOSSES, SUSTAINED AS A RESULT OF INJURY TO ANY PERSON, OR LOSS OF OR DAMAGE TO PROPERTY, OR CLAIMS OF THIRD PARTIES, EVEN IF THE COMPANY OR AN AUTHORIZED REPRESENTATIVE OF THE COMPANY HAS BEEN ADVISED OF THE POSSIBILITY OF SUCH DAMAGES. IN NO EVENT SHALL LIABILITY OF THE COMPANY FOR DAMAGES WITH RESPECT TO THE SOFTWARE EXCEED THE AMOUNTS ACTUALLY PAID BY YOU, IF ANY, FOR THE SOFTWARE.

SOME JURISDICTIONS DO NOT ALLOW THE LIMITATION OF IMPLIED WARRANTIES OR LIABILITY FOR INCIDENTAL, INDIRECT, SPECIAL, OR CONSEQUENTIAL DAMAGES, SO THE ABOVE LIMITATIONS MAY NOT ALWAYS APPLY. THE WARRANTIES IN THIS AGREEMENT GIVE YOU SPECIFIC LEGAL RIGHTS AND YOU MAY ALSO HAVE OTHER RIGHTS WHICH VARY IN ACCORDANCE WITH LOCAL LAW.

ACKNOWLEDGMENT

YOU ACKNOWLEDGE THAT YOU HAVE READ THIS AGREEMENT, UNDERSTAND IT, AND AGREE TO BE BOUND BY ITS TERMS AND CONDITIONS. YOU ALSO AGREE THAT THIS AGREEMENT IS THE COMPLETE AND EXCLUSIVE STATEMENT OF THE AGREEMENT BETWEEN YOU AND THE COMPANY AND SUPERSEDES ALL PROPOSALS OR PRIOR AGREEMENTS, ORAL, OR WRITTEN, AND ANY OTHER COMMUNICATIONS BETWEEN YOU AND THE COMPANY OR ANY REPRESENTATIVE OF THE COMPANY RELATING TO THE SUBJECT MATTER OF THIS AGREEMENT.

Should you have any questions concerning this Agreement or if you wish to contact the Company for any reason, please contact in writing at the address below.

Robin Short
Prentice Hall PTR
One Lake Street, Upper Saddle River, New Jersey 07458

About the CD-ROM

The CD-ROM included with *Advanced DBA Certification Guide and Reference for DB2 Universal Database v8 for Linux, UNIX, and Windows* contains the following:

> DB2 Universal Database Enterprise Server Edition Version 8.1 for Windows Operating Environments
> DB2 Version 8 documentation in PDF format
> Sample scripts for monitoring and tuning your DB2 system

The version of DB2 on this CD-ROM can be used on Microsoft Windows® NT®/2000/2003. The documentation can be read on all operating systems supported by DB2 UDB. Some of the scripts provided require Perl or are shell scripts intended for Linux and UNIX environments.

A setup window will be opened by executing E:\DB2_ESE\SETUP.EXE. As well as allowing you to take a tour of the product and install it, this window will give access to useful installation prerequisites and release notes.

The DB2 product supplied with this book will need to be reinstalled after 180 days and will expire permanently on June 30, 2008.

License Agreement

Use of the software accompanying *Advanced DBA Certification Guide and Reference for DB2 Universal Database v8 for Linux, UNIX, and Windows* is subject to the terms of the License Agreement and Limited Warranty found on the previous page.

Technical Support

Prentice Hall does not offer technical support for any of the programs on the CD-ROM. However, if the CD-ROM is damaged, you may obtain a replacement copy by sending an email that describes the problem to: disc_exchange@prenhall.com